FINDING
— A —
HOME
FOR THE SOUL

FINDING
— A —
HOME
FOR THE SOUL

Interviews with Converts to Judaism

Catherine Hall Myrowitz

JASON ARONSON INC.
Northvale, New Jersey
London

This book was set in 10 pt. Times Roman by Alpha Graphics, Pittsfield, New Hampshire, and printed by Haddon Craftsmen in Scranton, Pennsylvania.

Library of Congress Cataloging-in-Publication Data

Myrowitz, Catherine Hall.
  Finding a home for the soul: interviews with converts to Judaism / Catherine Hall Myrowitz.
    p. cm.
  Includes bibliographical references.
  ISBN 1-56821-322-0
  1. Proselytes and proselyting. Jewish—Converts from Christianity—
Biography. 2. Jewish way of life. 3. Spiritual life—Judaism.
4. Judaism—Customs and practices. I. Title.
  BM729.P7M93 1995
  296.7'1—dc20   94-32903

Manufactured in the United States of America. Jason Aronson Inc. offers books and cassettes. For infor- mation and catalog write to Jason Aronson Inc., 230 Livingston Street, Northvale, New Jersey 07647.

To my father, *z'l*, May his memory be for a blessing.

To Elliott, *Ani le-dodi, ve-dodi li*—I am my beloved's and my beloved is mine.

To Rachel and David, May God bless you as He blessed Sarah, Rebecca, Rachel and Leah, Ephraim and Menasseh.

To the Jews of Jedzejow, Poland, including most members of the Myrowitz family, who were killed on Yom Kippur 1943. May their memory be for a blessing.

Contents

Foreword

James S. Rosen

"The Holy One, blessed be He, exiled Israel among the nations in order to increase their numbers with the addition of converts."

Babylonian Talmud, *Pesahim* 87b

It surprises many people to learn that much of classical Judaism held a very positive attitude toward proselytes. After all of history's bitter experience, unspeakable tales of persecution, and continuing anti-Semitism, many wonder why anyone would consciously choose to be Jewish.

Yet, tradition tells us the first Hebrew, Abraham, was himself a convert. The Messiah will ultimately come from the line of David, whose ancestry is directly linked to the most famous biblical convert, Ruth.

In our day, the man or woman who would freely choose Judaism is a person of much interest, scrutiny, and even mystery. After all, in the open society that is America, one might imagine that in the marketplace of ideas, Judaism would occupy a most modest stall indeed. It is a demanding way of life, time-consuming, filled with rich history, colorful languages (Yiddish, Ladino, and Hebrew), and a strong folk element destined to make nonadherents feel like outsiders. And yet, thousands have voluntarily adopted Judaism and continue to do so.

Their choice of Judaism comes at a crucial juncture in American Jewish history. As never before, the Jewish community fears freedom's most potent sting: assimilation. Precisely because Western civilization is so open, so tolerant of individual expression, intermarriage has become a fact of life with resultant shifts away from Jewish identity amongst children of these unions. Many Jews perceive not a small communal wound of lost Jewish loyalty, but a virtual hemorrhaging.

Countering this flow is the convert to Judaism, better known as the Jew by Choice. Are such Jews potent weapons in reversing the tide of assimilation? Researchers such as Egon Mayer, Brenda Forster and Joseph Tabachnik, Charles Silberman and Sergio Della Pergola have painstakingly documented the demographics, behavioral trends, and attitudes of Jews by Choice. Their conclusions vary from virtually unbounded optimism to more modest expectations of the potential contribution Jews by Choice might make to American Jewish life. Mayer, in particular, has called for vigorous outreach so that more might be invited to join Jewish ranks.

One thing is certain: Jews by Choice are a recognizable subgroup amongst American Jews. One-third of gentile partners in marriages involving a Jew ultimately convert to Judaism.

More recently, writers, scholars, rabbis, Jews and non-Jews alike have begun asking a fundamental question: "Just what does the inner life of the Jew by Choice look like?" Writers such as Lena Romanoff address the issue in their guidelines to helping Jews by Choice find a home within Judaism. But in this volume, Catherine Hall Myrowitz takes the question to a greater depth by allowing Jews by Choice to speak for themselves.

The testimonies contained in this book describe the life experiences, motivations, joys, and tribulations of those who have chosen Judaism as a path in their lives. They are voices we have but scantily acknowledged to date. Perhaps, preoccupied with our fears for the Jewish future, and ongoing nervousness over continual anti-Semitism, we have failed to learn what Jews by Choice have to teach.

The lesson is simple yet profound: Judaism offers a rich, deeply satisfying path in life and infuses existence with powerful values, intellectual and spiritual challenge, and great comfort in time of crisis.

Conversion to Judaism is indeed a process, though in its technical details rather simple. Traditional Jewish sources describe the need to offer discouragement but also embrace the sincere convert to Judaism. A course of study is required, followed by examination by a *Bet Din*, a court of Jewishly knowledgeable leaders; immersion in the *mikveh*, a pool of naturally gathered waters; and in the case of a male, where necessary, *brit milah*, ritual circumcision. Acceptance of the Commandments is crucial. The balance of discouragement and openness is expressed by the following source describing what the *Bet Din* is to say to the prospective Jew:

> "What reason have you for desiring to become a proselyte; do you not know that Israel at the present time is persecuted and oppressed, despised, harassed, and overcome by affliction?" If he replies, "I know and yet am unworthy," he is accepted forthwith and is given instruction in some minor and major commandments. (*Yebamot* 24b)

It is clear that throughout much of Jewish history, Jews were very open to receiving converts. Salo Baron, the dean of Jewish historians, numbers some eight million as Jews in the Roman Empire and attributes this largely to the active seeking of converts.*

Christianity, when it became the Roman state religion, prohibited conversion to Judaism, often on pain of death. Moreover, in our day openly seeking converts carries negative impressions of Bible-thumping, judgmental missionaries. Many point rightly to the classic Jewish statement that "the righteous of all nations have a share in the world to come." Salvation of the soul is not a Jewish monopoly. Still, the sincere proselyte was viewed by classic Judaism as a blessing.

The stories you are about to read make vividly clear that conversion is a process

---

*Salo Baron, *A Social and Religious History of the Jews: To the Beginning of the Christian Era*, vol. 1, 2nd ed. (New York: Columbia University Press, 1937, 1952, and Philadelphia: Jewish Publication Society) p. 170.

that far transcends the mechanics of learning, answering questions, and immersing. It embraces a genuine journey that is often complicated, occasionally discouraging, but mostly triumphant. Conversion is a process that begins so often before a first encounter with Jewish study and lasts far beyond the time when the last drops of *mikveh* water are dried from the body. For so many, the path to Judaism is a journey filled with constant spiritual search, uphill battles, notes of despair and of exultation.

What makes it such a difficult trek? Largely because secular ethnicity and not religion is the basis of Jewish identity for countless thousands of Jews. For much of the last forty years, an appeal to Israel or the Holocaust touched reservoirs of clearly held passions that all American Jews shared. A sense of peoplehood has predominated. One often hears that the definition of a Jew is that person who looks at the morning newspapers searching for Jewish names in stories of success or disaster.

In this context, both Jews by Choice and born Jews frequently ask: "How is it possible to be Jewish without an ethnic tie to Jewish peoplehood?" With no chicken soup memories and Yiddish phrases, with no pictures of bearded grandfathers from Eastern Europe, can one truly stake a claim as a Jew? The jokes, recipes, folklore, sighs, and knowing smiles bespeak a culture virtually unknown to this prospective Jew. The answer Jews by Choice provide to this challenge is that Judaism as a religion is the ultimate link to Jewish identity. Their religious devotion and searching is often far deeper and decisive in their lives than that of born Jewish spouses, friends, and associates. This creates diverse reactions of amazement, amusement, envy, anger, and admiration.

As such, Jews by Choice pose a direct and creative challenge to some very comfortably held assumptions about Jewish commitment and identity. They tell us what the intermarriage statistics reveal as well: secular ethnic identity alone will not secure the Jewish future. Assimilation has only increased with the weakening of religious expression.

All might benefit from the encounter with the "sincere proselyte," a contemporary, committed Jew by Choice. Just who is he or she? That man or woman who reminds us that peoplehood is but one of the triad upon which Jewish life is based— God and Torah are the other two. Lacking ethnic memories in Jewish peoplehood, Jews by Choice create their own memories by actively pursuing an attachment to the God and Torah of Israel through their behavior, sincerity, and depth of commitment. There are minimalists amongst them to be sure. Some enter the process of conversion to Judaism for purposes of marriage to a Jew and, possibly, placating Jewish in-laws. For some, the commitment never extends far beyond a step taken superficially to satisfy the needs of the moment.

Yet, countless others have embodied the rabbinic principle *"Mitoch sheloh lishmah, ba lishmah."* "What begins from lesser motives can evolve into a sincere expression undertaken for its own sake." Indeed, who can count the Jews by Choice who first encounter Judaism under the unanticipated circumstances of an intimate relationship with a Jew but who later undergo a clear personal transformation? In the midst of a growing relationship, they find themselves confronted not only with their love for a Jew but their growing attachment to Judaism that is as mysterious to them as it is to anyone else.

More importantly, for many Jews by Choice, marriage has been but one factor in the course of their journey. There are many other experiences, some tragic and some joyous, that have created this decision to join the Jewish People. Often, Jews by Choice experience difficult childhoods with ambivalent feelings toward their parents. Many have encountered death or serious illness of close ones. Religion had a role in their early lives. What is decisive is that many Jews by Choice recall a point at which they could no longer believe comfortably in the divinity of Jesus. Once that link has been severed, many feel open to the influences of other faiths.

There are many triggers that create an interest in Judaism. A reading of *The Diary of Anne Frank* or visit to the Holocaust Museum in Washington, a friendship with a Jew, a chance meeting with a rabbi or visit to a synagogue, the discovery of a Jewish ancestor in the family's past. Usually, over the course of many months or even years, a decision crystallizes: "This path is to be my path." Ruth's famous statement in the Bible to her mother-in-law, Naomi, "Your people shall be my people and your God my God," is one never taken lightly by Jews by Choice. It is revisited almost every day in all of its glory and challenge. Very often, Judaism emerges as a powerful answer to life's questions, a warm and fulfilling answer to gaping holes.

The stories you will read are honest and diverse, yet point to a common thread of commitment. These choosing Jews come from a variety of backgrounds and express their Jewishness in many different ways. Some find their home in the music and warm community of a synagogue or *havurah* or contemporary Jewish spiritual movement. Most revel in the intellectual challenge of a faith that encourages inquiry and free expression.

Jews by Choice are now synagogue presidents, some are leaders of Jewish communal organizations, some are rabbis, others cantors, some have attained a degree of knowledge that allows them to teach Talmud in the original Aramaic. It will be a degree of our own religious maturity when such attainments no longer seem remarkable. Many, of course, maintain professions in secular fields. Whatever their careers or lifestyles, Judaism has become a powerful force in their lives.

What are their hopes, their worries? First, that they will find acceptance by the community and by the people closest to them. They seek others to share the fullness of their Jewish living. As Jeff, whose story is included in this volume, says, "I wish more Jews knew how converts feel. I wish that they could share some of our enthusiasm sometimes. And I wish that they could see the world through our eyes. I think we're fortunate because we've seen things from the other side." Their second concern flows from their first. It is shared by every serious Jew. It is the question, "Will my children be Jewish? Will this commitment to Judaism live on past me?"

The collective voices of Jews by Choice beckon that we listen more carefully. First, for their sake. The conversion process itself is often lacking in meaning. Contact with rabbis, teachers, and Jewish leaders, the trip to the *mikveh*, questioning by the *Bet Din*, the myriad of Jewish experiences that predate formal conversion—each of these discrete moments is filled with deep emotional meaning for Jews by Choice. We often underestimate the depth of their meaning for them. We often are too routine and mechanical in our approach to prospective Jews. They are telling us that outreach must be more sophisticated and continual and that warmth and welcome are still sorely lacking within our communities.

Their words remain most challenging when directed to us as a community. Says one, "My observance of *mitzvot* is always in process." How many Jews born and raised in their religion would make a similar statement? "I am a returnee, not a convert," says another. To make up for the loss of Christmas, Jews by Choice infuse Sukkot and Hanukkah with great meaning. Many send their children to Jewish day schools and study along with them. They tell us straight out, "Jewish nonobservance is unhealthy." They are not perfect exemplars of Jewish behavior in every sense, yet for so many, life is a way of seeing the *mitzvot*, the Commandments, as keys to a relationship with God and an existence of meaning.

No one is better qualified to edit and present these personal stories of choice than Catherine Hall Myrowitz. I've had the privilege of knowing her and her family for several years. She is sensitive to all the pitfalls and potential in a chosen journey to Judaism, for she has undertaken it herself. She asks the questions that need to be asked of others because she has put them to herself. Cathy demonstrates personally what a rich Jewish life might look like to those who seek it. She does this so naturally and so thoroughly that for some time, I did not know that she was a Jew by Choice and not by birth. That status is, of course, irrelevant. Some irrelevancies are worthy of celebration.

A prayer in the daily liturgy asks God for divine blessings upon the righteous proselyte of every generation. All tradition has ever asked of Jews by Choice is that they be sincere and committed in thought and deed. These days, that is all that Jews by Choice ask of the Jewish community. Whether or not their voices are heeded will be a measure of our commitment to translating Judaism's message into the language of both today and tomorrow.

Preface

Nearly four years ago I read an article in the Baltimore *Jewish Times* concerning the difficulty of keeping many Jews interested in Judaism. It was December and, coincidentally, a non-Jewish friend asked me why we, unlike another Jewish family she knew, did not celebrate both Hanukkah and Christmas? Would it make a difference to anyone—Jewish or gentile—I wondered, to know about the journey I have taken to arrive where I am today, living my life as a Jewish woman and how grateful I am to have *become* Jewish?

Just out of curiosity to see what it would look like in black and white, I began to write my story, getting up before dawn each day to write for a few hours before my family awakened. Over a *Shabbat* dinner I mentioned my efforts to some friends who suggested I write a book about myself and others who had converted! Me?—write a book? Ever so tentatively I began working on this possibility. I tried not to think about "book" but just concentrated on whom it would be good to interview.

I quickly discovered that, yes, there were many more people than even I had imagined who shared my positive experience of finding a home in Judaism. It seemed important, therefore, to get a variety of stories with as many perspectives on the experience of conversion as possible, an approach enthusiastically encouraged by Arthur Kurzweil when I submitted my proposal to Jason Aronson Inc.

I knew that the surface facts of my story could lead some people to conclude, "Oh, she met a nice Jewish boy, so she converted." I assumed that just as the story of my search for a living faith has many twists and turns, so too would the stories of others, and I was never wrong. I discovered to my endless surprise and delight that there are no hard-and-fast snap judgments to be made about any of the more than sixty people whom I interviewed for the book.

Since this is not a scholarly study, my efforts at finding people to interview were also not very scientific. In fact, attempts at a formal, logical search, one of which involved contacting Jewish communal agencies, were not particularly successful. I received few responses to the letters and materials I sent nor to my follow-up phone calls. There were exceptions. Dr. Lucy Steinitz, the executive director of the Baltimore Jewish Family Services, has been enormously helpful to me and very supportive of my endeavor, as well as Beth Land Hecht, coordinator for the Project on Intermarriage. Staff members from several other JFS agencies contacted me with one or two referrals. Another ineffectual effort was to put a letter to the editor in various Jewish newspapers across the country. Either the letters never appeared, or they were not eloquent enough to elicit even a single person I could interview. It was obvious that a formal, organizational approach to this subject was not going to work.

So I went back to the *hamishe* approach of calling this one who has a friend who knows somebody or a rabbi who maybe has the names of a few people. Ultimately, the contacts that proved the most fruitful were personal contacts made by friends or community leaders who knew me and those who gave me the opportunity to explain my project.

My only qualification for referrals was that the convert be actively involved in leading a Jewish life. It is a blessing to know that almost every contact person had more people to refer to me than I could possibly have interviewed.

I made it a policy *not* to contact a potential interviewee directly since this is a violation of Jewish custom and because an intermediary who had the confidence of the person could best present my project to him or her. Of the few attempts I made to do otherwise, most were met with a disaster of ruffled feathers and hurt feelings on both sides.

Once I was referred to the convert and able to speak directly, he or she was almost always enthusiastic about the opportunity to share his or her story. I then sent to each person information about the book, my story, and a list of questions to get the person started thinking in a more or less organized fashion about his or her experience (see appendix). The interviews themselves were very free flowing—often stream of consciousness—moving back and forth between recollections. People were often surprised by how much they had to say and how much they revealed about themselves, their hopes, dreams, fears. Most were very emotional, bringing forth laughter, tears, moments of despair or anger, and to the extent possible, I have retained painful as well as joyful details because we are each the sum of all our experiences.

With noted exceptions the majority of the interviews were conducted by me in person and were recorded on tape. Each interview lasted nearly two hours. Though I preferred to transcribe interview material myself, I eventually found this process was so lengthy and time consuming that I had to hire a transcriber.

With the transcribed interview on my computer, I edited out all the "uhms" and "ahhs" and "you knows" that pepper our spoken speech, and organized and rearranged the story so that it would read well as written material and flow from one idea to the next, though not necessarily always in chronological order. I always made an effort to preserve as much as possible the flavor of each individual's personal expression. I sent this first edited copy to the interviewee for comments, additions, and deletions.

There were several variations on this: As noted in their stories, "Ruth, Rachel, and Leah" gave me copies of the written portion of their *Bet Din*, and I reworked those into their interviews. Marcia Chertok, who lives in Israel, wrote her story, and she and I worked through the mail and fax to get it into its present form. Wave Korpi interviewed herself, and when I returned her edited manuscript she completely rewrote her story! Libby Bottero and Rebecca did similar extensive rewrites. One interviewee sat with me for five hours reworking her story, which was a satisfying experience for both of us.

Some people returned transcripts with spelling or grammatical errors checked, but essentially no revisions. Others deleted substantial portions of the material, either because they felt it was irrelevant or too revealing of their private life. Still others withdrew their stories completely, unwilling in the end to put their lives on such public display.

I offered each person the option of appearing under a pseudonym and a few chose to do this. Some used as their pseudonym one of the names they had contemplated as their Hebrew name. I also masked the identities of some people so that sensitive aspects of their stories could be told.

I am grateful to all the people whom I interviewed, for their interest in the project to begin with and for their trust in me and faith in the reader to treat their story with the respect due to another's unique life and spiritual quest.

From the first glimmer of an idea for this book, I have received the kind support of Rabbi Jim Rosen, who worked for many years with converts as associate rabbi at Baltimore's Chizuk Amuno Congregation. Now, as rabbi of the West Hartford, Connecticut, Beth El Temple, he continues that work and graciously agreed to write the foreword for *Finding a Home for the Soul*.

I received help from countless other people on this project, and my gratitude goes out to the proud friends and family of so many Jews by Choice, as well as the kind secretary, the thoughtful communal worker, and the tireless rabbi in Jewish communities across the country. My thanks to Daniel Mark Epstein for his encouragement and help with practical aspects of book publication. I am very appreciative of the assistance I received in Atlanta from our cousin, Aileen Smith, and in San Francisco from my longtime friend Kathi Wahed. Here at home I am always thankful to be a part of the East Bank Havurah and to those members who so willingly gave advice and editorial help, especially: Susan Atlas, Joyce Wolpert, Laurie Kovens, Judith Geller and Michael Raitzyk, Shelley and Dan Morhaim, Gideon and Linda Eisenberg, Marcia and Steve Glass-Siegel, and Becky Pepkowitz-Gilstrop. I am fortunate to belong to another community: the Friday Morning Group at the larger Foundation for Global Community, whose members support one another as we work together and individually to repair the world. Ever in my thoughts is my family—the Myrowitzs, Halls, Jim Witt—especially my mother, Norma, and my husband, Elliott, who believe in me, unfailingly.

Introduction

Finding a Home for the Soul is a collection of stories about people who search for greater meaning in life and discover Judaism's carefully wrought understanding and nurturing of the human spirit, manifested in ritual, prayer, and values. The stories will give the reader a feeling for the energy and love that people bring to Judaism and the varying yet deep satisfaction they take from it.

With *Finding a Home for the Soul,* I bring you, the reader, into the lives of people who graciously and courageously allowed the stories of their conversion and lives as Jews to be told. To each I owe a debt of gratitude, for without them and their generous participation my project would not have been possible. But more than that, I owe to each of these people a gentle reminder to all readers: Each story is a portrait, a *likeness* of the person, at a moment in time. It is *not* the person, him- or herself. Though this is as full a glimpse as one may ever get into a person's life, it is not everything there is to know about that person. I hope you will, therefore, feel *as if* you know each person, but understand that we cannot ever know any person completely, unequivocally.

As a social worker and psychotherapist by profession—and probably by inclination—I am fascinated to hear and I honor the details of people's lives. It is impracticable, however, to include within a book all the nuances of personal experience that people shared with me. It was a challenge, therefore, to delete material that was peripheral to the main themes of each person's story while remaining truthful to that person's individual expression. I hope that the words of each interviewee bring out the richness and fullness of lives thoughtfully lived. Nevertheless, these stories are but a moment in the life of each person. By the time you read this book, these people will have grown, retraced old patterns, or gone on to new ones. Their lives are, like Judaism, always in motion, always moving toward light and life, and, many would say, always toward God.

The stories don't follow in perfect progression. Our lives are not like that. Threads from childhood memories finally link up in adulthood with some experience that gives them completion. Jewish lives have always been remarkably full of mystery and miracles and almost-too-good-to-be-true coincidences, and so are the lives of many of those who convert.

My husband suggests that you read these stories as if you were lingering over a *Shabbat* meal, unhurried and content, getting to know a guest in your home. When we converts are asked about our conversions, we are often at a loss: "How much does this person really want to know? This is not an easy, quick thing to tell. Is this person really asking for the real story or just a glib pronouncement?" I asked each person to tell his or her story as if the reader really wanted to know, to understand, and was open to hear all the threads that must be followed to appreciate how someone comes to Judaism.

I have great aspirations for this book, guided by one simple enduring belief: Judaism is a beautiful religion and meaningful way of life that can bring a deep sense of spiritual connection to the Oneness we call *HaShem*—the Name.

My aspirations include: that those who are seeking Judaism, whether gentiles who are converting or born Jews who are returning, will find support for their quest in one or more of these stories; that families, both Jewish and non-Jewish, can read these stories and understand what it may mean for one of their members to choose Judaism; that the larger Jewish community will enjoy these affirmations of the blessing of leading a Jewish life and understand and value more fully those who come to Judaism; and that anyone who reads this book will have a deeper comprehension and appreciation of Judaism as seen through the eyes of those who have chosen it.

There are many wonderful books on *how* to convert to Judaism written by thoughtful, compassionate people, some of whom are themselves converts, all of whom are experts in conversion. There are also a few biographies of individual converts who have led extraordinary lives (see bibliography).

Finding a Home for the Soul is a book by and about the foremost authorities on leading *one* Jewish life. I wanted to tell the stories of "ordinary" people who make up the majority of those who convert to Judaism. We are people with whom most readers will be able to identify: we are your friends, family, neighbors, co-workers, and for fellow Jews, we are the people you *daven* with in *shul*; see at the kosher meat counter in the supermarket; wave to in the Hebrew school car pool line; serve with on committees; and stand together with for a *minyan* at a *shivah* house. Our stories attest that there is no one right way to be a convert and no one right way to be Jewish. There have been many delightful surprises and many gratifying affirmations in this project. I have been surprised at the variety of experience reflected in these stories, and gratified that my assumptions about the experience of conversion have been borne out by so many people.

My only criteria in seeking people to be interviewed were that the individual sees him- or herself as a committed Jew, and since I usually was referred by a third party, the community sees the interviewee that way, as well. I also assumed that commitment to Judaism would be expressed in the "practice" of Judaism to one degree or another. This reflects my bias that being Jewish—whether born or converted—is more than just "being," it is also "doing."

I received far more suggestions of people across the United States and in Israel than I could interview or include in the book. The number and scope of my interviews were limited only by time, energy, and money. If I had more of these resources, without a doubt I would have met many more wonderful people who would have lent new dimensions to the experience of conversion.

I have formed here a community of people, and just as in any community, there are some who are stronger in some areas and weaker in others. Most of us will not become "noted converts of the twentieth century." No one story is the definitive story of conversion to Judaism. To me that represents one of the many appealing aspects of Judaism—we are not judged by how well we measure up to some image of the "perfect" Jew, and though we may strive for an ideal that is meaningful to us, we can have a deeply satisfying Jewish life without achieving "perfection."

Though this is not a work of scholarly research (please see the preface for the process I used to contact and interview people), I included stories that would reflect the wide variety of Jewish expression and experience. There are no statistics to be gleaned from these pages to make recommendations, justify the funding of projects, or confirm theories, yet there are some recurring themes that are noteworthy, if only anecdotal.

There are no "leaps of faith" in these stories. People become Jewish gradually, which is both encouraged by tradition and, in truth, the only way to become Jewish. A few people in my project wondered about the use of the term *spiritual* or *spirituality* in talking about Judaism, while others profess no belief in God at all. As one rabbi said to me, those terms, as well as the belief in a personal God, have always been part of and belong in Judaism but have been used so long and so loudly in the larger culture to describe other forms of religious expression that they seem foreign to some, though not all, Jews.

Spiritual growth and spiritual experience in Judaism is both traditional and contemporary. Most of my interviewees encountered some spiritual experience in their coming to Judaism. This was described by some as a connection to those who perished in the Holocaust, by others as a second soul coming into them during the *mikveh*, in the miraculous *besherit** nature of their lives that led them to become Jewish, in the ongoing relationship and communication with God, and in countless other ways.

I imagined myself interviewing people who were settled and satisfied with their Jewish lives. I should have known, as is true in my own life, that if we do not continue to grow, we "die." There are, therefore, many stories that include dramatic shifts in people's lives as they strive to attain greater Jewish expression and deeper appreciation of their soul's quest. This includes people who have become increasingly traditionally observant, and others who are now less observant while remaining strongly identified as Jews and connected to their communities.

Very few people agonized about leaving their former faith, if they were connected to one to begin with. Most often they had left their childhood family religion behind years ago, often during adolescence. Many did not actively search for religion and some despaired that religion could ever be made meaningful enough to include it in their lives.

Some people had very negative experiences with their former religion. Others grew up happy in the Christianity practiced in their families but never felt committed to

*Derived from the root "to cut out," *besherit* is "to cut out in advance," i.e., preordained and therefore not just on this earthly plane.

the Trinitarian view of God. The fact that there are at least an equal number who have a neutral or positive view of their Christian upbringing suggests to me that conversion to Judaism is based on more than just dissatisfaction. It is also apparent that attitudes about one's religion have more to do with the way it is presented by parental and religious authorities and characteristics of the individual than with the actual doctrine of the religion.

I felt compelled to retain negative or positive comments that people made about their former religion, since their evaluations are completely personal and individual, just as their interpretation of Judaism is personal and individual. I also did not "correct" descriptions of Jewish practice, since I am not an authority on it and because I try to respect the wide variety of individual observance of *Yiddishkeit*.

Many people converted from Catholicism. Both Catholicism and Judaism are rich in rituals. A person who has left Catholicism may discover that ritual is a familiar anchor for new religious beliefs and values. Converts are often surprised to find the Jewish origin of many Christian rituals—the wine and *hallah* became the "blood and body of Christ"; the *mikveh* became the baptism; searching for the *hametz* became searching for Easter eggs (and these rituals have earlier antecedents and parallels in other cultures). Many of these Catholic families of origin involved intermarriage with a non-Catholic who may or may not have converted to Catholicism.

Readers will note that many interviewees grew up in families that were, for lack of a better term, "dysfunctional." As a professional social worker and psychotherapist, I believe that family dysfunction—broadly defined as the chronic or acute failure of a family to meet the emotional, physical, and/or mental needs of one or more of its members—occurs on a continuum and affects all families at one time or another. There is a cartoon that says it all: a banner proclaims "Adult Children of Functional Families Annual Convention" and only two people are in the audience. Nevertheless, it is a sad truth in our society that too many families are not functioning for the well-being of their members too much of the time.

It is important to note, however, that the majority of the people interviewed came to Judaism *after* having resolved earlier difficulties in their lives, and it is especially heartening that in Judaism they find a way of life that continues to promote their own health and well-being and that of their families.

Many converts would like to be more observant and feel deterred by their born Jewish spouses. A rabbi with whom I spoke said that the most challenging question he asks prospective converts is not the one they expect: "Will you be Jewish if—God forbid—your husband/wife dies or you are divorced?" Instead he asks, "What will you do if your born-Jewish husband/wife says, 'You've converted; it's enough. I don't want all this Jewish stuff in my life'?" The rabbi said he's gotten only one good answer: "Get a *get!*"

The reader will find many stories in which the convert's interest in leading a more fully Jewish life is the conduit by which the born Jewish spouse and sometimes even the extended Jewish family become more committed to Judaism.

Time and again, interviewees stressed the importance of community and a place in that community—for convert and born Jew alike! "One Jew is no Jew," as the saying goes.

The first and most difficult "community" gap for converts to bridge is the most obvious: they did not come from a Jewish family. Since so much of Jewish religious life centers around home rituals and celebrations, converts have found unique ways to supply the missing experiences. Naturally, many marry into Jewish families, though that may not always be the ideal setting in which to learn about Judaism because of physical (or psychological!) distance, and sadly, because many Jewish families simply do not know or no longer practice Jewish traditions. Some converts, especially those who are single, have adopted themselves into a Jewish family. Others learn through books, by observation, and hit and miss experimentation. Others join a group in their synagogue or community that, even if it does not actually teach Jewish practices, at least provides nurturance, support, and a feeling of belonging to the new Jew. For me and others in the book, *havurot** or *havurah*-like groups in synagogues provided opportunities to develop Jewish identity and experience the yearly cycle in a small, family-like group setting.

To address these issues, some communities offer participants in their "Introduction to Judaism" classes the opportunity to be paired with a family for a year.

One rabbi with whom I spoke came up with a unique idea to bring together new Jews and born Jews. Wouldn't it be provocative, he thought, to bring together his adult Intro to Judaism class and the teenage confirmation class at his synagogue? Although they are coming from completely different perspectives, both are making commitments to be Jews. What a unique opportunity for the two groups to share impressions when both are at stages of their lives to express openly what's really in their hearts. The rabbi was astounded when his idea met with angry and vociferous opposition from parents who feared such a plan would encourage interdating and intermarriage! It is possible, the rabbi thinks, that many born Jews are not aware that the memberships of most congregations—Reform and Conservative, especially— include a large number of converts, many of whom hold leadership positions.

Judaism and the Jewish people have been ambivalent about converts, though there were periods in Jewish history in which Jews actively sought proselytes. There are many injunctions in Torah and Talmud on the proper treatment of converts. The *Encyclopaedia Judaica* is full of stories of converts—famous and infamous—throughout history. One assumes that the ambivalence of later ages grew out of the persecution of Jews after they were forced out of *Eretz Yisrael*. In some Diaspora communities, gentiles threatened Jews with severe punishment, even death, for accepting converts to Judaism. Sometimes converts betrayed the Jewish communities that had accepted them. One can imagine that out of such fears grew the tradition many of us

---

Havurot is plural for *havurah*, which literally means group of friends. Some synagogues sponsor *havurot* in order for people to develop a stronger sense of community within a very large congregation.

have experienced—being turned away three times before anyone would speak to us of conversion.

There have always been some individuals and groups who were more warmly welcoming of converts than others. But it is a mistake to assume that the response is divided along liberal and traditional lines. One might expect to find greater acceptance of the convert among religiously liberal or secular Jews. However, sometimes these folks count their genetic and cultural heritage to be far more significant than their religious heritage. Consequently, since a non-Jew cannot become "genetically" Jewish—whatever that may mean—or easily culturally Jewish, liberal or secular Jews often dismiss converts. On the other hand, although Orthodox communities may make conversion more challenging for Jews by Choice, once people have converted they are likely to be accepted without question, and without reference to their former status. This can go to the extreme in some Orthodox groups that the convert is to have no further contact with his or her birth family—obviously a holdover from a time when such contact could prove extremely dangerous to the Jewish community.

The results of a recent demographic study* have sent a shock wave through the Jewish community. While the study showed that there are approximately 185,000 converts to Judaism in the United States, it also suggested that an equal number of born Jews have converted out. Furthermore, a substantial portion of Jewish persons (in some communities as great as 70 percent) are marrying non-Jewish partners. Children in these families are far less likely to be raised as Jews (22 percent) than in families in which the born-gentile spouse converts to Judaism (99 percent) (*Survey*, p. 16). To some Jewish leaders concerned with the continuity of the Jewish people, these statistics suggest the need for a more vigorous effort to encourage conversion, both for gentiles already married to Jews and anyone else interested in Judaism.

Although many of the people in the book have experienced isolated incidents of negativism directed at them and their conversion, most report warm—though sometimes puzzled—welcoming from both individuals and the Jewish community at large. Most interviewees were happiest and most satisfied in adjusting to Jewish life once they found a group or groups to join. They felt that acceptance depended in equal measure on how much effort and goodwill they put forth as on the welcome they perceived from others.

Surprisingly, few of the Jews by Choice I interviewed, even those who chose to convert after marriage to a born Jew, experienced the shunning by the Jewish family that, according to Jewish lore, is supposed to greet the non-Jew and his or her Jewish spouse. The non-Jewish family, though occasionally marked by reservation and even antagonism, was similarly accepting. This has something to do with the general increased openness of society to diversity, the increased assimilation of Jews, the postponement of marriage by career-oriented young people that leads parents to welcome any reasonably appropriate suitor, and other factors. I also feel that the overreaction

---

*Highlights of the CJF 1990 National Jewish Population Survey. A publication of the Council of Jewish Federations.

of Jewish as well as non-Jewish families, when it occurs, has more to do with personality, family dynamics, and family history than with actual religious and cultural tenets. When you put all of that together, it can create a potentially unpleasant, if not explosive, situation.

With all the ambivalence toward the convert, the Jewish community has historically regarded with antipathy the marriage of a born Jew to a non-Jew and has seen this union as "lost" to the Jewish people. It is especially noteworthy, therefore, that many of the people in my book converted to Judaism *after* marriage to a Jew. There is also a significant number of people who chose Judaism in the absence of a romantic relationship with a born Jew. This latter circumstance has been deemed the sign of a "genuine" conversion. I can agree with that, but I think to stop there does an injustice to the bonds between people that are one of the hallmarks of Jewish life.

Many converts have searched, often unconsciously, for a faith-based lifestyle, and it is only when they meet, fall in love, and decide to marry a Jew that they can be fully open to the possibility of becoming Jewish themselves. Though some may have been unwilling to convert at first, they agreed to raise children Jewishly in the belief that it is better to have just one religion practiced in the family. They then found that participating in Jewish family life had meaning for them beyond anything they had imagined, and that they had yearned for this and could now feel themselves a part of it.

My attitude, therefore, is that conversion is merely a point on a continuum of being Jewish, and the path that leads to the *mikveh* should not be more significant than the life led after emerging from the waters. The *mikveh*, in a sense, gives you the "legal" right to be a Jew, just as birth to a Jewish family gives the born Jew a right to be Jewish. In this age, it is how we live our lives after those events that makes us Jewish.

There is a saying that the true test of a genuine conversion is not whether the individual will be Jewish, not whether her children will be Jewish, but "Will the grandchildren be Jewish?" With that in mind, I set out to try to find converts who are currently *bubbes* and *zadies*. I am sure there are many converts who are *kvelling* over their grandchildren's Hebrew school plays and *bar* and *bat mitzvahs*. I am sorry I did not get to meet more of them (Marcia Chertok is the only grandparent as of this writing) so that they could share their stories with you, the reader. If you know such people, let them know that their lives have been a blessing on the Jewish people. We should all, born Jew and convert alike, look forward to watching our grandchildren grow into vibrant Jews.

The terms *Jew by Choice* and *convert* are used interchangeably. There are also *proselyte* and *ger* or *gioret*. Jew by Choice was ostensibly an improvement over convert, since it implied proactiveness and assertion of identity on the part of the new Jew, whereas convert is more passive. People seem to have a variety of opinions on what they prefer—thus the saying "Two Jews, three opinions." Some object to making any reference to the way a person becomes a Jew. Others are simply nonplussed by references to the fact that they or anyone else was not born Jewish. Most converts or Jews by Choice only feel like they are in that category for a period of time. Many report that their Jewish identity is so much a part of them and the way they live their lives that it is a rare occurrence for them to even think about ever having been non-Jewish. How a person responds to references about her or his status depends on individual personality and the circumstances under which such a reference occurs.

What one gets out of Judaism is—like almost anything in life—at least directly proportional to what one is willing to put in. Actually, my experience and that of others has been that from what we put into observance, the community, learning, and so forth we reap far more rewards. If one puts in goodwill and warm embrace, that is what one gets back. At the same time, it doesn't do much good to keep going back seeking acceptance from someone or some group that is never going to accept you.

There is always such a world of possibilities in Judaism that it would be impossible for a single person to absorb it all or do it all, so the importance of sharing resources as well as deriving support and sustenance in community is even greater. I believe the experience of living in community is what determines in large part the quality of the experience of the convert, and so in order to feel Judaism to the fullest, it is important for the new Jew to find a community that reinforces those areas of *Yiddishkeit* that are vital for him or her.

But the Jew, be she convert or born, is ultimately alone with her thoughts and feelings and it is at this level that we really become Jewish—although all the rest supports that. I think it is important to be willing to continue to risk, to challenge oneself, to deepen commitment to Judaism—after all it doesn't come "naturally," so to speak. We make it "natural" with each affirmation of our Jewishness.

What does it feel like to be a Jew? Often I feel as if wrapped up in a luminous garment—a prayer shawl. As if I have an extra layer to protect me from this sometimes-mad world. Being Jewish feels, too, like having a leg up in appreciating all the goodness that life makes possible.

I know where I am, who I am—I am grounded in the daily round of Jewish life. No matter what my worry or woe, I can find solace for it somewhere in Jewish teaching or practice. When it is time to celebrate the passages of my family's life, there is an abundance of blessings. To understand mortality and immortality, I have *Kaddish*; to feel the comfort of cycles, I have *Shabbat*, Rosh Hodesh,* and the holidays; to discipline my eating, I have *kashrut*.

Yes, it can feel confining to give up cheeseburgers forever or place limits on one's weekly schedule in order to observe *Shabbat*. We Americans, especially, have a horror of being fenced in. But there is a reason for observance beyond the ritualized keeping of the *mitzvot* (commandments). It is to deepen commitment, understanding, to

---

*New Moon, the first of each month according to the lunar calendar. Rosh Hodesh celebrations have been developed by Jewish women who see this time marker as uniquely related to women's own cycles.

"get" it at a deeper level. In this relentlessly secular, deconsecrated world joining the centuries-old ritual life of Judaism can be a transcendent experience.

For these and so many other reasons, I like being able to define myself as Jewish. I like tightening the circle around myself that gives me a distinct place in the scheme of things. I like feeling as if I belong to something bigger than myself—but not too big, so I still feel counted and important. I like being energetically involved in a life that few people choose to live—though I would not choose it just for that. I like feeling *and* acting on the responsibility that doesn't start or stop with me for making this world a better place. The puzzle to me is not why people become Jewish, but why more people don't become Jewish.

1

Finding a Home for My Soul

Catherine Hall Myrowitz

I remember asking someone the date of the *mikveh* when she "became" Jewish. She could not recall, she said; it had been some years back, and she had never kept count. I had not been to the *mikveh* yet but was preparing for that event—which includes an interview with the three rabbis of the *Bet Din* who ask you questions to satisfy themselves that you understand the principles and practices of Judaism. That date loomed prominently in my mind, and I could not imagine ever forgetting it. Now, if I sit and think about it I can recall that it was in 1982 and that it was before Pesah. However, although a marriage ceremony is the legal and dramatic status marker recognizable by all, you really make your marriage from everything that came before and everything that comes after. It is the same with conversion. The *mikveh* was a symbol of commitment, but the commitment started years before the legal act and continues years after. Both matter, but in different ways.

The lifetime of many people may include a reevaluation and recommitment to the faith of their family or community. But most people do not leave behind both faith and culture, so it is difficult for them to understand what it is like for the convert to Judaism. There is no one event that triggered my interest in Judaism, and my decision to convert was really the bringing to fruition of the disparate threads and paths my life has taken, as I believe is true of so many other Jews by Choice, that ultimately led me to the fulfilling life I lead today as a Jew.

I knew very little about Judaism when, as a nineteen-year-old, I made my first inquiries into the conversion process. I just knew that Judaism would be right for me, that I would love it once I was "there," and that foresight proved absolutely true many years later when I finally did convert. The more I learned about Judaism the more was confirmed and reconfirmed what I had always intuitively known about myself: I was meant to be a Jew.

After the *mikveh*, I felt newborn and vulnerable. In some sense I was this new entity but I was an adult. This wasn't just another transition, like graduating from college—my soul and my life were transforming. The range of my emotions mirrored the depth and breadth of this experience for me for the next year or so. I felt protective, a little defensive, and a lot scared. I also felt centered, on-course, at peace. This was right and proper. I had finally done it—done the thing that had brought me to the place I knew I wanted and needed to be probably since I was a child. I felt triumphant and special.

Although I believe that my conversion to Judaism is genuine, perhaps some day "righteous," there are some things that just won't convert and some that simply can't. While I feel deeply connected and a part of the spiritual tradition of Judaism, my place within the culture sometimes feels tenuous, and with the ancestral "peoplehood" and heritage even more so. I do not have experiences and memories like my husband—though in some ways his upbringing was more apple-pie American than mine, although both his parents are immigrants and observant in the Orthodox tradition. Because we are so close and share so much of our recent and current lives, I sometimes catch myself being puzzled and surprised that he did not celebrate Christmas, as I did. Just a little trick of the mind—but it speaks volumes about my differentness and the one reality that remains unchanged: how I grew up.

Yet, ironically, it is because of the way I was raised—in an open, loving home that embraced cultural diversity—that made it possible for me to choose Judaism. There were no deep ties to religious tradition or to a church, and that (although hardly the only factor) made it both easy and necessary for me to convert. My parents were not surprised and were supportive of my decision.

The things that connect me to my past are not nearly so strong as the things that connect me to my current life. There are, nevertheless, certain fond memories of childhood that cannot be recaptured or duplicated for my children—or myself! And there are certain fond memories that my children will have that are new to me—that's not particularly unusual given our modern culture—and many, of course, have absolutely nothing to do with Judaism. My two favorite foods, my mother's fried chicken and her mincemeat cookies, are off-limits for me as much because of being vegetarian as because of *kashrut* (she could fry a kosher chicken, although I doubt that there is kosher mincemeat!). And my children's excitement over the first snowfall of the year (and mine too!) has no similar attachment in my California childhood.

We send our children to a Jewish day school because I want help in transmitting all the nurturing nuances of Jewish life and experience—and I get to be part of that, too. Recently, my daughter, who excels in all school subjects, got her highest marks in Jewish law and customs, and my son proudly practiced his line—"*siman tov u'mazal tov*" (auspicious signs and good fortune)—for the program in which all the first graders were presented with their first *siddur*. I understand that my children are the bridge between my past and my present—they are my genetic link to our Jewish heritage.

One of the distinct advantages of having children is that one can relive one's childhood through them and make improvements as needed for both the children and for oneself. Still, I would not replace my past with the life that I am living now. I would not be who I am otherwise, so I am grateful for both.

Both Jews and gentiles are concerned about how I could give up Christmas, and that season was for some years the time I thought most about the fact that I was not born Jewish. With each passing year it becomes a more distant, though fond, memory.

A friend of mine, also a convert, likens Christmas to a great *Shabbat*. It is a day, like *Shabbat,* when time stands still, when the whole family is together mainly to *be* together, when the cares and concerns of ordinary life stop; there is no place to go, no stores are open, no one is driving on the streets. But it happens only once a year, and that is the secret of Christmas, how to understand it—it happens only once a year. On that one day there is an obligation to create magic, a magical feeling of having everything you have ever wanted: love, connection, wealth. Sometimes it worked, sometimes it didn't. When it worked it was wonderful, when it didn't, well, it might be awful but you could look forward with hope to next year. As a child on the afternoon of Christmas Day I would think, "Oh! Now we have to wait 365 more days for Christmas to come again." What a letdown.

Nevertheless, I believed in Santa Claus long after other children had not only caught on but grown cynical. There were no religious connections for me, but now I see the myth of Santa Claus as an expression of the need to have faith, trust, belief. Christmas itself was not a religious holiday for our family, and although we received presents, of course, the occasion was never one for all-out spending to satisfy every whim or fantasy. My mother really disliked the holiday due to the unhappy memories she had from her Depression-era childhood. For my father, traditions of any kind were simply not rational and, therefore, optional.

The celebrations in my family's calendar were therefore primarily family celebrations and had meaning only as defined by our family. For example, Thanksgiving week was made more special because my father's birthday, November 25, coincided with the holiday. Our family's observances can hardly compare to the celebrations, rooted in Torah and history, that occur throughout the Jewish calendar, giving a sense of transcendence to the individual Jewish family's "Tradition!" of which Tevye of *Fiddler on the Roof* so fervently sings.

Imparting tradition of any kind was not "traditional" in my family. Just as Tevye's daughters began to see new possibilities in the changing conditions of their world, the Depression-era and World War II disruptions that my parents' generation suffered almost demanded that people leave behind their past—good or bad—and look to the future.

As I got older I became the "Christmas spirit" in our household. I enjoyed the ritual of giving that began with Thanksgiving, and I planned lengthy lists of Christmas cards to send and cookies to bake and give away. Mostly, though, I was merely embellishing on the real meaning imparted to me by my parents—holidays were just a good reason for spending time with the people you cared about and who cared about you.

If Christmas is a reminder of what I have left behind, Pesah shines as a beacon for the direction my life has taken. I am most likely to reflect on becoming Jewish when I am right in the middle of cleaning and changing my kitchen over to make it *Pesadikh.* During the elaborate and thorough preparations for Pesah, I do say to myself, sometimes only half in jest, "Why do I do this?"—but as the first *seder* begins, I sigh with relief as if I, too, had made it out of Egypt.

With this and other experiences, I have often wondered, "Do I feel this way because I am a convert?" Not according to the following story a rabbi told at a Pesah service: A Jewish merchant thinks his business would do a little better if he converted to Christianity. So he and his wife convert, and, lo and behold, business is worse because now neither the gentiles nor the Jews will buy from him. He tells his wife they might as well convert back. "Fine," she says, "but could we wait till after Pesah?"

Pesah, when all is said and done—literally—is my favorite holiday. In a very different way from Rosh Hashanah and Yom Kippur it is a cleaning out of the soul. The weeks of preparation beforehand and the week of Pesah itself are really a time to reevaluate what you prize in the material world and what you can leave behind. I find myself looking forward to Pesah with some apprehension, knowing that I will not get everything done that I would like and knowing that I will have to find a way to make that all right. But I know, too, that Pesah will always do what it is supposed to with my soul, and I will emerge refreshed, renewed in spirit, and grateful.

As I consider all that Jewish religious life provides, the small daily observances, including *kashrut, Shabbat* every week to renew the family spirit, and a festival every so often to make a grander connection to the Source of life, I realize that my thoughts are rarely on what I have given up but on all that I have gained.

And Jewish life is a process always in process. You can't just *be* Jewish, you are always *becoming* Jewish. I see that even for those who are born Jews, as my husband was. He continues to renew his commitment and find new avenues to express himself as a Jew. If you stop struggling and growing with anything that you do, you stop "be-ing" that, and it becomes a factoid and not a living thing. And Judaism is a religion to be lived.

I know now that I have always been in search of religion and of God. I separate the two because I believe religion exists without God and God can be found without religion. There is yet another important element as well: spirituality—as I define it, feeling the presence of God in everything. Even with God in religion, spirituality can be elusive. However, for this human, all three were imperative and even followed a natural evolutionary course.

When I was four years old, our family moved to Madrid. My parents, who worked for the U.S. government there, had very advanced ideas about how Americans should behave in a foreign country. For five years we lived as much as possible like Spaniards, and it was my parents' fondest desire that their children should learn to speak Spanish fluently. To this end my younger brother and I attended Spanish schools, the best of which, my parents were told, were Catholic convent schools.

I had a mixed experience in the schools. While some nuns were extremely loving and nurturing, others felt a reawakening of the spirit of the Inquisition when faced with the infidel posing as an American, nominally Protestant, little girl. For years after the experience in the last school, which was horrible, I would cross a street rather than walk on the same side as a nun. Nevertheless, there were some aspects of a religious life that had a positive impact on me.

Spain in the 1950s was a country deeply steeped in religious life and bitter remembrance of their Civil War of the 1930s, which was recalled as if it were yesterday. I became fluent in Spanish practically overnight, and this gave me access to chats with the neighbors who, marveling at my precocity with their language, shared their lives with me. This included reminiscences of the hardships of the war—"We were so hungry we ate banana peels" (very impressive to a little girl)—and glimpses into a religion that informed every moment of every day.

The Spanish calendar was centered on celebrations and observances of Catholic religious events. People carried rosaries in their pockets for use on the bus or in the subways. Laden with grocery bags, they popped into the neighborhood church for confession or prayer. First communions were extremely solemn and lavishly celebrated with processions of little girls and boys, looking like miniature brides and grooms, closing down whole streets in the middle of the day. Even the herbal plaster that our maids insisted should be applied to my chest when I had a particularly bad cold was blessed, somehow, by a saint. (I didn't feel particularly blessed when it finally had to be torn off my chest like an enormous Band-Aid.) Everybody had two birthdays: their own birthdate and the day of their patron saint.

As this life comes back to me in memories after almost forty years, it seems clear to me that there was something deeply soothing about having religion guide one's days and weeks and months—even for a visitor.

Between school and my cross-cultural dialogues, I assumed that I was Catholic. I was shocked when my parents told me this was not so. I was especially disappointed when I found out that Protestants did not have saints cards, which were collected and exchanged among the schoolgirls just like baseball cards here in the States—"I'll give you two Maria Teresas for one Maria de los Dolores with the plastic tears."

Shortly thereafter, my parents took me to the nondenominational Protestant services held at the Torrejon Air Force Base in a makeshift chapel in the auditorium—the same room in which I'd seen a magician turn Kleenex into ice cream a few weeks before.

A profoundly altering experience occurred when I was nine or ten years old and back in the United States. My parents took us to see *Judgment at Nuremberg* at a drive-in movie. The idea was that we would fall asleep out of boredom, but instead I watched the movie transfixed. The film about the trials of Nazi criminals includes actual footage of the death camps. The monstrous and horrible things that I had seen were actual events and not mere science fiction fabrications that could be dismissed with other scary movies. For months after seeing this film I had waking and sleeping nightmares, and I became convinced that I had been in a concentration camp; why else should this continue to be so vivid and disturbing to me?

After a five-year hiatus back in the States, my father decided to take us overseas again, this time to a place physically closer to home but culturally light-years away—Brazil. Nothing in the materials provided to "acculturate" foreigners prepared us for the extremes of poverty and desperation we encountered there. The sheer brutality of life in the northeastern Brazilian city of Recife devastated us at first, but we eventually learned to cope, mostly, it is sad to say, by deadening ourselves to the misery around us.

My family's apartment was brand-new and modern by Recife standards, though we spent three months without running water, had no electricity on Sundays, and never had a phone. Across the very busy Avenina Boa Viagem (Good Voyage Avenue) was the ocean and the beautiful white beach ringed by the reefs for which Recife is named. Far out past the third reef one could see sharks on the prowl for unwary "Jangadeiros," fishermen on their precarious balsa log rafts. Each Sunday, Boa Viagem would become clogged with carloads of city folks on their way to spend the day at the beach. And each Sunday, right in front of our apartment, someone would be killed or maimed by a speeding, reckless driver. We eventually stopped looking out the front windows. We became habituated to the poverty and disease everywhere—my first experience with homelessness, which is now so commonplace in the United States. My mother attempted to do something by working in an orphanage and helping artists who had been imprisoned because of their political views. In contrast to this setting were the incredibly gracious upper-class Brazilians who were among our friends. Through one of these friendships, I decided to attend a Brazilian girls' school, which, as in Spain, was a Catholic convent. My social-work career may have begun when I wrote a paper, in Portuguese, concerning the advantages of family planning. Fearing an international incident, my parents called the school and requested that the paper be returned to us, unread.

The experience of life in Brazil had lasting repercussions on my life. This was manifested by my obsession with finding out who God was—if of course God existed, and the evidence seemed scanty where I was living.

One of my quests, which seems superficial but symbolized what was going on internally, was my need to find just the right cross to wear. Would it be a crude, wooden one purchased at the "feira," the street market? Or a jeweled one from the Dutch miner turned precious-stone dealer? Or perhaps a simple gold cross on the thinnest of chains, unobtrusive but evident? I simply could not put Jesus and God together. I read *The Robe*, that melodrama of rational deification, and *The Magnificent Obsession*. I talked my parents' ears off and tried to get them to define God. I attended the makeshift church at the library of the American School, but that was in part motivated by a boy I was interested in and thereby sullied the purity of purpose that I supposed should mark my search for God.

We left Brazil before I came to any conclusions. I never did buy a cross.

Our return to the United States was punctuated by a trip through the South to visit my father's family in northern Florida farm country. After leaving behind the horrific living conditions of most Brazilians, I was stunned to discover U.S. poverty that rivaled Brazil's. It really poked a hole in the self-righteous proclamations of Americans in Brazil, including mine, and began my own experience of disillusionment—and eventual renewal—that marked the 1960s.

But for the next two years, my life was typical for a high school student. I had a very close group of friends, one of whom was Jewish. Lani (Ilana) shared with us not only the dancing, music, and food that marked her culture, but more importantly a view of life that was joyous, liberating, and grounded in proud tradition. Several of us from that group graduated early from high school, and Lani planned to live in Israel until college started the following fall. I got very excited about her descriptions of *kibbutz* life, and my parents allowed me to investigate the possibility of going to Israel, but finally decided that they were too concerned about my safety. It was a decision they always regretted.

Although my family was loving and close it had one flaw—a major one for me. My parents, especially my father, had a boundless belief in the future, and my mother, especially, had the ability to endure the unendurable for the present, based on her certainty that the future would be better. This model of existence required concentrating on positive feelings and pretending that sorrow and pain did not exist, or at least ignoring them.

Sometimes this denial went on for months or years at a time, as when my mother developed cancer and was an invalid for months. My aunt came to take care of us, and life continued as if there wasn't a very sick woman on the couch day after day. It never occurred to anyone, as it would today, that we should discuss these issues or that our anxieties or anger might need an outlet. My parents really believed that it was a greater kindness not to "burden" children with "adult" problems. But children know and bear so much more than adults ever imagine. I spent the second half of seventh grade very depressed, silently terrified my mother would die and never able to express to anyone my fears.

When I was in college, my parents' method of coping with life stopped working for me. Although by all external measures I was a high-functioning and successful person, I felt a constant sadness I could not shake. After I graduated from college, I found a well-paid job and got into psychotherapy. I see this now as the beginning of my spiritual quest.

One evening during these years, the hundredth anniversary of the birth of Einstein was celebrated by our local PBS station. For some reason I was struck by the explanation of the theory of relativity and its implications for the way we view the universe and even "reality." These ideas resonated strongly in me and were "proof" to me that God really did exist. This was very exciting. Belief had been so elusive for me, and now I could believe! I decided I should explore religion anew, and I thought that the best thing to do would be to start from my own background.

Early in my college career, I *had* explored conversion to Judaism. I had been a part of a group called "People for Israel" and was friends with many Israelis and American Jews, one of whom was my roommate for a time. She suggested that I talk to her rabbi and attend services with her parents at their synagogue, which I did. The rabbi was wonderful, but the synagogue didn't seem much different from the Episcopal church I had attended as a child, and I realized that Judaism and I were not ready for each other.

So for the year after the Einstein program, I spent a lot of time reading and attending various churches, from the Episcopal church of my youth, with its lovely but remote service, to the more rousing fundamentalist churches held in movie theaters on Sunday mornings, where people testified, "Jesus Christ is my personal savior." I attended the Unitarian/Universalist society but although they professed the unity of God, they steadfastly avoided the mention of God. I did like the U/U involvement in social issues. The stumbling block that nagged me throughout this search was my inability, try though I might, to believe in Jesus as deity. I read, I studied, I prayed, I contemplated, I talked with my friends, and I could not do it. Yet my belief in God deepened.

During this period I was also involved in learning sign language and working as an advocate in the deaf community. I decided to attend graduate school and was very pleased to be accepted at the University of Maryland, since it would put me close to Gallaudet University. For the first year the curriculum of the social work program pretty much precluded normal life, but I managed to attend one meeting of the Ethical Society, which appealed to me because of its emphasis on values so much like those of social work itself. At midyear, I moved into a new apartment in what I was soon to discover is the Jewish neighborhood in town. I remember that the abundance of synagogues and even my first forays into the merchant district were enchanting to me. (My mother had the same reaction when she came to visit, so there *is* something tangibly different and engaging about this area.) One of my favorite places to eat was a slightly grungy deli that seemed to me steeped in an air of a different world.

So by the time I was introduced to the East Bank Havurah, I was really ready for everything it had to offer.

Probably the most significant single entity that affected my conversion was the *havurah*, which I joined in the summer of 1980. I found out about it through people I had met at a wedding of mutual friends. The wedding was interfaith—Jewish and Catholic—and it became a lively topic of discussion during the reception with my newly met acquaintances, who invited me to attend a *havurah Shabbat* get-together the next week.

Later that weekend I was at a party talking about the lovely wedding I had just attended. A tall, quiet, handsome man sitting across the circle was listening to my animated description, and in a few days he called me to ask me for a date. That was Elliott, the man who would become my husband. Weeks later he told me of a dream he'd had about an old friend from childhood days, and I realized that one of my new friends from the wedding and the *havurah* was his long-lost friend, Harold.

Although all these events seemed distinctly separate at the time, they eventually became so blessedly interconnected that the only way to describe what occurred is to say *besherit*—it was meant to be. Harold and his fiancée, Louise, who also converted, became our close friends. We danced together at our weddings, attended our *brises* and baby namings, and sat together at *shivahs*. Although our paths in Judaism have parted, since they now follow a *hasidic* way of life, we remain deeply connected to each other.

For many months my participation in the *havurah* was an activity I did on my own. Shortly after joining, I attended a *havurah*-sponsored retreat in the western Maryland countryside. My group arrived too late for Friday night services and almost too late for dinner, but the next morning many of us arose at dawn to walk to a nearby meadow still misty and wet with dew to do the *birkhot hashahar*.* In what was to become a *havurah* "tradition," the *brakhahs* were done with movements—each person either creating or following the leader with some bodily expression of praise and gratitude to God.

On the way back from the meadow I chatted with another retreat participant about how being out in the country like this reminded me of my grandparents' farm in Idaho. "Oh," he said, "I didn't know there were any Jews in Idaho!" That was my first experience of the sometimes not-so-subtle probing of my background that people undertake to figure out if I'm Jewish.

I know that for most of the participants at that retreat the weekend was a challenge of one kind or another. For me it was a challenge in a hundred ways, and yet, although I recall feeling a range of emotions from scared to bored to elated, I did not turn away then or since.

I was fortunate to join the *havurah* at a time when all of the people who came were in the throes of renewal. The atmosphere of the *havurah* was joyous, open, compassionate, accepting. We all sought a grounding in traditional Judaism without locking our souls into rituals before we could trust their meaning. It was a perfect place to be a convert because there I "grew up" Jewishly. I rarely felt that everybody but me knew the right page, the right melody—even the people who did know made it okay to be a beginner. Everyone had something to offer—even me. My seeking out Judaism had deep meaning for some who were coming back after turning away.

The first thing I noticed about the *havurah* was that God or "*HaShem*" figured prominently in people's conversations. People talked as if they knew God personally, as if God were a member of the family—albeit a very important one—a partner in the mystery of life. Submission to God's will did not require self-abnegation but faith that what was righteous in oneself would move one with the path of God, whatever that might be.

And the paths that led people to the *havurah* were so varied as to defy generalization. (This is still the case.) Therefore, the *havurah*, without formal agreement, was nonjudgmental. Who could know the pain or joy that took someone away from Judaism or the pain or joy that brought him back? Who could judge the wisdom of someone's passion for a psalm or another's revulsion to it? All the answers are not known by anyone—only that staying on the path toward God is the answer.

The *havurah* is like a family as much as it is like a synagogue, and it became my Jewish family. I found and still find within it all that I had been seeking in a religious life—God, religion, values, ethics, a way of life, social action, spirituality, and community.

---

*The early morning blessings are "a series of blessings that deal with the body, freedom and bounty, and gratitude for waking up to a new day. This section [of the prayerbook] is designed to help people move from the physical waking up each morning to a spiritual reawakening. It tries to ease you into the prayer service [which follows]" (Strassfeld and Strassfeld, *The Second Jewish Catalog*, p. 270).

Before joining the *havurah*, days and weeks rolled into one another, their meaning determined by the external world. But as I slowly began to observe *Shabbat*, the rhythm of the week completely changed. Ritual changed the rhythm of my life.

By the time I decided to attend a conversion class, I had already been *davening* for over a year with the *havurah*. My decision to seek an Orthodox conversion was both pragmatic and nonrational. I wanted my conversion to be accepted by the most scrutinizing elements of society: the rabbis in Israel and Elliott's family. I was also drawn to Orthodoxy just because it was more stringent and unbending: it seemed to provide a ballast for my as yet ethereal Jewishness.

Over the years, the locus of authority for the authenticity of my Judaism has evolved. A friend recently told me a story he heard from his rabbi: If I am looking over at my neighbor and I am disturbed by his lack of *Shabbat* observance, then I must ask myself what is lacking in my *Shabbat* observance. My Jewishness has always meant looking inward while being part of the increasingly larger Jewish circles in which I live. But the core is always me and God struggling and searching for the right path for my soul to take.

If the *havurah* almost universally welcomed me with open arms, there were no such emotions in my husband's family. All family members are now lovingly connected and involved in our lives, but this was not so at the outset of Elliott's and my interest in each other.

Everything that made my family open to my embrace of Judaism and my choice of a husband from a different culture and religion—mainly the belief that it was necessary and often desirable for children to do something different from their parents— was simply nonexistent in Elliott's family.

Despite my understanding of these things and my desire to be understanding, I was saddened and bewildered by the response of Elliott's family. For the first year and a half of my relationship with Elliott, I was never privy to any of the behavior that has since come to typify our interactions with the family—the warmth, humor, loving concern, and eager involvement in each other's lives. And although it was very hard for me it was truly harder for Elliott, who, with emotional strength and determination, held on both to me and to his family, refusing to let go of either. We had to be sure about each other, we had to really get to know each other, because we would continue to stand alone until the family came around. We plumbed the depths of feeling, attachment, and commitment.

My parents, who by this time lived in Washington State and were therefore aware only of the little we chose to tell them about the state of affairs here, were instrumental in the healing of the two families. My mother recounts the story of a visit to our family doctor she made before coming back east for the wedding. She told him that Cathy was engaged but that there was a problem—the groom-to-be is Jewish. The doctor huffily said he didn't see that that was a problem; he knew many nice Jewish boys, including himself! "But Doctor," said my mother, "the problem is not with *us*, it's with *them*."

Things with the family began to soften after the *mikveh*. I recall a social occasion in which my future mother-in-law recounted to me a conversation she'd just had with a friend. Upon being told that the "girl" over there was Elliott's fiancée, the woman said "Well, she's pretty, but is she Jewish?" My mother-in-law was pleased to reply positively *and* pleased to tell me she was pleased.

When my parents came for the wedding, they met Elliott's family for the first time. My mother behaved as if nothing untoward had ever happened and dove right into the spirit of things. My dad and father-in-law discovered they both knew a thing or two about slivovitz (plum brandy). My parents' open, warm embrace of everyone was a soothing balm that encouraged me to relax my guard. My mother told me she hoped I would call my new in-laws "Mom and Dad," and both she and my father treated Elliott as if he were *their* prodigal son, too, and called him "Elli" as his parents do. Without a doubt, my parents and Elliott's parents have enjoyed the warmest in-law relationship in our families.

It was, therefore, with my parents' gentle persuasion that I began to heal the wounds of the previous two years. In the past, anyone who had deeply hurt me, I merely cut out of my life. This was a new experience for me: to forgive without an apology, to remember and go on anew. Good skills for the newly Jewish.

Now, I cannot imagine anyone who has a warmer, more loving relationship with her mother- and father-in-law than I do or a more cordial extended family.

Barely a year after we were married, we had a baby and my father died. These three life events, following so closely on one another, bonded me more firmly to Judaism and reaffirmed for me the wisdom of Jewish ritual and community life.

My father and I were very close. He was a nineties father in the fifties: he was available and involved in all his children's lives—not that this involvement was always welcome, of course! As his children grew older and remained unmarried, he became increasingly anxious about becoming a grandfather. When I got pregnant unexpectedly soon after our marriage, my parents became happily involved in giving advice and planning for their role in their first grandchild's life. We made elaborate plans for them to come to the East Coast and spend three months with us after the baby's birth.

I was disturbed, however, as my parents delayed their trip east, for what seemed to me to be flimsy and evasive reasons on my father's part. Our delight when they finally arrived could not mask the disturbing sight of my father's haggard appearance—clearly, he was ill. But they were full of bubbly news of the purchase of the new sailboat on which they planned to live in the Olympic Sound, and my father helped us put together the crib, a task we'd saved just for his suddenly not-so-nimble hands.

Our daughter, Rachel, was born beautiful and healthy, to the delight of both families. Although she was not my in-laws' first grandchild, she was the first girl. I ignored my father-in-law when, through tears of happiness, he teased, "Don't worry, next time it will be a boy!" My father, concerned that he might have something contagious, felt he should not hold the baby.

Rachel's naming took place in the home of the *havurah* members with the largest space. Elliott and I had planned for hours what we would say. We made up a psalm by taking meaningful verses from various other psalms to make an acrostic of Rachel's name. The *havurah* had just begun to have babies, so there was lots of joy and energy borne of experience and hopes. We had a Torah by then, and my in-laws participated, as did my mother; my father was too ill to attend. The joyous celebration and moving participation of all the *havurah* mitigated my in-laws' concerns at the "unorthodox" nature of the service, and my mother recounted for my father every detail of this wondrously different ceremony. Shortly after that my father was diagnosed with terminal cancer.

Rachel and I spent every day of the next five months with my parents—most of the time in hospitals whose relaxed visitation policies suggested how near death he really was.

On the day of my father's death I called the only funeral home I knew of—the Jewish one. I carefully explained that I was Jewish but my father was not, and I was assured several times that they would, indeed, care for his body. Several hours later the funeral home called back and said that they could not take my father's body and had returned it to the hospital. I was furious. I felt betrayed—and I had no idea what to do next. I was embarrassed to have to explain this news to my mother, but she calmly and kindly insisted, "Do not think of it another moment." I was amazed at her continued fortitude for reconciliation.

Although my mother did not want a funeral, as my father no doubt requested, she did want a memorial service. The rabbi who married us graciously conducted the service in his home with many of our friends attending. We then flew down to Florida where my father was buried next to his parents in a cemetery in a tiny town in the northern part of the state where generations of Halls have been farmers and our family still owns land.

The night of our return home, the *havurah* gathered at the same home where our *Sheva Brachas** had been held and where Rachie had been named, so that I could say *Kaddish* for the first time. When we arrived, the room was filled with people. People shared their impressions of my father and their own stories of bereavement, as we often do on such occasions in the *havurah*. I recounted a great blessing from my father. When we lived in Brazil a close friend of my father's had died and his daughter grieved heavily, berating herself for not being a better daughter. My father was upset by this and told me that when he died he wanted me to know that I had always been the daughter he wanted and never to feel guilty for anything I thought I might have done.

Death is, after all, hardest on the living. I was never more grateful for Judaism, therefore, than after my father's death. The opportunity to say *Kaddish*, which I chose to do once a week at the *havurah*, meant so much. It was a balm to my immediate hurt feelings; later, it was a confrontation with my denial; now it has become a bridge

---

*The *Sheva Brachas* are recited during the wedding ceremony, and then traditionally for seven nights afterward when the bride and groom are feted by friends. We got together for one festive meal with friends the week after our marriage.

between us as his presence fades from my life; and of course *Kaddish* is an affirmation of the completeness of the universe that I understand as God. *Yizkor* and *Yartzeit* provide a continued confirmation that he was vital to my life and still is, in memory.

I felt sad for the other members of my family because they did not have the safety net of religious belief to care for them in the first year of their bereavement—to reach those regions of feeling that only faith can heal. I understand now that for religion to have any solace, it must be practiced even when you don't think you "need" it. The reality for me is that I "need" it every day and I am grateful every day that I am Jewish because Judaism is an "Every Day" religion.

Year has passed into year, their flow marked by the celebrations and commemorations of the Jewish calendar. We increase our involvement each year in ritual, community, learning, and *tikkun olam*. My son, David's, *bris* was the most recent major life-cycle event in our nuclear family and probably the last time that my Jewish identity faced any serious confrontation.

Our home was filled with the happy sounds of friends and family, and as David was brought down the steps, a friend quieted the crowd by beginning to sing with haunting melody the verse from Psalm 27, *"Ahalt sha'alti me'et HaShem"*:

One thing have I asked of the Lord, this do I desire:
That I may dwell in the house of the Lord
All the days of my life,
To behold the graciousness of the Lord,
And to enter into God's sanctuary.

I realized at this moment, as I had similarly with Rachel's naming, but more so than with any other ritual that involved only the dedication of my own soul—more than *huppah*, more than *mikveh*, more than *Shabbat* candles—that I was a Jewish woman, joining generations of faith-full Jewish mothers, and that the sacrifice of my son's foreskin was a covenant I made, not just for myself, but for him and all our descendants. It was a memorable moment.

2

I Was There

Ginny

More and more I have come to the understanding that whether or not the convert is accepted by his or her family or by the Jewish or gentile community is more a matter of interpersonal dynamics, family history, and individual personalities than Jewish law or Christian beliefs.

As Ginny tells her story, it is clear that the motivation to become Jewish came from something beyond herself, another place, another time. Ginny exerted her ability to make a decision and chose to follow this deeply felt longing, which in some way came from the Holocaust.

But those around us, who should be closest to us, are not always ready to accept where we must go. Our choices are never without consequences.

Jewish teachings tell us both to rock the boat and keep still; to be modern and carefully tend the heritage; to be for ourselves and for others; to wrestle with God and accept God's plan. In the struggle to find a balance we must discover both the truth and a way to be true to ourselves.

When I was growing up, my parents put a lot of value on the family and the importance of education, very similar to Jewish values. If you put my parents and my husband's parents side by side, they'd agree on almost everything except the fact that one was Catholic and one was Jewish. My family, however, had this problem with following through. A family event or holiday was planned because it was so important to my mother that everybody get together, but somewhere along the line it would just fall apart, and it would be miserable, and everybody would be just sitting there. My husband's family carried it off, for some reason. I think that is a lot of what brought me to Judaism—the friends and family, the aspects of being in the home with the family together.

There's more of a pattern or ritual for people getting together in Jewish families. In Christianity it's more of a free-for-all. We had Sunday afternoon dinners. That was our tradition, but there was no ritual around it, no written-down tradition that this is what you do; whereas on Friday night, you light candles and there are lots of things to say other than grace, which took all of thirty seconds in our family. The built-in home rituals are a major difference. In Christianity, there really aren't any that I can think of. Where did the rituals go? What did the Puritans do? They must have had rituals.

Growing up, I had several Jewish friends. My elementary school was predominantly Catholic—Irish Catholic—but there were maybe four or five Jewish children

14

in my grade to whom I always felt very attracted. I felt admiration for them and felt drawn to them. That started my interest in Judaism, although I didn't make the connection at the time that what made them attractive was their Jewishness. I was fascinated with what they did and when I went to their houses, I was really interested in what was different and what that felt like. It was probably just that everything around me was so Irish Catholic that it was nice to see something different. I was just an observer when I went to my friends' to play, and I asked some questions. I have always been an observer.

The next thing that made an impression on me happened in high school. I went on a summer trip to Europe when I was fifteen. Most of the other kids on the trip were Jewish. I am not sure exactly what effect that had—it just *was*. The major thing that did affect me was that we went to the Anne Frank house.

There were things that had touched me about Judaism before, but if I had to point to where it started consciously it was definitely that visit. I sat in the house for a long time. For some reason, it was not crowded that day, and I sat in a room by myself. I had this overwhelming feeling of connection with something—something really, really affected me. I don't know what it was. I would like to think that there was some connection to the events and people back then. There were all those lost souls, and somehow there was a reason for my feeling of connection. That was the beginning.

I didn't feel my conversion was something that I *chose*. It was like it chose me. From that point on (at Anne Frank's house), it was as if something was driving me toward Judaism, and I really had no choice. I mean, I did, but it was something that was very compelling for me to do. Whether it was to make amends for those souls or whether there really is some kind of . . . *I was there*. My parents were there. There are times that I feel that maybe my real parents were there. Maybe I should have been born to somebody who was killed there. I don't know. I don't tend to buy into that kind of stuff normally, but it is a gut feeling. It just felt right.

I've probably said this out loud to maybe three people in my life. It is not something I normally say, just because I think people will look at me strangely. I always had dreams, lots of different ones, about being in the Holocaust. If they were all the same dream, I guess it would be a better story, but I have had lots and lots of dreams about the Holocaust. That has reinforced my feeling that I was there or some part of me was there.

I came back terribly depressed from that trip. I felt lost and could not connect back to my family or back to school. It was really a very difficult time. I was going into my junior year, so it was time to think about college. I ended up applying to Brandeis plus a few others, and I got into all the schools that I had applied to. It wasn't a very hard decision—I chose Brandeis. Again, it was that I had to. I kept trying to think of the other schools and what it would be like there, but I just couldn't picture myself any place else but Brandeis.

I knew from the day I got there that I went there to convert. When I walked on campus, it was like, "Yeah, that is why I am here." I think almost immediately I started connecting to anyone who would tell me anything at all about Judaism and tried to get as much information as I could. It is a great place to go and learn. There are all different levels of Jewish life going on—from the very intellectual, to the services, to arts and crafts. You could do anything you wanted. That certainly helped to end my depression. I felt at home.

At Brandeis, I started going to Saturday services. The kids who go to services voluntarily in college are probably a select few who are pretty knowledgeable. I'm glad I found the services. They were in a beautiful chapel. There were three chapels around a pond. One was Protestant. One was Catholic. One was Jewish. The first two were totally unused. In the Jewish chapel were student-led Saturday morning services, and women led services and read from the Torah. This really clicked for me because the services—the whole experience—were so wonderful. There were also Friday night services, and afterward somebody would have an *oneg*, and everybody was invited; then we had dinner together at the cafeteria. Arrangements were made beforehand so nobody had to pay—you didn't have to carry anything. It was so easy, and it was all right there. It was such a nice community—nothing you can find in real life that I have discovered. And I've tried.

I got to Brandeis wanting to ask everybody everything that I could think of and, eventually, connected with a few people strongly—people who were willing to share their knowledge. I met my husband there, and our relationship started with sharing a lot about where we were coming from and what I was doing with Judaism. He was very willing to sit and talk about Judaism. I learned a lot of what I knew from him, and he was also helpful in directing me to different people and pulling me into the community. He was very accepting. Whether it was because of him or whether other people were like that, too—I felt accepted. It always surprised me that people were so accepting. I thought they would look at me and say, "Who is this person that wants to be part of our lives?" I didn't know that people would take me seriously and really want to share even before I converted or made a commitment. I knew that there was a tradition not to encourage conversion and the traditional turning away three times, and I expected that from my peers for some reason.

Going back to my parents' home in the summers was always very difficult. I felt very comfortable at Brandeis because I belonged. I was there a year and then decided to start to convert—I needed time to get into it. I was just deciding which direction to go in the conversion process and what I really wanted to study when the war of 1973 broke out. That scared me. I think that was the only time that I can recall a strong feeling of doubt about whether this was the right thing to do. I thought, if I convert, my children are going to be Jewish, and do I have the right to make this decision for them and put them in jeopardy and danger? It was never a hesitation on my part so much as what I wanted to choose for my children.

There was a Reform rabbi at Brandeis with whom I talked a lot about converting. He would have done it, and it would have been very special. But I decided that I wanted an Orthodox conversion because I didn't want anyone saying somewhere down the road, "Wait a minute! You are not Jewish and your children are not Jewish." I ended up studying with a well-known rabbi in Boston. Of course, he thought I should know how to keep kosher, the purity laws. I remember discussing how to *kasher* liver. Lighting candles—I needed to know the blessings. It took six months of meeting once a week. I learned less than nothing. I already knew everything he taught me, and I knew where to find out what I didn't know. So, the actual conversion process was not particularly rewarding.

I was nineteen at the time. My family's reaction was that they finally reacted, and they were extremely angry. My family is not particularly good at communication. My mother talked, but she kept telling me what my father thought, and he never once said one word to me about it. I don't know if what my mother told me was really what he thought, or she felt it would have more power if she said it came from him. They talked about disowning me. They were paying a good chunk of my college tuition, and they weren't going to do it anymore. There was all kinds of talk, but then everything got back to normal. Nobody ever took a strong stand; nevertheless, our relationship was damaged. They were very angry and hurt, which was understandable. If my child decided to convert to Catholicism, I would have a little bit of trouble with it. I am sure it was hard for them.

My grandfather died within the week I converted. He was my mother's father. That was a very difficult time. A lot of events surrounding his death were happening on Saturdays, and I had already made a decision to be *Shomer Shabbat*. I had no idea what to do—whether or not I should stand my ground. I didn't actually miss the funeral or the wake, but my mother wanted me to shop with her on Saturday for a dress and do other necessary errands. I had been practicing being *Shomer Shabbat*, and I was new in my practice, but it was a commitment. It was the first *Shabbat*, and I decided not to shop with my mother. I think that God would have understood if I had gone, but I couldn't do it at the time. You make your decisions.

It was a hard time with my family. To this day, my way of life is still a conflict. And there are times when I don't feel very comfortable bringing my Jewishness into the family. The kosher issue is an ongoing problem. I guess even Jews have that problem sometimes between Jewish families. So, it may not be anything unusual. For a lot of years I stood my ground and would not eat anything at any family member's house except nonmeat items, and there were times at Passover that I wouldn't eat anything—like Easter, every year. That's the way the calendar seemed to fall. I would have a drink of water and nothing else and you could just see in my mother's face that she was furious. I guess there is no right way. My family tends to ignore difference or not talk about conflict. It was my way of saying, "There really is something going on here, guys. We can't just totally ignore this."

I am the youngest of five children. I have three older brothers and a sister. They have all responded differently to me. My sister has been the most supportive, and she is probably the most religious. She married someone who is Polish Catholic, and they observe a lot of those traditions. On Christmas Eve they do a wonderful dinner where they have the *host*, and they bring it to be blessed by the priest. They have the priest bless the house at Easter, and he comes and writes in chalk on the doorposts.

The foods that they have are traditional Polish dishes and coincidentally are very similar to Jewish food. My brother-in-law and my husband are very similar in a lot of ways. They even have similar looks—dark, wavy, curly hair. So my sister has been very accepting and supportive. Whatever I want is fine, and she'll come and join. She is the only family member who came to my children's *brises*.

For two of my brothers, religion touches their lives, but it is something that is very secondary to them. I doubt that they attend mass or do other religious things. They have taken my father's stand basically and talked very little or not at all about my conversion. If I bring it up, they have no reaction. The brother who is closest in age and temperament to me and with whom I had a close relationship growing up is fairly religious. I believe his family attends church regularly, and I know he believes in God. He was really very angry when I converted. He said, "How can you not believe in Jesus!" He couldn't understand how I could not accept all the Catholic teachings.

I don't know that I ever did. I rejected Catholicism at such a young age that I don't know if I ever had a mature enought understanding of what it was to say that I accepted it or not. I had religious-school training—catechism. My father was active in the church. He is an educator by profession and for many years ran the church's high-school study program. I did all that until I was between fourteen and sixteen, but none of it ever rang true with me. We first learned about going to confession at around age seven and were told that if you go to confession then all your sin is cleared away. If you die without sin, you go right to heaven. On my way home after going to confession, I would take the route—forbidden by my mother—that required crossing train tracks. I can remember going through a period of wishing that I would get hit by a train after I went to confession so that I would die and go right to heaven. Obviously I bought into Catholicism at that young age. But it just never felt good. It always felt scary. It was never comforting. No part of it was ever comforting or safe. Of course the flaw in that story was that since I was told to never cross the tracks going home, I was committing a sin by disobeying my mother before the train would hit me! Later on I realized that.

What *has* been hard to leave behind is the hope of ever sharing a more meaningful life with my family members, like sharing holidays. It had never been there, and I doubt it ever could have been, but there was always the hope. This realization hit me the Christmas after I came back from Europe. We had this beautiful manger that had been passed down from generation to generation. It was probably a hundred years old. It was all wood and had a little attic and doors that opened. It was just beautiful. Each year, I had been the one who set it up. No one would have even brought it down from the attic unless I said, "Bring it down." That year they brought down all the Christmas tree ornaments and all the lights to put on the tree. I didn't say anything, and nobody brought down the manger. I just remember sitting there thinking, "What is the point—the point of the Christmas tree and the point of the manger? How can they just ignore what the point of this whole thing is? There is no acknowledgment of what is important here?" I don't think the manger was ever set up in my family after I stopped doing it. I don't ever remember seeing it.

My husband's parents were very rejecting when I first started dating him. They wouldn't talk to me, so they wouldn't have known what my feelings were. I would walk in the house, and his parents would walk upstairs, not even saying so much as "hello" to me. At Yom Kippur I fasted. I guess he must have told them, and for some reason that had an effect on them. After that they started talking to me and were then very accepting. Maybe they decided that I was really serious. I knew a few other families in which the son married a non-Jew or even somebody who converted and the parents were never accepting. I guess that is not unusual. But once I made the commitment and, particularly, when I converted, they became very supportive and very accepting. We never talked about their initial rejection. I guess they are about as communicative as my family when it comes to the really rough issues.

Still, it has been a rocky relationship with my husband's family. In some ways, they have been very nice to us, but at the moment, we are not particularly close. My husband is the oldest, and his relationship with his parents has not been without conflict. After their second son got married, our relationship deteriorated a great deal. He married someone whose background is very similar to his parents. His wife is somewhat religious. My feeling was that I was good enough until the "real thing" came along and things were never the same with his parents after that. Maybe it was just my insecurity, but you can sit and listen to how wonderful someone is for only so long before you start to think. For example, they would invite her family over, but once, when we had been married for about four years, I asked to invite a brother who would be alone for Thanksgiving. My mother-in-law's reaction was that she didn't want a stranger in the house. When things like that happened, I felt I had been put in my place. Still, I know that this has mostly to do with my husband's conflict with them.

My in-laws are gradually becoming more Orthodox, and there is conflict between our observance and theirs. I don't think they are able to see that both our families live our lives according to the rhythms and cycles of the Jewish year, although we may express it differently. I haven't told them that I am doing a *bat mitzvah* this Saturday, and I am reading from the Torah. My father-in-law would think that that was not right. He would say that it is a show and doesn't mean anything. I knew I couldn't handle that so I didn't tell them.

When my mother died last year, I was at a complete loss over what to do—how to observe that. Obviously, I needed to go through a Catholic wake and mass, which was very hard. Then, I got back here and I didn't know what part of mourning, if any, to observe. I still never have come to any comfortable resolution about it. Talk about a difficult experience! I talked with both of the rabbis at our synagogue. They both encouraged me to say *Kaddish*. I did, maybe once a week, but not as consistently as I probably should have to really have an effect. Partly it was my ambivalence over what my mother would have wanted. I just had this feeling that if my mother could see me saying *Kaddish* for her—well, I just couldn't imagine her reaction. I kept trying to tell myself that this is for *me*. There were some things I could do—I put her name in the Wings of Memory book for Rosh Hashanah—and others that I couldn't. It has been difficult.

The experience of my mother's death, however, made clear to me again how wrong Catholic tradition is for me. There was no period of mourning. The funeral was on a Thursday and that weekend my sister left for a week-long business trip in San Francisco. About six weeks later she had a big fiftieth birthday party for her husband. My whole family went, and I felt that I should be there, but I just couldn't do it. It made no sense to me. My parents' fiftieth anniversary had been a month before my mother died, and we tried to do something for that, and it hadn't worked out, obviously. Shortly after my brother-in-law's party, my husband and his brothers were planning a fortieth anniversary party for their parents. Again, I felt like I just could not do that. I just didn't feel up to those celebrations.

What I decided to do at that point was follow the laws—that I should not attend a function with live music. I knew it didn't feel right so I decided that was the best thing to do. The only thing I asked of the family was that they not have entertainment at the party. His brothers were absolutely furious. How could they not have entertainment, they said. They wanted a catered hall with entertainment, and they wanted all of us to be hosts. If it could just have been a house party or if they had just *invited* me to it—maybe. But the feeling of throwing a party at that point in my life— I just couldn't do it. I am sure they thought that I should have gone along. In their defense, I guess, the two brothers and their wives have never experienced a loss. I know that they don't in any way comprehend. Some people immediately do, even if they have not had the experience, but other people don't understand. I guess it is good for them that they don't. I don't know. Both of our families live in a distant city so these issues only come up long distance.

It has been difficult figuring out how to be comfortable with the life-cycle events. Some of that has not come very naturally. Planning a Jewish wedding. *Brises.* I felt that other people probably just knew what to do, but that I had to be very careful not to do the wrong thing.

In my life here in Baltimore, with the circle of friends and connections that I've made, I feel I'm doing the *right* thing. The day school my children attend, the preschool where I work, and the congregation to which we belong are all one community. A lot of my life is centered around the things that go on there. It feels like a very comfortable place to be and the right place to be. And I feel accepted in the larger Jewish community. When we came to Baltimore nine years ago, I had already been a Jew for ten years. I came here very much feeling Jewish, and we came with the intention of leading a Jewish life. My first job was for the *Jewish Times.* We immediately got an apartment right next to a temple. We reached out to the Jewish community. I think that especially in Baltimore I just feel so normal being Jewish that I don't feel like a convert most of the time.

A few isolated instances of nonacceptance have surprised me. Ninety percent of the time nobody looks at me any differently—or maybe they do and I just don't see it because I don't look at myself any differently than someone who was born Jewish. You look at my face and my name—I guess that anyone with half a brain would immediately realize I am not a born Jew. But when I meet people it isn't something that I think to discuss.

People sometimes say, "Oh, you know more than a real Jew does." And I want to say, "But I am a real Jew!" Sometimes I do more than you do, and sometimes I do less.

I feel that being Jewish is such a deep gut feeling that I don't know how you can encourage someone to be Jewish. The tradition obviously has been not to proselytize. To think about doing that for some reason goes against my feelings about Judaism and what Judaism is. I feel it has to be something that just comes.

I have a friend who was not Jewish and married someone who was Jewish. Right before she had her first child, she did a Reform conversion because she felt there should be one religion in the house but really didn't feel any of it. She was very comfortable with Jews and within the Jewish community but did not herself really *feel* Jewish. She didn't feel Christian either. Then her husband started becoming much more religious, and he has now become very Orthodox. They separated for a while and are separated at the moment but are trying to get back together. She did an Orthodox conversion for him. I respect and understand that she wants to have her family together. They love each other; they are compatible. It is just the religious issues.

Seeing how much religion affects what goes on with this couple, I really question whether someone can be Jewish without really feeling it. So, I am not so sure that reaching out is right. To reach out to someone who may be thinking about it already is different; I think the community does that to a certain extent. They have introduction-to-Judaism classes. I'm not sure, but I believe the rabbis don't really turn people away—although the tradition is to send them away three times. I feel that if somebody is showing an interest, there should be outreach to that person. Since it is hard to be part of what in some ways is a closed community, there could be ways to make people feel more comfortable in finding out about it.

It feels very uncomfortable to be with someone who is Orthodox and have them not accept or acknowledge that I am Jewish or that my observance can be different. It is a real problem and not just for converts. Part of my difficulty is that I can see myself leading that life. At the same time, there are parts that wouldn't work for me. If I could find a community that was very religious—like *"frum* Conservative." The problem with the Conservative movement is that there is not much of a community. How can you be *Shomer Shabbat* and Conservative? It just doesn't work. Even if there are sanctions for it, there is no community. It is the rabbis who are observant, period. I don't know how the rabbis and their families do it. I often wonder how they maintain that lifestyle. It seems to be very isolating. On *Shabbat* in the Orthodox community, you go to someone else's house—you share *Shabbat* with the community. When you drive a car to go to synagogue, the feeling is much harder to maintain. My goal was to live within walking distance of our congregation, but we couldn't afford any of the houses. We are about four miles away, so I have to drive ten minutes in order to get there. Once I walked and came back on Saturday afternoon. It is a challenge. I usually don't need the challenge.

I am a lot less observant now than I was at the beginning. I still feel drawn to being more observant, and sometimes I think if it were just me making the decisions for our family or had married someone who was religious, I could be very Orthodox. Every time I start to take on a new tradition or a new law, I feel this pull to do more and more and more. I never feel very comfortable where I am. I feel I should be doing a little bit more, but I don't. If my husband were more interested, maybe it would be easier. But it isn't just that. We also have a lot of problems with Orthodoxy and the role of the woman. Ultimately, that is the reason I couldn't be Orthodox.

I make an effort to be as observant as possible, and I truly love all the home rituals—Friday night dinners, Passover. We love doing *seders*. We build a *sukkah* when we can. Someone once said that a child who has a *sukkah* never misses a Christmas tree, and I think there is a lot to be said for that. When you see the kids enjoying it and inviting friends over, it is just so nice and special. It is what I always wanted for my family.

So, while I fluctuate back and forth, I think I am now in a direction of becoming more observant. I am doing it in the adult *bar/bat mitzvah* class that will culminate, appropriately, this Saturday (near Shavuot*). That has reawakened my urges to make observance more a part of my life. In the beginning I felt I had to do more than anybody else. Maybe part of my drive to become more religious was to prove that I was really Jewish. At this point, I feel that I am really Jewish. I don't think of myself as a convert. I think of myself as a Jew, as if I were always a Jew. I don't feel I have to be better than any other Jew. I do what I want to do and what is comfortable and what is right.

I do remember my roots sometimes in a meeting when everyone says, "Talk about your Hebrew school experiences." Intellectually, that jars me. It is like, "Oh, yeah, I don't have that." But, there is always something that I can share even though it is not the Sunday school experience, because I *did* go to classes to learn about Judaism. It is different, but it is still my process. Of course I don't have the family history that everybody else has, the kids' songs, camp. There are a lot of times that I am hesitant to say something about the law if somebody asks a question. I think I know the answer, and often I *do* know the answer. But I am always afraid to come off as an authority because I feel maybe there was something I missed when I was eight that everyone else learned when they were eight. It is a jarring experience when I remember that I wasn't born Jewish. My kids sometimes will say something about it, and I say, "Oh, yeah. That's right. I wasn't . . ." It does feel funny that I am the only one in the family who has celebrated Christmas, and nobody else shared that. They sometimes will look at me and say, "Well, what was it like—was it as wonderful as it seems?" Yes and no. More no. Much more no.

Though Catholicism was something that never did anything for me, I honestly don't know if growing up Jewish would have been different for me. From what Jewish friends tell me about growing up with the religion, I don't know if I would have

---

*Shavuot is the holiday on which the story of Ruth, the biblical convert, is read.

found anything. I think a lot of it was just the way religion was presented to children back then.

Now I teach in our congregation's preschool, although not the religious part of the day. The way the religion is presented to the children is through songs and stories. It looks very comforting to me, but I'm not sure how it feels as a three- or four- or five-year-old. It is hard to know sometimes. My children seem to have a very positive attitude about being Jewish. The fact that they cannot have a Christmas tree bothers them occasionally. "Well, you had one when you were little." Aside from that minor issue, I think they feel very special. It is something special to be Jewish. There is a rich history. There are lots of connections. There are heroes and there are all the things that kids love. You tell them the story of Hanukkah, and they pretend to be Judah Maccabee. They can act it out and they do. I think that now the educators are doing it *right* by appealing to what kids like—and they love to hear stories.

3

Just Like Everyone Else

Roberta Kramer

Many of the people who come to Judaism as adults report that they never felt quite right in the religion of their birth, sometimes not even quite right in their family. What is it like then for someone who is adopted at birth by Jewish parents and who is not, in a sense, biologically Jewish?

Roberta, raised in a loving home by parents who fully integrated her into the extended family and Jewish community, has never felt anything but completely Jewish—just like everyone else—and, for that matter, never gave her identity a second thought. Then, while being interviewed for an article on adoption, the editor of the Jewish newspaper called into question the authenticity not only of her conversion, but that of her adopted daughter's as well. Roberta was angry and shaken. No one had ever before in her life implied that she was not truly Jewish.

I grew up in a neighborhood in which I thought people were either Jewish or Catholic. The two children who lived next door to me were Jewish and adopted. We were very close to this family. The children were my parents' godchildren, and I called the parents "Aunt" and "Uncle."

My husband always thought I had an enormous family, when in fact many of the different people I had learned to call "aunt" and "uncle" were not relatives. That probably says a lot about my parents' attitudes about adoption and how one relates to and includes people as family members.

I always remember having a strong sense of being Jewish, and for as long as I can recall, I also knew I was adopted. It was just a fact, like "I am female; I have brown hair; I am Jewish; I was adopted."

I was adopted into a family and became part of that family. My family was Jewish, and therefore I was raised as Jewish as if I had been my parents' biological child. I don't think my parents did anything any differently because I was adopted, and I didn't think about my adoption much, and I still don't.

When you are growing up, you don't necessarily think of your situation as unique. You just assume that the way your family and the others around you do things is the norm. I didn't realize until I was a teenager, for example, that there were other ways of practicing Judaism than the way our family did. Now I know that we probably were not all that observant; on the other hand, it never occurred to me to be interested in any religion other than Judaism.

Our family was affiliated with a Conservative congregation. My father never went to synagogue, but my mother and I did. We celebrated holidays and festivals at home, like everybody else we knew.

My father's family was very unobservant. Although he certainly considered himself a Jew, I don't think he had any real feeling for religious ritual. If we went to a *shivah*, he would participate in the *minyan*. He attended my *bat mitzvah* and those of our family and friends, but other than that he had no urge to go to synagogue.

My mother's family was a bit more observant. Her parents were Polish immigrants, and from them she learned Yiddish and Polish. Her family was very poor, and she was not able to finish high school because she went to work to help support the family. She did not have the opportunity for a formal Jewish education, either, and learned observance and traditions from her parents' practices.

My parents had a book on adoption written in the 1940s that was in two parts, one for the parents and one for the child. The book is no longer in print, but I would love to find a copy and read the wisdom that guided my mother back then. I remember once, when I must have been about six years old, asking her a question about my "real" mother. She responded, "I *am* your real mother." There was no hesitation, no question there. Then I rephrased my question about the woman who "borned" me.

I did not look anything like either of my parents. They both had green eyes, and mine are brown. By the time I was thirteen, I was taller than both of them. Even if they hadn't discussed my adoption as I grew up, my first biology class would have made me aware that they were not my biological parents.

There have been times when it would have been convenient to know about my biological family history, especially for medical reasons. As an only child, I always wanted siblings, and it would be interesting to see people who do look like me. Nevertheless, finding my birth family has never been important to me, even after my parents passed away.

It is my belief that I was born to someone who was not married, and that, in the early 1950s, it was probably a *shandeh*, a disgrace. It must have been very hard to place her baby for adoption. I imagine that after all these years she must have married and had a family. Having me, this person from the past, pop into her life could be upsetting, as well as disruptive, especially when she might prefer not to remember.

Now that I am an adoptive mother of two children, there are many questions I would like to ask of my parents. Unfortunately, they both passed away before my children were born. My parents did such a good job of making me feel absolutely part of the family. The circumstance of my birth was insignificant. Becoming their daughter was the important event, and the start of our life as a family. I hope we are able to give our children the same feeling of unconditional love and acceptance.

My "aunt," who lived next door, tells a great story that illustrates that point. She and her daughter, who was a teenager or young adult at the time, went to a new dentist and had to fill out medical history forms. She noticed that her daughter was busy filling out all the family history information: "maternal grandfather died of cancer," "uncle had heart disease." When my aunt questioned what she was doing, my cousin responded that she was giving the requested information. My aunt had to remind her that there was no biological relationship, and they both enjoyed a good laugh.

The family becomes so much a part of your being that it doesn't matter that there is no genetic connection. That is how my husband and I, and the other adoptive parents we know, feel—these are *our children*. And if I can speak for my own parents, I am sure they would say the same thing.

Some people will occasionally say to me, "Oh, you don't look Jewish." This always takes me by surprise, and I still haven't come up with a good response. I feel my soul is Jewish, and doubt I would feel any differently if I were my parents' biological child. I had a wrenching experience, though, in which my status as a Jew was questioned, and just recalling the incident still shakes me up.

My husband and I and another couple had been invited to be interviewed by the local Jewish community newspaper for an article on adoption, which, as far as I know, was never published.

The interviewer was Orthodox. As we described our daughter's *mikveh*, presided over by a Conservative rabbi, he interjected, "She could never live in Israel as a Jew. We would never accept her." He then questioned whether or not I had been converted as an infant and under whose auspices. Further questioning ensued on the topic of our marriage, synagogue affiliation, and so forth, all with reference to my having been adopted and the manner of my conversion.

The focus of the interview shifted—from a discussion of our domestic and the other couple's international adoption, and the integration of our children into our families and the Jewish community—to what felt like an Inquisition.

My Jewish identity had never before been questioned in any Jewish setting, and I never recall being asked to authenticate my status as a Jew. My parents had never discussed conversion with me, and I didn't know about the *mikveh* and conversion until it was discussed in our home study prior to our daughter's adoption.

When it was time to do our son's *mikveh*, we went to an Orthodox rabbi because I wanted to spare my children the rejection I felt the night of that interview. Both children now have Orthodox conversion certificates.

I went to Hebrew school and my *bat mitzvah* was a rite of passage for me, as were those of my friends, and I studied very hard to do well. It was an achievement, but I remember sort of giggling at my mother crying in the front row as I read my *haftarah*. I studied and prepared for my *bat mitzvah* mainly for my parents, and I stopped going to Hebrew school after that year. I'm kind of sorry that I didn't continue, but at that point, it wasn't as important and meaningful to me as I consider it now.

I am much more syngagogue-oriented than my husband. When he was young, his family kept kosher, and his uncle was the Hebrew-school principal. His mother says, "he was dragged to *shul* one too many times as a child," and therefore doesn't want to be too involved now.

As of now, our children's Jewish education comes from practices centered around the home. We read books with Jewish themes and stories about the holidays as well as doing activity books and listening to music tapes. When they are older, they will attend Hebrew school.

I would like to re-create the things I enjoyed about our families' Jewish traditions. My mother passed away nine years before our daughter was born. She was really the spirit of all the holidays, which haven't felt the same since she has been gone. Mom had such enthusiasm for all the preparations. She loved to cook and was the proverbial "Jewish mother" in the kitchen. While we spend holidays with my husband's family now, their traditions, although warm and enjoyable, are different, and I still feel the loss.

When my parents passed away, I said *Kaddish*, and I observe their *Yartzeits*. When it was time to say *Kaddish* for Mom, I remembered how she would light the *Yartzeit* candles at home for her parents. I began saying *Kaddish* at home. Every morning I would come down to the kitchen, watch the sun rise, and say my prayers.

Because I was adopted, it was natural for me to contemplate adoption when we decided to have children. After I miscarried for the first time, I told my husband I wanted to start looking into adoption. He agreed, once he realized how much he wanted to be a parent, too.

In the era of my adoption, most adoptions were domestic and did not cross racial boundaries. Now parents are adopting children internationally and across all racial and ethnic lines. The biology of our children does not make a difference in how we feel about them, or how we will raise them. They are our family, and we'll share our beliefs with them. We hope they will embrace our way of life and enjoy our traditions as we do.

I hope that the love of our children will help us be more tolerant and respectful of all people, and that we can teach our children to do the same. I pray every day that we can make the world a better place where all of our children can live in peace.

4

Among the "People of the Book"

Susan Frank

Judaism could be said to be a religion of action, but not everyone lives her Judaism that way. Rabbi Susan Frank feels deeply at home in Judaism, its history, language, and teachings. She has identified as a Jew for most of her life, though her observance is more intellectual than physical. Sue describes in loving detail her five years attending rabbinical school, where she pursued her fascination with language, especially medieval Jewish poetry, by "digging into the text and worrying words to pieces to figure out how they fit into rhythms that then made meaning."

Sue's life is very much in keeping with the tradition of study of Torah, Talmud, and rabbinic writings throughout the ages. She immerses herself fully in the words, loving not only *what* is said but *how* it is said. Although we Jews have been called "the People of the Book"—better said "books"—it is the humanity inherent in Judaism that informs Sue's life and the way she conducts herself in all her interactions.

In 1976 we came to Philadelphia, where I attended the Reconstructionist Rabbinical College. Ken, my husband, got a job here so that I could do that. The RRC required that students also complete an advanced degree in a secular institution. Thus, I enrolled both at RRC and Temple University, in the religion department, along with several other rabbinical students. I was in some very good company with people who wanted to comprehend the various modern-day expressions of Judaism, and of Christianity as well. We gave each other moral support.

I was not interested in pursuing a degree for its own sake at Temple, but I figured I would write a dissertation if I could find someone with whom I could work well. Gerard Sloyan, a Catholic priest, was there, and he, like me, loves old languages, such as Latin and Greek. Classical languages were my undergraduate work. I was looking for a way to use that experience to make some contribution to Christian/Jewish studies.

Dr. Sloyan became my mentor—no doubt about it—and backed me up when I said I was interested in studying Paul and Paul's letters. I had never read that "junk." Even as a child at Episcopalian Sunday school, no one had asked me to read the New Testament material, now called the apostolic writings. I read Paul's letters with Dr. Sloyan and an excellent bunch of graduate students. When we got to the Letter to Romans, I said "Oh, my God, this is wonderful!" Because Paul seems to be saying, in Chapters 9–11, that his friends out in the field shouldn't be overly concerned with the Jews. God has his own plan for the Jews, and it will work out in time. Paul seems to be saying "leave them alone."

I became intrigued by this, since it seemed to run cross-current to the general mood of the church militant, who banged the Jews on their collective heads and said, "Convert!" I decided that a revealing way to look at this might be to study what Christian commentators had to say about the Letter to Romans. The Christians, like the Jews, studied their scriptures, "turned and turned in them," as they say, and tried to draw out contemporary wisdom. I looked at some of the best Roman churchmen to see how they understood this text. I had fun because so much of the source material was in Latin, and it hadn't been translated yet. This gave me a little virgin field, which was important to find for my dissertation. I was reading Aquinas, among others. The finest minds of the Church seemed to be saying, "That's right, we don't have to bother the Jews. We can leave them alone. God will figure this out in His own good time." So I wrote up my findings.

Many of our modern Jewish–Christian hassles come out of a huge backlog of stereotypical thinking. It is typical of people to be intellectually lazy; to operate with stereotypes and to repeat the same old boring short versions of everything. Much of our dullness is modern in origin. I am such a believer in history and text because they give us clues to the way people's minds worked as far back as we can find written work. It is then that you can see all the humanity and complexity of a topic.

Since I was a child, I have looked at Christianity as if I were a Jew. This is when I had a great friend, a grandmother down the street. What we recognized in each other—I was ten and she was in her eighties—was that we were both "religious." We were drawn to worship, and we loved to go to churches. We visited every church in town. I loved to go just to learn the hymns. There was the atmosphere and the mood. People were sitting still for a while in a beautiful place with others with whom they were kind of emotionally in tune, and they were thinking about things a little larger than their ordinary concerns. At that age, I caught on very quickly that I didn't believe in Jesus, whatever that was about, and all this nonsense about there being "One Way" and that we must accept Jesus as our personal savior. It did not compute, and I rejected it very early.

Commitment to a religion has to do with what you love. I believe that you are born with these tendencies. My husband is a good example of the born Jew who attended Hebrew school but wanted to be outside chasing bugs and playing with his friends instead. He paid his dues, and then he moved away from Judaism. I was drawn to Jewishness and was lucky enough to be able to approach it on my own terms without someone telling me how. I was shy and scared of everything, as adolescents are, but I knew I loved this, and it gave me the courage to seek it.

Although I didn't know any actual Jews during most of my growing up, when I was a junior in high school, a Jewish family moved in across a field from us. I remember visiting them just to say "Hi" and feeling terribly shy about talking to them. Then I discovered that they were not really into their Jewishness, and I thought, "I'm not going to bother them too much since this is not their thing." But they did give me a book, Louis Browne's classic *Wisdom of Israel*. That just knocked me flat. I read it; I loved it; it was full of bits and pieces of every rabbinic genius text you could think of. I made another good find in a local bookstore. One day I walked in and there was R. Travers Herford's edition of *Pirkei Avot*, Sayings of the Fathers. That became my little handbook. I lugged it around with me, even on a trip to South Carolina to visit my grandparents for Christmas. Every piece of it hit me right. What I loved was the humanity and the solidity of it. "Who is wise? He who learns from every man." It was on the money—compared to anything I heard Christians saying. It was my heart song.

My family is the kind of family that whatever you are interested in, however peculiar or alien to them, they will show an interest. Maybe all they can do is be amused, but they'll appreciate it as they can. People would try to find me books or to listen when I had something to say. I remember particularly when my grandfather was dying, my grandmother and I had left my grandfather's room—that was the last time I saw him—and she said, "Take good care of the Hebrew." She knew I was trying to teach myself Hebrew. That she would think of it at that time really touched me.

My father has his own special wisdom—a biologist's experience. He'll sit in front of the TV news and go into a rant about what's wrong with the world. Overpopulation, as far as he's concerned, that's the worst, and the world is too venal and stupid to figure this out, so we are just going to grow ourselves off the planet! Religion is mostly nonsense. In a lot of ways, he is right. All he has to do is see a picture of the pope and he's off! But he was very tolerant of my interest. He would let me try to explain why I thought the Jewish offering had merit, and why I could find a place in it. I didn't want him to mistake me for a traditional sort of Jew, a Jew who had a lot invested in a belief in God or one of the Jews who had enormous investment in the survival, at any cost, of the Jewish people.

I was always cutting out my own very particular Jewish identity. I found myself at the end almost saying, "I am a Jew whether or not Jews will say I am a Jew." I began to feel that I had the right to do that, which is a statement I know would be very offensive to many people. But I laid my claim. I could reconcile my family values with Judaism because Judaism is big enough. "If I go looking," I thought, "I will find precedents. I don't even have to pretend that I am unique; I'll find people who have said and thought everything I might ever say or think, and who are proud to be Jews."

In that regard, I was fortunate to have grown up in an unusual place: Woods Hole is a community of scientists and their kids. They were curious and respectful of differences. Few of them were religious. Some would say that science was their religion, but I have problems with that statement. I argue that the attitudes and behaviors of religious people belong in a very different box than do the activities and mind tracks of scientists. I think it is worth keeping them separate and figuring out why they are different. Science and religion impact on each other profoundly, but there is a distortion effect: what you bring to an investigation is liable to alter it in ways that you can't guess or anticipate. An optimistic, clockwork God kind of believer who teaches molecular genetics might influence his own results in ways I can't even guess, as opposed to, say, a skeptical atheist trying to keep a very hard objective stance. This is not to say that a believer can't be a good scientist—just that there might be some accidental mixing.

Despite the openness in our community, there occurred an incident that stirred up a huge controversy that I found very compelling. My sister, four years older, considered joining an outfit called the "Rainbow Girls." A Jewish girl in her class was not allowed to join. There was a big hoo-ha in the town, and that was the first time I'd ever encountered any discrimination in the basic sense of "this person is Jewish so she can't do this." She was being differentiated and set aside.

The effect this incident had was to remind me to take very seriously any Jewish declaration I might make. In the conversion document that I was eventually to sign there was a phrase, "Do you throw your lot in with the Jewish people?" I realized that once I declared myself Jewish in front of the Jewish community, I would have to stick to it even in the face of setbacks. I knew that there were consequences of being Jewish but nothing earth shattering. I did more laughing about the stupid Rainbow Girls than about the problem of getting into the Rainbow Girls if you were black, Jewish, or whatever. This also showed me that the little hassles of the Jew in America were pretty small compared to what I'd been reading or seeing on TV about Europe in the war.

I had a gruesome fascination with that whole period of Germany. Grappling with the Holocaust has to do with plumbing the dimensions of what it means to be human. Most of us would like to imagine that we are gentle; we can't be pushed past certain bounds of behavior—but to be presented with the spectacle of the Holocaust! Some Jews will not talk about that era or look at it on TV or read about it. I find that I still want to let it be present. Because these things did happen, and we are capable of them. I try to keep the knowledge of the Holocaust on an eye-level shelf. For me, processing the Holocaust mentally and emotionally takes the form of the movie *Shoah*, keeping the document at hand. I realize that in my sweet, privileged life I've not even been *hit* by somebody else, but these things can go on. American children not drawn to European history could have a similar confrontation with the documentation of lynching in the South—facing that people you know or live with were capable of these acts.

I have dreams that evoke my emotional response—since I tend to intellectualize experience otherwise. I had a series of dreams after I read John Hersey's *The Wall* in high school. (The wonder that a non-Jew could write this massively researched novel full of characters whom I found very believable!) His characters portray the series of events that led to the creation of the Warsaw ghetto, its existence, eventual destruction, and the escape of those last few people through the sewers. It fascinated me; I remember drawing little pictures—I've still got them somewhere—of how I imagined the characters in this book. I had dreams of being among those Warsaw ghetto rebels holding off the SS troops in the fire. The dreams would end with me being shot. I guess I was identifying somehow with the people of that time. On a deeper level of interpretation, I was saying, "Let me be among those victimized—if there has to be a choice—and not among the victimizers." I've always had a terror of abusing power. I wonder if this is a common thread among those who become Jewish?

Since my childhood, religion in general and Judaism in particular is where I loved to concern myself. I was drawn to history and Latin in high school. Intellectually, I wanted to know where things came from. I couldn't do math, wasn't too good at science, but I sure could read, and I sure could bullshit about religion and philosophy. My friends and I loved to do that and wonder about how we came to be and who we were.

When we were thirteen years old, about ten of us were choosing some kind of religious stance. I chose Judaism; two friends were getting baptized as Baptists. Another said, "I am an atheist!" Another set herself on the path to become an impoverished wandering evangelist. We would hang out together in the basement of the local Congregational church, which had a wonderful youth worker. He was ready to listen to us talk about religion. We were very fortunate to have this refuge. We could leave school, where no one was particularly interested in going into this, and go to the church. Leon would take us to places we didn't have access to otherwise. There was not a synagogue in Woods Hole, where I grew up. He put us in a car and took us to services at the synagogue in Hyannis, twenty miles down the road. It was the first time I saw a Torah. So exciting! I went to my first synagogue service when I was just about *bat mitzvah* age.

One of my seminal Jewish experiences in high school was when my friends decided that we needed to have a Passover *seder*—my first! We didn't have any Jews to help us, except that someone knew a Jewish scientist's family in Woods Hole, and they loaned us a little paper Maxwell House *Haggadah*. We decided to have our *seder* at Beth's house—Beth is the Catholic. So Chelsea made us the most atrocious meat loaf—she knew she couldn't put bread in it, so it was like a rock. We had the "delicious" Passover meat loaf, and we got what we could of the ritual foods. We made our own cut-and-paste *Haggadah*, and I learned the song *"Dayenu."* I had recorded the tune from a Jewish Publication Society TV show called *The Eternal Light*. It was a joyous *seder*. My friends were saying, "We love you; and we'll do this thing with you!"

I had a funny sort of overbearing confidence in view of the fact that I was afraid of everything else. "I want to be Jewish so much that I'll make it up as I go along." I knew that I'd have to wait till college to get some mainstream Jewish guidance. I went to Smith, my mother's school. The Latin department was great and the rabbi was great. I will always be grateful for them both.

I found the courage to walk up to Helen Hills Chapel and look up Rabbi Yechiael Lander, who is still there. I told him that I wanted to be a Jew. He is a very courtly, kind person. He could see how scared I was, so he went slowly and kindly. He explained that normally when a convert approaches, a rabbi might push him or her off a couple of times, but he said, "I can see you're pretty serious." So he worked up reading lists for me, and let me come each week and talk about whatever I was reading and thought was interesting. Eventually, he decided that I could go through conversion. He rounded up a few people from the Northampton congregation. I remember buying bagels and cream cheese and bringing them up to the chapel for *Kiddush* after. And I signed that little paper about throwing in my lot with the Jewish people. It was a Reform conversion, but at the time what was important to me was that it was with Rabbi Lander. He is my rabbi.

I finished at Smith and decided to go to graduate school in Latin and Greek down in Chapel Hill, where I enjoyed the Hillel House. It wasn't until I decided to go to Israel that I thought I should go through a second conversion, even though I felt myself to be Jewish. I hoped it wouldn't hurt Rabbi Lander's feelings, but I figured I'd better go through a *Bet Din* and *tevillah* so I wouldn't have hassles about my Jewishness. It's sort of like getting your passport. When I applied to RRC it came up. I don't think they would have rejected me without that, but they might have asked me to go through a *mikveh* ceremony.

A rabbi back on Cape Cod arranged for a *mikveh* in Boston. He was Reform also, but he had enough of a network to be able to make the arrangements. He knew Rabbi Lander and felt that if Rabbi Lander said I was okay, then I was okay.

I took a summer job in Woods Hole sorting marine invertebrates for a scientist studying oil spills, and earned enough money to send myself to Israel in 1975. The whole thing cost $1,000, thanks to the Kibbutz Aliyah organization. They sent me off to Kibbutz Ruchama. It was mind-blowing, crazy, weird, and fun. But after six months, I was glad to leave and come home.

My experience there is hard to describe. I wasn't afraid of hard work. But when I went to this *kibbutz*, I learned what it was to be a second- or third-class citizen, the status of the volunteers and *ulpan* students. I was disappointed to see that the women of the *kibbutz* had retreated from their socialist ideals. They weren't in the fields, they were in the children's houses. They were doing kitchen maintenance, and the volunteer women were doing the "shit" maintenance. I found myself relegated to cleaning the steam table in the dining hall day after day. Where was the diversity of labor? I also found myself enormously lonely, which was a new one for me. We were never assigned to the *kibbutz* families we'd been promised. I kept asking because I wanted to link up with someone, but we were pretty much dumped in our barracks and abandoned. I had one or two close friends, but the *kibbutzniks* were hard to meet. This was a large *kibbutz* and people seemed to have their social structures set.

Yet I was glad to see the mix of people among the volunteers. I met an amazing young woman from Germany who was not Jewish—a big strong girl who'd come to that *kibbutz* to do her thing. I learned the "Internationale" from her.

I realized that although I myself might not want to be ritually observant, I also didn't want to be on a *kibbutz* where they made fun of the synagogue. I made my first gaffe when I came onto the *kibbutz* by asking, "Where's the *shul*?" and they laughed. Maybe I should have known better—but gee! There was a wedding on the *kibbutz*, and they had to import a "black hat" rabbi. Some people made fun of him.

We had a *kushi* on the *kibbutz*, an Ethiopian Jew, and people talked about him behind his back because he was black. These little sour notes were disturbing.

It seemed to me that at least the Israelis I knew were like unhappy adolescents. They hadn't sorted out their relationships, so there was unhappiness and anger. It was hard for an outsider to figure how to fit in when people were flailing around so. The old *vatikim* from Poland, the founders, wouldn't speak Yiddish, because they'd put that behind them. I found myself among people who had put away their past and seemed to be living in a very narrow materialistic present, yet they attributed a lot of meaning to this.

Here was the *kibbutz* movement, Israel building itself. I was looking for a little transcendence, I guess, and did not find it in this setting. In the United States, life is so luxurious, materially and intellectually. We have room to sit and contemplate what kind of Jew we want to be. In Israel, many seem too harried to bother with all that.

I was met constantly with the attitude from Israelis, "Why would you want to become Jewish?" Something I thought much about when I was young was, "How could somebody not be thrilled with this heritage?" One of my fantasies was that I would find a Jew in my family tree. All I could think of was that if I were born into Jewishness, I would be so proud of it.

I am fortunate to have been one of those women of the generation where, if you had the right kind of parents, they said, "Do what you love. Be happy. Don't worry about getting a job." I took them at their word and was a perpetual student. After Israel, I said, what's next? Rabbinical school! I can study Hebrew; I can study history; let's go.

I was so naive! I wrote to about five colleges that I got from some list. Conservative. I wrote to the Jewish Theological Seminary. I wrote to Hebrew Union College. I wrote to a *yeshivah* in New Jersey. And I wrote to the Reconstructionist Rabbinical College. I got back nice letters. The *yeshivah* wrote a sweet letter—I think I've saved it—"We don't train women for the rabbinate, but you are welcome to come and study with us." JTS, of course, at that time had to turn me away.

I got back a wonderful letter from RRC. So I wrote them and they published my application in their magazine! I was thrilled. I had found my home! As I started to learn about Reconstructionism, I realized, "This is the place for me!"

At the time I went to the Reconstructionist College, there still seemed to be a big opening for people who didn't have much use for "God-talk." I was more interested in Jewish culture, the Jewish people, language, and history, than in reading much about theology. Things have changed at RRC. Students have now come who are profoundly religious and talented and interested in exploring the spiritual dimension. But I came with a group of people who were ready to grip ideas—grammar—the rocks of it. This was profoundly interesting.

It was a five-year course. I entered in 1976 and finished in 1981. There was the Bible year, the Rabbinic year, then Medieval, then Modern, and finally, Contemporary. If you came without much Hebrew, then you were asked to spend an additional year in Israel getting your Hebrew up to speed. Each year was nicely assembled with history and language courses. They would try to put in pastoral courses around the edges: how to get along with people; how to give a sermon.

I went to fulfill my heart, not as a vocation. I've always known that I'm not easy in front of crowds and don't have what that takes. I'm a one-to-one type. I knew I'd find a way to contribute—it just wouldn't be in the pulpit, and I didn't particularly want to teach. I'd tried teaching at almost every level and discovered that it was not fulfilling. For me the only kind of teaching I would have enjoyed would have been to teach those profoundly interested in what I had to offer. I have no interest in grading people who are just mucking through requirements. I can't imagine being bothered—I'd rather work at McDonald's. I'd rather teach somebody who loves what I have to offer and not be paid. The old, "Don't make an ax out of the Torah." You earn your living at some trade and teach as an avocation. If you find students who love what they're doing, then they are teaching you; it's not just a cliché.

One of the most rewarding things about rabbinical school was that with my classical languages background, I actually sometimes made a contribution. We had a marvelous teacher there, an observant Jew. He was an anomaly at the college but most welcome. He could read Talmud! Wonder of wonders to hear a learned Jew interpret that very difficult Aramaic! I quickly had a rewarding bond with him because he was fascinated by language. He could tell me about Hebrew and Aramaic, and I could tell him about Latin and Greek.

Each year was distinct and very much a new adventure. I think of each year in terms of the instructors who led each one. Rabbi Caine in the Bible year was a towering figure. He had a reputation as a very demanding teacher. He inspired many of us, and I learned an enormous amount from him. He felt a responsibility to convey a certain body of knowledge. He had to take people who hadn't studied a lot of Hebrew and didn't know which end was up in a Torah, and turn them into respectable rabbis.

Then there was the robust, cheerful teacher who led the Rabbinic year. He was not the intellectual that Caine was, but a friendly, ebullient character who could help bring out what you had to offer.

In the Medieval year, a woman turned up to teach, an elegant Romanian, Vera Moreen. I realized that I had met her back at Smith at High Holiday services in the Helen Hills Chapel. A beautiful young woman sitting near me began to cry at one point, and I spoke with her. I learned that she was from Romania. I never saw her again until I met her as my professor at RRC!

That was a wonderful year for me because she taught a course in medieval Hebrew poetry. I was fascinated to realize how much the great Hebrew poets of the Golden Age in Spain owed to Arab poets. It was a beautiful mesh of cultures that occurred in medieval Spain. I wrote a translation of one of these poems and began to feel like I was grasping its beautiful, intricate diction. These poets' minds were stocked with all the classical tropes of their period. You can read these poems on a hundred different levels. For example, there is a fabulous poem that seems to be written by a man to a boy about the delicious juice from the palate of his mouth. It might be God's sweet dew but it might be something else too—and it can be many meanings together.

In the Modern year, we had another exciting, demanding instructor. There were just three of us in the class. In my studies, I had always sort of hung back in the ancient past so it helped to be brought into the modern period. I found that Dr. Poppel elicited much that I didn't know I could offer. He would ask you to read something and give you a chance in class to cough up a few minutes of reaction. He was enormously appreciative if you came up with something. He also was good at reproving people who were lazy. It's hard to find a good editor nowadays, hard to find a good critic, somebody who'll tell you, "No, that's really not your best." He was good at that.

What most easily brought me out of the ancient past were personal documents, contemporary to their time, written descriptions of, say, the founding of the State of Israel, the Theodor Herzl work. Poppel himself was an expert on Central Europe. He was fascinated by the process of assimilation of the Jews, especially in Germany. The peculiar circumstances that brought the Jews out of their traditional ghetto lifestyle into the mainstream of society—the whole enlightenment process—then made them so vulnerable to what came next. It's just a small point, but I remember I heard it from this class, that one reason the Jews of Europe were so vulnerable to the Nazi machine was that the communities had submitted themselves to be regulated and registered, so governments knew who the Jews were and where they lived. That helped me better understand the structures that permitted the extraction of the Jews from Holland and France and why the old Jewish lady over in the Philadelphia Geriatric Center "won't sign nuttin'." There's a legacy of mistrust of government.

At the college, we seemed to alternate moods for these years. Bible was demanding. Rabbinic was cheerful, friendly. Medieval was exciting. Modern was demanding again. Then came Contemporary, and there was this big sigh of relief, like senior year in high school when everybody's relaxing. Dr. Weiner was very gentle; it was almost as if he felt, "You guys have been through a lot. We'll study, but we'll take it a little easier." It was a cheerful year. It reminded me that it is a good idea to keep your head in our own time frame, too—watching the day-to-day news.

Reconstructionists attempt to hold together many of the layers of history and the contemporary world. If you are praying or examining a Jewish principle or cultural artifact, you are doing so with an awareness that it may have had different meanings at various periods. Reconstructionism is an archetypically American movement because of its founder, Mordecai Kaplan. He was an immigrant to this country from Russia and trained at the Jewish Theological Seminary, where he taught. He felt there wasn't a place for him to express his Jewishness in this country. He wanted very much to relate to his setting—it wasn't just a matter of bringing his food and his clothes and his language from the old country and plunking them down in a New York neighborhood. It was more like "I am going to be an American and face the challenges that brings to my Jewishness."

While I was at RRC, I got a job helping out in the library, which suited me to the hilt. The librarian at that time, Jennifer Gabriel, was my ideal. I had never met a woman like her—brains, sense, she knew how to handle people. Dora Nathanson, the library assistant, represented to me the mothering Jewish culture. She always had recipes and stories of growing up in Philadelphia and her life with her husband running their small store.

When I finished at RRC, I was invited to stay on as the librarian and get a library degree at Drexel. If I have a vocation, it is to be a reference librarian in a busy academic setting. So I found this happy niche and did that for five years. But I wasn't moving on my dissertation for Temple, and I realized that finishing that degree was a lifelong goal also. I left the RRC library and finished my dissertation in 1990.

As time goes on, I think that the Reform, Conservative, and Reconstructionist movements sometimes give the appearance of converging, certainly as the JTS admits women to ordination, and the Reform movement admits a greater variety of outlooks on the State of Israel. The things that might have been platform essentials for each movement become more negotiable, so it may be harder to tell differences. It would still be hard for me to happily be a rabbi in the Reform movement because of its "God" focus.

God plays very little role in my Judaism. I can be moved by things, I can be lifted up. I've always been attracted to Jewish spiritual folklore—like the theme of the "thirty-six hidden saints." I am much more inclined to be moved by the extraordinary small things people do out of the blue that make life worth living. I am not inclined to attribute that to a "god." I find the minute that I have to talk about "Him" or "Her," I start to feel like an idiot.

Some might say to me, "If you don't believe in God, you can't be a Jew." And I could say back, "You're wrong. Certainly, I can." When I came to the RRC, I felt confirmed in that. On the other hand, I feel that I lead a spiritual life—but not a God-centered one.

I do worship, actually, very little. When I do, on selected occasions, it means a lot to me. Contact with the Torah, holding it, and reading it moves me. I had a recurring dream my junior year of college while I was in Rome studying Latin. In my dream, I would wander down to the Jewish ghetto in Rome and find the great synagogue deserted and dark. Nevertheless, I would find myself very much at home there. I would enter it, walk up the stairs, and in a cozy attic room, I would find a desk, like in a *yeshivah* room. There was a very large book open on the table, and the page was shining, but the black letters stood out in contrast. I approached it. For me, it comes back to the Torah, and although in no way do I believe God wrote this, or even one person, Moses, it *is* something the Jewish people created. When I contemplate the enduring dedication of these people to this text and the subsequent layers of readings, I am greatly moved.

More than the actual text of the Torah, I love the rabbinic layer—what I can grasp of it. For some reason the Torah text and the fact of being a Jew, say in exile or at a great talmudic academy, elicited from these minds a human wisdom that I find astonishing. I don't see it in any other tradition. The Greeks had a certain kind of worldly wisdom. The Romans were practical and sensible. But nobody comes up with the stuff the rabbis did.

There is a rabbinic notion that you can, in fact, find salvation if you aren't a Jew. You must observe certain basic requirements known as the Noahide laws. What this confirms for me is that, for the rabbis, there is a basic shared humanity that reaches around the world. If you live in Papua New Guinea, you could be all right and you don't have to be a Jew, too. I don't have to send a missionary over there to make you say, "I accept Jesus Christ as my personal savior." You can just stay there and do what you do and you are fine. Sort of what Paul was telling his peers about the Jews: "Leave them alone." I like the idea of looking at people with "soft eyes"; I think you *can* find that in Judaism. You can find the rigid outlook, too, but I think we can elect to steer around that. When I assert my right to choose, I am going to steer around the hardline stuff.

The notion of having the right to choose comes from Judaism. There's an acceptance of responsibility to see things as clearly as you can with as much integrity as you have and then to stick by that, even when, as Kipling says, "The whole round world's against you." You take your stand, yet you might make a mistake. Take Moses leading the people in the desert. His worst times are when he doesn't trust his instincts. He fails to have trust in "God," which for me is a metaphor for his being on the right track in his thinking and then acting accordingly.

It has been interesting to look historically at Jews in crisis, like Jews in the ghetto situation. The leader of the Jews in the Warsaw ghetto, who wrote heartbreaking entries in his diary, was constantly being asked to do things that he knew were wrong. He'd make a concession, always weighing the benefit to his community. It was wrenching. He finally got to the point where the dissonance between his heart and what was being asked of him was too great, and he came apart. But I do think that part of a Jew's job is to constantly be making choices and committing himself. Spinoza had to do this. I found him to be a soul brother in this sense: He wanted to talk about pantheism instead of a personal god in the traditional Jewish sense. He was ostracized from the synagogue.

I often think that it is the job of the Jew to accept ostracism if he has taken a stand that others find controversial. Somebody like me is not likely to prove controversial because I am not making any great statements. What I am asking for is a gentling of judgment. I've always appreciated in other people a willingness to be a little off balance. The most tedious thing is to be set on a track and not to be self-questioning. As the philosopher said, "The unexamined life isn't worth living." The comfortable, self-satisfied life is a bore. I am afraid that some Jews, as much as other religious people, are precisely setting themselves up for complacency with their vegetarianism, their strict dogmas, their observant lifestyles. I think some build themselves little, safe homes, and they say, "This is how we all should live." The only thing I find myself wanting to scold other people for is what the old rabbis called *sinat hinom*, "baseless hate," malicious acts that contribute to the deterioration of relationships or happiness or our ability to live together.

Judaism seems to work exceedingly well to provide us with a deep acceptance of humanity. There is something nice about Mordecai Kaplan's pushing aside the old motto "The Jews are the chosen people." Jews seem to have a special aptitude for religion—however defined—or spirituality. You can look at different groups of people and say they have certain gifts. Why not lay claim to ours? I'd like to think of the contemporary Jew as standing here with an open but responsible mind. Being Jewish seems to give me that power—that Archimedean place to stand—to be able to say certain things, things *I* could not say from inside Christianity.

5

God, Prayer, and Community
"Penina"

Penina's two young sons live secure in the belief that nearly 100 percent of the world is Jewish—and in their young world that is true.

How different is the sense of their place in the world from their mother's experience growing up in the South, where just the assumption that her great-grandmother was a Jew barred her from certain clubs in school. Nevertheless Penina's father, himself a devout Christian, embued her with an appreciation of Jewish values that may have been handed down to him from his grandmother.

Perhaps even more importantly, her father gave Penina permission to leave the religious life that no longer satisfied her, while imploring her never to abandon God, prayer, and community. Even though Penina's early adult life had more challenges than she might have wished, in the course of it she found Judaism and rediscovered the wisdom of her father.

From the earliest time I can remember, we were told by my father that we were part Jewish but not to tell anyone. His grandmother was a woman named Judith Harman, who, as the family story goes, was a rabbi's daughter who married my great-grandfather, converted to Catholicism, and changed her name to Christina. Her children retained some sense of being Jewish, as did the next generation. My father's family were merchants and landowners, and it was a business liability to be Jewish in the South, so if some sense of Jewish identity was retained, it was private, not public. Nevertheless, there were clubs in school they weren't invited to join because they were seen as Jewish.

My father's mother died when he was seven. Her name was Lila, a Hebrew name. My father, though not a Jew, had very great regard for Jewish ethics, Jewish devotion to learning, and Jewish communal values: the Jews take care of people in their community; they would not knowingly let someone go hungry, would not knowingly let a bright child go uneducated. While I was growing up, I heard of these very positive characteristics of Jewish people. I don't know whether he got it from his mother, but there were other relatives in his generation who shared those views. That sense of Jewishness was there in the family even after his mother was gone, and I feel some connection and continuity in that. Interestingly, in my generation on my father's side, three or four have married Jews; two of us have converted.

My father studied the Talmud in English translation. I don't know why my father carried on that tradition, because he was a very active Episcopalian. He was a lay

reader in a little country church about thirty-five miles beyond the city limits. I remember sitting in a pew in white gloves and hat listening to my father read the gos-
pels and deliver sermons. I was very, very impressed. Religious commitment was
just part of the fiber of our family—a multicolor fiber on my father's side.

On my mother's side of the family, it was much simpler. They had always been
Catholic and very devout. Now my mother, who lives with us, has Alzheimer's dis-
ease and wakes up every morning saying, "What time is mass?"

My parents did not attend each other's churches. You can't get much closer to
Catholicism than Episcopalian, but it was a pretty grand divide nonetheless.

I was educated as a Catholic—thirteen years in Catholic schools from kindergarten through twelfth grade. When I was around fourteen or fifteen, I started reading
early feminist writings about Margaret Sanger and the early birth-control movement.
It definitely made sense to me, but it caused a great deal of discontent with Catholicism.

There's a great deal of doctrine that you were supposed to accept in Catholicism:
these are the things you do, these are the things you don't do. I never thought about
Jesus as God or personal savior, and it wasn't what I was taught in Catholic school.
I was taught a little bit about the New Testament and about a few characters and stories in the Old Testament. You weren't encouraged to engage yourself with text. I
was taught catechism—the basic stuff you have to know as a Catholic: this is how
you live, these are the things Catholics do, and these are things Catholics avoid doing.

When I was in high school, I announced to my mother that I was abandoning
Catholic belief, and, further, that I didn't believe in God. This was on a Sunday on
the way to church. As we were arguing, she stopped the car and said, "Well, if you
mean it, get out of this car." So I got out of the car and walked home. I did not go to
mass again. My father sat down with me and said, "It's not material to me in which
religion you find your home. What's important is devotion to God and that prayer be
a part of your life. If you want to go to the Quaker meeting house, if you want to visit
with the Unitarians, if you want to go to the synagogue, I know people in all these
places. I will call, and they will welcome you, but don't divorce yourself from the
religious community."

In my early twenties a couple of critical events occurred that made it clear to me
that, while I might have thought I didn't believe in God or religion, I needed it. A
relative's child drowned in a boating accident. While they were searching for him,
my response was to pray; not on my knees, but in my heart, I very clearly addressed
some conception of the deity. When my father had a stroke, again my immediate
response was to pray. In my first year of graduate school I worked in a state mental
hospital where one patient attacked another patient and mortally wounded him. My
response was to pray—in my heart, not on my knees. So something very fundamental was there—an acknowledgment that I needed God, that the potential losses were
meaningless without the context of a loving God.

When my marriage to a fellow graduate student failed and I was raising a little
boy on my own, it became very real to me that I needed some higher moral authority

than myself to give a moral structure to this child. "Because I said so; because I say it's right" is not a sufficient rationale for a growing person.

These events happened over a period of years and made me ripe for affiliating with a religious community. There was also a sense in me of being part Jewish, though I did not know what meaning that might have in my life.

When I was in graduate school, all of the people who were my friends were Jews—though most were not strongly identified religiously. My second husband, a Jew, was a "red diaper" baby, and socialism was the family version of Judaism. Even though he was not interested in the religious aspect of Judaism, he was interested in marrying a Jew.

When I had started to study for conversion, I told him, "I don't know where this will lead. I can look into this because you request it, but I can't do it according to your definition. I can only do it according the things that make sense for me. Maybe that means I won't convert, and maybe it means that a year from now I'll be covering my hair."

I quickly decided that Reform Judaism was not for me. The lack of certainty was unsettling. I then went to the assistant director of the campus Hillel, and said, "I'm in love with a Jewish man and I'm thinking about marrying him. I have an interest in Judaism independent of that. I would like to study to see if it is possible for me to convert." He said there are some things that are really central to being Jewish: *Shabbat*, *kashrut*, *tzedakah*, devotion to the State of Israel; go read these books and come back. When I told him I wanted to learn to read Hebrew, he referred me to a programmed text for fourth graders that was wonderful. But there were a lot of things he didn't tell me about. He didn't mention the laws of family purity and neither did the Conservative rabbi that I took up my studies with at the campus where I did my postdoctoral work.

I spoke with this rabbi at great length and he said, "You know what you're talking about, you know what you're getting into, I would be willing to perform this conversion." But I wanted to study a little more, and he gave me more books to read, which we then discussed. There was still not much emphasis on *halakhah*.

I went through with the conversion under Conservative auspices, and about eleven months after that, I married. The marriage lasted less than a year. My husband was not interested in the religious observance to which I had, in the process of my studies, become committed. He proceeded to undercut my religious observance and undercut my parenting. My son was in a day school and my husband would say to him, "This is nonsense, you don't have to do this, you don't have to study."

I joined a Conservative synagogue, though my husband would not attend. I spoke to the rabbi about the various problems in my marriage. He said, "You converted to Judaism, you didn't convert to a life of subjugation to this man's definition of how you should live. This isn't a healthy situation." We divorced and I continued my involvement with the Jewish community.

Although I had had a Conservative conversion and a wedding performed by a Conservative rabbi, I wanted an Orthodox *get*. I didn't want there to be any question. I was young—not yet thirty—and I wanted to be able to remarry. I had one child; I wanted to have more children, and I wanted to do that within the Jewish community without question. I was becoming more observant, not less observant, my identity as a Jewish woman was pretty firm, and by then I understood enough about the risks to my status and my children's status if I didn't get a proper *get*.

I had to get letters from lawyers and make some threats because a woman can't issue a *get*. A *shaliah* was sent to the *Bet Din* near where my ex-husband now lived. I eventually received a *pittur*, the document that certifies that the *get* has been issued and the woman is free to remarry. I was treated very, very kindly by this group of Orthodox rabbis who knew that I was a *ger* and that I had converted under Conservative auspices. I felt no judgment from them.

It was a hard time; it was really painful. The egalitarian *havurah* and the Conservative congregation of which I was a member were very, very supportive of me as a fairly recent convert who had unfortunately gone through a divorce and found herself, again, supporting a child alone. The rabbi was always available to me if I needed to talk to him. I made a number of very close friends, and I was involved in daily and weekly observances. On Saturday afternoon and evening there was a very small group that got together for *seudah shlishit* and *Minhah/Maariv*.

There is of course the fear that if a convert is no longer married to a Jew, she will also no longer be Jewish. So it was fortunate that I had this community—my own Jewish community. It helped that a number of the people had seen me go through this evolution. And, as time went on, I was increasing my observance—a process that has been going on for a number of years.

A friend whom I invited over for *Shabbat* dinner asked if she might bring someone she had already invited to join her. I said, of course, bring him, and that was how I met my husband. For our second "date" we met in *shul*, then he came over for *Shabbat* lunch, and we went to a movie after *Shabbat* was over. He was not *Shomer Shabbat* at that time, though I was. He had a Jewish education though he didn't go to *yeshivah*. He had shown some interest and talent in Hebrew and in college got involved in Hillel. When he was doing his postdoctoral work, he lived in a community where there were very few Jews, and as one of the fewer still who could read Torah, he became a regular *leyner* there. Now back east, he became part of the community I was involved with, which gave him the opportunity to continue to do some of the things, Jewishly, that he was coming to love: lead services, *leyn*, study.

After we married and our first son was born, I happened to meet the attendant of the *mikveh*, quite by accident. One of her many children coincidentally had the same name as my son, and as I was running down the street chasing my son and calling his name she stopped to ask me why I was calling *her* child. We began to talk. She wondered why she didn't know me, since she was the "*mikveh* lady" (the attendant at the *mikveh* who helps women prepare for their immersion and oversees it to make sure it is kosher) and would have met me if I had been attending the *mikveh* regularly. I was embarrassed. My husband and I did not at that time practice *taharat hamishpahah*.

We were invited to this family's home a number of times for *Shabbat* dinner,

Shabbat lunch. My discomfort grew. I realized that if I'm embarrassed by my lack of observance, it means that this is a *mitzvah* we are ready to take on, whether we think it's easy or not. As a psychologist, I knew that a feeling of shame comes out of the sense of doing or not doing something that you've internalized a standard for. We started observing *taharat hamishpahah*.

This put me in regular contact with the *mikveh* attendant, and she began to speak to me about conversion. She was very nice but very insistent: "I know that you think your conversion is valid, but you need to understand that it is not considered so in the Orthodox community." My husband and I discussed the issue and finally decided that it was something I should do again—not because I didn't feel Jewish but because we were moving in the direction of Orthodoxy, and my status as a Jew was questionable, fairly or not, in that community. By then we were trying to conceive another child, and I wanted it to be born unquestionably Jewish. My child and I underwent the conversion and then my husband and I were remarried.

The day of the *mikveh*, we had very explicit instructions from the rabbi that my husband and I, as halakhically unmarried individuals, couldn't close the front door of the house. We got witnesses and signed another *ketubah* that afternoon, and were married that very day. I regarded this whole process very much as a formality—although perhaps one is not supposed to think of it that way. I did it far more to protect my kids than to change my sense of being Jewish, because it didn't.

Before the idea came for my second conversion, we had been in the process of finding a more traditional synagogue with which to become affiliated. To this day, my husband continues to participate in services weekly at the Conservative congregation as a *leyner* and occasionally as service leader. We still love and are friends with many of the people in the egalitarian *minyan*, but there came a point at which the unpredictability of the services there was too disconcerting. Would they *daven Musaf* or would they not *daven Musaf*? They didn't do it because it makes the service last too long—not a satisfactory response to us. This had been a wonderful, nurturing community for us for many years, but ultimately our needs changed.

There's a very authoritarian component in my personality, and before I was prone to question, the sense that this is the right way, this is the "Catholic" way, was very comforting. I've come back to some of these strictures—but through a very different route. Judaism is a system that has less insistence that you must believe exactly a certain way. What is far more important is the way you live your life. I have found that concept a more comfortable rationalization for a structured life.

We decided we should see if we would feel at home in one of the local Orthodox congregations. One of the nominal Orthodox congregations was very warm and welcoming to us, but some people would drive to *shul* and others would not. Our children even noticed this and asked us to explain. We were looking for a certain normative level of observance within a community. Another congregation was too right-wing, and we felt it promoted divisiveness rather than unity in the Jewish community.

When we *davened* with the congregation that we now have joined, it felt as if there was a certain chemistry with the rabbi. It helped also that there were several families that had belonged to the Conservative congregation and a couple that had been active in the *havurah*. When I approached him later about the conversion, I learned that he was the only Orthodox rabbi who has a decent relationship with the rabbi of the Conservative congregation where I had been for ten years.

I don't know whether he contacted the Conservative rabbi about me or not, but I told the rabbi about my relationship with the *shomerit* (lit. "guardian") of the *mikveh* and the impact that she had on us. I said, look, I am an observant Jew, these are the *mitzvot* that we observe. He convened the *Bet Din*, they questioned me, they questioned my husband at great length. By then we were both known in the community. It's a small town and even smaller Jewish community. It's sort of like living in a fishbowl; people may not know exactly what you put in your pot, but they've got a pretty good idea. That has a lot of disadvantages but it wasn't problematic.

But I can't imagine a Jewish life lived in isolation from a community. For a long time in graduate school I celebrated *Shabbat* in isolation. Life continues without community, but it's infinitely more satisfying within a community and infinitely easier with a community. There is a feeling of connection with the people we see in *shul*. There are people with whom we share the routines of *Shabbat* and *yom tov*, with whom we speak and who genuinely ask: How are you? We know enough about their lives. We can offer assistance to each other that might not be asked for. It's a life that's worth living. My children feel a part of a network with people that I don't recall as a child. That social cohesiveness is an enormous resource in times of potential or real trouble.

We became a part of that community five years ago, and we've been continuing on our path, but not without some bumps over trivia. What do you clean your dishes with on *Shabbat*? Is it really important?

What has been more of a challenge is addressing the needs of all the members of our "blended" family. My mother lives with us because, of my siblings, we are the best situated to care for her. Her illness has raised a lot of issues, and she remains a devout Catholic. Sometimes the two combined create a little havoc at home. One day my youngest son announced, "Grandma says I'm really a Catholic, and she'll baptize me." We've had to throw away a lot of flatware and china because she mixes things up in the kitchen. I'm quite confident that it's far more important to treat a parent with dignity than to worry about mistakes in the kitchen. We always treat her with love and respect, but when she says something that is very contrary to what we believe and want the children to believe, we have to confront that. And that's sometimes difficult.

Because of our living arrangements, there are people who know that I'm a *ger* who might not otherwise have known. My synagogue skills are pretty good. I look Irish but in this community, people don't come up and say, you don't look Jewish, though some did in the Conservative community. I'm not ashamed of not having been born Jewish, but it's just easier to avoid the questions. So most people who know us well have been to lunch here and had mother ask, "What time is mass tomorrow?"

The real challenge is for my children and how malleable they will see religious identity. Our oldest went to the *mikveh* with me and he is old enough to remember that. But he never asks, why did you do this, what prompted it? It is just a given for him, this is how we live, it's a good way to live, and it makes sense. My husband was speaking about a colleague's wife who might become Jewish, and our little one said, if she's not Jewish, she can't become Jewish. We just looked at each other because he clearly knows his grandmother is not Jewish and that I am. Does he not make connections between these facts? It won't stay that way forever.

My son from my first marriage converted with me when I went through the Conservative conversion. Although he attended day school for a couple of years, I was not able to give him the support I now could in Hebrew and other subjects. He transferred to a public school. He went to afternoon Hebrew school through his *bar mitzvah*. At his insistence, his Jewish education stopped there. I was fortunate that his father, from whom I had been amicably divorced, was very supportive of my raising him as a Jew. When my son was in high school, his father and current wife, for whom I have a lot of respect, located a synagogue for him to attend for *Shabbat* and the holy days when he lived with them for a year.

There *were* conflicts with my son, especially in high school. We wouldn't let him go out Friday nights, and to this day, we will not let him use a car on *Shabbat*. When he was younger, taking care of his little brothers in the afternoon, he might take them to a *treif* restaurant where he would let them have only a Coke. But the little brother would say, "I want some pizza, too." And he would say, "It's not kosher; you can't have it." "Don't tell Mama!" was the little brother's response. Now, he would take them only to a kosher restaurant—that's the difference between being a teenager and being a young adult. Now, he understands and doesn't in any way undermine us with his siblings and is generally respectful of our observance. He regards himself as a Jew and says, "Maybe later, maybe when I'm old, I'll be religious but it doesn't make sense to me now." The young women he dates are by and large Jewish.

I'd *like* to say that I dealt with these conflicts with patience and understanding; sometimes that was true, but not always. We try to be moderate. We aren't going to facilitate certain things for him, but we're not going to say, you can't live here if you do this. We try to make our position clear and try to treat him with the same respect we expect to be treated with. And I think that's the best way to leave the door open for him to come back.

My younger children don't understand that the rest of the world isn't Jewish. If you asked my nine-year-old how many people in the world are Jewish, he'd say millions and millions and millions. What percent? He'd say 100 percent, 95 percent. He feels safe in a world that's not safe, and that enables children to grow up much stronger. There's a predictability in our way of life that I think is very comforting. Jewish observance permeates all aspects of our life from the financial decisions that we make to how we eat our meals to how we furnish our bedroom. My children know that there are things we do that are more important than satisfaction of their own needs. They believe in the strength of their parents, as all children do, but when they are older and question our strength as all young people do, there'll be something behind us that makes sense and is still a source of strength and wisdom.

Judaism allows me to confront the vicissitudes of human life, the inevitability of loss, without my heart breaking. It nurtures me and strengthens me in a way that nothing else ever has. There is a way one is supposed to live, a way one is supposed to act, and there is justification for it in the centuries of writings that are the Torah and the Talmud. Prayer offers a structure for asking God for wisdom in the context of a complicated life. Thanking God on *Shabbat* makes sense because you have felt God's love at work. Knowing that there is more than myself to rely upon, more than another frail human, makes an enormous difference.

6

I Am a Part of Abraham

Doit Shotts

Doit met with me right after morning *minyan*, wearing a dark *yarmulke* over his white hair. A friend of his once said, "Oh, you don't have to wear a *yarmulke* at my house!" But Doit does not wear his *yarmulke* for his friends, he wears it for himself, a reminder of his life as a committed Jew.

"I was looking for something, and I found it in Judaism. Now I want to give of myself back to it." For the past thirty years, and now, in the tradition of retirees in synagogues around the world, Doit is doing just that at Agudas Achim, his congregation in Alexandria, Virginia. He serves on the board, attends morning or afternoon *minyan*, and with his wife, Marion, participates in various synagogue activities. But he considers one of the most important goals the nurturing of the hearts and souls of those who are bereaved, through the careful attention to the needs of those who are sitting *shivah*, knowing only too well what it means to have the support of friends when you must say *Kaddish*.

While I was growing up on a farm, my parents were not very religious. There was a belief in God. There was occasional going to church but not very frequently. Christmas was casually observed. I knew less than nothing about Judaism. In the community in which I lived there were no Jews. As time passed, I realized there was something in Christianity that I was missing. I just couldn't connect with a lot of things that were being taught. I finally realized that there were things I couldn't accept—that Jesus was born from a virgin, that he was the son of God—and I didn't like the idea of having an intermediary to God.

I was single until I was thirty-one. While I was serving in the Navy in London, I met and married a wonderful woman who was also serving in the U.S. Navy. We were married in a civil ceremony in London. Even though she was Jewish, raised in an observant home, she didn't ask me to convert. Her example of Jewish living and celebration of the Jewish holidays throughout the early years of our marriage had a definite impact on me.

I grew very close with Marion's British relatives, and we became very good friends. They welcomed me, and we just had a great time.

Our oldest child, Marvin, was born in London at the U.S. Air Force Hospital, Ruislip, England. With help from the USAF Jewish chaplain and Marion's relatives, I arranged for Marvin's ritual circumcision, at the hospital because Marion was still a patient.

I remained a non-Jew until after my transfer to San Diego. When we arrived there, we started attending services at a local synagogue and at the Jewish chapel on the navy base. We had wanted to become more involved Jewishly and I was able to observe and learn. I became comfortable with the Jewish Bible; it made sense. Also, I liked being able to express myself to one entity. I found that very satisfying.

There was a wonderful Jewish chaplain, Rabbi Lebeau, at the Naval Training Center in San Diego. He accepted me, never questioning why I was there. We had many discussions. One day, right before Passover, he and his wife said, "Come to our house for the *seder*." It was a wonderful *seder*, in which I was fully included.

One day, I telephoned the rabbi for an appointment. I really needed to talk to him, philosophically, about a few things. We talked and talked. I told him, "I would like to study with you with the desire to convert." He wanted to know if I knew what I was saying. I told him that I did. He then asked me some questions, one of which was, "Do you believe in God?" The answer was, "Sure. Yes!" Would I be able to reject Jesus as the son of God? I said, "It would be very easy for me to reject that belief because I never accepted it in the first place." He agreed that I might study with him.

After about a year of study—Hebrew, history, the Bible, and so on—he said I was ready. I agreed. There were several more steps for me: a ritual circumcision at the naval hospital in San Diego by a Jewish surgeon, supervised by the rabbi.

After my immersion in the *mikveh*, I was given my Jewish name, "Dovit." I took "Dovit" because I thought the David in the Bible was a kind person.

Marion and I were then married in the Jewish chapel.

Together, Rabbi Lebeau and I *kashered* our kitchen. It took a little bit of my getting used to, keeping separate dishes, but it really wasn't difficult. There is a lot of meaning for me in keeping kosher. It sets me apart and reminds me of the Jews' covenant with God. It's not just a Jewish "style" of life, but links me with the generations in the past as well as the present.

After my conversion, Chaplain Lebeau was released from active duty, and I became a lay leader at the Jewish chapel at the Naval Training Center for the navy and marine corps recruits. I was able to do this, even though I was new to Judaism, because the work I did in the navy, specializing in training, gave me a rapport with people. I helped organize the High Holiday services for the Jewish recruits, and explained to the navy the importance of having a rabbi to lead them. A rabbi was found, and I helped him conduct part of the services. We had a full house!

From San Diego, we went to Norfolk, Virginia, which involved sea duty. One of my assignments involved going out on a nuclear submarine. We were submerged for a couple of weeks, and, in fact, I spent Passover that year down under. I was the only Jew on board.

Before I left for the submarine, Marion contacted the Jewish chaplain, who made arrangements for all the *kosher for Pesah* food to be sent to the submarine. Everyone on the submarine was very hospitable to me. They made sure to give me plates and silverware that had never been used, and they even *kashered* a couple of trays. I had been rather apprehensive, not knowing how it would all work out. I brought some *Haggadahs* with me, and I invited anyone who wanted to to join me. They asked questions and I answered. They were very nice, very accommodating, and it was fun.

The navy is very, very positive about religion and tries to accommodate its service personnel. Over the years, officers and the senior enlisted people have been made aware of the requirements of the various religions. Shipmates of mine didn't question my religion, but they would ask questions—they were curious. So we would sit and have long conversations. I'd like to feel that I enlightened them about Judaism.

I believe in myself. I found that if I'm going to learn and continue to learn about myself and Judaism, I've got to get in there and do things. Not just read—I love to read and I do read—but if I don't put it into action, I'm really not going to amount to much. I became more outgoing. To be involved, you can't stand back. You've got to get in there and do it. By doing it, you meet a lot of wonderful people.

It's in me to continue to seek. I think it's a fact that I *found* myself in Judaism and I'm trying to give as much back as I can. Before becoming Jewish, I was just kind of wandering. I was questioning, I couldn't accept. In Judaism, I found something I could accept.

The fact that Judaism is a religion of actions is very positive. You can do what you need to do at whatever level you want to reach. And there are so many opportunities for involvement. Have I made mistakes? Yes, of course. But one thing Chaplain Lebeau told me, "Don't be embarrassed. We all make mistakes, including me, and we can learn by them." I have taken that philosophy.

We moved to the Washington, D.C., area in the late 1960s, and we've been involved with Agudas Achim since then. We could have continued to attend services in a military chapel but chose not to. I like the continuity at Agudas Achim. Since I retired, I go to *minyan* as often as possible.

I like *davening*. It's very—how can I describe it—it's like I'm communing with God, and it's just a warm, fuzzy feeling. I like the repetition. It's not that I don't insert some of my own prayers; I do. I have my own quiet meditations that I do here. But I also like that structure. There are differences each day, season to season, holiday to holiday. It gives me a sense that this day is special and the next day is special—they are the same, but different.

The Torah service is my favorite part. Here I stand, connected with everyone from many, many years ago. I'm a part of those generations. I feel like I *am* genetically connected. I am now whole, and I am a part of Abraham.

I always look forward to *Shabbat* and all of the holidays. There's always something different in each one, something that I've overlooked. I read something that I've read many times before and something new occurs to me that I hadn't thought of before.

The holiday that really fascinates me, the one I really like, although I like them all, is *Sukkot*—dwelling in the *sukkah*. I relate to it because I lived on a farm in my youth.

I also make a special effort to attend *minyans* in homes of mourning—*shivah* houses. It has special meaning for me, reminding me of when we sat *shivah*. It was comforting to have friends there with us.

Marion and I also try to support Jewish causes, including the Jewish Theological Seminary (JTS). We are active in getting Jews in northern Virginia involved in learning about the seminary, the kinds of programs it provides—besides training all of our rabbis, our cantors, our teachers. In addition to supporting JTS financially, I think it is good for Jews to go to New York and visit JTS, maybe even to study a little bit there.

I like going into the rare book library at JTS. It's the oldest Jewish library in the United States. I have really enjoyed looking at the collection of Torah scrolls from various countries throughout the world.

In the Conservative movement, Judaism evolves. I like the fact that tradition can be made to work for modern Jews. Just one example of a small interpretation that is important to me is being able to drive to synagogue on *Shabbat* and not feel guilty.

I also think it was long overdue when JTS started to ordain female rabbis and cantors. I feel that there should not be this "men-only club" in the Jewish religion.

I didn't start being active in our synagogue right away, but a few years after we'd joined, I asked to serve on the synagogue board of directors. Soon after, I got a phone call, "Hey, Doit. We'd like for you to be on the board." And that's how my very active participation in the synagogue got started.

Being on the board of directors at Agudas Achim is fun, time consuming, *and* a learning experience. You have to get along with people, but once in a while, make sure you assert yourself. You have to speak up. If you don't like how something is being done and you don't assert yourself, it's going to be done that way, and then it'll be too late.

One task that I have taken on that I think is essential is notifying people when there has been a death in the family of a member of the congregation. Sometimes, I just find out by chance. It can be hurtful at such a sensitive time when things don't get communicated properly.

We belong to a small *havurah* group devoted mostly to supporting social networks. I look forward someday to being part of a *havurah* that would be more devoted to religious issues and study. It would solidify a lot of activities in the synagogue.

Acceptance of me as a Jew has been fairly universal. Once in a while, something will come up in a conversation that makes things rather awkward. I find that if I don't say something, then it gets uncomfortable. So, under those circumstances, I do say, "I'm sure you don't know this but I was not born Jewish." Sometimes people are quite surprised. I do feel, though, that my status as a Jew is not information that people have a right to just to satisfy their own curiosity.

Once a challenging situation arose in which someone asked me out of the blue, "You're a convert, aren't you?" That is insensitive. Of course, I answered truthfully. When the person didn't ask anything else, I had to wonder, "Why did you ask in the first place?" I had to assume that this person was not aware of the custom that it is not appropriate to ask someone if he or she is a convert.

I think there are some in the community who think that most converts came to Judaism because of their mates. And I'd like them to know that's not true, that's not true at all. Marion did not encourage me in any way. She didn't even know that I was going to ask Rabbi Lebeau about conversion until I got home from my lunch with him, and I told her what took place. I know she was pleased.

My parents didn't reject me. I was already an adult and away in the navy, and I never got home that much. I tried to explain my conversion to them, but I don't really think it got through. *And that was okay.* My oldest brother is a minister. Although he accepted my conversion, he couldn't figure out how I could reject Jesus.

The Holocaust period has always disturbed me but not to the point where I rejected God. I'm not sure that I really understand all the messages that are there. One of the lessons I've learned, though, is that God gave each one of us the ability to think, to do things, to question, to argue—and I think some of that was missing during that period in Europe. But trying to understand why it happened is nearly impossible.

I hope to visit Israel to really observe, learn, and feel. I do not want to just sightsee and then return home. I have a feeling I'd want to live there.

Marion and I had two children; unfortunately, both are deceased. Our youngest son, Robert, was born at the Naval Hospital in San Diego with a heart defect. His survival was very short. Marvin, our oldest boy, lived to the age of ten and then died of cancer. It took a long time to get over his death. I know Judaism had a lot to do with my recovery from that loss. Judaism is incredibly nurturing to the mourner. Of course, we struggled. We have a lot of good friends who helped us to get back into the mainstream. I believe God didn't mean for me to mourn all my life, but that doesn't mean that I don't miss my sons.

I remember the good things about Marvin, and that helps. He was a really great boy. We had him enrolled in Jewish day schools both in San Diego and in Norfolk. He would help me get through some of my struggles with learning Jewish rituals. He would say, "No, Dad. Dad, it's this way." We had a great time.

7

From a *Shidukh* in Glasgow

Victor Tynes

On Vic Tynes's desk at the Equal Employment Opportunity Commission in Washington, D.C., is a picture of his wife, his son—tall, like his father—in a basketball uniform, and his guitar. In addition to working at the EEOC as a lawyer, Vic is a rock and roll guitarist, and he teases his wife that he *could* make a living in Israel as a musician if they were to move there!

Vic's ancestry is pure, melting pot America, and his community growing up was African-American. He speaks with candor and compassion about what it is like to be 90 percent non-African genetically, and 100 percent African-American socially—the latter controlled by society's blinders concerning human beings of color. In telling his story, Vic also challenges us to look deeply into our hearts to understand "Who is a Jew?"

After a spiritual quest that took him from his grandfather's Baptist church, to Hinduism, then to a Muslim mosque, he discovered that Judaism spoke to him from his soul—a beckoning through the generations to return again.

When I was five, my father started teaching me high spiritual principles, mostly from Eastern religions. We correctly call it mysticism, but we sometimes very horribly call it "occult," which is really bad. I have come to realize that the ideas my father was teaching me are similar to the principles one finds in *Kabbalah*. This learning was on the side, though, because I was born into a family of practicing Baptists. My grandfather and my great-grandfather before him were Baptist ministers. Even though the Baptist religion didn't really appeal to my father, he attended and had his family attend my grandfather's church rather than besmirch the family name. But on the side my father would teach me these other principles.

Once I was old enough to start reading, I read little bits about various religions, and when I was about eighteen or twenty I went beyond what my father taught me. When I was twenty-nine or thirty, it suddenly occurred to me that although I had done all this studying of Eastern religions and Christian metaphysics, the one religion I hadn't studied was Judaism. So I found a guy who worked with me—who now is my best friend—who I thought was Jewish and I said, "Listen, if I want to find out something about Judaism, what do I do?" And he said, "Well, I really don't know what to tell you other than to suggest you go talk to my rabbi."

So I did that. The rabbi told me, just as a preliminary step, to get Max Dimont's, *Jews, God and History*. Normally, when I am reading a book, I start out, read a little

53

bit, and if it sounds like something I already know something about, I skip and go to the next part. This time I was just enraptured with the book. There was something odd about it that I really couldn't put my finger on. As I got toward the end, I realized this book was talking about *me*. I couldn't figure out how that could be. So as I was musing to myself, "This is an insane notion," a voice within me said, "No, it's not. You are a Jew." I responded—out loud—"What! You've got to be kidding." When I did that I realized that I was veering off into the metaphysical level of things, and I was having an experience at a different level of consciousness. I had learned years before not to take those experiences lightly. I realized how rare they are, and how in most practices people have had to use an enormous amount of disciplined meditation to get to those points. I knew this was significant—a miracle.

I finished reading the book. I went back to the rabbi for more information. And I told him, "I have been told by the divine creative force that I am a Jew, and if I am a Jew then I must practice as a Jew." I said, "Please don't take me through the routine. I know you have to dissuade me three times. Consider yourself having tried to dissuade me once more so we can count it as three, and we've gone through the legalisms so I can get started on the process." He still felt that I was in too much of a hurry and wanted to tell me about the challenges I would face. I didn't want to hear any of that. All I wanted to do was to go ahead with the conversion so I could go on the pathway that was obviously set for me.

I started taking classes and attending synagogue. Fortunately this was a Reform synagogue. I say "fortunately" because it can be a real culture shock to go from a religion where you have no real requirements other than belief, to one in which you have physical ritual requirements as well as a different language. Little by little I started becoming aware of holidays—no more two-holidays-a-year. Even though I had given up on Christianity when I was seventeen, I had been going along with some of the usuals like exchanging gifts at Christmas, but I resented it. I felt Christmas had become a very commercial thing that was polluting my spirituality.

Class lasted about three months and then it took another four months before the *Bet Din*. Once I completed that, and I was official, everything was fine, and I just continued my educational process.

My realization that I am Jewish was a miracle. Miracles are still happening every day, but I believe that people have forgotten how to recognize them. A rabbi I know sometimes has me tell the story of how I first got the message, because people don't believe that God can speak to them anymore. They believe that God is an unseen force that never communicates in our lifetime. If that was the case, we would really be in bad shape for fulfilling our responsibility of bringing the world to the oneness. We would be at a great disadvantage with other peoples who still communicate with God and get answers. To remind everybody that it is possible, the rabbi has me give my testimonial.

Once I converted, my family began to divulge all our Jewish connections.

I was born in Washington and raised in North Carolina, where my mother's family is from. My mother's first job on leaving high school, before she went to college, was working for a Jewish judge from Florida who vacationed in North Carolina. Through her job, my mother became familiar with Jewish people and Jewish practices. I used to wonder why my mother liked to eat this very dry bread, like crackers. It was *matzah*, of course. After I converted, family members began to recall these experiences, and my conversion put their memories in perspective. They could see what kind of influences Jewish culture had had on our family.

But the most amazing revelation came from my father. About two weeks after my conversion ceremony, my father gave me a brass *menorah* that he had had since his days in New York. And with his gift came this story: My dad's mother's mother was one of the first children born into the Jewish community in Glasgow, Scotland. In the 1840s, Jews coming to America from Poland had to go through Scotland and some didn't have the money to continue on their journey, so they settled there. My great-grandmother was born shortly after that. When she grew up she was a leader in the Jewish community and met a Native American in Glasgow who was a shipper from Virginia. They got married and had my grandmother. Even though my grandmother attended Christian school back in Virginia, she was never baptized. Later, she married a Baptist minister, but we found out that she never converted to Christianity, for what reason, nobody knew. In the Baptist church in order for you to be considered a Christian you *have* to be baptized.

My grandmother, evidentally, felt her Jewish ancestry was not something to talk about. I can understand that; that was southeastern Virginia, and there just weren't any Jews down there. She never told her children that they were of Jewish ancestry unless they asked. So the only ones who knew were my Aunt Margaret and my Uncle Jacob, because they were the only ones who asked about their family history. My Uncle Jacob went to Scotland and met some of the relatives. Uncle Jake always had a *mezuzah* on his door. I asked him what it was and where it came from and he said, "It's a *mezuzah*; the people who lived here before me left it." If there was ever a stereotypically Jewish-looking person, it was my Uncle Jacob. But I never understood his connection to the Jewish community—it seemed all his friends were Jewish—until I was older and found my own connection.

When I was a kid my first real girlfriend was the daughter of a rabbi whose congregation was started in the mid-1800s. Apparently, a Jewish master liberated his slaves, and as part of his bequest to them (which included land) he gave them religious instruction and converted them to Judaism. Ever since 1846 they have been practicing Judaism, and there are small groups of them in four or five cities. This slave owner followed the duties of a Jewish father by offering them training in a profession, religion, and— swimming! All the people in this family were great swimmers at a time when African-American people often didn't know how to swim. I never will forget telling my supervisor at a grocery store where I worked that my girlfriend was Jewish. He had a fit because he thought she was white, and down south in 1966 you didn't do that; you could die for such an infraction.

In my senior year in high school, everybody wrote in my yearbook about my interest in Hinduism. A Hare Krishna at the airport had given me a copy of the *Bhagavad*

Gita. I asked my dad what I should do; he said give them some money. The guy said a dollar would do, and he gave me the hardbound book. I started reading it, and since I was already rebelling against Christianity, I adopted some of the practice of Hinduism. It fit in well with some of the principles of metaphysics my dad had already taught me.

The big problem I had with Hinduism was the multiple deities. I understood, however, that the reason for multiple deities was to provide the rank and file with a simple means of recognizing the various characteristics of God.

We Jews, on the other hand, identify the characteristics without the need to personify each one individually. One of the main things we did for the world was to come to know an invisible God. As a result people had to deal with the concept of spirit. If you read our sages, God is one, indivisible. And if God is one, God cannot be severed from us. God has to be *everything*.

A buddy of mine and I were talking at work about the Trinity and how the Romans abused people by forcing them to believe in a trifold manifestation when Jesus himself had never said that that was the case and always fought it when people attempted to deify him. But in order for the Romans to cause people to take up this new religion, they had to be able to concretize more than one entity so that the people could say, "Yeah, this is familiar. And these gods are kind of special because they all operate in more than one place; they can operate anywhere."

For a long time I would try to spread the message to Christians that they were being misled. Then I realized that I was unintentionally doing more damage than good because I was asking them to change their belief system. One should never consciously attack another's beliefs. It is preferable to provide people with facts and then allow them to develop the interest in examining their beliefs themselves.

For a very short period while I was in law school here in D.C., I attended the Nation of Islam mosque. Thinking about that time made me realize in retrospect something that a rabbi friend of mine said: that we Jews made a mistake in not proselytizing to the African-American community. The Muslims have done what we should have done. Islam is a religion of discipline, and discipline cures a lot of problems that any ghettoized people have. However, I couldn't continue with the Nation of Islam because it is fundamentally racist. In order to counteract the racism of the society, Elijah Mohammed felt it was necessary to fill the African-American people with their own sense of superiority. I have a real problem with that. I found myself, as in Christianity, going along with some of the nonracist but also questionable things that were being said in order to get to the meatier issues. I read the Koran. After going three or four times, I couldn't stand it and couldn't go anymore.

My venture into Islam was interesting, but it was in no way comparable to being a Jew. I was born a Jew. I just didn't realize it, so I had to go wandering for a long time. The Torah has a line: "If you turn your back on me, O Israel, I shall remember you even unto the third or fourth generation." And I am the third or fourth generation, depending on who you look at as the last practitioner. I find a lot of converts have had a similar experience—although people who have Jewish blood I don't call converts; I call them "returnees." I am a returnee, not a convert. My thinking didn't change because of my conversion. Rather, I found labels for feelings and concepts I've had since childhood.

My conversion or return was motivated purely by religious interest. Many people I meet who are converts decided to convert because of somebody they were enamoured with. When I started this process, I had a girlfriend who was not Jewish. We parted company, in part because of my Judaism. She had attended synagogue with me for a time and people thought we were married. One day, she turned on the radio, and some evangelist was on. I started criticizing him because I hate the way they use religion for self-aggrandizement. I can have a little compassion for the ignorant ones who say "send me the money" because they don't know any better than to be a money grubber. But when it's someone who is articulate and well-versed in the Bible and has probably studied peripheral texts and should know better, then it really bothers me. That's the kind of guy this was. We were listening to him, and I said, "He has just prostituted everything we are taught about the practice of religion." My friend got very upset. We parted company because she couldn't give up her dependence on Bible-thumping. We were incompatible. I wasn't going to turn away from Judaism. God had commanded me to do this.

I used to believe, as some people still do, that you and your partner don't have to be members of the same religion. That's fine if you are a member of a religion that doesn't require anything from you. But if you are a member of a religion that requires practices and observances, there is no way you can have a partner who is doing something different. Muslims are told that if you must marry out of the faith, marry a Jew because she will never serve you pork. Not eating pork is so important to them that they would marry a Jew instead of a Christian. Practices are very important. You can imagine: the High Holidays come; they're giving you trouble at work about taking off or you've got a schedule that is oppressive, and your boss says to you, "You don't have to do that religious stuff, so what?" You need support at home to deal with that.

I knew that my destiny would be to marry someone who was Jewish. I didn't really give it a whole lot of thought, at first. I dated women who weren't Jewish and some who were. Then I met my wife.

One Friday evening, my buddy Lionel and I were in the synagogue. Sitting apart from us was a guy we had befriended who was from Trinidad. He had expressed an interest in Judaism and had come to synagogue. We were impressed that this guy, coming from a different culture, had been interested in becoming Jewish. This fellow was sitting to my left about twenty feet away and I was trying to get his attention to say, "How are you doing?" to make him feel welcome. But every time I turned to try to get his attention, I was looking into my wife's face. It never occurred to me that *she* was looking at *me*.

Judy had come with friends to hear Flori Jagoda, a Ladino performer, originally from Yugoslavia. She is very popular here in Washington, D.C., among people who are familiar with Jewish music. Flori Jagoda plays the guitar and sings Ladino songs and does a seminar. I had come to synagogue that night just for the services and to hear Flori Jagoda, whose performance took the place of the sermon. Judy had been invited for the whole evening, which included dinner. During services, she was sitting with mutual friends and unbeknown to me she had said to them, "Who is that guy over there? He looks like he is really *davening*." Her friend said, "That's Vic. I'll introduce you to him later." But it turned out I approached her before that ever happened.

People always try to tell our Jewish kids: "Go to synagogue and you might meet somebody you really like." The kids always say, "Nah, it will be boring." To all my friends who are always whining, "There are no good men/women around," I say, "Go to synagogue. You don't know who you might meet." When you are *not* looking is likely to be the time you will meet somebody.

All of us have a connection to one another, and we just don't know how to lock into that. This is why I believe so strongly in metaphysics. All we do is make choices between things that are interconnected—whether we are aware of that or not—and circumstances occur that make things either more or less available to us at the time. My father had told me this. I laugh now about that because he said to me, "You are going to meet a woman in synagogue; she is going to have brown eyes and brown hair." What foresight!

Judy and I immediately hit it off. After a week, I stopped dating anybody else. Within a month, I had told her I intended to marry her. We got married about two years after that. My father had advised me to wait that long—which I had not done when I had married before—to test whether our relationship really had longevity. We live in a "McDonald's" society. Everybody wants everything right away. So people often miss the opportunity to really get to know each other. We were older— my wife is older than me—and two years was very critical for us. It was difficult to wait that long, but it turned out to make sense because we had both had relationships before that weren't happy, and we were both a little cautious. My wife was inspired, though, that I was willing to commit myself so early on. That was a little less than a year after I had converted.

It may sound odd, but I hadn't really thought much about the fact that most of the people in my faith group and my peoplehood happened to be of European extraction. On the other hand, I hadn't completely gotten over the problems I faced from the fear that I had about being in public places with a woman who was of European descent. That comes from being raised in the South in a black community. The woman I dated just before I met my wife really helped me to resolve that. Now, of course, I have met so many people who are European whose complexions are very brown in comparison to mine.

One of the worst things that happens in our society is that we don't really know a lot about each other. This is bad. I remember being in high school and kids wanted to put their hands on my hair to see what it felt like, and I did the same thing to them. I never knew that straight hair could be coarse and hard to the touch. I always thought that all straight hair was silky. I never realized that hair as curly as mine can be soft. There are a lot of simple things we don't know about each other. We learn to be divided.

I began to learn that I was different from what I perceived myself to be. My wife was different from what I perceived her to be. We are not what we are taught to believe we are in this society. We are very different from the people on television. People are much more homogeneous than differentiated. The biggest differences I see between people are based on economics. Those differences are scary. Poverty has always bothered me, but now we are allowing class divisions to become potentially lethal.

I was speaking with a Hispanic guy at the EEOC's recent Hispanic festival and I said to him, "Isn't it funny how in our society being a member of a color minority is considered to be a pollutant." He was shocked but because he was a sociologist he was immediately fascinated. (Sociologists are constantly accumulating data.) We explored this a little. He said, "Why do you say that?" I said, "Because I am about six to eight percent African, but people call me black because there is a presumption that black operates like ink in a glass of water. As soon as you put one drop of ink in the glass, it changes everything. I resent that point of view because it says that genetics is irrelevant and that there is some polluting factor in being of African descent. I honor all of my heritages, and I put them in the perspective that they each deserve. I am black, more so because of the fact that I was raised in a black neighborhood, and, therefore, I have some social characteristics that emanate from my childhood, rather than being black because I am primarily of African ancestry."

In our society, being part African makes you black, unless it is not physically obvious and you don't talk about it. I have a friend for whom it is not physically obvious. One of her great-grandparents was half black. It is impossible to tell that from her physical traits. A black man was saying that she is a white woman pretending to be black to get special privileges. He didn't understand. I said to him, "Let me tell you something, that 'pretend' black woman is about twice as 'black' as I am." He was shocked.

I knew a guy who was one-eighth Indian—barely enough for him to qualify to be on the reservation. He had accepted himself all his life as white. When he found out about his Native American ancestry, the first people he told said, "Just drop it; it's not important; it's only an eighth." He persisted in telling people. Pretty soon he found out he wasn't getting promotions. He had to file an EEO complaint. So, here is a challenge that I give every white person in the country, even if you are blond with blue eyes: if you want to know what it is to be black, tell all your friends you just discovered that your grandmother was a black woman. Recognize that if you carry this through, it will affect you for the rest of your life. You will discover what it is like to have a constant barrage of messages telling you that you are inferior—a constant, neverending barrage of negative information. There are a lot of people who have African-American or Native American ancestry who are divorced from it because it is very inconvenient.

Some people wanted to dissuade me from becoming a "double minority" by adopting a Jewish life. They said, "People push you aside for your racial minority status, and now they'll do it because of your religious minority status." The impact on me has actually been the opposite. I generally get introduced to people as being Jewish.

As a result, I have been able to observe something that almost no minorities within this society get to observe: the experience of what it is like to be white.

A few years ago I worked with a guy who was Polish. I was a source of pride to him because his wife was Jewish. One day he said something to another person about my being like his wife because I was Jewish and that person said, "Is your wife also black?" The guy said, "What the heck are you talking about?"—only in stronger language. And the person replied, "Well, Vic Tynes is black." So he asked me, "Are you black?" And I said, "Well, part, yeah; and I used to call myself black because that was all I really knew about myself." He started to laugh and said, "You know, I didn't even see it." Because I was Jewish, he automatically assumed that I was of European extraction. Most people aren't familiar with Ethiopian Jews, Cochin Jews, the Chinese Jews, the Japanese Jews.

If you are European and Jewish you could say to yourself, I could be Italian and somebody might call me names; or Polish, or Irish, but you still have majority status, from the standpoint that if you don't say anything and your last name doesn't end in "-berg" or "-sky" you can coast. I suspect that a lot of people are coasting—and they don't even realize it.

In contrast, old people still remember what it was like when society wouldn't let Jews "coast." My father-in-law, may he rest in peace, used to tell me stories about how they wouldn't let him be an officer in the military, even though he had qualifications superior to the guys they did promote. People are afraid of what they don't understand and we, as Jews, represent something people don't understand. They are getting less afraid of us because, for the most part, we are becoming more like them. We are not the guys with the *peyus*; we look indistinguishable.

I take great pride in the fact that we as Jews are not a racial group, we are a "peoplehood." We transcend physical differences. If we don't learn anything else from the Bosnians, it should be this: these ideas of differentness are not logical, they are emotional. In the former Yugoslavia are three groups of people who look identical, whose names are very similar, who five years ago were intermarried, and all of a sudden they are so strategically different. I think they are nuts. You say to yourself, "Where did this junk come from?" What we need is an invasion from outer space so that people will realize that everybody has two eyes, two ears, a nose. I say to people, "Pretend you are a dog for a day. What difference does a dog see between people?"

I have one son, who is eighteen and attends the University of Michigan. He went to a Catholic high school—that was the only religious education I could get his mother to agree to, although his mother is not a practitioner of any religion. She says she is agnostic. My son likes the shock value of telling people, "My dad is Jewish." (And he can go me one better as far as personal ethnic diversity is concerned because he's part Chinese as well.) For a time it was a seduction for me, too. The shock value was absolutely fun. My son takes great pride in the fact that we are not pigeonholeable. He also takes great pride in his African heritage.

I can say, I am African, Jewish, Scottish, Irish, English, Native American. I've gotten to the point where I don't bend to the pressure to overcompensate for my black heritage. I put it in its perspective as one phase of my existence. The predominant phase of my existence is being Jewish because it permeates my whole being. There are times literally when I forget the differences in my identification. My wife stops me sometimes and says, "Which *we* are you talking about now?" My *we* is always situational. There are very few "*we*'s" that I am not a part of.

When I am among Jews my *we* is a very intense spiritual as well as a physical feeling of we. If I see any differences it is only for the purpose of understanding history, it is not for the purpose of distinguishing or differentiating. Among Jews who are conscious that I am a Jew, I have suffered very little singling out or any level of disrespect. From time to time, it does occur, but it has always been somebody who I could have anticipated would treat anybody differently or rudely.

I think it takes about five to seven years to build up the self-confidence in your Jewish identity not to even think about it. The most difficult thing for people converting is acclimating to a Jewish community that demands your involvement, from a society where everything is very loose and not as disciplined. One thing that distinguishes us as Jews is that we take personal responsibility for the state of the world. We take personal responsibility for doing *mitzvot*. If the world goes to "you-know-where" in a handbasket, it is our fault. It is not the fault of some presence that is manipulating things like a marionette. Since the rest of the world functions on the basis of concepts of divine providence, it is very difficult for people to get used to the level of personal responsibility that we take for granted.

It took me at least a year to condition myself to reading my calendar often enough to be sure I didn't miss a holiday. Fortunately, my rabbi was very loving in that respect. He would say, "You can do it next year." He believed in a graduated process of observance, and he felt that observance should be meaningful to you. If it's not meaningful and you are just doing it because everybody else is doing it, it's not good.

Now that I am in the Conservative movement, I have grown to believe that sometimes observance is good whether or not it has meaning for you, initially, just to get you in the habit of doing it. Later, you develop understanding. Helping converts to understand why they have to do things is very important—and it's also good for born Jews! I know so many people who are born into Judaism who have rote knowledge—they don't understand *why* they are doing things. That's scary. We'll lose the whole faith if no one knows why we are doing things. We each have to take responsibility for being as knowledgeable as possible.

For my part, I'd like to learn how to read Hebrew better and faster. If you don't know what you are saying it becomes like that Buddhist practice of repeating the same thing over and over again. Eventually, what you say is less important than your intonation. I see a lot of people doing that, and I don't want to get to that point. It is one of our modern tragedies. Because if you don't know what you are saying, are you really praying? That is the question.

I was fortunate this year that one of my colleagues at work belongs to my synagogue and is interested in metaphysics, which we are able to discuss in the context of Judaism. The two of us are going to try to raise our consciousness levels more by studying *Kabbalah* and the *Zohar* together and maybe getting a class going.

If we don't all try to make opportunities like this, we Jews may lose five thousand years of knowledge because so many young people could care less about our history. Of Western peoples, we have the longest memory. It is very important for us to retain a memory base, or we are going to commit the same mistakes again. My own personal responsibility has to be that I learn more about what I am doing.

When I was single I would go to synagogue several times a week. My wife was not very religiously observant, so as a family we are at a median from the point where she was and where I was. My wife knows a lot about ritual and practice, but she was raised in a traditional home that believed women didn't need to know the reasons behind things—my library of Jewish books was bigger than hers, for example. So she knew practices, but not the religious reasons. As a result, when she left home, anything that she didn't do at home with her folks, she didn't worry about that much. Now she participates a lot more. She readapted very quickly to practices from her childhood—we always celebrate *Shabbat* at home, we light *Shabbat* candles. I do the *brakhot*. She has *Yartzeit* and *Yizkor* for her father, and I for my mother, and she is involved in the sisterhood. We like to go to *shul* on Friday nights and don't often go on Saturday, although Saturday is admittedly a much more fulfilling experience. We celebrate the holidays. We have Jewish objects in our home. But we don't always refrain from everything that we are supposed to refrain from—I have to be honest about that. We don't keep kosher. One problem is that our house is small, and it would be difficult. Sometime in the future, we may. When we are older we will become more observant, I am sure.

We have been to Israel, and I loved it! My wife says it is too expensive to live in Israel, otherwise I'd like to be living there now. In spite of Judy's concern about the finances, I was impressed that her relatives seemed not to be overly concerned about money—because the highest status comes from what you know, not from what you own. I felt a level of connection with history there that you don't feel here. Jewishness is a matter of course there. You feel a spirituality that is absolutely incredible. You can go around and touch things that have existed for eons, and I feel that I could contribute to the continuity of that process.

Converts as a group have this contribution to make: we don't take Judaism for granted. Sometimes born Jews have forgotten the value of Judaism. There were some understandable reasons for this. As people with European ancestry, Jews could have access to everything; but if people find out you are a Jew, your access might be diminished. There are clubs that won't have you. People begin to notice this in their teen and post-teen years, and it shapes their thinking about the effect of being openly Jewish. Whereas we who come to it later in life are free of all that. We came into Judaism accepting whatever plusses or minuses there were. One idea we might adapt from the traditions of Baptists is that you are not allowed to call yourself a Baptist until you make an *open* confirmation that this is what you want.

We have a thousand-year fear of proselytizing, which I am always encouraging the rabbis to discard. Somebody's got to say, yes, Mainz, Germany, happened in the year 1000 or whatever, and that is the last time any religious organization *officially* slaughtered us for proselytizing. We can do it now. We can get on TV just as others do and let people know about some *real* "good news"—something other than send a preacher twenty bucks. We have just as much right to go out and proselytize as anyone else. But let's face it, when gentiles went out and slaughtered thousands of our people, it made a lasting impression on Jews. So I understand why the rabbis back then said no more proselytizing. But we need to do it now to fulfill our responsibility. We don't have to say, "What you are doing is bad." What we could say is, "These are the facts that five thousand years of continuous knowledge have taught us. These things may help you to understand the good things you are trying to accomplish." If we just did that, we'd change the world. I think we need some Jewish evangelists.

In becoming Jewish, I have gained the universe. The great misfortune in growing up in the African-American community in the United States was that people had been trained in slavery not to honor education as much as they would have otherwise. They were trained to seek to survive before they sought to enrich themselves intellectually. You find this is also true among many Native Americans. Being a bookworm is not looked upon as an honorable thing. It is looked upon as trying to be "white." Thank God this is changing. I've always been a person who was desperate for new knowledge. When I finally found this people who hallow knowledge above everything else, my soul was free! Now I could use perfect English and be appreciated for it. I didn't have to use "corn pone" speech to survive. Now I could openly say that most of the time I'd rather get my hands on something to read than go dancing. My world was opened up to a people who saw deeper meaning in human existence than anyone else around because their perception is five thousand years old. "VT found home."

8

Building Community

Darlene Feldstein

Unbeknown to her, Darlene's parents regularly sent part of the family's mea-
ger resources to support the civil-rights movement. She was amazed to learn
of this as an adult because she could recall times when their family of seven
lived on a very tight budget. "Why didn't you tell us about this?" "We didn't
want to brag," they said. Darlene feels that this sense of community responsibility is an important part of her children's Jewish education.

In fact, commitment to family, community, and Jewish education has been
at the center of Darlene's life as a Jew for many years. Each enhances the other
and provides a spiritual grounding for her, her husband, and their two daughters, as well as other lives they touch.

Given that much of her life is involved in participating Jewishly, it is perhaps surprising to learn that Darlene was not interested in converting to Judaism when she and her husband married. Studying and "doing" Judaism for many
years eventually evolved into a comfortableness and security with the rituals
and holidays that reflect the values of a Jewish life and led to her conversion.

When Sonia, my elder daughter, started kindergarten at the neighborhood
public school, I became aware of the fact that she was really a minority in
her class, one of two Jewish children in a class of thirty-one or thirty-two.
Little things would come up. At the tender age of five, she was having to explain that
we don't celebrate Christmas. On the one hand, I was proud that she was so articulate about it. On the other hand, I detected that she had a sense, at such a young age,
that she was not like everyone else. This realization made me feel sad. While, indeed,
there are advantages to minority status, for example, increased sensitivity to other
peoples, I believe that having a deep awareness of your minority status is not really
the best for building self-esteem in a five- or six-year-old.

I wanted my children to be like I was. I never questioned whether I belonged. I
never experienced what Alan Dershowitz, author of *Chutzpah*, refers to as feeling
like a guest in someone else's home. In one of her books, Fay Moskowitz, one of my
favorite authors, refers to a boyfriend she had as a young girl; he exuded that attitude
of generations of being in the majority culture. My father's ancestors came to America
in the 1600s, so I know what she was talking about: always belonging, living secure
in the knowledge that you are supposed to be here. I happen to think this attitude
assists in building self-esteem, particularly in young children. As you are older, it is

easier and a more appropriate time to become aware of the fact that you are different and that not everyone is like you.

The sense of belonging is something that has really helped me in my life. The stronger base children have—in feeling they know where they've come from, they know what's at home, they know who they are—the better. In this day and age, we don't have the old structure of extended family helping out—even if Mother is working out of the home. A lot of kids don't have a community.

Sonia had gone to a Jewish nursery school, and it had been a wonderful environment: the nursery school, what we did at home and in our synagogue, and our friends all reinforced our identity as Jews. There was a noticeable difference when she started in the public schools. Wouldn't it be nice, I thought, to extend that wonderful nourishing Jewish environment, even just a couple of years. That's when I first started thinking about the prospect of a Jewish day school.

There is an Orthodox Jewish day school in the community, but I had heard from a number of people that there could be questions about the authenticity of my non-Orthodox conversion. Since my motivation for considering a Jewish day school was to ensure an environment where my child would not feel "different," this school would not meet my needs.

When I discussed this dilemma with my friends who were at the Jewish nursery school where my younger daughter was enrolled, I found a number of other parents who were also interested in the idea of starting a non-Orthodox day school. The first community meeting of over thirty interested individuals was in our home. During the meeting everyone stated why they were there, and what they were envisioning. We were energized by the knowledge that everyone was in agreement about the type of Jewish day school our community needed!

It took a little less than two years of planning to establish the new school. The doors to the school opened at the JCC four years ago with thirty-one students, kindergarten through second. Now the school has ninety-three students, kindergarten through fifth.

I have worked on most of the committees to help find the site, establish the office, raise funds, hire teachers—the myriad of tasks necessary to start a school! I've been active on the board of directors as an officer for the past two years. My husband was the first president, a role he held for two years.

My children have been involved in the whole process. In addition to receiving a Jewish education, it's important that they observe our activities in participating in and building the Jewish community. The downside, of course, is that we are out at meetings all too often, though we try to keep evening meetings to a minimum.

I have always hoped that the school would be a comfortable place for interfaith families. I wanted the school to be a place where adults also learn about Judaism. I see the school as a good place for couples who have agreed to raise their children as Jews, even if a spouse has not converted. A Jewish day school is a wonderful place to build community because it provides a place for the child and the entire family to learn about Judaism and live Jewishly.

I continue to learn with my chilren, especially the Hebrew language. I took a year of Hebrew when my daughter was in kindergarten because I could see I would soon not be able to help her with her homework. We've done a number of workshops for parents to help better understand the holidays. I have learned, both from experts and from my friends, ways of strengthening our Jewish practices.

When I look back on the process of my coming to Judaism, I do not see myself as someone who was looking for spirituality, meaning, or a new community. I had the rich spiritual tradition of the community in which I had been raised.

My mother was Catholic, my father, Episcopalian, and I'd been raised Catholic until I was thirteen. At that time my mother did not agree with the church's stance on birth control, and so she painfully left Catholicism to join my father's church. When my family first went to my father's church, as the oldest of five children I was the only one who was reluctant to change. My parents agreed to take me to the Catholic church for services while they attended the Episcopal church. Shortly after this time my family moved to a new community and I joined them at the Episcopal church. As a college student I always went to either Protestant or Catholic churches, depending upon which community was the most active in social-action activities.

I was challenged by issues relating to Jesus and Christianity when I was in high school and college. I saw a big difference between the Catholic literal understanding of such things as the virgin birth, Jesus' existence, and the resurrection, and the Protestant perspective, which tended to explain Jesus in more metaphorical terms. For example, the resurrection was referred to as a time of starting anew. I became accustomed to seeking explanations that had meaning for me within the Christian religion.

When I met my husband, he suggested that I might think about converting. When I asked him why, he said that he just thought it might be a good idea. I pressed him by asking many questions: "How would I be better if I converted? What would you like more about me? What do Jews believe about the afterlife? What do you believe about sin? What do you believe about resurrection?" He had problems articulating the "Jewish position" regarding Christian concepts that were important to me. He'd had a good Reform Jewish education, although I could tell he was embarrassed that he couldn't offer better responses to my questions. Though he was not sure how to respond to my questions, he was clear that he wanted to raise his children as Jews. At the time I thought, "Well, Judaism has the Old Testament, that's part of my tradition. It should be familiar to me." So I agreed, "We'll raise the children Jewish, but I won't convert because it seems to me that would be like saying 'I'm black' or 'I'm Asian.'" I felt that I couldn't be something that I wasn't, even with a ceremony.

"Maybe we can take classes together," Steve suggested. And that's how it got started. We've been taking classes on some aspect of Judaism during all the fifteen years of our marriage. Studying is a part of our relationship that's very important and has enriched our marriage.

We began with a series of classes, some at Stanford, before we were married. It was never my intention to leave Christianity and join Judaism. The reason I first started studying was to learn more what Jews believe, so that I could pass that on to my children. Over a period of time, I came to realize that there is a wide range of Jewish belief. There's no one thing that I could say that all Jews believe, other than that Jews believe in one God—*if* they believe in God. I found that Judaism was unlike Christianity, in its focus on behavior rather than belief in defining one's religiosity.

There were challenges in the process of establishing our "religious" practices, like the first Christmas Steve and I were together. For some reason, in all the talking we had done, we never talked about what we'd do at Christmas time. When the season approached, I said that I was going to get a Christmas tree.

I rarely see Steve get really ruffled or angry, so his response to my announcement was totally unexpected. "A Christmas tree reminds me of the Holocaust, the pogroms, the Crusades! Everything bad that Christians have ever done to Jews is exemplified for me in the Christmas tree!" I was stunned. His reaction was so strong. I said, "I just like it because it smells good, but if you feel this strongly about it, I don't think we should have one—certainly you don't think so."

So I didn't buy a Christmas tree. I did feel I was sacrificing, but I knew that I had hit a nerve that even he hadn't anticipated. I don't know if he could have foreseen how he would respond.

Shortly after this discussion, I came home one night to the wonderful smell of pine. I looked around. There was no tree, but Steve had gone to the Christmas tree lot and gathered up all the branches that were on the ground and put them around the house so that I could come home to the scent. I thought it was such a nice thing for him to do, and for the first two or three years, we had pine branches around the house at Christmastime.

Another issue for me had to do with the difficulties in reconciling the Catholic position with what I was doing in my work with Planned Parenthood: distributing birth control and helping to set up an abortion clinic. The first thing I wanted to look into when I started studying Judaism was the Jewish position on birth control and abortion.

I found that there was a whole spectrum of views. There were some positions from the Orthodox that were just as adamant as the Catholic Church against abortion, though their argument came from a different perspective. The Orthodox position has more to do with the concern of not "spilling the seed" rather than that the fetus is a human life. The concern in the Catholic Church is that the child be baptized, otherwise it is doomed forever to a limbo category of a life between heaven and hell. It's a theological problem. In Judaism, I found that there was a range of positions from "abortion on demand" to a prohibition against abortion in most cases.

What I appreciated about Jewish positions was the struggle exemplified in the dialogue. Like so many things in life, the truth lies somewhere in the struggle with the issue, in the process of prioritizing values. This struggle with all issues in Judaism was intellectually attractive to me.

I've been studying Talmud for four to five years now, and I've been amazed at the dialogue that goes on—within the Talmud *and* our classroom discussion. There's always the minority voice, and, even if that's not really the ultimate decision, it's still retained in the literature. It's still written down, it's still acknowledged, so that it may speak to someone at a later time, in a later age. Through Talmud study I have discovered that understanding often comes in the process of the struggle to find guidance.

If you look at history, there's no good reason for Jews to have survived all that they've lived through—all that *we've* lived through. The Jewish tradition encourages people to think, to grapple with problems, to get an education, to respect different points of view—qualities that are essential to survival, to adaptation, to life. Do we always achieve this ideal? No, but it is an ideal that is modeled in Jewish writing.

At some point, years after my wedding, I realized that I wasn't Christian anymore because I had had contact with the Christian religion, except for occasions with my family. Other than that, everything in my life was Jewish. Judaism was a large part of my life, and all my friends were Jewish. By the time I had the conversion ceremony, it was a public marking, because I had already been "becoming" Jewish over a period of years.

We joined a synagogue and a *havurah* so that we would have a community. I lit *Shabbat* candles and we celebrated the Jewish holidays. I practiced these rituals so that I would be familiar with them and the celebrations when I had children. With time, the rituals started becoming familiar and took on their own meaning for me. It occurred to me that it would appear hypocritical to my children to have them participate in the Jewish community while I "stood back" and watched. I decided I wanted to convert before I became pregnant with my first child, and I went to the *mikveh* three days before our daughter was born. The rabbi kept wanting me to read one more book, one more book. Finally, my husband said, "Enough! The baby's due. She will convert before the baby's born."

My conversion included a four-hour written examination, a meeting with the *Bet Din*, and then a trip to the *mikveh*. Actually, our rabbi had never gone to the *mikveh* as part of a conversion ceremony before. I told him at the end of this process of studying—for me it had really been seven years, even though only one year with him—that the process merited a degree in Judaic Studies! However, I explained that for me a spiritual aspect was missing.

The rabbi listened to my comments and suggested that I think of ways to make the process more meaningful in a spiritual way. I decided to go to the *mikveh*. The *mikveh* closest to our home was run by the *hasidim*, and they wouldn't allow me to be converted there because the rabbi who was converting me was affiliated with the Reform movement. I found another *mikveh*, which provided the meaningful experience for which I had hoped.

During my conversion studies, the rabbi insisted that I always be connected to the Jewish community. Since I don't have memories as a child of Jewish grandparents or Jewish relatives or Jewish holidays, they cannot define my Judaism. The only way to define my Judaism is by living it, practicing every day. I agree with the rabbi, I need to *do* Jewish things in order to be Jewish. Involvement in our community's day school is a part of this commitment.

The pain and problems for interfaith or converted couples are often most intense during December. My experience is that after celebrating the High Holidays; throwing a big community party for Rosh Hashanah; having pre– and post–Yom Kippur meals with my family; building a *sukkah* and observing Sukkot (particularly sleeping there with the neighborhood children!); celebrating Simhat Torah in the synagogue; having Thanksgiving and, of course, Hanukkah, by the time Christmas comes around I am tired of celebrating. Fully celebrating these Jewish holidays is my antidote to the "December dilemma" problem. By the time I get to Christmas, I'm ready for a break. I have already done all the cooking and celebrating and festivities with the families. Gradually—I don't even remember when it was—I didn't even miss the Christmas odors of the pine branches. My celebratory needs were met with all the rich Jewish holidays.

Shabbat is my favorite "holy day" because it comes every week and because I feel that I need a day of rest. *Shabbat* enables such nice things to happen in the family. The kids like talking a long time at dinner. We have a custom of going around the table on *Shabbat* and sharing with each other the best thing that happened during that week and the worst thing. We spend time listening rather than being in a hurry to get the table cleared and the dishes done. The lights are dim, and the ambience is quiet. We have a long dinner, and my husband and I drink a glass of wine. It's a good time to sit back and think about how much I have to be grateful for, experiencing the moment, and listening to my children speaking. It seems like such a simple thing, but I love having *Shabbat*.

We do try very hard to keep *Shabbat* sacred, special, and quiet. We always have Friday night dinner together as a family, with rare exceptions. Both of our mothers know that they can just show up for *Shabbat* dinner. Occasionally, we go to friends with our children. Friday night is always family time together. Saturday I try to make separate from the rest of the week. Otherwise, the weeks and days and years kind of run together and pass so quickly. *Shabbat* is a time that I am more conscious of the fact that time is passing.

Ritual is wonderful for children. It just automatically gives a specialness to whatever is being done. Lighting candles, lighting the *menorah*, doing a *seder*. Repetition of the holiday observances creates wonderful touchstones for children. Ritual also is a catalyst for new insights.

When my father died, suddenly, of a heart attack, I was grateful to be involved in my *havurah*. My mother had a service at the church that my family had attended. Everyone in the *havurah* came for the service at the church, which was an hour's drive from our community. My whole family sat together in the same pew, but when they went up to receive communion during the service, I didn't go with them. I stayed in the congregation with my community! I don't know if my friends knew how much their presence meant to me at the time. It could have been a very lonely time, but it was not, because I was supported by my community. The community saw me as a Jew, saw me as theirs, and came and shared that with me.

I sat *shivah* for the seven days. I was the only one from my family, of course. It so happened that it was five weeks after my daughter had been born. So I stayed at home with my mother to receive people. For thirty days, I didn't go anywhere socially. Once again the rituals made so much sense. It was so pragmatic, so practical, and so comforting in terms of helping me grieve and adjust to the change in my life.

At our synagogue my father's name is read at his *Yartzeit*, and we always go to that service. My father would have smiled if he were in the room. I can just feel his presence. He would have appreciated it. I've always felt that whatever I was involved with Jewishly, my father would have been very proud of. Before he died, he had often helped me with my various Jewish community projects.

I'd have to say that one of my pet peeves is when Jewish community leaders list intermarriage among the great perils befalling the Jewish people. While I know that most intermarried couples do not choose to raise their children solely as Jews, that is not always the case. My husband and I were intermarried and look at the result: my husband has continued his Jewish education as an adult; I have chosen Judaism; we are raising two children Jewishly. We are very involved in the JCC, the synagogue, the Federation, and we helped start a new Jewish day school. We support our local Jewish organizations with our time and money. *This* is the result of an interfaith marriage.

9

Rejection and Acceptance

Terry Kallet

The rejection that Terry felt as a child and young adult from the religious community in which she grew up made her sensitive to the ways people have of distinguishing between who is and is not acceptable. As her own children grew up, Terry could see that the messages from religious groups ran parallel to the secular culture purveyed on television, over neither of which she felt she had any control. These influences contrasted so sharply with the philosophy of Martin Buber and other Jewish writers that in life—whether spiritual or secular—relationship is paramount. After years of exploring Judaism, Terry decided that it was time her family found a synagogue to affiliate with.

The Kallets' synagogue is located on Mercer Island in Lake Washington across a floating bridge from Seattle. Bnai Torah is nestled in a wooded cul de sac in a community of small and unique homes. The synagogue is also small and architecturally beautiful. The *bimah* is in a large open area in which chairs can be rearranged to suit the needs of the congregation.

Terry, who met with me in the board room, is the assistant director for education. It is a position she regards with both confidence and humility. Her confidence comes from her long and determined quest for spiritual centeredness for her family; her humility is a reflection of the deep honor and respect she feels for the teachings and values of Judaism and the community of people that sustains them.

In bringing her family and born Jewish husband back to Judaism, Terry discovered she could gain acceptance on her own terms.

My coming to Judaism was a very long and slow process. My experiences with Catholicism helped me appreciate the beauty of community and philosophy in Judaism. I was surprised to discover that Judaism articulated what I had personally come to believe, but my belief and commitment to Judaism was a growing toward rather than a reaction against something else.

If you can think of Catholicism as being organized into Reform, Conservative, and Orthodox, I grew up in a family that was considered an "orthodox" Catholic family, and I attended twelve years of religious school. I never felt comfortable in school, even in grade school. I was so uncomfortable by the eighth grade, I literally wasn't speaking to anybody in the school. I went on to high school, which was an academically oriented school and really quite good. They never got around to teaching Christian theology, however. We read things like the Vatican II documents, and although we studied the Old Testament, we never did get into the New Testament. At that time I was beginning to be very critical in my thinking about what I was reading and learning.

I remember two things very clearly from being at high school. One was learning about Hanukkah and about the Jewish holidays and the other was wishing that we had holidays that were as beautiful and meaningful. The holidays that we had, I thought, were ridiculous, stupid, and fantasy. The whole notion of Christ's birth and his conception and Mary and all of that—I thought that was such a fantasy story that it had no relevancy to what I thought might be the real meaning for Christianity, and I just couldn't relate to it. It just seemed crazy. In our religion classes, we *did* have to memorize these long lists of sins dealing with sex and whether or not you kissed a boy while thinking about sex or not thinking about sex—whether it was a sin or not a sin. I memorized them just like anybody else, and I would get them all right and then I would write on the bottom of the paper, "This is all a bunch of crap, and I don't intend to live my life this way." I guess I was into honesty, and I was naive enough to be surprised that I got failing grades. I started questioning the validity and truthfulness of everything that was said.

The thing that was really kind of a turning point for me was learning about the Holocaust and starting to question how an organized religion could support and perpetrate this. There was an attitude of anti-Semitism that was pervasive in Catholicism at the time of the Holocaust. It was in the church, though not necessarily with individual Catholics. As a child, I was told that the Jews killed Jesus, and anti-Semitism was a part of the community I grew up in. It was lumped with a whole lot of other things—McCarthyism still had its tendrils in this community. The fathers of some people I went to school with had to go to Canada because they were professors at the university teaching Marxism and other "dangerous" subjects.

Many years later these same Christian anti-Semitic beliefs were to come back to plague my family. My son, Nathan, came home from preschool at age three and said, "Protect me from Daddy!" I said, "Why, why, what happened?" His preschool teacher had told him that the Jews killed Jesus and that Jesus was the son of a Jew. So my own son went home thinking that because his father was Jewish and he was the son of a Jew, therefore Daddy was going to kill him. This whole conversation happened while I was preparing a *seder*!

An early turning point for me was that when I was in second grade my father died of a heart attack. All of a sudden the community became rejecting of our family because we were different from everybody else. If you didn't have a nuclear family, you weren't really accepted as part of the community. That is how America was at that time. The messages I got from the nuns who taught us and from the other kids in my class were that I didn't fit in and that I wasn't a part of them anymore. People would try to match my mother up with men regardless of how appropriate they were. She was accused of having affairs and other "inappropriate" behavior because she was a single woman. Supposedly, everybody's husband became vulnerable.

It wasn't hard for me to leave Catholicism when I went to university. I felt that it just wasn't relevant, and during my college years the church was taking a stance of supporting the Vietnam War. On a more personal level, I was living at a boarding house in which another Catholic girl was living. She was quite promiscuous but believed that because she attended church every day she was a better person. There was just too much hypocrisy. At about this time I was engaged to a nice Catholic boy. He had the right credentials and background to fit into my mother's view of what was acceptable, but she didn't approve of how we conducted our relationship. For many very sad and complicated reasons, we broke off our engagement.

After this I went through a long period of nihilism—"life really has no meaning and there is no way to understand life's meaning and you shouldn't even bother to look at it"—that is kind of a rootless search. I was an art student at that time and was involved in radical politics and trying to define my own lifestyle. I was also studying a lot of philosophy. Once I was looking through the bookstore and came upon Martin Buber's book *I and Thou*. I found myself agreeing with Buber's point of view on life. Essentially, I reorganized my thinking and my life parallel with his belief structure.

It has been a very important way for me to think about the world, and it is a Jewish point of view. It affected my approach to dealing with the tragedies of my early life—to transcend the individual events, learn what I could, and use them to become a better human being. The alternative was to be consumed and destroyed by them. This is not unlike the history of the Jews.

My view of the world starts with a belief that I do not have to understand the nature of God. I finally decided a few years ago that it is arrogant for me, with a finite mind, to understand something that is clearly beyond the realm of human experience. That is not to say that it is not there, that it is not real, that I am not capable of having a relationship with God—but I do not have to know everything.

Another important aspect is that *relationship* is really paramount— paying attention to relationships and not objectifying people. My belief and my practice of Judaism includes all of that because Judaism has a lot to say about the nature of relationships and about separation and coming together.

I find all of this very rational and very distinct. Judaism has a lot of room for diversity and acceptance of minority opinion. It is okay with me that the Orthodox community has a different point of view toward me than I have toward them. That is fine. In essence, I think Judaism has an inclusive quality to it. I guess my worldview is also colored by what I know and experience as a Jew. The way to be in the world. Although it is a challenge, I try to accept things for how I actually see them and not how I would like to see them.

An essential part of my enjoyment of Judaism is its acceptance of humanness— of who humans are and not just in the sense of recognizing human nature for its sexuality but also its other aspects. The Jewish concept of justice is vital to me. The Christian notion of turning the other cheek, it seems to me, teaches people how to be good victims rather than how to achieve justice in a situation in which there is conflict.

That is really important in the modern world, and something I deal with on a professional level. We have two sets of teachers, the day-school teachers and the Sunday-school teachers, and if something happens, like the classroom gets messed up, how do you create justice that both sides can live with? It's not just about how do you forgive and forget.

I was contemplating issues such as these when I met the man who would become my husband. I was an art student, and he was a professor of music at that time. We met while folk dancing. He is a born Jew, but was not at that time committed to leading a Jewish life.

My mom was not very happy when we became engaged and encouraged us to wait a while before we got married. She was very upset through most of the planning—mainly it was the little things she wasn't happy with, like the music. I couldn't wear a white dress, she insisted; I should wear an off-white dress because I wasn't really a virgin. It was crazy. We married on Saturday, spent Sunday sight-seeing with his parents, and had to go back to work on Monday. I would *not* do that again. My advice to anybody is, "Get out of town. Don't hang around. Everybody needs a honeymoon." At least our families were polite to one another.

About three years later, we had our first child. We were living in Philadelphia at that time, but I had returned to Seattle to complete my master's degree and teaching credentials. While finishing up, I stayed with my mother, and my husband joined me when he finished his academic year as a professor. Our son Nathan was born three weeks late, just as my master's work was done.

At this time I was still trying to fit in to the Catholic Church, and my husband didn't want anything to do with Judaism. I felt that it was important to be a part of something, and even though I didn't really believe in Catholicism, we had Nathan baptized. I went through the motions to keep peace in the family, essentially with my mother, but it was a horrible experience. They wouldn't let us do it in the church itself because this was a "mixed" child. The priest wouldn't do it. A lay sister or some other lay person did it. To me it just represented the whole hypocrisy of the way the church handled things. Afterward, while I was somewhere else nursing the baby, my mother and my husband got into an argument. My mother threw him out of the house and told him never to come back. So, we packed up and went back to Philadelphia.

Children really precipitate a lot of these issues. I decided that this was truly crazy, and I didn't belong in the Catholic Church. I didn't want my children involved in it. So, I started studying a lot. I had some friends—a couple; the wife was a Jew by Choice. They were moving into Orthodoxy. She had initially converted through Reform Judaism and now was moving into Orthodoxy and very shortly thereafter moved to Israel where they have been the last sixteen years. They sent me boxes of books, and I would read my way through the box and send it back, and they would send me a new box.

The more I learned, the more fascinated I became, the more committed I became, and the more certain I was that this is what I wanted for myself. At first, my husband was somewhat oblivious. Then I started keeping a kosher kitchen and observing

Shabbat. We observed only Jewish holidays. He was just sort of perplexed by all of this. He just didn't know what to make of it.

We moved back to Seattle before our third child was born and lived in a community full of incredible Christian fundamentalists. There is a big Bible college nearby and about three or four denominations that take a point of view slightly different from one another but still fundamentalist. These people are very active in the community, and my children had some very difficult experiences.

My children then became the objects of everybody's desire to convert them to whatever their denomination was. The people across the street were Pentecostal Catholics and would speak in tongues and fall down in a faint on the floor. It was really a dramatic thing. As our children got older, though, we celebrated only Jewish holidays. We would go to my mother's on Christmas Day, but we celebrated Hanukkah at home. We celebrated Passover.

My children had some vague ideas that they were Jewish but didn't know what it meant. The issue of religion just became more and more complicated, and I finally forced the situation. I was concerned that several things were happening: that my children were being educated about spirituality by other people over whom I had no control, and that they were being socialized into a moral and value system through television. Furthermore, their father's ambivalence about Judaism affected how we dealt with these issues. I finally came to a realization that the concerns my husband had about religion could best be worked out in therapy, and I convinced him to go to a therapist.

We were then able to make the decision to start looking around for a community to affiliate with, and we found Bnai Torah. We were really comfortable with Rabbi Mirel and with the community. Then, I went through a formal conversion with the rabbi. So, the conversion process has been fairly recent—about four years ago. But, if you ask me, I have lived my entire adult life as a Jew.

It doesn't seem like it was only four years ago that we became members of Bnai Torah—it seems like all of our life ago. Joining this congregation got us involved in a new community, even though I had a lot of fears about acceptance and rejection in the process. I brought that up with Rabbi Mirel when we met with him before joining the congregation. His answer startled me almost to the point of being offended. He said, "If you feel that you are being discriminated against in this community, it is coming from you. It is in your head. It is not coming from the community." I did not want to hear that—that I was the problem. But my experience with the community has shown me that he was exactly right.

Usually Rabbi Mirel is not so direct about things, but I think he was very wise. He understands the psychological process of conversion pretty well. I now see that he wanted to make clear that what you bring into a situation also sets you up. For example, I spent this past summer at the university taking intensive Hebrew. My class had a number of Orthodox women, some from *Chabad*. There was a time I might have expected that they would feel uncomfortable because first, I am from Reform Judaism and second, I am a Jew by Choice, and I know that the Orthodox community has some points of view about "who is a Jew." Well, I didn't experience any of that. I felt a tremendous amount of acceptance and enjoyment from those women.

It may be that the Jewish community here in the Northwest is a little bit different from those in other parts of the country, though it is true that the debate about Orthodoxy as the correct standard has begun in this community. Even so, last year on a retreat that included individuals from the Orthodox, Conservative, Reconstructionist, and Reform communities, there was acceptance, tolerance, and understanding. It was truly one of the most wonderful experiences I have ever had with people coming together to form a group. The facilitators told us that very rarely are they in a community in which there is so little friction between different groups of Jews when they are thrown together to interact physically, emotionally, and spiritually with one another.

From time to time, I do have concerns about what other people think, especially now in my position in the temple. People tend to view me not only as an administrator but also as a spiritual leader in some way, so I approach my job with a great deal of humility. I don't think that I am the expert in any sense, but a fellow learner. If people felt that they did not like me, or if they were uncomfortable with me as a Jew by Choice, they kept it to themselves. No one has ever said anything or treated me in a way that would make me feel that I was a second-class citizen or not a real Jew.

For our children, it was hard at first to become integrated into the community. They were, at that time, thirteen, eleven, and nine and decided that they didn't want to be in religious school the first year we were members there. So, we required them to attend every Friday night. For a year we all attended every Friday night and quite a few Saturday morning services. The following year they enrolled in Hebrew school. We did not require them to have a *bar mitzvah*, and my oldest son chose not to do that, although he is very much involved. They are all active in the temple youth group—one son holds an office in the group—and they went to Jewish camp this summer. I feel that they are very well integrated into the community. The two younger children decided to have *bar mitzvahs*. Allen had his when he was fourteen. It was a really wonderful experience for him. He has tremendous depth to him, and he made it a very spiritual event. The youngest one had his *bar mitzvah* this past January. He was a little more "traditional" in that he didn't have the same depth of understanding. But he did a nice job. And they both *chose* to do this.

My husband has become very involved, too—totally involved. He is cochair of religious practices this year. He taught Hebrew in the Hebrew school this year and has taught ninth grade there for the past few years. He reads all the time. He has, in a sense, gotten in touch with all of the positive aspects of Judaism. I am not sure what had been preventing him from being in touch with those positive feelings before, but he was able to reconnect to Judaism in a religious way, and it has really been wonderful.

My involvement has been total, too. The rabbi is someone to whom it is very difficult to say "no." When I went through the conversion process, he told me I needed to get involved in the temple in some way. So, I ended up as the chairman of adult education, for which I felt totally inadequate and totally overwhelmed. I didn't know anybody in the community, so I had no informal network to pull from to put things together. I spent two or three years struggling with adult education, but it is now doing well and has a lot of committee members and another chairman.

Eventually, I started at Bnai Torah as a teacher. I had wanted to go back to work and had been at home primarily painting and was broke. Art doesn't pay. So, I taught fourth grade and applied for the job as assistant director of education. I didn't get it the first time, but the second time around I did.

I see education as a way to address the dilemma we are all facing—assimilation. The recent demographic study showed that 60 percent of those who identify themselves as Jewish in the Seattle area are unaffiliated, and a majority of them live in one particular area, Belleview. I think this represents an opportunity for Jewish education because one of the reasons people join congregations and become affiliated for the most part is the Hebrew school. What that has said to me is that our supplementary schools need to be very strong. They need to be very professional. They need to be a real force for education, not just for children but for families, by taking an inclusive approach to education.

After I formally became Jewish, my mother decided that I was no longer a part of her family. We have since resolved that and are rebuilding a relationship. It was a very painful process for me. One of the things that I often do when I try to solve a problem is to spend time with the Talmud. There is a section in the Talmud that talks about the Jew by Choice, although, of course, they don't call us that—it's the "righteous *ger*." The rabbis say something to the effect that converts need to be treated with care and concern by the community because they have no other family. I think that is important because quite often, even though there is acceptance, even though my mother has come to an acceptance, it is different. Maybe it is not the same anymore as in talmudic times, when you needed the Jewish community as your family because you were cut off. But even if there is a lot of understanding from your family, you still may be cut off from them because you no longer share their values or feelings or points of view.

10

There's a Lot of Love in This House

Maryanne Ehrlich

Few people speak with the kind of self-assurance that Maryanne does, yet without the judgmentalness that can sometimes mark people of conviction. As a very young woman thirty years ago, Maryanne had to stand up to her family and state quite plainly that the life she was choosing was within her right to decide for herself. It took two years to heal the rift that then ensued between her and her parents. She knew her father had come to peace with the issue when on a visit to meet his new granddaughter, he confided to Maryanne's mother-in-law, "There's a lot of love in this house."

With clear-headedness, goodwill, and occasional to-the-point wit, Maryanne has lived her adult life as a Jewish woman, mother, and wife. As her children have grown up, she has taken an increasingly active role in the activities of her synagogue and in planning for the future of the Reform movement, which she wants to see become more vibrant and responsive to the changing world around it.

My great, great, great . . . grandfather on my mother's side was George Washington's drummer boy. We have a lithograph from a newspaper that's in a museum in Pennsylvania documenting that. My father's parents were immigrants from Germany in the late 1800s. They belonged to the Moravian sect of Christianity, whose headquarters are in Bethlehem, Pennsylvania, where my father was born and raised. When I recall going to that big church as a child, it reminds me very much of a Quaker meetinghouse because it is explicitly plain with a very simple form of worship. My mother's family belonged to what would now be called the United Church of Christ. This was pretty simple Protestantism. My parents came from very conservative backgrounds. We had relatives from various parts of the family who were every denomination. My mother has second cousins, like sisters to her, who are Jewish. Being Jewish, therefore, was never something foreign to me as a young child.

I was raised in a small, quiet family community in suburban Philadelphia in which there was no ghetto of any group. Consequently, we had every kind of religion represented in our neighborhood. We had several Jewish neighbors. In the wintertime, a very beautiful floral display would arrive at our neighbor's, a gift from a relative. If there was no one home at their house, my mother would take it in from the florist. The Sterns called it a "Hanukkah bush." It was not a Christmas tree, just a display of flowers. It might have just been a tradition peculiar to that family because I don't know of anybody Jewish in my adult life who has ever had anything like that. Later on, I wondered if this was to replace a Christmas tree. Maybe to pacify their youngsters they felt they had to have something decorative at that time of the year. I don't know. The point is that I was exposed to a variety of people from different religions. I remember going to the Stern children's weddings and their synagogue. It was always a very positive experience.

The first time I remember questioning my Christian background I was about twelve years old and our church had a class for young people who were going to be confirmed at age thirteen. Fifteen or twenty of us sat around a large table and studied the New Testament. I was always the one who questioned everything. At one point, the minister of the church looked at me rather disparagingly, and I could tell that he was not happy with the line of questioning I was pursuing. I was very frustrated because he couldn't give me an answer that would content me. I asked him about the miracle of the birth of Jesus and the fact that he was then considered to be the founder of Christianity. "How could he be considered the founder of Christianity if in fact he was born Jewish? What proof do you have that this was the immaculate conception? I come from a more scientific background, and I do not accept that such an event could have happened. Nobody can prove that." The minister said to me, "Well, it is a matter of faith." And I kept my mouth shut because I knew I had better at that point. Being thrown out of the class, at my tender age, was something my parents would not have been able to comprehend.

I was always raised to be a very independent thinker, and later on my parents may have questioned themselves, "What did we do wrong?" At thirteen, I was confirmed. I just thought I'd go along with the rest of the crowd and be a good little thirteen-year-old and not give my parents any flak.

As time went on, I really questioned religion more and more. I learned more, and I read more. When I was in high school, I took a wonderful course from an outstanding teacher—"History of the Religions of the World." In discovering what the various religions were about, a whole wonderful realm of possibilities was opened for me. Just because you are born into one religion doesn't mean you have to stay. You are free to choose what you truly believe. The more I read about the different religions, the more I read about Judaism, the more fascinated I became, and the more disenchanted I became with Christianity. As I progressed, I really thought that there were tenets in the Jewish teachings that I could firmly be happy in believing and going forth with for the rest of my life, setting a code of ethics for me. So much that I read was continually positive. There was never anything that I read that I doubted—oh, maybe certain stories that are in the Old Testament. Are these really valid? But as far as the true belief and the day-to-day living with the religion, I felt there was nothing there, seriously, that I questioned the way I was questioning Christianity.

I attended Wilson College, a very small women's school in Pennsylvania. It is affiliated with the Presbyterian Church. My best girlfriend's mother went there. I visited Wilson, and I liked what I saw, and I loved the young women who were students there. I really liked the atmosphere; then I realized that this was a very

Christian-oriented school and they had mandatory chapel—which, actually, most of the time was extremely creative: a modern dance group, people reading poetry, someone performing an original piece of music. Maybe once or twice a week there would be a regular religious service but the rest of the time it was pretty free.

You had to take Old Testament and New Testament as a prerequisite for graduation—one course freshman year, one course sophomore year. Old Testament was first, and I really was drawn to that. I started going to the little Conservative *shul* in the town. There were very few Jewish girls at Wilson, but I met one or two. I also met my husband my first year at college. It never occurred to me that there was ever going to be any kind of problem with the fact that he was Jewish. In my sophomore year when I took the New Testament course, I realized, "I do not believe in Christianity." It was passé for me, and I knew I could not hold on to that for the rest of my life.

Gary was a couple of years ahead of me and was going to be graduating at the end of my sophomore year. We began talking about the possibility of spending our lives together. I told him, "There is not going to be a problem as far as religion is concerned because I want to convert to Judaism." He was sort of surprised to hear that on the one hand, but he really wasn't because he knew my feelings from all the interesting discussions we'd had. He respected whatever my decision was, but he never ever asked me, "Would you consider converting to Judaism?" This was never an issue. His parents were very concerned he was dating a woman who was not Jewish. His grandparents were all Orthodox, although his parents were not.

I was adamant about converting to Judaism before we got married. I came down to Baltimore one weekend in my junior year to talk with his family's rabbi. I had a couple of meetings with him and of course he tried to persuade me otherwise. Finally, I said, "Look, let's stop this go-round. I really want to convert to Judaism; just give me a list of books to read. It's going to have to be long-distance because I can only come down to Baltimore about once a month." He did this, and I did the studying on my own. If I had questions, I'd jot them down and see him once a month to discuss them. This was the head rabbi of a very large congregation, and there weren't a lot of people converting—I was it. So it was a one-on-one situation, and we had a very nice relationship.

I knew my parents would not approve of my conversion. I had dangled the idea in front of them a few times, and I got some very negative feedback. In fact, I got a lot of negative feedback *before* I even started mentioning it. It is fascinating to me that even though we had Jewish relatives, my parents said to me, "We don't want you to date Gary any more." I said, "Why? He's a fine young man." "We just think it's too difficult; there's a difference of religions. His family is not going to want you, and you'll be a pariah. Blah, blah, blah." The family member who was Jewish was my grandmother's contemporary. She married someone Jewish. Half of her children decided to be Jewish and half decided to be gentile. It was a real mishmash.

I was so taken aback at my parents' reaction. There had never been a negative discussion around our dinner table or in our home about somebody Jewish. Yet when my parents began to perceive that I was falling in love with Gary, they started to get really shaken. My father forbade me to see him. I thought, "This is really ridiculous. I know who I am; I know what I am; I know what I want. My parents are wrong." I was lucky to have the maturity to step back and see that. I'm not quite sure where I got that! They threatened. "We won't send you back to college." I said, "Fine, I'll borrow the money from my uncle John," who had no daughters and thought I was the sun, moon, and stars. Of course, my father couldn't handle that so I went back to college.

My husband's parents were equally displeased. When Gary wanted to bring me home to meet his parents the first time, he called his mother and said, "Hi, I think I'd like to come home next weekend, would it be okay?" "Sure! Come on home, we'd love to see you." "I'd like to bring a young lady." He had never, ever brought a girl through the front door! So my mother-in-law said, "What's her name?" Gary told her. "What's her ancestry?" So my husband said, "Swiss near the German border!" (This quip had something to do with the fact that his mother did not like German Jews!) It was really sort of humorous. His mother said, "Don't bring her home!" and hung up on him. About an hour and a half passed, and she called him back and said, "I made a mistake. You can come home and bring her with you."

I think curiosity overwhelmed her. My mother-in-law is a wonderful person, though there have been challenging moments in the development of our relationship. My father-in-law is the salt of the earth. He was very gracious; when I left, he was lovely: "It was so nice to meet you, and I really look forward to seeing you again." I knew I had a foot in the door and was on the right path. This was not "good cop/bad cop." This was their real personalities. I am sure they discussed that they should be a perfect lady and gentleman: "We're not going to get into any discussions; we're not going to get in the way; we're just going to be nice." We did nothing together with them that weekend except the Friday evening *Shabbat* dinner. That was it. My husband knew what the limitations were; he reads them very well.

As I said, my mother-in-law didn't like German Jews. Generations ago, her family and her husband's family were originally from Germany, but they had immigrated east to Russia and Lithuania and Latvia. When my mother-in-law's grandfather came through western Europe, he stopped at relatives in Germany—this man was trudging on foot—and they would not take him in. He became a stowaway on a cargo ship that docked in New York and somehow got to Baltimore because there were relatives here. Each one would earn money and try to bring the next one over. There are some wonderful stories that my mother-in-law has shared with all of us, and we keep begging her to write them down. I'm not as clear about how my father-in-law's grandfather got here.

The divisions in Baltimore between the German Jews and the Eastern European Jews reinforced my in-laws' feelings about how their relatives were treated by the German relatives. The German Jews here only wanted to assimilate. They didn't want to be called "German Jews," they only wanted to be "Americans." Consequently a lot of German Jews who came here early—and I've heard lots of stories from friends about this—did not want to have anything to do with the Russian Jews. They didn't even want to be called or referred to as Jews. They were Americans now and that is what they wanted to be known as. The Jews who left Germany were already very assimilated *"erev"*–World War II. The problem was that they were too assimilated, and the ones who stayed in Germany thought they were safe from persecution. That tells you something about the dangers of assimilation.

So in the beginning, we had some rough spots on both sides of the family. In fact, when I came home from college at the end of my junior year, I announced to my parents: "I have something very important to discuss with you," and they said, "Let's go out to dinner!" They thought that was a safer setting—everyone had to behave properly because we were out in public. There would be no histrionics!

"I am in love with Gary, and he is in love with me. We are planning to get married after I graduate from college next year. I know that this is not your choice, and it is probably not his parents' choice either, but it is our choice for each other, and that is what's really important. We would like you to be part of our happiness, and we hope that you can be." Thud! It was as if I dropped a twelve-ton brick. There was utter silence. I had decided I was not going to Mickey-Mouse around about this. It was an important part of my life, and they had to know that.

My father wanted to know where we would get married. "You have to know it is not going to be in a church," I said. "I do not feel comfortable getting married in a church; that's not an important place for me anymore. I would like to be married on neutral ground, so that it would be acceptable for both his parents and you." I knew if I said to them that I was planning to convert to Judaism, the door would be open, and I'd be out. I didn't want to have any conflict that really wasn't necessary. They didn't comprehend why I wanted to convert, and, anyway, it is such a personal decision, they didn't need to be a part of it. I did not want to have a fighting match the whole summer.

We officially became engaged right before New Year's. Gary and my father took a long walk in the snow, and Gary formally asked my father for my hand in marriage. Later that evening we were talking it over and Gary told me, "You know, your father would really like you to be married in his church," and I said, "Forget it! That's not going to be a part of it. I want to convert to Judaism. You know what *I* want." My plan was to get married by a judge, a friend of my father's, then come back to Baltimore to be married by the rabbi. Gary said, "How are we going to do this?" I said, "I'll figure it out!"

At the beginning of the summer when we were to be married, I had a private conversion ceremony in the rabbi's study. I was so excited that it is almost a blur, and I remember little about it. There were so many other things that I was dealing with that summer and a lot of different emotions. I just remember feeling a great sigh of relief when it was over. It wasn't until the rabbi performed our wedding ceremony, under the *huppah*, that I really felt the impact of my decision. I realized then that I was a part of Jewish tradition. That was emotionally very moving to me.

Between my husband taking the national boards of medicine and my starting a teaching position, we had only two weeks to get married and go on a honeymoon.

We got married on a Wednesday at noon. It was a lovely small wedding—about 100 people. We had our closest relatives and closest friends. His whole family came to the first wedding; some of them knew about the second wedding, which my parents did not know about.

The judge performed a lovely nondenominational ceremony for us. We told him exactly what we wanted. He was very gracious about everything. We had a champagne luncheon afterward. Then we drove off in our VW convertible, with almost everybody thinking they were sending us on to our honeymoon. It was such an emotional release to get out of that scene that when we got to Baltimore, I burst into tears. My poor husband was beside himself: "What's the matter?" I sobbed, "You have to admit, dear, this is a pretty emotional day!" "Yes," he said, "I know! You are right! But what's the matter?" He thought maybe I was feeling I'd done something wrong. I was really filled up, and it had just begun to hit me that finally the two of us were free to spend our lives together the way we wanted to. It felt like a departure for me—it felt very symbolic to me. I cried for about a half an hour, then I was fine.

We went to his parents' and just relaxed for about an hour. Then about eight o'clock the rabbi performed a lovely ceremony for us in his study. By that time I just couldn't wait to have it all over with and get away from everybody else. We left from there for our honeymoon in Martha's Vineyard. When I look back on that day, I wonder how I had the stamina to go through with all the emotional drain. Most men just don't dwell on the emotional part of the day. As they grow older they may reflect back on it and realize the emotions involved. But as a twenty-five- or twenty-six-year-old, it doesn't hit them in the same way.

We were married about a year, and I went to stay with my folks for the weekend because a girlfriend was getting married. Gary was in his last year of medical school and on call that weekend, so he couldn't go. I went out to dinner after the wedding with my parents. During the course of the evening's conversation at the dinner table with my parents, my father, out of the blue, point-blank asked me, "Are you Jewish?" I thought to myself, "I can't lie because this is too important a part of my life." I realized that an explosion was coming. "Yes, I am," I said, "but before you say another word or ask another question, I have to tell you something. Please give me the courtesy of letting me say what I have to say. My decision to become Jewish has been one hundred percent totally my doing. Nobody influenced me to do this. This is something that I have been thinking about for nearly the last ten years of my life. It has been a very personal decision, not a snap decision—nor a decision I had a lot of difficulty making. Once I began to realize what I truly believed in from a religious standpoint, the decision was very easy for me to make. I know that you are having a lot of difficulty understanding this, but please try. We all pray to the same God, we just do it in a different way. I hope you can understand that."

I'm not sure what sparked this confrontation. Maybe they had inklings of it for quite a while. Maybe it was the fact that I didn't want to get married by their family minister, whom I had known all my life. I knew there would come a time when I would have to face up to the reality of the effect on them of the decision that I made.

I knew that regardless of how difficult it would be, I had to be up front with that, eventually. I wasn't prepared for it then, though. My father started to become very verbally abusive, not loud, because we were in the restaurant. I looked at the two of them and said, "You are my parents, and I love you, but we are having a tremendous problem right now. I am leaving because it is neither necessary nor appropriate to make a scene here. When you can somehow understand this decision that I have made, you can let me know. But I will not sit here and listen to your abuse."

I got up from the table and left and immediately started to drive back to Baltimore, even though I'd planned to leave the next day. It was pouring rain. I was so upset and the driving conditions were terrible—big trucks roaring past the little VW. When I got home I told Gary what happened. He went to the telephone, dialed my parents, got my father on the line, and gave him an earful in three terse sentences. With very special words, he told my father exactly what he thought of him for doing this to me. He hung up. He said to me, "You are my wife, and nobody is going to ever treat you like that!" My husband is nonviolent in all things, but he will fight to the end for his wife and his children. There's no gray when it comes to us.

We sat up and talked a lot that night. About a day later my father called me, and he apologized. It was obvious that he was very, very angry, and we really had a rift. I did not see my parents from that time until after our first child was born. I would call my mother when I knew she was home by herself. She and I kept in communication. I never talked to my father.

What it really boiled down to was that they took my leading a Jewish life as a personal affront. That was pretty common in their generation. They wondered, "What did we do wrong?" It so happened that I was the only one among all their friends and in their whole family who had decided to change her religion. I was like the pariah with my immediate family. Forget about the fact that they had Jewish relatives— that didn't even enter into it. They were so provincial in their train of thought that they just couldn't see a few degrees one way or another. It was sad. I felt sorry for *them* because they were the ones who were losing out.

I always described my father as a very European gentleman: very formal, elegant, rigid, and very bright—and always in control. He came to the breakfast table in a suit, a starched white shirt, and tie, and never took the jacket off. We had a home at the beach for years, but I think I saw my father in a bathing suit twice. My mother liked the beach, and was out on the beach all day long with us kids. On the other hand, how many people do you know who have read the *Encyclopaedia Britannica* from cover to cover? He read everything.

I never stopped writing to my parents and I never stopped sending them birthday cards. I kept up the communication because I knew as the years went by, they would probably feel that they were losing out on a part of my life. I knew for my father this must be very difficult, since I was his favorite, and I also knew that my mother must be giving him a fit. My mother and I had had a wonderful relationship. Although the response from my father might have been predictable, it was not something I expected from my family. Even though my maternal grandmother only met Gary once, had she lived, this kind of behavior would never have sat with her. She was very bright and very ecumenical; a woman before her time.

After all this healed up, which it did eventually, our four parents had the best relationship of any of their children's in-laws. Basically, it took a grandchild and the softening of positions to effect a reconciliation—and that didn't happen for two years.

During the Vietnam War, Gary was stationed on a military base in northern Maine. I got a lot of positive Jewish reinforcement up there—an ironic way to get it and an ironic place to get it. The base medical and dental personnel were, to a large degree, Jewish. We had a traveling rabbi who used to come once a month. We'd all have him in our homes for dinner. We did everything a certain way so that the food would be kosher. We had a good community; everybody became like family to one another because all of our families were so far away. Whenever anyone had a baby naming or a *bris*, everyone came out for it.

I had lost my first pregnancy, so when Randy was born after I was six weeks in Maine, my in-laws were on the next plane up. They brought up the *yarmulkes* and, in dry ice, all the hors d'oeuvres. The Ob-Gyn who delivered Randy happened to be a Conservative Jew from California whose parents had been Orthodox, and he knew what to do for a *bris*. He had his father ship the *bris* board ahead of time because there were other young Jewish wives up there who also were pregnant. So besides being the obstetrician, Steve was quite busy as the *mohel*. The *bris* was in our little house up on the base, and was attended by all of these people I didn't know because I'd been there only six weeks. My husband was assigned to the medical squadron and was the flight surgeon for the fighter squadron, who behaved like a bunch of cowboys! They were riotous. A lot of the people who came had never been to a *bris* because a lot of them weren't Jewish.

Our son's *bris* was the first *bris* that *I* had ever attended. I remember certain aspects of it vividly. All the women were made to stay downstairs, and the circumcision was upstairs in the baby's nursery. Our bedroom was next to that, and my mother-in-law and my closest woman friend in Maine sat on either side of me, each holding one of my hands. The doors were open so I could hear everything. I had such a feeling—a tremendous, awesome feeling. It was almost overwhelming. For the first time it really hit me that I was a Jewish mother; "I have this incredible responsibility to raise this child Jewishly." It was a very special moment—but it was also very frightening.

In Maine, winter was from October to May, and you had to go to the second story of your house to see across the street because the snow piled up to 160 or so inches. We dug tunnels from the front door to the street. So here we all were, and what was there to do? Of all the Jewish women at the air force base in Maine, I was the only one who was a Jew by Choice. They had all grown up in Jewish families, with Jewish mothers. We would trade recipes, and how many Jewish recipes did I have? I was new to this whole thing anyway.

As it happened, I did have some recipes from Gary's mother and grandmother, to whom I had managed to endear myself after an odd beginning. His grandmother was a particularly wonderful *bubbe*—a *real bubbe*—who lived with his parents. When I had come that first time to be introduced to my future in-laws, they had moved *bubbe* out of the house for the weekend so she wouldn't be upset to meet me. She didn't know what was going on! We were to sit around and laugh about this later. When she eventually met me, she knew that her adored grandson loved me. I kept a small set of kosher dinnerware and pots so that whenever she came to visit she could eat with us and be comfortable. She kept kosher in her daughter's house, but her daughter did not keep kosher. That was amazing! They did it very successfully. She was pleased that I liked to cook and take good care of her wonderful Gary. I was willing to learn, and I wanted her to teach me things. She thought I was wonderful, too.

So in Maine I was able to put all this to good use and I learned how to bake— mandel bread; Jewish apple cake. In fact, a lot of the women learned how to cook and bake in Maine, even though they'd grown up in Jewish homes, because for a number of us it was the first time in our married careers we weren't working. We all entertained each other in our homes. We all celebrated the holidays together. We would have the rabbi over for dinner, then we'd go to the nondenominational chapel for services, and afterward meet at one of our homes for an *oneg Shabbat*, for which we would all do the baking. It was a wonderful young Jewish community, and we've remained very close to two of the couples from that period.

The day Randy was born, I told Gary that he had to call my mother, and let her know that I was okay and the baby was okay. That was very difficult for him to do, but he did it. A couple of days later a box of baby clothes arrived and a letter with a nice check. I sat down with my husband and said that since I had corresponded with my parents during these two years, I no longer had a bone to pick with them. "You picked up the phone and you defended me, but in doing so you caused a rift between you and my parents. I would like you to heal that as best you can so that they, too, can be a part of our children's future. This is their grandchild as much as it is your parents' grandchild, and it's only fair that they should be given the opportunity. Whatever way they respond to this is another story, but you make the entree." He said, "I'll do it for you, but I won't ever do it for anybody else." And I said, "Well, I understand that!" So he sat down and he wrote a very outstanding letter, and my father, interestingly enough, responded with an equally fine letter.

So, after our baby's birth, my parents decided to take a trip to Maine the follow- ing spring. My father refused to fly due to a bad experience he had had once, so they were going to drive and didn't want to do that in the winter. They spent a week with us after two years of separation. The apprehension and anxiety of their visit was definitely worse than the visit itself. I wondered how they would greet me and how I would greet them for the first time. Somehow, everyone just kind of forgot any animosity. Nobody ever spoke of our rift again. We just picked up the pieces where they had been left and built a new relationship. It worked out amazingly well, espe- cially when I look back and think how it could have been. They had had enough time to focus on what was really important in life. As my father said in his letter and reit- erated when he came to visit, what any parent wants is for his child to be happy.

Our daughter, Alison, was born ten days before we left Maine. My husband stayed in Maine to close the house out and take care of all the moving, and I flew to Baltimore with a toddler, the dog, and a ten-day-old infant. My darling father-in-law met me in Boston and as we were about to board the plane to Baltimore, we got fogged in in Boston for five hours.

My parents came down as soon as we moved into our newly built house in Baltimore because they hadn't yet seen Alison. My mother said, "Just tell me what can I do for you?" That's the kind of mother she was anyway. She was a great help for the three days they were there. My in-laws came over, and we all had dinner together. My father said to my mother-in-law during the course of that evening (she told me afterward), "There's a lot of love in this house. It is very special to come here and feel that." She felt he'd really come full circle, and so did I. What else could he have said that would have made me know that it was okay with him. What mattered was that Gary and I had a wonderful happy life together, and anyone could see that.

It was hard on my mother to be separated from me during the two years and especially at the time of my first child's birth, but my mother was a stoic—like the Rock of Gibraltar—emotionally. Years later, I was able to appreciate this stoicism during the three years that she was ill and going downhill; I was amazed at the inner-strength she mustered and the positive memories that she gave to me. We did a lot of talking during my weekly visits to her in those years. From her vantage point, I had not done anything wrong. With my father, a lot of things were left unsaid that I would have liked to have been able to discuss with him. When he was terminally ill, I know that I was a tremendous help to him in a lot of ways—as far as making decisions medically, in easing his discomfort, and also in helping my mother as far as easing his passing for her.

For the past thirty years, the way I've been living my Jewish life has been mostly as a mother! I definitely was the leader in our family in observing Jewish traditions. When we came back to Baltimore, I looked at my husband and said, "We have two children—I think it is time to join a temple. I'd like to join, and I want the children to go to Sunday school. I want them to have a place that they could say, 'this is my temple, this is where I worship.'" When the children were really little, Gary would say, "Do I have to go?" And I looked at him and said, "Are you their father?" That's all I ever said—he got in the car, and we went. I always enjoyed reading to the children about the holidays from the time the kids were really, really little: *My First Book of Hanukkah*, *My First Book of Passover*. We still have these books and now read them to our nieces and nephews.

We always observed the holidays and from the time we came back to Baltimore from Maine, my mother-in-law and I would split doing the holidays. I would do this one in my home, and she would do that one in her home. Now that my mother-in-law is older, I've done all the holidays for the past fifteen years. The families are bigger, and I have the space; I really enjoy cooking; and I like the preparations. But the real reason I wanted to do it myself here at home was so that our children would have the memories of holidays spent in their home with their family members: cousins, aunts, uncles, and grandparents. As they grew older, these memories would be very near and dear to them. I remember that the times together with my family during the holidays were always special regardless of whether or not I could believe in them as far as the religious content was concerned. Jewish holidays are so much more family oriented anyway, and there are more of them, so you have more opportunity!

For the last few years it's just been hit or miss when the children can be home for the holidays because they are all in colleges out of town. Sometimes the logistics are just too problematical. Last year was Sarah's, our youngest's, first year away at college. Suddenly she realized that it was the first time in her eighteen years that she wasn't going to be home for the holidays with her parents, and she was feeling very nostalgic. About a week after school started she called me. "What am I going to do for the holidays?" I told her, "Get out the phone book right now while you're talking to me; look in the yellow pages and see what kind of *shuls* there are; pick up the phone and call them; tell them who you are and where you are; and what you want to do, and I guarantee you you'll be able to go to services." I said, "Have you met any friends who are Jewish?" "Yes," she said. "Meredith, my best friend here, is Jewish." "Good, you take her too." And she went.

Burlington has a fair Jewish population and the University of Vermont does as well, so I was teasing her, "Why don't you date any Jewish fellas? How come it's always these Irish fellas?" She said, "I'm not looking to get married yet, so don't worry about it." "Why don't you go to the Jewish things?" "Well, they don't have any, Mother." But the newsletter came, and I see now they have a Hillel, so I underlined it with a red magic marker!

When we first joined the temple, I realized that the only people I knew were my husband's family and some of their friends, so I joined the sisterhood, and I was fairly active there for quite a few years. I started to become more active in the workings of the temple about ten years ago. I'd been asked various times when the kids were younger to be on the board, and I said no. But I told them to keep my name in reserve, and they kept asking and now I've been on the board for about four years. Over the years, I've helped to decorate the *sukkah* on the *bimah*; I've often helped with the *Oneg Shabbat* or when the cantors have some kind of special concert. I was chairperson of the social-action committee for three years and did a lot of terrific projects, with national recognition from the UAHC (Union of American Hebrew Congregations) on some of the things that we did. We've done a lot of innovative programs: handgun control, a homeless shelter, letter-writing campaigns for the state legislature, and at the federal level, various political activities. That is really a forte of mine because I had a double major in college and one was in political science. Now I am secretary of the executive board of the temple.

My involvement has become broader and my commitment to Judaism has become stronger. The only reason I am serving on the board is because I'd like to see Reform Judaism grow and be prolific in the future. I think there are some more changes that need to be contemplated. One of the major issues, about which I have done some reading, and there has certainly been a lot of discussion in the community, is the issue of interfaith marriages. The numbers are against us. In over 50 percent of marriages involving a born Jew the other partner is not Jewish. I've talked to the rabbis, and I am not happy with a lot of their answers. I would never want a rabbi or a cantor to feel pressured into changing his or her ethical philosophy about marrying or not marrying a couple. It has to come from them from the point of view that "Look, this young couple is going to get married anyway. The chances that they are going to be Jewish are nil if no one Jewish marries them. The chances might only be 5 or 10 percent if somebody does. But 5 or 10 percent is better than nothing." If a congregation has a very active outreach program, I think it is negative for the clergy at that particular congregation to refuse to marry an interfaith couple. If we do not embrace them on the most important occasion at the beginning of their lives together, then how can we say to them, "Oh, but we want you to bring your children here and go to religious school." That is an unrealistic expectation if we are not involved at the beginning.

I don't say that across the hoard every interfaith couple should be able to be married by a member of the Jewish clergy. I think that there should be restrictions and guidelines. I think that if a family has been active and supportive in temple life for a number of years, and the children have become *bar* or *bat mitzvah* and really do know that they want to maintain and perpetuate their Jewishness, just because they happen to fall in love with someone who isn't Jewish shouldn't be a barrier to them to still feel comfortable and welcome in the temple where they grew up. One of the criteria would be that these people would agree to raise their children as Jews. What is the point of being married by a Jewish clergyperson if you do not want to perpetuate the Jewish tradition? If your children aren't Jewish, how are you going to perpetuate it? If it is meaningful for the mother of the potential Jewish children to be married by a member of the Jewish clergy, that's where it counts—or if it is meaningful to the young Jewish man, and his wife thinks, well, maybe I'll convert, but I am not ready yet. Sadly, I know of families who have left various congregations in this community because their children were turned away.

Today's world is such a secular world, and so many people are brought up non-religiously. They celebrate Christmas because it is the commercial thing to do, but they don't go to a church; their family never belonged to one; they don't know where they are coming from except they think they have Christian roots. If one person in that relationship feels their Jewishness strongly enough to want to be married by a rabbi or a cantor, then it shouldn't be such a difficult thing to accomplish. The barriers shouldn't be there.

We had a very interesting discussion a couple of weeks ago about a nephew who is to marry a non-Jew. What if the wedding was in a church? We are a very close-knit family and everybody is very bright and very opinionated. All the younger generation are mostly young adults now, and they really join in. No one is at a loss for words. My mother-in-law, who is this child's grandmother, said she would not attend.

Randy, my oldest son, had been dating a non-Jewish young woman whom he was quite serious about, but when he saw her and her family's observance of Christmas he knew that he could not marry someone who was not Jewish. Nevertheless, his response to his grandmother's refusal to attend the non-Jewish marriage of one of his cousins was "I don't think it is anybody else's business what kind of a religious scenario people want to be married in as long as the people have agreed and that is what makes them happy. I think it would be a tragedy to jeopardize a grandchild's happiness on a day that is supposed to be the beginning of his future with his significant other. To have that kind of a negative impact is really, really tragic."

Randy's current girlfriend was a part of this discussion. She added that she had dated a non-Jewish young man and approached her grandparents about the idea of marrying him. They told her that even though they weren't thrilled with the idea, they certainly would be part of her wedding day because they loved her and this was an important time for her.

I reminded my mother-in-law of the diversity of experience in our own family. I have three sisters-in-law. One has been divorced twice—both were marriages to Jewish men. One who married late is pregnant with her first child, and although the husband's background is Catholic, their children will be Jewish. They were married by a Reform rabbi in Chicago. These were two adults, independent, earning their living—very well, I might add. They didn't ask permission from anybody. They said, "This is what we are doing, and this is when it's going to be, hope you'll be there." The youngest sister-in-law is married to a man who's father is Jewish, but for all practical purposes this young man has not been a practicing Jew his entire life. Nevertheless, he considered himself Jewish when he met my sister-in-law. They were married by our rabbi because a Conservative rabbi would not marry them. My brother-in-law knew very little about being Jewish, but he is now learning with his young children.

"Let's be honest," I said to my mother-in-law, "if it had been up to your son, my husband, your grandchildren would never have had *bar* or *bat mitzvahs*. I was the one who demanded that." She said, "We're well aware of that and we're very grateful to you! We talk about you all over town and you know it!"

What came up in the discussion was that you have to set the example for your children to try to live a Jewish life by providing them a home life in keeping with Jewish tradition—whether Reform, Conservative, or Orthodox. You make it clear that it is an important tradition to maintain. If you do that and your children grow up and become adults and they make decisions, it comes down to this: if it is somebody Jewish they want to marry, it is easier, and if it is somebody who isn't Jewish—well, that is not the parents' decision. I grew up and made a decision for myself and, therefore, how could I ever stand in the way of my children saying, "I'm going to marry someone, and that person is not Jewish"? My only hope is that I have instilled in our children that they are Jewish and that it is an important part of their life, and that they value it to that extent and want to perpetuate that tradition.

Randy definitely does. Alison does. She has a wonderful, wonderful young man whom I think she will marry. He is not Jewish. He is from a Christian family, but he considers himself an agnostic. He has gone to services with her. He has known from their second date that Alison is Jewish, that any children she would have would be

Jewish, and so there are no surprises there. I have discussed with my children that if you choose someone to marry who is not Jewish, you have got to talk about how you are going to raise your children—before you get married. I gave them examples of couples that we know whose families have varying religious expressions. I said, "You know most of these young people, you tell me which ones are mixed up and which ones have their feet squarely planted." The kids can peg it right on the nose. They said that there is no doubt that when a child is brought up in a family with one religion practiced in the home, the kids are better off. Definitely. And all the sociological studies show that, too.

I have also pointed out to them that if they marry someone who is not Jewish, they may not be able to be married by the clergy they have grown up with. Alison has told her boyfriend that she wants to be married by a rabbi, and he does not have any qualms about that. He just asked, for his parents' benefit, would it be a very religious ceremony? And I said it will be a ceremony the way you want it to be. It would be wonderful if you can be married by one of the clergymen that we all know. That would be the nicest scenario. The most important thing, though, is that the two of you are happy with each other.

Over the thirty years of being Jewish I have been to just about every major *shul* in this community. I have never felt different, I have never felt non-Jewish. I have never been treated that way. Never. I personally feel very comfortable. When I go to an Orthodox synagogue, I wear a hat, although, I have to say, most of my born-Jewish friends don't. I am honoring their tradition. I am respectful of their tradition. I may not love it, but in this tradition that is what they prefer you to do.

I am not intimidated by any of the other denominations. I am obviously more comfortable in a Reform or Conservative setting than an Orthodox one. Had I married somebody who was Orthodox, I would not have practiced Orthodoxy. On my own, I would have practiced Reform because it fits well with my personal beliefs. I like the idea of families worshiping together. There are certain aspects of Orthodoxy that, as a young, modern woman, I find repulsive and unacceptable. I don't like the idea that women are not really considered as important as men amongst the Orthodox—or even within the Conservative movement to a large degree. It's right there in their prayer books that somebody who is retarded is accepted in a *minyan*, but not a woman. Nevertheless, I have attended many services in Orthodox synagogues for friends' and family's life-cycle events, and I am able to fit in and feel comfortable.

I have been extraordinarily offended, however, as I am sure others have, by the assumption too frequently expressed or implied that "Oh, well, you converted because you married someone Jewish." The process of making the decision and becoming Jewish is one of the most important decisions I ever made in my life—and one of the best decisions I ever made for myself. I think that most born-Jewish people take conversion rather lightly, and they take for granted their own Jewishness. I have heard comments over the years that I have found offensive. When someone asks me, I let them know that I converted to Judaism because it was a very personal decision that I came to before I married my husband. "Oh!" is the kind of answer you get to that.

When people hear an in-depth version of how I got to be Jewish, for the most part they have respect and a kind of admiration for the process I have undergone, and it becomes more meaningful for them. One time we were on vacation at a lovely resort we've been going to for many years. A lot of people who go there happen to be Jewish, and over the course of the years we've developed some good friends there. One couple, both of whom are Jewish, have four children and are not practicing Jews at this time in their lives, yet they feel their Jewish roots very strongly. They support a couple of different schools in Israel and have been there several times. One evening they asked me, "What made you decide to become Jewish?" There were eight of us at the table. I looked at my watch and said, "Well, we haven't had dessert yet, how long do you have?" An hour and a half later, I was fascinated to feel them almost magnetically drawn to my story as I was telling it. They had never known a convert or had never heard the in-depth story of someone's venture into Judaism. They were mesmerized. It was a revelation to them. By some of the things they asked me, I know that they felt my experience caused them to examine their experience and practice of Judaism and may have caused them to be more religiously Jewish.

One of the main reasons I go to services is that I really want to. I just want to go and sit and participate and read sections of the prayer book and the various teachings. It is a very refreshing aspect to being Jewish, and I can do this in any *shul*—it doesn't have to be mine. I feel very much at home, very content and very much at peace with myself—though not always with the world around me. I have always had a belief in a supreme being—"God," for lack of a better term—and I feel that there is an overall plan. The Jewish people have tried to carry out the teachings that have come down from the prophets and from whoever has had the "ear" of God, so to speak.

One of the most beautiful aspects of Judaism and one of the most beautiful teachings of Judaism is to do *mitzvot*. This is something I take seriously and try to incorporate into my daily life. A small example occurred recently. I know a woman who is just starting out in law school—she's a couple of years younger than I, she has a family of three young adult children, she's had a couple of different careers, and has always been very active. But no matter how bright you are, that first week in law school can be pretty overwhelming. I called another friend of mine who is a second- or third-year law student, and I said to her, "I am going to give you the name and number of someone new to law school; maybe you could give her a call and just give her a little boost." We came back from an outing and found that my friend who was starting law school had left a message on the machine: "You did it again! You did another *mitzvah*!" My husband said, "Look at how happy you made her; you can just hear it in her voice!"

It is so wonderful to be a part of a tradition that teaches us to be responsible for one another in a very practical, everyday way so that you don't have to feel that it has to be a special time to do a nice thing for someone. And I've really tried to teach this to my children by example—by being a living example.

11

Mohelet

Bente Yael Hoegsberg

Bente's story goes against the conventional wisdom that says a convert will not continue practicing Judaism if the marriage to a born Jew ends. In fact, Bente completed her conversion process *after* she was divorced.

Bente met her husband when both were college students traveling abroad. For many years they led an international life in which religion played little role in their lives. They agreed their children would be taught ethical and moral values but not a religion. As they settled down in the United States and began to plan a family, Bente was shocked to learn that her nominally Jewish husband would insist upon a ritual circumcision for any son born to them.

For Bente, who was not Jewish and lacked the support of faith and community, her sons' circumcisions were wrenching experiences. Thus began her journey in Judaism, which demands from parents this mark of commitment no matter how far they may have strayed from a traditional Jewish life.

What we do with the adversity in our lives depends on so many factors—personality, age, opportunity. As converts our responses to the inconsistencies that can be found in Judaism—as in all areas of human endeavor—are affected by all that has happened in our lives beforehand. Unwilling to be overwhelmed by having incomprehensible religious beliefs imposed upon her, Bente took control by studying Judaism, and after conversion, becoming a *mohelet*. To her amazement she found Judaism a welcome refuge in which her most anguished doubts might find expression and even the potential of spiritual redemption.

I do not know why or exactly when I decided to become Jewish. Decided is not the correct term. Rather, when I *knew* that I was Jewish. There was no doubt in my mind. I *felt* Jewish. I belonged among Jews.

I was brought up and lived in Denmark until I was twenty-five years old. Denmark has a state church, Lutheran, to which over 90 percent of the population belongs. Religion to most people meant being baptized, confirmed, married, and buried. I, on the other hand, was brought up Catholic, quite strictly. My mother was German and Catholic. We were, in a homogeneous, nominally religious society, different: foreign *and* churchgoing.

When I was a child I thought I liked going to Catholic church, singing the songs. My mother was very religious and very strict. But I thought it was more just a convention. She was very critical toward others who didn't do the right thing. Later, after I was grown, I learned that she lived in a way that didn't follow church rules. I got very angry with her about that—she made me believe something that she didn't even follow.

I had a very difficult relationship with my mother. I always tried to be a good, dutiful daughter and please my parents. But I never succeeded, especially with my mother—my father was absent most of the time.

When I was sixteen or so I started feeling it was a lot of crap in church and in school. You weren't supposed to be sexually active, have sexual thoughts. And I thought that being a good person had nothing to do with whether you had sex with somebody or not. When I was eighteen, I had a boyfriend and I wanted to sleep with him, but I couldn't because my mother wouldn't let me. I moved out which caused a major break with my mother which hasn't ever been healed.

So, at age eighteen, I dissociated myself from the church and for many years felt no need for religion. Religion was, to me, something for weaklings, "opium for the people." Being moral and ethical seemed sufficient. I did not consider myself an atheist, but whether God existed or not was really of no interest.

My parents were divorced when I was twenty-two. It was then that I understood that they had "pretended" much of the time. The effect this had on me was as if everything that held me up from my childhood disappeared.

My husband and I met while traveling in Russia. I was there studying, but really it was to get a nice, cheap vacation. Jonny was a serious college student at that time. A year and a half later, I traveled to Central Asia, and we ran into each other in Tashkent. It was in March and there were no tourists there. When I was in the United States traveling more than a year later, Jonny said that he would meet me and show me around. Six months later he came to Denmark, and we were married in the Copenhagen Town Hall.

I was twenty-five, and I had never met a Jew before I met Jonny. Jews were the Holocaust and Israel. In World War II the Danes viewed Jews as Danes first and Jews second, and they were very active in saving Danish Jews. Now I know that there were people who were famous in Denmark who were Jewish, but growing up, I had had neither positive nor negative experiences with Jews. Jonny's background was non-religious, materialistic—the suburbs in New Jersey. I didn't know what it was to be Jewish and certainly wasn't going to get it from him.

After I finished medical school, Jonny was an exchange student and we spent a year in Russia. We lived in Virginia for a year while he clerked for a judge. Later, he worked in New York and I got a residency there. At that time we were leading a very secular, international life.

At first Jonny's family regarded me as a total stranger and outsider. They would use a Yiddish word and then explain it to me, but because of my German background I could understand many of the Yiddish words the family used, and the food was also familiar. And since I had religious training, I knew some of the Old Testament stories far better than any of the family did. That felt strange to me.

Jonny's family had a strong sense of Jewish identity, and it puzzled me that this was completely separated from the religion. Oddly, my feeling for Judaism started awakening through my husband and his family when they were acting in ways I thought were *not* Jewish. By this time I had learned a little about Jewish history and religion, feeling a strange familiarity.

At the *bar mitzvah* of my husband's nephew, the ceremony in the Reform temple, I found myself upset by the apparent lack of interest in the religious part. Later, I also found disturbing that at the elaborate party, lobsters were served. Why should it have mattered to me? I ate these foods, so why should I care? The realization that I did care, that it did upset me, was really even more unsettling. And I started, reluctantly, to look at my religious feelings. I frequently tried to talk myself out of this ridiculous interest in religion.

In fact, Jonny and I had agreed that we would bring up any children we might have without religion. We felt that teaching them moral values would suffice. When the issue of circumcision came up, we had the only serious disagreement in the first seven years of our marriage.

In my country, circumcision was unheard of, except among the few uneducated, Muslim foreign workers. I considered it the mutilation of infant boys—barbaric! As a resident in obstetrics and gynecology in New York, I saw circumcision almost universally practiced. I spent more time convincing women *not* to do this cruel thing than it would have taken to do the circumcision—although I did feel that performing a circumcision out of religious conviction was okay. Since Jonny did not follow *any* of the other rules of Jewish law—and even thought observant Jews ridiculous—when it came to my son, I said, "Over my dead body!" "If he's Jewish, he has to," Jonny said. "But you are not particularly Jewish. You don't ever go to temple; you don't do anything; you don't keep kosher. Why is circumcision more important than keeping kosher?" He didn't know. He still is not able to say why that is important. "It's for the Jewish identity." But according to some Jews these kids aren't even Jewish.

To this day, I still do not understand why circumcision is so much more important than the other *mitzvot* among nonreligious Jews.

Three years after I started my residency, my first child was born in Denmark while I was on my vacation. I was quite alone in New York except for Jonny. By giving birth in Denmark I could be with my family and the baby would have dual citizenship. He was named Samuel; it was important to me that he have a Jewish name. We came back when our son was four or five weeks old and continued our circumcision argument. Finally I said, "Okay, you can go ahead and have him circumcised," so Jonny took him to my obstetrician—a Jewish obstetrician—and had him circumcised. I suffered greatly, certainly more than my son, and vowed I would never allow this again.

Our second son was born eighteen months later and was named Joseph. I refused to have him circumcised. But then Jonny acted as if Josie didn't exist. He was extremely involved in the first child, taking care of him; he was really close to him. Even his mother noticed Jonny's behavior toward the new baby, which was unusual.

Finally, it occurred to me that maybe it was because he wasn't circumcised. I raised it with him; he denied that he was treating the second baby differently from the first. I couldn't get through to him at all. He's not good at examining what's going on inside himself. He thinks that if he ignores things, they will be okay. So, I took the baby to be circumcised, this time in the hospital, with anesthesia, because he was ten months old. And Jonny's relationship with this child improved. And I felt—rather than understood—some big, underlying meaning of circumcision.

I don't know how I could have thought that it would be possible to raise the children without religion. When they were a little older, I started taking the kids to the Jewish Community Center for nursery school and kindergarten. I signed them up for after-school programs, for religious education—very Reform religious, though. The initiative always came from me, but Jonny approved, always. I eagerly participated in the parents' activities. There I met Rachel Cowan, recently ordained as a rabbi and also a convert, and Daphna Soltes, whose father was the rabbi at Jonny's childhood temple. I felt inspired by these two bright, enthusiastic women, who seemed to integrate spirituality and Judaism with modern life.

I began to light *Shabbat* candles and to celebrate the Jewish holidays. This included taking the boys to children's services at Jonny's family's temple in New Jersey. My husband approved of all this, but never took the initiative. Since he was action-oriented in most things, that was unusual for him. Using the children's religious education as an excuse, I learned myself. I read in a haphazard way whatever I could find and started living differently. I fasted on Yom Kippur, had *matzah* for *Pesah*, and didn't mind the mild ridicule from my husband. Our marriage, however, was becoming severely strained, and during these years we separated and were divorced.

Although legally separated, we continued to live together for several years. I wanted to leave earlier but then Jonny got a restraining order. Jonny went to the judge and said, "My wife is crazy and an unfit parent. Prevent her from taking the kids." They issue these orders automatically. I had actually already rented a house and moved. I had to move back because otherwise it would have been like abducting the children, and he would automatically get them. One of the reasons he listed in the ten pages of proof that I was an unfit mother was the arguments we had had about circumcision. I thought it was so strange that he put that in there. That I think circumcision is barbaric proves that I am crazy?

Then we had to meet with a court-appointed child psychiatrist to see if I was indeed a crazy and an unfit parent. Of course I wasn't. The psychiatrist concluded that we were both fit parents—even a husband who accuses a wife of being an unfit parent, because that had nothing to do with parenting the kids. The psychiatrist was actually very helpful. He said you can figure this out yourselves; you do not need to go to court. Finally we got divorced, and I could move out. We had joint custody and joint residence.

The failure of our marriage affected me deeply. There were few bright days. Being able to keep kosher when I was finally able to move into my own apartment was a good thing that I am still happy about.

Our joint custody is working out very well. There is no problem. We talk about everything beforehand. He's busy, and I'm busy. We tell the kids ahead of time where they are going to be. We are very flexible because sometimes they miss the other parent, so I'll call him up and say, "Jonny, this one misses you tonight," and that child goes over there. We are now, surprisingly, very good friends, so much so that the kids have trouble understanding why we aren't together. It is sort of a paradox. We get along; we talk daily about everything. The kids cannot manipulate us.

Amid all this pain and difficulty I converted. While Jonny and I were separated but still living together, I started studying. I got more and more interested and felt also that it was the right thing for me. I wanted to have a kosher kitchen, which was a little difficult, but one way of dealing with this was to become vegetarian. Throughout all this my husband thought I was absolutely crazy. To him I was cuckoo like the Orthodox.

I worked at Albert Einstein Hospital and had friends who were observant Jews, and that is where I learned about Jewish laws and customs. I spoke to them about conversion, but mostly I did not discuss this with others. Among nonreligious Jews I found prevalent the attitude "you won't really be Jewish anyway"; among observant Jews, "you are only Jewish if you live like we do"; and from others, "are you crazy, what are you doing that for?" One friend wanted to know why it wasn't enough for me that I *felt* Jewish. Officially belonging was important to me.

Two friends at the hospital—one Israeli and a *ba'al teshuvah* Lubavitcher—thought very much that I should convert to Orthodoxy for the practical reasons. I didn't want to have my conversion questioned by anybody. I could imagine that maybe I would go to Israel, and I wouldn't want them saying, "You are not Jewish." I also didn't feel that I belonged in Reform Judaism at all because it seemed very frivolous: the organ music, the rabbis dressed in black robes who looked like Protestants, and the "thou art"—pretend Christian—oh! give me a break, I couldn't stand it.

So I went to an Orthodox rabbi who asked me questions and discouraged me, as they are supposed to do, three times. "You don't want to do this, and we don't want to do it either." The study for my conversion was a great disappointment to me because it wasn't learning. It was rote memorization of some facts, and they didn't want argument and discussion. Questions were not appreciated, especially critical ones. I remember one session that involved the carrying of things on *Shabbat*. The rabbi explained that it is allowed to carry a key, if the key is made into a brooch. I felt it was hypocritical. I got the message, though, that if I did not shut up, my readiness for conversion would be in question. The reading we did was interesting in itself, but the interpretations, discussions, were missing.

Most of those in the class were getting married and were in a hurry to convert. It was obvious that this was simply a practical matter in order to get married. So I had the suspicion that this was a "conversion mill." And it was very expensive. It cost $1,500. But I just thought, let me get through with this. Somehow it was important for me to have the formality. It makes you a member of the club. One of the things that upset me about my conversion is that written in Hebrew on my certificate is the admonition that I may not marry a *kohen*—which they never told me. At least they should have put it in the English part too.

The conversion itself was in a small *mikveh* in Brooklyn. The woman at the *mikveh* thought that I was being converted because I was getting married. She was really amazed that I wasn't. The *Bet Din* was there—oh, God, it could have been eastern Poland. They sat there with their hats on. It was warm, and they were bored, and seemed to have no interest in being there. I remember hoping that they were at least paid for their inconvenience. They asked me a question or two; then in the *mikveh*, it was really weird going in there with these guys looking through the door. So it wasn't a great spiritual experience. Although I must say that I read the *Shema*, and I thought, "That is a powerful thing"—it still is. And that was that. My Jewish identity was not changed by that experience, but now the formalities were in order.

When I converted, I of course wanted to have my kids at the *mikveh*, converted along with me. Jonny absolutely would not have that. "These kids are Jewish," he said, "according to Reform—that's the majority of American Jews, and the majority of Jews in the world feel that way—so they are Jewish." I feel that *halakhah* is stronger than an opinion from the Reform movement, but I realized that the resulting schism, were I to force the issue, would have outweighed the benefits. The children will have to figure this out for themselves, later.

The reaction from my family has been generally supportive. One of my sisters with whom I am very close gave a speech at my fortieth birthday party, saying she thought it was wonderful that I had converted to Judaism. When my father writes to me he uses my Hebrew name, because he saw that on my professional card. I liked that; it is a sign of respect. I haven't told my mom per se that I have converted, but she knows it because I changed my name, and my niece, to whom I write frequently, shares news about me with her grandmother.

People know I am Jewish now because I have a very Jewish identity. I just act as if I were always Jewish, and I rarely tell people that I am converted. At a meeting recently at the Conservative synagogue I attend, a man, prompted by my "non-Jewish" looks, asked me: "Are you really Jewish, I mean one hundred percent?" And I said, "Yes, one hundred percent!" When people hear I am from Denmark, they say, "Oh, there aren't many Jews in Denmark." And I say, "No, there aren't." Once at the children's Hebrew school the parents were meeting with some of the teachers and a rabbi, and we talked a little about this. The father of one of the teachers was a rabbi, and he used to say that it was always the converted wife that took the most care and was the best parent religiously, but that they were very much looked down upon. I have gotten support from my Israeli friend and my Lubavitcher friend and from Rabbi Cowan. She was always very nice and supportive. Being a convert herself, she seemed to understand. But most people are not very welcoming. I think their negative attitudes come from a lack of knowledge. People should read what the Torah says about converts. They are closer to God, it says somewhere—I can't remember the place that that comes from. But converts are mentioned several times and are regarded as Jews—highly regarded. The general community should just keep that in mind.

Right now my kids go to a Reform, fancy schmancy New York synagogue. Jonny would like the children to become *bar mitzvah* in the Reform synagogue, but I won't agree. He wants the children to be raised in the religion—but not as much religion as I would like. Recently, though, he's seen some of the benefits of deeper observance.

I went out for the first night of Passover with the kids to some friends, and the second night they were supposed to go to their grandmother's with their dad. But Jonny felt uncomfortable with some of the company invited and he said, "Okay, I'll just stay home." I felt sorry for him because I know he appreciates these holidays even if he doesn't do much for them. So I said, "You can come to our house." I made the *seder* the second night. I don't like to cook particularly, but I made the *seder* because I think the kids should have the second *seder*. We read the *Haggadahs*; the kids take it very seriously, and it was very nice. They read their parts, and we discussed some of the issues. They found the *afikomen*. They were into the celebration.

I feel my children's religious upbringing is inadequate. This is partly because I feel that I am still fumbling and learning, and partly because their father feels differently about Jewish living. For example, I asked the children not to eat ham and shrimp when they are with me. Invariably they would say, "But Dad lets us." Out of respect for me, they will keep kosher when with me. Averting conflicts over religious issues is probably more important than what they eat. In addition to wanting them to have a much better religious education, I would like to keep Saturday a sort of quiet day but that seems to be impossible. I read them stories from the *Mishnah* and read Bible stories. My youngest son, whose name is Joseph, loves the story about Joseph, whose brothers maltreat him—he can identify with that, he thinks! And then Joseph ends up the boss. We read that many times.

I took the children to Elat Chayyim—a retreat sponsored by the Jewish Renewal Movement. I got the brochure from I-don't-know-which mailing list, and I thought that it sounded really exciting. I couldn't go to any of the week-long things, which I wanted to, so I just went there for the weekend. I loved it; I had a wonderful time. The kids were so critical at first. They wanted to know if they had room service there! They looked at the people and said, "Is this a vegetarian place?" They said, "We won't have anything to eat for the whole weekend." They had such a good time—and they loved the food.

About two years ago, one of my residents took a course to become a *mohel*. As soon as I learned about it, I questioned him, looked through his book, and made him tell me what it was he learned. I am now studying to become a *mohelet* at the Hebrew Union College, and the night of the class has become the highlight of my week. Considering my earlier feeling about circumcision, it is perhaps strange that I would do this. The reasons are several. It gives me a chance to study, and if I see the deep spiritual (rather than traditional) connection between circumcision and being Jewish, maybe I'll make peace with that issue by connecting on a deeper level. This is also a way for me to share something that is important and dear to me with others. The closeness and even elation I have felt with others when talking about religious issues, or even saying *brakhot*, is difficult to describe but very significant.

I like to teach, in all different ways: formal teaching, but also by acting and by showing. I often feel in my work as an obstetrician that I can show interns the spiritual matter that birth is. It's rare, but it happens: they get a glimpse that it is not just cutting the episiotomy, turning the head around, getting the shoulder out—there is more to it. And I prefer to be a catalyst rather than just give out facts. To be a *mohelet*, therefore, would bring together many aspects of my life. Like birth, a *bris* is a highly charged situation, a time when people's hearts are open and they are receptive—even for people who come from a more secular perspective, there comes a point when their interest turns to more religious matters. There is hardly a better time than a *bris*, I think, to share with others.

In the *brit milah* class, we are seven, one man and six women. Some midwives, one pediatrician, a family practitioner, and I am the only obstetrician. Everybody is really there for his or her own spiritual reasons, which makes it such a good group always. I wasn't the only one in the course who thought circumcision was barbaric. Everybody there—most of them do circumcisions already—feels the same way. They all had their sons circumcised, but they still had problems with it. I think we are all there to come to peace with it.

We have excellent lectures and interesting discussions. One of the senior rabbinical students who came told us that every time you study Torah, you should say a prayer. He said these study sessions were like studying Torah and we should say a prayer. Everybody really liked that! We have some of the teachers from the seminary, biblical scholars in different fields. One person tells about the ceremony itself—how it compares among Conservative, Orthodox, and Reform. They encourage us to do our own thing. We all have these doubts about doing it—not the circumcision itself, but that we are responsible in this spiritual affair. We can have a big influence on people.

I recently had some practical experiences that brought into focus the importance of my decision to become a *mohel*. I went to a friend's son's circumcision, and, oh, I was so upset. The rabbi said that when the baby's crying it is not because it hurts. Oh, give me a break, of course it hurts! Don't lie to us. I can't stand that. Let's be honest. Then I had a patient recently who had been on bed rest since twenty weeks because her water had broken. When she finally delivered a healthy child, she asked me to come to do the circumcision at her home. But I told her, "I am not a *mohel*, yet." She said, "That is okay; the cantor will come and do the blessings." It was strange to do this, but it went well.

The course is over in May, and I am sorry about that because it is so good. Then we will go on a list of people who need a *mohel*—people who are in mixed marriages or who are not religious who think that they want "something." There is some organization to educate people to become *mohels*—to take circumcision out of the hands of the doctors and make it a more spiritual event. This organization is having a meeting in Jerusalem next year. So our group is hoping to go. That will make my third trip to Israel.

I can't imagine being a *mohel* without knowing Hebrew, so I am going to start studying Hebrew, which I've wanted to do for a long time. I will get the course cata-log from the Jewish Theological Seminary and see what they have to offer. It sounds like they have some very good courses, and sometimes you can just sit in on them. An Israeli friend of mine was teasing me that perhaps I will become a rabbi—and perhaps I will.

One of the things I love about Judaism is the ethics—for every step in life, every situation—and it is so human, too. There is an openness about discussion—it is a tradition to study the texts and discuss them and have opinions. The Orthodox don't allow you that anymore, except for the chosen few men who make the decisions, and then they tell the rest what is right. I don't think that that fits in the spirit of Judaism, though I am sure they could give me twenty reasons why I am wrong.

Everybody has to fit in their place and my place is somewhere in the middle. Maybe my friends who are Orthodox don't think so, but for me it feels that I am leading an authentic Jewish life. Right now this is the level that I can do. If I did much more, then I feel that I would be fake. My observance is very natural and, in a way, low key. I couldn't think of not eating *matzah* during the Passover week that has just gone by. When I moved into a new office recently, I put a *mezuzah* on the door. To me that is very important. I use my Hebrew name, Yael, as my middle name, and I plan to make it legal because that is meaningful to me. I chose "Yael" by looking over a list that my Israeli friend gave me. I chose one that sounded nice. It is the name of a kind of goat that you find in the desert. When I was in Israel last year, in May, I saw them.

12

"Guard Your Soul Carefully"

John Bonavita

The words above from Deuteronomy are engraved in the Holocaust Museum and were quoted by John in the speech he wrote for his *bar mitzvah*, which he celebrated shortly after his visit to the museum.

In coming to Judaism, John, like many of us in the post-Holocaust, post-Sputnik generation, has come to realize that rational and intellectual answers to the meaning of life are not always enough. We need, John says, permission to explore our spirituality—and we need to do that, he adds, in a supportive community. Yet, before we can fully discover ourselves in community, we must discover who we are as individuals—and to do that, we must know what lies at the depth of our soul.

After years of denial and trying to lead a straight life as a conventionally married man, John realized a truth he had known about himself since he was a child: he is gay. Acceptance of that fact became a liberating force in John. In the ten-year relationship he has shared with Harold, it has been possible for John to nurture both of their spiritual lives: first, by encouraging his partner to rediscover the religion of his childhood, and then by choosing Judaism for himself as well.

Through their openness, loving-kindness, and dedication to community, John and Harold, separately and as a couple, have made a place for themselves in their synagogue and in the broader social circles in which they live and work.

Although the Holocaust Museum records the atrocities committed against Jews, it also tells us of the persecution of other groups: the Roma (Gypsies), leftists, the handicapped, and homosexuals. The Germans were especially cruel to anyone who fell into more than one of those groups. One of the lessons of the Holocaust Museum seems to be that prejudice against one group leads to prejudice against any and all of our diversity as human beings:

> Only guard yourself and guard your soul carefully, lest you forget the things that your eyes saw, and lest these things depart your heart all the days of your life.

I made my *bar mitzvah* at the Society Hill Synagogue in June of 1993. I began studying the previous fall on my own, not through a class. The prior year I learned how to do the *Musaf* and that took about three or four months. So I told the cantor I would do my *bar mitzvah* this year. It's sort of nice doing it as an adult because you can choose any time you want. So I chose June 5 because Harold's sister could get in from Memphis, and the whole family could be here. It was a convenient time for everybody, and there was nobody else scheduled, so I knew I didn't have to share the spotlight with anyone.

My *parashah* was *BeHaalothekha*, when the ark of the covenant is moving all over the Sinai peninsula. I gave a whole *shpiel* on the role of visual versus auditory communication. In that *parashah* the cloud of smoke and the funnel of fire move around all over the Sinai. So you've got the visual thing, which is very obvious, but at the same time there's always the trumpet sounding. Why the trumpet? Was the trumpet superfluous, was it not superfluous, how did it fit in? Then I came around to the idea of the trumpet as a manifestation of oral communication, which Jews have always done, partially because of tradition, partially because of injunctions against the visual. Then I worked in the Holocaust Museum, which is of course predominantly visual . . . very little of it is oral. I ended up suggesting: are we unwittingly entering a new post-modern–post-Holocaust paradigm in which we are merging the oral with the visual? Moses versus Aaron? Are we being blasphemous, or is this something that is going to work? Then I went back to the Torah portion and said that it obviously does work because in this whole *parashah* you really are mixing the oral with the visual. That was a nice full-circle argument.

My father and mother were there and also a lot of relatives. My father gave a wonderful speech as I stood there on the *bimah*; I had no idea what he was going to say. He had a little piece of paper about the size of a 3 x 5 index card. I always surprise him, he said, because I am always doing something unexpected, but he knows that I am always very thoughtful about what I do, so I must have good reasons for things. When I told him that I was going to do my *bar mitzvah*, he was a little bewildered because he thinks that only thirteen-year-old kids make *bar mitzvahs*. But he was very moved by it and by the way that both Harold and I had been accepted by the congregation, and how we really seemed to have found ourselves as individuals. He really was quite pleased about it. He brought tears to most of the people in the audience. I couldn't look because I was quite choked up. He was terrific.

As adult children, one of the things that we are always wistful about is that our parents never see us as real adults. They always see us as kids. They never see our mature relationships with other people. They see what we've accomplished only through their eyes but not through our eyes. At my *bar mitzvah*, my parents were able to see what I had accomplished and saw me with all my adult friends and how they reacted toward me. It was a wonderful experience for me, and they loved it.

My family used to live just outside New York; now they live on the Jersey shore. My family is Italian Catholic, but they predominantly think of themselves as Italian. The Catholic part is almost an afterthought. Lots of people who are Italian probably don't understand that. My mother has always been moderately religious; my father has always been irreligious and has always viewed religion with a jaundiced eye. His family came from southern Italy; they were very poor and very radical in their politics. My mother's family has been in this country for a long time, which is something unusual for Italians. They came from northern Italy and were much more traditional. My parents had a mixed marriage in a sense. It was like a Russian Jew marrying a German Jew. They came from very different social backgrounds.

My father was a shopkeeper. He owned a clothing store. I used to go over with him to Seventh Avenue (the clothing district in New York City, which has historically been predominantly Jewish) every Wednesday to go shopping. Everything he would get from Seventh Avenue was always addressed "Bonavitz" rather than "Bonavita." I guess they assumed somebody in that profession couldn't be Italian—we must have spelled the name wrong!

My childhood was very ethnic. Until I was five years old most people I knew were Italian and had an Italian accent. As in most cases, our parents didn't want us to speak Italian. They wanted us to speak English—but from working in the store I learned Italian. The county was very ethnic: it was Italian, it was Jewish, and it was German, although they had started moving out. And that was basically who I knew. Then I switched from public school to a Catholic school and most of the people were Irish; there were very few Italians. That felt foreign to me, coming from a neighborhood that was one-third Italian and one-third Jewish. (By the way, the basic critical issue that distinguishes Catholics from Jews is whether or not you go to camp. Italian boys don't go to camp because their mothers don't want to let them go out of the house. Jewish mothers send their kids to camp because they can't wait to get rid of them. When Harold and I were first together, the first thing I noticed that was really discordant was that it was February and he was reading the *New York Times* to try to find a sports camp for the dogs. I was upset about that. These are Italian dogs, and they are not going to camp!)

My first conception of my religion was that it was separate from me. The Italian kids were always made to feel different at school. We were always second class. Religion was something that was taught by Irish Catholic nuns, and I always felt that Italians really didn't get it right, and that our Catholicism was always sort of part pagan. The reality is that Italian Catholicism really *is* very pagan, and it's a lot of fun. It really has absolutely nothing to do with Irish Catholicism. It was disconcerting to me because religion became something that was really sort of "other," something that was not in our family but was outside, something we should conform to. I was ashamed about it as a kid; maybe we weren't really doing it the right way. I don't think that lasted very long. Everybody I knew in the neighborhood was exactly the same as us; it was when I went to school that we were different.

We didn't celebrate all of the Catholic holidays. Easter was just an excuse to get new clothes—of course, that was part of my father's business. We celebrated American holidays, but they were always very Italianized. Thanksgiving and Christmas were wonderful events that lasted forever. You basically sat around the table for eight hours talking and eating one course after another of Italian delicacies. It was fabulous. At Thanksgiving the turkey was always immolated in the oven and nobody really cared about it. We had to have it because we were in this country. Our family's idea of cooking a turkey was that if you should have it in the oven for five hours at 300 degrees, why waste the time? Put it in the oven for three hours at 500 degrees because it's the same multiplication. One year my Aunt Tillie decided she'd had enough of this Italian stuff—we were going to have a real American Thanksgiving this year, a turkey with chestnut stuffing. About an hour after she put the turkey in the oven there was this enormous explosion—she had put the stuffing in the turkey with the chestnuts whole, without taking the shells off. Enough of these American dinners—we were not fated to have American Thanksgiving. That was it, and we got back to the real stuff.

I felt more Catholic by the time I went to a Jesuit prep school. I am happy that I got a Jesuit education because the Jesuits were remarkable. They are an aberration in Catholicism because they are very intellectual. At that point in my life, I began to question what everything was about. The times were radical enough and the younger Jesuits were raising the question themselves—how does Christian belief fit in with modern existential philosophy? Is there really an afterlife? What is the purpose of ethics? Is the only reason to be ethical or do good that you are going to be rewarded for it? Can ethics exist in a vacuum? Those were the kind of questions that began to obsess me.

For a really long time I sort of gave up on religion. Faith was something that was not all that important—to me or even to the Jesuits. They would almost be ashamed to discuss faith because it was so anti-intellectual. I always thought of faith as being something much more Protestant than Catholic. It feels very out-in-left-field to me. Catholicism, especially in the very highest circles, among people like the Jesuits, has always been a very intellectual exercise.

In Protestantism faith is very much about the relationship between the individual and God, so it is very nonintellectual and emotional. There have been some articles recently about places like Brazil becoming increasingly Protestant because the intellectual aspect of Catholicism doesn't appeal to poor people, especially when their lives are hideous. What appeals to people when they don't have any other hope or help in life is this pure leap of faith.

For me, the Trinity, the divinity of Jesus, was almost a given. The history of Christianity, and specifically Catholicism, has been rife with all kinds of schisms and controversies about the Trinity. The best way to think about that was *not* to think about it because it never made any sense. Who wanted to get involved in another controversy? There are many foundations for Catholicism, and the divinity of Christ is only one. There were other beliefs and ways you could feel connected to the religion without that one. Just as the belief in God is not central to Judaism.

The rabbi in our synagogue, Rabbi Ivan Caine, former dean of the Reconstructionist Rabbinical College, said there are left-wing agnostics and right-wing agnostics and you go back and forth in your life being a left-wing and right-wing agnostic, so big deal! It's sort of a nice way to look at it in the sense that whether you believe in God or not you're probably going to go back and forth between the two extremes during your life if you are a thinking person. Why get exercised about it?

I graduated from the Jesuit high school full of questions and radical ideas, and I went to Duke because I had a cousin who was a doctor there. My mother's father was completely mystified. He thought they were crazy to send me down there. I should be going to the University of Pennsylvania. He was probably right. Duke was a Protestant school. It was in the South. It was so different. I came from New York, and in North Carolina there was all this green stuff. What was I doing there? I didn't graduate from Duke, but I did quite well, very high in my class, and it was a hard school. I transferred to St. Jo's in Philadelphia. I never really understood, at the time, why I did that, but I know now.

I was coming out then. The process of coming out for me was a very hard process because I didn't want to be gay. At several times in my life it was terrible. One time was in the eighth grade, and I tried to speak to my father. I knew then, and I found it very scary. My father had me talk to a psychiatrist. Unfortunately, he was a friend of the family and said, "Oh, it's just a stage." I felt that he didn't really understand. Then I had the same kind of problem when I was in high school. When I was all alone in college, I found that I was confronted with it again. It was something that I couldn't run away from, and I didn't realize it at the time. I went to St. Jo's. It was like high school—it was very safe for me. And my sexual orientation was something I was basically able to put away.

I went to Penn for medical school, and I was still confronted with the same issues. I got married. I spoke to my wife about being gay and that I didn't want to be and that I wanted to get married and maybe this would work. We were married for eleven years. We tried to have kids but couldn't because she had had peritonitis as a child. She had a couple of operations, but she couldn't get pregnant. About eleven years into the marriage, I started letting down my defenses about being gay. I was in therapy at the time, and I began to ask, "Why torture myself?" Mary Ann forced the issue. She said, "This is not working, and we are not going to have kids." She made the decision for me. I would never have done it. That is a horrible thing to say: she made the decision. But it was the smartest thing to do. About a year after that I met Harold.

That was 1983. We went together for about six months and then moved in together. It was strange, though, being divorced from Mary Ann, because she was always my best friend. You think you are going to be with somebody the rest of your life and all of a sudden you're not. We didn't hate each other when we got divorced. It was just terribly sad. We are still good friends, and she is friends with Harold. You hear about this—people who come out and are friendly with their ex-spouses—and you sort of get cynical about it. But in reality it's true. The two of us care very much about each other. But we also have to be separate. If we get too close to each other, it becomes uncomfortable because the interdependencies come up again. We are friendly but we are not involved in each other's lives too much. We both need to develop our own lives. But I make sure I am there if she ever needs me.

My brother is gay. He came out twenty years ago. He was married and living in Italy. In the family, I have always been the "good" son and my brother always the "bad" son. I never did anything wrong. I was always the golden boy. It was hard coming out to my parents for two reasons: it meant giving up the notion that I was the good son, and it meant they were not going to have grandchildren.

There is a funny story about coming out to my parents. The day Harold moved into my house, my father called me up and said, "I am coming to Philadelphia and stop over at your house." I said, "You can't come today!" because the movers were there. He said, "What do you mean I can't come today? I'm coming." Two hours later he's there. All of Harold's furniture was in the back yard. Harold was upstairs, and I wouldn't let my father upstairs. We were trying to hide an entire half a household while my father was there, and he never caught on.

Another story has to do with how my parents felt about Harold once they finally met him. Later the same year that Harold moved in, the whole family was invited for Thanksgiving. It would have been unfair if everybody in the family knew who Harold was except my parents, so I had to come out to them. And it was hard. They knew, and they didn't know. They knew because I'd talked to them when I was an adolescent, but I never really talked to them about it afterward. It was a disappointment to them. A major problem for parents is worrying about what their friends are going to think. And the other problem, of course, is not having grandchildren.

The funny thing is that my parents get along with Harold much better than they ever got along with Mary Ann. She was a WASP and they could not relate to her at all. The Italian family structure is similar to the Jewish family structure; they knew how to relate to Harold and vice versa. Their relationship with Harold has none of the tension that existed between Mary Ann and them, and I don't have to be in the middle any more. So it is very easy.

Harold and I have worked very hard on our relationship. I think both of us had preconceived notions that gay relationships wouldn't work. We were always afraid that it was going to fall apart. Both of us had issues with intimacy and dependency. It's hard to be a gay couple, not having many role models and not having structure. But we've made it work.

It was purely incidental that I was not Jewish and that Harold was. There is supposedly a slight skew in the incidence of Italians and Jews being gay on the East Coast. It's probably just because there are lots of Jews and Italians in East Coast cities. So the odds of meeting somebody who is Jewish or Italian are higher.

When I met Harold at a dinner party given by a friend, before he had even moved to Philadelphia, I said, "I can't believe you're Jewish and you're from Memphis." I learned that right after the Civil War, the Jewish community in Memphis was decimated in a yellow-fever epidemic, and its population dropped to a quarter. The German Jews fled Memphis and moved to St. Louis. Baron Hirsch* established villages on free land available in Memphis and other places like that. The Russian Jews replaced

---

*Baron Maurice de Hirsch, a German financier and philanthropist, was the originator of the Jewish Colonization Association, which enabled the resettlement of Jews throughout the world.

the German Jews in the middle of nowhere. A lot of them became peddlers throughout the mid-South. The southern gentility thought that handling money was somehow disgusting, so they were landowners. The Jews were the merchants and did commerce. You look all over Mississippi and Alabama and there's lots of Jews in these little towns. As their children have become educated, they want to move to bigger cities and the Jewish populations in those little towns are going down to nothing.

Five years ago, for Harold's stepmother's eightieth birthday, we went to Memphis, and I met a lot of his family members. I'd never met Jews from Alabama or Mississippi in my life. To hear Jews speaking in a southern accent, with names like Peggy Sue Pinstein and Holly Sue Goldman, was beyond my comprehension! There was a wonderful story recently on National Public Radio and in the Jewish *Forward* about the Jews in the last Orthodox synagogue in Greenwood, Mississippi. The rabbi is the sheriff and his name is "Bubba." He was wonderful on the radio, and when I finally saw a picture of him, I was expecting this skinny guy, but he is a big heavyset guy with a beard, with his nightstick and a *tallit* on.

Harold grew up in an Orthodox family in Memphis, left that and became very secularly Jewish. He really had a lot of conflict about being Jewish and gay and never felt very comfortable. He was a lawyer, gave up law, got his Ph.D. in social-service administration at the University of Chicago, and after a couple of years began to work for Jewish Family and Children's Service in Philadelphia. He came to Philadelphia and took that job precisely to reconnect with being Jewish.

When Harold moved to Philadelphia two months after we'd met at the dinner party, we started going out. He worked in program development for JFCS (Jewish Family and Children's Service). Within a couple of months he became vice-president and within two years the director. When they asked him to apply to be director, he said, "I am a gay man. I'm in a relationship, and I don't want to have any problems. If there are problems, I am not going to put my hat in the ring." His board was really amazingly enlightened—not that they said, "There's no problem." They thought about it a little bit and said no, that's not going to make any difference.

I think when people know gay people and work around them all the time and get friendly with them, there is a breakdown of prejudice so that people aren't "other"; people are the same. I think it's worked the same way in the synagogue.

I got us involved in the synagogue in the first place. Even though he'd gotten free tickets through his job, Harold would not even attend High Holiday services. When we first started attending services, I had to encourage Harold to go: "It's not going to be the end of the world if you go. If you hate it, you hate it, but let's go." And it was okay—he didn't die! And I knew this is what he wanted, at some level. And that turned out to be true for me, too.

About four or five years ago issues about spirituality began to come up for me. I was feeling unfulfilled spiritually, and I needed to somehow connect to something outside myself. The intellectual or rational way of looking at the world wasn't what I thought was meaningful anymore. That was okay when I was a kid, but I started feeling there was something more to life now. I had to give myself permission to explore that side before I was able to look into Judaism.

I started reading, because I always start by reading. And I began talking to Rabbi Caine every couple of weeks. It was very tentative initially. I told Harold: this is okay, we are going to join, I am going to take this seriously. About two and a half years ago, I began studying with the rabbi to convert. Luckily I missed the conversion classes so I didn't have to do it with other people. Studying with the rabbi on my own was great!

In some part, this had to do with Harold and my being Jewish *together*. But there was also a part of not wanting to admit that. On the other hand we could admit to ourselves that the spiritual side is a very important issue and crucial in life. It is very helpful to sharing as a couple if you speak the same language. We are not trying to be the same, but it is important to be able to share something.

My studying in preparation for the conversion took three or four months. I read tons of books. I'd go back to Rabbi Caine every few weeks and talk with him for about an hour. He was very interested in getting me to learn how to read Hebrew. I went to the *Bet Din*, three rabbis plus Ivan. The conversion class had just finished, so I hooked up with them for these rituals. They were mostly a bunch of young kids who were converting because they were getting married. I was different. And I said to Ivan, "Do you think my being gay is going to be an issue?" I wasn't sure whether he was being disingenuous, but he said, "Gee, I hadn't thought of it." "They're going to ask me why I am converting, and I can't really hide something so crucial."

The three rabbis were somewhat taken aback initially, but all of a sudden it was okay. They asked a very thought-provoking question: "If Harold were to die would you still consider yourself Jewish?" I think that's probably a question they ask everybody. I said, "Of course, because I'm not doing it for him, I'm doing it for myself." That was the most interesting question I was asked. It seemed particularly applicable because we are not going to have children. For most couples the conversion is due somehow to raising the kids. Here we are, a couple who is obviously not going to have children—so what is going to keep me Jewish if not my kids? I was really expecting more intellectual questions. Most questions were about why are you doing this; have you really thought about it? I was a little nervous but it was okay.

I went to the *mikveh* the next week. I had these concepts of what it would be like. I thought it would be this steamy eastern European bath. It was this little dinky place in Cherry Hill, New Jersey, in a basement, sort of dank, and there was a little pool. There were all these little kids who were there because their mother had just converted, so they obviously weren't born Jewish. They couldn't figure out why they were in the *mikveh*. They kept saying, "We're Jewish; why are we here?" And once they finally got into the *mikveh* they wouldn't get out of the water.

Right after these rituals, there was my "debut" at the synagogue in which I touched the Torah and had an *aliyah*. That was quite nice.

We had been introduced to our synagogue through the efforts of the concierge of our building, a former cantor whose voice went bad. He's also gay. When we first moved into the building, we got little notes under the door that the synagogue was looking for prospective members and would we be interested in going to services. Ronnie obviously gave them our names. We were astounded, actually, that they came after us because even the most liberal Reform synagogue in the area didn't have a membership that would be right for us. We would have to join the Reform congregation as individuals, not as a couple. But Society Hill Synagogue came after us. We courted with them for a couple of years and discussed it, and when we finally joined, we joined as a couple. There must have been some people who were surprised, but no one ever let us know. People basically treat us as a couple. It happened so naturally. But that is our synagogue, and it does not negate the ambivalence that the rabbinate in general feels about gay Jews.

At my *bar mitzvah* there were a number of friends who got *aliyahs*. I wanted to have couples come up to the *bimah*, but ended up just with individuals. The problem was that three of the couples that were going to have *aliyahs* were gay couples. The rabbi said, "Well, you know they are not married, so if we do that we change the by-laws of the synagogue." It was a month before the *bar mitzvah*, and I had not known of this before. The rabbi said, "How can I do this for a gay couple who is not married if I can't do this for a straight couple that is not married?" And I said, "Well it's not the same because we don't have the option; we can't get married, but I'm not going to embarrass you and make a big production of it." So he said, "How then do you really define being married as a gay couple?" I said I didn't know.

We finally came to a definition: if with a divorce you risk the same amount of loss as a straight couple, then in reality you are a married couple. Everything that Harold and I own is in both names. If we were to get "divorced" or split up, everything would be straight down the middle. It would be extremely painful financially. That's looking at the negative side. But you can't define a marriage by the negative, you have to somehow define it by the positive. One of the things I'd like to do with the board is slowly but surely bring this issue up and see whether or not we can do anything about it. Not a commitment ceremony—I'm not sure that they mean anything. But the other issue is whether a gay couple can have an *aliyah* together, because that's something that's important. I hope gradually people will come around to accept it.

Society Hill is a very nice synagogue. It is named after the part of town that was renovated in the sixties. Lots of people moved into the city at the time of regentrification and formed a synagogue.

Originally it was a Congregationalist church built by the same person who built the White House. It is a beautiful, beautiful, very austere building. It became a Baptist church in the 1840s; around 1902 it became a synagogue and it was called the old Romanian Shul. In the cantor's office are all the articles of confederation required by the city at that time, and all these pictures of wonderful Romanian guys with moustaches. It was this very *hamishe* synagogue for about forty or fifty years, serving an aging group of immigrants, with murals of palm trees painted on the sides. I am assuming lots of synagogues of that era had these murals depicting people's conceptions of what Palestine would look like. I would have liked to have seen the murals, but the synagogue was refurbished, and they got rid of the palm trees.

Twenty-five years ago it became the current congregation, and it was very different because this was sort of a "yuppified" area. The synagogue is Conservative/Reconstructionist.

Four hundred families are members, but since we are in a downtown area we've got about a 10 percent turnover each year. Maintaining membership is one of the biggest problems of the synagogue. With the change in demographics in the city, lots of people are leaving. The question is what's going to happen to the synagogue? Is it going to be able to maintain membership? I am on the board, and I am also the cochair of the membership/program committee—which I was coerced into since I didn't know anything about either of those issues! Part of what I do is a lot of outreach, a lot of advertising. Anybody who moves into an apartment building we try to get. We've actually been able to maintain membership fairly well.

I really like the people in the congregation. They are sort of all over the place professionally, financially, and also Jewishly—from people who are very conservative to people who are not conservative at all. The only common thread is that people are basically willing to live with other people. This congregation has enabled Harold and me to be a part of a bigger community. That has been quite important—as important as anything intellectual.

Most of what I've been doing the first two years is being part of the community. We meet once a month for something called the "support committee" for people with various family issues. People who come to the committee meet first with the rabbi, then they come to us to discuss their situation. The synagogue wanted us for the committee because Harold is the head of JFCS and I am a doctor; there's also a lawyer on the committee. It gets us very actively involved in people's lives in the synagogue. There have been a couple of people whose mothers have become demented, and the question is how to get them evaluated and get them care. There was a couple who were involved in the care of a person in the community who was ill and had no family. All they wanted was emotional support and validation to continue dealing with a difficult situation. There have been other situations that have to do with challenges to people's boundaries—how do you keep giving and being open and at the same time put limits on the expectations people have of you, including your own expectations of yourself? Concerns that come up run the whole gamut from psychological to legal issues.

Converting to Judaism has changed me a lot. I have dropped my embarrassment about allowing myself to be spiritual. I've decided to allow myself to think about whether or not there is a God. I am not afraid of that anymore. I'm still not sure about belief, but in a different way. I am one person in the universe. Whether or not I believe in God is a moot point. The Old Testament Jews were smart when they talked about not being able to conceptualize who God is, as opposed to the New Testament Christians. For humans to try to decide there is a god that is like a person we can relate to is almost blasphemous. God to the early Jews was something that was ineffable and still is to us. I don't have to be embarrassed by belief and not-knowingness because I am in exactly the same position as the ancient Jews.

Judaism is unique in the sense that it focuses on you as a part of a community but also on you as an individual relating to both community and God. Your job as a Jew, basically, is to make God's world a better world than when you entered it. That is a very good dictum to live with. It is also important to me that there is this: "Be as smart as you can and ask questions." That's one of the things that's so unique about being Jewish.

13

Everything Has Its *Midrash*

Yehoshua ben Avraham

His blond hair and blue eyes don't immediately suggest his identity to some people, but if "Jews are like everyone else—only more so," Yehoshua, whose English name is Jeff, is certainly Jewish. He sits on the edge of his seat, looks you right in the eye, and speaks intensely of his life as a Jew.

"I wish born Jews knew how converts feel. I wish that they could share some of our enthusiasm sometimes. And I wish they could see the world through our eyes. We're fortunate because we've seen things from the other side."

Jeff is in his last year of residency as a surgeon, and most of his life has been devoted to those qualities that have made him successful as a physician. Judaism has taught Jeff to look beyond the "facts" of a case, the obvious sequence of events—life unfolds in real time, he says; its meaning can be understood only through metaphor or *midrash*. Most eloquent in Jeff's story is the voice that speaks for his soul, telling of the experiences that occur between the facts of a life, weaving the "*midrash*" that explains who he has become.

There's no beginning, really, it's been that kind of journey.

I really don't know when I finally converted. I'm sure it was a couple of years ago, but it seems like a lot longer because of all that has happened in the last few years. Laura and I got married, started a family, I went to medical school. We lived a lifetime in just the last year because Laura was treated for cancer. So if you ask me how long I've been Jewish, in a way it seems I've always been Jewish.

I always believed in God. I was raised to believe in Jesus, nominally at least. My parents would occasionally take us to Sunday school at a Lutheran church. We celebrated Christian holidays. But I always felt uncomfortable in church—as if I didn't belong there. I felt I had to put on my best and watch the way I talked—just "act like a Christian," whatever that might be.

My last brush with Christianity just didn't take. I was a probation counselor at a juvenile center in Orange County, California. Almost all the counselors there were Christian. For a while, I really got into it. I really felt that I belonged there, though not to their church. Finally, though, I realized I couldn't adhere to the demands on Christians to proselytize and to witness. I could not do that. I never felt comfortable with it.

Now, after several years of studying Torah, in a way I never studied the New Testament, I wonder how I could have ever believed. My concept of God is so different. Knowing what I know now makes me think that Christianity couldn't be further from the truth, though I would never argue the point with a Christian. They are happy with their belief, and it's great for them, and I wouldn't want to make them feel bad.

I do struggle with integrating my past with what I am right now. Although I feel wholly Jewish, I also feel that I'm too valuable to leave any part of me behind. There's too much that was good in my life before I converted that is still a part of my life now, like my side of the family, who are all gentiles. I don't want a part back there and a part here and a part in the future. Being able to tell my story is part of the process of bringing it all together for me.

When my wife and I were married, she wanted a Jewish wedding—not because she was religious, but she'd been to gentile weddings and a Jewish wedding is what she wanted. We found a rabbi to perform the ceremony who was himself a convert to Judaism. We took some classes, but I wasn't immediately taken with it. The first Rosh Hashanah I went to, I wrote in my diary, was just a lot of standing up and sitting down.

As time went on it became pretty clear to me that I wasn't a Christian, but I had a nagging feeling, like there was something wrong, something missing. "What am I supposed to believe in? What would happen if I died? Would I be 'saved'?" It is interesting that now as a Jew, I never think about those issues. Life is about the here and now. Today. And I never think about the hereafter.

I don't recall any discussions Laura and I may have had about how we would raise our children. We both just assumed it would be as Jews, and when my daughter was five we enrolled her in Sunday school at Bet Haverim (House of Fellowship), the Reform synagogue we'd joined when we came to Davis so that I could attend the University of California medical school.

In most Reform temples there is a Friday night service and that is it. At Bet Haverim there are Saturday morning services all in Hebrew; we even used Birnbaum's Orthodox *siddur*. So when I decided to attend services on Saturday morning, just out of interest, I felt as if I were dropped onto another planet. I didn't understand anything. But I kept going back, although I hadn't made the decision to convert yet. I was attracted by the melodies. I learned to read Hebrew, and I learned the service. You just catch on after a while. There are only so many words in the *siddur*, and they're repeated and repeated.

My study for conversion was typical of the way I had approached other subjects of interest to me through the years. My wife would joke that she would always know where to look for me in the bookstore, depending on my latest interest. I would study until I had learned everything possible about it. I would become an "expert" on computers, for example, then get tired of that and move on to something else. But in Judaism, you can study for a lifetime and never become a master.

After my conversion, the first time I was called up for an *aliyah* was wonderful. When I could be counted for *minyan*, I really felt I belonged. Now, when I *leyn* the Torah, I feel this is my heritage. I feel that I am connected to Israel and the Jews of Israel and every other Jew. I feel that Abraham is my spiritual father.

Our *minyan* is really geared to participation, and on a good *Shabbat* we get ten to twenty people, so everyone *has* to join in. Our rabbi now, David Feder, is a great guy, more approachable than the previous rabbi, for whom I, nevertheless, had a great deal of respect. One thing about Rabbi Feder, though—and he is the first to admit it—he can't carry a tune. So he doesn't lead services very often. He doesn't chant, doesn't do the *nusah*, though of course he knows Hebrew very well.

So I've learned to *leyn* the Torah, which we read on a triennial cycle, as many Conservative *shuls* do. Each *Shabbat* a third of the Torah portion is read, so we complete the whole Torah every three years. It has encouraged participation, and we can get a lot more people to read Torah.

When I decided I wanted to learn the *haftarah*, one of the guys in the *shul* made me a tape of the trope and wrote it all out. I picked a *haftarah* that I thought was very short, but it turned out to be *Shabbat Rosh Hodesh* and the *haftarah* was actually much longer, but I was already committed. I studied for hours and hours to be the *maftir* one *Shabbat*. These days, it takes me just about an hour to prepare to read Torah. I just read the Hebrew, then go through it and read with the trope, then read it from the *tikkun* without the trope. The melody helps you to remember the Hebrew.

Somehow this all just clicked with me. Not that it happened all at once, but you do get over the self-consciousness. At first saying the prayer before putting on the *tallit*, and kissing it, was uncomfortable for me. Now it *means* something to me. Touching the Torah with the *tzitzit* when it comes by—it felt fake and awkward. Now it doesn't, it feels right. "*B'rikh hu*"—to say that during *Kaddish*—it felt weird. Now I would miss *not* saying it. Learning to *leyn* has helped me to feel a part of the congregation; I end up being an important part and people count on me. I don't feel like an outsider at all. I even have a key to the temple, I have the alarm code—it's my place! I don't feel so uptight or like I have to be on my best behavior. I feel comfortable here. That is the first time I've felt like that in a religious setting.

The things that I thought at first were negatives turned out to be positives. (That's been my life experience in general for the last several years.) I thought Jews would be more spiritual—whatever that was. At least, I expected people to be as enthused as I was. As it turns out, it was right in front of my face, but I didn't see it or take it as such. I've learned that spirituality in Judaism has wide variation in both individual and communal expression. At first I wondered, "Why can't everyone be quiet and pray together?" No one does! Everyone's in a different part at any given time, drifting in, then drifting out again. The *shatz*, or *shaliah tzibbur*, at some point brings everyone together at the beginning or end of a section. We say the *Shema* together, and then we drift out and we drift in. Now I love to pray that way. It's more free-form. It's less rigid.

Participating so fully in services has demystified them and made them more accessible to me. Maybe at first it took away a little bit of the sparkle of experiencing ritual as something "on high." On the other hand, it became real for me, and I came to appreciate that *we*—each individual Jew—make this happen. Judaism just doesn't go on all by itself. You can't sit there and just receive. We're necessary partners of God. We need God but God needs us, too.

The rabbis say you should approach God only if you're in a prayerful mood, and the *Pesukei D'zimrah* are a warm up. Sometimes when you *daven*, your mind wanders and you wonder what's wrong with you. You have to get out of yourself and into the ritual and it brings you right back. With such a little bit of effort come so many rewards.

Most converts are adults, which shows that if you want to educate yourself as a Jew, you can start at any age. That's really important. I walked in cold, and I didn't know anything. I wish other Jews knew how easy it was, once you start, and how accepting people are. Sometimes when I am acting as *gabbai* I'll see someone who is new to the *shul* and I'll always offer them an *aliyah*. Often, they're mortified. I wonder if that's why they don't come to *shul*—because someone is going to ask them to do something and they feel embarrassed they won't know what to do? Perhaps they fear they will be judged. I feel that a judgmental attitude doesn't have any place in Judaism; it doesn't fit in with any of the classical teachings. I wish they knew that it's just not that hard, and if they make a mistake, we're not going to be mad at them, at least that's been my experience.

And I've made mistakes! There's a woman in our *shul*, a Holocaust survivor, who likes very much to be called up for an *aliyah*. So I always make sure I do. She is called to the Torah as Miriam bat Haim Shlomo. The first time I called her up I said, Miriam bat Haim v'Shlomo—daughter of two men! And everyone cracked up. In another instance, I was unaware that there were two men who have the same Hebrew name, Michael ben Moshe, which I called out, and they both stood up. What to do? I had one man come up; then the other I called up as Michael ben Moshe *hazakein*, the elder. People who understood the Hebrew laughed. I like that about our congregation, especially because I know it's not the same everywhere.

Some people might think that is too informal, but I believe that some of what we need to experience from spirituality comes from how we treat each other. Part of God's plan is that we are supposed to help each other. We do live in a world where evil exists, but whether evil wins out over good has to do with what we do. We're the instruments of that triumph. Not God up there waving a wand.

Our *shul* recently started a Young Family *Shabbat* service once a month that is early enough to accommodate really little kids. My son is four—always moving, wanting to play, and he's disruptive. I don't want to deprive him of the benefit of going to *shul*, but in the regular services, some people complain about all the little kids running around. I have respect for other people's needs, but God forbid my children would ever not feel comfortable in a synagogue. I liked it when someone said, "We should all be quiet so we can hear the children."

The Torah has been another revelation to me. In my Christian background, it was either the word of God or nothing. Now, I have discovered that it can be understood at so many different levels: as a historical account, as a mystical experience, as a guide for living, or just an incredible story. It's valid at all those levels.

I use to hear people say they "read" the Bible—in the same way they might say,

"I read a novel." Jews study it—every word. Every *letter* means something. The translation really can't do justice to the Hebrew language, and the way it is used. Look at the English and count how many words are in a sentence, then look at the Hebrew. It is so compact and economical, yet so full of meaning. In the Torah portion in which Joseph is in Pharaoh's prison interpreting dreams for the wine steward and the baker, he tells the first one, "This is what your dream means. In three days Pharaoh will lift your head up—and redeem you." And sure enough it happens. To the next guy he says the exact same thing in Hebrew, "In three days time Pharaoh will lift your head up—from yourself, from your body." You would never understand the subtlety of that from the English. It means, he'll cut your head off, but he uses the same words, "lift your head up." You miss all those things.

Torah is very terse, it's very brief. It says, "They slew them." It doesn't make a judgment, for the most part. Tamar has to dress up as a prostitute to seduce Judah. He finds out she's pregnant and says, "Bring her to me and have her burned." But she has his staff and signet, proof he is the father, so she says, "Okay, I'm here." The Torah doesn't editorialize. It doesn't say, "So this means that Judah was such a bad guy." There is *midrash* to fill in the meaning. When the *malakhim* visit Abraham, he runs to get them some food—and at that point there's a *midrash* that breaks off to describe what happened next, because he didn't just go get a lamb and come back. That wasn't all that happened, because that time was real, but the Torah can't tell you every single thing about it, so the *midrash* fleshes it out. Then the *midrash* brings you back to exactly the same point and lets the Torah continue.

I've learned that everything has its *midrash*. When we look at someone's life, *midrash* is what fills in between the facts. There's much more to everything in the world than is apparent so I carry with me the metaphor of Torah and *midrash*.

The study of Torah, therefore, has taught me to let go of expectations. Most of my life I have been encouraged and rewarded for that side of myself that is more dominant: the mathematician, the scientist, the doctor. I considered myself pretty concrete. Poetry, literature always eluded me. If it didn't rhyme, I didn't get it. I didn't have the capacity to find the meaning beyond just what was obvious, written down, concrete. Now I get a glimpse that there is something else, there's something deeper, there's something that's maybe right in front of me. Sometimes, if I look too hard, I won't find it, but if I don't expect it, it will be there. That surprises me less and less all the time. I think there is a part of me—my softer side, maybe my more feminine side—that wants to be expressed. Judaism has given me that capacity. In Judaism, there is a structured way to be unstructured.

Being Jewish has also affected the way I see my role as a doctor. As a head and neck surgeon, I treat a lot of cancer patients and often, when I operate, I never know exactly what I am going to find. Now, in my last year of residency, I have come to the realization that I can't do it all myself. I ask God to help me help people. I never did that before. My patients sometimes ask me to pray with them, and sometimes the nurses will join us. I always agree because I think it is a good thing, and it makes everyone feel good. We just hold hands and say a prayer. Sometimes I'll say the prayer because I think Jewish prayers can be acceptable to Christians, since they all begin by praising God and recognizing God as the source of all power. I ask Him to guide me and to guide everyone in there to bring a speedy and complete recovery. It's really powerful.

We joke that my wife didn't marry a Jewish doctor, but she ended up with one! I am much more religiously observant than my wife. She is a cultural Jew; religion is not very important to her or her family. They eat pork, and I say, "I can't believe it!" Sometimes I wish they were more religious, then I think, if they were, maybe my wife and I never would have gotten together. If they were more religious, she wouldn't have even conceived of marrying a gentile and her parents might have forbidden it.

Religious or not, her family has been a blessing. They've really brought me something, just because of who they are. My own father died when I was twelve. We lost everything. It was really hard. Horrible. From the vantage point now of being a father of a ten-year-old child, I think I understand more fully how devastating it was for me. I didn't even know how to tie a tie or any of the stuff fathers teach sons. My father-in-law has been incredibly good to me. He has been like my father. I love him so much. He treats me like a son—to the point that he can bawl me out just like he would his other son if I've done something unwise.

Sometimes I ask myself, "What was it that was guiding me to become a Jew?" Through my extended family, I've gotten the message that I was created a Jew just as much as anyone else. When we think about time, we say the past is back there, the present is here, and the future is over there, as if these were actual places. But God creates every moment—everything that we do, every word that comes out of our mouths—we're all constantly being created. In this moment, God can create me to be a Jew, so I don't feel any less a Jew than someone who was born to it.

I've also come to believe that God works in my life through other people. There are so many people who have enriched my life and helped me turn one way or the other. I see that people in my life sometimes fit the Jewish concept of angels—"angel" is the way it gets translated, but the Hebrew words really have distinct connotations. "*Malakh*," as in the story of Abraham, is a messenger, and a *malakh* can be a person. My wife is definitely a *malakh* in my life. We've been married thirteen years and every once in a while, I'll look over at her and wonder to myself, "Who is this? Who's this person? Who did I end up with? How would this have all come about if I had married another wife?" We just fit. And I thank God for her.

Her illness has really made me appreciate every single moment. Time almost seems like an enemy to me because I don't know if she's cured or not, and neither does anyone else. Breast cancer can come back any time. Chances are that it won't, but it could. It could come back twenty years later. I know more about it than I ever wanted to know. But it's just one more thing that's really made me live in the here and now—sometimes I don't even want to go to sleep, I just want to live right now with her.

One thing I like to think about in the future is that in 1995, we will be living in Israel for six months. I will be working there with a surgeon who referred an Israeli police officer to our center here in California for surgery. I am looking forward to going for many reasons, but one is that I have always wanted to feel comfortable wearing a *yarmulke* every day. I couldn't do that at work here, but if I can't feel comfortable in Israel wearing a *yarmulke*, where could I? For me, it's a sign of reverence to God, to wear a *yarmulke*, and it identifies me as a Jew.

Being a Jew, for me, is an act of reverence to God.

14

A Foundation for Life

Leslie Breland

When Leslie and her boss were in Washington, D.C., on business, they had a few hours before their meeting began and decided to go to the Holocaust Museum. They just managed to get into the museum and were given the identity cards all guests receive upon entry. Leslie was amazed to discover the card she was given was that of a Seventh Day Adventist who had married a Jewish man in the concentration camps. When she showed the card to her secretary, also a Seventh Day Adventist, this woman seemed to think the name sounded familiar, and, indeed, her parents knew the woman and her story of survival in Germany.

To Leslie, this was just one more in a series of coincidences that marked her coming to Judaism. And though this journey has had some very painful and disappointing twists and turns, she says, "I didn't come this far to stop."

As an African-American and a Jew, Leslie feels deeply the shared experience of oppression coming from both her heritages, and she has found in Judaism a foundation, an anchor from which her spirit may fly free.

More than twenty years ago, I was engaged to be married, the wedding invitations were already printed up, but my fiancé and I had a terrible argument over the phone and our relationship broke up. I never saw him again. Then, about three years ago, my mother was returning from a Unity Church convention in Kansas City. She saw a tall, handsome black man get on the airplane and discovered that he was the long-lost Jesse whom I had at one time planned to marry. She talked to him and gave him my phone number. He called me and told me that he was now an Orthodox Jew, having converted to Judaism twenty-five years ago. We talked for a long time and found we had so many views in common. He was in the process of getting a divorce, and I was ending a ten-year relationship. We agreed to get to know each other again.

When Jesse described his conversion and life as an observant Jew, it brought back to my memory thoughts of the grandmother with whom I grew up. My lineage is Jewish; my grandmother's father was Jewish, and, in fact, three of my four great-grandfathers were Jewish. Although I don't think her mother and father ever married, my grandmother was aware of her heritage and wanted me and my cousins to know about Passover, Hanukkah, and what little other knowledge she had. When I met Jesse again after all the years, and he introduced me to Judaism, I felt that a circle had been completed.

Years before she died, my grandmother gave me a pair of candlesticks that she knew I had always loved as a child. With my fingers, I used to trace the design in their base, but it wasn't until the first time that I used them to light the Sabbath candles that I saw the design was the Star of David. You could see the design in the candlesticks only when looking down from above—the position you would be in when lighting candles!

When Jesse and I discussed getting married, it was no problem for me to begin to study for conversion. And Jesse was so helpful because he was so knowledgeable.

I have always considered myself a very spiritual person, but not a churchgoer. There was always something missing for me in church, but I also had a feeling that I wanted to get involved deeply in religion. I could never visualize or grasp the idea of going through another person—the pope, saints, Jesus Christ—to get to God. I have always felt there was this link between me and God, that I could talk to Him. When I discovered the depth of Judaism, I said this is what I have been looking for. It was like going back to the beginning. There was something very solid, something very soothing that I was getting in touch with when I began my studies. It is still very new to me, and I am still in a continuous process of learning.

My husband-to-be was known as a scholar in his synagogue in the Midwest. He was well respected and had a lot of time to give to study and to helping around the synagogue. It turned out that his rabbi of twenty years knew the rabbi I studied with for conversion. Jesse had also become a follower and friend of Meir Kahane—a fact I'm not sure I would have liked. He had two wonderful children, whom I met and fell in love with, and I was looking forward to the role of stepmother. He had been, he said, a pilot for TWA for fourteen years. I was looking forward to being a part of Jesse's life, and, initially, my pursuit of Judaism was to enable me to be closer to him.

The process of my Jewish education was fortuitous as well. A girlfriend, who is herself a nonobservant Jew, suggested that I pick up the Jewish newspaper to see what might be offered in the community. There was a Hebrew class starting the very next week at Beth Jacob, an Orthodox synagogue. Perfect timing! Then when I was at another synagogue, Shearith Israel, looking for a book that Jesse had recommended, *Song of Sarah*, concerning feminine spirituality, I ran into a friend from my Hebrew class. She and I talked, and I told her that I was looking for a rabbi to begin conversion studies with. My friend said, "Why don't you talk with the rabbi of this synagogue?" and who should walk in at that very moment but Rabbi Kunis himself. I liked him immediately, probably because, as I later found out, he was from Brooklyn, where I had lived, and there was a New Yorkness about him that clicked with me. We talked, and he said to come to his class the next week. I started to attend Shearith Israel as well as attending classes and having weekly discussions with Rabbi Kunis. Since that time I have developed a very close relationship with him and his wife and children. I have always felt so welcomed by him, and his wife has graciously given me an open invitation to join his family for *Shabbat*, which I often do.

My learning really accelerated at that point, and I was amazed at how much I already knew, apparently things my grandmother had shared with me. To me, learning about Judaism was like going back to the beginning, the true roots of not only my family line but the spiritual foundation. I was immersed in reading, and attending classes and synagogue. As I got to know Jewish people in a religious setting I realized that, looking back all through my life, the people I selected as friends and who chose me for friendship as well were mostly Jewish. I learned a lot with Jesse in our phone conversations. Since I knew it was important to be able to walk to synagogue, I began looking for a house near Shearith Israel for us to live in after we were married.

I did all the planning for the wedding, since Jesse was still in the Midwest. I read everything I could about Jewish weddings. I wrote the wedding program because there were so many non-Jews invited, and I wanted everybody to know what was going on. We were delighted that his rabbi would fly to Atlanta and join Rabbi Kunis in performing the ceremony. The wedding was set for a Wednesday (Tuesdays and Wednesdays, Jesse told me, were particularly propitious days for weddings in the tradition). It was a year and a day after his first phone call, September 2, 1992—9/2/92—even the numbers seemed to line up! It was to be a glorious celebration with 225 people in attendance. Over the years in my life in Atlanta as an executive for a big corporation, my circle of friends and acquaintances had grown quite large and included some notable people. Now I also counted as my friends the wonderful people I had met in the synagogue. There were people from all the different parts of our lives. My wedding pictures, encased in a beautiful book that was a gift from a friend, show that it was truly a happy occasion, full of hope and promise—two mature lives joined together by family, community, and religion.

Jesse had just turned fifty and I was forty-six. He had been my first love, and now we weren't kids anymore. This seemed to mark the foundation of stability and a way of life that I would lead for the rest of my life. I do see Jesse as the catalyst for many good things that have occurred in my life.

I look back at the first happy months we spent together, and I can see, now, that there were some indications that all was not right. Jesse was extremely meticulous—far more than I—about such small things as washing the dishes immediately after eating, even on *Shabbat*. He was very particular about how his furniture should be arranged, allowing me to have little say in the matter. When I moved some things around in the spare bedroom to accommodate a visit from his two daughters, he became very angry. Most disturbing of all, he was making little or no financial contribution to our household. Nevertheless, the fall holidays were wonderful. In October, we had gone back to visit his community in the Midwest, where we were invited to stay with his rabbi's family. It seemed that there was just one celebration after another, with me happily planning and cooking for all of them, culminating in Thanksgiving and Hanukkah with his daughters and my mother joining us.

By January, though, things seemed to be getting worse with Jesse. I went to Rabbi Kunis and told him of my concerns, and he took Jesse aside to talk to him. Then, through a series of sad and painful circumstances I came to understand that I had been misled by Jesse, and he had, it seemed, misled not only me but the other people in his life. I took this information to my rabbi and began the process of getting a divorce from Jesse.

I also called Jesse's rabbi and told him everything. He was shocked and disillusioned by my story and what he had now heard from others who had approached him. He told me, "I'll make sure that you get a *get*." And he did.

My marriage ended—almost before it had begun. Had Jesse not entered my life, I would not have converted to Judaism, because this was simply not the direction my life was going at the time we met. Yet because he came into my life, I found what I was looking for. It was as though he took my hand and came into my life and out—staying just long enough to help me get on the track that I needed. In spite of all of the sadness of the loss of a marriage, I am also able to see that I am now a part of a communal family.

My adjustment to being Jewish began before my marriage, and my learning continues. Finding time to take all the classes I'd like to take is a problem, but the learning itself is not. Keeping kosher, cleaning for Pesah, for example, was difficult at first, but you learn.

Judaism is so logical on so many levels, and I am, if anything, a head person. I find fascinating the discussions about the difficult decisions that must be made in life. Judaism is so humane; there is compassion for people and their circumstances that comes before the hard-and-fast rule. For example, the rabbi was saying that even if you are *Shomer Shabbat*, if you become so ill you must see a doctor, then you have to go to the doctor; you don't say, "I can't drive because it is *Shabbat*." Judaism is life promoting. The laws are there to guide your life, but you also must use your head as you move toward life.

When Jesse and I were together, it was helpful to me that he was so well versed in all that goes into living a Jewish life; however, he was very strict about so many things. I am now learning from others that there is a kind of temperance that goes with observance. When Jesse was here, we walked the two miles to *shul*. Now I drive to *shul* because I don't have anyone to walk with. It is more important to be at *shul*, to me, than how I get there.

I have become kinder. I don't know if it's because I'm getting older, but my mind is different. My way of seeing things is progressively getting different. I always thought of myself as a wonderfully understanding person, but I'm even more so than before. I'm not as critical of things.

I find more of my life is functioning around the synagogue. I was asked to be on the board. I said, "Are you kidding?" They said, "No, we want you, we want you." This sense of communal family. I'm very involved in fund-raising and the membership committee. I take my class on Sunday morning, and I'm one of the regulars for services.

Our *shul* is considered "traditional," and we offer what I've come to understand is a unique seating arrangement. There is a women's section, a men's section, and a section where men and women sit together. I sit behind the *mehitzah*. I have a friend who sits there with me when she comes by herself and in the mixed seating section when her father comes with her. There's no judgment made about where you choose to sit.

Jesse explained to me that the reason men and women should sit apart is that women are such a distraction. "But," I said, "women are able to concentrate, why can't men?" "Well, women affect men differently," was his reply. I liked better the way the rabbi spoke of it. "Women," he said, "are of a higher spiritual order than men. Women are innately nurturing; they are not warmongers; they deal with life on another level. Men need laws to discipline and guide them. In the creation of the world, God made man, then He made woman: each level of creation is higher." But never have I felt a sense of one group above the other or below the other in our synagogue.

I think we have a very unique synagogue. We are in town, very urban, with such a good mixture of age groups from the very young to the very old. We recently celebrated the members who have been with the synagogue for fifty years and are still going strong. There were more than twenty of them! Some of the singles complain that they don't get invited for lunch after services, so there is an informal committee that makes sure that everyone has some place to go. I've encouraged my single friends to make opportunities for themselves. I guess I am fortunate that I have always been able to make myself comfortable in strange situations. I'm not afraid to go up to someone and start talking.

It is rarely on my mind that I am the only black Jew in the synagogue. Actually, I am no longer the only one, but I've been in so many situations in my life in which I was the only black person that it doesn't loom large for me. It is funny that sometimes I'll be talking to a person and catch our reflections in a mirror and realize that there is a difference. Part of that has to do with growing up in New York among so many different kinds of people.

In terms of saying am I a black or am I a Jew, I'm not there yet. I choose to say that I can't choose one from the other, although my physical presence is dominant. On a philosophical level, it shows the dimensions of Judaism—every nationality can be Jewish. Judaism is on a religious level, a national level, a cultural level—it is unique from that standpoint because it can and does share all.

I find it so interesting that there are so many born Jews who don't practice their Jewishness. The Jewish wife of a friend has teased me about doing my "Jewish thing" and wanted to know, now that I am divorced, if I'd like to come over for a pork roll. I declined. I suppose that is a reflection of a way of thinking that says a convert is not "really" Jewish. Then when they hear of my ancestry, they say, "Oh!" What I want to let people know is that I was looking for a spiritual foundation and I found it. If they are looking, it is there for them, too. In this world of disorder and loss of humanity, Judaism offers a thousands-year-old tradition, a foundation for a sense of being, and sense of what is right and wrong. Jews have survived all these centuries of chaos, and we are still here. *That* impressed me.

15

A Long and Winding Road

Alberta Weinberg

Alberta is a striking woman in her early fifties who met with me in her office at the Jewish Federation of Greater Seattle. She had recently become the principal of the Community High School of Jewish Studies. Seattle has a small but diverse and cohesive Jewish community. Its openness and acceptance of diversity was a pleasant surprise to me. "You know," said Alberta, "there are enormous differences between the East Coast and the West Coast."

Jews came to Seattle in the days of the wagon trains. Some Jewish communal organizations in Seattle are over a century old and were founded by concerned Jewish women. Jewish Family Services recently celebrated its centennial, and the current executive director is Alberta's husband, Ken.

Alberta is forthright and passionate in speaking about conversion, her life as a Jew, and her place in the Jewish community. Her interest in Judaism was at first intellectual, then she was drawn by the way in which the home-based nature of Jewish ritual makes the daily become holy. She revels in the way in which Judaism puts these ideals and values to work in the community, in terms of our individual and collective responsibility for ourselves and each other.

Periodically there will be something in the community pertaining to the conversion process, and someone will say, "Oh, well, let's ask Alberta." I will be startled because I no longer think of myself as a convert. In my mind I think of myself as a Jew. If anyone asks me about my religious identity, I don't respond, "I am a Jew by Choice," I say, "I'm Jewish." Of course, that is what Jewish law also says. Once the conversion takes place, it is not correct to refer to the person's previous status. Which isn't to say that I am embarrassed or find it difficult to talk about being a Jew by Choice. I make the point that choosing to be Jewish is really what born Jews do when they make the decision to join BBYO (B'nai B'rith Youth Organization) or go to the high school of Jewish studies or finish Sunday school confirmation. They are *choosing* to be Jewish.

My grandparents were Methodist and very devout. I don't mean fundamentalist, but real pillars in their church. I was very close to my grandparents. In fact, I lived with them for a year during my junior-high days because my family was moving from one community to another, and I wanted to finish junior high where I was. My grandparents made a very profound impression on me—not so much in a Christologic sense but in the sense that religion and spirituality were a foundation for a good person's life, and that doing good deeds and being a moral and ethical person were concerns that religion gave to you.

My grandparents were more of an influence on me by their openness and kindness than my own parents, who were lackadaisical Christians. My family belonged to a church, and our parents would drop us at Sunday school—sort of the classic situation that certainly happens in any denomination. I know very well that there are many Jewish parents who drop their children off at *shul* and go to read the paper, have lunch, play golf, or whatever it may be. That is sort of how my parents were. They were dedicated to our going to Sunday school, but they were less dedicated about their own attendance.

I was pretty independent. I was the oldest of five kids, and I had a lot of responsibility for taking care of my siblings. I was also a serious student and won awards. Studying and getting information was something that came naturally to me. In my senior year of high school, I was an exchange student in Mexico. I loved it; it was one of the highlights of my young life. What that did for me, looking at it in terms of this discussion, is that it allowed me to step outside my community and my family and get a sense of myself in another context. It really opened up my mind that I could be something different—that I wasn't just a product of my family but was accepted and loved in this new context for just being me. That was a very liberating experience for me, because I was born into this large family with a very authoritarian father. My mother was very much role-bound even though she was a working woman.

During my college years, I began to take classes in comparative religion. I am sure, at least on a subconscious level, that I was very dissatisfied with the Christianity I had been exposed to—that I wasn't feeling very firmly grounded in the notion of a man who was God and a woman who had a magical conception; that this didn't resonate for me or even make a whole lot of sense. At the same time, I had a Jewish roommate my first year in college. Even though while growing up I had a close friend whose father was Jewish, college was the first time I really got to know Jews. It was at that period that I probably stopped regarding myself as a Christian. I had a need for a spiritual life, but I didn't think it was going to come through the route of the Methodist or Lutheran or Episcopalian or whatever church.

During college, I met and subsequently married my first husband, "David," who was a Jew by birth. Interestingly enough, he was entirely secular and never had a *bar mitzvah*. David's father was born in Jerusalem and came to New York as a child. His mother was born in Cairo. So he had this wonderful family background of Yiddish-speaking and Ladino-speaking grandparents—Ashkenazic and Sephardic. But when David's parents left New York, they left being Jewish behind—not an uncommon experience for western-moving Jews. They got to California and then just sort of—well, they changed their name from "Braunstein" to Brown. They tried to become plain old Americans—so their children got nothing Jewish whatsoever—and I believe this ended up being a loss for them.

David and I had two sons, Peter and Nick. I didn't take the formal steps of conversion at that time, and there was no interest whatsoever on David's part in my doing so. There was a lot of conflict because my parents were involved with the children and sending them Christmas presents, even though we had stopped celebrating Christmas. At that point, it just seemed meaningless to me. So, for the nine years of our marriage, we didn't celebrate much of anything. Of course, the kids knew about Christmas trees and Christmas presents and all of that.

While we were married, I finished up my B.A. and got my teaching credential in California. After our divorce, I started teaching. On my first job, I met a Jewish New Yorker who was a coteacher. Ken and I team-taught a class one year, and we got to be very good friends—not romantic friends but good friends. At that time, Santa Barbara didn't have a formal Jewish community. So Ken belonged to a *havurah* with a lot of ex–New Yorkers. I joined the group and got to hang out with Jews, and Judaism became increasingly more interesting and important to me. Ken was dating a Jewish woman at this time. We were all great friends, and I thought for sure that they were going to get married. Ken would have told you, emphatically, that he would never even date a non-Jew.

If I had not fallen in love with Ken, would I have converted to Judaism? That is the question that some people ask. I think there is a very strong possibility that I would have converted to Judaism, because I had already embarked on that road prior to being involved with Ken. My first husband was Jewish. I felt that the children deserved an opportunity to know that culture, that tradition. But certainly, I can't deny the fact that Ken's being Jewish was very significant. First, I intellectually appreciated Judaism; then, when I got to know Jewish life, I appreciated that. The two things came together and really made sense to me. I had Jewish friends—born-Jewish friends— who said to me, "You're crazy to convert to Judaism. Why do you want to do that?" It was funny. They didn't see all the things in Judaism that I saw.

When I was in college taking comparative-religion classes and reading about Judaism, there was complete resonance. I also liked and still like that Jewish observance is home based. You can go to *shul*, but it is what goes on in the home that's important. Jewish religious practice is about ritualizing and sanctifying the everyday. There is something about that concept that is so appealing to me in an aesthetic and a spiritual sense and in a pragmatic way. How you live your life. How you treat people. How you treat your family. What you do in your community. I'm not saying that those aren't values in the Christian or Buddhist or Islamic communities. However, they are not values that I was exposed to in my home, but ones that I *did* find in Judaism, and they have become integral to my life.

I can't imagine another way of living. I can't imagine not giving and not actively working to make your community a better place. It is an internalized driving force. It is not something that you just feel good about one day of the year and say, "Oh gosh, I am going to write a check out." It is an everyday commitment. Of course, I was very fortunate to marry someone who has a positive Jewish identity and has made Jewish communal work his professional life. Our friends—all of our Jewish friends, in fact—are really remarkable and wonderful people, each one in his or her own way, who enrich our lives.

From 1975 to 1977 Ken and I lived together in Berkeley. At that time, I started taking classes at Hillel. They call them Introduction to Judaism, and they are the first step in the conversion process. Then, when we moved to Seattle, I began classes with a rabbi. I had a Reform conversion, and my younger son, Nick, who moved to Seattle with us, chose to have a conversion at the same time. He is strongly identified as a Jew, became *bar mitzvah* and went to Israel with USY (United Synagogue Youth). My older son was in high school and living with his father in Santa Barbara. Even he, who didn't have a more formal Jewish education, regards himself as a Jew. If you ask him, he will say, "I am Jewish."

When it came time for Nick's *bar mitzvah*, Ken said, "You know, I would really like to be married to you. When we go up on the *bimah*, I would like to be able to say that this is my son—my stepson. Let's get married." A childhood friend of Ken's had become a Conservative rabbi. We were his first marriage. (In fact, he subsequently came to Seattle for six years and was the rabbi of the congregation of which we are members.) Although I had had a Reform conversion, our rabbi friend thought that it would be good if I would go through a Conservative conversion—and at the Jewish Theological Seminary. He would set it up for me at JTS because he had just graduated from the seminary. Actually, it was very appealing to me because I had wanted to have the *mikveh* experience. I felt that the symbolism of immersion was important, and *mikveh* wasn't a part of my Reform conversion. We were married in Ken's childhood congregation, Whitestone Hebrew Center, in Whitestone, New York.

I went to New York about a week early and went to JTS for the *Bet Din* and a ritual immersion in the *mikveh*. That was a very significant experience for me. I think having the testimony in the *Bet Din and* the *mikveh* is a very important step. I feel that the Reform movement is making a mistake in its conversion format because there is symbolism that is absolutely undeniable about the immersion. In their efforts to be modern or whatever, they have thrown out some important things, and in doing so they are depriving converts of a meaningful experience. The ceremony with the Reform rabbi was very nice, but it was done in his office with two or three members of his congregation and us. One could say it was intimate, or one could say it was secretive. There was no announcement to the congregation as is done in our Conservative synagogue, where there is a welcome by the whole congregation to the Jew by Choice. It is an honoring as opposed to a clandestine kind of thing.

I used to think that conversion, since it is a private decision, should not be announced. Now, I think that conversions should be a celebration. If we really do want to do outreach, and we really do want conversionary marriages to be good ones, then we must fully embrace the convert. There must be a ritual and a celebration—a *simhah*. We are giving a name to a new Jew. I think that a public celebration is very important. It can have special significance. A woman, a convert, writing in *SH'MA*, said she liked to believe that converts were taking the place of all the lost souls in the Holocaust. That was a very powerful idea for me. It has always stayed with me, and I am moved when I speak of it.

The Jewish community needs to understand that if we are going to survive and keep on converting armies of people—which most congregations are engaged in doing—we must make the ritual of conversion important. I think having good Jews from the moment of conversion and for the rest of their lives is what counts. Not just getting them to the *huppah* (I hate to imply that all Jews convert in order to get married, but I think a lot do). It's what happens after the *huppah* that matters most. We have to look at their children, and all the rest of the things that happen afterwards.

I do a lot of things that many born Jews don't do. We have a kosher home. I *want* to have a kosher home. It is not that I am trying to prove anything to anybody. I cast no judgments on those who don't keep kosher. Keeping kosher speaks to me. Again, it is the business of making the daily become holy. You think about what you eat; you think about the preparation of what you eat. It is a discipline. This is important to me. So much of Jewish practice takes place at home and, as I've said, that is one of the parts of being Jewish that I like so much.

Judaism has enriched my life beyond anything I have ever imagined. I never guessed when I took the step to convert that it would have such far-reaching implications. It affects every aspect of my life. I think I have become a better family member because I am Jewish. I have learned the Jewish way of doing things: staying in touch; closeness; not letting time pass without talking; the observance of all kinds of holidays, birthdays, anniversaries in a meaningful way.

There were many years in which my parents had enormous difficulty accepting my husband's—both of my husbands'—and my lifestyle. And my parents (my father just recently passed away) are not particularly demonstrative.

One of the most striking differences between Jewish and non-Jewish practices was brought home to me at my father's funeral. What I experienced was a service that was devoid of any kind of personal solace. There was no opportunity for cathartic expression. There was no structure for grieving—no *shivah*. A person dies; they are put in a box; words are spoken; you see the box sitting by a hole in the ground; more words are spoken; and everyone leaves. Then you go back to the home and have something to eat, and everybody goes away, and that is it. There is no organized way for the community and the family to share in the grieving process.

I could not wait to get back home because my friends had made *shivah* arrangements for me. The day I got home from my father's funeral, two dear friends met me with groceries and a *shivah* candle. They had the rabbi lined up, and a *minyan* planned.

I thought about all my siblings who were going back to their respective homes without these comforts. My mother was fortunate that my youngest sister could stay with her for a while so at least she didn't have to go back home alone. The one good thing about the funeral was that I was able to sit around with my siblings for two days after the burial and talk with them about my feelings. I told them what I was going home to and why I was comforted by that knowledge. I think that may have been the first time in their lives that they really ever understood what being Jewish meant to me—what concrete things about my life were different from theirs.

Shivah and then the first month after the death—*shloshim*—gives you an opportunity to feel whatever you need to feel by being identified to the congregation as a mourner. That is just so important. Knowing that for a year every time you are in *shul* you will stand up again and say *Kaddish*.

I told my mother about *shivah* in quite a lot of detail. I believe it really made a profound impression on her. I don't think she has ever really let herself deal with my being Jewish. She appears to accept it, and she can talk about it; she refers to our holidays, and she doesn't send Christmas cards. She has learned this sort of outward behavior, but I don't think she has ever understood that my life is really different. She likes to think that my being Jewish is all because of Ken. She has it in her mind that, "Well, she wants to have a good marriage. Ken is Jewish. He works in the Jewish community, and gee! I guess it's a good idea for Alberta to be Jewish." That is what may go through her mind. Now, after Dad's funeral, she really understands that my being Jewishly observant has nothing to do with Ken.

I have experienced only one incident of the prejudice that is sometimes present in the Jewish community regarding converts. It was at a dinner party—a very nice dinner party. Everyone there was well educated and urbane. One of the men was talking about his son who attended an Orthodox day school. He said something like, "There's this little blond who has a crush on him. She looks just like a *shikseh*." Then there was a silence. He looked at me, and his face turned bright red, and he said, "I am so sorry I said that. Please forgive me." It was interesting because, first of all, I'm not a *shikseh*, but it did reveal a prejudice. I am willing to bet that that was the last time he used that expression, because he is a very thoughtful, good person. It was probably an old habit, and it slipped out. My being there made him see what a stupid thing it is to say. That it is as bad as saying, "He looks like a kike." He realized that what he said was very ugly, you could tell that he was honestly embarrassed. Afterward, I saw him at a couple of different events and he would invariably say, "I can't tell you how many times I have thought about what I said and how inappropriate it was, and how deeply I apologize, and how much I respect and like you." That was the only time in almost twenty-five years that I have had an experience like that.

In fact, I have had the converse. In a setting in which I might have occasion to say something like, "Well, as a matter of fact, I am a Jew by Choice," people are utterly disbelieving. They say, "What? What?" Even Israelis. I have lots of Israeli friends, and it astonishes me that they seem to have little context in which to deal with converts. Israelis probably don't know many Jews by Choice, and they just don't know that much about conversion. I honestly can't say that I have had any terribly embarrassing situations, but I once had doubts about myself. There were times when I was asked to serve on a committee or be part of an observance and said to myself, "How can I possibly do this? Gee, I don't know how to do this or that." *Now*, if I don't know how, I'll just ask someone, "How do you do this?" I also found out that nine-tenths of most born Jews don't know how either. In many ways, I am far more knowledgeable than born Jews. In fact, my friends used to kid me that they were going to chip in and send me to rabbinical school because I was clearly the best-qualified person of anyone they knew!

I have friends and colleagues in the Orthodox community. I know that in their heart of hearts they don't think I am 100 percent Jewish because I have not had an Orthodox conversion—even though they have never shared those thoughts with me, and they have never behaved in any way to make me feel less than Jewish. I have a working relationship with a *Chabad* rabbi. He has always been warm and friendly to me, so much so that it has even crossed my mind that he doesn't know that I am a convert. I think he must know. It is not a secret in this community. There has never even been the slightest inkling that he has anything other than the greatest respect and admiration for me.

It's partly just my personality that's made me comfortable in the Jewish community. As a convert, you can't have a chip on your shoulder. You have to be whole-hearted, and you have to work at it. The first thing one needs to do is to get educated. If the rabbi who is part of the conversionary process hasn't insisted that you read and study, then do it yourself. The other thing to do is to join the community, and do Jewish stuff. You have to do it in your home. You have to do it with your friends. I think that most Jews are very accepting, and they will bend over backward to help you in whatever way they can. Leading a Jewish life also has to be a decision that you and your spouse make.

Do you have to prove yourself? Probably in a way you do. You have to prove that you are sincere. Yes, I think you do. Not to prove it to show anybody, but you have to manifest something that shows you didn't do it just to please somebody's mother. Maybe you have to prove it to *yourself.*

People who are converting to please someone or who are marrying a Jew without converting had better not get married until they work this out. That is my advice. If you intend to celebrate religion in your home, you had better decide which one, and you need to decide it now because a lot of people think that the issue will go away, but as soon as they have a child it intensifies—logarithmically.

On the other hand, I also don't think that it serves the Jewish community well to alienate either the born Jew or the non-Jew. I think it is very important that we do outreach, that we are welcoming, and that we encourage—if not pressure—intermarried people to learn about Judaism. We need to keep half the partnership and possibly the children of that partnership for Judaism. We are not going to do that if we alienate the non-Jew, and we might get another Jew. I have known cases in which people were married ten years, and then there was a conversion. I know one woman who converted prior to her daughter's *bat mitzvah.* Do you want to know what the impetus was? The *bat mitzvah,* of course! Her daughter *chose* Judaism, had a conversion, and she wanted a *bat mitzvah.* The mother then took the step to convert as well. So, it can happen.

My husband always teases me and says I would never make it as a social worker because I have such strong opinions and voice them. I have a hard time accepting the anger at the Jewish community that comes from the intermarried. I think, "What *hutzpah!* You are angry at the Jewish community? Here we are doing everything we can possibly do—running schools, programs, JCCs, raising money, doing everything that is possible to do to ensure the continuance of the Jewish people, and you are mad because we're unhappy that you have chosen not to have a Jewish family and not to raise your children as Jews! You want us to say that everything you are doing is wonderful, and that we love you, and we love your lifestyle, and that it is okay? What! Are you crazy? It is not okay!" But, they are angry. I read about the *Parve* group, and I thought, "Well, all right. Fine. It meets their needs." I'll bet you they spend a lot of time being really angry in these groups. Maybe if they work through their anger, they will come to a place where they can begin to see what the other side is.

We have two sons (from my first marriage). One is almost twenty-nine, and one is thirty-two. Ken and I spend a lot of time talking about what happens if they don't marry Jews or if they marry someone who is not willing or is not interested in converting to Judaism. It bothers me. I would like to have Jewish daughters-in-law. I would like to have Jewish grandchildren. Ken would like that. Our sons know that. We have been clear about our feelings on this topic. They both have had non-Jewish women friends. I know they are adults, and they will do whatever they like. We have been friendly and pleasant to their women friends, but we have always given a consistent message: "She is very nice, but we hope you will marry a Jewish woman or someone who will convert to Judaism."

I think the one thing that I would want understood by the larger Jewish community about me as a convert is that I am 100 percent, wholeheartedly, unequivocally Jewish. I am never going to not be Jewish. You know, there is that feeling that when the chips are down, converts will bail out. My husband teases me about which of the two of us would "bail out" if things got tough for the Jews. He knows that if there was ever a question, I would be the last person to deny being Jewish. He may doubt himself, but he never doubts me.

16

Shabbat and Dafina
Rebecca

As a child, Rebecca had once contemplated conversion to Judaism, but by the time she met Michel, while she was a college student in France, religion was something she thought she had left behind. Her eventual decision to convert, however, was made easier by her earlier interest. She and Michel were married and settled in France.

With her conversion papers in hand, Rebecca, at age twenty-two, walked into the Moroccan-Sephardic Jewish culture of Michel's family, which was led by his iron-willed and loving mother. She and Michel lived with the family for a while, and Rebecca had a total immersion experience of running a Jewish household and observing the weekly rhythms of *Shabbat* and Dafina—the traditional Moroccan dish that is the centerpiece of the *Shabbat* noonday meal.

I'm from North Carolina originally, the third of five children born into a family that can trace its roots back to the Revolutionary War. We were not a very religious family, although we did go to church very frequently. The Presbyterian church was a part of our lives; in fact, as children we often played in the churchyard, which was situated on four or five acres near our home.

I attended Sunday school as a child and learned a great deal about the Old Testament, which I enjoyed very much—I particularly loved the story of Rebecca. The Protestant religion is less demanding than, say, Catholicism and especially Judaism. Mostly, you are just supposed to have faith. I do remember that my grandmother followed the injunction against work on the Sabbath—she did all her cooking on Saturday for Sunday.

I had developed an interest in Judaism as a child, the result of my friendship with the two Jewish families in our small Southern town. One of my mother's closest friends was Jewish, and I had spent a great deal of time with them from infancy. Jackie, the daughter, and I were playing together one day, and I asked her something about Jesus—we were no more than five or six years old. She informed me that her family didn't believe in Jesus. I never knew that could be! And I asked, "What do you mean?" and she replied simply, "We're Jewish." I was quite startled at Jackie's pride in her Jewishness. That was my first introduction to Judaism, as I recall.

There are bits and pieces of memories I have about being in their house. They had a *mezuzah* on the door, and I was very impressed with the "Happy Hanukkah" decoration on their fireplace—right next to their Christmas tree! There was a Jewish calendar in their kitchen that I used to gaze at with interest as I ate at their table. Their house exuded a warmth and cohesiveness that I loved to be around, more than any other home I visited. There was almost something mystical about their family life, even with my youthful perception. Perhaps it was the devotion Jewish families feel and demonstrate for their children.

When I was in seventh grade, I had a very good teacher who was already preparing us for college. She allowed us great leeway in choosing a subject for our term papers, and I chose to write about the Jewish holidays. After I did my term paper, I announced to my mother and father that I was going to convert to Judaism. I felt very sincere about it. My mother became very upset and she discouraged me. So I just put that idea on the back burner and didn't think about it any more for a long time.

In college, my interests were in math and languages—French in particular. I spent my junior year studying in France and resolved that, in an effort to totally immerse myself in the language, I would associate only with French-speaking students and not with the other Americans in the program. By November I was very lonely, but I stubbornly kept to my resolution. Then in January, I met Michel. We started going out together, mostly to the French movies, sometimes to museums and even once to a medieval village. We sometimes sat and sipped espressos in sidewalk cafés. We talked about anything and everything and we became the best of friends over the five months that ensued. He was Jewish and I was not and we did not intend to fall in love. Matters of the heart are not so easily directed.

How Michel and I met is an interesting story. It happened because of a friendship I had developed with a French girl at the university. She sat next to me in a logic class and we became friendly, since I often assisted her with the assignments. She in turn helped me with French.

The French normally do not use biblical (Old Testament) names for their children. Rather, this is a practice generally reserved by the Jewish population. My name, Rebecca, therefore was a mistaken signal to my friend, and she simply assumed or chose to believe that I was an American Jew.

One Friday night, she invited me for dinner at her home. For my part, I did not know that she was Jewish, but as the *Kiddush* and the *Hamotzi* were recited, I understood. As I gazed around the table, it became apparent to me that I was a "stranger" to them, and I felt suddenly unwelcome. When asked, I admitted that I was not Jewish, and one of the brothers in her large family joked, "Well, that's okay; we're going to convert you!" That relieved some of the tension but I sensed that the father regretted my presence, sitting as I was in the seat of honor next to him. Perhaps he harbored a mistaken concern that I might mock this Jewish tradition rather than appreciate its beauty. Nevertheless, we all enjoyed the family's traditional Friday night dinner of couscous along with other salads so telling of their Tunisian origins. And once again, I sensed that intangible quality of family unity and devotion that I had felt once before in the home of my childhood friend on another continent, in another land. The next day, my friend introduced me to Michel. She knew then that I was not Jewish, but for whatever reason she did not share that knowledge with him.

As I got to know Michel, I found that, although he was not particularly religiously observant, he had very strong feelings about God and about his Jewish religion. The effect that had on me was to reignite the spark that had been dormant since I was an early teen. I also understood something that I hadn't understood before about the Jewish religion, and that was the feeling that my husband had for the Jewish people and his attachment to the State of Israel. In addition, on several occasions in France I was exposed to something I had not experienced in the United States: tangible evidence of what happened in the Holocaust. There were a number of photographic exhibitions, and I had visited many of them as well as the concentration camp that was near Strasbourg, France. The latter visit occurred well before I met Michel and, unmistakably, it represented for me a solemn but graphic three-dimensional exposé of the dark side of human possibilities. Today, I cannot understand how anyone could deny that such atrocities took place.

When the time came for me to return to the United States early that summer, we realized that our friendship had flourished into a serious courtship, and we were not ready to sever our relationship as I boarded the train to Paris. Michel visited the United States late that summer and met my parents. My mother and father liked him right away. When I returned to the university at Chapel Hill that fall to finish school, Michel returned to France. Although we had begun to think of the possibility of marriage, Michel never asked me to convert. Since I had already felt the impetus to convert many years before, I began to turn this matter over in my mind once again. I thought long and hard about it and whether or not I would complete the process even if I did not marry Michel. When I was sure within my heart that I would, I was ready to begin. I was not, however, prepared for the events that would unfold.

I wrote once and then again to a rabbi at a synagogue that I knew of not far from my home, but he never responded. Returning to Chapel Hill, I located the campus Hillel House and introduced myself to the rabbi. I explained to him that I wanted to convert and asked him if he would help me. He tried to dissuade me, but I insisted that I was sure of what I was about to undertake and explained how I had previously written to another rabbi who had ignored my letters. He finally relented and invited me to join a conversion class that he was starting that very week. I realized that I was not alone in what I was doing.

With Michel back in France, I had the whole year to study, both for my degree and my conversion. Every Friday night, the campus Hillel sponsored a *Shabbat* dinner, with services afterward and also on Saturday morning. I didn't go to the services very often on Saturday morning because I liked to sleep in too much, but I truly enjoyed the fellowship of the *Oneg Shabbat*. I studied Hebrew there and was delighted to discover that I recognized the *Shema** prayer I had heard when, as a child,

---

*"Hear O Israel, the Lord our God, the Lord is One." Rabbi Hayim Halevy Donin, in *To Be a Jew*, says that the *Shema* is not, technically, a prayer but a "declaration of faith. It is an affirmation of the unity of God that reminds us of our obligations to Him" (p. 164).

I had accompanied my friend, Jackie, to her synagogue for services. I recalled that most of the words ended in the "ah" sound.

There was one thing that I found particularly disconcerting. In the conversion classes, the rabbi recommended that we not reveal to the other Jewish students that we were converts. On the one hand, I understood that he did not want us to be labeled as such because he believed that label stays with you. I followed his advice, but still it bothered me. I like to be straightforward and honest, and for the first time in my life I was being asked not to be open and honest about who I was. I didn't like it.

It was during this period that I totally ruptured any remaining feelings I had for my Christian upbringing. I bought a lot of books on Judaism and read them all, with the intensity generally reserved for a university course. One afternoon, I was sitting in bed reading some of this material when I had a vision. It was the image of Jesus that was portrayed in a picture in my home as a child. The image was there but wasn't there; I could see it and yet not see it and then "pffffft," it was gone. I have never shared that story with anyone, nor can I explain it. I understood it as something of an "ending," and any doubts about what I was doing were gone.

As I undertook my immersion into the Jewish campus community, I began to have glimpses of what it was like to be Jewish in a non-Jewish world. I remember the awkward feeling of having to explain to a professor that I would have to miss an exam because of the High Holidays and how she had expressed annoyance with that. Then, just as I was learning about Israel's wartorn history, the Yom Kippur war erupted. I began to have worries about the American political position as the Arab oil embargo took effect and for the first time knew what it was like to have a dual allegiance.

Michel and I wrote to each other long letters every other day. I still have a stack of them. I shared with him my feeling about what I was going through and often interjected Hebrew phrases that I was learning at Hillel. That winter break, I visited him in France. It was at the airport arrival gate that he proposed to me, and I accepted. I had not yet met his parents. They had been actively discouraging Michel from continuing the relationship and were not very pleased at the prospect of having a convert as a daughter-in-law. For my part, I was hurt and felt rejected by people who did not really know me, but I was optimistic that things would eventually work out. In the spring of that year, Michel left his family to come to the United States.

It was also at that time of year that I believed myself ready to formalize the conversion. The rabbi explained to me that there were two ways he could arrange it: a Reform conversion or conversion according to *halakhah*, which involved going before a *Bet Din* and immersion in the *mikveh*. He also explained to me what the consequences of both could be. I preferred to have a halakhic conversion.

Michel was present for the conversion ritual. I was nervous and afraid when I went before the *Bet Din* but I found that they were kind and understanding of me. Afterward, Michel and I prepared a celebratory meal. It was something simple—probably involving spaghetti. What I do remember is that he roasted some peppers, a salad treat he'd learned to prepare at home. "I hate bell peppers," I said. "But you're going to love this!" he replied. My first introduction to his Moroccan-Sephardic cuisine: roasted peppers with olive oil, lemon juice, and garlic. Delicious!

Looking back on it, the only thing about our wedding ceremony, held at the Carolina Inn, that was traditionally Jewish was the *huppah* and the breaking of the glass. The Hillel rabbi, of whom I had grown fond over the year of studying with him, performed the ceremony. My in-laws back in France requested that we send them copies of my conversion papers. They then had those reviewed by their rabbi, who then consulted with the chief rabbi of France, who concluded that it was indeed proper and acceptable. So when Michel and I arrived back in France, his parents organized a second marriage ceremony. We now had a real *ketubah*.

I was twenty-two years old and meeting Michel's parents for the first time. My father-in-law met us at the airport in Lyon. His demeanor was such that I realized that while he may have resigned himself to the events that had transpired, he had suffered a big disappointment: a convert was not the kind of Jewish girl he had envisioned for his son. Inwardly, I accepted that he would probably never change these deep-seated feelings. My mother-in-law reserved a warmer reception for us. When she hugged me for the first time, I knew that I had an ally and that everything would eventually be all right.

The day I walked into their home, I stepped into a Sephardic culture I had only had a glimpse of one Friday night more than a year earlier when someone I hardly knew casually predicted my eventual conversion. It was the world of the French-speaking North African Jews who had fled to France in the late fifties and sixties. It was a culture within a culture; a Jewish way of life with an oriental flavor, spicing its distinctive cuisine, transcending its music, and most of all, molding a very different way of thinking. It is through my mother-in-law that I was able to bridge the chasm separating me from them, not only because I was a convert, but because I was, after all, an American.

I cannot begin to describe all the things I had to learn and all the adjustments I had to make. It was as if I had come into a marriage with a tabula rasa. My mother-in-law took charge of teaching me how to cook and equipping my kitchen in preparation for when we moved out on our own. We had to purchase everything: dishes, plates, utensils, pots—the whole works. She is a very strong-willed person and in the interest of making sure that I did things properly she would let me have no say in the choices about what to buy. She insisted, for example, that I buy dishes of the Corning Ware type because of their practicality, especially in keeping a kosher kitchen according to her standards: you could use them for milk or meat, reheat in them, and therefore only needed one set of dishes. I learned much from her and grew to love her very much, but I was too young to know how to manage her need for control. If I was not careful, discussions would end up in arguments that I, of course, could never win. This was a lesson in diplomacy.

It was in the kitchen, however, that we collaborated and our friendship grew. There she taught me to prepare the flavorful dishes whose aroma would permeate my home, the same scents that greeted me as I crossed the threshold of their home for the first time. It was a Moroccan cuisine with her own special twist and an occasional touch of France. These are the dishes that my own children would learn to savor at home in Atlanta, where we sometimes wonder in awe just how many other Americans might be lucky enough to know them. Our most prized creation in the kitchen is the "dafina." This succulent masterpiece is cooked in an oven starting Friday afternoon until Saturday noon. In Morocco, it was taken in its big pot to a large community oven to bake. Depending on how much you slipped the attendant, he'd put it in the best spot in the oven or not the best spot, if the tip was not big. A great deal of speculation surrounded the anticipated return Saturday at noon as to how the dafina was going to turn out. Would it be nicely cooked with an unctuous sauce or too soupy? Judgment was handed down as its contents of chick-peas, garlic, meat, saffron rice, spicy wheat berries, potatoes, and eggs were separated and passed around. *Shabbat* and dafina became a central part of our lives.

After Michel and I were married, formal instruction in Judaica ceased for me. I certainly absorbed a lot by osmosis and here again, my mother-in-law played a major role. She is a talented storyteller, and over the years she spent many hours relating to me the stories of her own life and spinning enchanting tales that are Moroccan in origin, dealing with mysticism, God, and the Jewish religion. Through them, I became acquainted with the anonymous donor, the evil eye, and the *magid* (pronounced with a hard *g*). The notion of the *magid* can best be explained as the personification of negative and positive events that guide an individual toward misfortune or opportunity. As I understood it, the *magid* was fatalism. I have ambivalent feelings about this because I continue to believe in the concept of "free will"; that through choice, individuals exert great influence over personal destiny. When I reflect back on all the events that transpired during this period of my life I cannot help but wonder: Was it the *magid* that had guided me through the sequence of events that led me to my present situation or was it the result of my own personal choices? Passive participation or proactive choice; perhaps it can be *understood* within the context of one concept and *explained* within the context of the other.

My mother-in-law was greatly influenced by her own father-in-law, who was a rabbi. He was a tall gentleman, stern and proud. He spent many afternoons sharing his rabbinical knowledge with her in the seven years during and following the Occupation that she and her husband resided in the same home with him. He taught her how a woman should conduct herself with her husband, how best to bring up her children, what to consider when choosing a neighborhood to live in, and other such matters as may be learned in the *Shulhan Arukh*. They conversed in "Judeo-Arabe," a highly poetic language of the North African Jews. He believed that one must use the mind to reason over and judge religious matters. For example, he said if he had been invited to someone's home, once there, it would be offensive to refuse refreshments and to cast doubts about the hosts' degree of *kashrut* observance. Furthermore, he reasoned that should they knowingly offer nonkosher food to him under the pretext that it was kosher, then the transgression was theirs, not his. He also assured her that if she, the very "earth" of her family, always kept kosher, then as a result her very home would be guaranteed a solid foundation. All of this and more, she in turned shared with me.

After almost four years of such an enriching experience, Michel and I returned to live in the United States. We chose to settle in Atlanta when we learned that a sizable Sephardic community had a synagogue there. In France, we almost never attended services, but here we instinctively knew that being alone and isolated in a strange city meant that we would appreciate the affiliation even if we didn't attend services on a weekly basis. We continued to keep kosher as we had in France, with Corelle dishes no less, but the Moroccan-Sephardic culture as we had lived it in France was elusive, and soon I was spending more time in the car than in the kitchen. The stress of managing a family and a career took its toll. We were feeling more and more like American Jews.

My husband worked on Saturdays, at first, and I had small children to care for. Therefore, in our early years in Atlanta, we rarely attended services. When I did, I felt a great sense of inadequacy, not knowing the Hebrew prayers or how to conduct myself there. I found that I was constantly losing my place in the *siddur*, sometimes standing when everyone else was sitting, and feeling awfully self-conscious. Over time, we managed to become more regular in our attendance, and I slowly made progress. It was so slow, in fact, that I was not even aware of it until my mother-in-law, on a recent visit, remarked at how well I knew the service and the prayers. Indeed, I was now keeping her turned to the right page, my fingers underlining the Hebrew words for her.

One by one, my children grew up. We joined car pools and drove back and forth to Hebrew school. *Bar* and *bat mitzvahs* came and went. At the same time, I was beginning to ask myself questions. What are my children really getting from all of this? When they grow up, will they desire to be "good" Jews? I assumed that they were learning the concepts of the Jewish religion at Sunday school, and perhaps they did, but I realized that I had abdicated responsibility and had not actively imparted these concepts myself. I really did not know how. I recognized that while I was a good parent, I lacked good Jewish parenting skills.

Reading one book opened my eyes: *Cultural Literacy*, by E. D. Hirsch. While Mr. Hirsch is mainly concerned with American cultural literacy, I focused on transferring what he asserted to the Jewish family experience, especially vis-à-vis my children. The book reminds us that children learn almost everything about their culture by the ages of twelve or thirteen, and isn't it interesting, then, that this is when rites of passage occur in many cultures—the Jewish *bar/bat mitzvah* for example—to mark them as full-fledged members. Reading on, I became aware how important are even the very small actions that we undertake on a daily basis, which ingrain in our children a sense of our culture. This becomes their "baggage," enabling them to transmit a culture to their own children. "And you shall teach them diligently. . . ."

This presents a particular challenge, and a convert who comes into this as an adult will be at a disadvantage. The cultural baggage from his own childhood contains precious few tools to help him transcend the generations. My own childhood experiences, of course, were void of Jewish meaning. At holidays, it's like having cultural amnesia, only there was nothing there in the first place—no childhood memories to sustain me and no traditions from my own past that I could share with or duplicate for my children. On the other hand, I realized, if I were to suddenly go back to being a Christian again, I could organize Christmas festivities almost without having to think about it, even though it has been twenty-one years since I last celebrated this holiday.

How different it is for me in trying to remember, from year to year, all the different things to do for Rosh Hashanah and Pesah. It just wasn't ingrained in me from childhood, therefore it doesn't come automatically. And then, I began to wonder. Within a Jewish context, what experiences in our family have made their impression on my own children? What special events will they remember when they are grown? What traditions would they seek to share and instill in their own children? What I began to fear was that their Jewish cultural baggage was very light indeed.

It was at this point that I realized, among other things, that to be a Jewish family you have to do Jewish things and do them together if you can. I endeavored to take steps to enhance our Jewish experience. I also wanted to reach our children through their senses. The logical first step was *hallah* baking. We now bake *hallahs* almost every Friday. I even adapted an old recipe to develop a quick-rise method that could be prepared in a matter of minutes using a food processor. By the time rising is done, our youngest daughter has returned from school, and she sometimes "paints" them with egg and "sprinkles" them with sesame seeds just before baking in the oven. This is a wonderful way to welcome the *Shabbat* bride,* with the aroma and the taste of fresh-baked bread set upon the table! A logical next step is building a *sukkah*. This could be a great family event—building, decorating, and using it together.

There are challenges, too, in working around the differences in religion with our extended family. It has been difficult, at times, for me to reconcile our Jewish observances with my parents' Christianity. Although I am grateful that my parents supported my conversion, it is a fact that they don't understand the life that I lead nor do they fathom the complexities of the Jewish religion. My father has been most accepting. He believes that his own grandfather was Jewish, a peddler passing through who met and married my father's grandmother. When I told my father-in-law about the possible heritage of my great-grandfather, he asked what his name was. Ebenezer, I said, pronounced in French as in Ibn Ezra. Our surname, he explained, is a derivative of this Jewish name. For some reason, my father-in-law found reassurance in that.

Some people have said they had a Jewish soul in their body and their conversion was really a "return." I felt that way. Maybe my great-grandfather really was Jewish, and perhaps, through me, his soul is returning to its source. Maybe not. Neverthe-

---

*We greet the Sabbath as if "she" were a bride; the Sabbath is the time when the *Shekhinah*, the feminine aspect of God, dwells among us.

less, I feel totally at home and at ease in what I have done. I've had no regrets since I embarked upon this journey. Some of the problems I encountered along the way have been resolved and others linger. I am still sensitive to the possibility of doubts about my sincerity, and the hurt and rejection I endured will never be completely forgotten. But I will continue to seek knowledge about my chosen heritage and use that knowledge not only to express my Jewishness but to better the person that I am.

17

Acceptance in the Promised Land

Gerry Gilstrop

Gerry began the process of conversion when he was fifteen, and he spent several months in Israel when he was a junior in high school. There for the first time in his life Gerry experienced a level of personal acceptance never available to him as a man of color in the United States. "In a ghetto situation," Gerry says, "you have to have society's permission to leave. You have to prove you are 'worthy' to leave. If the acid test of your 'worthiness' is the color of your skin, you can't ever get out."

In Israel, he found considerations of race to be of secondary importance. In Orthodox Judaism he discovered that a person's acceptability and status in the community is judged primarily on one's observance of the *mitzvot*, level of knowledge, and sense of commitment to an observant lifestyle.

Now, many years later, Gerry is married and the stepfather of his wife Becky's two sons. He has developed a loving relationship with these children as he has led his family back to a more traditional Jewish life.

W hen I was fourteen my grandfather died of complications arising from his already life-threatening case of skin cancer. He was actually my step-grandfather because he was the second husband of my maternal grandmother. But the lack of biological ties between us did not diminish the stature he had achieved within our family. He was the patriarch; a father figure who kept the family together and served as its moral force. I was so overwhelmed with grief for him that my family feared, however mistakenly, that I might commit suicide.

The summer that my grandfather died, I went to San Diego to visit my father. My parents had been divorced when I was a small child, and I had seen little of my father through the years. My father is African-American and his wife at that time was of Czechoslovakian descent. Their blended family included her two teenaged boys from a previous marriage and their own child, a girl, of African-American and Czech heritage.

My father's enthusiasm for exercise helped lift me out of my depression, and his attitudes toward religion gave me something to think about. He was down on religion and believed it was used as a means to exploit African-Americans. At the end of the summer, when I returned to the fundamentalist Bible school where I was a student, I found the church's constant diatribes against anyone of another faith upsetting me profoundly.

Ironically, it was my reaction to my parents' divorce that had led to my enrollment in this school in the first place. Following the divorce, my mother and I came east to live in Baltimore near my maternal grandparents. My father remained in California. As adults, both my parents had become Catholic at least partly because the Church afforded opportunities for African-American children to get the kind of private education not available elsewhere in the 1960s. When my mother and I arrived in Baltimore, I was sent to Catholic school. Now, from an adult perspective, I believe that my grief and rage over the divorce led directly to behavior problems that got me kicked out of two parochial schools. I began third grade in a secular private school that caters to Ivy League aspirants. This was intended to help me, but it did not, and I was expelled after the fifth grade.

At this point, my grandmother intervened and insisted that I be placed in the academy of a fundamentalist church. I followed that church's doctrine for several years, finding its emphasis on the all-powerfulness of God to be reassuring in some ways. But in the months following my grandfather's death and my subsequent visit to my father, I began to question that which had been held "unquestionable" in the dogma of the school. I began to question the whole premise of Christian "love."

Seeking answers, I took advantage of the public library to read anything I could find on other religions. What I was searching for was not necessarily a different faith to join but whether I could find the vocabulary I needed to articulate my own belief in God and explain my own place in the cosmos. Monotheism seemed like the right place to start, and I looked into Islam and the Nation of Islam. I never did attend any Islamic functions, however. The culture and lifestyle felt foreign to me. I also felt that growing up in mainstream America had made me too Westernized to entertain Eastern religions.

Then I turned to Judaism, and I liked what I read. After learning that "Torah" differed from "Bible," I decided that I needed to know which, if any, of the Christian versions of the Bible were actually accurate and true. The only way to do this, I reasoned, was to be able to read the Torah in the original. So, I checked out some books in the library and began to teach myself Hebrew.

The next year was both calamitous and fortuitous for me. My mother worked for Social Security, and we lived in Section 8 housing. By the middle of the school year my mother's financial situation had deteriorated to such an extent that she was unable to pay the tuition at the academy. One day I went to school and was promptly sent home with the tuition bill. They told me not to return until it was paid. My mother was optimistic that soon she would have enough money to pay the bill and send me back or find another Christian school in which to enroll me. But she did neither, and for the next two or three months, I sat at home watching TV. One day, out of sheer boredom and frustration, I walked over to the nearest public junior-high school and enrolled myself.

The anarchy of the first day of public school was a complete shock to someone accustomed to the uniformity and discipline of nine years of private education.

By the time I was fifteen, it was clear to me that I needed to connect with the larger

Jewish community in order to continue studying and growing. I found out about the Baltimore Hebrew University (then Baltimore Hebrew College). Since I didn't have any money for the bus, I walked the ten miles from my home and signed up for night-time adult *ulpan* courses in intensive Hebrew. I couldn't take the daytime courses that I wanted because, of course, I was still in the ninth grade!

My conversion process began when I was sixteen. The Reform rabbi I contacted never showed up for our interview, so I switched gears and sought out a highly es-teemed Orthodox rabbi in town, Rabbi Menachem Feldman. He met with me, laid out a list of requirements for conversion, and paired me with a *havrusa*—a study partner. But there were constant interruptions to my studies.

My family was temporarily displaced during this period, and we were moving around a lot. That, added to the fact that I was still a minor, initially made it difficult for me to meet the rabbi's requirement that I find a way to live and study in the Jew-ish community full-time. The "study" in itself consisted of learning about Jewish culture, values, and the holidays. I didn't have to learn a lot about the holidays be-cause I had already read so much about them.

What appealed to me most about Judaism was that here was a regulated lifestyle that actually reflected one's beliefs and morality. The calendar, the rituals, and so forth all support Jewish values and ideals. There is internal consistency to the sys-tem: monotheism (the belief that you have to answer to an ultimate authority), linked to the knowledge that you are responsible for your own actions (not opting out with, "The devil made me do it!"). There are certain times, both personal and communal, that are set aside as holy times to remind us of our relationship to God—to Israel and to the world. All this made sense to me.

The study partner the rabbi chose was an African-American man. He was much older than me but had a background similar to my own. He came from a well-educated family out West. He was extremely intelligent and articulate. At that time he was either finishing medical school or doing his internship in pathology. His family, unlike my own, were avowed atheists. He had grown up with atheism as the central dogma of his life, but at some point had begun to question that. Superficially, however, our similarities were marked. He remains stringently Orthodox (*mahmir*) and still resides in this community.

At the time, I didn't think much about the appropriateness of being paired off with someone whose background was so much like mine. For me, it was a color-blind issue because this person had information that I desperately wanted to learn. Gener-ally, during our learning sessions, he was very rational and structured, but sometimes he would go off onto a mystical tangent. Our discussions would become very eso-teric. At that time my knowledge was so limited that sometimes I simply couldn't follow him, but we managed to survive that. I learned a great deal. I don't know what the rabbi had in mind when he paired me up with this man—whether he thought color would be a bonding issue or not. For me it wasn't. It had more to do with finding a *havrusa* with compatible behaviors and outlook.

Meanwhile, in the BHU *ulpan* class, my conversational Hebrew was developing nicely. I was coming to understand a bit about the unique relationship between the land of Israel, and the Jews of the Diaspora, and Israelis. I decided I needed to go to Israel.

So one day, I repeated my long walk from home to the Jewish Community Center and presented myself to the Israeli government's *shaliah* (agent for immigration who helps people making *aliyah* to Israel). His office was a green metal trailer set up on the JCC's parking lot.

I'll never forget the look on his face when I walked in and said, "I have to go to Israel. How do I do it?"

His eyes bugged out, his jaw dropped, and he stammered, "Uh, uh . . . I guess kids your age go to work on a *kibbutz* with a ZOA (Zionist Organization of America) program." "Fine," I said, "What's the ZOA and how do I sign up?"

He sent me on another hike across town to the ZOA office. The staff there was equally stunned to see a young African-American kid walk in with such a request. But, when they found out that I was not only conversant in Hebrew but also fluent in Spanish, they warmed to the task and found a program for me on an Argentinian *kibbutz* near Gaza. I borrowed money for the trip from my father and a cousin and left Baltimore in the middle of my junior year in high school.

I made five visits to Israel between the ages of sixteen and twenty. Religious observance assumed a more concrete form for me while in Israel because Judaism revolves around *Eretz Yisrael*, Jerusalem, and the festivals that are associated with the land. Being there put these things into context for me. Those visits also intensified my desire to finish up the conversion process and not to remain in a kind of religious limbo.

I enjoyed Israeli society in many ways more than American society. It's more direct and honest, I think. People don't put on so much of a "face." There isn't such a high value placed on what I call "Anglo" behaviors: displaying a calm demeanor all the time; pretending that everything in the world is civilized and nice people don't struggle with problems; believing that "privilege" can protect you.

From my point of view as a young person seeking identity as a Jew, life in Israel was much more natural.

Probably, Israeli culture is much more in line with the family cultural traits I grew up with. There is an informality there that is lacking in the States. Israel has a greater sense of social egalitarianism; each Jew is seen as a legitimate part of the political process regardless of whether you are rich or poor, well educated or not well educated at all. It's not perfect egalitarianism (without addressing the issues of Arab Israelis, Palestinians, and women, who certainly have to struggle against prejudice and abridgment of rights), but "inclusionism" is much more noticeable there than what we have here in the dominant society, or even in the microcosm of the Jewish community. In Israel, there's a strong emphasis and expectation of stable family relationships. Things tend to be more socially conservative in regard to religion and social behavior. Unfortunately this sometimes means that women too often do all the work at home, but the networks of interpersonal and extended family support *are* stronger.

In Israel the color of my skin was not the same kind of issue it is here in America. It was right before the Ethiopian airlift and I was still somewhat of a novelty to a lot of people. Israelis were familiar with black students from sub-Saharan Africa coming to study at the universities and to work on *kibbutzim*. But they didn't get too many black Jews. Actually, there were Jews in Israel darker than me—Cochin Jews from India, and Yemenites who were obviously darker in skin color than I was. I was actually much more attractive to people—physically attractive, that is—because I was a novelty. It was an interesting perspective for me. I think it helped my self-esteem. In Israel there is not just one way to look in order to be accepted into the majority culture.

On the other hand, I have had a few experiences here in America in which Jews have treated me in ways that were personally challenging. Things have happened to me from both sides—from observant and nonobservant people. I am sure it has to do with the racism and social stratification that is endemic to America. One *Shabbat*, long after my conversion, I attended services at a local non-Orthodox synagogue out of respect for a friend, a Conservative rabbi, who was speaking there. I took a *tallit* from the rack and was putting it on, when the woman who was acting as an usher rushed over and started to pull it off me. She kept pulling if off from the right and I kept pulling it back on from the left. After a few long seconds of this tug-of-war, I asked her why she was doing this, and she replied, "Because you don't need one." I said, "Why don't I need one?" And she said, "Because you're not Jewish." I said, "I *am* Jewish." She was taken aback and obviously perplexed. An Israeli friend from an observant home had accompanied me that day, and she was appalled at the woman's behavior.

On the other side, when I am walking in the Orthodox community, *frum* women will often veer away from me and rush across the street as I walk in their direction. They really are afraid of me. And hearing religious people talk about the *shvartzes* (Yiddish for "black") in denigrating tones, at the very table where my wife, children, or I are seated, constantly astonishes and distresses me. What do they think I am? People often act without thinking their actions through.

The entire course of my conversion was spread out over four to five years. Between my family's moves, my travels to Israel, and commuting to work in Washington, D.C., after my last trip, I didn't have a contiguous chunk of time to deal with study and the conversion process. Even though I had a good amount of the prerequisite knowledge, my conversion still took many years. In a way, I think that showed the rabbis that I wasn't just a kid rushing into something. And, I guess, it showed my tenacity.

I finally went to the *mikveh* on a Sunday, a week before Rosh Hashanah, the 24th of *Elul* 5745. I was twenty years old. The *mikveh* looked kind of like a spa, though it was not as fancy as the new *mikveh* in Baltimore. I was excited, I was nervous, but afterwards it felt anticlimactic. I felt like saying to the friend who'd accompanied me, "Are we there yet?" There was no blinding shaft of light streaming through a window, no burst of song from a heavenly choir—like you hear about in stories of

Catholic conversions. It was, instead, very simple, very soft. At that time I was renting a room from a very wonderful *mahmir* Orthodox family, and they immediately invited me to join their family for Rosh Hashanah.

Going to the *mikveh*—the formal conversion—opened a lot of doors for me. I was no longer someone to be hugged and pushed away at the same time. Jews are not allowed to push away a person who wants to convert, if they persist. However, there's a social-religious ambivalence in the Orthodox community toward people who are studying for conversion but haven't yet become a *ger* or *gioret*. Besides the usual doubts about their sanity or their ulterior motives, the community recognizes that while they are not yet halakhically Jewish, they are no longer an integral part of the religious group they were born into either. It's an awkward and lonely period for the convert. Making it more difficult, those studying for conversion are not obligated to keep all the *mitzvot*. Therefore, the people in the Jewish community aren't obliged to include them in certain activities. Following my conversion I became genuinely a member of the Jewish community. As a Jew, I now had to fulfill certain familial obligations, but since I had no family—no Jewish family, that is—I basically had become an orphan . . . someone to be cared for.

I got lots of invitations for *Shabbat* and the *hagim*. Many people who knew me or knew *of* me went out of their way to be friendly. It wasn't long before people asked me when I was going to get married and began trying to arrange things for me in that way. However, that didn't go very well, because at the time I didn't want to get married. Traditionally, by eighteen or twenty, in the Orthodox community, most men are married. Certainly by the time you are twenty-five, people are wondering, "What are you waiting around for?" So here I was, already twenty and unmarried. The community's obligation to me was to help me find a wife, and that may have made them a bit nervous. Attempts were made by well-intentioned people in the community to find appropriate women for me to meet. Everybody felt that they should, of course, be observant and *also* be black. This led to a number of awkward moments as the same woman was introduced and reintroduced to me by different people. As for my concerns, I didn't want to repeat the mistakes my parents had made and create an unhappy life by rushing into an involvement, so I decided not to pursue marriage at that time.

I had had virtually no exposure to the other branches of Judaism. My decision to become Orthodox was to some extent colored by the prejudices of people within the Orthodox community and also by what I saw of Jews who were not Orthodox. Non-Orthodox Jews seemed to know absolutely nothing about traditional rites. Orthodoxy is an ordered world. I now consider myself part of "modern Orthodoxy"—in Israel it is called *kippat rugah*, which means, literally, "knitted *yarmulke*." This perspective says that one can continue to live in modern culture while maintaining traditional values and practices. You don't have to give up one or the other.

There are some groups within Orthodoxy that do not believe that. But I feel it is viable—some people call it the "YU" (Yeshiva University) approach, which holds that Torah and science are not mutually exclusive. I just don't believe that you should be isolated from the "real" world. You should have the fortitude to stand up to the larger world strengthened by your values and what you practice. I know that often that is easier said than done with the influences of television, movies, marketing, and the media. Nevertheless, for many people on the more liberal side of Judaism, even "modern Orthodoxy" seems fanatic.

Because these distinctions are becoming more entrenched and divisive, I worry now about the future of Judaism in America. It seems to me that Judaism here is following the path Christianity took in the fifteenth and sixteenth centuries in Europe. It is splintering into virtually separate religions in a way similar to what happened during the Protestant Reformation. The responsibility for the breach lies with all of us, so every Jew bears responsibility for the healing. I think every Jew has something to offer, and every Jew has areas to improve him- or herself in some way—if that weren't so, we wouldn't need *Mashiah*. I think the various groups in Judaism can get along and should get along together to cooperate on certain core issues, for example, creating some minimal standards of Jewish behavior. I may not agree with the point of view of certain groups, but there surely are ways we can interact for the common good of the Jewish people.

After I converted, I initially drifted away a little from traditional Judaism for various reasons. Leading a traditional life meets with some obstacles that can seem insurmountable. Taking time off from work in order to observe the holidays or to get home in time for *Shabbat* can seem too hard—actually, overwhelming sometimes. You have to use vacation time and arrange your schedule to leave early on Friday afternoon. That has been a big hassle for me, even more so recently, since I am working on my B.S., as well as working full time.

Food is another challenge. I love to eat, and I enjoy eating out. I don't call myself a gourmet but I *do* like the food I eat to look good and taste good . . . and sometimes the food from the kosher restaurants in this area leaves a lot to be desired in that department! It would be great to be able to get kosher Indian food or kosher Vietnamese cuisine, or kosher sushi! Things like that really pose challenges to integrating a modern and traditional lifestyle.

I first spoke to my future wife, Becky, on the phone when I was looking for an apartment. She had placed an ad for "room and board in exchange for child care and light housekeeping" in the housing section of the Jewish Information Service. She sounded nice but my work schedule didn't mesh with hers, so nothing came of it. Later that summer, on the night of Tisha B'Av, Becky called a mutual friend with whom I was staying. She was very distraught because her house had been broken into once again and was now surrounded by police. As an ardent feminist and single mother of two, she was a bit chagrined to have to be calling our friend to "get men into the house," but he and I set up camp there for a few days until the police were persuaded to organize a stakeout and the perpetrator was eventually apprehended. Becky and I laughed when we realized that we'd spoken to each other on the phone months before about her ad.

Becky is a warm and welcoming person and always has a houseful of interesting people. I joined a bunch of other people from the neighborhood who would routinely hang out at her house talking, studying together, or watching TV (contingent on parental permission, she made her TV available to the *frum* kids in the area who wanted to watch sports). I had a meal at her house once with friends and I remember that she went out of her way to prepare something kosher that I could eat.

Meanwhile, the daily 5 A.M. train commute I was making to Washington, D.C., was wearing me down physically and interfering with my ability to study and connect with people Jewishly. I shared my concerns with Becky, and she reiterated her proposal for room and board in exchange for child care. "Of all the people who responded to the ad, you were the kindest, gentlest, nicest-sounding one," she said. "Now that we are friends, I still feel the same way."

Halakhically, such an arrangement presented a problem. We struggled with the physical adjustments required to create an acceptable environment for a single man to live in the same house with a woman. Her father counseled her against the arrangement, regaling her with numerous story lines from turn-of-the-century Yiddish theater in which the landlady ends up marrying the boarder! We discussed that possibility and then laughed it off. We were, we told each other, very, very different. We had our own lives, and we were interested in other people.

We did become very good and supportive friends and the four of us really functioned as an extended family in a low-key way. Becky tried her hand to fix me up with someone suitable, and I assessed the appropriateness of each fellow she dated— finding each one to be lacking!

Several years passed in this manner, and we gradually found that our personal styles were beginning to merge. She began making adjustments to keep a more kosher kitchen (until then I'd been existing on a lot of tuna fish, and *Shabbat* meals at other people's houses), and I attended services occasionally at the East Bank Havurah an egalitarian *minyan* where she and the boys were active.

My future father-in-law had been right all along, of course. Having supported each other as housemates through lost jobs, lost loves, the children's nighttime attacks of asthma and illness, one day we both realized that the best person in the world for each of us was already living in the same house. Five years after we'd first spoken on the phone, we announced our engagement.

Nevertheless, I had some serious concerns about the fact that Becky was not *Shomer Shabbat*. I wanted her to become more observant—incrementally. Things like keeping kosher, observing the laws of family purity, keeping *Shabbat* and the holidays fully were very important to me. Other than that, I didn't have a lot of "requirements." Her children, Chad and Ben, both from a former marriage, would live with us. I wanted the boys and any other children we might be able to have—with God's help—to be raised in a traditional household. We all had some adjustments and compromises to make. We continue to work together on it, day by day.

Some people let me know that marrying such a nontraditional, progressive woman might be damaging to my growing sense of *Yiddishkeit*, or my standing in the Orthodox community. But I knew about Becky's background and her character, and I wasn't worried.

Becky comes from an extended family with a very strong rabbinical tradition in Russia. One branch of her family, now living in England, is considered prominent in the Orthodox rabbinate to this day. When her maternal grandfather came to this country at age seventeen, he was already ordained as a rabbi. He died at the age of forty-two, and the second generation gradually became Americanized. While Jewish, they didn't stay tied to Orthodoxy in the same way. Becky's father's family is descended from Rav Kook, but by her grandmother's generation they had become very assimilated. Interestingly, however, some of her paternal cousins have become real pillars in the Reform movement.

Due to her father's work in the nuclear industry, Becky's family often lived in rural areas with small Jewish communities or none at all. But her mother carried on the family's rabbinic tradition by finding Jews wherever they lived. She single-handedly started a Reform synagogue in rural Pennsylvania and served as principal of the religious school. She also served for years as a leader in Hadassah. From my perspective, Becky grew up with a lot of Jewish flavor or *tam*, so to speak, but she didn't get a lot of Jewish education in the traditional sense. Becky's commitment to education, Judaism, and social action, however, is unquestionable. As a special educator and advocate, she has taught for years in various Jewish settings, as well as serving briefly as the Jewish "chaplain" at Gallaudet University for the Deaf in Washington, D.C.

I have always felt more drawn to the Sephardic practice of Judaism, while Becky's background is Ashkenazic.* There is a lot more emotional outpouring in Sephardic Judaism. If you go to a Sephardic synagogue you will see people running up the aisle to kiss the Torah—actually hugging and kissing the Torah—not just touching the Torah with their *tallit* or fingers. It's much more sensuous, much more demonstrative. And coming from an ethnic family, as I do, it feels very familiar to me. I can *daven* in any *shul*, but I prefer to be in the kind of effusive situation I've found most often in a Sephardic synagogue. Becky and I attended a Sephardic synagogue in Rockville, Maryland, during our engagement, and we had the honor of having that rabbi, Rabbi Yossef Chai Kasorla, perform our wedding.

When we got married, we didn't have any money for a fancy wedding. We really didn't want anything posh anyway, so it just involved notifying relatives and enlisting the help of our wonderful friends from the *havurah* and elsewhere. We rented the auditorium at the Hebrew University. We didn't hire a caterer, so the biggest thing logistically was having affordable, kosher food that everyone could eat and enjoy.

We involved Chad and Ben in the wedding by asking them to create a "coming

---

*Sephardic Jews are descendants of Spanish and Portuguese Jews expelled from the Iberian peninsula in 1492. *Ashkenazim* generally share the Jewish cultural heritage that originated among German Jews and spread through their descendants to Eastern Europe.

together" ceremony for our new family, based on the idea that a *Havdalah* candle's intertwining wicks yield more light and heat than do the same number of single candles standing alone. Ben, aged eight, chose long tapers, one black, one yellow, and two brown to represent the color of our respective hair, and Chad, aged nine, wrote the words. We lit each candle separately and then leaned them together until the flames merged. The result was a "roaring" success with a tower of flame that shot up so high we thought the *huppah* would catch fire! There was a lot of joyous laughter under the *huppah* that day.

A wide variety of Jewish and non-Jewish people attended our wedding—a real cornucopia, in fact. There was one man who looked like Jesus, or so said the people who were very observant and lived mainly in the *yeshivah* world. My father-in-law's wonderful comment was, "I've never been in a room with so many different kinds of Jews. They cover the whole spectrum, all the way from Lubavitchers—to me!" Many of the prominent *rabbanim* in town came to the *huppah*. Becky says that's because they like me, but I still think it was because of the special place a *ger* holds as an "orphan" in the community. Either way, it felt very nice because, since our wedding was at the end of December, more friends and relatives had come from Becky's side than from mine.

My wedding gift to Becky was a copy of the "*eshet hayil*"—the description of the "valiant woman" as created by Avraham Cohen, a local artist, calligrapher, and illuminator. As I said to the wedding guests, "That's what Becky really is!" I presented her also with an illuminated *ketubah* made by a fellow up in New Jersey. It was very unusual, and I felt it was a nice solidifying point for the marriage.

So, like everyone else in the world, I'm still in process. Being an observant Jew, a husband, and a father is challenge enough for anyone, but being a "Black Jew" in America makes it that much harder. It can be a fragmenting, dualistic experience, because this society won't let you be both at the same time. The party line says you must be one—or the other. That message, constantly announced loud and clear from all sides—observant, nonobservant, black, and white—is particularly painful for my stepsons. But we are persevering, and letting them all know, "It isn't so!"

18

Teshuvah in a Jewish Family

Ann Blonder

"When biology meets theology, biology wins." So quipped Lena Romanoff, author of *Your People, My People*, at a workshop on intermarriage. Among Jews, intermarriage has been feared as provoking the loss of another, precious Jew. But we should not give up on theology so soon. It tends to follow its own natural course—one might even say, its own God-given course.

What if an intermarriage results in not only the creation of a new Jew but also the return to Judaism of a whole family?

That is the direction Ann Blonder would like to see her family take. It has been painfully slow, she will tell you, but in her conversion to Judaism, Ann discovered a richness that she feels compelled to share with her assimilated Jewish husband and in-laws.

By following her own sense of God's purpose in her life, Ann may bring with her other Jews who perhaps would not have come on their own.

Oh, I would be kosher in a minute. My husband takes issue with it. "You're getting too extreme," he says. How am I extreme? This is my religion; keeping kosher is stated in the Torah. It's just such a simple thing to do.

I married into a wonderful family. God gave me my mother-in-law and my Jewish family, because my mother was all I had, and she died after I was married. My Jewish family is not religiously observant, yet they are very active in the community and have a great reputation. I wish they were more observant. I'm constantly saying, "Excuse me, I believe this family is *Jewish*. Let me explain what we do here." It is interesting that I'm my husband's teacher.

Recently we celebrated a relative's birthday at a friend's house, and to my surprise the party was held on Friday night, even though we are all Jewish. Ordinarily, I never make plans to go out on Friday night, but this party was a must. When we arrived I said "*Shabbat Shalom*," and the host's response was, "Oh, we didn't even realize it was." I was really taken aback. Why couldn't they just have responded politely with "*Shabbat Shalom*" and let it go at that. It shouldn't have surprised me then that there was *treif* (unkosher) food everywhere. I looked at my husband and said, "Don't you dare eat one bite!"

Of course, I grew up with all that, but since I've been Jewish, every year I get more sensitive. I cannot do things anymore that I used to just take for granted. Now

I feel, if you must eat shrimp, at least do that on Thursday night, but not on Friday. And please don't have me at your home if you're going to do that.

After this party, my husband and I went out for a drink and a talk. I told Mike, "I guess every year I'm growing" in my relationship with him and my children. But my religion is the forefront. To keep kosher is the next step. There are so many people I can't invite to our house because I don't keep kosher. On the other hand, our best friends don't keep kosher, and they think I'm completely crazy. To me, though, it is not *just* another thing to do; I'm doing it because it's a covenant with God. It's the same as conversion. You just can't "kind of" convert. You've got to really get involved.

I didn't convert until after we'd been married for a year and a half. I converted in a Reform synagogue and the rabbi said I didn't have to go to the *mikveh*. I turned to Michael and said, "Well, wait a second. When I go to Israel, will I be acknowledged as a Jew?" And he said, "Well, probably not in Israel." And I said, "Well, what if we had girls, and their husbands won't marry them if I don't go to the *mikveh*?" "Oh, they will, Ann." I said, "Well, how do you know that? We don't know that. I'm going to the *mikveh*!"

The day I went the heat was off, and the water was freezing. As I was immersing myself, I yelled to the rabbi, "There's no heat!" "I didn't want to tell you, Ann. You'd be so nervous." As a former Catholic my first thought was, oh, for sure I'm being punished for this!

I was raised in a very Catholic family. I went to Catholic school. I was scared of the nuns, and I knew when I was a little kid that I could *not* really be Catholic. I felt that I was in the wrong religion. I would sweat. The priests and nuns made me so nervous. I didn't think that they were real. Nobody could be that good. I was always so bad, so I could stay away from them. I think I spent most of my school years in the corner. I would do anything to get in trouble. My mother finally took me out of parochial school. When my father told me at sixteen that I didn't have to go to church anymore, I never went back. I hated it. Now, I go to synagogue every Saturday, and I love it!

I know now that church and God are different; religion and God are different. When I was being raised a Catholic, the last thing I wanted to do was to be around God. Now I want to get more connected to God. There are certain things in life one must do to commit to God. There are ways you can do that—through a little bit of discipline and sacrifice. By keeping kosher, by keeping *Shabbat*—to me that's a pure way of doing it.

I think that I should have been born into a Jewish family with Jewish parents. My father is a devout Catholic and is very supportive of my leading a Jewish life. As a divorcé, of course, he can't take any sacraments. Here is a man who goes to church every week and does all the right things, but a divorce is a no-no, and if you've done a no-no in Catholicism, you are punished for life. You can't atone for your sins and start anew. Once you've slid, you've slid. When I was growing up, I had as my philosophy, "If I just keep sliding, maybe I can get away from it." That is not to say the religion is not great for someone else. I have wonderful friends who are Catholic. It is great for them. It's just not for me.

Michael and I are both natives of Georgia. But when I was growing up, I didn't know any Jews and just assumed everybody was the same as me. Our family belonged to country clubs, and I was a debutante. "Coming out" is very upper-class. Here you are, this is the pick of the litter. That kind of feeling. I didn't like that either. I could not conform. My date for the parties was a hippie with long hair—instead of the preferred preppie blond. I'd wear killer purple tights when my mother thought I should wear white or black. So I'd sneak them in my bag. My father insisted that I attend Mt. Vernon College in Washington, D.C.—WASP City—instead of the University of Georgia where I wanted to go. I spent two years in D.C. working for WAFT—Women's Area Feminist Theatre—so I wouldn't have to be on campus. When I became a Jew, all of this need to be rebellious disappeared. I feel most comfortable with Jewish people.

What was also true about my upbringing that people didn't know or acknowledge was that my family was very dysfunctional. When people ask me if I miss Christmas, I have to say, honestly, that I never really cared for it. In a family with substance-abuse problems, Christmas can be very chaotic. When people talk about Christmas as a wonderful time for being with the family, I weep. Now I can enjoy friends' Christmas celebrations, but it is not something I miss in my own life.

Easter, though, does have special memories. The Easter-egg hunt and pretty dresses. My mother was a great seamstress. She was very sick when I was married and died before I converted. She was a Presbyterian, although she never went to church. I think my conversion would have been all right with her. When I first started talking to my dad about it, he said that he thought it was wonderful. "The best thing you can do for your family," he said, "is to have one religion and raise your child with those convictions." I respected that tremendously. A lot of parents would be up in arms as if by choosing a different religion you were denying what they taught you.

Other people I knew from childhood have not been so accepting. My father's friends would say, "Dave, how can you let her do this?" Certain members of my family tried to persuade me not to convert. One of my brothers just couldn't believe that I was giving up Jesus Christ. People have a hard time understanding how I can deny that belief. But I'm not "denying" Jesus. I just don't think he was the son of God. I think that he existed as a great prophet. I *can* agree on that.

My twin brother, Bobby, actually set me up on my first date with my husband. Bobby and I are close, and I was concerned how he would feel when I converted. For years he never said anything to me. He's not great about talking and especially about confrontation. He and my husband are very close friends, and one day when he was over, he said, "So you're still converted, right?" And I said, "Yeah, Bobby, I'm still Jewish." He said, "Well, that's good. That's good, Ann." That was his blessing. I knew he was thinking, "You must be doing something right, because you're both happy, your kids look happy." But it took him a long time.

Interestingly enough, my oldest brother, who was like a father to me growing up, married a Jewish woman. They live in New York and are raising their son as a Jew, although my brother never converted.

On Michael's side of the family, his oldest sister, Dale, converted to Christianity when she was in high school. She's now married to a very conservative guy and raises her children as Christians. I've always felt that she was the most religious Jewish child in Michael's family, but out of rebellion, she got involved in a cult and converted without her parents knowing it. Some people say to me, "Well, you converted and she converted, so what's the difference?" I didn't convert out of rebellion.

Just recently, Michael's brother, Scott, who had always been very troubled, committed suicide. It was a tragedy, devastating to the family. We were all gathered together at Michael's parents' house to sit *shivah*. It was amazing to me to see the response of the Jewish community. For years, Lois and Jerry have given so much of their time and energy to the community. People came every day—sometimes we had as many as one hundred in the house. So, the *shivah* process was exhausting, but also comforting and extremely cleansing, a way of saying good-bye.

When we were first talking about getting married, Michael said, "Oh, it doesn't matter. You can raise our kids Catholic." And I said, "Ugh! How much fun can we have?" Then I met his parents, and I looked at Michael. "Mike, I'm not sure if you are aware of this, but you're Jewish. Do you know this? You have a *Jewish* family." During further discussions of our marriage plans, he said, "I *am* Jewish. I really don't think I could be anything else." I said, "That's good. That's good that you feel that way."

But I didn't convert just to get married. It was I who was going to change my entire life. I had to do some deep soul searching.

When I went to speak to a rabbi, I was so amazed. "Wow! This person is so normal. I can talk to him. He speaks normally. He is married. I could be friends with this person." It was like the lights just went on for me. The conversion classes, though, were sort of like marriage counseling instead of connecting to God. So I didn't love that part of it.

After I converted, I would attend services at a Reform temple, and I would sit and think, "I feel nothing. Why am I not connecting here?" It's too Reform, too nonreligious for me. Now I go to a Conservative synagogue, and I love it. When I go on Saturdays, I feel great, and people know me, including the rabbi. But when I first went to meet the rabbi there, I was a nervous wreck because I still thought a rabbi would be like a priest.

As a child, I was afraid of religion. Even though I'm comfortable being Jewish, I'm still afraid of the religious aspect of it. I don't have the roots to be confident—or even someone close to me to ask about it. I can't turn to my husband for help because although he knows he's Jewish and loves it, he is not knowledgeable about Jewish religious practice. When I go to synagogue, it's all in Hebrew with some English. I know some of it, I don't know all of it, but it doesn't matter. At first, though, I wouldn't even say the prayers out loud, and I always sit in the back. I say to myself, "Next year, I need to move up three more rows. Come on, Ann, if you moved up three, by the time you're sixty, you'll be right up in front!"

But I am gaining confidence. I feel a spirituality. I know that *kashrut* is next. Whatever God is doing, it's like He's telling me that this is my next step. My heart agrees. I'm doing things little by little. This has to be my evolution. Our house will never be a very religiously observant home, but we can be more consistent.

After my marriage, I joined my mother for a Junior League meeting. I realized, "I'm in the wrong place. This is not my world anymore. I have to be in a Jewish organization." I walked out and never went back.

So I called my mother-in-law, and said, "Lo, I have to get into a Jewish group. What do I do? I don't want to play mah-jongg." She said, "Join Brandeis."* So I did. A very close friend of mine, also a convert, was the president that year. After twiddling my thumbs for a long while, being seated at luncheons next to the gentile women married to Jewish guys, I said, "This doesn't make any sense. I need to get to know some Jewish girlfriends." I called my friend, the president, and said, "Can I volunteer to do something?" "Oh, sure. You want to work on the book sale?" Of course I didn't know what I was getting into at the time!

I always felt very welcomed and was always signed up for all the hard work. But socially, I was not invited to any parties or other get-togethers in the Jewish community. This had nothing to do with me. It was because Michael had few Jewish friends. Most of his friends from college are gentiles. So I started to get to know Jewish couples, and we slowly became friends with them. Now, of course, Michael's more involved in the Jewish community, with our children's school and other things.

Our children attend a Conservative Jewish day school. I made this decision before we had children. Michael had attended public school and then Hebrew school afternoons and weekends. He hated it. Why should our children do what he hated? But who was going to teach them the things they needed to know? I don't have a Jewish history, a Jewish past. If you don't have a *bubbe* coming over with chicken soup on Friday night, who's going to give the children what they need? Michael can't because his family didn't give him many stories.

I'm very proud of the fact that the children attend a Jewish day school. It makes me feel good, and they love it. Michael and I are both very involved. I do anything they ask of me: fund-raisers, the ad-campaign book and silent auction for the founders' dinner, the bistro night where artists come to sell their work, and I've worked as a teacher's aide in the classroom. I'm a professional volunteer! I have a very comfortable life, and I'm not one to sit still. I really believe that it is important for me to give back to the community, since it has been extremely generous to me.

Being Jewish is not easy. Sometimes I'm asked to speak about my conversion and life as a Jew. People come up afterward, sometimes in tears, saying that their son or daughter is going to marry a gentile and they wish that person felt as I do. That makes me sad. "You don't want them to be Jewish unless they want to be Jewish," I tell them. Given my background and my life, this was just a natural course for me. A

---

*A women's social service organization that, among other activities, conducts annual book fairs.

friend of mine told me that a theater agent in New York who knew me before I was married wasn't surprised when he heard that I had converted and was raising a Jewish family. "I knew she was going to marry a Jewish guy! I knew she was always Jewish, that girl." He saw what was going to happen to me!

The hardest thing for me about being Jewish is talking everybody else in the family into being Jewish. After all the dysfunction in my early life, one of the things that appealed to me so much about Judaism is that it's very stable, very sensible, and practical. It's not, "Let's go on Sunday to pray"; it's a day-to-day thing. I can lock into that, and take a step further with *kashrut*. For me, that is another extension toward God. My husband doesn't understand. He is already so grounded. He doesn't need to extend one more step to God. He already feels what he feels. I think he'll get there. I just keep slowly at it—not putting too much pressure on him.

19

Tumah and *Taharah*

Rivkah Libby Bottero

When Libby met me in Eugene, Oregon, she had just returned from a work-shop on Jewish women's spirituality with Rabbi Leila Gal Berner, her congregation's *Shabbaton* guest. Libby had enjoyed the morning's lecture and discussion on issues of Judaism and feminism; she was especially impressed by the rabbi's depth of knowledge as well as the depth of her compassion and concern for others, including her responses to the heartfelt questions of individual children in her congregation. As represented by the teachings of this liberal woman rabbi, Libby's soul has evolved, finding stability in tradition and freedom in creative new rituals, through living life to facing death—from *tumah* to *taharah*.*

In my family, my father was an Episcopalian and my mother was a convert to Catholicism. My mother wanted something in her life that had more depth and meaning for her than the Protestant denomination into which she had been born. She had always been drawn to the Church and became a very liberal and social-activist Catholic. So, when I chose to become Jewish, my parents understood my feelings, and I didn't have any trouble at all with my family. They are very accepting, open-minded, and open-hearted folks. I feel very blessed to have such a loving family.

During the years when I was growing up and attending various churches, I often had a feeling that I didn't quite fit in as a Christian, that I didn't quite belong, but I didn't know why. By the age of twelve or thirteen, the time for "confirmation of faith," I was really struggling with certain aspects of church doctrine, such as the Trinity, but I had to follow my own conscience. Finally, I just had to say, "Okay, God, I don't know what you want me to do, but I don't think this is it, so you're just going to have to let me know, and I'll keep searching."

The other feeling that I had for as long as I could remember was that I'd been alive before and died during the Holocaust. I knew this with some inner certainty

---

Tumah and *taharah* refer to states of *ritual* impurity and *ritual* purification, respectively. The *First Jewish Catalog* (p. 167) notes: "Tumah is the result of our confrontation with the fact of our own mortality. It is the going down into darkness. Taharah is the result of our reaffirmation of our own immortality. It is the reentry into light." Immersion in the *mikveh*, "simulates the original living water, the primal sea from which all life comes" (ibid., p. 170) and results in the state of *taharah*.

from an early age, and it did not seem unusual to me. I was happy to have another chance at life.

I was born in 1947 and grew up in the military, so every kid I knew had a dad who'd been in World War II. Many soldiers had seen the camps and knew what happened there. When we were stationed in Europe in the mid-fifties, we went to Dachau. Military families and schools made sure that we children knew the truth about the war and its aims. Later, when I was an adolescent in the United States, I went to a civilian public school for the first time. It was a shock to me to discover that some people didn't have much understanding or concern about the Holocaust and other aspects of the war, such as the Japanese internment camps in this country—things that I assumed everyone knew. This really disturbed me, the attitude of turning a blind eye toward evil in the world; it was so foreign to the values and environment in which I'd grown up.

Several years ago, we had a Pacific Northwest Jewish Women's Conference at a *moshav* in Oregon, Shivtei Shalom (Living in Peace). Rabbi Ayla Grafstein made a video there about Jews by Choice called *Bat Sarah* (Daughter of Sarah). Most of us had been born shortly after World War II and although we all came from different backgrounds on our paths to Judaism, a common theme in the stories of the women in that group was the sense many of us had of having been in the Holocaust. Few of us were very much surprised by that.

Recently at the Jewish Renewal Kallah, I met Rabbi Ze'ev Chaim Feyer, an extraordinary teacher from Atlanta. He is deeply interested in the stories and spiritual journeys of people who felt reincarnated from the Holocaust. He'd had similar experiences himself and really understood. This was an affirmation of what has been an important part of my Jewish identity.

When I was eighteen I married a man who happened to be Jewish. He was trying to get away from his fairly traditional family, but I didn't realize that at the time. Although the marriage did not work out, I've remained close with his family, who are really fine people. The first Pesah *seder* I ever attended was at the home of his Aunt Ruth and Uncle Harry. It was a wonderful experience for me, and, in fact, Pesah is still my favorite of all the Jewish holidays! Unfortunately, it did not please my husband that I found interesting what he was attempting to reject.

At nineteen, I became pregnant. We were living in Seattle and didn't have any money, but I was just so happy to be pregnant and full of life. Many women will be able to identify with the deep insights and feelings that I experienced during pregnancy. Suddenly, I felt intimately connected to all life in the universe—those flowers in the garden, the stars in the sky, this baby inside—they're all connected. And I was really thirsting for some way to express those feelings for the greater Life Force that were at the core of my being.

One Friday night after seeing a movie, we were walking down the street past a building with lights in the windows and people singing. I said to my husband, "Oh, I have to go in there! I know that song!" I didn't even know it was a synagogue, but I was drawn inside, irresistibly, and my husband followed me reluctantly. The song the people were singing was *"Adon Olam"* ("Lord of the World," a traditional *Shabbat* song), and I can still remember the moment of hearing it. It seemed as if all these candles (actually just electric *menorahs*) were lit up, stretching back and back through time, and my candle was there too! Then I understood: "Ohhhh! This is what I've been looking for!" I had made that deal with God a few years before: "You're going to have to show me." And now my prayer was being answered. I was so thrilled, and my soul just opened up. There was a very familiar feeling like when you meet someone and it's as if you've always known them, or you go some place, and it seems you've been there before. I knew I was home.

I began to attend services at that little *shul* every *Shabbat* morning, and I met with the rabbi there, Rabbi Maurice Corson, every week. Of course, he tried to discourage me at first, but I was determined to convert. I'll never forget the first book he gave me; it was Abraham Joshua Heschel's *The Earth Is the Lord's* and *The Sabbath* in one volume. I loved it and proceeded to read everything I could find by Heschel. Every week I'd come to the rabbi's office, and he'd give me more wonderful books to read, and we'd talk. That *shul* is long gone now, and I'm sad to say that I've lost track of Rabbi Corson, but I'd very much like to reconnect with him.

In the spring of 1968, about three weeks before my son, Asher, was born, I went to the *mikveh* for the first time. I was really looking forward to this. It was truly awesome. I just loved the experience, and I've been going to the *mikveh* ever since. After the *mikveh* we returned to the synagogue to sign the conversion papers. It was a Sunday morning. The night before there had been a wedding at the synagogue and the *huppah* was still up. The rabbi was so sweet; he said, "Well, as long as we've got three *Shomer Shabbat* witnesses here, and you're going to have this baby and you've just come from the *mikveh*, the *huppah* will only take five minutes." So, he married us, we signed the *ketubah*, and the witnesses all signed. A month later we celebrated Asher's *brit milah*, done by the *mohel* at our apartment in Seattle.

This was all very wonderful for me, but my husband was very distressed. He did not feel ready to handle the responsibilities of being a husband or a father, nor did he want to have anything to do with Judaism at that time. A few weeks later he left. So as a single mother with a new baby, I returned to the San Francisco Bay Area, where my family lived, and they helped me out a lot. Fortunately, a bad marriage did not dissuade me from Judaism.

I wanted to explore the many worlds of Jewish experience. I was just on the first steps of my journey, so I began going to different synagogues and different denominations around the Bay Area. Eventually I found the House of Love and Prayer, which had been founded the year before by Rabbi Shlomo Carlebach in San Francisco.

Rabbis are first and foremost teachers and some few have the gift to be spiritual leaders. Throughout history there have been rabbis who have been shining lights and have gathered about them followers whom they have inspired and who have inspired them—in Judaism spiritual enlightenment is definitely a two-way street. There have been many Jewish spiritual teachers who have had an effect on my life. As a young person at a vulnerable and receptive time of my life, three stand out now in my memory: Reb Shlomo, Rabbi Zalman Schachter-Shalomi, and Rabbi David Din, may his memory be for a blessing.

It was 1968, and young people were flocking to San Francisco from all over the country in search of free love, free dope, spiritual enlightenment, communal living, protesting the draft, and social change. Shlomo saw that many Jews were yearning for a meaningful spiritual path, yet were looking everywhere but Judaism. He wanted to open people's hearts and minds to the depths of Jewish life, to turn us on to Torah. He did it through music, storytelling, Jewish mysticism, serving God with joy, and a nonjudgmental acceptance of people, wherever they might be on their spiritual journey.

Rabbi Shlomo Carlebach is a great teacher and a master at giving "soul food," knowing what each holy beggar needs. It is my great privilege to know Reb Shlomo and to have lived at the House of Love and Prayer for a couple of years. Some of the people I met there are still among my close friends; it's a unique and wonderful community and the source of many blessings in my life, for which I'm very grateful. Shlomo also did a very big favor for me. When my conversion papers were lost in a fire, Shlomo went with me to the old San Francisco *mikveh* and redid the immersion ceremony and provided me with a new conversion certificate. This may not seem like a big deal here, but one really needs it in Israel, as I would come to find out.

Reb Zalman, sometimes referred to as the "father" of the *havurah*/Jewish Renewal movement and founder of P'nai Or, is one of Shlomo's oldest colleagues and friends from *yeshivah* days. Zalman's great genius, vision, and scholarship, his support for creative rituals and *havurot* such as the Berkeley Aquarian Minyan, his strong commitment to making tradition accessible and relevant, his wisdom and humor and love for *klal Yisrael*, all contribute to an exciting vibrant growing Jewish Renewal community. It is also my privilege and honor to know Reb Zalman as both teacher and friend over the years. It was Zalman who taught me how to lay *tefillin*. Now twenty years later, as an example of the *tikkun olam* of eco-kosher vegetarianism (*kashrut* based on ecological concerns), Zalman has suggested that those of us who object to the use of leather make our *tefillin* from nonanimal sources instead of giving up the *mitzvot* of *tefillin*.

These two rabbis are great lights of our generation, and both of these great souls, Zalman and Shlomo, continue to have a profound impact on my life.

Rabbi David Din was yet another teacher who was an inspiration to me. He helped bring many *baalei teshuvah* close to the Holy One through his teachings of the Torah, *Kabbalah*, meditation, and observance of *mitzvot*. David had a beautiful, compassionate, luminous *neshamah* (soul), despite his personal suffering. He, too, was a student of Shlomo and Zalman, founder of Sha'arei Ora (Gates of Light) Community for Judaic and Mystical Studies, and my much-beloved soul brother. *Barukh HaShem*, his loving presence is felt beyond space and time.

In 1970, I decided to go to Israel. First, of course, I wanted to go to all those holy places, especially Jerusalem. Second, I had been an *agunah*, an abandoned wife, for two years, and I was seeking a *get*, a religious divorce, from my husband, who now lived in Israel. In a complete reversal from his earlier disdain of Jewish practice while he and I were together, he had become a Lubavitcher* during a period of deep depression in his life. I believe the world of the *Chabad hasidim* offered him some structure and security when he was in the grip of inner chaos and despair, and he has remained in this community for more than twenty years. But his newfound commitment to Orthodoxy in Israel, added to his complex personality, made what could have been a relatively simple process quite complicated.

According to Orthodox *halakhah*, the right of divorce is given only to the husband, not the wife, and the woman must receive a *get* from her husband. It does not matter what the circumstances of the separation are—that he abused her, left her, refused to suppport the family. And a woman is not able to remarry, should she wish to, without a *get*. Some women are trapped or, in Hebrew, "anchored," for the rest of their lives by recalcitrant husbands and the unsympathetic Israeli religious courts, who for reasons of political control insist on upholding the letter of the law. Women have no rights on this issue in the religious courts, and the extortion of large sums of money from a woman's family is not uncommon in order to effect the issuing of the *get* from the husband.

This was my first introduction to the political and social injustice of the system of religious courts in Israel. Coming from the United States, where there is a Constitution guaranteeing separation of church and state, I was dismayed to find out that a civil divorce was not possible, that women and children had no rights whatsoever. Absolute authority resided in the patriarchy. I was appalled by the abuse and corruption of the Orthodox rabbis, by the humiliating and costly ordeal.

After several months I did eventually succeed in obtaining a *get* from my husband at the *Bet Din* in Yerushalayim. If I had to do it over again, I wouldn't allow myself to be so intimidated; in fact, today, I would simply write *him* a *get* after obtaining a civil decree. That whole experience and the suffering it caused really opened my eyes to the traditional power structure and was probably responsible for turning me into a Jewish feminist.

I left Israel and tried living in a traditional community in New York for a while but was very unhappy. After that, I left Orthodoxy over issues of sexism, racism, and lack of environmental concern in the religious fundamentalist worldview. I returned to the West Coast, went to nursing school, got a job in a hospital, and tried to get on with my life. By the time my son was in second or third grade, I wanted a more peaceful, healthy place for us to be, so we moved to Oregon in 1976 and we've been here ever since.

When we first moved to Oregon, we were living in a rural area, and I was not very involved in the local Jewish community. My observance fluctuated somewhat over time, but certain things I held on to, like keeping kosher, lighting *Shabbat* candles and saying *Kiddush*, and observing *mikveh* by going to rivers and the ocean. Other things, such as wearing *tzitzit* and laying *tefillin*, I let go of or did less often. After a

---

*Lubavitchers are a branch of hasidic Judaism.

while, I began to look around for a rabbi who could teach my son what he would need to know for his *bar mitzvah*, and also I wanted to find a Jewish community where I felt comfortable again.

Eventually, we joined Temple Beth Israel in Eugene, Oregon. Our rabbi at TBI, Rabbi Myron Kinberg, is Reconstructionist, and his wife, Alice Haya Kinberg, is very much a feminist. Together they involve themselves in all kinds of social justice and peace issues. Alice and Myron Kinberg epitomize for me the ideal of Jewish commitment to *tikkun olam,* repair of the world, and *kedushah,* holiness in daily life. It was wonderful to come here and participate in an egalitarian *minyan,* to read from the *sefer Torah*! (the Torah scroll).

Especially important in any Jewish community is the formation of a *hevrah kadishah,* (lit. "holy friendship"), the people of the community who prepare the body after death for burial, and that was one of the first areas in which I became involved. As a nurse, I've worked with dying patients, so it seemed natural to extend care by washing and preparing the body, sometimes helping to dig the grave and bury the individual as well. One cannot look death in the face without facing one's own mortality in the most intimate way. Most of the people serving in our *hevrah kadishah* tend to be in the healing professions, perhaps because we are already familiar with the dying process.

The essence of the *taharah*, purification, is washing the body; then we dress the person in a plain white cotton or linen shroud. Traditional prayers and customs are part of the ritual ceremony and we generally use plain wooden coffins made by a member of our congregation.

Recently, a close friend passed away after a long illness. He had lived for many years on a farm outside of town. His friends and family were at home with him during his last few days. He died at about eight in the morning with his family at his bedside. The *hevrah kadishah* carried him outside and performed the *taharah* under a nearby oak tree; then he was wrapped in a white cotton sheet. His son made a simple plywood litter that we used to carry his father up the hill to a section of the property that had been dedicated as a cemetery. A neighbor came with a backhoe and dug the grave; into the grave, one of his daughters scattered straw and wool from the sheep he had raised. Several rabbis were there, including another daughter, and people shared some of their memories of him during the service. Then we lowered him down into the earth with ropes, and everyone took turns with the shovels. By four in the afternoon, the burial was completed and we walked back to the house together for a meal of consolation. It's very meaningful to participate so directly, somewhat like being at a home birth, and it's a great comfort to the families.

I also joined a Rosh Hodesh group in Eugene and met a wonderful circle of intelligent, sensitive Jewish women who enjoyed God-wrestling/Goddess-worshiping and supporting one another. Some of these women are also involved in the *hevrah kadishah* and we sometimes accompany each other to *mikveh*, whether natural streams, springs, or hot tubs filled with rainwater. *Mikveh* is such a deep experience, immersing in the life-giving, womb-waters of our Mother, and I'm so happy to share it with my friends. Reb Nachman, a famous *hasidic* rabbi of the late eighteenth century, taught that *mikveh* water is connected to the rivers coming out of Gan Eden, the Garden of Eden, and to the Oneness of God—such deep and beautiful spiritual symbolism! I suppose it is no surprise that there is an overlapping group of us sisters sharing in all these areas—we often celebrate those intimate moments of life together in prayer and song, from birth to death. Sometimes we need to create our own feminist rituals when it is not provided for in the tradition, for times such as miscarriage or abortion, adoption, menarche and menopause, and so on. We encourage and empower each other and we learn together.

About ten years ago, I met a wonderful man, my soul mate, best friend, and lover: Joseph! He, too, is a convert to Judaism, so we really appreciate making a Jewish home together. When we first met in the Goodwill Store in Corvallis, it was as if we really knew, "This is it! You're the one I've been looking for all my life!" The funny thing is that our kids were friends, and for years we lived only a few blocks from each other, but I guess we met at the right time because we've been happy together ever since.

I am reminded of the *hasidic* story of a poor man who dreamed that he should go to Krakow to find his treasure. When he got to the bridge of the city, a guard laughed at him and said that he'd also had a dream about a man from his village who found a treasure under the stove of his own little house. Of course when the man returned to his village sure enough there was the treasure right under his roof the whole time!

When we got married in the courtyard of the synagogue, it seemed like all the angels in heaven were blessing us along with our families, friends, and rabbis. Like many couples, we used an egalitarian *ketubah*, which is a meaningful contract for us. It is hard to express in words how wonderful it is, what a deep sense of contentment we share, and what a joy it is to be with someone who shares the same values. Our love continues to be a garden of blessings for us, thank God.

Joseph already had several grown children when we met. His daughter, Rebecca, got married about a year after we did. When we received the invitation we realized the wedding date was on Yom Kippur. We called to congratulate the happy couple and said, "You probably don't realize it, but the date you picked is Yom Kippur." "Yes," she said. "You told us it was the holiest day of the whole year and that the wedding day is supposed to be like Yom Kippur—that's partly why we chose it!" So, of course, we went and it was the highest Yom Kippur ever, a taste of the messianic age. Joseph's son, Jacob, is a chef and had made a wedding cake and on top the hands of the high priest giving the priestly blessing in white icing. The officiating minister was a former Hell's Angel who arrived on his Harley-Davidson. The wedding was on a high bluff overlooking the great Columbia River at a replica of Stonehenge built by Sam Hill as a memorial to the fallen soldiers of World War I. Simply glorious. It was the only time we've not fasted on Yom Kippur, yet we could hear "*kadosh, kadosh, kadosh*" (holy, holy, holy).

Joseph and I have worked on some projects together such as researching and putting together a guide for the *hevrah kadishah*. Now, we're working on a guide for how to build your own *mikveh*, a project close to both our hearts. Most *mikvaot* today are controlled by the Orthodox, who often will not allow their use for conversions by non-Orthodox rabbis, nor do they permit unmarried women to use the *mikveh*, although men can use it whenever they want. We envision a more open and "user-friendly" *mikveh*, without the power trips. I still think that one of the best introductions to *tumah*, *taharah*, and *mikveh* is Rachel Adler's article in the *First Jewish Catalog*.

Joseph and I also had the opportunity recently to study Hebrew together at Ulpan Akiva* in Netanya, Israel, which is an extraordinary place where Jews, Muslims, and Christians come together to learn to communicate with each other.

Being a Jewish woman is such a core part of my identity, I can't even imagine what my life might be like had I not converted to Judaism, or to use Mordecai Kaplan's term, Jewish civilization, which I believe is flourishing. I am not so worried about assimilation and Jews "marrying out." That has happened throughout history. I rejoice in the realistic and ethical decisions of the Reform movement to include patrilineal descent and for Jewish communities to become more welcoming of gays/lesbians, interfaith, and nontraditional families. And I think that converts bring perspectives of cultural diversity along with our commitment to Judaism, which enriches the vast and beautiful tapestry of Jewish life. My own life has been deeply enriched by the teachers and friends I've met along this spiritual path, for which I'm very grateful.

I feel very blessed.

---

*Hebrew school named after Rabbi Akiva, an early Jewish scholar who had a famous school in nearby Safed and who was murdered by the Romans.

20

"The Convertible"

Martin Disney

I interviewed Marty Disney in the office I use for my psychotherapy practice. He sat on the edge of the paisley couch with his overcoat folded in a neat package on his lap, politely refusing my offer to hang the coat for him. I felt Marty might bolt at any minute. At first, I wondered if he was nervous about the interview, but later it occurred to me that this must be his posture at the interviews he conducts in the homes of victims or perpetrators of crimes in his job as homicide detective for the Baltimore city police.

It is intense and depressing work, and Marty and the other detectives blow off tension with hard-edged humor. When he became a Jew, his police buddies dubbed him "the convertible."

Marty is a large man, beefy. The kind of person you would want to avoid in a dark alley—or hide behind if the going got rough. As we talked, he did relax, but he stayed on the edge of his seat with his coat, ready to leave in a hurry if things got ugly and out of hand.

If the picture of his professional life is like a mug shot, by contrast, his view of life as a Jew is a technicolor vision, bringing glimpses of order, justice, and peace to his existence. As many Jews by Choice do, he rues the pulls away from observance and looks forward to Monday, February 27, of the year 2000, his retirement date from the police force, when he will be able to live more fully as a Jew.

When I was a child, my mother, a born Lutheran, went through a period in which she was searching for a religion. She took us to various services: Episcopalian, Baptist. We went to every religion except Catholicism and Judaism. She was toying with, I guess, getting more involved in religion, but not in the strict sense both of those faiths would mandate. She was looking for more of a social community. So I saw everything from revivals to people speaking in tongues—it was a real eye-opener. When I was about eleven years old we joined the Reformation Lutheran Church that was a couple of blocks from our house. She had started out Lutheran and came back to it.

Through most of my adolescence, my Sunday-school teacher was a born Jew who converted to Christianity. So in December, we learned about Christmas *and* Hanukkah, and then we learned about Easter *and* Pesah. I vividly remember playing *dreidl* in church and eating potato *latkes*. My mind was stimulated by Judaism—the family aspects and the tradition and the heritage and the fact that the people are very proud and very determined. My teacher was in her fifties then. I never really found out why she left Judaism, but she was a very prominent image during my adolescent period.

In my teens, I began reading about Judaism but on a very superficial plane. It was interesting research, and it was a little flare in my head, but there was no conception of switching religions at that point. I wasn't going to tell my parents, "Look, I want to convert to Judaism." That just wouldn't have gone over too well when I was fifteen years old. In fact, I was very involved in the church and at different points I was thinking about going into the seminary.

I did believe in Christ as savior when I was young. As I grew older I started thinking of him more as a very charismatic man who lived in a time when people needed something to believe in. He was probably very learned—a very wise rabbi—and a tremendous public speaker. I think he was a breath of fresh air, not the "one and only." Miracles? I don't have any idea. I think a lot of things are exaggerated over time, and there are any number of explanations for things that he did. He definitely was real, but as the son of God? I'm certainly not qualified to debate on that. My own belief is he was just a very knowledgeable, charismatic person.

I don't think Christians as a whole spend time thinking about their religion, but neither do the majority of Jews. In my opinion, however, Judaism is more of a way of life than Christianity. Growing up, I saw many Christians going to church on Sunday, and moments before leaving they would "check" their Christianity at the door, to be picked up again the following Sunday. I don't believe the community of Christians is spending a lot of time pondering the divinity of Christ. I'm not speaking of the devoutly religious. In all religions the devout clearly have their own agendas. But the everyday church-going Christian, believer in the Father, Son, and the Holy Ghost, is not spending a large part of every day thinking about it. Anyway, this is my thinking and how I rationalize things in my mind.

I think most of us leave religion for a period of time—things get kind of hazy with religion from about eighteen to twenty-five. I went into the service, and I married a Catholic girl in a Lutheran church. Her parents didn't come because they didn't like me. We had a baby, Sarah, who was baptized in the Lutheran church. Colleen, my former wife, never did belong to any specific church. She had gone to Catholic schools and had a good Catholic education in a strict religious environment but got no reinforcement at home. Like many people she got saturated to a point where she needed a break. So when the idea of religion between the two of us did come up, she was fine attending services in the Lutheran church. We didn't go often, but we did some Bible study groups and things like that.

Midway through my twenties, though, I began thinking about Judaism again and started to seek out more information about conversion. I mentioned it to Colleen a couple of times, and she said, "Well, if you really want to that's fine, but I won't and it's going to be a very difficult thing." So it was put on hold again, and I didn't really do anything about it.

What I was beginning to realize was that my religion just wasn't fulfilling to me.

I had this feeling that your religious life also ties in with your daily life, and as a Christian I always felt that you live your Christianity on Sundays and on major holidays; the rest of the time you're pretty much on your own. As a Jew, you pretty much live your religion on a daily basis, and it's a deep inner feeling—a perception—that is different for everyone who is Jewish. And I'm sure every Christian has a different perception of their religion. Christianity just wasn't that much of a commitment for me. That's probably what was the catalyst for my eventual conversion.

I joined the police department in 1980, so I've worked there the major portion of my adult life. Through my work off and on I'd meet Jewish people, not necessarily Orthodox or very religious people. I began to have a pretty good idea of what to expect and what the religion was going to be about. The possibility of becoming Jewish was there all the while lying dormant in my brain. And I always remember that woman—the Sunday-school teacher.

So, I began reading. I read *To Be a Jew*, and I've read most of the *Jewish Books of Why*. Just about this time my first marriage ended—for a lot of reasons. My schedule at work is horrendous, her work schedule . . . and we just drifted apart over the years. With the marriage over, I could pretty much do as I wanted for the first time.

About a year later, I met Debbie, who is a born Jew. We were working out at the same gym. We started talking right away about being Jewish, and I started talking to her about my desire for conversion. She went through a double master's program in social work and Jewish studies. I figured that since she has broader knowledge than most Jews because she has a degree in Jewish history, she might have a little more of an inside track on this conversion business. She had a wealth of books, as you can imagine.

Debbie was amazed that anyone would want to convert to Judaism. I get amazement a lot: "Why would you want to do this?" I don't understand why anyone questions it, but then again, I would question why anyone would want to convert to being a Lutheran. Anyway, Debbie put me in touch with Rabbi Jim Rosen, whom she knew from working at Chizuk Amuno. I talked with Jim, and he tried to discourage me. Basically he wanted to let me know that it's not something you want to do on a whim. The process of conversion itself is long, and it takes a degree of responsibility and commitment. He wanted to find out my sincerity level and what kind of commitment I was willing to make.

So, I enrolled in an Introduction to Judaism class, which Debbie and I attended together. And I studied with Jim Rosen every couple of weeks. About six months later he told me I was ready. I said, "Wait a minute! No, no—I don't know anything yet." He said, "Yes, you are ready."

So, in March of 1988, I went through the ritual of circumcision. That in and of itself was a harrowing experience. It's just a small cut—just to get a drop of blood. But it's a definite thing to remember!

Then you go to the *Bet Din*. I walked down the hall to meet with these three rabbis who were going to grill me on my knowledge for the next hour, and I was thinking, "If I fail, I've just been cut for nothing. I'm going to go back and get an aggravated assault warrant for the *mohel* and rough him up!" But no—I went through the tribunal and did really well. It was the first time in my life I felt I was really "on." They were asking questions, and I was very comfortable giving the answers. I was very relaxed, and, after about two minutes into it, all my fears and anxieties just started to melt, and I was actively engaging them in discussions. The two other rabbis besides Jim Rosen complimented me on my knowledge—and that was pretty special! It was a very gratifying feeling. Then I went to the *mikveh* and into one of the chapels to say the *Shema* and that was it. It was a very positive experience.

I had been apprehensive, of course, because I didn't know everything. But you don't realize that you'll never know everything. Having been a Lutheran, I already knew a lot about religion. And what does that denomination date back to—the 1500s? So what you have in the Lutheran religion is four hundred years old. In Judaism, what you have is thousands of years old with many, many, many different interpretations. As a prospective convert, you don't know that you'll never know it all. But you think you should and you might, so that when they tell you that you're ready to convert, you say, "Give me a break. I don't feel comfortable with all this." But it was absolutely a very positive experience. It felt like a whole shadow of doubt about my direction had been lifted after that. It was one of the best feelings I've ever experienced besides the birth of my children.

Debbie's mother and father accepted me right off, and her sister and brother did as well. In fact, when I went through the conversion process, her mother sent me flowers. It was a bouquet tied to a can of chicken soup for the circumcision part. They have been very supportive. I don't think her dad fully understands why I converted. He grew up in what I would consider a "wing-it" type of Jewish family. They had ham in the house, and it was go and do your *bar mitzvah*, and that's about it. Debbie's mom grew up in an Orthodox household. And Debbie grew up attending a Conservative *shul*.

Debbie and I were married a year after my conversion. We have two children now, Adina and Jordan. Sarah, my oldest, is eleven, and she lives with her mom not far from me. Colleen wanted Sarah to convert to her religion, Catholicism. Sarah lives with her mother so it makes sense. I'm a strong believer in a good religious foundation, whatever it is. When the child is of legal age she can make a decision about what she wants for the rest of her life. So I went with Colleen and Sarah to see the priest. And he asked Sarah, "Do you know why you're here?" And she said, "Yes." "Can you tell me why you want to be a Catholic?" Sarah said she didn't want to be a Catholic; "I want to be a Jew." Sarah was nine at the time, and I had just converted. Her mother looked at me as if this was all my fault. But I told Sarah, "Look, you live with your mom; you have to go with your mom's religion now. Whenever you come over to my house, you can have *Shabbat* dinner with us and say your prayers. Learn both religions, but your religion is going to be Catholicism, and you'll have a real strong knowledge of what's going on through that religion, and when you're old enough then you can make your own choices."

The priest was pretty nice. Pretty modern. He had been to some functions with some sort of Catholic–Jewish dialogue, so he was into going to Friday night services from time to time. He wasn't in shock and crossing himself as an older priest might have done. So there wasn't too much of a problem there. Sarah went through the conversion process into Catholicism and had her holy communion and things like that. I was there for that. I'm not up on the Catholic religion that much, but she has gone through different stages of her precatechism. She now goes to Notre Dame Prep, so I'll have two in Hebrew school and one in Catholic school.

As far as the relationship with my parents goes, I think it's pretty typical of the firstborn son—them against me. We fought until I was old enough to leave. After I left, then they wanted a relationship. I have some bad memories, some lasting scars, that are for *me* to deal with, to work through. I developed a very bad habit in relationships, and my career feeds off of it: keeping people at arm's length. I build walls and block people out. It's a hard habit to break because I can insulate myself from being hurt. Anyway, my parents seem to be changing, and I, too, see that I must make an effort—for them and for my children. I will not, however, be vulnerable.

My mother wasn't surprised at my conversion. She said, "Well, you don't surprise me; you always did go ahead and do what you set out to do." What did surprise her was that I didn't tell them I was going through the process. I just said, "I did it"; I didn't say anything else. My father was baptized a Catholic but he never went to church. Then they got involved in the Lutheran church. Now I think they go to the church up the street, mainly to accumulate some friends. They pretty much lost their friends thoughout the years and don't have a whole lot of people besides themselves. So I think going to church is more of a social thing, and that's fine.

I'm very close to my aunt and my grandmother. My aunt, whom I expected to be very shocked, was actually pretty cool about the whole thing. In fact, she had been to a couple of *Shabbat* dinners and even had been to a *seder*. It really amazed me because nobody ever knew about that. When she was working, she had had a boss who was Jewish, and after my uncle died in 1965, this guy became kind of close to my aunt, although she never got involved with anyone but my uncle. But apparently she had gone to his family's house for some *Shabbat* dinners and some *seders*. When I told her, I was at her house helping her to clean out her basement. And I decided I was going to tell her, since I hadn't told anyone. She was making me lunch and she said, "Does this mean you won't eat the ham sandwich I just made for you?" And I said, "Well, for you, I'll do it, but this will be the last time; I won't do it any longer."

My grandmother, on the other hand, was very surprised. I didn't tell her for a long time, and that hurt her, I think, because she already knew. She found out from her sister and my mother and everybody else, I'm sure. When I finally did tell her, she let me know how upset she was that I had not told her before.

There's some anti-Semitism in my family. That just extends back to their German heritage and their probable ignorance of people different from themselves, be it Jews, be it blacks, be it Japanese. It doesn't really matter; they are all lumped into the same group—them against us. I don't know why I'm different, not prejudiced. I think it's my laid-back personality and the fact that before I became a cop, everybody was my friend. I made friends very easily and talked to everyone—it didn't matter who they were.

Now I'm very cynical. The police work has done quite a bit to me. I meet people and because of what I see on a day-to-day basis, I assume initially that they are evil until they prove otherwise. I see the horrendous things that people are capable of. The people I deal with every day are basically the dregs of the earth, and it's a shame. They have all sorts of extenuating circumstances that make them the people that they are. I see that, I understand that, but, come on, let's get with the program. You've got kids with guns—eleven and twelve years old—shooting people because they want to know what it feels like. The young kids have no conscience whatsoever, no remorse. They become heroes in their peer groups for "capping"—shooting—someone. We are losing whole generations of people. It's beyond me. This business really drags you down and makes you a pessimist on life and very cynical.

The job is just incredible in so many ways. I generally work from seventy-five to ninety hours a week. I've already worked 800 hours of overtime this year. The national average for homicide detectives is three to five murders a year; I've been out on seventeen so far this year. That's not to mention the suicides, the serious assaults, the extortions, bomb threats, school threats, and threats on political officials and everything else we go out on. It is pretty exciting work, and it's where most officers want to get to. So it's the pinnacle of my career, and it's quite a commitment. I've got eight years left to do, then I can retire. I plan on retiring the 27th of February, 2000—that's a Monday. I will go out with twenty years and do something else. In the meantime, it would be good if I was religious and could study a bit more.

I think you can find some solace and some support from religion. The trouble is finding time. The family aspect of religion gives me my sustenance, my support to go on from day to day. I look at the family as the main aspect of this whole thing. The time I'm not working, I'm with my family doing things as a family. Two of my children are growing up knowing they are Jewish and practicing as much as their mother involves them. She shows them my picture and says, "This is your dad, and you might see him next Saturday."

It was the demands of my job that made me decide to choose a Conservative rather than an Orthodox conversion. Sometimes in the back of my mind I toy with the idea that I will seek out Orthodoxy because I think it's more strict and it structures your life more. I want to find something that I can totally live by and mold the rest of my life around. My ideal is to be religious, and one meaning of that is to be religiously observant: studying, fulfilling the obligations of the religion by keeping one's head covered, wearing *tzitzit*, and obeying the laws—living for the religion. You *can* do all of that as a Conservative Jew; as an Orthodox Jew you *have* to do all that—there's no time off. On the other hand, Reform just never held any interest for me—not covering your head in synagogue and having music and things like that. It's too liberal for me. I want more of the religion itself, which I know you can get as a Conservative Jew. If I could, I would go every morning to *daven*.

But on the other hand, if you say you're religious, you can also be religious and never be seen in a synagogue. I believe that, but, in my mind, I'm not actively religious because I don't study, and this religion more than any other that I know of requires study, and that is good. I enjoy that, and I kick myself that I don't have the time to devote to it right now.

Maybe the trade-off is my public-safety job. Maybe because I'm committed to guarding life and property, I'm allowed a little deviation from the laws. It's all I know that can justify my nonobservance of *Shabbat* or keeping kosher. We keep kosher at home, but I don't while I'm at work because there are very few places at three in the morning where you can eat kosher, and I am *not* a vegetarian. On the one hand it's give and take, and on the other it's hard to justify sometimes. Basically that is the way I do business right now; that's just my life right now. It is just very difficult to squeeze a lot in.

We did go to Israel this past August. It was my first trip and Debbie's sixth, so she was my tour guide. As Debbie and I often do, we researched what we wanted to do, and we hit just about everything I wanted to see, both in the Christian sections and in the Jewish sections. It was neat because I showed Debbie some Christian things that she wasn't familiar with, and we had some pretty good discussions.

My sister-in-law got married over there; that was the occasion for going. The whole family went and stayed on the *moshav*—a state farm—about forty miles south of the Kinneret. It was August, very hot, no air conditioning on the *moshav*. We took the two children with us. We stayed on the *moshav* most of the time and then rented a car and used it as home base.

My brother-in-law Shmulek's family is from Iraq—his mother is Kurdish—and they came to Israel in 1952. They are fantastic, warm, beautiful people, and their culture, the things that they do, are just beyond belief. Shmulek is one of eight, and six of the eight speak English. His dad, though, doesn't speak a word of English and neither does his mother. Every morning I got up with Shmulek's dad, and we prayed and I wore the *tefillin* for the first time. He put them on me and showed me things, and every evening we prayed again. It was very, very fulfilling. It was a step out of my culture; out of my busy life. I enjoyed going to *shul* on *Shabbat* and coming back to this huge meal that Mom and the rest of the women had prepared, then lounging around most of the day, playing volleyball, and then coming back in and having the evening to look forward to. It was a great time—just a fantastic trip. I could do it again and hope to soon.

As I have grown older and probably become more insightful, I feel that God is within everyone. We must try to get beyond all that makes us different and attempt to rejoice in those differences. We are all born with a certain amount of spiritual potential, and as we grow older we make the decisions as to what to do to nurture it. We are all equal at birth; and yes, some of us have positive circumstances, some of us have negative circumstances. But we all have the option to be spiritually responsible—to seek out whatever degree of spirituality we want.

I think of religion as a mountain, and we are all climbing the same mountain. We all start out at different points at the base, and we can't see each other. As we get closer and closer to the summit, we all see the same thing. I take great comfort in that. I was thinking about it one night when I was working—I needed to think of something.

21

Hashgahah Pratit: Arranged by Divine Wisdom

Ruth and Avi Eastman

When I finally met Avi, after speaking to him several times on the phone, I was surprised and delighted to find that he was the same "Avi" who worked at the organic food co-op we both belonged to. His invariably kind and calm presence was especially welcome when things got hectic, as they often did, with moms and dads hurrying to get produce, and little kids being helpful or, sometimes, not so helpful.

It was Ruth who warmly greeted me at the door to their apartment and ushered me into the neatly crowded living space that lovingly reflects the lives of the six people who call it home. On the walls and shelves are beautiful ritual objects. Near the head of their dining room table are the framed photographs of the three rabbis who have guided them, and whose lives, one senses soon after getting to know the Eastmans, have been enriched in return.

Avi's story:

Prior to the conversion I was a Methodist. That's what the dog tags I wore in the army said. When I was a teenager—around fourteen—I was in the Boy Scouts. I had to work in the church for a year to earn an award, a little metal eagle that says "God and Country." Because I was there every Sunday and worked during the week helping to clean up the church, I began to notice the phoniness, I would call it. Most people drove up and just dropped their children off and roared on to do shopping or watch the ball games on TV. It was a Sunday baby-sitting service. It seemed to me that was wrong. Then I noticed that in an hour's talk the minister spent only about five or ten minutes addressing some real moral issue. The rest of the time was spent singing hymns, asking for money, singing some more hymns, asking for more money. Most of the people there were asleep—most of the men slept anyway. I began having serious doubts, and I began asking questions.

I was reading both the Old and the New Testaments. You were told to just pay attention to the New Testament; you don't have to worry about the other thing. As it got to the end of that year, I said, "This doesn't sit with me. I accept that there probably was a Creator in the world, but organized religion doesn't hold the answer for me." I pulled back, and my parents never forced me into any kind of Sunday school. I really didn't spend any more time in a church until I got married, at age twenty.

And that was the last time I was back in the church again for a long time. I got to a point where I believed that God may have created the world but He was physically done and was off creating new and better worlds. This is heaven or hell depending on how we make it here on earth; this life is it.

I held to that line until my mother died of cancer in 1982 when I was thirty-two and she was fifty-two. This is when I started to come to grips with what happens after death because it became very important for me that there be somewhere for her to go. I was still not able to turn back to a church for the answers. On the day when she was buried I ended up standing outside throwing rocks at God. That was the first realization that He was out there because He threw them back and He's much more accurate. Every one hit me right on the head. That started a quest of a kind. I had to have answers. I needed God and a place for people who died to be other than just dead.

I was crazy about my mother, and I am still crazy about her. We were very close. She divorced my father when I was two years old, so I really never knew him. For many years, she and my grandmother raised me. Then she met my stepdad and married him. My grandmother lived with us until she died, which occurred when I was stationed in Korea and was on a mission in which they could not notify me. So I didn't know until I came home. I had actually written her a letter, which was lying on my dresser. I thought I could just send it to her when I got back.

I held myself responsible for my mother's death. Most people feel that way when they have someone who dies of cancer, especially when it is a smoking-related illness. I was the favorite son; maybe I should have put more pressure on her to quit. She had slowed down her smoking, but continued working stressful jobs. Maybe I should have said more often during those last three years, "Mom, pull it up; we are going to lose you," but I didn't. We accepted, "Mom's Mom." Even when I was told by my stepdad in total secrecy that she was very sick, the fact was she had outlived what the doctors predicted. I attribute that to her orneriness. She just wasn't going to die until her last child was eighteen years old. After she died, it was a very tough time for me, emotionally. I was very frustrated and angry with everything including my family and severed all relations with them. It was a very tough time for all of us. Ruth has since patched up most of those relationships.

From that point, though, I began to think in terms of an entity called God and that there's got to be something beyond this life. Still, I had difficulties anytime I went back into a church, because it just didn't feel comfortable. I got a divorce from my first wife, and my eldest son lived with Ruth and me. It began to bother me a little bit that my son felt that the only thing he had to fear was the law and me—and not necessarily in that order. My son is a good person, but his concept of right and wrong was like the new American idea of just get away with as much as you can; if you don't get caught, it is okay. That wasn't good. I thought we'd done all right as parents, but his attitude bothered me. I wondered what was missing from his life? What experience in *my* life had given *me* concepts to hold on to? I realized that what I had gained from the church was the idea that there is something out there beyond you. There is something checking things off as you go through life. When you put God in the picture you can't "get away" with things.

So we made a foray back to a Lutheran church on the post at Fort Huachuca, where I was stationed in the military. I walked in, spent an hour, walked out, and said, "Not here!" It's as though you put on a piece of clothing that is just too tight. It looks okay on you, but if you move around it binds in a way that only you know about. I had the same feeling in church. There was a binding, something that just didn't fit.

One day on a temporary-duty mission in D.C., I called back home, and Ruth told me she'd been talking to a Jewish guy on post about her Jewish background and interest in religion. "They've invited me to come to their services on Friday night. Do you mind if I go?" she asked. I didn't mind a bit. Ruth then went to a Reform temple in Sierra Vista, Arizona, and had a good time there. They opened their doors to her. They were remarkable people and very kind from the beginning with Ruth and our baby, Joshua, including them in events during the many times I was out of town. One Friday night, I went with them. I was struck with how comfortable I suddenly felt—just the reverse of how I'd felt in church. I didn't know exactly why. The people were very nice; they were struggling very hard to hold on to *Yiddishkeit* as they see it. It felt good. One of the prayers that struck me, which I read in the English, turned out to be the *Shema* ("Hear O Israel, the Lord our God, the Lord is One"). It puts an emphasis on teaching your children—this was my emphasis because Joshua was my concern. I said, this is it! This is what I have been looking for. Services were held every other week, and we attended for a year.

I never considered that I could be Jewish. I went through all the things that somebody does who is spiritually seeking: I did Tao; I fiddled a little bit with Zen; I wished I were an American Indian for a while, and worshiped the Great Spirit. When Ruth and I met, we found that we had the same books. Our search had been almost identical. I was looking for something. But even so, my tagging along in *Yiddishkeit* was solely because I loved my wife: whatever she did, if I could assist it, I'd do it. I was standing back.

With my mother's death, even the issue of celebrating Christmas was gone. That had been an extremely beautiful and pleasant time. For a while in Arizona, Ruth and I had a Christmas tree, but it grew uncomfortable for her to deal with it with Joshua, trying to teach him meaning in something that meant nothing to us.

We went to Germany. I had spoken to a rabbi on one of my trips there about conversion, but the military tries to avoid the issue of conversion from the aspect of who's valid and who's not because all three different denominations of rabbis are represented. So the military had mandated among the chaplaincy, "Don't do conversions." I didn't have much hope when we got there, but we checked in. I considered all along that Ruth was Jewish because her father was Jewish, although according to Orthodox laws we understood this wasn't so. Nevertheless, she and Joshua were accepted as Jews by that little rogue community in Sierra Vista. By the time we were in Germany, Ruth was doing *Kiddush* and other Sabbath observances, but I didn't know much of what was going on. Since I wasn't Jewish, this didn't seem to be the thing for me to do.

We went to services at Rosh Hashanah in Frankfurt, and the baby and I both got bored so I took him downstairs and started playing boogie woogie on the piano, which apparently carried upstairs. The chaplain's assistant came down and said, "Stop that! Don't you know what this is all about?" She turned out to be a wonderful lady whom we would get to know better, but at the time she was chewing me out. For a major in the Army to be chewed out by an E-4 is a little tough to take, but she was right, and I had to let it go.

The year 1988 was the fiftieth anniversary of Kristallnacht.* The rabbi stationed in Frankfurt sent a letter to all the people who identified as Jewish (probably only about six families including us), announcing that he would come to speak about Kristallnacht and the Holocaust. Then everyone would proceed together to the dedication of this new synagogue that the Germans had rebuilt in Darmstadt. The Germans had been rebuilding synagogues throughout the country to express that they were sorry about what they did.

When you are in Germany you can't help but feel that you are walking on the memories of the Jews who lived there—literally— because one of the things the Nazis did was to grind up the bones of the Holocaust victims to scatter on the ground for fertilizer. As you open yourself up Jewishly in Germany, you realize that there is a hurt there that has never been repaired, and I don't think it will ever be repaired in that country.

Most of the Jews who live there now are very old, most nonreligious. I am not sure why the German government pressed to have all these synagogues built because I think in time they will just become Jewish museums in those towns. In Darmstadt, the *shul* I eventually attended was Conservative/Reform, but it was the closest one to me—about two and one-half miles from my house. I could walk on a *Shabbat* morning once a month, the only time they got together. The community just isn't strong enough to support more.

It is still very uncomfortable to be Jewish in Germany. They ran a hate poll while we were there. I find it interesting to live in a country that runs a hate poll. At the time of the poll 57 percent of the Germans hated the Turks. Jews came in second at 25 percent, Americans came in at 13 percent—I guess I was like a 38 percent! It was nice that all of a sudden we were second. Terrible things continued to happen there when the Berlin Wall came down.

Nevertheless, the occasion of the rabbi's Kristallnacht talk and the dedication ceremony sounded like a nice event to attend. So Ruth and I went and we were the only two who showed up. (Army chaplains of all denominations are used to doing many enthusiastic things and having nobody there to share the enthusiasm. The army

---

*The Night of Broken Glass, in which massive vandalism of Jewish communities was staged by Nazis.

is a very hard audience to deal with. Either you are not allowed time off for something as "silly" as religion or you just want to spend any free time in some other way.) It turned into a two-hour session on us. The rabbi was Rabbi Sachs, whose picture we have up in our dining room. I had to return to work, but the rabbi invited Ruth to attend the dedication of the synagogue in a special ceremony for survivors of Darmstadt whom the Germans had flown in from the various parts of the world.

Ruth and Rabbi Sachs talked more after the reception. He said, "I can see your husband is searching. Encourage him to come with you to my class." Ruth was surprised at what the rabbi had said. "Searching?" she thought, "My husband is the most stable person I know. The rabbi doesn't know him at all." She shared these observations with me and I said, "The rabbi is absolutely correct. I am trying to find some answers."

Although the class was scheduled at a time I could not attend regularly, I accompanied Ruth to some classes just to be supportive of her interest. After a couple of classes I realized that there were answers there for me too. Whether Ruth went or not, I had to be there. Sensing the strength of my motivation, Rabbi Sachs changed the meeting time so I could continue to attend the class—a surprising thing for him to do, considering that there were several other people in the class.

Ruth and I were blessed because we both caught fire at the same time. Sometimes when I was bogged down, I had my wife and *HaShem* to pull me along. But before the conversion, I had to resolve many things, chief of which was the question in my mind, "Why me, why now?"

The Jews in the military were spread out throughout Germany and once a year there was a conference to bring people together so they didn't feel so all alone. Many rabbis from Israel came to speak at this conference. To my question of "Why me, why now?" one of these rabbis said, "We hold that a *neshamah* had to come back because something needed to be repaired, there was something that has to happen. For whatever reason, your soul came back at this time, and you've been carrying it all along, but now is when it needed to come out." That was the explanation for the fire. I've never called myself a religious person. Did I believe in God? Yes, but it ended there. If you are a good person, doing your best, it's going to be okay. To suddenly feel as if I had a void filled was very unusual for me.

I also heard the story that the Torah was offered to many different people. In all the other nations, there was only a minority that said, "We want this!" In those nations the majority ruled, and the minority didn't get the Torah. So converts are those souls finally returning to where they wanted to be. That helped me to understand.

Our first real issue came up when I said to Rabbi Sachs, "Wait a minute! Aren't you supposed to turn me away three times?" He answered, "The Torah will turn you away." When I look at it now, he was absolutely correct, the Torah will do it. We were all of a sudden working against some timetables. Rabbi Sachs was leaving the military in eleven months, and with the wear and tear of army life, trying to get through an Orthodox conversion in less than a year was difficult. Rabbi Sachs was very patient and very willing to teach.

Soon after we began classes, Rabbi Sachs wanted us to come to his house one Friday night just to experience our first real *Shabbat* with them. From our house to the rabbi's would take forty-five minutes driving and by the time we could get there, *Shabbat* would already have started. One *erev Shabbat* we had finally been able to arrange our schedules, and as I was about to call the rabbi, I turned to Ruth and said, "Is this a test? He's testing us to see if we are going to break the rules." We had already taken on many of the *mitzvot* of *Shabbat,* and we weren't traveling any more on *Shabbat.* I said to the rabbi, "Are you testing us?" He said, "No! I'm not testing you. Just come. Just come now. We want you here." Even when we got there, I was still worried that he was going to come out and say that we would be unacceptable as Jews. But all he really wanted was for us to begin truly experiencing a little bit of what *Shabbat* is about.

Ruth: We had originally wanted an Orthodox conversion, not to live an Orthodox life, but so that our children would be recognized as Jews no matter where they lived. As we continued to learn, we didn't know at what point we would say, "No, that is not valid for us." We just grew to love the *mitzvot* and the things we were learning about.

Avi: As you try to take on more of the laws, you are challenged. The one that was difficult for me was family purity. "What do you mean there is a period of time I can't touch this woman?" The rabbi said, "That's just the law." For a half a month! As we were taught these laws, and we took them on, we did it with the attitude, "We'll try. If it is just not going to work, it's not going to work." I still gripe about it, I still want to talk to somebody from way back when who had the idea here, but in the end, as always, we found the beauty in the observance. It is a remarkable thing when you think about it. That beyond all the bonds of husband and wife there is a time you have to deal with this person just as a person. You can talk but you are not touching anymore. It brings to mind all those times when I had to travel, and how excited and happy I was to return to my wife after a week of traveling. *Taharat hamishpahah* is not unlike that. When we started to look at it that way, it was really beautiful.

We began to observe the laws of *kashrut* and the laws for me to *daven* and use *tefillin.* When Ruth began to cover her hair, we found that her hair became something that was just between her and me. I really grew to appreciate that. All the observances were added, but in the end, nothing changed—our lives just became enhanced.

We had started to eat kosher about five weeks after Rabbi Sachs's class began. A few weeks later we did a topsy-turvy in the kitchen and got rid of dishes—that was tough on me, looking at good things going out the door. By the time of the *Bet Din* we had really been living a kosher life. One week before the *mikveh*, Rabbi Daum said, "You've got a week to blow it all out. Do whatever you want to do, get it done with, because after the *mikveh* you can no longer do these things." On the way home in the car, we had a great conversation. Before we began keeping kosher, I loved Cordon Bleu—that's schnitzel (pork) and cheese all wrapped together. Escargot! German wines were excellent; none of them kosher, needless to say. Then we got to thinking what we'd have to do to go out and eat these things. I'd have to take off my *kippah*; she would need to uncover her hair.

Ruth: That already would be like taking off my shirt, God forbid, it would be that uncomfortable at that point because I'd been covering my hair for so long. It's funny how you can train your mind to accept a different way of thinking.

Avi: We went through all that we would have to do to do these things, but the final kicker was that Michael, our baby who was in the womb, had never known nonkosher food. We didn't want to feed him *treif*. And in the end we couldn't do it ourselves anyway because it would be too weird for us. So we did nothing different from what we had done before or now.

Ruth: Several times we had been encouraged to not quite keep all the *mitzvot*. "Don't observe the Sabbath completely." To take on all the *mitzvot* would not be right somehow, because we weren't Jews, yet. I don't know exactly the reason, but I am sure there is a *halakhah* behind it. We tried, anyway, but fortunately we are still learning to keep the *mitzvot*, so we know we must have messed up something in those days: the lights go on—whoops—the lights go off!

Avi: So, we already saw ourselves as Jewish, and we were getting closer and closer to when we were going before the *Bet Din*. God forbid we would die! What would happen to our souls? We were not Jewish yet! The Jewish community would not be able to bury us, but at this point we didn't see ourselves as Christians either. We felt if there really is a "limbo," as Catholics believe, we were in it. That was a huge fear— besides facing the *Bet Din*.

Rabbi Aharon Daum, the chief rabbi of Frankfurt, would do our conversion, although Rabbi Sachs had taught the classes. The German rabbi who was also working with us on the conversion said that he wanted to test us before we went to the *Bet Din* in Dusseldorf. He said, "Come to my office for twenty minutes, and I'll ask some questions. If you are ready, we will set the date." So we said, "Twenty minutes, what could be so bad?"

Ruth: We had met this rabbi before, and he was our first "black hat" rabbi. He seemed very imposing and very frightening. He was just so Orthodox. We were terribly afraid that he was going to recognize us for the "frauds" we feared we might seem. Somehow we were not going to be allowed into the club. We felt a lot of apprehension, therefore, in going to meet him. Even the twenty minutes did not look appetizing.

Avi: It lasted two and one-half hours. He took us through the paces. Ruth did an outstanding job on the questions of *kashrut* and the things that a woman has to do. We held our own on all the other laws, but the Hebrew was the worst. He handed us the *siddur* and said to read *Ritzei* (the paragraph for *Shabbat* in the blessings after meals). Because I had done most of the *bentsching* in English up to that time, I couldn't even find *Ritzei*. Rabbi Sachs helped me. I read that first line so slowly, I believe I saw the German rabbi's beard grow. Ruth did okay, but we were both sweating. I assumed at the time that we were both washed up. What would have been sad about that is that Rabbi Sachs was leaving the country and a new chaplain might not have carried through with this.

Ruth: The reason all of this had been necessary was that Rabbi Hochwald of Dusseldorf, who would be the third for the *Bet Din*, was very old and not well. Rabbi Daum was concerned about taking up his time and making the trip unnecessarily.

Avi: He wanted to make sure that the people who were being trained in his area were truly ready. They especially wanted us to get Rabbi Hochwald's name on our conversion papers because it is a name well known in Israel. Rabbi Sachs, a chaplain in the U.S. Army, not too many people know. They didn't want to take up Rabbi Hochwald's time if we weren't ready.

Rabbi Daum surprised us. He flipped his calendar and said, "Okay, when do you think we should go?" Rabbi Sachs said he wasn't surprised, but I think he was. During *hol hamoed* Sukkot (the intermediate days of the festival of Sukkot) we went to the *Bet Din*. We were still worried. Rabbi Sachs and the *rebbetzin* (rabbi's wife) drove us to Dusseldorf and were very reassuring. We couldn't calm down: "We're disappointing students; we're sorry we let you down." One of the other people in our class went also. So we went through another hour of questioning with the *Bet Din*, but we could see that we already had two allies who knew how prepared we were.

Rabbi Hochwald was a remarkable individual, very kind. His questions still probe to the depth of the knowledge that we have. There were a few questions we couldn't answer. For me, they asked the laws of *tefillin*; the laws of the *yom tovim*; for Ruth the laws of the kitchen, all the things that she was going to deal with specifically; the laws of family purity (because if it is left to the man, he will botch it in a heartbeat). Again we had to read something, but this time we picked something with which we were familiar. I still botched a little bit because I was so nervous.

We had to go to the *mikveh*, and Joshua had to go too. We had heard a horror story of another child who'd recently gone to the *mikveh* who'd had such a hard time going under the water. Joshua, who was two and a half, had just recently developed a fear of water. The bathtub was a wrestling match. So we were anxious. But in the *mikveh*, he was perfect. It was as if he knew—or at least his *neshamah* knew—"This is important for me." He went under water completely; he came up not crying. I was talking to him all the time: "I'm going to let go of you, you are going to be by yourself for a minute, but I'll pull you right out." Not a tear came out of him, and he said the *brakhah* (blessing) right afterward, perfectly. The rabbis really thought he was something!

When I went into the *mikveh*, it was the first time—we now know from all of our reading—I was to do a *mitzvah*. As I was about to go underwater—it's tough enough to be a man with three other men standing there watching you naked in this water—Rabbi Hochwald said in such a gentle way, "I am envious of you." I stopped. "Why are you envious of me?" "Because you are about to do a blessing I will never get to do in my lifetime." He also said, "Know that, when you come out of the water, you come out as a Jew. From then on no matter what you may decide, whether you want to go back or become a Buddhist, you are going to be judged on the final day as a Jew." Then I was asked, "Do you accept that?" And, of course, I did.

Rabbi Daum gently reminded us that "after the *mikveh*, what was before is no more," referring to our marriage. I joked that we would live in sin, but we had already arranged with Rabbi Sachs to have a marriage ceremony. Ruth and I separated for seven days, which is part of the traditional preparation for a marriage ceremony, although it wasn't strictly necessary in our case. Ruth and the baby went to live with Rabbi Sachs and his wife for the seven days. I could talk to her on the phone, I had to go through the rabbi and *rebbetzin* to get to her. That was a remarkable time.

Ruth: One day we even had a conversation through the bedroom door. It was so romantic!

Avi: Then we had the wedding, and that in itself was a trip. I left the house with fifty minutes to make the forty-five minute journey to Frankfurt. It was no big deal, a big highway—the Autobahn. That particular day the "*stau* (traffic jam) of all *staus*" hit the Frankfurt Autobahn, the result of a massive accident north of the city. Traffic was backed up twenty miles. I realized I was in trouble. The "man-to-be" wasn't going to "be" there. I did something I'd not tried before, drive through the heart of Frankfurt and during rush hour. I actually got to the *shul* with minutes to spare, but Rabbi Sachs and a few others also caught in the traffic did not arrive for three hours.

Ruth: The beauty of a Jewish wedding is that the bride and groom are the guests of honor; they are not responsible, as in a civil or Christian wedding, to take care of the guests. I was in a special room, being waited on and cared for. I knew everything was going to be fine because everyone out there was bustling and worrying. In another situation, I would have been as overwrought as everyone else.

Avi: The wedding went well. At the time we were married, Ruth was carrying our son Michael, who was due in three months. I think it would have made a funny picture for me to be under the *huppah* with a gun pointed at my back!

Ruth: It was funny seeing me lifted up in my chair during the dancing. Someone from the men's circle had to come over to help when they started to lose me. They didn't want to drop the pregnant bride on the floor.

It wasn't a huge wedding. It was just the people who attended the chapel. People in a chapel situation in the military are in so many different stages of learning. There were very few religious people. So people didn't know what to do. For the *bedeken* (the veiling of the bride by the groom), when they led my husband in, Rabbi Sachs had the ability, by himself, to seem like five of Avi's best *yeshivah* buddies—all the noise they would make and all the revelry. He was a one-man party. He was charismatic enough with members of the community so that they would catch fire and do whatever he was doing. People were very enthusiastic, and it made a very nice wedding.

Avi: Shortly after our wedding, Rabbi Sachs left the military and Germany.

It is still amazing to me the speed with which I got involved and how much it became very important for me to grab hold of it. Now my frustration is that I am not learning fast enough. I've got to accept that Ruth and I are about five-years-old in this religion. So I am probably doing pretty well as a five-year-old reader, but as a forty-four-year-old man, I feel I am really at a terrible level.

Ruth's story:

My father was Jewish and my mother was brought up Catholic, but although she went to Catholic school for a while, she was not very observant. I was raised as an open-minded sort of person with Christian overtones. My mother always believed in two things that mean a lot to me: instead of fighting about the differences between one another, people should celebrate their differences. And she said, "Any path to God is the right one."

My father's family escaped from Warsaw when he was four years old, in a group of 200,000, just before the ghetto was closed down. When I was very young, just a few months old, I had a naming ceremony at Pesah in Cuba, where my grandparents lived. My mother didn't know at the time that it was a baby naming, but we've pieced together her various memories of the time and realized that was what it was. My grandparents insisted on telling her many stories; they went over them and over them so that she would remember, but she didn't know what any of them meant. As was the case with many immigrants, they were trying to recall traditions of which they had only partial understanding.

The woman I was named for *was* religious. "Ruth" comes from my paternal great-grandmother, and I know this story about her: My father's family was the seventh wealthiest family in Warsaw. They waited too long to leave. They had sewn jewels into the linings of their clothing and had gathered all the family together on this big farm. It was just moments too late. The Nazis came and gathered everybody. Ruth, my great-grandmother, was there when the Nazis were going to take one of the children, a mentally retarded girl, to the woods and get rid of her right there. Ruth understood what was going on and said, "I'll go with the child."

I know only that story about her and I'd like to do some research and learn more about my family. The strength of her spirit meant a lot to me. I was given her name at my naming ceremony, and it is now my legal name also.

My father was in the military, and shortly after I was born in California, we went to Germany. My father left my mother when I was very young, and I have not seen him since then. I grew up in eastern Washington State in a town called Ephrata. There weren't very many Jews there. My mother made it possible for me to identify with my Jewishness. She helped me to remember my heritage by telling me the stories my grandparents had told her. When I was three, another relative gave me a little Star of David, and I cherished it.

I don't remember becoming religiously aware until I was about ten years old and I started thinking of myself as Jewish. It was easy to do in that town because there was nobody to contradict me. Somewhere along the line, I realized that I was not Jewish, although I don't know when I knew that. As Avi has mentioned, it didn't occur to me that I could actually become officially Jewish. I always thought of myself as half-Jewish. It is a strange thing to live on a fence when you are half-Jewish and half-Christian, though according to Orthodox law that concept doesn't exist. I had relatives who had died in the Holocaust but I couldn't claim them as a Jew, I could only claim them as relatives. There is a disjointed feeling to that. I've read many articles about people in the same situation. I taught Torah school in Germany for a while to small children, and there is this real feeling that this issue of "half-Jewish–half-Christian" must be resolved. Both my sister and I, who are children of the same father, had to deal with this. She is wrestling with it now. My younger siblings are from my mother's marriage to my stepfather and therefore are not affected by these identity dilemmas.

My stepfather was Lutheran, so we went to a Lutheran Bible school. It never really took. I went through a lot of searching. I went through being a Jesus-freak as a teenager and trying to find an answer there. I was always in pursuit of a spiritual home. Finally, I gave it up because I wasn't finding any answers. So I decided I must be an agnostic, and I lived happily in that belief for many years.

Years later, Avi and I came to an important realization when we were watching a TV program in which a high school student was being interviewed by his principal. The young person said, "Why should I stay in school and work hard to become a principal and earn eight hundred dollars a week like you do, when I can sell crack cocaine on the street and get eight hundred dollars a day?" Avi and I were raising his teenage son at the time. We thought, "If that is the kind of world we are bringing our kids up in, being a secular humanist is not going to be enough weight to carry us." That was the beginning of our pursuing religion.

When we were stationed in Arizona, I had a very sweet Christian friend who listened to my struggle and my questions about where I wanted to go religiously. She actually gave us our first Union prayer books. She was very close friends with some Jewish people in the military community, and she said, "I have just the person for you to talk to!" I called this gentleman up and told him I'd love to attend services. "I am not Jewish—would you mind? My father was Jewish." I was often apologizing for my presence in Jewish surroundings: "I am not one of you—but I am, kind of." At this time not everyone in the Reform movement agreed on patrilineage, but they still accepted us. Nevertheless, I wanted to convert and wanted to find out how to go about that. I didn't want my husband to convert. I didn't see any reason for him to do that. For just me to convert and for him to be supportive would have been fine.

On December 7, 1987—that date sticks in my mind, I think that is when the Intifada started; maybe God was trying to make a counterbalance by gathering a few more of us around—there was a race for Soviet Jewry, and Avi had signed up to do this run. Avi always felt a tie with the Jewish community and had been to Israel several times.

So my husband signed up for the run for Soviet Jewry. He paid his five dollars, and then for some work-related reason couldn't make the run. He's always been the more spiritual of the two of us, and if he makes a spiritual commitment he sticks to it. He went ahead and did the run on a different day so that he could say he had earned his T-shirt. I am a little more pragmatic, I think. Once I had missed the run I would have just let it go. So, we went to pick up his T-shirt at the JCC in Tucson, and that is how we met Margie Fenton, an amazing older woman who has eyes that look right into you. She was the president of the JCC.

She started asking me all these questions. I immediately told her, "Well, I'm not Jewish." She wondered what I was doing there. "My father was Jewish. . . ." She started giving me information and treating me as a Jew. Suddenly, something happened inside me, and I said, "Wow! This is possible; I really could become a Jew!"

She gave me a couple of books about a woman who had survived the Holocaust and a woman who had helped build Israel. They were very moving books. I finally felt that I had found a niche, a toehold in something, and I suddenly realized I really wanted to be there. This was an answer to the question—I didn't know the question, but I knew that this was the answer. I went to a couple of functions, and I'd see her there and she treated me in such a strange way—like a new relative in the family. She would sit me next to her, and she would say to people, "This young woman is going to be very busy in our community." She made me feel so welcome and that I could be part of the Jewish community.

We kept trying to learn more and more. I wanted to convert, and the question arose then about Joshua's status. Of course, he would have to convert with me, but there was the question of circumcision.

By eleven months, Joshua was still not circumcised. We were told that if I wanted to convert, of course Joshua would have to convert with me—Avi wouldn't have to. No matter how nonreligious the people were, everyone said that Joshua would have to have a circumcision, which would now be far more complicated surgery and would cost about $900. Even people who are very far away from their faith still hang on to the *brit milah*. We just weren't that committed, and I didn't understand why it was so important; now, of course, I do.

Joshua was born at a time during which medical fashion held that circumcision was optional. In fact, they gave you a form that you had to sign in which it was said that 1 percent of all babies who are circumcised bleed to death. When my husband was born everybody got circumcised, so we hadn't given it much thought until we got that form. I read it, called Avi, and we wanted to get more information. All the information was "anti" at that time. So then my husband got to go through his personal *akeidah*.* Was it right to put his son under the knife for what seemed, at the time, merely for cosmetics? Was it right to put this baby under anesthesia, perhaps risking his life, God forbid, just for me and my tenuous grasp on my heritage? We didn't see any of the spiritual implications back in Sierra Vista. We said, "We can't see any real reason to do this." So we didn't do it.

I had already resolved by this time that the circumcision was the right thing to do; that I would trust in God, whom I had finally decided I was going to believe in again. (He thinks that's very big of me, I am sure! He believes in me, too!) After reading the daily prayers containing the line "the uncircumcised shall not abide," I was convinced, but I felt that this was something Avi needed to decide on his own.

Avi: The line really refers to idolaters, but every time I would read that line my son would pop into my mind. I knew I needed to resolve it.

Ruth: We had Joshua's surgery in Germany. The military hospital would not do it. We went to a German hospital. The *mohel* was present, and two rabbis and friends. (We felt very privileged, especially in retrospect now that we know more, that both

*Binding; referring to the binding of Isaac, when Abraham is told to sacrifice a ram instead of his son.

rabbis attended so many events in our lives, because it wasn't halakhically necessary for them both to be present. But it was very important to them. Spiritually they
are like our father and uncle—Sachs and Daum, the chief rabbi of Frankfurt. We were
important to them also. We see that now much more than we did then. We just assumed that they were following the proper "form." Now we see that we were their
"children.")

I am somewhat reluctant to include in Avi's and my story this portion about Joshua,
because it is a major *mitzvah* not to embarrass a fellow Jew. He is seven years old
now, and it may not matter to him to have the details of his conversion discussed in
front of what could be a large audience. As he gets older, I have to consider whether
this would embarrass him. It has a great deal of meaning to Avi and me, but at what
point does this become his story and for him to decide how and where to tell it?

And it was concern for our children that brought us to religion, to begin with.
Children do get people back to their religion. When we decided that we needed religion on our side, I decided that I would have to teach myself to believe in God or at
least manifest a belief in God for the sake of my kids. It was a very arduous struggle—
thank God it has been successful. It took me a long time.

There is a very valid sociological explanation for this—I've spoken with other
people in my age group, and we feel that, when we were growing up in America,
spirituality was really pushed aside. In 1957, when I was born, Sputnik had just gone
up. It suddenly became very important that education be very rational and very competitive with the Soviets. The value was to be smart and rational. You were to swal-
low Darwin's theory hook, line, and sinker, but anything spiritual was just a little
too flaky. So developing my spiritual self was a really big struggle. As time went by
and I really wanted it, the belief came—not without help, though. Some good books
helped; one called *Permission to Believe* sealed it for me. It is a very fine little book
by Lawrence Kenilman. I usually have it on my shelf, but I give it away all the time.
It has four different rational approaches that tell you it is okay to believe, to have
faith. You come away understanding that people who believe in scientific theories,
Darwinism for example, really have a lot of "faith" in those concepts. It helps when
you can look through the glass from the other end and see it a little bit differently.

Avi: There are now two books out by two different scholars who discuss Darwinism and Creationism in terms of each other. Their conclusion is that we are really
dealing with time and space. What science says and what the Torah says both work.
This was very helpful to us.

Ruth: The author of one book has moved to Israel, leaving a position at M.I.T.—
not an easy thing to do. Hearing him helped me to solidify my belief and, I am sure,
to enhance my husband's. I believe very strongly in *hashgahah pratit* (providence),
and I see many times throughout our lives where we were put in a position to meet
somebody—meeting and hearing the author of this book speak was one of these.
Finding our way to live in Baltimore was another.

Avi: We came to Baltimore on the recommendation of a rabbi we met when we
were in Germany. We moved here in September 1991, when I retired from the mili-

tary after twenty years. I joined for two years and got lost for two decades. Ruth, in her efficient way, wrote to the cities we were considering—Seattle, Baltimore, Kansas City. It was very big in Ruth's book to have a restaurant or two in town, after being in Germany and doing all the cooking or having to go to someone's house. We knew New York was too much. We made a decision based on *Yiddishkeit* to come to Baltimore. Also, the military was encouraged to come to this area because Maryland was a booming state. Ruth wrote a letter to Rabbi Porter, the founder of Etz Chaim Center for Jewish Studies, who happened to make a trip to Germany and personally called us. He joked, "Now I don't want you to expect for me to answer every one of your letters in person!" He was there with his mother after the Berlin Wall came down for a chance to see where she had grown up. He gave us names of people to contact for help, and suggested we try Rabbi Goldberger's *shul*. A lot of help came to us from so many strange places that you knew God's hand was working. We got names of people who referred us to others in the community.

Ruth: It is such a family network. It doesn't matter how famous a person is or whatever. You are hand carried from one family member to another and taken care of. This happened here in the States and in Israel, where we visited after leaving Germany. We had reservations for the first night in Israel. Friends had said, "Drop by anytime you are in Israel," and after the first night we didn't have to worry about meals or a place to stay and were very well cared for.

Avi: I had first gone to Israel in 1981 and 1982. A Baptist chaplain in the military had made a connection with a reserve military chaplain who lived in Israel and had a tour company. This rabbi had made an offer to other military chaplains that if they came to Israel and used his tour service, he would make sure they had a good tour of the country. For all religions, Israel is such a holy place. I had a wonderful time on both my trips. I had already considered that I would like to live in Israel. I liked the attitude of the people and I liked the atmosphere of the country. And now, we know the *kedushah* of the country—it has a special holiness. It was a more peaceful time, during the first trip anyway.

In 1982 I was visiting a *kibbutz* on a tour stop on the Israel-Lebanon border as the tanks were rolling in. Two things I noticed when I arrived: the *kibbutz* was guarded by the young men on the *kibbutz*, but suddenly about midday the guarding changed and it was the old men with weapons walking around. Later that night I couldn't sleep and I noticed that the older men still were on guard. I asked what happened to the young men. "Oh, they are gone," was the reply. I heard the rumbling of what I knew to be tanks. The men said, "Oh, there are no tanks out there." I said, "Look, I was in an armored unit in the army and I know what a tank sounds like, and that is not just one tank, it is a bunch of tanks out there. Why are they rolling?" Well, the next morning, I could see that they had entered Lebanon, and you could see that the Palestinian guerrillas had left weapons littering the ground as they fled backward so fast from the Israeli military. The young men who had been guarding the *kibbutz* had all been called up in their reserve units.

It was at another point that I got introduced to what I now understand as a national sadness. There was a man I spoke with who had been there in 1948; he had survived the horrors of Europe to come to Palestine to fight again. He said, "You know, in 1948 I hoped that that was a last time a Jew would have to pick up weapons in anger. It saddens me that we are raising a nation for war." Children are particular targets of violence, and in Jericho we saw a woman teacher carrying an M-16 to class. The principal carries a shotgun and a .45, and there is an Israeli soldier who patrols to protect this group of children.

All these things struck me—the very nature of these people fighting is like the last of the frontiersmen. These people are still etching out a place for themselves in a hostile frontier.

I met again with the chaplain from Israel when we were both involved in the Gulf conflict. He volunteered to go to Saudi Arabia, knowing that there would be Jews there in need of a chaplain. When I met up with him again in 1991, I was able to reintroduce myself as a Jew.

Ruth: Our reception in Israel was mirrored by the warmth of our welcome to Baltimore—like coming to the bosom of your family. We arrived near Rosh Hashanah, and I didn't cook a holiday meal or any other meal for two months. Throughout the holidays we were taken care of. I was pregnant with Aryeh then, and my friend Bryna said, "Oh, the baby is due right between Purim and Pesah, you'll never be able to do Pesah, I'll make Pesah for you." I didn't take that seriously—that's too much work already.

Time went by and the baby was born right on schedule. I discovered that I just didn't have the strength to do all the cooking. I could get the main meals done, but that would be it. Maybe God would forgive me, but we wouldn't have side dishes, we wouldn't have desserts. My husband was very understanding; everybody else was very understanding. Suddenly, three days before Pesah, my friend arrived with a huge box of side dishes and desserts. This is the kind of people who are in the community.

Avi: I was amazed at the reception we have gotten in the Jewish community. I was the first to arrive in Baltimore, and Bryna took me into her house right away. I had to look for a place for us to live and start looking for work. Bryna had already made appointments for me before I even arrived. In the military there is a program for families to sponsor new families. But I was never sponsored as well as I was coming into this Jewish community. It was amazing to me to have five o'clock come around and someone would arrive at our door with a hot meal. Some of these people we've never seen again. We finally had to let people know that we were ready to resume our own cooking.

Ruth: Thank God we've been able to reciprocate by making meals for others who have had babies and so on.

Avi: And from the very beginning we were very active in our Jewish community. Ruth has done some wonderful things. In Germany at the Rosh Hashanah after we had converted, the new rabbi's wife had had to fly back to the States, and she had asked us to look in on the rabbi and maybe bring him some meals, fearing he would not take care of himself. Ruth cooked the meals inside the military chapel where there was a kosher kitchen. We were going to cook for our family, the rabbi, and a couple of guests. Then the first night someone found out that Ruth was cooking, and I think we ended up with about twenty people. What amazed me was that she had prepared the food with ten people in mind and the meal stretched and none of us went hungry. That happened again the second night. People got wind of this—there's cooking going on in the *shul*!

Ruth: It was a miracle. There was an elderly man also. Every *Shabbat* he would get in past the military guards without identification and come and eat, and the rabbis found out it was really his only solid meal during the week. He had too much pride to let anyone persuade him to come home with them. Rabbi Sachs finally did once, and we were honored to have him at the table. So during Rosh Hashanah, he also joined us on the last night, and there wasn't so much food for that meal. I was so worried that he would not get enough. I hinted to people, "Maybe you won't take seconds, let him eat enough." But there was enough; there was always enough. It was really a miracle. He went home with a full belly and everyone else did too.

Avi: With all the loving support of the Baltimore Jewish community, we made a quick adjustment, and to her credit, so did my mother-in-law, who continues to live with us. Almost as soon as we arrived, there was a family who needed child care. The mother had died very young, leaving several young children. My mother helped out there until complications with her diabetes prevented her from working.

Ruth: My mother has been remarkable. As I said, she has always believed that any path to God is the right one. She herself doesn't have any use for organized religion. She has a spiritual connection of her own. She is very much like Avi in the depth of her spirituality. In fact, she said when we were married, "If anything were to happen to this relationship, *he* can still write to me." She very much loves her son-in-law, which of course makes it very comfortable to live together.

She is my best student. She learns everything, she coaches the children to say their *brakhot* (pl. for blessing). If she is helping with a meal and is concerned about *kashrut*, she asks. She eats only kosher in the house. In Germany, when we were first starting to keep kosher, she said she was going to keep kosher too and stop eating bratwurst, which she loved. I told her, "Someday the kids will catch you eating a bratwurst. We are not going to pretend that you are somebody you are not. They will learn to accept you as you." This is wonderful because our children accept non-Jews; they accept that non-Jews don't have the same rules, and that doesn't make them less worthy of respect. My mother has really helped facilitate that education for them.

Avi: Across the board our families have been very accepting. The biggest issue we've had is that our families and friends want to learn—they want to figure out how to cook for us. We have to tell them that it is easier if they come to us. A big problem we ran into in the military was that non-Jews would come to our house to eat and they wanted to reciprocate, and it just couldn't be done. One individual went to the trouble to build a separate, brand-new cupboard in his house for us. We have been blessed all along, on both the Jewish and non-Jewish side, of people accepting us. And Bubbe has been the example for everyone. She knows the *brakhahs* as well as the boys do.

Ruth: At one time my mother said she wanted to convert for the children's sake. I discouraged her because even most rabbis would since she wasn't converting for herself. I told her, the kids will grow up and move away and you'll still be expected to light candles and do all this. If it is not yours, it is not fair for you to do it. But if you ever come to the conclusion that this is what you want, I'll be in your corner, and I'll teach you, although you probably won't have much to learn because you've been living the life already. I think she was a little bit relieved because she is really very content with who and what she is.

Avi: You are told you don't have to tell anybody that you are a convert. We don't put any binds on Bubbe, so she will wander out the door on a *Shabbat* to go walking and shopping, because it is her day. People will be here for *Shabbat* who may not know that we are converts and you can just see them wondering, "Where is she going?" And we explain that she is not Jewish, and then that starts a whole conversation.

Ruth: We could leave it in people's minds and then people have to wrestle with giving her the benefit of the doubt. Maybe she is a Jew but she is not observant, and we thought that would be worse because it would give them a bad impression of her.

Avi: No one has ever been unkind to us. I have been treated from the beginning as a Jew. But there is no way around the conversion issue. This is what happens to me nine times out of ten: Someone will say, "Where are you from?" and I'll say, "Kansas City." And all of a sudden they'll start naming all these Jewish people they know from Kansas City, and there are not that many Jews there, and they'll say, "How could you not know him?!" "Well, see, at the time I was a Methodist." "What?" It shuts the door on conversations.

There is nothing I can say. Perhaps individual Jews should be kinder to converts; be less inquisitive, because I think the wholeness of what a convert brings to Judaism is really beautiful. Sometimes what I think they bring is a bridge. The job of Jews, as we are being taught, is to bring the world into a similar thought process. We are supposed to be guides and teachers and examples for people to follow. It is very easy from being on the other side to look at this side and say, "I can't ever do that; I can't ever be this." But suddenly there is a whole bunch of us who are coming across who are like little bridges. We have a unique status with a non-Jewish mother in the house. As we pursue our path spiritually, we must be cognizant also of our relatives who are not Jewish—especially the woman who lives in this house with us who is very precious to us, and my stepfather, and other relatives, and accept them for who they are and what they bring when they come to our house. We are a bridge of understanding between these two worlds.

A non-Jewish couple we stayed with recently were full of questions. I felt some envy of the man who is a full colonel in the Army and is doing quite well; he's got a remarkable career and is a great person. And he told me, "I am envious of you because you have made a commitment to something I could never commit to." He sees himself in a finite world.

There is an interesting story connected with this man. In 1986, his daughter from a previous marriage had developed a rare form of cancer; only seventeen other cases had been recorded in the United States and none had survived. The prognosis was that she would die soon. Ruth got a call from this man. He is a very strong man, but this was very tough. Ruth made a promise with God that if this child survived, then we would get more religion in our house. The girl is very much alive today, the cancer is totally gone, and she is in total remission. She is an active teenager, going windsurfing and sailing, and we are Jews.

Sometimes when we are having a hard time with an issue of *halakhah*, we'll call him and tease him that it is his fault. Ultimately, though, on issues of *halakhah* that I don't agree with—I follow them. In the end I follow them.

The German *shul* was the first time I dealt with issues of *halakhah* that I didn't agree with. All the rabbis told me, you can't go to that *shul* and *daven*. You are an Orthodox person and that is not an Orthodox *shul*. But they had asked me because on the days they did have services they needed a tenth man, and I was it. I said, "Isn't that important?" The whole issue was that the women sat on one side of the synagogue and the men on the other but there was no partition.

Ruth: They happened to have a beautiful gallery but nobody but me used it.

Avi: That was a tough issue for me. I tried to do what was right from both perspectives. I *davened* behind a pole, so I couldn't see to the right of me. I could never be called to the Torah because that would bring me out to the middle of the room. I wanted to say, "Where I *daven* is my issue. Whether I do it at home alone or I do it with other men isn't that important. How do you teach these people something if I never show up? I was walking to *shul* to form the *minyan* they needed." One of the last functions we attended at that *shul* was Purim, and I could drive Ruth and the kids there in the car. Many questions then ensued: "Why didn't we come more often? Why didn't we bring the kids?" They were starved for the company of children because there were so few in their community. We then explained to them that we could not travel on *Shabbat* in the car or use the stroller. It was at this point that their rabbi explained to them the various laws of *Shabbat*. So we cannot know what effect our presence had on the people there.

Our relationship with *HaShem* is in its infancy. Right now I have in me the acceptance that everything I am supposed to do is with *yirat HaShem*—in fear and love of *HaShem*. There were thirty-nine years of my life in which I didn't have this—God was my copilot, my "amigo"; we both had important jobs, but we were together in it; flying side by side—that put us on a parallel. If we are in a sense equal, it makes it hard to accept God's will. But Ruth helps me to remember the true relationship with God. The car breaking down, for example. There is a reason for this, and, *Barukh HaShem* it was only the car. Perhaps I wasn't paying attention to something earlier in the day or maybe the car needed to break down to avoid something—say an accident—farther down the road. Ruth reminds me that the interruption of my plans is not the focus. God's plan—which we may not see—is the focus. So I would say that my relationship with God is a growing thing right now, and God willing, He's patient.

I can't think of a world without God—otherwise it is all madness, there is no purpose to anything here, there is no purpose to being good. A friend of mine had a bumper sticker of which he was quite proud: "He with the most toys when he dies, wins." It was all based on material gain. We are now trying to pare down our possessions, trying to get rid of things. I was in that cycle before. I've lived that American dream. I was pursuing getting things, and prestige, and then finally realized that in the end all you are left with is nothing. My mother, God rest her soul, worked hard for many, many years and in the end she died. She and my dad worked hard to get us all the things we needed—but the one thing we needed the most was time with her. I am sorry for that. We are working toward that goal.

Ruth: I used to believe, when I was younger, that true freedom meant having no boundaries and doing whatever you wanted to. That was being an American girl—that was everything. Now, I think I have learned that you can't be truly free unless you have some boundaries to work within. True freedom or true power means rising above our own petty cravings to be what we are taught God wants us to be. We have a long way to go.

I don't think anything is unique about me. Those of us who are Jewish, whether we were born Jewish or are Jews by Choice, have always had a Jewish *neshamah* (soul) or been part of a Jewish *neshamah*, and we come into the world at God's choosing—whether born into the world or steered down a path toward Judaism.

It is very good to be part of something that is so connected. It is good to think that if I do one small kindness here, it might save the life of an Israeli soldier in Lebanon. Everything we do is interconnected. That makes us very much a family. Rav Yisroel Miller says that if just the religious Jews—just a handful of religious Jews—would be truly kind to one another, it would have a ripple effect. Soon not-religious Jews and religious Jews would have kindness toward one another; and eventually this would ripple out to the whole world. That puts something in front of me that I can do. I can't bring world peace by myself. When you don't have a belief in God, it all seems like too much. It's too much to fix. In the movie *The Year of Living Dangerously* a socially conscious character comes to the realization that the only thing you can do is just take care of the person that God puts in your path. Adding that idea to *HaShem* as I see Him in *Yiddishkeit*, that's exactly what we have to do. If each of us takes that course, eventually the world will be repaired. I can do small things.

I see my connection to *HaShem* also through the children. I see how they are becoming such spiritual and amazing little people—very individually and very differently.

Avi: When I was asking the question "Why me?" as I became a Jew, I wondered about what awesome mission I might be required for. The rabbi said, "It may not be you. You may be just the vessel, the bridge that is bringing your son or maybe a grandson or daughter or granddaughter. You've got to accept that you may be stumbling forever while trying to learn. Once you converted you did what God wanted and the next step is the real step." This keeps me very humble. I have been granted the grace of the years I have been allotted to live. In those I have to continue to try to grow—because even if it is my kids for whom all this was really meant, they've got to see their *abba* (Hebrew for "father") setting a good example.

For my Jewish name, I wasn't sure what I would pick. The rabbi said it is not usual but if you took the name Abraham, then when your son Joshua is called to the Torah he will be Joshua ben Abraham. If I picked the name, say, "Shimshon," he would also be called to the Torah as Joshua ben Abraham; but Michael would be called to the Torah as Michael ben Shimshon.

As it is I, like the name. I like the patriarch Abraham. If I can be like him in a small degree, I will have achieved what I need to achieve.

22

In the Rabbi's *Shul*

"Shlomit"

"Shlomit" has gently steered her family toward an increasingly Orthodox way
of life. This path did not always follow seamlessly from decision to completion, in part because an observant life is a progression, not an end point.
"Shlomit" needed to discover what her center was in the new world she had
entered upon her marriage to a Jewish man. Yet she also had to balance her
drive to find her place in Judaism with her close-knit family's desire to be involved in her life.

I grew up in a Roman Catholic family in a working-class area of an East Coast
city. We are Eastern European, very ethnic, and the Christian holidays were very
rich and alive. There were no Jews living in my part of the city. When I was
growing up, it was expected that I would go to Sunday school and church every week.
My grandparents were very religious Catholics, and although my parents were not
very religious, my father was a very spiritual man. He taught Sunday school, and he
always taught the Old Testament. When my two brothers and I were children he would
read us the Bible and the Old Testament.

I can remember from a very early age the experience of being in church—I must
have been about five years old—and when I would look up at the cross, I was very
aware that I was struggling in my acceptance of Jesus as God. I was *afraid* of Jesus
on the cross. I was afraid of it because it was very graphic, but it was my secret and
I kept it to myself. In adolescence, I was very consciously aware that this was a *man*—
how can he be God?—and grappling with that. I did not share my feelings because
there was not a lot of encouragement for having alternative religious ideas, but my
breaking away in my teenage years coincided with the family's general recession
from the Church.

When my mother would tell me to go to confession, I finally reached a point that
I said, "I am not going to talk to another person about my sins—this man is an intermediary for me? If I have a sin against another person, I'll deal with that person. If
I have a sin with God, I'll deal with God." Imagine my amazement to learn about
teshuvah when I was starting to study for conversion: if you have a sin against a person
you deal with the person; if you have a sin against God you deal with God. I said,
"I'm home! This is what I felt all along."

I was always interested in the way other religions and cultures were expressed. I
went to friends' churches of various denominations of Christianity. These experi-

ences reaffirmed for me that I had been monotheistic and never believed in the Trinity. There wasn't much of a shift when I came to Judaism. I said, "Oh, this is right; this describes me." I always believed in God even though there were times when I struggled with the possibility of God's existence—how can I think of something of which I have no direct evidence? I really just have to go on a leap of faith here.

In my early twenties I met my husband. I had dated a lot before I met "Ze'ev"—even a couple of Jewish guys who were very secular, so that religious issues never came up. At first, I didn't even know they were Jewish. Once I knew, it was an interesting difference, not really significant to me, though I was curious about it. These weren't lasting relationships, anyway.

Then I met my husband through work. There is a wonderful story in the tradition that when a soul is sent down from heaven, it contains both male and female characteristics; the male elements enter a boy baby, the female, a girl baby; and if they be worthy, God reunites them, in marriage. It quickly became apparent that we were soul mates. We had a relatively short courtship and were married.

Ze'ev's family is very secular and very strongly identified as Jews. The family was very assimilated into American culture, although they did not have much contact with non-Jews. They came to the United States prior to the big wave of immigration from Europe. The family had historically been devoted to the Reform movement and its ideals.

In my husband's generation none have married Jews, and I am the only non-Jew who converted. So we are the last link—literally. In his family, the actual observance of ritual was minimal. Going to *shul* was for the High Holidays and for *Yartzeit*. His mother insisted on lighting Hanukkah candles. My husband's religious education consisted only of Sunday school. He had a formal *bar mitzvah* ceremony and then confirmation.

Although my husband had an active and thoughtful relationship with *HaShem*, it was not one bound in ritual. He attended a private secular prep school for most of middle school and upper school. Ze'ev is a very gentle person and very religiously tolerant, so it was not controversial or an act of rebellion for him to marry a non-Jew. He still considered himself Jewish, and he didn't feel that his marriage to me had any bearing on his Jewish identity.

At the time of our marriage I did not give much attention to the issue of our differing religions. I waited until about a year after the marriage to convert. When we were going to be married, I called a priest at the nearest Catholic church. He said, "I can't marry you. No Catholic priest is going to marry you! We're going to excommunicate you!" The cantor of my husband's Reform temple also declined. He said, "We can't do it; that is our policy. Why don't you consider conversion?" And I said, "Absolutely not! I will not do that just to get married. If I am going to make any changes, it is going to be well thought out."

I was twenty-two at this time. We were finally referred to a cantor who was willing to do interfaith marriages; and we were married under a *huppah* in Ze'ev's family home.

My adjustment to married life was complicated by difficulties I experienced adjusting to moving from a working-class Catholic background to a middle-class, nearly exclusively Jewish neighborhood. I was trying to figure out "Who am I?" in this different world. During this period of adjustment to such a dramatic shift in my circumstances, I had a need to view my efforts to become a part of the community in a spiritual light. I really started thinking about converting. I was feeling the need to strengthen my relationship with *HaShem*, which had been growing over the years, in a more formal way with some kind of religious structure—not only for myself but also for the marriage and the fact that we wanted to have children. It was important for us to be religiously consistent with the children. I discussed our options with my husband, but he was not interested in pursuing anything outside of Judaism. So I called the cantor from Ze'ev's temple and began the process of learning that eventually led to a Reform conversion.

Through Orthodox friends I learned that there would be questions about the validity of the conversion halakhically, although I had gone to the *mikveh*. The year after my daughter was born, I contacted an Orthodox rabbi, who told me he really didn't do conversions. The rabbi to whom he referred me never returned my calls. Since I did not feel comfortable exploring this further in the Orthodox community, I just put it on the side for a while, though I knew it was something I would eventually pursue.

After my Reform conversion, my husband and I started keeping kosher, and we went to temple quite regularly, but it was so big, and there were not many young people there. It was very difficult to make connections, and we didn't feel a sense of community. So our observance was primarily home based.

When my daughter was born, *my* family became much more actively involved in our day-to-day lives. With so many people coming and going through our house, it became impossible to monitor the level of *kashrut*. Our attempts to keep kosher lapsed during this period because of the complications we were experiencing trying to accommodate my family's interest in supporting us by preparing meals for us and inviting us to share meals with them. Eventually, we made a conscious decision that it is more important to allow the family to be part of our lives than to observe the *halakhah* of *kashrut* now.

We were young, new to marriage, new as parents, and trying to be observant in the absence of a supportive community. Our commitment to observance was made more tentative by our feeling that we couldn't push this with our families. So we became very lax. At the same time I was also moved to call an Orthodox rabbi because I was very worried about the status of our children. I felt our children had to be Jewish, without any question. For a while, I didn't do anything about that issue. I had another child. We still observed holidays, and my daughter went to a religious nursery school. She had Jewish friends.

I was becoming increasingly concerned about how much of our religious focus we had relinquished, about how easily one can be drawn into assimilation, and I was very ambivalent about my status as a Jew, and of course my children's. To complicate matters these issues were also caught up in the normal separation that one must go through in establishing a home and family life separate from one's parents. I felt that an Orthodox conversion would be the first step in providing a framework to address all of my concerns.

An added dimension to this was that my husband was uncomfortable with what he knew about Orthodoxy. He felt that the adjustment for the family would be too great, that it would require too great a sacrifice to become *Shomer Shabbat*. "I know I'm Jewish," was his response, though he was supportive of my interest in doing more on my own. But I quickly realized that observance is not like a hobby—it requires the commitment and involvement of the whole family.

At about that time, I was getting to know better a woman who had previously been only an acquaintance. She's *frum*, but I had not known that. I felt comfortable with her in discussing my interest in becoming more observant.

I was invited to her home for *Shabbat* and also to her *shul*, which was led by a hasidic rebbe. So, I drove there, and because I knew this congregation would not drive after *Shabbat* had started, I hid my car on a side street. There was such warmth at this *shul*. I just loved it there. I was nearly in tears. I met the rabbi, though he intimidated me a little at first. Then we went back to my friend's house, and I stayed for *Kiddush*. When I arrived back home, my kids were sitting in front of the TV; there were lights on all over the house. It was like having a bubble burst. I felt sick inside. It's *Shabbat*, and look at my house! This is what we do at the end of the week— veg out!

So I started going back maybe every two weeks. I'd drive my car down, hide it, go to services, and come home. It was really bothering me to do this alone, and I told my husband. Despite his concerns and mixed feelings, he was willing to accompany me to *shul*. But Ze'ev was not touched by the atmosphere in the same way I had been. His Hebrew was rusty and he had difficulty following the service. It was somewhat intimidating to him, and he was concerned, if we were to join this *shul*, about how this level of observance might set him apart from the rest of the world. Still, he was intrigued by the intensity of the *davening*.

This congregation is very warm and welcoming, and as we got to know more people, the issue of my status as a Jew came up very quickly. People were very supportive of my interest in an Orthodox conversion, and they encouraged me to discuss this with the rabbi. I was also aware that in order to participate fully as a family in all the activities of this *shul* and community, a halakhic conversion was essential. I became aware of how charged this issue is, and how the understanding of "Who is a Jew" is interpreted differently by the various segments of the Jewish community, including individuals within the Orthodox community. Eventually, as a result of considering the various points of view, I came to see myself as halakhically not Jewish, which was a very strange thing because certainly I had internalized my identity as a Jew. Finally, I went to the rabbi and began to learn and go through the process for conversion again.

The rabbi was really wonderful. He knew that my husband was having difficulty. He said, "Just take it slow," and I added, "Otherwise, I'll be religious and not have a marriage." He acknowledged my concern. I never had the experience of his advising me to do anything inconsistent, but he would inform me of the proper observance, while also communicating that only I knew what I was able and needed to do at any given point. He was very, very wise.

A few months after I had my first meeting with the rabbi, Ze'ev and I went to see him as a couple. My husband was honest with me about his struggles in this process, and I encouraged him to express this openly with the rabbi. The rabbi helped us to see that at this time it was important for our relationship as a couple to shift the focus I had developed concerning my conversion to focus instead on the family's need to become connected with our move toward a religious life. He suggested we put the conversion "on the back burner." He did not communicate a sense of urgency.

This was at first hard for me to hear. I *did* feel a sense of urgency. Why should my status be affected by my husband's hesitation? I wanted to speak to the rabbi again to make this point more strongly. For some reason I had difficulty in getting in touch with him, and by the time I did reach him, I realized that he was absolutely right, and I told him so. I had come to appreciate the wisdom of the rabbi's advice to go slowly, and I was able to give Ze'ev some latitude. It was a revelation to me that I could be at peace with a different level of progress than I felt my soul was demanding.

My response to Ze'ev's reticence went from "We have to do this!" to "Well, if you don't want to do that now, that's okay; maybe in the future we will." I stopped pushing, and he really responded. He started becoming more interested in learning and attended classes.

As a family we began doing those *mitzvot* with which we were comfortable. The first thing we did was *Shabbat*. My husband said, yes, this could be kind of nice because right now we come in kind of pooped on Friday night—we get Chinese food or pizza—and it would be nice to do something together as a family. This was near Pesah, so we decided to *kasher* everything so we would be *Pesadikh*. It was a very busy time! My husband really likes keeping kosher. He said, "This is the thing I like to do! This really identifies me as a Jew." He even started keeping kosher at work. *Kashrut* was never a problem for him. With *Shabbat*, we gradually learned more about the laws of observance to sanctify the day, and as we were ready we included more aspects of observance. We started with the things that we knew how to do, like the cooking and the lights. We're still learning; "Oh, we should do this; we shouldn't do that."

My goal is to be halakhically observant. I have certain limitations right now. I know who I am, and I know myself, and I know my family situation. There are some things I just can't do at this moment in time. It's going to be too much of a struggle, now. But the intention and goal is that we will get to these things. While my husband and family were moving along at their own pace, on a personal level I was feeling an even greater eagerness to move ahead. I was comfortable with covering my hair, which is part of a Jewish woman's observance of the *miztvot* of modesty or *sniyes*. This is the *derekh*—the way—of my community, and it also represented a significant spiritual practice for me.

I felt very relieved after the Orthodox conversion. My two children converted on the same day—it was kind of a package deal! What was different about this second conversion was that I converted into a community. A few days later the rabbi called—as he often does for no special reason—just to see how things were going. This was just a continuation of the relationship we had already established with the rabbi and that is enjoyed by all the members of our community. He knows my family—my whole family—he knows what is going on in our lives, he is always available to us.

Our oldest child was already attending a secular school when we began this process, and Hebrew school in the afternoons. We knew that once I converted, she would be attending an Orthodox day school. She would initially have a lot of catching up to do. Ze'ev began studying with her, teaching her *parashot*. I never cease to be delighted at how adaptable our children have been. They have gone from being secular little kids to observing *Shabbat*. Working with our daughter really changed things around for both Ze'ev and me.

It quickly became apparent that the process of becoming religiously observant wasn't just about our own individual spiritual quest—not a self-absorbed spiritual learning; this was really about *survival*, about our family's reconnection with our Jewish heritage that I pray will continue into future generations. Let's teach this to our children—that was the mandate. The importance of bringing our family back to Judaism put a whole different light on whatever differences Ze'ev and I might have had at the beginning. The whole process became something that we were doing together for a higher purpose.

My relationship with God had been a consistent one but as I have grown spiritually and especially with my conversions, it has intensified. It is a very personal, deep communication that goes on all the time. In my *davening* is that ongoing communication. I turn everything over to God—I try to. I try to be very conscious of the source of everything. A religious life is not just rote observance of *halakhah*; it is your whole intention in doing things. It's not just something that I do that is separate from my life, it's really part of my life—when I'm gardening or in my interactions with my children.

Life gets pretty miserable when I'm not centered on God. I think sometimes that you do forget and you get complacent or you may have a day when you are just into yourself. The *halakhah*, the *mitzvot* that you do everyday bring you back. Simple things. You can express your gratitude to God for life and for the most basic blessings—you say a *brakhah* in gratitude that your body works like it does because of *HaShem*. There is a *brakhah* for when you see a beautiful sight; when you wash and you eat and you *bentsch*. The *mitzvot* keep you in relationship to God all the time, they give the relationship a structure. They are paths to holiness, and if you follow them, you can't go too far astray. I like that too. To pay attention to a *mezuzah*. You get a paycheck and you know you have to give part of it away. Just being human, it's so easy to see yourself as the center and to forget where things come from. That's what I like about the *mitzvot*. They are there to keep you connected all the time, to always keep *HaShem* there with you.

In my work, which involves complex issues about human nature, we are not trained to address spiritual issues. I find in the people I work with a deep and sometimes hard-to-express desire to explore those realms, and I am comfortable to go there with them. I try to be open to asking for help from *HaShem* in my work. I know that there are limitations to what I can do, so I ask for support—perhaps only to help me think more clearly about what I can do.

My family of origin has gradually come to accommodate the changes we've made in our lives. They have realized that we still can maintain a close relationship, but at the same time, Ze'ev and I are different and are leading a life separate from them that does not necessarily diminish the strength of our bond with them.

Ze'ev's family is like many born-Jewish families. I've noticed that it is sometimes difficult for Jews who are not Orthodox to understand a friend or family member's move to a more observant lifestyle. When you add to this other issues—leaving certain family traditions behind, changing habits that your parents valued and took for granted—things become more difficult. In the end, though, I think it boils down to whether or not you can accept your chidren being different from you, yet still be deeply connected. And this connection is felt in both our families.

I have had a sense for a long time that there are just some people who need to be Jewish, who feel as if their soul is Jewish and this is where they need to be. At this point, I couldn't live without Judaism. It would be like taking away my essence. I believe that God does know who all the Jews in the world for all time are going to be, and we converts are included among them. Why we weren't born Jews, I don't know. When I came to Judaism I said, this is really me. Yes, I met and married a Jewish man, but I searched this out on my own and brought it into our lives. Did I convert *because* I married a Jewish man or did I marry a Jewish man *because* I needed to convert?

There is a great deal of sincerity among people who convert and there is a great spiritual yearning to be Jewish. There is so much to learn from somebody who converts because we have made these choices to do this. We come to the religion fresh. We have a perspective of God that we developed as adults, which all of us must do in order to have authentic religious lives—Jewish or non-Jewish.

My family had lunch one *Shabbat* with a man who is particularly brilliant in his field of endeavor. He is a very practical, scientific person, and it was a surprise to have him say to me, "Your *neshamah* was there at Sinai because all the souls who would become Jews were there."

23

When Is *Shabbat* Over in the Land of the Midnight Sun?

Gloria

Gloria's fascination with history and culture has taken her all over the world. No matter what country she is in, she takes time to find out about the Jewish community and its customs and loves to go for services at the local *shul*. Her commitment to *Yiddishkeit* began as a teenager, over thirty years ago.

Gloria remembers how when she was a little girl everyone looked forward to the visits of her great-aunt from New York, who would carry in her suitcase enormous loads of Jewish rye bread. Gloria heard once that this aunt had married a Jewish man—or was she herself Jewish?

Was that why Gloria, at the age of sixteen, decided to become a Jew? Was there some ancestral spark waiting to be lit? If there is the right combination of experiences that touch you, does that spark become a flame?

I converted the day before I graduated high school, over thirty years ago.

I grew up in Bucks County, outside of Philadelphia, and for the last couple of years of high school, my family lived in the city in a predominantly Jewish neighborhood. The high school I attended was big—3,000 kids—and I would say 80 percent were Jews, maybe more.

I was brought up Protestant and confirmed in the Lutheran Church. My mother was involved in church activities, and I remember when I was younger going to church every Sunday and participating in Bible school. My father wasn't really that religious.

When I was thirteen and going through the confirmation class, I started to question things that didn't make sense to me. There were a number of things about Christianity that I had difficulty believing: the immaculate conception, the resurrection, the divinity of Jesus. My doubts may have just been part of my need to analyze everything. But I was not supposed to question. You were told, "That's it; that's the way it is." One of the things that appealed to me about Judaism was that there was no problem with questioning. It's not wrong, and you're not looked down upon, at least I haven't run into that.

Although a lot of things didn't make sense, I had grown up knowing that religion was important, so it wasn't just a matter of saying, "I don't want any religion." There were, however, some religions that would not have been acceptable due to the climate of prejudice in which I was brought up. For example, some of the Protestant points of view with which I was familiar were negative about Catholicism. But that was a different time.

This attitude, though, affected me when I was studying religion by influencing my elimination of Catholicism. I did an analysis of various other religions, reading up on them, anything from Buddhism to Confucianism to Catholicism. I also investigated different Protestant denominations. I had belonged to the girl's part of the Masonic Lodge, a group called "Rainbow Girls." As one part of socializing, we would go to different churches. I was not moved by what I saw and learned. Sometimes, I went to a synagogue, or I had discussions with Jewish friends. But people just didn't convert to Judaism back then.

In my later teens our family doctor was Jewish, and I often baby-sat for his family. I had a discussion with him and his wife once, and I said, "I think I want to become Jewish." And he said, "Well, no, people don't do that." But he also said, "Okay, I will call my rabbi, and I will have him sit down and talk to you." He set up the appointment with his rabbi. I was sixteen, I had a car, and I drove myself to meet with him.

I didn't know until awhile later that the rabbi had called my mother. He talked to her and asked, "Do you know that your daughter is doing this? How do you feel about this? Should I discourage her? What is your position?" My mother said that studying Judaism was my decision.

I visited the rabbi every week for a period of several months. We would have a discussion for an hour or two. Although he was an Orthodox rabbi, and one of several in his family, his synagogue was Conservative. He was about the same age as the doctor, probably in his thirties, and also had young children. At his home, I watched his wife *kasher* meat and do other things in the household. One time during Passover, the rabbi said he had to go do an inspection for the local dairy, so I went along with him. Eventually the rabbi said, "I guess maybe you need to get involved in some kind of course." He contacted the rabbinic board for information, and I signed up for a class and went twice a week for about a year.

The classes were in Center-City Philadelphia, so I would stay overnight at my grandparents', who lived farther down in the city. Neither of my grandparents objected to what I was doing; in fact, my grandfather said it was fascinating.

The class I attended was made up of perhaps a dozen people who were interested in converting for various reasons. I think some because they were getting married. There were some people who were looking at being Jewish and had Jewish boyfriends or girlfriends and just wanted to be able to relate more. I was the youngest person there. I could see that there was much to be gained by being with a group of people with similar situations and an opportunity to learn from more than one person. We had three different rabbis as teachers. We covered various topics: Hebrew, prayer, the Bible, and various other things. We were advised that if you don't understand, you ask. I was interested in the classes, and I questioned.

It all made sense. It was a challenge, though I really didn't realize then how involved Judaism is. This course was really just an overview, strictly the bare basics. There was a lot of discussion. We learned the basic prayers, attended services at various synagogues, and, before the *mikveh*, we went before the board of rabbis to be questioned. We signed a statement that we were doing this by choice and not being forced to do it. We had to pick a Jewish/Hebrew name. I'm sure there were reasons why I picked "Leah" for my Hebrew name, but now I can't remember them.

I converted the day before I graduated from high school. There was a big ceremony for all the people in the class, held at the Philadelphia synagogue designed by Frank Lloyd Wright. There were speeches by the people who were involved in the class, and the rabbis gave speeches. We were allowed to invite family members and friends. My mother and my grandmother attended.

It was really difficult for a lot of people to understand why I had converted. My Jewish friends were supportive but puzzled. "Why do you want to become Jewish?" they asked. Their response was not really negative, they just took their Jewishness for granted. They were growing up in a Jewish neighborhood, had had Jewish friends for ever and ever, but couldn't understand why somebody would want to be Jewish intentionally! For me, it was in that environment that my interest began.

My situation as a convert was kind of unusual. I used to light candles on Friday night at my mother's house. I was not eating certain things, but she didn't have too much problem with that. My father did object, but my parents were in the process of divorce and he soon moved out.

After I graduated high school, I went to college at Temple University. I would go out only with people who were Jewish, but just because you're Jewish doesn't mean that you're even halfway observant. I had thought that if you were Jewish, you went to synagogue or participated in Jewish activities. I found out that that wasn't always the case.

I dated and became seriously involved with a Jewish man who was to become my husband. His parents strongly objected because I wasn't a born Jew, though they were not observant themselves. They were not active in a synagogue, but his father did take him to see a rabbi and had the rabbi try to talk him out of seeing me. He was not allowed to come to my house, and he could never have the family car if he was going out with me. They stopped paying for his college. It was a very nasty situation.

We did decide to get married, but if my mother was going to do the wedding, his parents wouldn't come. Finally his parents said, "We'll come, but we'll make the wedding." The wedding itself was small, the way they wanted, with a big reception afterward. It turned out his father, as a manufacturer, could get business tax write-offs by having his clients from Macy's and Gimbel's as his guests for the wedding.

I was about twenty-one when I got married, and my husband was a little bit older. Though his parents always expected us to spend the holidays with them, I really had an increasingly difficult time maintaining any kind of Jewish identity because he was not religious at all. He was Jewish in name only and nothing else, so I became Jewish in name only, too. We didn't belong to a synagogue or go to one very often. We lit candles occasionally, but that was it.

It was a very negative feeling, but I thought, well, maybe this is true of all Jewish people. I was confused but didn't know whom to turn to at that point, and we began to have other problems. He became overly friendly with somebody he was working with. Then we moved from Philadelphia down to Washington. We had been married for ten years and I was pregnant with my son when we finally joined a synagogue—because I wanted to. I became active in the sisterhood. We met people with whom I'm still friendly, and we'd go to services with them once a month or so. But any other time I'd say I wanted to go to services, he'd say, "No, I don't want to deal with that nonsense." He ridiculed my preparations for Passover. "I don't believe in this stuff," he said. And I thought to myself, "I don't need this—his behavior or his criticism."

My children were very young—Mark was five and Rebecca about two and a half—when I decided to get a divorce. I had to do it. I was working, I had a good job, and I was used to doing things on my own. The kids have grown up with me, and I have made ours a Jewish household. Their father does not tell anybody he's Jewish. He will not take off for holidays, and has always tried to undermine my efforts at raising the children as Jews. It was extremely difficult when the kids were involved in religious-school activities because he would tell them, "You don't have to go to Hebrew School."

Rebecca went to Jewish day school from kindergarten through sixth grade. That school was not in existence when Mark was younger, but he went to Hebrew school, and they both had *bar* and *bat mitzvahs*. We've been to Israel. My daughter is very involved with being Jewish, and both of my kids went to Jewish camps.

When I was free to be the kind of Jew I wanted to be, our observances at home increased. We keep kosher at home, although we don't have separate dishes. I became more involved in our synagogue. I'm now on the board of directors and co–vice president of ways and means of the sisterhood. I subscribe to various Jewish magazines and books. And I made sure we attended services more frequently. The kids went to Sunday school and junior congregation. Rebecca is probably more religious than Mark, but before he takes out milk at dinner, Mark will say, "Can I have this?" I'll say, "No, you can't because we are having meat for dinner." And he says, "Oh, okay." And that's it; he puts it back. Sometimes Mark will say, "I don't think I want to be Jewish." I'll say, "You don't have a choice; your mother is Jewish." And then he'll go on to something else.

Being a single Jewish parent can be difficult because of time and financial pressures. I was fortunate to have a career that allowed me to belong to a synagogue, to send my daughter to a private school. A lot of single parents might say it's not worth it or, yes, they'll identify as Jews but don't have the time or the energy to belong to a synagogue or to get involved. It would be so much easier to say, "Hey, I don't feel like getting up on Saturday, or I need the day to run around doing things." But I see being Jewish as very family oriented and also very communal. My children do not have a lot of family—no aunts, no cousins—so I hope that they will see the community in the synagogue can be for them an extended Jewish family.

Our rabbi is great and so is the congregation. It's a real community. There's a big mix of people in all age groups. We have a sense of togetherness; people caring about each other. I'm getting a lot out of it, but I think you can get out of something only if you put into it. If you get involved, it's there for the asking. It is important to me to be a part of a group, the friendships, and being able to share things with others who have a mutual background and understanding. On the other hand, you don't have to fit into a mold. You're allowed to express yourself. In Judaism, there is room to be yourself.

When I was divorced, people who knew I converted asked, "Well, are you still going to be Jewish now that you're getting a divorce?" "I was Jewish before I got married so why shouldn't I stay Jewish?" A lot of people think that most people convert just because they're getting married or they're involved with someone.

I feel more accepted now, and I've been Jewish so long that when I tell somebody I'm not a born Jew, they don't believe it. "How can you not be Jewish?" In fact, at my daughter's *bat mitzvah*, which was only two years ago, there were people who did not know that I had converted. During his talk to Rebecca the rabbi said something about "your mother chose Judaism," and people expressed their surprise to me afterwards.

Now, I am sometimes in the unique position of sharing my knowledge with my friends who are born Jews and who don't have the practical knowledge of how to run a Jewish household. They will ask me about something to do with the kitchen— can you do this, can you do that. I can tell them, "Well, I think this is how it goes, and this is the reason behind it." It helps to have been a home-economics major, but I have also either cochaired or chaired or worked with the Sukkot luncheon at our synagogue for about twelve or fourteen years. I've learned by doing, as well as by studying.

I have a lot of confidence as a Jew, but it's been so long—thirty years. It takes a lot of energy to convert, and even after the conversion, it takes a lot of energy to be Jewish. For example, I travel a lot, and although I'm not strictly kosher, I do worry about what they serve on airplanes. So I always call up the airline and say, "I want kosher food." But it has been through my travels that I have been able to experience a broader perspective of Jewish life.

Each trip I take, I always wind up at a synagogue in a foreign country. I have been to synagogues in St. Thomas and Finland and Sweden and Denmark and Toronto. In Toronto, we wanted to have lunch rather late on a Friday afternoon. From downtown to get to the Jewish area is a $30 cab ride, and when we finally got to a restaurant, they were shutting down: "*Shabbat* is coming!"

In St. Thomas there is a Sephardic synagogue with a dirt floor. The building is all wooden. The rabbi is Reform and from somewhere in the United States.

In Finland, sundown in June or July is really late. So I asked, "How do you know when *Shabbat* is over? When do you do *Havdalah*?" "We just do it Sunday or Sunday afternoon." I didn't know that it is permissible to do *Havdalah* until Tuesday! The Jewish community in Finland is small, but they support numerous facilities: a day school, nursing homes, and many other things. That experience impressed upon me how important it is that each of us contribute to Jewish institutions and always make donations to the people in the local community.

When I was in Denmark, I got everybody out of bed at six in the morning to go to the *minyan* at the synagogue. All the men there had on tall silk hats, and instead of making me go upstairs because I was a woman, I was allowed to sit behind the palm trees and flowers in the back. The rabbi from this synagogue is the chief rabbi of Copenhagen, and he came to Washington, D.C., recently to celebrate the fiftieth anniversary of the rescue of Denmark's Jews. The Jewish community in Denmark is very small, but it's also supported by the government over there. Danes declare their religious affiliation on the tax return, and a certain amount of taxes goes to support religious organizations.

In Curaçao there is a Dutch synagogue, a very old building that looks like the other Dutch Island houses from the outside. It was a yellow building with black and white marble floors in the courtyard.

Visiting these communities worldwide reinforces my own sense of what it means to be Jewish. Being Jewish can be many things. It's a culture, a language, a community, a people. For me, God is in all of these things. That's something I think about.

24

Judaism Is a Journey— Not a Destination

Michael Lawson

It has been said, "Life is not a problem to be solved but a mystery to be lived." Michael Lawson is open to the mystery of life, its twists and turns, the new possibilities offered by deeper experience. He thoughtfully explores his spirituality through his and his family's increasing commitment to leading an observant Jewish life.

Michael has found that spiritual insights come from disparate sources: a charismatic Unitarian minister; a Reform rabbi who was born in England and now leads a congregation in Albuquerque; the B'nai Isaac *shul* in South Dakota where seventeen families keep alive their traditions beside Native Americans who are struggling to preserve their culture; and now the wit, intellect, and spiritual presence of his rabbi at Congregation Agudas Achim in Arlington. For Michael there is wisdom in both the scholarship of the Reform movement and the fervent faith of the Lubavitchers. What he sometimes finds challenging is the negativity Jews often show toward each other.

Many converts are, like Michael, gratified, and often surprised, to learn that Judaism expects, even requires, that Jews be of this earth even as we seek higher spiritual planes, for which we are all considered to have the potential. We are commanded to enjoy the pleasures and joys life brings and even have prayers to celebrate and acknowledge those, just as we are to acknowledge the hardships and sorrows that are part of being human. Judaism teaches that the more fully we become part of the cycles of the seasons, the cycles of life, the more we can see God in everything.

Michael, himself, trusts absolutes without being an absolutist. He does not know with certainty what will be around the next corner, but he is firm in his belief that he will live fully now, always evolving and open to the gifts a new level of observance will bring.

Coming to Judaism was an evolution for me.

I first converted in 1975, after Marcia and I had been married for a few years. I've actually gone through two conversions. I'll probably go through three! I started with Reform, and then in 1991 I went through a Conservative conversion. I am happy with where I am in Judaism now, but I don't know if I would have taken this direction if I had not married a Jewish woman. It has taken twenty years, and it has been an evolution for both of us.

My father was killed in World War II, and I was raised primarily by my mother in a small town in Michigan where my father's family was well-known. My grandfather was the postmaster. Although my mother came from a very fundamentalist, Pentecostal southern background, the church that I grew up in was Methodist—middle of the road Protestant. My mother is still a very religious person and has now become a born-again Christian in the charismatic movement. She is remarkable in that she always let her children do their own thing, make their own choices. This has not been easy for her because we've sort of gone on different paths.

When I was ten, she married a Catholic, and I have two half sisters who are ten and twelve years younger than I am. My mother and stepfather were married in a Catholic ceremony, and my mother promised to raise their daughters as Catholics. My sisters attended Catholic school until high school. Now, one of my sisters is a nominal Protestant and the other is probably a nominal Catholic, but religion is not the center of either one's life. Although I don't think my mother completely understands some of the choices I've made, she does like and respect the fact that we have a religion-centered home.

I used to go to church camp in the summer. Michigan has beautiful lakes where we would have morning meditations and campfire services at night. The spirituality of all that really touched me and I felt a very personal relationship with God, in the Protestant tradition. I wanted my children to have the opportunity of such an experience so this summer we sent our daughter to a Ramah camp in New England. It was a great experience for her, and she can't wait to go back. Her knowledge of Judaism grew so much in the short time she was there. I just knew she would feel a religious aspect of being at camp. It will be the same with my son too, because he is naturally spiritual. My son really picks up on everything and enjoys every aspect of Judaism that he knows about. He and God already have a very personal relationship.

It was my college study of the early church that caused me to question the divinity of Christ. I was disillusioned by how much Christ seemed to be a fabrication of Peter and Paul, the disciples, and the early Roman churches. I was surprised to learn about the kinds of manipulation that went on during those early days of Christianity. I began to question the need for an intermediary to God. At the same time, partly as a result of studying science, I began to doubt that there was an afterlife.

Later, I discovered that Jewish philosophy says you should live your life as if it is its own reward. There are no guarantees after you are gone. The only thing you will leave is the memory and reputation you develop while you are on the earth. That was very appealing to me.

This exploration and development of a personal philosophy was coming together while I was meeting Jewish people for the first time. Their lives were different; there seemed to be a lot of stress on family values and education and on being successful. Even though they weren't particularly religious Jews, these values really made them better people.

Before I finished college, I went into the air force for four years. At the time, I was having identity problems. I changed colleges or majors every semester or so. I needed to get focused and I was going to be drafted anyway, so I decided to enlist. While I was in the military, I heard about a branch of the University of Nebraska in Omaha that had pioneered the "Bootstrap Program" to help servicemen get college degrees. People could take six months' temporary duty away from the service and get a degree. By this time I knew I wanted to major in history. I could get my degree and then go to graduate school.

While I was matriculating, I met a Jewish guy from Omaha who was also in the Bootstrap Program. We were in the library one night, and he introduced me to a woman he'd gone to high school with who was teaching at the university. That was Marcia. She and I really hit it off, and, within a year, we were married.

Marcia came from an "American Orthodox" background—that's the way she described it; I don't know if that is an official term or not. There is no *mehitzah* in their *shul* in Omaha, but they are affiliated with the Orthodox movement and they retained other traditions.

Marcia says I swept her off her feet, and at the time, it wasn't an issue for her that I wasn't Jewish. I think she had regrets about that later. Now, I think it is difficult for her to understand some of the things that she did at that point of her life—like going to the Unitarian church. But she was attracted by the charismatic minister, and I was, too. At that time she was ready to reject many of her family's traditions and the way they viewed her. She had had some negative experiences with the rabbi at her home synagogue. In hindsight, though, she would have done some things differently—one being not to have gotten married the same year her father died. Also, she probably would have tried harder to find somebody to marry us who was Jewish.

There was no rabbi in Nebraska, then, who would marry us. There was a Jewish judge who would have been willing to marry us in the hotel. But I said, "No, I want some kind of religious sanction," so we were married by the minister of the Unitarian church we had been attending. We were very much enthralled by him, and Unitarianism was sort of where I was intellectually—questioning the deity of Christ. We also went to High Holiday services, so our religious life was pretty eclectic.

Her family was a little cool toward me, initially, particularly her sister and brother-in-law, although that relationship has grown closer over the years. Marcia's mother has more of a Jewish cultural identity, but for her father the spiritual aspect of Judaism was the focus which may explain how they responded to me. I didn't get to know Marcia's father very well, though I did have a private conversation with him the first time we met. Afterward he told her mother, "That's who Marcia's going to marry, so you better learn to live with it."

When Marcia and I had been married for four years, we lived in New Mexico, where I was in graduate school. We were involved in a *havurah* there and had gotten to know a wonderful Reform rabbi who had grown up in England. At the time I made the decision to convert, I was a graduate assistant at the university for a course on Jewish history. The rabbi meshed that course with my preparation for conversion.

My conversion ceremony didn't involve a *bris* or *mikveh* or *Bet Din*, only studying about Judaism in general and the Reform movement in particular.

After that, I worked for the Bureau of Indian Affairs for many years—we call it my "foreign service" duty—and for a few years we lived in a small town in South Dakota, where our daughter was born. The town had about 26,000 people, with a small Jewish community. It was amazing to me! The *shul*, B'nai Isaac, was an old converted Methodist church—George McGovern's father had once been a minister there. It had been a synagogue since 1917 and was affiliated with the Conservative movement. The *shul* was maintained by the seventeen or so Jewish families that lived, permanently, in the region. There had been a rabbi at one point, but not when we were there. We flew in rabbinical students from the Seminary for High Holiday and other services. This congregation became the bridge from Reform—the only branch of Judaism I had known—to a more traditional observance of Judaism. And it was the only show in town!

The congregation was primarily composed of merchant families who had department stores or salvage businesses—they were the long-term families. Then there was a group of transient people, such as physicians who worked for the Indian Health Service. There was such a sense of community—it was like a *havurah*—and it was easy to become very involved. Everyone was very helpful and very accepting, and open to just about anything you wanted to do. We were invited to different families' homes for all the holidays. If you patronized their stores you got a "Jewish" discount!

Although we did not at that time keep kosher, there were very *frum* families who had their meat flown in. They maintained a very strong Jewish identity. The sisterhood was always winning awards because, per capita, they always got the most participation and contributions!

Despite living in a small town, these were pretty worldly people. The older folks left every winter for Florida or Arizona or California. Most of the adult children had gone off to become professionals and did not return, but there was usually at least one who stayed to take over the family business that had been established by grandparents or great-grandparents.

There wasn't much anti-Semitism in the town, and all the families were respected in the community. We always joked that we knew all the Indians and Jews in the area. At times, we even brought the two communities together. At my daughter's naming we invited all my Indian friends from work. They had never seen anything like this. And I attended some of their family events as well.

South Dakota was not a place where I would want to spend the rest of my life, but it was good for the years we were there. I was back there recently, and, sad to say, the Jewish community continues to dwindle.

We lived near our current *shul* in Virginia for a long time before we joined. For a while, we attended services at the George Washington University Hillel, but we wanted to get the kids more involved. We needed to decide whether we would go to a Conservative or Reform *shul*. When we met the rabbi at Agudas Achim, that convinced us.

Part of the draw toward Judaism has been the charisma of the three spiritual leaders who have influenced me: first the Unitarian minister; then the rabbi in Albuquerque; and probably foremost, Jack Moline, who is my rabbi now. Each of these men seemed to be close to God, and by becoming close to them, spiritually, I could get closer to God as well. Even though my current rabbi sometimes comes across as very "hip," there is no doubt, if you know him, that he is a very spiritual person. All three of these men are worldly and also very intellectual. They also have a good sense of humor—that is important to spirituality!

Having a personal relationship with God and spirituality is very important to me, but I don't know if it is distinctly Jewish. Is my relationship with God any different now than it was when I was a kid at Methodist church camp? It is just that the medium is different. I left Christianity, not God. What I need from religion I can find in Judaism. Marcia certainly can. She is very happy—it has really become the focus of her life, and the kids are well established in the religion.

I am very happy with the place we've arrived, as a family. I grew up in a house that was divided by religion. Everyone would get up on Sunday morning, and my stepfather and half-sisters would go to mass, and my mother and I would go to Methodist services. It wasn't particularly negative—we still had a sense of family, but it seems to me that in mixed marriages there should be some compromise worked out so that there is a uniform approach to religion. Raising kids is a crapshoot no matter what you do, but it is best to give them one coherent message.

My particular philosophy is that if you give children something that is fairly structured, when they do break away they aren't going to go too far. I see kids who were raised without any structure, without any religious ideas, and I'm not surprised that they run off and become Hare Krishnas or New Age people. They are searching for that thing they didn't have. They had all kinds of diversity, but they didn't have structure.

In both Marcia's and my experience—maybe it is just a phenomenon of our generation—we had pretty narrowly structured values presented to us. We went through a period in the sixties when we rebelled far away from that, but we are back to some form of it now. Even the experimentation we did back then was not very far afield. They seemed like big, bold steps at the time, but compared to the options today, they weren't.

When Marcia and I decided to celebrate our twentieth anniversary by renewing our vows, I knew that the rabbi would require me to undergo a Conservative conversion before he would perform the ceremony. Rabbi Moline recognized that I had been practicing Judaism for nearly twenty years and that I was a very active member of the congregation, so there were only ritual requirements.

The *bris* was interesting. A member of the congregation who is an Ob-Gyn and a *mohel* had donated his services as a *mohel* to be auctioned off as part of a fundraiser at my son's preschool. The auction participants were to put their names on a list for the things they wished to bid on, and the list was circulated around. I put my name on the list to bid for the *mohel*. Everybody assumed, of course, that Marcia must be pregnant. What else would you need a *mohel* for? The *mohel* was surprised, too. This was the first time that he had done an adult, and certainly there were very few males sitting in his waiting room waiting for their appointments!

It was wonderful to have our children at our wedding! We invited all our friends to the reception, catered by a kosher Chinese restaurant that has since gone out of business.

Conversion to Judaism is a very personal choice. Unlike other kinds of conversion, there is no one proselytizing anyone to become Jewish. Part of the process is to make you aware of the reality of what you are about to do and to discourage you from making this step—mostly so you don't have any regrets afterward.

I've never felt any stigma about being a convert in my congregation, and I've not heard too many negative comments about converts. I think there is a more open environment now. However fully one wants to participate in Judaism, it has been my experience that people are very accepting and helpful.

The first time I met Marcia's sister and brother-in-law, though, it was as if I wasn't there, but that relationship has evolved through the years. Now that we both have families and we're both at the same points spiritually, we get along really well.

My brother-in-law comes from an ultra-Orthodox background, and until recently he always maintained that tradition. That began to change when he and his family moved to a new city a few years ago for an important job he had taken there. They had trouble finding a spiritual home, so they affiliated with a Reconstructionist synagogue as the best alternative, and their daughter had her *bat mitzvah* there. Recently, they found an old Orthodox *shul* that was dying out. The congregation had decided to affiliate with the Conservative movement and bring in a rabbi from the Conservative seminary. My brother-in-law has some problems with that, but he really likes the community that developed there, and during the interim before they hired the rabbi he led the services.

So now we are all meeting in the middle at the same place. We've grown a lot closer together, and I don't worry about them anymore. I think they accept me as Jewish, although they were indifferent about the first, Reform, conversion. After the second conversion, they came to our wedding, and when I went to their daughter's *bat mitzvah*, they gave me an *aliyah. That* is the most open, dramatic sign of their acceptance.

In terms of *my* family accepting me and the choices I've made, I think my mother has, although, really, deep down she doesn't understand it. Her religion is so focused on the afterlife, she doesn't understand how I would deny myself that—I will be damned and go to hell. She has tried to learn about Judaism, but a lot of her information has come through the messianic Jews for Jesus movement, so her knowledge is kind of slanted. She sees programs about world rallies held in Israel and talks with the messianic Jews who come to her church. She doesn't understand why I couldn't make that leap as well, although it does help her understand how Judaism is different. She sends us appropriate Jewish holiday cards. We don't flaunt it, but our children certainly *do* flaunt their Jewish identity—there's no denying that! She's pretty accepting of that.

I have a lot of respect for anyone who places a high value on living a spiritual life—no matter what religion it is, across the board. There is a lot that I've learned about Judaism from Lubavitchers and just as much from Reform publications. I respect them all. What I don't understand is the nonacceptance of the ultra-Orthodox by people who otherwise place importance on Judaism. They think of them in almost negative terms. On the other hand, I don't understand the attitudes coming the other way: the *hasidic* people not accepting anyone who is trying to be spiritually Jewish, no matter how they are doing that.

Closer to home, I am also disturbed by the critical nature of many people in my own congregation. Some of these people are just generally negative people, and I notice that they are negative about just about everything. We have had to learn to distance ourselves from the naysayers—even though we'd rather they distanced themselves from us!

It has been a learning experience to discover people's differing needs when it comes to religion and spirituality. We had two sets of friends who were shopping around for a synagogue. We shared with them that although we are very enthusiastic about Agudas, we realize it is not for everyone. One couple thought they would be more comfortable in a Reform synagogue because the husband is Hispanic and has never converted. We recommended a Reform temple we thought they'd like. They hated it. It wasn't for them; too big, the people were too flashy. Our *shul*, on the other hand, is kind of a *hamishe* place—there's not a lot of glitzy, show-off things going on there. The couple wanted to try it out. They are drawn into it because their kid wants to be there all the time. The wife has had the support of the rabbi through the recent death of her mother. I don't know if the husband will ever convert—but he is there, and he is supportive.

Then there is the other couple. She and her husband both come from Conservative Jewish backgrounds, as a matter of fact, so we went through the whole thing again— "come to Agudas, although it may not be for you . . ." We thought they would have the same kind of experience as our other friends. They came to services, met the people at the religious school. The wife was embarrassed to tell me afterward that it was "too religious" for her, and it was inconvenient! She wanted to go to services that were only an hour long and a Sunday school that was only an hour and a half.

I guess I didn't realize the extent that we have become more observant, the extent to which Jack Moline has prodded us in that direction, and how much support there is in that community for increasing involvement.

Every year we do a little more that makes us more observant. It is interesting how little things add up, if you take one little thing at a time. We decided that we wanted to keep kosher and we went to talk to the rabbi about it. He said, "Whatever you do, don't go 'whole hog' tomorrow. Start with this: just try not mixing milk with meat— see how that goes. Then just try to have only kosher products in your home. If you get comfortable with that, then— this is the hard part—try not mixing milk and meat when you eat out. If you are comfortable with that, try having separate utensils and plates at home for milk and meat."

So the whole family got involved. My son became the "kosher cop" because he'd go shopping with us and he'd be checking for all the *hekshers*—"Dad, you can't get this. There's no sign on it." "Yeah, but Dave, it doesn't have any nonkosher ingredients." "No, Dad, we can't get this." It has become a family thing—a family commitment. I think the kids have to be reminded that this is *not* just a test of their will power, but that it is a way to honor God and keep the commandments.

My favorite Jewish holiday is the one I just had—whichever one that is. We just had a wonderful Sukkot. Maybe it is because fall is my favorite season; I like the whole idea of a harvest festival. Although we haven't yet built our own *sukkah*, we will—I went to a workshop on how to build one. We have some neighbors who built a wonderful one in which twenty people could eat. On a crisp night it was just great to be there.

It is getting easier and easier for me to fast every year—for Yom Kippur and the minor fast days. I don't know what there is about that. Each year you can remember back to the year before—you could do it then, you can do it now.

We are actually getting more involved in the minor holidays, the minor fasts that we didn't observe before. There is always a higher step you can take. We are doing it by increments, and it is a lifelong process. Perfection of observance is an unattainable goal—and anyway, they say Judaism is not a destination, it is a journey. It is so intellectually and spiritually challenging that there is no reason why you can't always be challenged by it—maybe to the point where you perpetually feel inferior! That is the danger. You see the people whom you respect as learned, observant people asking the same questions you are in their relationships with God. They don't feel that they've attained the level they want to achieve either. Everybody's spiritual path is so distinct. That is why I don't know if I can say that my spiritual path is distinctly "Jewish." I don't know that for sure.

While I have a Jewish identity, I don't have that feeling of possibly becoming a victim because of being a Jew. I don't have the fear that my father-in-law had that there would be the equivalent of an American pogrom. That had been his experience when he left Poland as a young man. He was always convinced that, well, we have it pretty good here now, but it could end at any moment, and we've certainly seen that in other places. I think that doesn't affect me, both because I am a convert and because I am of a different generation.

I really believe in Israel and am supportive of it, although as part of my air-force experience I lived in an Arab country. I don't have the hatred of Arabs that drives much of Jewish policy. I was someone who long ago supported peace accords along the lines of the ones that have developed recently. I think I now understand the differences on both sides—but what is striking, I think, are the similarities between Arabs and Jews.

We are soon going to have new neighbors who are from Saudi Arabia. He is a professor of Islam and has kids who are our kids' ages. So we are going to have our own peace accords here! That is what I hope will happen, anyway.

25

Naming a Soul

Uriel Hadassah Wave Korpi

I have a vivid memory of Uriel *davening*—hair and *tallit* flowing—at Elat Chayyim, the Jewish Renewal Movement's retreat center in New York State. This was Elat Chayyim's first year and my husband, children, and I had come up for the week-long Family Arts Camp. We participated in classes led by talented people who encouraged us to express Jewish spirituality through various art forms—including comedy! We feasted on gourmet vegetarian food and enjoyed the camaraderie of a diverse group of Jewish people from around the country, among whom was Uriel.

She was the only Jew, she said, in an isolated town in northern Calfornia. The year she lived in Bernie was for Uriel a time of deepening her understanding of the commitment she had made to become a Jew.

Much in the way of our biblical foreparents, during the years of exploration of the unfolding of her spiritual path, Uriel had been moved by the naming of her soul that came as an inspiration to her at each bend in her journey. Finally, in the Jewish Renewal Movement, all the disparate threads of her search were brought together, and through the evolving, dynamic, yet deeply rooted religious expression that is Judaism she became "Uriel Hadassah."

My spiritual journey has been much like putting together pieces of a puzzle. At times it was apparent that the pieces were falling into place beautifully, and at other times it was only later, upon reflection, that I could see how it all fit together.

I was born Catherine Marie Mitchell ("Sissy" to my family), the second child and first daughter of Tom and Adeline. My father and mother, along with many others of their era, were products of the grinding poverty of the Depression. With the one exception of their poverty, you would be hard-pressed to find any other similarity in their background. My father was one of two children raised in semi-isolation in the middle of a flat, dry West Texas plain. His family was a Southern Baptist clan of Irish-English-Welsh descent. My mother grew up in the middle of Denver, Colorado, number eight in a family of ten with dramatic, expressive Spanish-Catholic roots.

They met in "postwar-land-of-opportunity" California and within three months of their first date were married. Seven years later they had five children. We lived in a small town called Pittsburg, east of Berkeley, California. My father was in the general construction department of Pacific Gas and Electric, and was often "on the road."

My mom was a "professional" mother and always kept us, and the house, clean and neat. My parents created a tight family unit, within which their six children developed quite normally (a sixth was born to them seven years after they thought that they had finished their family). My childhood was placid, secure, and relatively uneventful. Although my father was often absent, my mother was always there. I never questioned my parents' love for me, it was just a given.

I was secure in my role as eldest sister. I made up skits and songs, then directed my "troupe" of three younger sisters as we entertained our parents for various birthdays, anniversaries, and holidays. My older brother was shy and reserved and seldom took part in our little family "productions." My mother always said, "Your sisters are your best friends," and we were very close growing up. I am proud to be able to say that I was a kind and generous older sister, sharing freely my "first discoveries" and "inside tips" on being a big kid, as well as my material possessions. There were, of course, times when I resented being so tightly woven together, but most of the time I was very happy and proud to be one of "the Mitchell sisters."

I did most of the things a reasonably self-assured, outgoing lower-middle-class kid did in the late fifties and early sixties. I went to public school, played with the neighborhood kids, and went home to a meat-and-potatoes meal after Dad got home from work. Besides my family, I had several close and faithful friends throughout my school years. In high school, I usually held a class office and some "rah-rah" position. Always family, friends, and community have been important and fulfilling to me. My positive experiences of such, I believe, created a fertile ground for the blooming of my Jewishness.

My mother raised us as Catholics. We went to church sporadically, usually at her urging, though she generally did not attend. I went to catechism classes, made my "first holy communion" at seven, and at the age of thirteen made my confirmation (similar to a *bar/bat mitzvah*). For the most part I enjoyed going to church. When I was between eight and twelve our family went to a large old-fashioned church in Pittsburg called St. Peter Martyr. There were stained glass, statues, votive candles, incense, and mystery. I loved saying the Rosary (Catholic holy beads) and listening to the Latin chants, hymns, and prayers. The mysterious ambience and aura of the Catholic Church of the late fifties suited my desire for private contemplation. It dawns on me now just how much my experience of religion in my youth was such a private one. The specifics of the religion did not hold much meaning for me. I really did not relate to, or have a profound sense of, Jesus. Rather, it was the peace I felt surrounded in the mystery and contemplation of God. My favorite line from our catechism was: "Who is God? God is love. Where is God? God is everywhere."

The Catholic Church began to change during my early teens. Gone was the Latin and the incense and with it the sense of mystery and awe. Services had become dry and boring and no longer held any appeal. I was changing, too. As I moved into adolescence, my churchgoing decreased dramatically. Catechism class was no longer required and going to confession was a thing of the past for me. It was difficult to resist the excitement and liberating "free-for-all" of Telegraph Avenue and the Haight-

Ashbury of the late sixties. Traditional religion just couldn't compete. Thinking or *feeling* about spiritually oriented subjects was not a part of my teenhood reality, until a major crisis struck our family when I was nineteen.

My older brother was killed in Vietnam as the first humans prepared to walk on the moon, July 19, 1969. His death became a major milestone on my spiritual journey. Seeing my brother's face behind glass, lying in a coffin, was a shattering experience. In my daze and disbelief I began to wonder, in a way I had never wondered before, about life and death and God. Although I was not yet on an *active* spiritual search, my brother's death impacted me on a deep and profound spiritual level that revealed itself as time went by.

The family cohesiveness that was such an integral part of my life disintegrated before my eyes. In the aftermath of this family upheaval, the possibility of marriage, and getting out of my sad and troubled home, seemed more appealing. Just seven short months after my brother's funeral, I married my high-school sweetheart in a "white church wedding" with 200 guests. It seemed the perfect antidote for all the "bad" things that had been happening to our family. My Catholic wedding essentially was the end of my formal relationship with the church.

My marriage, born out of the sorrow and chaos of that time in my family, lasted two years. We were both immature and our marriage had no firm foundation; it was merely a continuation of our high-school "going-steady" relationship. There was no planning for the future, no dreams, no visions. I left the marriage in a dramatic and destructive fashion and entered what I consider to be my "dark period," which lasted about two years.

During this period I was periodically depressed and consistently self-indulgent. I worked at numerous jobs, none of them satisfying. I bummed around and eventually ended up in Golden, Colorado, where, emotionally and physically depleted, I became seriously ill. After several weeks in bed and with the care and support of my roommates, I started to emerge out of the fog of the previous two years. I felt the illness to be my "wake-up call." I was grateful to be shaken out of my stupor and was inspired and reenergized to create some stability in my life once again.

Back on the northern California coast I had a job that enabled me to work outdoors. Discovering the beauty and physical challenge of the rugged coastline was an inspiration and a delight. I experienced a sense of peace and mystery and awe that I hadn't felt in a very long time. The wilderness opened up a whole new world of experience for me as well as the desire to experience this "spiritual" high in a more conscious manner.

I was looking for a sign directing my next step, and I found it, literally, in August of 1976 in an ice-cream store in San Francisco. A notice beckoned to me from a bulletin board in the back of the store: "Man, Woman, Nature—Wilderness as Healer —Songs, Chants, Herb-Gathering, Native-American Ritual." On impulse I wrote down the phone number. I telephoned the next day, and after two preparatory meetings, found myself a short time later on an ocean beach with a group of people, preparing for a week-long hike into a wilderness area.

During that trip I did a three-day vision quest completely alone. It seemed important to me to really challenge myself in a way I had not done before, so I didn't bring a sleeping bag or any food with me. I spent my mornings walking and meditating on the ocean and the afternoons gathering wood to keep me warm through the long night. How amazing those three days and nights were! I had never really been alone in my life. What an incredible revelation! I loved it. I composed my first song/chant on that trip:

Here I sit on the edge of the earth
watching the waves chasing land-ward.
Each mighty crash seems to fill my heart
with acceptance of my infinity,
with acceptance of my mortality.
Be gentle, be brave, be fearful not to love.
Then you will find the peace beyond understanding.

I left the ocean behind and took with me a new name. I became "Wave" on that backpacking trip. Wave represented a woman of courage and love and peace, and I was inspired to become her.

I jumped or rather catapulted into the next phase of my life with exuberance and inquisitiveness. I entered a program in psycho-ecology through Sonoma State College in northern California. I lived and studied for nine months with a group of fellow seekers in the little, timeless coastal town of Mendocino. There, we explored the unconscious through dreams and creative expression as well as Native American spiritual studies and practices. We became very "tribal" and community oriented, both with respect to community living and service to the community. I finished my studies in Mendocino and left with the desire to find my "tribe."

My interest in Native American spirituality took me back to Colorado. From 1977 to 1980 I attended Ft. Lewis College in Durango in southwest Colorado. Durango is on the edge of the Southern Ute Indian Reservation and close to the Navajo Reservation. I thought that being close to Native American lands and peoples would bring me to my spiritual home. This proved not to be the case. Although during my years in Durango I involved myself peripherally with Native American spiritual activities, it was not satisfying. I loved the philosophy, prayers, chanting, music, and rituals, but the community/tribal connection was missing. I felt like an Anglo *trying* to act Indian. During this period of my life I also discovered and participated in Sufi* dancing and Sufi songs and chants. I thought perhaps it held some potential for me as a spiritual path, but again, something was missing and my interest flagged.

That fall in Cambridge, Massachusetts, on a visit to my sister, I had my first major experience of anything Jewish when I joined the Harvard-Radcliffe Hillel Choir. I read an ad announcing tryouts for the choir in the Harvard school newspaper, and commandeered my sister to come along and try out also. We both got in. The choir became for me the highlight of my time on the East Coast.

---

*Islamic mysticism that has been inspirational to many Jews throughout history.

Music has always been a source of inspiration and solace and healing for me. Not necessarily listening to music as much as singing myself, either other people's compositions or my own. Although until I was twenty-six, I had not been aware of ever meeting a Jewish person, I had loved "Jewish/Hebrew" music whenever I came across it. In our fourth-grade music book, nestled in among all the Christmas carols, was "O Hanukkah, O Hanukkah, Come Light the Menorah." I was mesmerized by the tune and the words and was always requesting it, even after the fourth grade when it was no longer in our music books. In my sophomore year in high school, the choir I was in performed *"Hava Nagila,"* and that became an all-time favorite of mine, as did *"Shalom Haverim"* and *"Hinay Matov"* (favorites of my psycho-ecology group). Of course I did not connect any of this to anything spiritual; they were just inspiring and exotic songs that I loved to sing. My reaction to the bits and pieces of Hebrew music that I had heard up until this point was minor compared to my total absorption and enthusiasm with singing the Hebrew music in the Hillel Choir in the winter of 1981.

We sang only Hebrew liturgical music, most of which was from the High Holiday services. The fact that it was sacred music did not make a conscious impression on me, but I was completely carried away by the sounds of the words and the haunting melodies and the complexity of the harmonies. I had sung many types of music over the years with choirs and choruses, but none had ever impacted me as deeply.

I didn't connect my experience in the Hillel Choir with Jewish spirituality at the time. I now believe it was clearly a spiritual experience, offered to me in a form that "spoke" to me—vocal music. Up until that time I had "consciously" known only four or five Jewish people, and my knowledge of Judaism was nearly nonexistent. I believed either you were Jewish or you weren't. In my mind it had nothing to do with spirituality. Of course, I knew Judaism was a religion, but not a religion you could *become* or practice, but something you just *were*, like being Spanish or American. Toward the end of my time with the Hillel Choir, the meaning of the words we were singing started to make an impression. I was interested in knowing more about the religion that produced such exquisite music, but it was a while yet before an opportunity presented itself for me to do so. First, though, I was going to have to go back to the beginning.

A Navajo friend from the Southwest came to visit me upon my return to California. Annie is a teacher of Navajo spirituality, and she showed me the special healing objects from the medicine bag around her neck, explaining their significance to me. She told me that the Navajo "love to share our spiritual teachings with whomever is interested, particularly the Anglos, but we don't want you to take on our tradition as your own. You must find it in your own culture, you must dig deep into your own roots and find your spiritual home there."

Her statement affected me very deeply. I was morose for weeks after that. Christianity was the only spiritual home I had known in my own culture, and so I followed Annie's advice and took a second look at the religious tradition of my youth. I went to some Catholic services. I attended some Charismatic Christian services. I went to Jehovah's Witness Bible-study classes. I halfheartedly investigated the Moonies, which operated under the guise of the Creative Community Project. I was beginning to think perhaps I was never going to find a spiritual home and that my practice was just going to be eclectic and private. *Still* I did not see Judaism as a possibility. In my mind it was grouped in the foreign cultural traditions and not of my own culture. What a hardhead! Judaism, it seems, was going to have to find *me*, because I certainly wasn't coming any closer to finding *it*.

In the summer of 1986 my sister and I attended a lecture given by a psychologist named Stanley Kellerman at the San Francisco Jewish Community Center. Kellerman does a lot of work in the field of death and dying and having just gone through my grandmother's home death, I was interested in finding out more about the spiritual aspects of dying. During a break in the lecture, my sister and I were talking and a man came up to us and broke into our conversation. He began debating with us about the lecturer. He was criticizing Kellerman, and I was defending him. We exchanged small talk for a few minutes, which included our names and where we lived. The break ended, and we went back to listen to the lecture. After the lecture was over, the man who had conversed with us during the break hollered to me across the room, over the heads of many people, "What's a nice Jewish girl like you doing living in Martinez (a very white, middle-class suburb of the East Bay area)?" I replied, as he approached through the crowd, "I'm not Jewish." He said, "Oh, sure you are." I replied again, "No, I'm not." Little did I know at that time that this fortuitous meeting would finally bring me home to Jewish spirituality and that from the start it would feel like I arrived at a place where I had been before.

The man I met at the lecture, Martin, telephoned and we ended up dating. During our first date, he invited me to a Jewish High Holiday service, to be held later that week (this was the week between Rosh Hashanah and Yom Kippur). My response to his invitation was, "Don't you have to be Jewish to attend one of your services?" "Oh no," he said and proceeded to tell me a little about Judaism, Jewish Renewal in particular, and his experiences with Reb Shlomo Carlebach. I was fascinated and agreed to go to services with him.

An irrevocable shift took place in me when I walked into the Yom Kippur day service sponsored by the Aquarian Minyan of Berkeley. Before me was a roomful of 350–400 people singing and praying with joy and devotion: "Who are we? We're beings of light and truth, infinite wisdom, eternal goodness." The service moved from that (in the *Ashamnu**) into *Avinu Malkeinu*† and into mysterious and thrilling melo-

---

*The *Ashamnu* is the communal confessional prayer that is said in the first person plural because, as Michael Strassfeld says in *The Jewish Holidays* (New York: Harper & Row, 1985, p. 114), "Even though each of us is asking atonement for his or her own sins, it is important to feel part of and responsible for the whole community of Israel."

†*Avinu Malkeinu*, "Our Parent, Our King, reach out to us with grace even though we have not done enough to deserve grace; act toward us with gentle righteousness and with loving-kindness—so as to save us" (Arthur Waskow, *Seasons of Our Joy: A Celebration of Modern Jewish Renewal* [New York: Bantam Books, 1982], p. 12).

dies and prayers and rituals that totally captivated me and engaged me in a journey that, I now know, will carry me to the end of my life (and, perhaps, beyond). The English translations of the prayers spoke to my deepest spiritual longings and desires: "misguided attitudes of ourselves and others cut us off from the core of our being . . . even in the midst of darkness we can always return to the real foundation of life . . . we take responsibility to continually evolve our lives towards greater truth."

One of the prayers that was sung at that first service was the "Angel" prayer sung to a Shlomo Carlebach melody. The name of the angel, Uriel, leapt out at me from the page, as the sound of the melodic name beckoned to me. I became Uriel, in my heart, during that first service. Four years later when I found the second part of my name, Hadassah, all my doubts came to rest as I chose, with a full and certain heart, to become a Jew.

The shift I experienced was away from the *search*, toward a growing feeling of release and relief. That shift eventually led me into formal study and conversion, but at the time I just knew that I had found a major missing piece of the puzzle. I heard the "click," as if all the pieces finally fell into place, and I was grateful that at last I could rest.

I became a member of the Aquarian Minyan and learned about Judaism O.J.T. (on-the-job training). It was like finding a buried treasure, with each new shining jewel more delightful and beautiful than the last. I felt that I had finally found a practice that gave full expression to my range of emotions. There was a time for sorrow, for joy, poignancy, ecstasy, and even a place for addressing the darker emotions of jealousy, anger, and greed. My voice and music found rich and fertile ground in the Jewish liturgy within which to grow and blossom. There was such a feeling of security, and a vague familiarity, in the cycles of return. *Shabbat* keeps coming round, Yom Kippur keeps coming round, *Bereshit* (the first portion of the Torah) keeps coming round; I will listen to Lamentations in the heat of summer and Esther (the Megillah or story of Esther) in the last chill of winter. . . . I took to learning and leading prayers like a duck to water. I took great joy also in what some might consider to be the less "spiritual" tasks such as mopping the hall floor after Yom Kippur services or taking minutes at the Minyan's business meetings.

I also studied in more traditional, and some not-so-traditional, ways: Torah, Jewish Literature and Hebrew Letter Movements (*Otiyot*), Basic Judaism and Introductory *Kabbalah*. And from Martin I received an almost daily infusion of "things" Jewish and his love, support, and enthusiasm for my Jewish spiritual journey. I started studying the Holocaust on my own but was so shaken that I decided to wait until I could have enough time to do it justice. I knew facing the Holocaust would be difficult for me, and since I was in graduate school and working full-time, I was not left with much time to sink into powerful and dark emotions.

I became so enthralled and enmeshed with all that I was learning and doing that I lost perspective that I wasn't technically Jewish. It was rituals surrounding the Torah and because of *Kol Nidre* that I started seriously thinking about conversion.

My first experiences of the Torah were thrilling, and again imbedded within them was that sense of vague familiarity. As the Aquarian Minyan is Renewal-Egalitarian in orientation, *aliyot* to the Torah were usually in groups, thus giving as many people as possible the experience of being called to the Torah. As I was usually part of a group, it wasn't initially apparent to me that in traditional Judaism non-Jews are not called up to the Torah. As time went on and I was exposed more and more to the ritual, it became clear that there was something special about being called up to the Torah as a Jew: "*bat—*" (daughter of—) or "*bar—*" (son of—) somebody. I started fantasizing about what that would feel like and what that would mean to be known as a Jew and not just a person participating in Jewish spiritual practices. But then again, as I seemed to have full access to most rituals, and I even assisted in leading services, why would I want to make a formal conversion?

An incident occurred that challenged me to really start thinking about conversion. Our High Holidays planning committee was discussing possible individuals to sing "*Kol Nidre*" and someone suggested me. Someone else said, "But she isn't Jewish." "Oh, yeah, that's right, I forgot," was the reply. It took me by surprise.

One certainly does not consider conversion just to be able to sing "*Kol Nidre*," but for me it was a powerful catalyst that stimulated a constant flood of internal questions: I privately tried out the words "I am Jewish," shyly and with much trepidation. I went through many emotions. I felt like a fraud. How could I call myself a Jew? Look at the struggle, the prejudice these people have had to endure; how could I join with that history? Did I want to expose myself to possible anti-Semitism and rejection by the mainstream cultural groups on this planet? I was not comfortable with the exclusivity implied in the concept "chosen people" or the ritual of the *Kohanim*, still a revered practice for many Jews. I was saddened by the separation of women in traditional Judaism—the rationalization that "women are naturally more spiritual than men, and not as easily distracted from their spirituality" did in no way satisfy me. I could hardly imagine not participating in ritual around the Torah or not letting my voice soar in prayerful song.

At the same time I could not deny the love I felt for Judaism, and how deeply my life was affected by living Jewishly in community. Though I was reticent to take the step of commitment, I was no longer satisfied to be "just participating" in Jewish spirituality. Finally, an event occurred that allowed me, almost magically, to make this "leap of faith."

In May of 1989 Martin's mother was dying at home of cancer, and we flew to Texas to be at her side. It was a very meaningful experience for me. I was chanting the *Shema* during her last labored breaths, with my hands on her head and my Jewish star around her neck. She left this earthly plane surrounded by prayer and song and sweet and loving family and friends. After her death Martin and I were talking about her Hebrew name, which was Hadassah. I heard clearly in my head "Uriel Hadassah," and again there was an affirming "click."

Until that moment, I had been on a fruitless search to find my Hebrew name. I was advised by a respected Orthodox rabbi to use Uriella, as it was "not good to mix male and female genders in names." I tried to like Uriella, but it was never a fit. I decided it must not be my name after all and searched and prayed in earnest for another. With the linking together of Uriel and Hadassah, I knew my name had finally come to fruition. It felt as though the completion of my name was the gift of one Jewish soul to another.

When I found my name, I lost the continual anxiety I had been carrying about my decision whether or not to convert. Even though the internal debates continued and even though I had no fast and easy answers, it was no longer important that all my questions be answered *now*. I realized that I would be challenged and would struggle with the particulars of my faith, probably always, and that was okay. I finally decided I would never know what it truly felt like to be Jewish or what it meant to be called a Jew until I took the next step—leap. I truly desired to nurture and perpetuate this tradition, as I knew it, that had already given me so much. I was now sure that I wanted to make a formal conversion (an *immersion* is how I like to think of it) and was ready to make my proclamation that "I am a Jew" publicly.

My studying increased in intensity, and yes, I was asked to sing *"Kol Nidre."* I joyfully began learning the prayer in anticipation of leading the congregation as a newly birthed Jew.

As the week of my ceremony approached, I felt like a bride approaching her wedding day. As always there are last lingering doubts, but the excitement and the great love for the beloved carries one over the hurdles. And so it was for me. It was August 1990, in the week of Torah portion *Re'eh*. My ceremony took place in the northern Sierra Nevada Mountains in the midst of the Aquarian Minyan's annual "Joys of Jewishing" summer camp.

The *Bet Din* sat on a bench behind the large, long, old wooden table. They looked so serious in their *tallitot* and *tefillin*. They were my familiar and beloved teachers and friends, but at that moment, they solemnly took it upon themselves to investigate my sincerity and devotion toward becoming Jewish. They wished to know why I chose to become a member of this "tribe" and if I was aware of what "membership" entailed. They quizzed me on minor halakhic questions (sometimes in whimsical fashion); for example, "If you were cooking chicken soup and a blob of yogurt mysteriously flew into your soup pot, what would you do?" Surrounded by friendly witnesses, with sunlight streaming through the cracks of the roof, I felt vulnerable, scared, ecstatic, revealed, and renewed all at the same time. Standing alone, in front of the *Bet Din*, I felt as though I were participating in a most ancient ritual. Time stopped. I could have been anywhere. It was as though I was suspended in time and space. Outside the lodge, my friendly witnesses held me in a prayerful circle as we sang *"Dodi Li"* ("My Beloved," referring to the love God has for Israel) and *"Yevarekhekha HaShem mi-Tzion, urei b'tuv Yerushalayim"* ("May the Lord bless you from Zion, and may you see the prosperity of Jerusalem"). The giant doors to the lodge opened and the *Bet Din* emerged from the darkness into the sunlight and welcomed me as a new daughter of Zion. It was an exquisite moment, lovingly burned into my being for all time.

The next morning before dawn, I arose, and with the help of a friend, prepared for my *mikveh*. We trekked down the trail to the Yuba River in single file, my women friend-attendants and my rabbi-friend. Surrounded by the haunting echoes of the rabbi's chanted prayers coming from around a bend in the river, I immersed four times, taking my first *mikveh* as a Jew. The sun broke the horizon and sparkled on the ripples I had created, as I completed my prayers of gratitude and thankfulness. Again, there was the sense of timelessness, that ancient, primal quality. The next day was *Shabbat*, and beneath the whispering pines and surrounded by sweet and loving friends, I was called to the Torah as Uriel Hadassah *bat Sarah v' Avraham* (daughter of Sarah and Abraham).

Here I am four years later, still learning what it means to be Jewish. Since my first *aliyah* I have been able to "test" my sense of Jewishness while living in a small isolated town where I was the only Jew. It was an important time for me. I discovered that even without other Jews with whom to interact, even without a structured service to attend, I still *felt* Jewish. I was still able to embrace Judaism fully and deeply, on my own. I have learned so much these past two years in Ashland, Oregon, where I now live. I am an active part of a wonderful Jewish Renewal community, and am grateful to be part of a beautiful household where we fully bring *Shabbat* into the home. I have spent time in joyous communal worship and in isolated, extended private contemplation, and I still *feel* Jewish. I have prayed in an Orthodox *shul*, conversed with Orthodox people, and listened to Orthodox rabbis speak, and although *they* might not consider me Jewish, I *still* feel Jewish. For me, being Jewish is a feeling, usually an unexplainable feeling, that comes about through my relationship with the words of Jewish sacred texts and my struggle with their meaning. It comes about through my relationship with the sounds, symbols, and rituals that I regularly participate in. It comes about in the deepening exploration of my relationship as a Jew to Israel and to the Holocaust.

My constant prayer is to know my *truth* and then live it. No religious tradition has a corner on *the* truth. Although there is much beauty and truth in the Catholicism of my youth, I have found my *greater* truth in Judaism. It does not negate the truth of the Muslims, Christians, Sufis, or Buddhists. The challenge is to find where *all* truths are rooted in the *one* truth, whatever that may be. It is indeed a worthwhile exploration. The goal of the journey is the same regardless of the vehicle one chooses. I am on that journey, and Judaism has become my trusted and sturdy vehicle.

26

Thrice Blessed

Ellen Olmstead

In their book *Twice Blessed*, Andy Rose and Christine Balka explore the joy—and the pain—of being gay and Jewish. The stories of gays, Jews, *and* converts challenge us to expand our notions of the categories into which we place people.

Ellen is lesbian and Jewish—by conversion. The balancing act with these identities can sometimes be like a tightrope she walks—with whom is it safe to tell one, two, or all three? She leads an ethical, nurturing, and joyful life with her partner, Deborah, a born Jew.

Ellen found her values expressed well in the Jewish practices of *tzedakah*, *tefillah*, and Torah—charity, prayer, and study. She is dedicated, as is Deborah, to providing education and health care to underserved people in urban communities, both in their vocations as well as their acts of charity. Ellen became an active member of the synagogue she and Deborah now attend, and she continues to take courses of study in the Jewish community.

When I was a teenager my mother showed me photographs from when I was a child and we lived in Detroit, and said, "These were your best friends when we lived in Cambridge." All the kids that I was friends with were either black or Jewish. My parents had always chosen neighborhoods that were very culturally diverse. My father had gone to work on a fellowship in Nigeria shortly after my parents married, and I was born there. They had both come from very WASPy families, and living in Nigeria made them rethink things when they came back to this country. They weren't going to live in an all-white community because they hadn't done that for a while.

Just looking at that photo album, I realized that the really significant people in my life when I was in junior high and high school were Jewish. On a Friday I would be at their house, and they would invite me to stay for dinner. Some of my friends' parents did the blessings over the candles and *hamotzi* (blessing over bread), and they would explain things to me. Later, when I went to college I took courses in Jewish history.

When I was in junior high school my mother decided she wanted to belong to a church. We hadn't gone to church in my early childhood, but we had been christened—I still have this little cross with my teeth marks in it that I guess I tried to teethe on. Neither of my parents attended church when they were growing up—at least they never mentioned it. I think I understand now that my mother's interest in religion had partly to do with her disintegrating marriage.

We started attending a Congregational church when my youngest sister wasn't a baby anymore. She is ten years younger than me, and my mother finally had the energy to get everybody ready to go out on Sunday mornings. I must have been in seventh grade, and confirmation was in ninth grade. My mother wanted me to get involved in choir and youth group, but it didn't do anything for me.

My father would go to church with the family, but he would fall asleep, or he'd meditate. He'd gotten interested in TM (transcendental meditation) and had also gone to some Quaker meetings. He did Est (Erhard Seminars Training) too when I was in high school, and my mother told him he couldn't come in the house with those ideas! He just did his own thing, and I don't remember him ever sharing with me what his religious beliefs were. I'm pretty sure he never gave me the messages that "God's gonna see what you're doing" or "You shouldn't do this or that because it's a sin."

My mother was the powerhouse in the family, and I think she had the idea that religion had something to do with having a normal family, giving it some cohesiveness and structure. She was also big on family celebrations. She tried to instill in us the religious elements of the holidays like Christmas and Easter. But she was pretty relaxed about our involvement and didn't get aggressive when I didn't want to participate. One thing I did like about holidays was that my aunt and uncle and cousins would sit down together for huge meals and be at the dinner table for a long time talking. Even as little kids we'd be invited to have wine or beer and talk with the older folks. All this became more and more important to my mother as she was becoming stressed out and disillusioned about her marriage. When it fell apart and she decided to divorce, she went through a lot of hard times. She used church as a place to meditate and try to look at things on another plane, instead of getting bogged down in the material hardship.

My family is characterized by a history that everyone knows but no one is allowed to discuss. Both my parents came from very dysfunctional families. From an aunt I learned about the sad history of many of my relatives, but none of this was presented to me while I was growing up.

In sharp contrast, I have let everyone in my family know that I'm gay. Everyone knows that I live with Deborah and everyone knows that we want to adopt kids. And everyone knows that I converted. I don't keep any secrets from my family, and in a family not practiced in honesty and openness, that causes problems. It is only recently that my mother is able to make some acknowledgment of my relationship with Deborah. I have explained to her that I am happy; I have a good life. Sadly, this is not true of my younger sisters, who seem to be mirroring the problems of previous generations.

I was concerned about my mother's reaction to my conversion. I thought, "Oh, she is really going to see this as the ultimate betrayal." My actions had nothing to do with her, of course, but she was taking everything I did as a reflection on her. She surprised me by saying she thought it was really good that I had this spiritual life, and she was really happy for me.

My father didn't say anything about my conversion. If it had been a problem for him, he would have said something. He was pretty unconventional in the way that he was experimenting with things in his own life, so who was he to be telling me, "Oh, my God! You've betrayed the family." My parents had always been very close to Jews, and I remember my father introducing me to Jewish men and women at work whom he really liked or people he was going to go on a trip with. So I didn't expect a negative reaction from him.

I think I've always been very spiritual. I always believed that there is a God—a kind of tremendous force in the universe. And I've always been in awe of righteous people. And beautiful places. The area around Dartmouth, where I went to college, was simply gorgeous. Later, one of the main reasons I liked where we lived in western Massachusetts was that it was so beautiful. That was really my religion.

I was raised with values that coincide nicely with the things that I most like about Judaism: action instead of faith. I'm a very pragmatic person. Let's not have forty meetings to come up with a theory. I like to have a meeting where everybody says, "Okay, I'm going to do this, you're going to do this, you're going to do that. Let's go." That's kind of how I view Judaism—the social justice aspect—you see a problem, you act on it. Even though my parents disappointed me and seemed not to appreciate me when I became an adult, I know they did instill certain values in me. From as young as I can remember, I helped my mother with volunteer work. In college, I did Big Brother/Big Sister and tutoring as a volunteer. My fellowship teaching in Jersey City was as a volunteer.

Volunteering, giving money, sharing things that I have is the way I like to lead my life. Deborah and I practice *tzedakah*. We started doing that way before I thought about converting. I like that. I got those values from my parents.

I hadn't done anything religiously as an adult. When I went to college, I never went to church. I did go to a Quaker meeting with a friend down the hall. It was a social thing; first we'd go to brunch, then to the meeting; it had no religious significance. At Dartmouth I participated in some of the *seders* that the Hillel had because some of my friends were going and they invited me. Again that was social, not religious. I wasn't trying all these things out of any need to explore involvement in organized religion. My interest in converting came through learning and experiencing and living a Jewish life with Deborah.

The majority of people who were important in my life during the time when I became who I am—as an adolescent and when I went off to college—were all Jews. I don't want to generalize, but there is something pretty special about all of these people. They'd take time to explain what a *mezuzah* was or what holiday was coming up. I took courses in Jewish history, although at that time I didn't have any idea that I would convert. When I was a graduate assistant teaching literature courses, I made an effort to introduce my students to the works of Jewish writers. While studying for conversion, the rabbi said these are the things that you should know when you convert, and I already knew almost all the history and cultural stuff. Either I had been exposed to it because of the people I was with or I just went out and taught myself.

When Deborah and I met at the University of Massachusetts in the spring of 1985, she was finishing her undergrad degree, and I was working on a graduate degree. We met when Deborah placed out of a class I was teaching in women's studies. It was not a very positive introduction. I came in to tell the students my plans for the class, and Deborah was there to tell me she didn't think she needed a writing seminar and wanted to find a way to place out of it. Our relationship got on a more positive footing when we ran into each other at a meeting for the Student Center for Educational Research and Advocacy. The only chair available was next to Deborah. The center conducted workshops on antiracism and anti-Semitism, ran cultural programs, and had a network with different groups—like Hillel and AfroAm. They started a position for a gay and lesbian awareness educator, and I was selected for the job. Deborah and I taught a course together on images of Jews in popular films. Eventually, she and I became involved as a couple.

Just being around Deborah, I was experiencing more of Judaism. When we started living together, Deborah began to keep kosher, as her family did while she was growing up. In college, it had been hard for her to have a kosher household since she'd always lived with a group of other people. Now, living just with me, she could have more control, and she became more observant, including attending services more regularly.

Living together is a time to decide what you want for your home situation, and the household we established was a Jewish one. I wanted to make that work out for Deborah. I was really excited when she decided to keep a kosher home. I love learning things and exploring cultural stuff. There's a part of me that is fascinated by why do you do this and how do you do it. I wasn't particularly conscientious, and Deborah was the one who took the initiative to get things set up in the early years when we were getting together, but I enjoyed the rituals. I saw this as part of making my home—my family—with Deborah. We put up *mezuzot*, some of which Deborah had made. Deborah put together a gorgeous *Haggadah* and friends came over for a *seder*. We lit candles on *Shabbat*—we took turns.

I got a fellowship to Columbia in a graduate program and went to live in New York City alone. I saw Deborah on weekends, but I was really missing her and missing our home, so I was happy when she came down mid-year to live in New York. She had really looked forward to seeing the historic Jewish communities and to being able to buy kosher food easily; we'd go to the Lower East Side for brunch on Sundays. I had also discovered a gay and lesbian synagogue, Congregation Beth Simcha Torah. We went and were both very intrigued. Deborah had made a commitment to herself that she would go to services more regularly, but she didn't feel safe taking the subway there by herself back and forth on Friday nights. I made a promise to her that I would go with her so she could do that. That marked a big change for me.

For me Friday nights had always been a time to just let go—doing whatever felt like fun, sleeping in on Saturday morning—after working very hard all week. I wasn't used to the notion Deborah had about totally slowing down and then staying at home and studying something or taking a nap. That hadn't been part of my lifestyle.

The gay and lesbian congregation in New York was an incredible place. My experience with going to services in other places when it wasn't a holiday or *bar/bat mitzvah* was that there were not a lot of people there. But at CBST there were hundreds of people and barely enough seats. The Jews here were very knowledgeable and took turns leading services. People were singing at the top of their lungs. At services elsewhere, I had never experienced the joy these people felt in singing. I am not much of a singer, but here it was fun to join in. I started to pick up the melodies and the Hebrew—really just memorizing things. I was excited by it.

Their community was based on their Judaism, not on the fact that most members were gay and lesbian. A heterosexual family were members because they lived nearby, and they had their daughter's baby naming there. Since there was a lot of diversity in terms of people's backgrounds, members made an effort to connect spiritually with everyone. Spirituality was the center—not whether you identified as a gay or lesbian.

They were eager to involve us because there were few women who attended, although there was a women's service and women's dinner at CBST once a month. A lot of radical dykes came, but they wouldn't come back because they didn't want to be with the boys for the regular service. We would see them walking out. After a search for which they received many applicants, they hired a rabbi, Sharon Kleinbaum. A woman rabbi should help attract more women congregants. She was raised in an Orthodox home and received a Reconstructionist ordination, which pretty much reflects the range in the congregation's background and observance.

On the whole, though, the men at CBST were really a sweet group of guys, and they were clearly glad to have us. It was very affirming to look around and see all these gay folks. We were quite young compared to a lot of the other people, and it was good to be able to see what my life could be like twenty or thirty years down the road. I had never had a sense of that before. Since most of the gays I had known before were college students and very transient, it felt as though you could only be young and be a lesbian, as if it were just a phase in your life. At CBST there were people who had been in relationships together for years; who had homes, whose moms came with them to services sometimes. One couple who were very friendly to us were middle-aged themselves and had been together for twenty-five years. They were going to be cleaning out the house for Pesah and going to their mothers' for this or that *Shabbat* or holiday.

In my involvement with CBST, I learned more about Judasim. It wasn't really intentional—it was the same way I'd picked up things from having a home with Deborah. I felt like a more active participant in it. I would have flashes of real happiness when I was on the bus going home from services.

After a year in New York, Deborah got into Johns Hopkins University in an accelerated nursing program. She wanted to work with low-income women; I had made a commitment to work with African-American youth. We both wanted to live near a Jewish community—so Baltimore fit the bill better than the other options. Neither of us had ever been here before in our lives and the only things we'd heard from people were that there is nothing good to say about the place!

When we went *shul*-shopping in Baltimore we attended all the Reform, Conservative, Reconstructionist, and independent *shuls* in the area. We were looking for a place Deborah would want to go to services every week, and I was keeping an eye out for a place in which I could become more involved so I could approach the rabbi about conversion. July is a very slow time in the synagogue, therefore it is a pretty good gauge of how committed a community is if they have services and quite a few people show up. We would spend a long time before and after services just looking at the architecture—these enormous places—looking at the gifts that families had donated, historic *menorahs* and *mezuzot*. I'd never seen anything like it and Deborah hadn't either. I was in awe.

I was the one who got us our subscription to the *Jewish Times* because I'm the organizer. In fact, all of the Jewish mail comes to me. We read in the *Jewish Times* about the Institute of Jewish Studies sponsored by Reform, Conservative, Reconstructionist, and Orthodox synagogues. A course on ethics was the one we were most interested in, and it was taught by the two rabbis I was considering to approach about my conversion.

Then I read *Your People, My People* by Lena Romanoff, and that helped me decide that I wanted to have a Conservative rabbi to study with because if I followed through on the conversion it counted more. I didn't know where I'd be in the future, but if I studied with a Reform rabbi I wouldn't be able to join a Conservative synagogue.

I never considered an Orthodox conversion. First of all, I would have had to camouflage a major part of my identity and my most important personal relationship. Second, it is not egalitarian. I went to modern Orthodox services and that was interesting, but still, the history behind the separation of the seating is something I could not support. Why would I get involved in a segment of the religion that I couldn't wholeheartedly support and didn't really believe when I had dismissed for the same reasons the religion my mother was trying to give me? I also knew that there is nothing about me that is absolutely orthodox: these are the rules, and you do them. That just wouldn't fit my personality—it's just not the way I look at things. I'm a person who has to look and understand and maybe I have to make another explanation of why you should do it, at least to justify it to myself. So I took the next notch down!

Conservative Judaism is more than on the fence about gays and lesbians. A Conservative rabbi cannot be gay or lesbian—not openly. Gays and lesbians are not supposed to be in leadership positions. Gay and lesbian marriages are not something that a rabbi is going to perform. I knew all of that. I was concerned about that, but it wasn't going to have anything to do with my decision to convert with a Conservative rabbi.

I was very sensitive to the possibility that someone would think that I was doing this because of Deborah. It was especially important to clarify this for myself. If you look at society, I was part of all the privileged groups, except for being a woman and a lesbian—white, Anglo-Saxon, Protestant, ruling-class family, Ivy League school. In western Massachusetts there were a lot of people who were very sensitive to oppression and they were eager to grasp whatever part of their identity would put them in the group of "oppressed" instead of "oppressor." I identified as a WASP and never tried to deny or diminish that. I tried to reach out to people from my own background and work with them. I was wary that with my involvement in Judaism some people might think that I was trying to link into the "oppressed people" identity because that was "chic."

So I had to ask myself, "Are you doing this because of Deborah or because of you? If something happened with your relationship with Deborah, would you still pursue this?" And I realized that the answer was "Yes!" My study with the rabbi then became something I was doing for myself. I really wouldn't tell Deborah much about my conversations with him. I needed the space to explore it on my own.

There were hundreds of people in the institute classes, so at first I only knew the rabbi I wanted to study with in a distant way. Nevertheless, I thought he'd be a great person for me because of his personality. The other rabbi I was considering was not as self-revealing—though I agreed with a lot of his ideas—and I wondered what it would be like to develop a more intimate relationship with him in which something so core, so deep inside is being discussed. The rabbi I chose made himself much more vulnerable. He would share some personal anecdotes and he would also make fun of himself—which I do a lot. He was a peer for me in this way.

I came out to the rabbi the first time I met him. I had to think about it a little bit because I really liked and respected him when we were taking his class. It has been my experience, though, that if I don't say early on in a relationship that I am a lesbian, people develop certain assumptions about me. When I feel that we are becoming friends and getting closer, it sometimes changes things when I say that I am a lesbian. So, I thought it was better to risk it not being comfortable for us and both of us deciding to bag it from the beginning than to wait until I got invested in a relationship with him.

He seemed pretty nonplussed by it. I talked to him about an hour, and he didn't say anything about it. He asked me some questions. "Why are you here? Why did you come to me? Why this place? What do you know already?" Then he started to ask questions about my childhood, college years, whatever. He didn't ask about relationships but it seemed like the time to tell him about Deborah. He didn't seem flustered or like he was trying to be cool to cover up that inside he was a little uptight about it. He always asked me how Deborah was, how I was. When holidays were coming up or just passed, he'd ask what we'd done to celebrate them. He seemed pretty natural with that, and I thought it was just great. In retrospect, I was probably the first gay convert he worked with. There may be a few gay male members of his congregation and he knows they're gay and he's counseled them in some ways. Lesbians—I don't think so.

Study with the rabbi was great. It seemed to me that either we have a lot in common in the way we see things or he just has an incredible intuition about people. The books he recommended to me I treasure: Barry Holz's *Back to the Sources*; Irving Greenberg's *The Jewish Way*; a lot of Heschel; the book on *kashrut* published by the Conservative movement. He was even helpful when I'd come and ask him very concrete questions: about swordfish—is it kosher? About the microwave—can I put chicken in there to heat up if it's used for dairy, too?

Recently, in a class he was teaching he joked that people never come to him about the important questions in life: food, sex, and money, but all my conversations were about those issues. That is mainly a reflection of him, of his willingness to discuss the tough questions. I would never have talked to my own father about my sexuality and my relationship, and here I am talking to this guy, and he's the rabbi, and he's of the age that he could be my father. He would tell me about his children when I came to see him sometimes. He has a daughter my age who is in rabbinical school who is probably as opinionated as he is—as I am.

I'd see him about once a month, and this went on for a year. Finally, last fall, he said in our meeting, "I think you're ready for this." And I told him, "Deborah wants to be involved in some way." He misunderstood me. He thought what I was going to say was that the rituals that are established aren't enough, that I wanted some kind of ceremony in his synagogue, or I wanted an *aliyah* that Deborah was going to be involved with in some way. What I really wanted was for Deborah to come while I was going through the *Bet Din* and the *mikveh*, and for the brief service in the synagogue afterward. When he understood what I wanted, he said absolutely fine.

He gave me a big hug after I came out of the *mikveh* and after the service. There was another woman and a little baby who were at the *mikveh* on that day. He was holding the baby while the father was getting into a bathing suit to go into the *mikveh*, and he said something about how he wishes he'd spent more time with his kids when they were young. That was very touching. He was very warm, especially then.

I was nervous that day because I'd been in a graduate program, and I thought the *Bet Din* would be like a dissertation defense. I had been through exams for my degree—three professors, three rabbis. I taught myself how to read the Hebrew so I could read anything they gave me. I learned the names of all the Hebrew months; all the holidays; I knew everything. They hardly asked me anything. I was relieved, but later I kept thinking of the things they didn't ask me.

But I was very moved by the rituals. I wasn't really prepared for that. I was nervous about the *Bet Din*. I was a little shy about the *mikveh*—I didn't know what it would be like. But I felt really different afterward.

When I resolved that I was going to convert, I really did it. We were keeping a kosher vegetarian household at the time. When I was eating out, I was eating only chicken—at least I was trying to start narrowing down transgressions! On Friday nights we were lighting candles and having wine and *hallah*. We were observing the major holidays. We were practicing *tzedakah*.

Then I made a resolution. I was going to join a synagogue and get involved and attend services. I was going to continue the adult institute and any other kind of classes—lifelong learning. Before I converted I had been like the *Shabbat goy*—I carried the money if we were going to a movie; I'd drive if we went out to see the fall foliage. By Saturday afternoon I'd be restless and want to go out. So part of my resolution was that I would try on *Shabbat* not to do anything for which I needed to have money on me. We could walk to places; we could drive to see places, but I wasn't going to do any of the mundane things.

From our earlier *shul*-shopping, we had narrowed it down to just a few places. I went back to the *shuls* that I had kind of liked, but no place was perfect. Some that were okay were just too far away. Some were just too big. In others we were the only people under fifty. In one of the *shuls* near our home, people had been incredibly warm toward us. Before I converted, if I wasn't there they always asked, "Where is Ellen?" They became accustomed to seeing me after *oneg* to walk Deborah home because she doesn't want to walk alone. When I did go to services, people would come up to me afterward to encourage me to participate more because I knew more than many of the people there, and I sang loudly.

I wanted to be with people who really knew a lot more; I wanted to learn more; I wanted to be challenged. So I didn't feel that that was a place where I would grow Jewishly, although I felt comfortable socially. I really wanted more religious stuff.

I knew the first time I went into the other synagogue near our home that that was where I wanted to be. When we had first moved into that neighborhood, we fell in love with the architecture, especially of the old synagogues. I love history, and I like the idea of ties to things that are ancient. This synagogue is the only one still operating in that neighborhood, and it is magnificent. I felt it was very special—it gave me a sense of place. There were people a little closer to my age and lots of kids running around. The rabbi was very progressive. He didn't give a long, pompous sermon. It was provocative. I noticed that they had all these Reconstructionist *siddurs* downstairs. Even though they weren't using them upstairs, it was like a Conservative-Reconstructionist thing—that's different. And it was egalitarian. There were many women going up on the *bimah* doing things, and a lot of women being called up for an *aliyah*.

So I wanted to find out more about it, and I made an appointment with the rabbi, as it turned out, a week before my conversion. I wanted to ask him some questions because I was confused. Is this *shul* Conservative or Reconstructionist? When I met with the rabbi, he asked me to tell him about myself. The minute I said I was a lesbian and told him about my partner, he said, "Oh, do you want to join as a family?"

So he brought in the executive director of the synagogue for me to meet and said, "This is Ellen Olmstead. She wants to join, and we need to have a meeting of the board to ask if lesbian and gay couples can join as families." The rule was that if you want to join as a family you have to be married and both partners have to be Jewish. The only option for me was to join as an individual, unless Deborah and I could be considered a family. We can't get married, but is there any equivalent of that? It was not going to be a determining factor about whether I was going to join or not. And I didn't want it to seem that the first time I came in I was banging people over the head, saying, "Okay, the queers are here—you gotta change your policies."

I told the rabbi one of the reasons I want to join a *shul* is that we really want to have kids, and I believed that a Jewish way of life is a great way to raise kids. Also I had read about kids raised in families in which only one parent was Jewish and none of the results sounded good for the kids. So when I mentioned to him about adopting kids, the rabbi said, "Who are you going through?" And I said, "DSS (Department of Social Services); we want to adopt kids other people don't want." And he said, "Well, Jewish Family Services should be able to help you with adoption." And I told him that we'd already asked Jewish services, and they only help heterosexual married couples who are infertile. And he said, "Hold on a minute! So and so is a member of the congregation and an important staff person at JFS." So he got on the conference line, called the woman, and said, "Can't you help gays and lesbians to adopt?" It was beyond my control. She said, "I don't know; we never had anyone ask. We'd have to talk about it as a policy issue, but send them on over."

Then he asked me if I had thought about a commitment ceremony for Deborah and me. And I said, "Well, a little."

He was very nice. And he also told me about a group, ISO—In Search Of, for thirty-something folks. He said, "You really should come, and bring Deborah, because a lot of the people are married couples. I think you'll find those people are really supportive." He told me about all the things going on in the synagogue and sent me a letter upon my conversion. He is a very sweet man. He has really set the tone for me meeting people in the synagogue. When I've gone to the *oneg*, he's come over and introduced me to people.

The first time I met Deborah's family was at a *seder*. That was our introduction to each other, and it was very positive. Deborah is bisexual and had come out to her parents years before she met me. So they responded very well to our relationship. Deborah says that her relationship with her mother, which was always good, has actually gotten better because she goes home more often now. Her mom really likes me. Her father was a little more freaked out by the idea of our relationship at first, and he's the kind of guy who won't express it. Now, though, he gives me a big hug and kiss—and he doesn't really do that for other people.

When I shared with the family that I was planning to convert, Deborah's mother was very excited about it. She kept asking, "How is it going? When is it happening? I want to give you a gift!"—even though she had never really mentioned the fact of my not being Jewish before. Deborah says that her mother's enthusiasm for my conversion has to do with family. She's dying to have grandchildren, and we are her best shot. Her mother sees my conversion as making a real commitment to Deborah and the relationship—to making a Jewish family with the emphasis on *family*.

27

Starting Off "Good"

Kathleen

On the surface, the path Kathleen took to becoming Jewish might be considered "typical": nice Catholic girl falls in love with nice Jewish boy; she converts so they can get married. The power of stereotypes is that often there is *some* "truth" in them.

Looking beyond the surface, however, this bright and thoughtful woman had spent years questioning and being dissatisfied with her own religion. Meeting and marrying a Jewish man gave her an opportunity to contemplate the spiritual bounties Judaism had to offer; she might not have done so otherwise.

With wit, goodwill, and sometimes acerbic analysis, Kathleen describes her life and her embrace of Judaism—with one of its more appealing aspects to her: the central premise that we all start off "good."

This all started for me when I was in Boston where I met my future husband. Richard was the doctor who made rounds for the patients at the alcohol detoxification unit where I was a nurse. We started to date after we'd been friends for about a year. Initially, I was not committed to this relationship and was not aware of the role Judaism was to play in my life.

I was raised very Catholic. My parents go to church every Sunday and are really quite involved with Catholicism. I went to parochial schools not quite my whole life: Catholic grammar school; then public schools for a few years; then Catholic high school with nuns. It was an all-girl Catholic high school, taught by an order of nuns, women who had gone into the convent before or right after World War II. They were very traditional, and were children of immigrants to this country.

I began to have a lot of trouble with Catholicism in high school. It troubled me that you couldn't ask questions, that the person God loved the most was the one who never asked—I think of the story of doubting Thomas—and that if you believed without asking, God loved you more. The better person was the person who never asked a question. It didn't seem right, but in my house, I wasn't going to make an issue of it.

I went to church every Sunday, but I didn't understand how Catholicism was the better way. I didn't understand why God loved nuns more. God loved nuns and priests more because they saved themselves—physically. They are pure. They are special. God wants you to get married, and God wants you to have children, but He loves nuns and priests more. And don't do anything you would regret because then you could never be a nun and have this special relationship to God.

234

The biggest problem that I had was that if all the aspects of God are equal—the Father, the Son, and the Holy Ghost—why can't you pick who you are praying to? But you can't. You can only pray to one out of the three—Jesus Christ; he is the intermediary. Why couldn't you say "God" instead? I never liked being told that I had to do it a certain way.

The emphasis of Catholic education was on learning what it took to get into heaven and hell. There were things about that I just couldn't accept. One of the problems basic to Catholic education is that you never learn theology and you don't really learn history. As I got older, I realized that what passed for history and theology were simply what in Judaism are called *bubbemeises* ("grandmother stories" or old wives' tales). They were what the nuns were teaching you: not only did Mary get pregnant immaculately—everybody knows she got pregnant by the word of God—but, as one very sincere woman said, she didn't have to suffer the "indignity" of natural childbirth! It was dirty, so she gave birth to the baby immaculately, too. Now, I was a really nerdy high-school kid—I was not one of the movers and groovers. But even *I* knew that *that* way of looking at childbirth was not a great attitude.

When I left home at eighteen, I stopped going to church. If I went home for the week, I always avoided going home on Sunday. I didn't really confront my parents with it until I was about twenty-two. I got up one Sunday morning and put on a bathing suit and went out in the backyard while they were getting ready for church. There was quite an argument.

Although I consciously didn't participate in Catholicism, I didn't consciously leave it, and I guess I never really thought about *not* being Christian in some way. I had problems with being Catholic, but I had no contact with any Protestant religion. When I was growing up there were us Catholics—who we all knew were in the right—and then there were Protestants, who were only Protestant because they were too lazy to get up for church in the morning. If they weren't lazy, they would be Catholic. That is what I was taught, and as a child I believed that no Protestants went to church on Sunday. I was fascinated as an adult to discover that there were non-Catholics who went to church every week.

People don't realize that New York has neighborhoods. It used to. It doesn't really anymore. My parents grew up in the same neighborhood in New York and knew each other from childhood. My aunts and uncles all married people they grew up with. My parents' friends are people that they have known since they were children. One of my uncles and my father have been best friends since they were five years old. Everybody lived in "the neighborhood"; you married people in your neighborhood, and it was basically Irish. But my father wasn't. In fact, my father was an Episcopalian who converted to marry my mother. He had been quite involved in the Episcopal church. When my father came to ask for my mother's hand in marriage, my grandfather said, "If you will not become Catholic, I will not give my permission for her to marry you."

I did not make my husband go and ask permission to marry me. I was twenty-eight years old. I told my parents. He told his parents. My parents' response initially was "Why do you have to do this now? Why are you rushing into this?" Not the marriage—but the conversion. And I said, "Well, you know, when you and Dad got married and he had to become Catholic to marry you—it is like that." And my mother said to my father, "Yes, George. That is true."

My husband was quite committed to being Jewish. When he had his own apartment, he kept it kosher. He came from what might be described as a "Conservodox"* home. They kept kosher reasonably well, but they were not *Shomer Shabbat*, although my mother-in-law had grown up in a *Shomer Shabbat* home. My father-in-law's father owned a grocery store during the Depression—you just couldn't be *Shomer Shabbat*. My husband went to Hebrew school, then to Hebrew high school. After he started going out with me, he told me that the reason he was willing to date me was that I obviously was not committed to another religion. If I had been strongly committed to some form of Christianity, he could not have gone on with the relationship.

I never saw myself getting married young—like right out of college—so I was not unhappy not to be married at twenty-six. But at about that time I thought, "Well, gee, you know, I should be thinking about this. Do I want to go out with losers anymore?" I went out with very nice guys, but you knew that they weren't going anywhere or weren't marriage material. When I started going out with Richard, I had never really seriously considered marrying anybody before, so the issue of marriage really didn't come up right away. Eventually, though, he went back down to Baltimore from Boston to start work. I stayed in Boston for another six months while we decided what we were going to do—whether we would get married; whether I would move down to Baltimore. We decided and I moved down.

My conversion process began while I was still in Boston. I took a ten-week course on Judaism, and it was a good introduction. (Of course, they wanted our spouses to attend as well, because so many born Jews have such a little bit of Jewish education.) When I went to speak with the rabbi, I felt that maybe I didn't know what I was doing. Maybe this is frivolous; they are going to think I am not serious. I wasn't supposed to hear, but the couple ahead of me in the rabbi's office hadn't closed the door. They had been married for quite a while. They had children. She was Jewish and he wasn't, and he was not planning to convert. The rabbi asked them what they celebrated and, of course, they did everything: They did Hanukkah. They did Christmas. They did Easter. They did Passover. The rabbi very gently said, "Well, if your husband converts, there won't be any more Christmas in your house because there won't be anybody to celebrate Christmas." And the wife said, "I couldn't possibly not have a tree. I have to have a tree." And I thought, well, no matter what I say, it can't sound more stupid than that.

I never had a Christmas tree in my apartment. Well, I had it one year. It was a mess. I hated the leaves. I hated the needles. I hated the decorations. I never again had a tree. I never really got into it.

The class in Boston was very nice. Then, I moved to Washington, D.C., while

---

*Made-up term for a blend of Conservative and Orthodox observance.

Richard was in Baltimore studying for internal-medicine boards, for which he needed lots of time. I thought I would pick up the conversion process where I left off, but I was not allowed to meet with a rabbi unless I took the introduction-to-Judaism class in Washington.

So, I went through the course twice, and I was a real star the second time because I knew all the answers. Then, I met with a Conservative rabbi for a year, and I did a lot of reading. You can go to the eight-week course, go to the *mikveh*, and get married, but I wanted people to know that I was really serious about this. Even though I never was committed to being Catholic, I had gotten the message growing up in my house that religion was important. You didn't just *say* you were Catholic. You *were* Catholic. You went to church. You went to Catholic schools. You participated.

I told my parents about my marriage plans more than a year before Richard and I actually got married. I felt I needed to give them time to calm down. I couldn't say to them, "I am converting. I am getting married, and you are going to be there at the wedding in three months." I just felt that I couldn't do that to them. They needed time to come to terms with it. It wasn't so easy in the beginning. The first few visits home after I told my parents, they were quite upset. What would people think? They weren't upset because I wouldn't be "saved" or that the finger of God was going to get me. They didn't look at it from the very traditional point of view. Their thinking was "What will people think? They will think that we didn't do a good job. What will our relatives think?" I would be different and in their community people did the same things. I needed to give them time.

I finally did have to say to my parents, "This is what I am going to do. If you make my life miserable, I will stop coming home; or we can try to find our way through this. So you can choose." My parents, fortunately for me, made the right choice. They came to terms with it on their own. There isn't a lot you can do to help somebody go through the process of acceptance, I don't think. My mother was concerned because I had said my husband's parents were Orthodox. At the time, they seemed very Orthodox to me because they kept kosher. My mother knew that Orthodox women covered their hair and wore long sleeves, and that, as she would say, is "clannish." She was upset and afraid that I would not be accepted and would be unhappy because I would be left out. When I told her that I wasn't going to have to wear dresses all the time and that I wasn't going to have to wear long sleeves all the time and that I wasn't going to have to cover my hair, she really came to terms with it a lot better. My parents are not highly educated people, but they were much more open-minded than people I met later on.

From my parents' point of view, since I was converting to Judaism, they thought Richard's parents had the easier time of it. What could *they* possibly not be happy about with me? But, it is difficult. My father-in-law is first generation. My mother-in-law is actually third generation, but from a very traditional family. When my husband told his parents, they told him that he had to be the one to tell his grandmother—my mother-in-law's mother. It was like, "You are killing her—so you go and tell her and kill her."

I said to my husband, "How did your parents take it when you told them?" It was easier, first of all, because I had already gone to a class—I was "on my way," so to speak, which eased the blow a little bit. He also said, "Well, I am thirty. If I were twenty, my parents would say, 'Wait. You will meet somebody else.' But at thirty, they are afraid that they won't see any grandchildren. So it is easier for them now than it would have been ten years ago." I think that is probably not far from the truth.

After that my husband's family was nothing but welcoming. He has a large family, mostly from his mother's side. All of them were very supportive and really nice. Everybody gave me a kosher cookbook! I can make cocoa more ways than you can imagine.

There were rough spots—but they were minor, really, compared to some of the stories you hear about parents abandoning their children or not coming to the wedding. I have a friend who converted and even after the marriage, the mother-in-law made it difficult. She did not want this marriage no matter what, and she was going to make it as hard as possible, no matter what. I never had any of that from Richard's family.

Nevertheless, opposition did come from a place no one had considered. My father-in-law is a very kind man, and he wanted us to just speak with the rabbi of their synagogue even though we would not be married there—a courtesy call, so to speak. So we went to talk to the rabbi, and it was not a happy experience.

I was so proud that I had been working on the conversion for a year and a half, that I had gone to these courses, that I had read these books, and that I was demonstrating that I was serious about this. The rabbi looked at the list of books—three pages of books—and said, "None of these are any good. They are all Conservative and they are not good because it was a Conservative rabbi." He said that he couldn't possibly, possibly even start to talk to me until I lived a completely kosher, observant life for six months and then he could start instruction. And I said, "Excuse me. I have already ordered the invitations. I am getting married on December 28. This is it!"

Richard was sitting there. He is very quiet, and doesn't usually say anything until the end. I am more emotional about it. I said, "I don't understand. If I had been born a Reform Jew and had never gone to Hebrew school and didn't know anything, you would marry me without any hesitation." And he said, "Yes." I really operate on fairness, and this didn't seem fair to me. Then the rabbi said, "What would you do about the children visiting her parents?" And my husband said, "We would tell Kathleen's parents what the children could and couldn't eat." And he said, "Well, how do you know you could trust them?" I was on a roll by then. I said, "You think my mother is going to baptize these children in the sink, don't you? You think my mother has statues and she kisses their feet. My parents aren't even educated, and you are more superstitious than they are. You know less about my parents' religion than they know about yours." The rabbi then said to Richard, "Kathleen is a very confused little girl. She doesn't really know what she wants, and I think she should think about this more."

We went back to my father-in-law's house and I was really upset. My husband was very silent. This rabbi wasn't his favorite anyway. When we told him the story of the interview with the rabbi, my father-in-law hit the roof. He was furious. He called the rabbi the next day and said, "How dare you tell a child that she can never eat in her parents' house again! How could you turn a child against her parents? Remember Ruth! Remember Ruth! How could you say this to my daughter-in-law?"

By the time the wedding came, everybody had calmed down so that it really went very smoothly. My parents stood under the *huppah*. They really have been princes about this. The first year that my husband and I were married, my mother sent us a *Purim* card, and my husband said, "In my entire life, I have never seen a Purim card. Where does your mother find these things?" My mother calls before every holiday to say, "I know you have a holiday coming. When does it start?" They came down for my three daughters' baby namings, and for the oldest's *bat mitzvah*. My whole family came. I have been really happy with how much my family has supported me. They send Hanukkah presents, wrapped in Hanukkah wrap. They really have done well, and my husband's family has really done well also.

For my parents, had I converted and done nothing, they would have been quite upset. My parents really believe that religion is important and that participating in a religion gives you an ethical framework. My children go to a Jewish day school and keep kosher at home. My parents are happier about this than they would be if we did nothing.

As for myself, in the beginning I thought the big things were going to be a problem, religiously, I mean. I thought it was going to be whether I was really going to believe that Christ was God or not God. In Catholicism you make a decision about whether you think the pope is infallible. Whether Mary was assumed into heaven body and blood. Whether Christ was really God. If you die without being baptized, do you never go to heaven? These are the big theological concerns for Catholics. I thought I would have trouble coming to terms with theological issues, but I had already made those decisions before I got married. During the ten years living away from my parents, I had come to my own decisions. But it's the little things that get you—the really little things that you don't think about. They would sort of pop into your mind and you would think, "Gee, I never really thought about that."

For example, after we were married, we went to a wedding of a friend of mine from school. It was at the big Catholic church down in Bolton Hill. A big, gray stone Catholic church. It was the whole big nuptial mass—not just the wedding ceremony. The priest says, "In the name of the Father and of the Son and of the Holy Ghost." I was standing there, and after all these years, I started crossing myself and my husband turns to me and says, "What are you doing?" I said, "Oh, I forgot! I forgot." Or somebody Christian says that they are having a baby, and they aren't having it baptized. The first thought that came to me was that baby would never go to heaven. Then you think, "This is irrational." But you know what? It is the little things that come up—and Catholicism was a totally different culture, a different way of looking at the world.

I probably knew more about Judaism living in New York than I knew about being a Protestant because, after all, the Jews were so separate that you would never have to worry about them influencing you. In New York, Judaism is part of the culture. There was a very large Jewish community where we went in the summers. We stayed at the dividing line between the Jews and the Catholics, so that the concession on the boardwalk that was run by the city served *knishes* (stuffed dough). I thought everybody knew what a potato *knish* was. I knew that there was something called "kosher pizza," because for a really exotic treat we would walk down to the Jewish section and buy kosher pizza. Even though we didn't know what made it "kosher," we knew this was really fancy. Words, expressions that in New York are common idioms, I later found out are really Jewish expressions. Still, I never had any Jewish friends while growing up.

What is appealing to me about Judaism is that you get to be Jewish even if you don't believe every single thing. It is a different way of looking at the world. After we were married, I was complaining to my husband about something. I was moaning and groaning and really being a pain. He said, "You are such a martyr." And here is the difference in cultures: When I grew up, a martyr was somebody who never said a word, suffered in silence, and offered it up for the souls in purgatory. Somebody who complained was just a pain in the ass. In Jewish culture, somebody who suffers in silence is a jerk and the person who complains is the martyr.

When we first started going to synagogue, I could only relate it to mass. Mass was the magic part where you have the transformation. You have the bread and wine turned into body and blood and you *have* to be there for that. If you are not there for that part, it doesn't count at all. So, because mass is short, you get there at the beginning. It has the beginning, the middle, and the end, and then you go home. Well, we would go to synagogue, and I would say to Richard, "We have to get there at the beginning." He would say, "At 7:30 in the morning? Kathleen, no one gets there." Then I would get there, and I couldn't find my place in the prayer book. In the beginning I found it very upsetting that it wasn't organized. I wasn't there for the beginning, the middle, and the end.

We go to Beth Am, an unaffiliated synagogue in the city, but not on the holidays. We still go to the in-laws' Orthodox synagogue for Rosh Hashanah and Yom Kippur. I hate sitting separately, but three days a year makes them happy, and they have been very good to me. My husband sits with his father. They have been sitting in the same seats for thirty years.

I have found that the Jewish community is, for the most part, very accepting. I feel almost guilty because it has been very easy for me. Living in a large Jewish community and the fact that my husband had so many friends in Baltimore makes it a lot easier. When we were looking for houses, it didn't occur to me to look in an area that was predominantly Jewish. Richard was more interested in that than I was, so we ended up in Mount Washington. After I had children, I realized that it was much easier that there weren't other houses with Christmas lights. We could go look at houses with lights or we could go up to my parents' house and see the tree, but it is easier to be in a neighborhood where it isn't a big issue.

For me, Judaism gives an ethical framework to live within, and I think it gives you a way of looking at your life on earth in a more positive way. You are not always waiting for the good stuff to come. You have to make something out of the here and now. I think you come to terms better with being Jewish the more you participate. I don't understand how people can feel connected if they don't participate. The more you do, the more you will become a part of it. Because we do participate, it has made it easier for me to explain to my children what our family believes. If you haven't come to terms with it on your own, and if you are not sure about what you believe, I think it is very difficult to explain it. You really have to have a feel for the religion, and there are things that you don't realize that you don't know. You don't realize that scripture is interpreted and translated differently in the Christian Bible than in the Torah. The Christian Bible isn't just the Torah and some other stuff. They changed the Torah.

Participating in the religion gives you what people always talk about in Judaism: a sense of community and a sense of family. I don't understand not participating either as a convert or as a born Jew. But what I consider "not participating in any way" isn't how other people interpret it. My husband was raised Orthodox, so for him Reform is like Unitarian. For my part, coming from a religion with a lot of rituals, I do not get a lot of feeling from a Reform service. I just can't get into it very much, and I hate when rabbis wear robes. They should stand up there in a suit. They are regular guys. There is no "magic." The magic part was what I really had trouble coming to terms with in Christianity.

Since I wasn't born Jewish, I didn't learn all the things in childhood that sort of stick with you. The more you participate as an adult, the more you can understand how born Jews feel. I did not understand in the beginning why my husband never described his family as Polish. He always said that his family was Jewish living in Poland. My mother was Irish, but she was born in England. She always did describe herself as Irish, but it wasn't exactly the same as in my husband's family. There were similarities, and maybe that is why I could relate to the Polish-Jewish issue a little better, because as Catholics living in England my mother's family had to put down their religion on the employment form. You were the last hired, first fired. You were discriminated against. You were told to go back where you came from. You were foreigners. You didn't belong there, yet my mother and my grandmother were both born in England. But my mother can go back to the house she was born in. It is still standing. My husband's family—there is nothing to go back to. The more you learn about people's cultural backgrounds and experiences, the more you understand why people describe themselves in different ways. That is important to know because otherwise you really don't have a feel for everything else that goes on in the religion.

When it came time to decide on schools for our children, my husband said, "I want the children to go to a Jewish day school." And I said, "Absolutely not! I will never send my child to a parochial education." And he kept saying, "Believe me, without the nuns, it is different." And I said, "All right, I will send them one year to make you happy, but those children are out of there after that because I will never allow this." But it *is* different. It is very different.

Catholicism is so authoritarian. You have to believe it and you have to believe it in a certain way. You can't not believe any one part or else all the rest doesn't count. That was my biggest problem with Catholicism. Catholic education does not teach you religion as a child or how to interpret it. But it wasn't just that. I went to school with corporal punishment—with people who would hit you with a stick. They punched you. Kids had bloody noses. People were being slapped. I went to school with that! I remember graduating from high school and one of the nuns saying to me, "Oh, you will look back on this as the happiest time of your life." I remember that because all I could think of was that they couldn't do anything more to me. Other girls I went to school with had a very positive experience. For me, it wasn't. That was why I was opposed to day school for my children.

Although Jewish day school has provided an education for my children that I would not have been able to give them, if you don't do anything else, if you do it in a vacuum, it sort of just goes by the board. At the same time, the more you participate, especially at home, the more you learn. In my children's school, Beth Tfiloh, which is an Orthodox day school, the children are taught by people who are not Jewish at all; who are Jewish and not observant at all; who are Orthodox and some who are even more Orthodox. We handle these differences by explaining to the children that everyone has to make the decision about what is most meaningful in their life. If you think that being more observant will make your life more meaningful—we don't really discuss being less observant—that is a decision you will have to make as you grow up.

I cannot understand families who decide to celebrate all the holidays, Christian and Jewish, or people who go to the other extreme of never admitting that you ever believed anything different and cutting your children off from your past. I never went home for Christmas after I was married, even when I didn't have children. I went before or I went after and dropped the presents off for my family, but I did not go home on Christmas Day because then I never had to say I wasn't going home on Christmas Day when I had children. One year, though, the children were older, and I felt they were more set in what we did and what my parents did. We were going up the weekend before Christmas and my mother said, "Can I leave the tree for them to decorate?" I said, "Yes, that is fine."

There is an order to decorating a tree or else you can't do it. Not any religious order. You have to put the lights on first and make sure that there are no bare spots, and the big bulbs go toward the trunk because when the tree starts to die, the branches droop and the bulbs fall. The little ones go on the outside, and plastic, nonbreakable go at the bottom if you have a pet or young child. Your good ones go at the top. Tinsel goes on last. There is a whole order. So my children helped to decorate the tree, and when they got back to school, they talked about what they did over the break, and my daughter told not just that she decorated the tree, but the order of decorations. She went through all the minor details, and I knew this poor teacher was dying— a very nice teacher—and then my daughter happily said, "But of course we didn't stay because we are not Christian, we are Jewish. My grandmother is Christian and that is why she has a tree, but we aren't Christian so we didn't stay there."

What I particularly like about Beth Tfiloh is that, since most of the children come from a wide variety of non-Orthodox backgrounds, the school has been very nonjudgmental and really allows children to have a lot of discussion. Of course, some of the teachers are more simplistic in their beliefs than I would be comfortable with. As an example, one of my children came home and said, "Do you know that 5,000 years ago today was the flood?" Absolutely, today. I said, "Well, I am not going to tell you that it wasn't today, but I don't know." My answer was, "But the people who were there were so busy bailing out the boat that nobody had time to write down the date so we can hope it was today, we can think it was today, we can believe it was today. Some people are more sure that it was today than others. I am very unsure. The teacher is very sure. She may be right. I am just saying that I am not as sure as she is." My daughter came home a few weeks later saying, "Do you know that 5,700 years ago today was creation?" And I said, "Oh, really?" She said, "I know. The teacher wasn't there. Her father wasn't there. We don't know for sure." I told her, "That is right. We don't know for sure. If the teacher believes that it was 5,700 years ago today and that is meaningful for her, that is fine. But you see, in Judaism, you don't have to believe that. You have to make a choice, as you get older." I am not telling my child that the teacher is wrong and that you have to make this choice right now to agree with me or to agree with the teacher, the person who is feeding you or the person who is not feeding you.

I love history, and one year one of my daughters was learning about the Inquisition at school. She came home and told me about the Inquisition. Well, it was not what I had learned, and I was furious that the school was rewriting history , and I went up and told that rabbi that he was not to do this anymore and that I was furious! He was not to make the Jews the center of everything; he was not to rewrite history because that wasn't the way the Inquisition was! I really read him the riot act. He very nicely shook his head and said, "All right, all right." The next year one of my other children had to do a report on the Inquisition, and there aren't children's books on the Inquisition. So we went down to the Pratt, and we had to get adult books. I would sort of skim them and put in markers saying, "Read page 69; read page 93." As I read through the books, I realized that *I* was the one who had been taught rewritten history in Catholic school. My children were being taught what really happened. I wrote a note to the rabbi saying that I was completely sorry, and that I was the one who learned this completely differently from what actually happened.

The most important book I read was *Sunflower* by Simon Weisenthal. It is a very small book. In the book he is working in a forced labor camp cleaning up infected matter from hospitals. There is a German soldier who has been horribly burned and is dying. He wants to confess to Weisenthal and be forgiven for the mass murder he has committed. Weisenthal wrote this story, then sent the manuscript to different people to have them give their views on what he should have done. Should he forgive, could he forgive. In the responses you saw the range of how Christians look at the world, how Jews look at the world. There were some who wrote, saying, "Oh, yes. You should have forgiven him so he could have died a peaceful death." Christianity says that you always can be forgiven before you die or that God always forgives. But according to one writer—I think he was Jewish—there comes a point when He doesn't, even in Christianity. And as you are reading the story you think, "I wouldn't have forgiven him."

One of the most appealing things about Judaism to me is that you don't start off bad and that you are not always waiting to be punished. Every Jew begins on sort of an even footing and you can get better. I think people don't realize what a positive thing that is. Maybe they don't realize it because they haven't lived under the other system. I can understand people converting into Judaism. I see it as a much more life-affirming, much more positive way of looking at your life. Judaism seems much more human to me. It puts participation in the religion into the hands of each individual Jew. In Christianity, especially with Catholicism, the ritual and the magic can be done only by special people, and that keeps you on the outside. You are always subject to the person who can do the magic thing, and of course that is the person who is better—the priest or the nun—who will tell you what to do. There is a joke about two Jews on a desert island who have three synagogues: the one he goes to, the one I go to, and the one we would never step foot in! I find that to be a positive aspect of Judaism—that there is a discussion and a choice. Not just a choice between Reform or Conservative or Reconstructionist or Orthodox, but within each there is a choice. The basis for all of it is that you are responsible for yourself.

28

Shades of Gray

"Chava"

As the conversion classes she agreed to attend proceeded, Chava discovered that the religion she was studying in order to be married to her husband was meaningful to her, too.

At first Chava and Aharon, who had once been strictly religiously observant, practiced only those rituals that they felt enhanced their life together. When they decided to live in Israel for a year, Chava was confronted with Judaism according to *halakhah*, and her development as a Jew was caught up between her own desire for acceptance and security and her husband's struggles about leading an observant life.

It has always been clear to me that the quality of the practice of any discipline is dependent on such diverse factors as personal psychological characteristics, opportunity, relationship, history, cultural time frame—the list goes on. Chava's embrace of Judaism paralleled an equally strong process that she was beginning to undergo in healing the wounds of her troubled childhood growing up in a dysfunctional family.

What happens when a person from a family in which rules are aribtrary, chaotic, and authoritarian tries to fit into a religion whose rules are arbitrary, regular, and authentic? The regularity can be soothing, the arbitrariness feels familiar, but there is confusion about what must be followed unquestioningly in order to survive, in the first case, and what one is willing to undertake in the pursuit of a life of devotion to a higher authority who in this case is . . . God.

As she rebuilds her internal life, Chava has gained the confidence to reexamine her commitment to Judaism, find her place as a Jew, and make a meaningful Jewish life together with her husband. The process, Chava says, has been one of teaching two people who see things in black and white to see life in shades of gray.

Most of the members of my family are in one way or another alcoholics and none of them are in recovery. My dad started drinking when he was very young—in high school, then in college, in the navy, and it kept snowballing. He said that he felt pressured to marry my mom because all his friends were marrying when they got out of the navy, so he just went along with it. He came to realize that he really didn't love my mom, but by that time he had three kids and a fourth one on the way. He was never faithful to my mother and he drank a lot and stayed out late at night at bars.

My mother dealt with that by starting to drink herself. She never went out to bars, but every night she had two or three Jack Daniels, and her whole behavior changed. She became very belligerent, violent. She'd never been the adult in my growing up. When my dad left, I was the one working and cleaning the house, paying the bills. She would never take over and do any of that. It still plays a big part in our relationship, though now I'm finally not doing that.

Until I was eight or nine years old, my father was an electrical engineer and was president of a company. Then he tried to go out on his own and that was when things started to fall apart in my family. My father has a thing about gambling. He would gamble absolutely everything on a business deal and then the project wouldn't go through. He was finally caught in Utah, and actually spent some time in jail for swindling people.

My parents wanted to live a very extravagant life—driving a Mercedes; I had three or four horses; I showed horses all summer. There was no limit, yet there was no money to support it—it was other people's money. We constantly moved—twelve times in eight years—because we kept getting evicted. I would show up at the barn and my horses would be gone—sold at auction. There was absolutely no stability whatsoever. They never would say, "Okay, we have X amount of money, where should this money go? To pay the heat, to buy food." Instead my father would spend it on something completely unnecessary—a Xerox machine. So we'd sit there with no electricity, but with all this equipment and all this stuff. It was just ridiculous. In a way my gambler father finally gambled away his family. Growing up that way, it took me a long time to trust in any stable situation.

I would say my family's motto was very much "everyone for himself," and just recently I've realized how much violence there was. There was such high tension all the time that came out as complete frustration. My father was either physically or emotionally violent with my mother; then she would beat up on us, or he would. It was a completely out-of-control household. There were no limits, no boundaries, not really any caring for anybody else. You just tried to survive. My mother always talks about how proud she is to have raised survivors. To myself, I say, "Everyone survived—what? Is that the point?" That's how I look at my childhood: "Well, I survived it, and thank God I don't have to go back to it." Thank God I had animals. I had lots of dogs, and I had horses, and when they were taken I was able to ride other people's horses. I worked with kids, teaching riding, and so I had some release in spending energy in a way that I absolutely loved. If I hadn't had those things, I'm not sure what would have happened.

When I was very young, we went to church. My mother used to teach Sunday school in the Lutheran Church. My sisters went through confirmation. We used to get all dressed up and go to Easter services. Then suddenly, we stopped. I remember my mom saying she was fed up with the hypocrisy in the church and everybody in it. That was about the time when my little brother was born and things were starting to really fall apart at home. I was nine at the time, and I never stepped foot into a church until college. There was never any discussion about religion: what beliefs are, what God is, no teaching of any of that.

In college I went to a few churches seeking solace, I suppose, because I was falling apart. I had gotten a full scholarship to play field hockey, but I hurt my knee in a game and the coach told me to get back in or I'd lose my scholarship. My knee was so badly injured (to this day I am still undergoing surgery to repair it) that I could no longer play for the school, and I was kicked out of school because I'd lost my scholarship. I didn't have any money, and I didn't know what to do. I was searching for help, and I went to all these churches, but nothing really made sense.

I eventually moved to Boston to work and get back in school. I had all these plans and was feeling good about taking charge of my life in this way. But, I began getting migraine headaches and one particularly severe one sent me into the hospital. My ex-boyfriend's roommate, Aharon, felt very sorry for me because I didn't know anyone in Boston. So he came and visited me. I was sitting in a dark hospital room, my left side paralyzed; I couldn't see out of my left eye. We talked for two or three hours. It was the first time in my life I had had a truly honest conversation with someone. We just became friends. There were a lot of changes going on for both of us. He had just lost his father. We were both grasping for that security and that family we were both desperately missing. We each needed someone to listen to our story. These issues are at the root of our pursuit of a religiously observant life.

On our first date Aharon said that he eventually wanted to live in Israel, so if I could deal with that we could keep going out. He also said he would never marry someone who wasn't Jewish. So right from the start he set the tone. I thought, "Well, Israel sounds good. I'm into moving around." The part about not marrying someone who wasn't Jewish didn't even faze me. Then as we got much more serious and began talking about marriage, he kept bringing it up. I realized that I was against converting if he was only going to love me if I was Jewish. I wanted him to love me as I was and see if our relationship could work on that basis. I didn't understand the dynamic that I can see behind it now—the sense of tradition and the sense of not giving anything up. But it was really hard and I finally consented to go to some classes that the Reform and Conservative rabbis gave.

By the time I started taking these classes, we had known each other about eight months. I had to drive for two hours just to get to the class, and at first, I insisted that Aharon come with me. A wonderful woman rabbi taught the classes, and she presented the philosophical side of Judaism as well as the traditions in a wonderful spiritual way. This was really my first education in organized religion, and the fact that a religion could be so family oriented was news to me. We even went on field trips to a Jewish funeral home and the *mikveh*. It wasn't long before I told Aharon he could stay home because this was something I was enjoying. It was something that really clicked. And I liked Aharon's family rabbi, who was working with me. We had a lot of good talks about various issues.

During college, Aharon had spent a year in Israel and studied for six months in an

Orthodox *yeshivah* in Jerusalem. On his return to the United States he found it too difficult to hold on to his Orthodox lifestyle, and it really didn't make much sense to him once he got away from the fold. But that influence was still there for him when he met me and while I was going through the conversion. He had the pressure of knowing that he'd given up something when he'd stopped being observant, and yet he didn't know what he wanted to take back.

Aharon's parents were actually scared to death he was going to become a black-hatter because he'd taken so strongly to the *yeshivah*. So, I guess his mother never worried that he would not marry someone who is Jewish. I think she knew that making the decision to convert had been a difficult process for me, and she was very supportive and very warm—always joked that now that I had gone through all these classes, I knew more than she did. At the same time I really tried to forge a relationship with her and encouraged her to share with me the family traditions. I've tried to collect all the family recipes. When we are down in Florida with her, we always use the candlesticks that her mother brought from Russia. That is another part of Judaism that I just love—the traditions that are passed on from family to family. To be a part of it, keeping the chain unbroken, is very meaningful to me.

I remember in eighth grade there were three Jewish boys in my class, and I was invited to their *bar mitzvahs*. I felt how comfortable it all was. There were all these relatives—a real family celebrating together. It was such a nice service. Judaism seemed like a safe nurturing place to be. Remembering these impressions years later when I was going through the crisis in college, I had thought of stopping by the Hillel to just see what's going on. I felt Judaism had a mysterious pull on me even then, though I still haven't quite discovered what that pull was. That is why it never surprised me that I ended up with someone Jewish.

Aharon and I lighted candles on Friday night, and I had begun baking *hallah*. Soon we started not answering the phone or watching TV so we could have just this night to ourselves. It was wonderful. We were just doing things that were special between the two of us and growing together. Judaism was exactly what I wanted, exactly what I had missed all my life—a long-standing, secure religion based on tradition and centered around the family. I really loved it and grasped on to it. And I went through the conversion—a Conservative conversion.

Three male rabbis watched over the process, and in retrospect, I wished I'd included the woman rabbi because I would have liked to have that female presence. The rabbis asked me why I wanted to do this, and I was incredibly nervous in front of them. It was very clear, though, that the conversion was my choice and that I would have gone through with it even if Aharon and I had ended our relationship. It felt right, although I don't think I understood more fully until recently why it felt right and safe, particularly for me.

After we got married we went to Israel for a year. That blew me out of the water. It was horrendous. I stuck out like a sore thumb. Nobody would believe I was Jewish—maybe because I didn't speak Hebrew or know much about the essence of Judaism or because I was blond-haired and blue-eyed. I kept thinking of my born-Jewish sister-in-law, with her highlighted hair and blue eyes, who looks just like I do. Would she have been questioned? And in Jerusalem I was confronted with the halakhic aspect of Judaism, about which I hadn't even a clue.

When Aharon decided to spend a few days in a *yeshivah* in Jerusalem, I thought I would take some women's classes to see how that was, but I was asked to leave because my conversion hadn't been Orthodox. In the eyes of the people who ran the *yeshivah*, I wasn't Jewish, and they don't allow non-Jews to study there. At this time in Israel the whole "Who is a Jew?" issue was the subject of demonstrations and hot debate. I didn't agree with them; I felt I was Jewish. But even though I was furious at this school for claiming I wasn't Jewish, inside myself, I had mixed feelings. Instead of standing up for myself and fighting the issue, I gave in and wanted to do anything that I could to fit into that community.

We started studying with a wonderful man, a very knowledgeable and very non-judgmental Lubavitcher rabbi, who was himself a *ba'al teshuvah*. He was very supportive of my going through an Orthodox conversion, not so much to make sure that I fit in with everyone else but for any children we might have, so that if we ever did live in Israel there wouldn't be any problem for them. The only thing I could hear was that this was for our kids; I could do it for them, for their future. The rabbi also suggested that I do the conversion when we returned to the States because it is much harder in Israel.

I look back now at the time we spent in Israel and I see the influence that Aharon had on me, stemming from his need to rediscover for himself what was meaningful. I had no understanding of what it was he was searching for, and I was too scared to say, "Wait a minute, this isn't for me." So I went along with him, without too much questioning. Our observance increased measurably, but without my understanding or really feeling wholehearted about what we were doing.

When we returned from Israel, I went through an Orthodox conversion. It was nonspiritual and unfulfilling. I would plan to meet with the rabbi for two hours, and he would either miss the appointment or come and talk about his frustrations that some people didn't like him. I had learned more through my Reform-Conservative studies, and of course, I learned a lot in Israel without even realizing it. It was just something I needed to do to get on paper, so the rabbi was doing it quickly—although not quickly enough for some people who were concerned that we didn't have a kosher marriage.

I learned this painfully through a conversation with some anonymous man who answered one of the 800-numbers out of New York—like 1-800-MITZVOT or 1-800-KOSHER. I don't know what I wanted or expected from the call I made, but the guy who answered started asking a lot of questions. I freely gave the information that I had converted or that I was working on a conversion. He was outraged that the rabbi hadn't done it in *one* day and then gone back and taught me things because, to this guy on the phone, we were living in sin. I didn't even know this person screaming at me over the phone that I wasn't the right kind of Jew yet. It was very easy for me to be derailed by anyone who told me I was doing it wrong.

Now, I have neighbors who are very right-wing Orthodox Jews and won't talk to me except to lecture me that, as a convert, I should be considered an orphan and have no other family except the Jewish community, and I should not maintain any relationship with my own family. Their fervency and the stringent observance they expect made me horribly upset; what should I do? I felt so lost, but at first I felt incapable of rejecting what they were saying outright.

I have learned, finally, that I am never going to please everybody. Up until recently I would try to do whatever requirements anyone presented because I wanted to be accepted as a Jew by everyone. I realize that that is not possible. I know now that I have to be what I feel is Jewish and feel comfortable with that. I still struggle with what "comfortable" means, though. I examine what I can and cannot give up in my life—right now, for example, I'm not going to cover my hair and I like to wear shorts and pants. I know that this may change and it might grow, but for right now this is what I want to do with it.

After the conversion ceremony the second time around, Aharon and I had to be remarried and were just going to do it in the rabbi's office. Some of the couples we had become close with put together a ceremony and a party at one of their homes. It was actually as special as my first marriage, having friends around for a celebration. I realized that that is what I love about Judaism—the friendship and community. And, perhaps most important to me, these were people for whom it did not matter whether I had converted or not; they liked me for who I was.

We then went from Massachusetts to a Native American reservation and hiked around the Southwest for four months. We rarely saw another person. On the reservation the people were trying to bring the Apache language back in the schools and teaching the children their history. These people are surrounded by memorials to the fallen soldiers and nothing to the fallen natives. It is a very skewed picture of what happened. It made me think about how I felt being Jewish. These people are trying desperately to hold on to their own traditions, and it was exactly what I was trying to do in finding my own sense of Judaism. To see the parallels was meaningful to me. A lot of people out there had never met a Jew, didn't know what they were, and really had very negative images of Jews. I found myself defending this faith and this person that I was. It was very enlightening.

After this adventure we moved to this city and were starved for Jewish community. We were just like sponges, soaking up as much as we could and before we knew it, we got caught up in this incredible wave of Orthodoxy. When we stopped and looked at each other we said, "Oh, my God, what is going on?" Even though there are some wonderful people here in the community, and it is in a sense very nonjudgmental, there is still a sense that you have to be mainstream. Maybe no one is putting pressure on you, but you get the feeling that there are things that you do to be a part of the group. If you want to fit into the community, you play by their rules whether or not you believe in everything.

We have also been a part of an egalitarian *havurah* that is attractive to me because it enables me to express myself Jewishly in a nonpressurized way. I don't think I'd ever been involved in an organization where there is such equality, and I enjoy being involved with women and men, together. That experience is something I've missed along the way in Judaism and otherwise, and I realize that that is very important to me.

But there is a safety in Orthodoxy that makes it very hard for me to break away from it. Given my background of chaotic family life, it is hard for me to trust myself and my ability to make decisions and follow through with them. Orthodoxy provides me with rules, boundaries, limits—and *I* don't have to set them. And I do have to set them in other areas of my life. Knowing what is right for me and trusting in making decisions for myself is the hard part for me. The *havurah*, for example, is something I like and trust, but it would mean leaving my security blanket of Orthodoxy—as problematical as that security blanket is for me sometimes.

In Israel we started keeping kosher. Friday nights were definitely always *Shomer Shabbat*. Saturdays were sometimes kind of mixed—we still went on hikes, but when we were home in our apartment, we were observant. We weren't involved in a community, and we were bored to tears at times. We have actually never been able to keep strictly *Shomer Shabbat* for more than a four-month period. We always end up getting so claustrophobic and so fed up with it all that we run out and go camping for the next four weekends and just say we can't do this.

Aharon felt incredibly guilty about this patchy observance. I, on the other hand, felt ambivalent for different reasons. At times I was very resentful that all this observance was being foisted onto my life, yet I didn't want to make too many waves with Aharon. Some of this is in part related to my own issues of never being able to have a different opinion from the people I am with. It has taken work and some time for me to realize that I've got my own opinions and I can be my own person and that that is not threatening nor am I going to get punished for it.

It is scary for me to be making my own life in Judaism, which is at times separate from Aharon's vision. On the one hand it is quite clear that I had to make a separation from my family—that being different from them was essential to my well-being. But what does being my own person different from Aharon mean?

Aharon and I are very similar. We were both real loners as kids and didn't have a lot of friends. We are very comfortable just having each other and doing a lot together. We do a lot of camping and hiking by ourselves. We've never really tried to be a part of a community and feel very uncomfortable with how to make friends and all that that involves. That tends to make us hang on to each other tighter.

It has been only recently that I have felt enough safety in the relationship to test the limits with Aharon of how far I can go away from being Jewishly observant. I told him that I was not sure I wanted to keep kosher outside the house. When we were on vacation I had a bowl of clam chowder. I was testing him but I was also testing me—do I really believe in this God that is not punishing? I still have this idea that if I don't do everything just right, if I am not the right kind of Jew, I will be punished for it. The idea of a punishing God clouded my whole Orthodox conversion and my attitude toward the acceptance of more *mitzvot*. In my mind it is still very black and white. You did everything or you did nothing, and you couldn't do nothing because you'd be punished. So you just had to dive in whether you believed or not.

All the testing the limits with *kashrut* and other observance is not a disrespect to Aharon; it's really just my way of making sure I'm doing what I'm supposed to be doing. I am making my own identity within Judaism and that may be different from Aharon's identity in Judaism. The fact that we are maybe each taking a little bit different path in Judaism I think has been very threatening for both of us. And we are realizing that it is okay to do that. It's important for me to find out that I can be different from Aharon and I can trust that he's not going to get angry, or he's not going to leave or I'm not going to get punished by him.

Aharon himself can't find comfort in the middle ground or at either extreme, which is a torturing place for him right now. It is hard to see. He gets incredibly anxious around *Shabbat*. There are paths in life he'd like to take—such as live in the country—that require him to moderate some of the ideals he holds for Jewish observance. Yet there is that fear that if you take one step over the threshold then of course your whole body is going to go—your toe isn't going to hang over the end. We both see things as pretty black and white—I never realized how much alike we are in that. We are trying to teach ourselves to see gray. It is not easy.

I've had to take a hard look at why I find myself in Orthodoxy. As I've said, there are nurturing qualities about it—but there is the flip side. The *mehitzah*, the rules proscribing contact between men and women, the rules about modesty in dress for women—these all provide a measure of comfort and security that can protect women from abusive men. I didn't have to worry about a man walking up to me and giving me an unwelcome hug. Orthodox men don't touch women who aren't their wives. But on the other hand, if it's hot and you wear shorts, you are "uncovered," you are "provocative," as my mother used to point out, and whatever ensues is your fault. How can it be a horrible thing to wear shorts? Given these messages, it's very hard for me to think of myself as a sexual female and have that be okay. I've hidden under the skirts of Orthodoxy because it's a very safe way, and I didn't have to deal with ambiguous situations. As I am working in psychotherapy on the issues of my dysfunctional family life, I am reexamining these things, and I'm wanting to assert myself and find a role for myself as a female without being told how it must be.

The result of this process has been that I have begun feeling much more comfortable in the community here as a Jew and not being afraid if people don't recognize that I'm Jewish. Now I feel much clearer that I don't bother with them and they don't bother with me. I'm finding people that I enjoy being around and that I can identify with.

Aharon and I have both taken a step back and said let's put the enjoyment back into this. We are discovering the things we do like and building again so it comes to mean something that we enjoy again. We recently spent *Shabbat* with friends who have been at this for fourteen years and just think of observance as a ladder that you slowly move up. If you find a rung you like, you stay there for a while. I need a reminder that this can be a slow process. It can be a nice slow exploration; especially since we don't have kids right now, the consistency factor doesn't have to be there. It feels much more comfortable now. It doesn't seem like it is a frantic searching. It is more like, "Okay, let's explore and see where this road takes us."

By the time I began conversion, I was really wanting what religion seemed to be offering, and I wondered what would have happened if I'd gotten it from somewhere else. Would that have made any difference? Was I at a point where I was really ready to accept religion or did Judaism really make a statement for me? The idea of one god made sense to me, but beyond that what do I really believe about God? Was the Torah God-given, or just inspired by God? Most of the laws about observance are rabbinic—versus what really is in the Torah—and are fences the rabbis built. Do I need to be bound to laws about my relationship to God that were made by other human beings? Once I converted I felt that I couldn't question any more, that I had to be so strong in my belief. I remember asking the rabbi of our *shul*, "I feel very uncomfortable because I have all these qualms and problems and issues with the religion, is it because I converted that I think I'm supposed to have no doubts? Is it okay for me to question?" He said, "You are not a Jew if you don't question." He said it's part of the struggle. That was such a relief. It was okay that I didn't have all this figured out.

29

That's Funny,
You Don't Look Scottish!

Steve McKerrow

"It looked like cat food; I swear it looked like cat food." That was Steve McKerrow's first reaction to gefilte fish, and the line he plans to use when he gets around to writing down the tale of his conversion. Steve envisions this book as a comedy because so many funny things have happened in his twenty years as a convert to Judaism.

Take the first time he met his wife's extended family, for example. Debbie, as a teenager, had developed a crush on a midshipman at the Naval Academy. Her parents had met him at their Annapolis synagogue and invited him home for *Shabbat* lunch. His name was also Steve. They dated for a while but nothing came of the relationship. Years later Debbie's parents had invited the whole *mishpohah* (family) to *Shabbat* dinner to meet her fiancé, Steve McKerrow, from New Mexico ("Where's his horse?" he felt they must be asking themselves). Debbie, terribly nervous and excited, announced, "I'd like you all to meet Steve Lieberman." After an embarrassing pause, she realized her mistake. Steve wanted to say, "I know you all would have liked to have Steve Lieberman here, but . . . it's—just—*me*." Debbie was mortified, but Steve thought it was a wonderful introduction. It cleared the air, and he met Debbie's aunts and uncles on a totally new plane.

"Obviously my name suggests my ancestry, but funny things happen when people don't realize you are Jewish and then suddenly they discover you *are*, and it's embarrassing. 'That's funny you don't look Scottish.' I always tell people that there are Jews in Scotland—there must be."

Steve wanted to formalize his identity as a Jew in time for his first child's birth. He can always remember precisely the date of his conversion since it was a month before Josh was born. Steve's decision has led to a lifelong devotion to his chosen religion.

I came to the decision to convert very gradually, after first expecting that I would never convert. When Debbie and I started to date in college, it became a concern fairly quickly. Debbie's parents were always on the more liberal side of Orthodoxy. But their synagogue had separate seating and women did not have a huge role there. Debbie had a "confirmation" but not a *bat mitzvah*. Even so, both she and her parents expected that she would marry somebody Jewish. And I wasn't. I was *definitively* not Jewish. I was nothing at the time.

I am a second-generation New Mexican. My mother was the granddaughter of Nebraskan farmers who had come to New Mexico in a covered wagon around the turn of the century. In New Mexico my grandfather became a furniture salesperson.

During World War II, my father was stationed at Kirtland Air Force Base in Albuquerque. Both my parents had been raised as Christian Scientists. My father's mother, the strong religious figure in their family, raised her family near Boston, the home of the Christian Science of Mary Baker Eddy, where the "mother church" is found. Albuquerque had an active Christian Science church where members welcomed servicemen. My grandmother invited my father home for lunch after church. There, he met my mother, who was only fourteen at the time. They married when she was sixteen. (One story I heard was that after they were married he signed her high-school report cards, since he was her legal guardian as well as her husband!) Apparently this was quite the scandal in the family, but my grandmother fiercely defended them. She recognized that it was right—and I guess it was, because my folks are still married and quite happy.

My father wanted to fly B-24 bombers but was excluded due to vision problems. When the air force discovered that he was a musician, they put him in the military-band unit. He spent the rest of the war traveling around from base to base, marching in parades and performing concerts for bond rallies. When he got out of the air force, he and my mother returned to live in Albuquerque. When I was six months old, there was an abortive experiment to go home to New England. He wanted to attend a music conservatory in Boston. This venture lasted all of six months, and back they went to New Mexico. Apparently my mother was mistreated by the family, creating a tremendous split that lasted for years.

The Christian Science Church is a lay-led organization. There is no equivalent to a priest or a rabbi. My parents served as "readers" in the church. I was born in a private Christian Science clinic with a midwife, and my older sister, Jan, was born in my grandmother's house, also with a midwife. Our life revolved around the church. But by the time my brother, Dan, was born, there had been some falling away, for he was born in a hospital with doctors attending.

But my parents were still devout; I have a vivid memory that I had to get a note from home to give to my teacher in first grade to exempt me from getting a polio shot in school because of religious beliefs. The whole class went down the hall to get their polio vaccines, and I stayed in the classroom. Everyone was afraid it was going to hurt, and as they came back one by one, they were rubbing their arms. A nasty little girl started quizzing me: "Why didn't you get it?" "Because of my religion." "Well, aren't you afraid you'll spend the rest of your life in an iron lung?" What do you say to that when you are in first grade? It was hard on me. Once, I burst an eardrum, and I was out of school for two weeks because we did not use antibiotics. The second time the polio vaccine was offered in school, I got it, but by then, things had changed drastically in my family.

By then, I wasn't in Sunday school anymore, and the family didn't attend church regularly. My parents were evolving into "free thinkers"—free of anything that was organized. The real catalyst to their breakaway from the church was the tragic death of my fourteen-year-old sister when I was twelve. She was walking home from school with a male classmate. They got into a quarrel when she refused to go out on a date with him. He hit her on the head with a rock, and she died. He was ultimately convicted and put away on a plea of insanity.

I bring this up because that was absolutely the breaking point between my parents and religion. How could something like that happen, particularly to people whose religion depended so wholly on absolute faith? Christian Science teaches that if you order your faith and thought processes properly, the reward is incredible: you will be free of ill health—in body and spirit. The flip side, however, it seems to me, is that if you do suffer those things it is a condemnation. Somehow you are faulty, you are to blame. I'm sure that my folks went through a lot of that. Yet random tragedy happens in life, and you can't predict it. But they couldn't fit it into that belief system.

At that point there was a fixed separation from anything religious in my life. It was a violent change in the sense that it was also a break from longtime friends. Well-meaning people said things to my parents that were meant to console but seemed hurtful and ridiculous. Our neighbors who were devout Catholics said, "Well, God must have had a reason, must have wanted your daughter in heaven." My mother snapped at her that no god would do that!

We never talked about religion per se. My parents came to the belief that religion is just a crutch. They wanted to get past religion's limits. They began reading about supernatural things—ESP, mediums—but were not obsessive.

My younger brother, my two much younger sisters, Melissa and Amanda (Amanda, born after Jan's death, will be thirty this year; she's a principal dancer with the American Ballet Theatre), and I were brought up from then on in a household that could be called "secular humanist." We were politically liberal, respectful and tolerant of other systems. Our home was filled with books. We began to go to doctors more regularly. I do remember my first visit to a dentist when I was twelve—that was very exciting for me! I'd been lucky up to that time, I guess. We started taking aspirin. Our drug cabinet had been bare before that time.

My memories after my sister's death are generally indistinct. (I had this same experience when my wife's mother died about two years ago. The whole year afterward is blurred in my memory. Debbie and I went to work and did all the things we were supposed to do, but as a family we turned inward then. It's like we were a stream just floating along.) I was in junior high, and a lot of my time was occupied in competitive swimming and diving. A lot of church and other friendships fell away. I remember being told, "It's just us now; we have to draw strength from each other."

I know my parents tried very hard not to be overprotective of us but didn't succeed. My brother and I, especially, were acutely conscious that if we were going to be late, phone home; if there was a problem, call. Having suffered a tragedy, my parents knew what *can* happen. It brought to reality the level of risk we are all in all the time—you could be hit by a car, your life can end violently. I am conscious that my parents bent over backward not to restrict us. I took part in a lot of physical activities. I went away on bus trips with the diving team. I got involved in risky pursuits—I learned scuba diving, went on hiking trips, did rock climbing. And I know my folks really had to grit their teeth and say, "He has to do this."

When I was sixteen, my family moved to Maryland. Up to the time my brother was born, my father made his living with his music. He had an orchestra that played in nightclubs around the area, earned a master's degree in music, and taught part-time at the University of New Mexico. Ultimately, though, he just wasn't making it financially, so he got a "straight" job. He worked for a heavy equipment company, first as a delivery driver, then in management. My earliest memory was that my father was a truck driver and trumpet player. Later, he took the civil service exam and became a government bureaucrat. But he kept his music in his life on weekends.

During most of my growing up, he had his own jazz band. New Mexico is an interesting place culturally: separate strata of Hispanics, American Indians, a very small black community, a whole layer of government-industrial complex people, and folks like us. My father's band always had people of different cultural backgrounds in it. "Unusual" people came in and out of our house. We were different from our neighbors in that way.

My first encounter with anything Jewish was when my father played for *bar mitzvahs*. He had a band member who was Jewish, and he introduced my father to Jewish food—bagels and lox. I didn't associate that food with Jewishness. That's just what my father ate on weekends. Later I would find the cultural aspects of Judaism harder to adopt than the religious ones. But bagels and lox I knew.

My parents were having difficulty in Albuquerque. Everything reminded them of my sister. My father started to look for civil-service opportunities elsewhere. For about a year, we were constantly looking at atlases as he applied for jobs around the country. Through friends, he finally heard about a job at the National Institutes of Health in Bethesda, applied, and got it. In the summer of 1964, we moved to Rockville, Maryland.

I hated it. I was ready to move back. I'd grown up in the West. I loved it out there. I found the East green and oppressive, very closed in. But my father thrived. Much to his surprise he had a flair for administration. Before he retired, he rose to a position as a chief administrative officer of two institutes at NIH.

I was already interested in journalism when I went to the University of Maryland. In ninth grade our class at a new junior high school in Albuquerque had created the school newspaper. From that moment I knew what I wanted to do. I became a reporter on the college paper and was assigned to interview Debbie. We were both juniors at that time. She was in student government and the first person ever to think of registering herself as a lobbyist at the state capital in Annapolis. This was the story. She was the youngest registered lobbyist in Maryland.

Months later, she joined the newspaper. She had lost interest in her theater major and took on journalism and public relations. By then, I was a middle-level editor.

She showed up one night to work at my copy desk. I said, "I know you; didn't I interview you?" At the time I had a steady girlfriend from high school. Everybody expected Bonnie and I would get married someday. Debbie and I were just friends. We liked each other just for our company—joking, asking questions of each other. There was none of that silly dating pressure. We knew each other for about six months, and I suddenly realized I liked this person better than anybody I knew. Happily it worked that way for her, too, so we went from being just friends to dating and were engaged within two months.

When I had originally interviewed her, part of the story was that she was Jewish. She had been very active in Young Judea, a Zionist youth group. You couldn't talk to her without learning really fast that she was a committed Jew. So I knew that.

My mother also knew that. I lived at home throughout college. One day I said I was going out to the movies. "With Bonnie?" No, I said, with this new girl. And I gave her name, Debbie Rosen, and my mother right away asked, "*Oh*, is she *Jewish?*"—exactly that way. I said, "Yeah, I think *so*," feeling challenged. Nothing was discussed further. For Debbie it was much harder. She had her mother saying, "Who is this man? He's not Jewish?"

I've always used the analogy that for me, Debbie was like color TV versus black and white. She is remarkably free and easy, in fact, the most interesting woman I know. There is something about Jewish women that is remarkably liberated—in spite of the paradox that within the Orthodox tradition you think of women as being second-class persons. We decided that religion was not a problem—for the two of us. We were very much in concert on our views on almost everything. Politically we seemed at about the same place. I suppose "secular humanism" described my beliefs—justice, tolerance. Secular humanism is a big part of Judaism. We both came to the same belief system from completely different places, which I found fascinating.

We decided that we could do fine. If other people objected, it was their problem. There was never the remotest consideration that I would become Jewish. When that was suggested by some member of her family, Debbie really bristled. "Why should he have to convert? Nobody should have to convert." Since I was no longer a part of a religious tradition at all, when Debbie said she'd like to raise our children as Jews, my response was, "Fine, sure, no problem." I instinctively felt kids ought to have an identity—it shouldn't just be as unstructured as mine had become.

Debbie's parents surprised us by being very welcoming to me. Her mother was a remarkable person and apparently recognized the genuineness of our affection and the commitment we felt toward each other. Not once did anyone ever try to talk Debbie out of marrying me, or about having me meet the rabbi so I could convert. I was a stubborn person at that point, and wouldn't have considered it if they'd asked.

We were actually engaged for a month before we told them. We scheduled the announcement for a *Shabbat* dinner. Boy, I was nervous. Debbie felt that I had to be the one to ask for her hand—she's very traditional in that way. I waited through the whole meal, and we got into a terrific argument about the Vietnam War. Debbie and her father were shouting at each other. Her mother was trying to make peace between the two of them, but at the same time voicing her own opinion!

I come from a family (German and Scottish) where conflict is not something easily done. Suddenly, I find myself at this dinner table with people shouting and screaming at each other. It was like a cliché in a Woody Allen movie. I was terribly upset. I didn't know that in this family, the style was to argue, scream, and get it all out. Ten minutes later everybody would be fine. If this had happened in my family, people would have stewed for weeks before peace was restored.

So, here I was, burdened with the announcement that we were engaged and I just didn't know what to do. Debbie gave me a kick under the table. Finally dessert was brought in; her mother and father sat down, and I stood up. I had to seize the initiative right then. "Now that I have you here, I have something to say." They knew it was coming. In fact, to this day I think her father knew and had been pulling my chain all along to get a reaction. I was expecting shouting. In fact, her mother said, "Your father has already talked to his doctor about his ulcer, and we can handle this." They had also been to their rabbi. They looked at me and said, "We think you are a wonderful person; you should know that we wish you were Jewish, but other than that we think you are a wonderful person." I said, "Well, I can understand that. I am not Jewish, but I love your daughter."

My family's response to our engagement was poor. My mother had a tantrum—that's the only way to describe it. I was too young; couldn't we just—my father actually said it—live together?

I was going outside to marry somebody from a different culture who was not what my folks had expected. From my mother's point of view, if I married into a Jewish family she would lose me. I didn't grasp that at all. The sum total of my knowledge of Jews came from my brother's friend who was Jewish: he wore a "beanie" and got presents for eight days in December. I was simply not aware of the *content* of the difficulty in both families.

On the other hand, my father understood. He grew up in a strict New England family, went out West and married a native New Mexican. That was a big part of why my mother was never accepted into his family, even though she was of their religion. For years, he didn't see his family. There was an enormous split. I remember the big deal when they finally came to New Mexico to make a reunion.

In a way, here I was making the same kind of break. We had a brief conversation in which he wanted to make sure that I was firm and sincere. "I'll deal with your mother. You and Debbie be happy." My mother didn't understand, but her objections were veiled in concerns about my youth and the starting of a career.

We went forward. Debbie wanted a Jewish wedding. I was perfectly happy to have that, but we had trouble finding a rabbi. We had to have the wedding in a hotel in Annapolis and finally located a rabbi who was a navy chaplain. He did mixed marriages on the side, I guess, to supplement his income. We had a lovely ceremony with the *huppah* and a light bulb—not a glass—that I stepped on. My brother was best man. My parents came and loved the ceremony. My mother told me that she found the ceremony very moving. I don't remember it. I remember my knees almost buckled standing there. I was very happy. I danced with my mother at the reception— that was the first time I'd ever danced with her. We had had a little bit of conflict over whether members of the wedding party had to wear *yarmulkes*. My brother and father said, "No way are we going to wear *yarmulkes*." Deb's father was a little upset by that. But, in the end everything was fine.

I had graduated from college in the spring of 1970 and took a job with United Press International in Cleveland. For the first time in my life I was living alone. Debbie and I were to be married in August. After the wedding, Debbie and I went to live in Cleveland. It was just a year from hell. My working hours were terrible and didn't mesh with Debbie's at all. We didn't see each other much; we didn't like Cleveland and didn't know anybody there. When we finally moved into our apartment after three months in the Howard Johnson's, our furniture was delayed. We bought a TV to get a box to eat dinner on. I sent out job applications—lots of them—and got a job as a news editor at the Montgomery County *Sentinel* outside of Washington, and we beat it back to Maryland.

In Cleveland, the High Holidays came around early, and Debbie wanted to go to services. Debbie needed to find a synagogue to go to services. I couldn't understand that she needed *tickets* to go to pray. She would patiently explain, and I would challenge her: What about this? What about that? Through that process, I learned a great deal. She went to her services; I didn't. I think I wasn't invited because of the ticket problem. She'd gotten one ticket from a friend of her mother's. But I was fascinated by the holidays.

I had not been involved in organized religion since I was twelve, and I had felt somewhat disdainful of the few religious services I'd attended at other people's churches. With Debbie—and Judaism—I found things more interesting. I measured what I was learning against previous experience. What was so inviting about Judaism is that it is permissible to question and doubt and argue and yet still be Jewish. It's almost fundamental! My perception is that at least in some Protestant denominations, if there is a tenet with which you disagree, you are not considered fully a member anymore. There is not the possibility of having the level of discussion that one can have in Judaism.

How we dealt with religious issues was remarkably free of "freight" for Debbie and me. When December rolled around in Cleveland, we did have some questions about what to do.

Christmas was the biggest time of the year in my family. The photo album has pictures of all of us greeting Santa Claus at the door of my grandmother's house. In Albuquerque there was a man who was a great Santa Claus. He had a real beard. You could arrange to have him come visit your house before Christmas.

Christmas was not a very religious celebration—we did not read the nativity story, for example. It was mostly just getting together and eating traditional foods—and getting big presents! My birthday is the day after Christmas and always got tangled up in those festivities. Christmas was like the pinnacle of the year. Even after my parents were no longer religious, Christmas was still a big secular event.

Debbie was equally curious about my traditions and Christmas. I think Jewish children growing up have a lot of trouble with that. It's such a force in this culture. It can't be easy to see this happening around you but not be part of it. We did not have a Christmas tree in Cleveland, though we did light Hanukkah candles. I worked Christmas Day. Since UPI is a wire service, somebody had to be on duty, and I volunteered to be the guy who worked that shift. I know now that is a very Jewish tradition. The brotherhood at our temple arranges to fill lots of jobs on Christmas Day in places like hospitals, for example.

My family has pretty much dropped Christmas out of their lives now, but when we were first back in Maryland we were eager to be included in the family traditions. Here they were bending over backward to say, "Oh, we know you don't celebrate Christmas, but if you want to come, I guess you can come." "Of course we'll come!" Christmas is no longer important to them, but Debbie and I miss being a part of *the* big family celebration in my family. Now, we have to go out of our way to make arrangements to get down there to give them their Christmas presents.

Debbie felt a need to be involved in a synagogue, so we joined the temple that her sister and brother-in-law attended. Although non-Jews could be members, I was told, "You can't serve on the board." Ha! Like I'd even want to! We started attending services a lot more regularly. We'd go Friday night, then have dinner with her sister and brother-in-law. I welcomed the experience as a chance to see things and satisfy my curiosity.

We also went to Debbie's parents' synagogue. I think that's probably when I had the gefilte-fish experience. An Orthodox synagogue, for someone with as little experience as I had, was totally incomprehensible—they could have been Druids. It was mystifying to me. I sat with my father-in-law. Much of it was in Hebrew, so I really didn't understand what was going on. He tried to help me follow along in the prayer book. Unlike Reform, Orthodox services proceed at a lot of different paces: some people race along with their prayers, some are slower. It's a lot less structured. I find it fascinating but still completely beyond me.

Since we were now members of a congregation, I attended my first High Holiday services that fall. I had the choice of seeing it as Debbie's thing and letting it go at that or participating. I chose to participate. From the very beginning of our relationship we have done things together, not separately. It just felt right to me, and again it was my curiosity to know more.

I was starting to read about Judaism a little bit, still without any conscious intention. I read Herman Wouk's *This Is My God*, which was on our bookshelf. I still think it is one of the best introductions to Judaism anyone could have. It is from the Orthodox perspective, but written from an intensely personal point of view.

Part of my drive to understand Judaism came from being with Debbie. She had a large, widespread family, and we attended a lot of family functions. I am sure I attended my first *bar mitzvah* during this period. I joined in on the cultural part of it because that was the fabric of our life. And in one sense, because I wasn't Jewish, I could have opted out. But I didn't. Debbie's family, almost to a person, were warm and welcoming, wonderful people.

I just grew more and more comfortable—with the family, with the culture. Suddenly, at some point, I found myself identifying with things from a Jewish perspective. For example, I started seeing the negative side of Christmas—the tremendous commercialism. I started remembering that awful feeling of the end of December and having to wait another long year for more presents. Christmas never quite measured up to what you expected. Even when you got what you wanted, it was never the payoff you'd hoped for. There was always a terrible emotional crash afterward.

I became conscious of bias and prejudice. I began to hear things in a different way. When we were in Cleveland there was an old teletype operator—a crusty old Irish guy nearing retirement. He made a slur about Jews. Suddenly I thought, "Wait a minute; he's talking about my wife here, and that's a generality, and it's wrong. What should I do?" I am proud of myself for having said, "Paul, that's an ugly thing to say, and it's wrong to boot." And he said, "What's your problem, McKerrow?" And I said, "My wife is Jewish, and I don't appreciate that kind of talk." He backed off. He thought he was safe with me, and he wasn't. I became aware of that. I started seeing things from that perspective.

Christians make a lot of assumptions about things because they are the majority culture. Debbie and our kids became quite active in consciousness-raising in the city public schools our children attended. Frequently we'd meet with teachers about including a Hanukkah component in December, although Debbie bristles at that solution because Hanukkah and Christmas are not parallel. The answer to overemphasizing Christmas is not to emphasize Hanukkah. I became aware of those issues.

But the real impetus for me to actively consider conversion was my first son, Josh. Debbie got pregnant with Josh when we'd been married two and a half years. We knew we wanted children, and when she did become pregnant, that was the catalyst for my decision. Debbie never said a thing to me about conversion. We already had agreed that when we had children, ours would be a Jewish household. I was comfortable with that. But suddenly I felt uncomfortable because I wasn't identified. I was bringing a child into the world who should have a father who stood for something.

Shortly thereafter I went to our very wonderful rabbi. He's the senior rabbi of a big congregation in Boston now. I asked him sort of diffidently, "Well, if I were to think about converting what would I have to do?" He was cool. "Study, basically. I'll give you a reading list; then, we'll get a schedule of meetings. So we'll talk, and you'll ask me questions, and at some point we'll see." It was no more than that. I didn't tell a lot of people; I just started learning. The rabbi did a smart thing: he gave me two Jewish history books. One is from a very liberal perspective and the other from a more traditional perspective. I read them back-to-back. What he was doing was showing me the difference in interpretation. I always admired him for that.

The rabbi's hobby was baking. Frequently while we were in discussion he'd jump up, run to the kitchen, pound some bread, and then return covered with flour. To this day, I associate the smell of bread baking in the oven with my conversion!

By this time, for all intents and purposes we were living a Jewish life. I found the experience of studying and questioning very stimulating in a way college hadn't been. My study for conversion was a wonderful process: read and question. I didn't realize it, but what I was doing was very similar to traditional Torah study—even though it was a different text.

I could ask the rabbi anything and challenge anything. I had problems with certain subjects. The first one was the *bris*—isn't this just a pagan ritual, just a vestige of some sacrifice? He didn't say it wasn't, exactly. He was a classic rabbi in the sense that he wouldn't give an answer. He would say, "Well, one school of thought would view it this way; another school would view it this way." He'd stake out the territory, then he would find a spot in the middle, somehow. As I now understand, this is also a very classic style of Torah study.

I have come to understand and appreciate the dietary laws, but I had trouble with them at first. What place do they have in the culture at this point? Our family doesn't follow them very closely, though I understand the function they have of enhancing normal acts and as a way to identify as a Jew. I don't think people keep kosher because God says they have to. I think people keep kosher because it gives them something back. I've often admired the ability of people to do that, though I've never quite been able to cross the line. We don't have pork or shellfish in our house, but we'll happily go out to a crab feast.

I drove Debbie crazy at first when I learned there were 613 *mitzvot*. To be a holy person, don't you have to obey all 613? Well, clearly, nobody does, but I wanted to know, how do you justify that? Her answer was, you find what works for you. So in her case she won't eat ham, but she loves bacon. "It's pork, Debbie, how can you eat bacon and not eat ham?" The answer is, "That's just the way I do it. I would feel bad eating ham but I feel fine eating bacon." She would draw the line at Canadian bacon. I would argue, "When we eat out your mother loves crab and your father won't eat it." Then of course I realized that none of them should have been eating in that restaurant to begin with, because it wasn't kosher!

I gradually began to understand how you find a level of spirituality that is meaningful to you. Individuals make these decisions because we have free choice. In an adult *bar mitzvah* class the rabbi put it very well. "Most people," he said, "misread the Adam and Eve story as the development of sin. The Jewish viewpoint would say that what they got was 'choice'—the burden of choosing how to behave and sometimes erring." I like that. You have the ability to choose what is meaningful to you and what enriches the lives of those around you, although you may not get it right all the time. I was also attracted to Judaism because Debbie explained that, "Yes, there are ideals to strive for, but we are all just human beings—even rabbis are just human beings. They are teachers and not necessarily endowed with a special spirituality." A divine representative overseeing our lives has never struck me as particularly important. What's important is how you live your life in relation to other people—particularly the people closest to you.

To this day, I find it rather remarkable that Debbie was so blasé about my not being Jewish. She was centered in her own identity and knew who she was—something that I have found is typical of many Jewish women. For her part, she has said that she somehow felt we were on that level where we could be frank with each other. I was the first boy with whom she could be honest about what movie she wanted to go see when asked what she wanted to do that evening.

To find myself comfortably identifying myself as a Jew is surprising sometimes. It happens to me at every High Holiday. At some point during the service I'll be standing there enveloped in that wonderful observance and suddenly I'll think, "This is *me*, little Stevie McKerrow. How did this happen?" I still find it really amazing, given the way my parents aggressively discouraged organized religion. But they encouraged open-mindedness, saying, "Read everything, delve into all kinds of things and then find yourself." I followed my parents' advice, and strangely enough it led me to Judaism.

I am a parent so I know guilt; you never feel you've done enough. There are disappointments. At the moment neither of my boys is particularly involved in Judaism. My oldest boy, Josh, studied through the high-school program at Baltimore Hebrew Congregation; he spent a summer in Israel. He could be a rabbi someday, but at the moment he is finding himself. He's a writer, a poet, a painter. He took a year off from college this past year. He's much like I am in that he is intellectually grappling with life.

My other son, Andy, went through his confirmation, walked out of the building, and said, "I don't want to ever come back." He had a conflict with the young rabbi at the temple. It was complicated and very saddening to me, but this was a rabbi who just didn't have the maturity himself to be leading fifteen-year-olds in intellectual discussions. He was very dogmatic. Fifteen-year-olds love to argue, and Andy particularly loves to have intellectual discussions. This rabbi just kept putting him down. So Andy's concept of Judaism became that it is rigid; a view we are slowly trying to alter. But he's almost an adult, and we said, "It is up to you what you do."

Even though I chose differently than my family, if my children chose something other than Judaism, I'd be disappointed. That is another surprise to me. Given my experience, how could I challenge them? I could say what Debbie's parents said: "I would wish that you find in being Jewish what I have found and that therefore the person you choose to be a partner in life would find the same thing." I think part of me thinks that somewhere down the line they might. Debbie certainly went into our relationship not knowing that I would ever find Judaism. She would tell you now that oh, yes, she knew at heart somehow; I didn't, and I don't see how she could have. I can only hope that I have for my boys the understanding that my father had for me when it comes time for them to settle down with someone.

I've been living a Jewish life for twenty years now. It didn't happen right away. It was slow. Although I grew comfortable with identifying myself as Jewish, the process of feeling it inside me was yet to come. I knew that time had arrived when I didn't have to work at it anymore. Others I've met through working with Jews by Choice have reported the same experience. Once you are formally converted you go through a period of not wanting anybody to question you. You want to submerge and be accepted and not be identified as a Jew by Choice; not have anybody look at your name and say, "McKerrow. McKerrow?" and you hear the wheels turning: "This is not Jewish from the beginning." It happens, all the time, and I became pretty aggressive about not feeling the need to satisfy others' curiosity. I'd just say, "Yeah, I'm Jewish." Jewish people aren't shy, though, and I would always answer a direct question. At some point that ceased to be so important. I am quite comfortable now with telling people who raise an eyebrow or something, "Yeah, I haven't always been Jewish," or "I'm a new Jew," or a line that I've always used in talks, "I was always a Jew by birth, I just didn't learn it till I was twenty-three." Which is glib but true as well.

30

This Is Where I Belong

Elsie Heyerman

Elsie converted eighteen years ago as a single person. Some time after her conversion, she was attending services at her Reform temple and met up with a Jewish couple she had known as a teenager. She has been a part of the lives Becky and Louis and their children ever since. They are her "Jewish family."

The richness of Jewish family traditions and home rituals is among the most appealing aspects of our religion and way of life. For single people—born Jew and convert alike—the "lack" of a family can rob home ritual observance of much of its luster. Given our images of the proper *Shabbat* table crowded around with family, how do you "feel" Jewish on Friday night if you are the only one to enjoy the *hallah*, wine, and festive meal? Single people solve the dilemmas they may have about Jewish home observance in a number of creative ways. Perhaps the most difficult first step is to banish the images of only one right way to be a Jewish family: I am a family of one; my community of friends is my family; and I am adopted by and adopt another Jewish family or families for my own.

Elsie has done all three of these things and has through the years carved out for herself a place of comfort in the Jewish community. It has been difficult at times to continue to feel rooted in her Jewish identity, but when she discovered her father's family in Belgium were Jews, she looked in the mirror and said to herself, "See, I was right all along!"

It's been more than eighteen years since I converted. I can remember that time vaguely, and as I look back now it seems almost amazing to me that I actually did something like that back then.

I was raised a very strict Catholic, and I always felt very uncomfortable with that when I was growing up. I never felt comfortable saying the words and performing the traditional things that our family did. We went to mass every Sunday, received communion, had confession, and celebrated all the holidays. My parents were very observant. They didn't have strong ethnic backgrounds; they were just very sincere about their Catholicism. But there was something about all of it that didn't ring true to me from the time I was very young. I felt very constrained by the words and the beliefs that I had been asked to accept.

The holy Trinity was especially difficult for me. The whole concept of this god who is an old man upstairs in heaven dictating to us the words that we were all sinners.

I was also uncomfortable with the notion that Catholics were better than everybody else—which is what I was taught. Sure, it was possible that you could be a sincere "something else" and possibly a good person, but we were better than everybody else because we were Catholic. Those "other" people were to be saved. The value of anybody who was not a Catholic was as a potential convert. If they were offered a chance to be converted, they should take it; if not, they were lost. That made me very uncomfortable. I don't know what a priest or a nun would tell you about what the doctrine is, but that was my experience of attitudes I was taught to believe.

My mother died when I was a senior in high school and my father got sick about that time. He died the year before I converted. My brothers and I were not close, so my family became fragmented.

When I was seventeen, I went to a local, four-year college. I joined a community of radical Catholics. In those days that was a very underground group. They really broke away from a lot of things that I had learned growing up, but there was still the issue of Jesus and other things in which I couldn't believe, and, in the end, I couldn't stay there. Even though I wanted to leave Catholicism behind, I was not comfortable having nothing. I looked around for something else.

My first job may have had something to do with my developing an interest in Judaism. I was working in an office with a lot of Jewish people. I had known almost no Jews while I was growing up, so everything I saw and heard, the whole culture, was foreign to me and I was very curious about it. I didn't know the first thing about the culture or the religion itself or what Jews believed. I asked a lot of questions, and the people I worked with were very welcoming to me. They exposed me to anything I wanted to know about. They invited me for holidays and *Shabbat* dinners. They were very Orthodox, and of course I didn't know what that meant then.

I don't think I was as aware of the community as I am now, but I *sensed* something that was very attractive to me. I realize that what made an impression on me was seeing these big families and all of this warmth, this tight community where all of these Jewish people lived together and were so open with each other.

The more I learned about the religion the more attraction it held for me. From the angle that I came in, it looked very free and very intellectually challenging. To me, it looked like a place where I could conceive of God the way I wanted to, and it fit my life in the way I wanted religion to fit. I would not have to have a set of rules that I was trying to adhere to but could never measure up to. It would accept me the way I was, and I never ever felt that before.

Once I got into the religion, of course, I realized that there was a lot more to it, and certainly a lot of Jews in the world wouldn't even consider me Jewish. But it was that initial conception of the religion that I found very attractive. I wanted to belong to something. I didn't know what that meant then, for me as a convert, but I knew that I wanted that.

There was a woman in the office who had converted and married into a Jewish family. She gave me books to read. I don't even remember what they were, except one, I think it was called *What Jews Believe*. It was a thin little book that I still have.

There were a lot of things that I understood and some that I didn't. I went to the library and got books out. I don't remember what I read back then. Then I had to find a rabbi. I don't know how I made that decision or how I was led to where I went.

I ended up at a large Reform temple and talked to the rabbi. I just told him that I wanted to convert. I worked with him for almost a year. He would give me things to read, and we got together once a week or twice a month and talked. I attended the Introduction to Judaism course, and I still have some of the books that we read in that class. One of the things the rabbi asked me was, "Why do you want to convert? You can come to services, you can celebrate the holidays and you can do everything. You don't have to convert to do that." I was just sure all the way along that this was what I wanted to do and that I did want to belong enough to convert.

All the way along, nobody had tried to discourage me, but I had not been pushed either. At the end of the year of study, I talked with the rabbi about what I wanted to do next. The rabbi said, "There is no rush. You can do it now. You can do it in a year." I wanted to have a ceremony, and one of the things I decided I wanted was to go to the *mikveh*, even though I was converting with a Reform rabbi. I don't know if it is still true, but in this city there was no *mikveh* that would take somebody who was converting with a Reform rabbi. So a group of us from the class went to a *mikveh* in a nearby community. The next day I had a very small ceremony just with the rabbi. If I were to do it today, I would have friends and family come. Back then it was very private and very scary, and I didn't have a lot of people to share it with at that time.

The people at my job were very supportive, and the woman who had given me the books was very happy for me. But I left that job for an extended trip to Europe two days after my conversion.

When I came back my life was very different. I had a new job and I wasn't in contact with those people from my old job anymore. I didn't quite know how to get started. I think I had envisioned that I would convert and all of a sudden, my life would be changed and I would be part of this community. I didn't envision how much work it would take. I floundered in the beginning, but I started going to services at the Reform temple.

I ran into a couple there for whom I had done baby-sitting when I was in high school, who lived on the street where I grew up. I hadn't seen them in many years. They didn't understand why I was at the temple. They thought they knew that I wasn't Jewish—or that I hadn't been Jewish. Once they learned that I had converted, they just took me in and started including me in their holidays and in their family. They are my closest friends now. Really, more like my family now. I was very lucky to have that and still am.

That was the beginning to my living a Jewish life and has become the springboard to everything else. Becky and Louis would have me over for *Shabbat* dinner and every holiday. They would encourage me to go to services, and they would find out every Jewish activity that they could think of and encourage me to participate. They put me in touch with all kinds of people.

The connection with this family is very important because it is not an experience you can go to a synagogue and necessarily get. Just the everyday things and preparing for the holidays and discussing what is going on in the Jewish community and hearing about their backgrounds and watching how they have created their life together. They come from very diverse Jewish backgrounds themselves. Louis is from a very Orthodox background and Becky from an absolutely nonreligious, just cultural background. Seeing how they have created their Jewish lives has helped me to see how I could do mine.

One thing that I have learned is that it is okay to try different things and see how they feel. It is important to have traditions and to keep doing them—and doing them and doing them. A lot of meaning comes from the repetition becoming history. After years of celebrating the holidays with them and using the same implements and preparing the same foods and trying some different things each year to try to reinvent the holiday a little bit—whatever the holiday is—I have learned from that. I have watched them try to accommodate each other and each other's backgrounds. That has been very good to see and has helped me a lot.

I think it has also been important for me to watch their kids grow up in that environment and see how important it has been for them to have this very close Jewish culture in their family. The children went to public schools, but also to Hebrew high school. I think a lot of their development and the skills they have learned have come from the experience they had in the Jewish community and with their family. Their leadership skills come from their involvement in the Jewish youth activities and that hasn't always been easy. I think it was hard for all three of them as Reform Jews to go to the Hebrew high school, which is very heavily Orthodox. That was a real challenge for them.

For me, it has been kind of a double problem to fit into the Jewish community, both because I didn't grow up in the culture and because I am a single person. When I first converted and for I-don't-know-how-many years afterward, I felt a great drive to kind of catch up and felt like everybody else had something that I couldn't take for granted yet. I felt I needed to read and study, take courses, go to services, experience every kind of experience that I could, be exposed to all the different branches of Judaism—in short, see and do everything.

Everything was new, and it was all very exciting at first. It took a long, long time, and I'm not sure it was any one thing that happened, but at this point I feel a part of the Jewish community even though I don't live in the community. I feel a little more like I can take it for granted. This is who I am, and I don't have to prove it to anybody or explain it to anybody. I can do what I want. I am still, though eighteen years later, making my own traditions and kind of finding my own place inside of myself in Judaism, but much less with any thought about what anybody else is thinking or about what anybody else is doing.

For example, how I treat Friday nights. For a long time, I spent a lot of Friday nights with Becky and Louis. That was wonderful, but we don't do that so much anymore. I had to look at the reality of what Friday nights are in my life. Sometimes I'm home and sometimes I'm not. I have had to decide for myself how I was going to make *Shabbat* every week even though I am alone and not always a part of a community on Friday night. I light candles every Friday evening, but sometimes I do it at eleven o'clock at night.

Holidays are a bit more of a struggle. I spend them with my friends, and that is wonderful, but it means that I have not developed my own holidays at home. I tried to do that a couple of times but have been disappointed. Everyone else has a family and I haven't been able to develop a little community "family" of my own yet. So up to now, I've spent the holidays with Becky and Louis. I make each holiday my own by bringing something, spending the day helping with the preparations, whatever those may be. But I have to pay attention to my observance because it is easy for me to let some of these things slide by and then come to regret it later.

I tried keeping kosher for a while and was very enthusiastic about doing it, and I really got caught up in all the physical aspects. Then I found that it really didn't have a lot of meaning for me, and I decided that I wouldn't keep doing it. Still, I am very glad I tried.

It has been difficult to find my place in a congregation. I belonged for a long time to the large Reform congregation where I studied for my conversion. After a time I found that I really didn't enjoy that congregation, and I was only continuing there because of my Jewish family. Although I am not their children's age, Becky and Louis have been like my Jewish parents. I was very aware when I was ready to leave the Reform temple that it was very much like leaving my family congregation and finding one for myself. Even though it was a hard decision to make, I needed to be someplace where I could take more of an adult role. I actually left twice. The first time I went to a more Conservative synagogue, then came back to the temple for a while. None of the experiences have been negative in any way. All of the places that I have attended, I have enjoyed and had a good experience.

I joined one of the local *havurahs*. When I first joined, it was a very exciting group of people for me. It was very stimulating in every way. The people in it were excited about things. Everything was a controversy. There was a lot of diversity in backgrounds. There were Reform Jews and converts. There were Orthodox Jews. With all kinds of Jews, nothing was easy! There was a discussion about every single thing we did, and it was very exciting for me to be a part of it. We studied a lot and we tried every kind of religious experience we could think of, and we socialized. We just did everything and it was wonderful for me. Gradually, though, the group changed and my association with them dissolved.

I am now a member of a Reconstructionist congregation, and although it took a while for me to find my place there, I am now very comfortable. One of the women in the *havurah* told me about it—in fact, it is the first thing I've found that has the same kind of feeling to it as the *havurah*—an openness that I hadn't experienced anywhere else. It is a small community—about fifty families. I like the size a lot. It is small enough that I feel I can find a place there. It is very open and accepting. Nobody is there looking at anybody's clothes or looking at where anybody went to school or anything like that.

We do a lot of discussing and a lot of activities, and I enjoy the services there. I've been there only a relatively short while, but I would like to get more involved, and there really seem to be a lot of opportunities to do that. They have a very strong social action committee, and that interests me. There seems to be a lot to do just in the running of the congregation, so I am just waiting and watching and looking for opportunities for things I can do.

It has been true for me that the most challenging thing about becoming a Jew has been to continue to be a Jew—to actively do it, to not let it rest, to continue to grow in it. There have been times when I have been very tired, and I just don't want to try anymore. I don't want to push it. There are so many other things that I can do with my time. It just takes so much energy to continue to keep up that aspect of my life. It is hard to do it alone, and I get tired of doing it alone. That has been a big challenge. Nevertheless, it is a strong commitment and whether I like what I am doing with it at any particular moment, it is something that I feel very committed to keeping alive in my life. There are times that I am very aware that I could just shut it off. I could not go to services. I could ignore everything about the Jewish community and not light candles and it would be easy—but in another sense it wouldn't be easy for me to allow that to happen.

A big part of the situation, as I mentioned before, is that I am a single person. I see other young Jewish single people who have the same conflict, who were born Jewish and grew up in the community. They, at times, are very torn about what they are doing, how much they are doing, and they get pressure. I don't get a lot of pressure from anybody about what I am or am not doing. For me at first there was the novelty of all the experiences I was having. Now that the novelty has worn off, it is just a part of my life.

The thing I was not aware of, and that there is no way for anybody to understand until they have done it, is to understand what it is like being on the other side. That has always been very difficult for me—from being in the mainstream of society to suddenly become part of a minority. I sometimes ask myself, if I had it to do over again, would I choose to do that to myself again? Given the pros of what I have been through, I would say yes, but that sensation—of being an outsider and having *chosen* that—has been particularly difficult. At times, it has been extremely lonely not to be a part of the mainstream. I have felt as if I were looking through a door back to the past, wishing I might go back there to be a part of that again. I know I am not a part of that world, and there is no going back to that. For a long time after I converted, though not often now, it was extremely difficult to go through each Christmas and know that even though I had a family and I could go and have Christmas with family, it wasn't mine anymore. It took years and years for that to change and for it to get easier.

At the same time, I think Judaism is where I have always belonged and that I was just born into the wrong place. I do believe that. My coming to Judaism is bigger than just me intellectually saying this looks good and this is what I think I will do. This was reaffirmed for me recently when my younger brother went to Belgium where my father's family is from and discovered that my father's family was Jewish over there, and we never knew it. One brother stayed there and one brother came here. The brother who came here converted to Catholicism. When I found that out, I just looked in the mirror and said, "Ha! See, I was right all along!" I just always felt like this is so much where I belong, and I didn't have to make myself "become."

When I was growing up, I knew only my mother's family. I didn't know my father's family. They lived in the Midwest, and we were never in touch with them except through letters. After my father died, I went out to the Midwest and met his family, and I remember having the overwhelming feeling of "this is where I am really from, this part of the family." My mother's family, whom I knew better, I have never felt close to or part of. Somehow, this is really where I come from—these people. I had a lot in common with them even though I had never met them before.

I know that my conversion looks like a rejection to a lot of Christians, but I never thought of it as a rejection. It has been me finding out where I should be. A lot of Christian people asked me over the years if it was hard to stop believing in Jesus and start believing that he isn't God. It was never that kind of question for me. As far as my family goes, when I told my father's sister I had converted, she didn't even bat an eyelash and thought it was fine. My brothers don't know that much about my conversion.

The only negative responses to my conversion that I have received from anyone have actually come from the Christian community. Once when someone heard I had converted he said, "Oh, well, you are not a real Jew." I have been fortunate in the Jewish community that people have always been very welcoming. The only thing that has ever irritated me is that sometimes people make more of a deal of it than I would like them to. I was once on a committee of our temple to do outreach to converts. We even started a group. But I never really felt comfortable with that. What I wanted was to feel a part of the mainstream Jewish community. I didn't want to be singled out. I didn't want to be called a "Jew by Choice." I didn't want a label. I just wanted to be Jewish. I have always been fortunate to find people who looked after me and welcomed me. Maybe I looked needy! But I think I just met people who were so willing to share.

When I look back, I can picture myself in that Introduction to Judaism course, and I see myself now and look back over the past eighteen years. It is hard to explain to somebody what that experience has been. Sometimes it amazes me that I did it not knowing at all what it would be like. I certainly didn't know how hard it was going to be, but I also didn't know how rewarding it would become. I didn't know how much a part of my life it would become or how it was going to shape my life. I thought that it was just going to be a thing—one little thing—in my life, and it really is not. It really is my whole life in a lot of ways because it is a framework for everything that I am. It is a structure that I operate within everyplace.

31

Coming Full Circle

Ruth, Rachel, and Leah

It is hard to capture an effervescent personality on paper, someone who has an irreverence for what's not important, and deep reverence for what is. But for Ruth, and her family, coming full circle has been an adventure of life-altering mystery—and funny asides.

When Ruth and her husband married, the greatest gift they could give themselves and especially their children was freedom from religion. The religions practiced in their respective, Methodist and Orthodox Judaism, homes had not been life affirming. Twenty-three years after they had been married, a life-threatening event brought the family in contact with Judaism, but it was Rachel and Leah who led the way to the family's full embrace of a Jewish life.

I spoke with mother and daughters the day after all three had been to the *mikveh*. (I have incorporated parts of written answers to the questionnaire they were given in preparation for the *Bet Din*.)

It was cold, wet, and quick. We had to be out of the *mikveh* before sundown, and there was a family before us. Even though it was rushed I felt so much love, support, and fellowship from the rabbi and the *Bet Din*. I couldn't stop smiling. I would have liked to have splashed around for a while, all the time exclaiming, "This is it!"

It was not only all the studying I did—we all had to do. I read everything I could get my hands on, but I still would walk into the study at *shul* and go crazy at the thought there were even more books, and I didn't yet know what was in them. I know I drove my friends to distraction with all my questions. Only converts and rabbis study like this, they would say. And it is true that my daughters and I pursued this with the kind of zest and vigor for Judaism that most people born and raised Jewish have a hard time imagining anyone else feeling.

But most amazing about our family's return to Judaism is that it would have seemed completely improbable twenty-five years ago when my husband and I first met.

I came from a family that was very active in the Methodist Church, and I participated fully in all the church-sponsored activities for children. I was, of course, given no other choice. Although I enjoyed the camaraderie of the group, I never fully believed in any of the teachings—the Virgin Mary, the stories of Christmas and Easter—though I did love the music and the hymns. I questioned, prayed, believed—but only in one God, and I spoke to Him daily.

As a child, I recall being told not to play with a boy because he was Jewish. I didn't even know what a Jew was, but I understood that it was different, although I couldn't see what that difference might be. Then in the Sunday school, I was taught that Jesus was a Jew and that he was the son of God. One night I told my mother that I would like to be a Jew so that I could be just like Jesus. This, I thought, would please her, since she considered herself to be a very religious person. Instead, she was angry. "The Jews killed Jesus," she said. "You must never make such a statement again." That made no sense to me, but I certainly was not going to argue with her. In view of her feelings, it amazed me that my mother could be good friends with a Jewish lady, Mrs. Abromivitz.

Basically, though, my parents did not approve of anyone who was not white, Anglo-Saxon, and Protestant. My father even wrote my sister out of his will for marrying a Catholic—and wrote her back in when she got a divorce! It was hard to understand how these feelings of bigotry and hatred could be reconciled with their deep devotion to Christianity.

These contradictions began for me a period of questioning that led me to realize that my thoughts and beliefs were always putting me at odds with my family.

In college, I was attracted to my husband long before I ever knew he was Jewish. He never asked me what my religion was either. Jewish life growing up in a very Orthodox home with immigrant parents had not been happy for him. When we did participate in his family's Jewish life, *I* felt more comfortable than he.

Our differences did not matter at all to my husband and me, though we quickly learned it mattered a great deal to our parents. His entire family boycotted our wedding. We were both just twenty-one when we got married. Since we were not communicating particularly well with his side of the family, nobody told me that my choice of Friday night for our wedding was absolutely unheard of. Now I understand why. It would matter to me too, now. His family did not entirely disown us—they didn't sit *shivah*, for example, as another generation might have done.

Once we were married we practiced no formal religion. We had both been forced into our religions by our parents, and we were rebelling against that fact. We participated in the various religious ceremonies of our families, but we relished the freedom from conformity, the freedom to choose not to be anything.

When our children came along, we thought this was a real gift we were giving them. No one would ever force them to be anything; they were free to choose, as we had never been. We discovered, though, our gift of freedom gave them the feeling they didn't belong anywhere. It is remarkable to me, therefore, that even as very small children they were naturally inclined toward their Jewish heritage. They did not like *treif* food, for example. They seemed to gravitate toward Jewish friends, as I had myself when growing up. And eventually, it was my daughters' interest in conversion that caught me up and brought me to a place I knew I belonged.

Our move to Sacramento from Los Angeles several years ago made possible many of the new directions our lives were to take. My husband made the decision to move here for all the reasons anyone wants to move out of L.A., but I hated the idea. I

loved L.A. and everything about my life there. Moving to Sacramento felt like being
sentenced to purgatory—a punishment for being bad, somehow. Now I realize that,
had we not come here, we never would have returned to Judaism, because life in
L.A.'s fast lane just didn't allow time for religion.

After we moved to Sacramento, my husband suffered a detached retina and had
to have surgery. Somehow when they were giving him the anesthesia, his breathing
stopped and he died on the operating table. Code red. Thank God they were doing
the procedure in the hospital, because they had to "jump start" him. But during that
time he had what could be described as an out-of-body experience. He heard chanting that he recognized as the High Holiday services. This event occurred in August,
and he made the decision to attend High Holiday services that fall for the first time
in nearly twenty-five years. And that started the whole thing off.

The family of my daughter's best friend offered my husband an extra ticket they
had for a seat at their congregation, Mosaic Law. Rabbi Moses spoke at one of those
services about welcoming the community and doing "spiritual outreach" to the children and grandchildren of mixed marriages. My husband came home very excited,
saying this is the place where we might even be welcome—when you come from a
mixed marriage, and both families are fighting that marriage, there's nothing in your
background that makes you feel that you would be welcome in either religion.

The girls began to attend Hebrew high school, and they wanted to make an appointment with Rabbi Moses to tell him that they were Jewish and wanted to be recognized as Jews. He told them, "No, you are not because your mother is not." When
we did go in to talk to him about conversion, I figured we were going to be thrown
out because we were all coming at it from such different points of view. I had been
in a marriage for twenty-three years in which religion wasn't a problem, and I didn't
want it to be a problem now. I wasn't going to convert, but I would help my daughters if that was what they wanted to do. My husband was saying that he was born and
raised Jewish and wanted to find his religion again. The girls were saying that they
were Jewish no matter what anyone said, and they just wanted to get their "pass-
ports" in order.

All of our friends said that we would all have to convert or no one could convert,
"that's just how this rabbi is." Instead, he made us members of the *shul*—limited
members, though—because he wanted us all to be able to participate and feel a part
of the process even if I did not convert.

One of the things the rabbi said *would* be a requirement, regardless of my status,
was that we keep a kosher home. My husband simply refused. To me it wasn't such
a big deal, but he just kept arguing with the rabbi. Finally, I said, "I am not the problem here. You two go at it," and I walked out of the meeting. Some of the things that
were coming up for my husband was that growing up Jewish to him was not a joyful
thing. It was "suffer, suffer, suffer, fast, suffer." That's how his family "celebrated"
Judaism. He remembers his mother ripping plates off the table and burying forks all
over the backyard—very much old-country Orthodox.

I said, "Look, if the girls want this and you are going to support them, we have to keep kosher. Either that or you're going to have to explain to them why they can't be Jewish." He couldn't do that. "You do what you want to do," he said—"You will anyway." He's right! Finally, we just quit asking him. We just made announcements. "Now we're kosher." "This week we're having *Shabbat* dinner." By then I had really gotten involved, and it was fascinating to me.

There were two other turning points for me; both sort of gave me permission to come to my decision to convert, but in very different ways.

We were invited to attend a birthday party of the daughter of very good friends of ours who live in Las Vegas. The Jewish community is very small and in Las Vegas everyone seems to know everyone else or is related to someone's aunt. It turned out there was a Lubavitch rabbi there who was a very good friend of friends of ours in Sacramento. They asked us to stop by to see him while we were in Las Vegas. Our Sacramento friends had met the rabbi when he was doing his "missionary" time (only looking for Jews to bring back to Judaism, of course) in Anchorage, Alaska, traveling around with a backpack and a bag of salami. Now he had his own *shul* in Las Vegas. They hadn't seen him in ten years and wanted us to take presents to his four children.

We met him at the Chabad House. As we introduced ourselves, I tried to shake hands with him. Big mistake. He jumped back. We were all scared and nervous and felt like we must not be welcome, but he invited us to come in and sit down. I don't know how he did it, but in three questions he very tactfully and quickly got to the heart of our life. He asked if the girls had had *bat mitzvahs*. They both said, "No" (because at the time they were still in the process of conversion). "And whose fault is that?" he asked. We all looked at my husband. His fault! From that point on we all relaxed, and he just talked to us for an hour and a half about so many things: mysticism, numerology—in fact, he gave Leah her Hebrew name.

One question had really been burning inside me that I had never been able to get answered to my satisfaction: how could you convert to be part of a "peoplehood"? I still had no plans for conversion, and that question was one of the reasons. My daughters after all had a sort of genetic way in; it seemed natural and normal for them to become Jewish, but how would I fit in?

The *rebbe* told me that upon your conversion, when you are in the *mikveh*, you receive your second, Jewish, soul. He believed that it is possible for a Jewish soul to be reborn and trapped in a body that ends up in a Christian family rather than a Jewish family. And that soul will end up searching for where it needs to be to feel at home. Once I heard that, it was as if somebody switched on the light for me. My whole life I had disagreed with everything my family believed in. The more I questioned their beliefs and values, the more at odds I would become with them. But where would that leave me then? Now I knew I could become a part of the *spiritual* peoplehood of Judaism.

As we were having this discussion with the *rebbe*, from out of nowhere came a desert storm. Thunder was rolling and crashing and lightning was flashing—as if the weather echoed the spiritual experience we were having talking to him!

In so much of what we were all going through there were glimmers of the mysticism that the Lubavitchers describe. I'd watch the girls light the candles, then soon I was doing it with them. When we celebrated *Shabbat* as a family there was a wonderful, warm feeling that we never felt in any other religious ceremony we'd ever been a part of. I loved to watch the candles burn, and I had read somewhere in one of the many books I had devoured that you get an extra soul on *Shabbat*. When the candles go out and the smoke rises up, the souls are returning to heaven. They can do that only if you really spiritually celebrated *Shabbat*.

The other experience that has really been a revelation to me has been watching the metamorphosis of my daughters—like bringing buds to bloom. It has been wonderful to see their zeal and commitment to this religion that at first didn't recognize them as Jews. They stood right up for themselves and told the rabbi it wasn't their fault that only matrilineal relationship counted in Judaism. Before I'd decided what to do for myself, I was reading everything they were reading, just so I'd know what was going on with them—it was all conversion, conversion, conversion! One day Rachel, my youngest, came to me after attending a USY (United Synagogue Youth) convention and said, "If you had experienced what I just experienced, you wouldn't hesitate. You would know that it was right."

I gave birth to them and they gave birth to me. They brought me to Judaism. My husband had married outside of his religion and his children brought all of us back. They connected the missing link. We have come full circle.

Rachel's Story (Age 15)

Even though our family didn't have any real religion, I have always considered myself Jewish. But when we joined the synagogue a couple of years ago, I discovered that I wasn't Jewish, and I wanted to change that.

My sister and I have been taking part in synagogue youth activities for a few years now, and everyone was so nice and welcoming to us. Hebrew school just felt more true to me than the Methodist Sunday school we had attended for a while when we were younger. The basic difference was that in Hebrew school you didn't have to have a set belief, and the teachers didn't say, "You have to believe." Instead, they said, "This is what we believe." It wasn't so pushy.

Our family did things in a very gradual way, so it didn't really feel like a big change. We've been keeping kosher now for several months, and it is something I plan to continue as I grow up. We have *Shabbat* dinners, and besides the rituals, it is a time for us all to sit down together, which we don't get to do very often. It's very nice, and hard to explain, too. We go to *Shabbat* services several times a month, and of course we are now observing all the holidays. This year we had a *sukkah* and a USY party here.

I go to public school, and I have always had a lot of Jewish friends, and a lot of Christian friends too. I liked the sense of family and pride that Jewish teenagers had in their religion. The majority of my Christian friends don't really share the same sense of pride for their religion. When my non-Jewish friends come over, they are interested and respectful of the way our kitchen is now. I answer their questions, and that's kind of fun.

The *mikveh* and *Bet Din* weren't what I expected. The rabbis and cantor all knew me, and what I was going to say. I guess I was hoping for something more meaningful and challenging. We were a little rushed, too, because there was another family ahead of us.

I'm in a confirmation class that will end this year. Next year in USY, I want to run for office in our local chapter. We're part of the New Frontier region, which includes northern California and Nevada. There's an international convention during winter break in Los Angeles, and all the regions of the world get together. I am definitely looking forward to that! And I may also get a chance to go on an Israel pilgrimage for six weeks next summer.

I think our family has had the best of everything. We celebrated Christmas, and we gave it up, and it was no big deal. It is so blown out of proportion and has so little meaning. Hanukkah has actual meaning. We weren't born into something, we got to choose it, and maybe, because of that, we feel more of a commitment.

Leah's Story (Age 17)

Although my father is a Jew, I did not discover Judaism until I was nine years old, when I met my cousins for the first time at a Hanukkah celebration. I had never been exposed to Hanukkah before, and my cousins explained the details to me along with a little information about their religion. Needless to say, I was curious.

The first synagogue service I attended was for the *bat mitzvah* of my oldest cousin, Dorie. Although it was held in a Reform synagogue, Hebrew prayers were used often throughout the service. I remember being awed by Dorie's ability to speak Hebrew. I tried to follow along with the transliterations in the prayer book. My cousin Darrin's *bar mitzvah* was the next chance I had to attend another service.

By that time, I was in high school, and when my friends—the majority of whom were Jewish—heard that I was attending a cousin's *bar mitzvah*, they insisted I start coming with them to Hebrew High and USY events. Not only did I have fun participating in these activities, I learned a lot also. It was through Hebrew High lectures that I learned that in the Conservative movement, a child is not considered Jewish unless she or he is born to a Jewish mother. Armed with this knowledge, I made the decision to seek conversion.

Beliefs and values are very personal, and I liked that in Judaism you are not questioned too closely on just what those are. In Judaism you can even doubt God's existence and still be a good Jew! Judaism stresses action far more than faith. Like many other teenagers, I have not come to any definite conclusions about what "faith" will look like for me, and I appreciate the freedom to learn, grow, and experience at my own pace. Having said that, I also like how valued tradition is in Judaism. Observance is intrinsically important to the religion, yet each person in the congregation is free to practice Judaism at any level that is comfortable for him or her. I entered the religion rather recently, knowing very little, but I have noticed that the level of my observance increases as my knowledge and awareness slowly increases.

We began keeping kosher several months ago. After our kitchen was *kashered*, there was an initial period of adjustment. Now, it is an accepted part of our daily lives. It really wasn't that difficult, and I've enjoyed it a lot so far. We observe *Shabbat* as a family with the traditional rituals of lighting candles, *hallah*, and reciting blessings and attending synagogue on Saturday and sometimes on Friday nights. In the future I would like to increase my *Shabbat* observance to extend to not writing, driving, or cooking on *Shabbat*.

One of the concepts that I find very meaningful is *tzedakah*, which literally means "righteousness" but translates into "charity." One is expected to give *tzedakah* cheerfully and sympathetically. In USY we have Social Action/*Tikkun Olam* fund-raisers, and everyone is expected to make a contribution.

In college, I look forward to studying Hebrew as a language and taking courses in Jewish studies. I've heard a lot about Hillel from my friends. It seems like that program really does help them to stay involved in Judaism once they've left home.

I didn't feel truly connected with Jews, as a people, until I began to learn to read Hebrew. The knowledge and use of Hebrew, and the services, traditions, and holidays of Judaism bind Jews together all over the world. As I become more skilled at reciting the prayers in Hebrew, I feel that my identification with the Jewish people gets stronger, and I have come to truly feel Jewish.

32

Judaism Is for Survivors

Ellen

We are commanded as Jews to choose life. The teachings of Judaism make it very clear that God intends that we live so that we may redeem ourselves and repair the world. When Ellen discovered her own strengths and determination, she was able to leave a troubled marriage and pursue her lifelong dream of becoming an architect. This period of self-renewal was also a time in which Ellen became open to the life-affirming values of Judaism that coincided so well with her personal ideals.

"I view my journey as a miracle. Through God's love enough miracles happened that I am where I am today."

Now in a strong and loving marriage, Ellen is carefully nurturing her family's commitment to a thoughtful increase in Jewish observance. With her involvement in leadership development through the Associated Jewish Community Federation, Ellen has found her niche in what she sees as the Jewish community's very effective efforts in *tikkun olam*—repair of the world.

My mother's initial reaction to my conversion was that she had failed to turn me into a good Christian. Even as a child, I was particularly interested in religion, the Bible, and God but didn't feel an affinity for Christ. I didn't understand who this person was that we were supposed to feel so close to, so I just ignored that part. I felt increasingly uncomfortable with my parents' very wealthy Presbyterian church in Grosse Pointe. It was a wonderful church with a beautiful facility and incredible music, but I didn't feel like it was "mine," and I refused to become confirmed.

I was always interested in God, and I was able to discuss religious issues with my mother from a very early age. She's a very open person herself and agreed that there were certain concepts that were difficult to accept, for example that those people who follow Christ go to heaven and the rest don't. It just didn't feel right to me. With certain things you have a sense of perceived truth; when you hear them you know if they are right or they don't feel right. Even in grade school, I knew this idea wasn't right.

I felt very strongly identified with the notion of God and prayer and living the right kind of life, but not so strongly with the idea of Christ as a personal savior. When I was in junior high I became very interested in a variety of religious expressions. I was a precocious reader and come from a family with a number of intellectuals—people to talk with about these things. Questioning was encouraged. That is important, I think. In Christianity, generally, you aren't supposed to question. Presbyterians are probably close to Reform in Judaism. In fact, my parents and my husband's parents, who are Reform, got along fine when they got together, probably because their worldview is, "This is the right way, but other people have their good things too." They had an openness to difference.

In my teenage years I became involved in yoga through an organization called Self-Realization Fellowship. A cousin with whom I am close is an artist and introduced me to the group. They conducted Sunday services at the Art Institute in Detroit, and I went with him. He is still involved in the group.

Self-Realization Fellowship was founded in the 1920s by an Indian yogi who came to this country. Its central premise is that Christianity and yoga are part of the same overall religion with the same God, and the ancient yogis were saying the same thing that Christ was saying. It is basically an attempt to blend the two religions. There was more of an emphasis on intellectual thought and discussion rather than on behavior, so it wasn't a cult at all. It bills itself as a science or a philosophy. I felt comfortable with those kinds of messages. My mother still felt in her heart that I hadn't stopped being a Christian.

That is where I met most of the Jews that I knew as a younger person. I grew up in a WASPy part of Detroit where there were no Jews who told you they were Jewish. There were no synagogues. The Jews I met in the yoga group weren't particularly Jewish or expounding the values of Judaism. I think most of them came from Reform homes. They were looking for spirituality, and I was looking for a system of thought to express the spirituality I already felt. The meditation and prayer fit and made sense to me. The yoga was good. I made a lot of friends in the group.

Although I didn't feel connected to Christ, I struggled with leaving Christianity, which had drummed into my head that salvation was found only in belief in Christ. The alternative was to be damned to eternal hell. So, "Okay, I believe!" It was a struggle unleashing that psychological hold. Even if you don't consider yourself a Christian, it is like you have been brainwashed, and it is hard to break out of that head lock. I remember praying to God, "If I am on the wrong track, if this is terrible, please, somehow, let me know. I can't see it all, but this seems right to me." I prayed like that for a long time. After a few years, I was convinced that it wasn't wrong; I was comfortable not being a Christian.

It was helpful that my family is not fundamentalist in personality or belief. They are a little eccentric, actually, in their intellectualism and philosophy, and in their personalities. They value education and thought. People like that are more questioning and more open. My mother assumed yoga was a phase, and she saw I wasn't getting crazy. Mostly, I was practicing the Hatha Yoga physical discipline and meditating, and I was a vegetarian, which was healthy for me because I am allergic to meat. There were positive benefits, and my mother saw that I was fine and she didn't worry.

My parents came from very well-to-do families, and in my mother's family, especially, there had been outstanding, wonderful people for generations back. There was a lot of wealth; there was a lot of education; there was a lot of prestige. I was told revered stories of family members who had stood up against slavery or had been missionaries in China. They put their lives on the line for their beliefs. In the face of this heritage, my parents felt that they weren't living up to their families' expectations. For complex reasons, my parents at times have been so preoccuppied with issues in their own lives that it limited their ability to focus on my and my sister's needs while we were growing up.

I should say that both of my parents have improved with age. They are happier now than they ever have been. We enjoy it when they come to visit us. Things have improved, and we have a pretty good relationship. The story has a very happy ending. But it was very difficult growing up. I had many emotional problems and lack of self-esteem. Some of that quite honestly may have affected my discomfort at church. I was always trying to work on myself, fix myself, improve myself, and that may have been a reason I was looking beyond the church and got involved in yoga.

Despite the distractions of the difficulties in my family, from the time I was in fifth grade I had had a career focus: I had wanted to be an architect. My parents took me to various architects to discuss my interest. They were very discouraging. I was told, "You can't be an architect; you're a woman." When it came time for me to go to college, I lived at home and saved money. At the local university, I studied everything, wondering what I could do, but I always came back to architecture. I started architecture school in Michigan at a small engineering school. I was frustrated because I had been attending Wayne State University, which had the libraries and the wonderful environment of a big university. In this small college there were about four women in a school full of engineering men, not an ideal situation. So, although I struggled with my lack of self-esteem and lack of money, at the same time I was growing more sure and focused about how to realize my college goals.

The next period of my life is difficult to describe because it was a particularly troubling time for me, though it was also the beginning of the personal growth that has led me to where I am today.

I was getting tired of Michigan and was ready to spread my wings and leave home. I had become involved in a relationship with my yoga teacher, and we were married. He was older than I, had been married before, and was supposedly in recovery from alcoholism.

This man and I decided that we would go to Arizona because the University of Arizona at Tucson had a wonderful architecture program. Also, he wanted to get a Ph.D. in addiction studies and there was a program for that at Arizona as well. I quit school entirely and just focused on working to save money to go there. We moved out to Arizona, and I worked there for a year to save money and become a resident so I could have in-state tuition. This endeavor was totally on my own shoulders.

We were very excited about living in the Southwest, but within weeks of moving, he began to drink again. I then realized he had been drinking on and off for a long time but had concealed it. Looking back now, I am amazed how little I knew about him and that I excused and ignored his behavior. Over the next three years we went through a terrible period. This wonderful person who was so bright and so knowledgeable and so caring and so in love with God also had a substance-abuse problem. When he became violent I said, "That is it; I am not sticking around for this." Going through that was the most painful, shattering experience of my entire life.

At the same time that everything was falling apart, I was picking myself up and going on. Through it all, I gained a lot of personal strength. I had been in counseling for about a year with a wonderful woman who was very helpful in putting my self-esteem back together. I had grown to understand the ways in which my background and my own personality influenced some of the choices I had made. I learned to heal myself and get on with my life.

When I moved out of that marriage, I was finally in architecture school, and I was on my own, but it was not easy. I had enough money to get through the month, and I had a job. I was—of all things—a cocktail waitress at a country-western bar. After all I had been through with someone else's substance abuse, here I was working around all this alcohol. But the money was good, and I certainly knew how to deal with drunks. I worked odd jobs, and even sold my plasma down at the university plasma center with all the homeless people. It was a very uphill climb. Looking back on the mosaic of all of this, just desperately trying to get enough money together, it was a very weird period. I earned more than an architecture degree; I earned a degree from the school of hard knocks.

But, I was doing it! I felt that the slate had been wiped clean inside. I left it all behind. Because this man had used all of the wonderful ideas from the yoga discipline to excuse his behavior, I simply could not buy it any more. "It may be fine for other people, but it's not for me. I have to look for something else for me. I know that I need my own philosophical framework." I also had made a decision to disconnect myself from AA and Al-Anon, really everything that related to my former life. I was completely on my own and wasn't part of anything anymore; what was I going to do? I didn't worry about it. I certainly was not going to get involved with anybody. I would just stay focused on getting through school, getting to work, and keeping a roof over my head. I loved architecture school, and I loved Tucson, and by this time I had many very good supportive friends who were wonderful. It was a scary period and yet a wonderful, exhilarating period. I felt that I was really on my way.

Through a group of friends in my apartment building, I met Rich. His roommate, Marty, was my sister's friend from Colorado. Sometimes during my divorce my sister would come down to help me, and she would discuss it with Marty. So Rich knew what I had been through, though a lot of time elapsed before we actually met. As far as I was concerned, Rich was just a friend and a nice guy to date. He was also three and a half years younger than me. After what I had been through, I wasn't going to let anything distract me from pursuing my goal of becoming an architect. I later found out that Rich wasn't thinking of me very seriously, either, in part because I wasn't Jewish.

Although Rich was Jewish, he didn't know much about it. When I'd ask him questions, he'd say, "I don't know." He had been raised in Reform and had been *bar mitzvah*, but his family was more involved in community activities than in synagogue attendance. Even so, when the High Holidays came around at an early point in our relationship, Rich searched out a synagogue because, he said, he "needed to go." I said, "Can I go? I really want to. Please, let's go." I liked it more than he did!

But I said to myself, "I don't want to be interested in this guy because he's Jewish. I want to find out about Judaism myself, and if he's a great guy and our relationship develops, fine." I didn't fall in love with a Jew and say, "Oh, I have to be Jewish, too." That wasn't the issue. I didn't trust myself to make an intelligent decision about getting involved again in a relationship or a religion. But I was so fascinated by it.

Tucson is not a hotbed of Jewish life, so in the absence of a community to become immersed in, I approached Judaism much more from an intellectual and philosophical standpoint. I went to the library and got out the encyclopedia and started reading about Judaism, and I just felt like "this is me!"

Then, I started a class at the Reform synagogue and took my time about it. I loved the class with the rabbi. There was a lot of reading. There were discussions with the eight other students. I loved going to synagogue. I loved the services. I loved the Hebrew. I didn't know what it meant, but the sound of it was wonderful. I loved the rituals. The more I experienced them, the more the magic in them was self-evident. It's amazing to realize that these rituals have been practiced for thousands of years. Through these experiences, I came to the decision on my own that I wanted to be Jewish.

I had always been impressed by the Jewish people I had known, though most were not very involved in the religion. There's a certain quality about Jews; it's almost as if Jews are more alive somehow, more intense; they are cranked up a couple of notches. If they are going to work, they work harder; if they want to pursue something, they really pursue it. There's a sense of duty. If something is wrong with the world, we really do need to fix it. Not everyone who is Jewish is this way, but I have noticed that in many Jews there is a richer experience of life. I was very much attracted by that, because I've always been an intense person.

The emphasis in Judaism on morality and righteous living was appealing and resonated with those aspects of Christianity I had always valued. I was also impressed with the sense of community and the imperative to care for one another—not just Jews, but others as well. I believed those things all my life but felt that I had been in a vacuum. I didn't know other people were really following an organized path to give expression to these values. When I discovered Judaism, there was a sense of recognition.

I remember being so concerned while growing up that there were so many problems in the world and so much pain. Here was a religion that not only said, "Yes, you can repair the world," but also, "You are *supposed* to repair the world!" This is what I had always believed. Then I found out what the Jewish organizations do for old people, for young people, for people without jobs, for people who need help. They are *doing* it. There's a crisis in Bosnia; they don't just stand around wringing their hands saying, "What should we do?" They fly in and bring medicine, and not only do they distribute it to Jews, they give it to the other people too. Ethiopian Jews are being slaughtered; they go in and they get them out. They act together as a group. The concept of *tzedakah* for many Jews is not a choice; it is "I have to give." You don't find that with other religions. Yes, some tithe and give, but only the very religious. Even Jews who aren't religious feel the *mitzvah* of giving.

I was attracted to the Jewish view of the world and of God as expressed by Leo Baeck, a scholar and Holocaust survivor, in his book *The Essence of Judaism*. There is one God, and we are connected to Him; there is no mediator or middleman. There is instead a sacred relationship, a covenant, with us and with God and with the people. Instead of it being "God and Jesus Christ and Holy Ghost," it is "God, me, the people, the world around me." It pulled together all the heretofore disparate parts of my life.

I feel that the relationship I have with God is something I was born with and have had all my life, and it has never changed, regardless of the way I worship. Being a Jew, however, *has* significantly changed my view of what God wants me to do.

As a small child, I had a notion that everyone started out with a pure white soul and every time you did something wrong it would get a little black mark on it and it would get darker and darker. It was like keeping score. Now, I don't see it that way at all. God created me and there is love there, and it is two-way. But it is not enough just to love God; you have to act; you need to be the best person you can be and reach out and do that work for God in the world. Be aware, learn, care. It is very hard to do that, sometimes. I think being Jewish is about being *and* doing.

After I made my decision to convert, Rich and I realized that we wanted to stay together. By the time we got married in 1986, we had known each other for four years. Ours has been a wonderful relationship, and I believe that the health and happiness of our marriage gives ample demonstration of the resiliancy of the human spirit.

The spring before we got married was the first time I took part in any religious activity with Rich's family. They didn't have a typical *Shabbat* dinner, though they did make sure to have a Passover *seder* each year. Rich and I were married in the family synagogue in New Jersey, after which we moved to northern Virginia.

We didn't know any Jews when we started working in Virginia. I told Rich, "We need to be part of a synagogue, let's go around to different synagogues and get involved." We started synagogue shopping and went to Friday night services at Reform temples. When we found out how expensive it was to join, we wavered. Rich felt we would not be in the area long since he was not interested in continuing to work for the federal government. Also at that time, due to some health considerations, physicians were telling us that we needed to get pregnant soon or risk never being able to do so. I told Rich that if we were going to have a child, we needed to belong to a synagogue, and I put my foot down. We joined a Reform synagogue and got involved in a *havurah* there.

The northern Virginia Jewish community is very fragmented compared to Baltimore. Most people living there don't have family in the area, so the *havurah* was a way to get people connected. We got involved in what started out as a young married couples' *havurah*, and it quickly turned into young married couples with children because everyone was having babies. It was fun for us because we met some interesting people who were becoming parents around the same time we were. One thing that we noticed was that most of these Reform Jews were married to people who were not Jewish; most of them didn't know very much about Judaism; most of them did things in ways that even I knew were wrong; they were Jewish mostly in identity only. I felt like something was missing, and in the end it wasn't very satisfying.

When we moved to Baltimore, I said, "You know, Rich, we met all these Reform Jews in northern Virginia who weren't very Jewish, and of all your friends from high school and college, there's only one who married another Jew and had a Jewish ceremony. They don't seem to know anything about Judaism, and although they might like being Jewish, they are not growing. Let's look around. Maybe being Conservative might be better for us." He agreed. So when Rebecca was old enough, we put her in preschool at Chizuk Amuno, a Conservative synagogue. We started getting involved there, and I loved it.

My original conversion had been Reform and had not involved the *mikveh*. So, when we decided to join the synagogue, I told Rich, "Maybe I'll have to go to the *mikveh*," and Rich said, "Well, I am not getting married again!" He was hot about that. I knew I wanted to take Rebecca to the *mikveh* in case she ever marries into a family that says, "We don't approve of your mother's conversion." If she has had a *mikveh* and she has been brought up the right way, then maybe that will help her. We went to talk to the rabbi at Chizuk Amuno.

The rabbi was lovely and immediately agreed to do it. He set up a *Bet Din* with the other rabbi from Chizuk Amuno and a rabbi from Beth El. He had told me that I needed to have the three things that were required for a conversion: the turning (to Judaism); the learning; and the ritual (of the *mikveh*). To him the only thing that was missing was the ritual and if we took care of that, everything would be fine. The rabbi rattled off the things I'd need to do and I said, "Wait a minute, write it down!" I had to learn the *Sheheheyanu*,* which I didn't know. "What is this prayer?" I said. "Oh," he said, "you don't know this?"

The *mikveh* was a wonderful experience, though the outer, physical reality of it is never the same as the internal, spiritual one. It was a hot day when we went to the *mikveh* with our two children. I had to take my contacts out before the immersion, and when I got out of the water, there was no time to put myself back together in the dressing room because there was another family waiting. I couldn't see; my hair was wet; my face was red, and there I was talking to these rabbis! It was comic, it really was. I'd like to go back for myself, privately, without an audience and without it being

---

*This blessing is a benediction of thanksgiving for God having brought us to this joyous point in time. It is said on many occasions: on the first day of a festival, at rites of passage, at recurrent events such as tasting a fruit for the first time in the season, and putting on a new article of clothing. In short, it may be used to mark any happy event in which we are moved to celebrate God's goodness and blessing.

a ceremony. I found it a very intriguing thing. A friend of mine who is Conservative and goes to the *mikveh* every month says that it is a wonderful thing for her, and she loves it. Other people I've talked with hate it, but they go because they feel they have to.

Rich's parents were very happy that I had converted, and I think that they would have been very unhappy if Rich had married someone who wasn't Jewish. I did not realize this in the early part of our relationship, which was good because I felt there was never any pressure on me about it. After we joined the synagogue in northern Virginia, Rich's dad said how glad he was that we had done that because it was so important, and Rich wondered, "Where did this come from?" He was surprised how much they cared. When we joined Chizuk Amuno and I went to the *mikveh*, my in-laws were so thrilled. I received a package one day, a gift of two gorgeous silver candlesticks. The card said, "We are so pleased with what you have been doing, and we wanted you to have these." They have been more and more excited with what we are doing. But then I was up in New Jersey and my mother-in-law was lighting the candles, and my daughter corrected her and said, "No, Nanna, do it this way." Now we are in this stage where we are becoming more observant than some others in the family—the flip side.

When I became involved in Judaism, all my mother could see was that I was dating a Jewish man and *that* must be the reason. But that was not so. After I converted to Judaism, my mother went to the minister because she was concerned that even if there is an afterlife for Jews, maybe it is not in the same place as for the Christians. These sorts of technical things can really throw you for a loop.

Since she is a student of the Old Testament, my mother eventually came to the realization that I had, actually, come back closer to her view of the world. Now she has been learning more about Judaism. When my children have grandparents' day at Chizuk Amuno Preschool, my parents go. They love it. They are very supportive, and they love my in-laws. They enjoyed our wedding. They loved coming to synagogue with us the night before. At the same time, I didn't call and invite them to my son's *bris*—mostly because they live in Michigan, but also because I felt that would be too much for them to deal with. They understand the idea of Passover and the notions of the various holidays. My husband would be uncomfortable with going home at Christmas, so we don't do that. As far as the practice of Judaism goes, we have kept our families quite separate. And I think the distance helps.

When we moved to Baltimore, my mother-in-law introduced us to a friend she's met through the Council of Jewish Federations and United Jewish Appeal. Carol was a real-estate agent, and she not only helped us find a house, she adopted us. She is a member of a modern Orthodox congregation, and she had these big family dinners Friday nights to which we were invited. They became our family here in Baltimore, and I laugh and say, "Rich, she is your Jewish mother-in-law." Most couples can say, "My family did it this way, and his family did it that way." We, of course, only have "his family did it," because mine didn't. So I do things for Friday night the way Carol does them; I have taken on some of her little traditions. With continued study and my exposure to modern Orthodoxy and Conservative Judaism, I began to understand the differing attitudes about halakhic requirements. It was this learning that had led me to feel that I needed to have the *mikveh*, though I realize that Orthodox does not acknowledge a Conservative conversion.

At this point in my life, I feel I have completed my conversion. Nevertheless, I realize that Judaism evolves, and I may not feel that way in ten years. For now, though, I feel very Jewish. I am very comfortable with Conservative Judaism. I like its emphasis on ritual and learning, while at the same time, it is open to discussion. To me it is really an ideal blend of tradition and modernity. Reform has done away with too much, and I don't think the emphasis on just Hebrew school is adequate. Our daughter, Rebecca, is attending day school, and although it is a big financial sacrifice for the family, it is important for her to get the background that I feel I cannot give her.

I definitely have pulled Rich along with me in my exploration of Judaism. He has come along because I have been so interested and passionate about it. Once he went to a *shivah* house to help form a *minyan* and he came back and said, "I felt like such a goy! I didn't know what to say; I didn't know what to do." Everyone was putting on all these ritual paraphernalia, and he'd never done it in his life. Even for my son's *bris*, my father-in-law had to dig up a *tallit* from somewhere. It is interesting to see the family struggle to get back into the rituals. Rich is brushing up on his Hebrew, which he can read, though he doesn't always know what it means. My daughter comes home from school with all these Hebrew words, and we say, "Oh, that's right!" and, aside to each other, "Is it?" But Rich cares about Judaism deeply, and I think that he is enjoying the process more than he is letting on.

The practice of Judaism has to blend with your family, otherwise it could cause real problems. I would like to keep kosher at home, but I don't know if it is worth it to alienate my husband in order to do so. I would want us to come to that decision as a married couple so we both feel comfortable about it. Even though he is less observant by nature than I am, he is stricter about the rules. If you are going to follow the rule, you've really got to follow it. His attitude is that if you are going to be kosher, you have to be kosher in and out of the home, and he is not ready to do that. I can see his point. On the other hand I think it is good to at least observe it in the home. The home is sacred and you are at least making that effort.

We add to our observance all the time. We light candles on *Shabbat*, we have *hallah* and wine. The children are very excited about it and love it. My two-year-old son runs for his *kippah*, which has Sesame Street characters on it. Over time as we add a little bit more, we will evolve. We have not run out of things to do to make ourselves increasingly observant! There are plenty of other areas besides *kashrut*.

I was able to take advantage of an opportunity for myself to learn more and get involved in the community. Associated Jewish Charities offers a two-year program called the Young Women's Leadership Council. The Associated is the umbrella organization that collects funds and plans and oversees the seventeen local organizations like the Jewish Community Center and Jewish Vocational Service. It also sends money to national causes like United Jewish Appeal, to international organizations, and to Israel. The program I joined is a part of AJC devoted to education. For two years a group of women meets once a month to hear speakers, such as a rabbi from CLAL (Center for Learning and Leadership), Shoshanah Cardin, a leader of the national Jewish community and now president of CLAL, and other very interesting people. Agency "spotlights" are presented, or perhaps a *devar Torah*. There are community service announcements, and then a little time to *shmooze* (chat), have coffee and a bagel, and meet with people in the community. It is open to the whole Jewish community, and there are some very observant as well as very nonobservant women who attend. I thought it was a great way to learn about the community and find opportunities for involvement.

The second year, I was asked to be cochair of the campaign, and this year they asked me to be chairperson. I think that it is a big vote of confidence from the community that a convert would be asked to be in a very highly visible position. Not only do I chair that group, I am responsible to all the forty-plus members within our group, nurturing them, encouraging them, and overseeing all the different subcommittees. There is a lot of work that goes into doing it. If I bring up "Oh, but I am a convert," they say, "Even better." It is my commitment to Judaism, not just the fact that I am a convert, that makes an impression on people.

Though my experience with the Associated has been wonderful, acceptance in the broader community presents challenges. Because I am blond and green-eyed, if I walk into a store in Pikesville, salespeople will often ignore me or not be very friendly. Then I'll make a comment like "I'm shopping for shoes for Passover for my daughter to go to the *seder*" or "I've got to run to pick up my daughter at Chizuk Amuno," and suddenly they are all over me, they are so friendly. And I think to myself, "Before they knew I was Jewish they didn't want to bother with me." It burns me; it gets me very upset.

There are times when I am waiting for my daughter outside the JCC, and all the women are talking and they are clearly not bothering with me. Either they think I'm somebody's *shikseh* wife or they all grew up together in Baltimore, and one way or another, I'm seen as an outsider. It is a little bit of a closed community that way. If you are just waiting for them to come to you, it is not going to happen because everybody here has years and years of relationships and everybody knows everybody else. I had to find a way around that, and I discovered that it is not a closed community if you come in from the top. If you say, "I love it here, and I want to get involved," it is a very welcoming community.

The fact is that unless you are actively involved in the community, you won't feel a part of it. I learned just recently that everybody feels a little like an outsider; it's not just the converts. You have to take an active role. Since then, I've felt very much a part of the community and very welcome.

It helps that it is my nature to get involved. I am a very warm person, I care about other people, I am able to communicate, I get excited about things and am very enthusiastic; I am an optimist. I feel that it is important to take action. Those attributes are all in my favor. I have a burning thing inside me about Judaism and that definitely makes it easier.

I do want the community to know that a Jew by Choice realizes how wonderful Judaism is; that is the one thing that is lost on many people who were born Jewish. People constantly say to me, "I grew up with this, and I take it for granted. You don't, and that's great." They might care about Judaism, but they don't realize how unique it is compared with what is out there in the rest of the world. The emphasis on community, the emphasis on *tikkun olam*, repair of the world. The history, the consciousness of a past and a future, the deep awareness of the totality of life involved in the religion and the relationship with God are so distinctive. Judaism is concerned about the past and the future but the connecting point is the present. This is not the waiting room, this is the real thing, not the dress rehearsal.

I think Jews by Choice help awaken some of that excitement in Jews who have taken it for granted. Sometimes people have said to me, "Why on earth would you choose to be a Jew; I didn't have a choice, I got stuck with it; why would you decide you want this?" I felt so sad, because they really were honest about that, they really wanted to know, "What on earth was it about Judaism that could possibly make anyone want to be Jewish?" I think it is a real failure on the part of the community to express what it is about Judaism that converts find so wonderful. I think we are healthy for Jewish identity. You may lose some Jews who don't care anything about being Jewish, but when you gain a convert who cares deeply, you are strengthening the religion.

I think more should be done to encourage converts to get involved in the community, because it is very hard to be a Jew without a community. I would like the rabbis to let people know that it is not enough to just go through the classes, that afterward they need to get involved, and that they are welcome at the Associated. The community needs to help that a little bit: here is a new Jew, let's stretch out our hands and go out of our way to welcome this person, invite him or her to your home. Look at the welcome they've given to Russian Jews. Do that for converts! "Come to our house for a *Shabbat* meal; see how we do it." The sisterhood sends you a form letter in the mail because you joined the synagogue; maybe have somebody give you a call.

My involvement with the Associated has enabled me to face the Holocaust. I could never stand to think about it when I was growing up because it was just so horrible. When I was campaign cochair for Young Leadership, we went to the Holocaust Museum for a tour before it was open to the public. We met with the scholar-in-residence there and were shown the scale model of all the exhibits and toured the building. That was a very moving experience for me, coming face-to-face with so much evil, and I realized that that may be why Jews are so intense. They don't have a choice, they have to be; that is the only way to be Jewish.

Having met and talked with many survivors now, I can identify with them. There's something in my psychology that feels like I've had to fight my way back too. Judaism is a good religion for people who are survivors. It is a very intense religion that doesn't give you easy and pat answers, and doesn't say, "Oh, everything is going to be fine." It says, "It's not fine, and what are we going to do about it?" That attitude is diametrically opposed to Christianity.

My journey has been a miracle. I am very lucky to have survived some of the early experiences of my life and to have arrived where I am today, with a wonderful family, a good life, and a fulfilling religion. I have always wanted to tell my story—even if it was only for myself and perhaps for my children, someday. I want to tell them that through God's love enough miracles happened to bring my life around.

33

*Hazzanit**

Ann Sachs

In Germany at the turn of the century, anti-Semitism ran very deep, though Jews moved more freely in society and felt an unprecedented degree of acceptance. Nevertheless, even among the most assimilated Jews who had left behind tradition and felt themselves to be fully German, there was the knowledge that their status would be different if they were identified as Christian. So some converted to Christianity, some out of conviction, some out of convenience. Once Hitler and the Nazis rose to power, however, conversion, no matter what its motivation, did not save anyone of Jewish ancestry.

When Ann Sachs's grandparents arrived in the United States, having barely escaped from Germany, they remained committed to the Lutheran Church, which they had joined as adults. While growing up, Ann knew of and felt pride in her Jewish ancestry, but the family was very active in the church, in which Ann was especially moved by music and sang in the choir.

Ann was a student in a music conservatory where she met Joel, a born Jew, who was to be her husband, and it was not difficult for her to decide to convert to Judaism. Through Jewish music and song Ann was able to envelop herself in Judaism, and she began to feel it from the inside out. As a cantor-in-training she is growing new roots in the tradition of her ancestors.

The process of becoming a cantor started during my preparation for my *bat mitzvah*. In order to feel Jewish, I needed to feel more comfortable and a "real" member of the Jewish community. By learning to read Hebrew better, I could do what other Jews do in the congregation. That in turn led me to study for my *bat mitzvah*. That was in 1984; I was eight-weeks pregnant, and I was so sick! It was the *worst* time to become *bat mitzvah*.

And that's sort of the story of my life—I've said yes to everything that comes along, whether I think I can do it or not. I end up doing things and finding out that I *can* do them.

I studied with a lot of people in the congregation. I took a course with Rabbi Martin Siegel, Ethics of the Fathers. And I studied with Siggi Rowe, the cantor emeritus, who offered, out of the goodness of his heart, to work with me on prayers. Sue Raymond, my tutor, was aware that I had a master's degree in music. Just as I was

---

*Hazzanit is the feminine Hebrew word for cantor.

about to have my baby, she called to say, "We need a choir director for the children's choir next year. Would you be interested in taking on that position?" I love choirs, and I had a very strong choral background. So, in spite of the fact that I knew only about eight Jewish songs, I said, yes, I'll do it.

Then I was asked to be cantor for a service because they couldn't afford to pay anybody. Rabbi Siegel said, "I think you can do the *Hatzi Kaddish* (the half *Kaddish* that marks the end of one section of the service), just get the melody from Judy Porecki or another cantor." So I did the *Hatzi Kaddish*. I could lead the *Aleinu* (the prayer at the end of the service that proclaims God the supreme ruler of the universe).

I wasn't called a "cantor"; I just provided some cantorial services. Then someone said, "I bet you could do my son or daughter's *bar/bat mitzvah*." One thing sort of led to another and that's how I fell into that role. I call myself a "developing" cantor.

How I fell into Judaism is a lot more difficult to tell.

My father was born in Munich. His parents were first cousins, both Jews, and they converted to Christianity around 1910. People always ask me why, and I always have to say I'm really not sure, even though my grandmother insisted they both did it out of conviction. A number of people have said they suspect his motivations to become a Christian were more political than religious; I believe Germany was very tolerant toward Jews in 1900, but in order to advance to a certain level, one really was better off being Christian than being Jewish.

My dad was never resentful of his German background, even though he had to leave Germany because the Nazis were counting Jews back through generations. I have known for as long as I can remember that he left because of his Jewish origins, and I've always felt some identity with the Holocaust as a result of that. My dad told me, "My parents saw when Hitler came to power that we were in trouble." He told stories about how when he was thirteen, kids would call him "Jude" and nasty names, though as far as I know my father never had to wear a star. At one point, my grandfather told my father not to tell anyone of his Jewish background, but somehow my dad let the cat out of the bag, which apparently was a very big mistake. When he was fourteen, still in Germany, he lost an eye. In spite of the pressure that was put on everybody to avoid Jews, his Boy Scout leader came to visit him in the hospital, even though he knew my father was of Jewish origin. To my dad, it was remarkable that this man had the courage to do such a thing.

My father had close contact as a child with his extended family, who had remained Jewish. They were very assimilated. I have a few objects of Judaica that were passed down through my grandmother. They were believed to be used in *seders*, but as far as I know, in my grandparents' generation no Jewish rituals were observed. So that's how far they were removed from practicing Judaism. I don't think they ever had a *seder*.

I knew my grandmother's sister. My great-aunt and my grandmother were unusually close. She worked for a wealthy Jewish lady in Philadelphia as a sort of companion, and when that lady died my aunt came to live with my grandparents. There was nothing Jewish about her in terms of her observance. But she wasn't Christian either.

Some of the extended Jewish family got out of Germany and settled in South America, others settled in the United States and still others in Israel. It's a tribute to my grandfather that they all managed to escape, because he had foreseen what was to come, though he and his wife didn't get out until 1939. Apparently the Gestapo was really after him.

My mother's family is also German, and her grandfather was a conservative Lutheran minister, but her father was much more open-minded and tolerant. My mother is probably the most religiously liberal in her family. There were some members of the family that were upset when I became a Jew, but not my parents.

From a religious point of view, my parents raised me with a very open attitude. Their message to me was, "You have to figure out for yourself what you believe." Although they loved Jesus and the traditions of Christianity, as did I, they questioned the divinity of Jesus. My mother would often say to me, "I'm not so sure that Mary was a virgin. The virgin birth doesn't make sense to me."

As I was growing up, this background was confusing to me. I think it muddled my identity somewhat. I have a vivid memory of a fight with one of my very closest friends because I told her I was part Jewish. And she said, "You can't be part Jewish. You're Christian, Ann. You go to a Lutheran church; you're Lutheran. You're not part Jewish." And I said, "Gail, my father was in the Holocaust, and his family is all Jewish. I am definitely part Jewish." Obviously it was something I was always really thinking about.

When I said the Apostles' Creed in church, I'd have to make up things to make it work for me. "I believe in God, the Father Almighty, maker of heaven and earth," that's fine. ". . . and in Jesus Christ, his only son, our Lord. . . ." His only son? Our Lord? I never really saw Jesus as an intermediary between me and God, or thought that we were different from Jesus, or that Jesus was different from us, that Jesus was God.

Jesus was certainly a good person. The things that he preached I never had any problem with. He certainly suffered, but I always felt that no matter how much Jesus suffered, I was responsible for my own actions, and I believed every person should be responsible and accountable for his or her own actions.

I also had problems with the idea that people go to hell if they don't believe in Jesus. Even though they're wonderful, good, giving people? Even if they are struggling to try to come to grips with what God is and who Jesus was? They go to hell? I felt that belief would hinder me from being a good person, and I think it hinders other people, too. I saw it as hypocrisy and egotistical for people who believe in Jesus to make themselves an exclusive club. A minister in our church, who had a lot of influence on me when I was a teenager, was thrown out of the church because he also questioned Jesus' divinity.

Many of the concepts of Christianity are lovely concepts, universal concepts. I still love the baby in the manger. But I finally just got tired of always squeezing my own philosophy into words that didn't give me full expression.

It is clear to me, though, that I needed religion and I liked ritual. It was the music and the beauty of the ceremonies that really appealed to me. As a child I loved to sing and sometimes when I was playing alone, I would take out a hymnal and pretend I was the minister and lead my congregation. Imagine a little girl doing this!

While prayer had always been difficult for me, music usually is not as filled with dogma. It is much more emotional, and through music, it is much easier to express your love and your passion. Religious music in particular was a very important tradition in my family.

When I decided to become Jewish, I didn't realize that, even though I could still listen to and sing that music, it would change—totally change—my feelings about it. I've never been able to separate the music from the words. To sing, ". . . for unto us a child is born, unto us a son is given," is still beautiful and brings tears to my eyes, but the joy and the energy are no longer there for me. Becoming Jewish changed the dimension of that music for me.

So at Christmastime, I feel sad, and I'm sure a lot of us who are converts go through the same thing, although perhaps less as time passes. I loved decorating the house and making it festive. I was the cookie baker. My parents still use some of the cookie ornaments that I made. I was the one who nurtured a lot of the rituals in my parents' home. That's translated well into being a Jewish mother, responsible for the home rituals.

Easter was definitely a major holiday. It was *the* spiritual holiday, as I think it is for most Christians. My family was very spiritually Christian. We went to services on Good Friday. There was a beautiful piece that they always sang a cappella at the end of the service, "Christ we do all adore thee," as they were veiling the cross, and the lights would go off. It just made you feel moved, very connected and very spiritual. I loved the way that song and the rituals could evoke the emotions. It's a very spiritual day. It's the day of repentance for Christians. I compare Easter to *Yom Kippur*.

The power of Christianity is its appeal to people on the most basic emotional level. They've got the icons, they've got the beautiful churches and the cathedrals and the music—everything to draw people in on an emotional level.

In some ways Judaism is more intellectual. But I don't agree with some who say that it's not extremely spiritual. It can be, and for me it definitely is. One reason I think I became a cantor is because I have always had a very strong connection between music and my spirituality, and people sense that when I sing. It helps them to connect with their own spirituality. I think many people find it easier to feel spiritual when they sing.

At first, my decision to become a Jew was very rational. I couldn't find my place in Christianity. I couldn't agree with the dogma. Intellectually, I agreed with everything that was expressed in Judaism. On the other hand I had a very strong emotional connection to Christianity, though not an intellectual one. It's been a long process to connect myself spiritually to Judaism, but as I look back I can see I had always felt a connection to Judaism, and I'm a great believer in fate.

I think that you have a path that you are meant to follow. All of the decisions that I had made about my life before I chose Judaism seemed arbitrary, but they ended up bringing me to a certain place. And there was a sense that I was driven, compelled to make certain decisions. There was absolutely no stopping me. It couldn't have happened any other way, and it was the best thing that could ever have happened to me.

As a freshman in college, I thought I would be a math major, but I was extremely unhappy. I began to feel a strong urge to study music, but the college had no music department, so I had to transfer. I do believe it was a spiritual need or yearning that drove me to become a musician. It was something I *had* to do, as if something were propelling me. I didn't listen to anybody but my own inner voice. At Peabody, I met my husband, Joel. I saw that he was the right person for me. I loved him. And I felt Judaism is where I was meant to be, though I'm not sure what all my motivations were for making that decision. Mainly, I just felt like I was Jewish.

I never had negative feelings about my Jewish ancestry. I felt sensitive and vulnerable. I don't necessarily think of those as being negative. Even though there were these moments of connection with Jewishness, I didn't know anything about Judaism.

There was one boy who was Jewish in our class of 500, and when I was home for my twentieth high-school reunion, he said to me, "I remember in fourth grade, Ann, they had asked me to bring a *menorah* to class. So, I brought it to class, and I told everybody about Hanukkah, and you were the only person who asked me any questions." Was that because I just thought it was interesting, or did I feel a connection?

Joel and I were introduced by another Jewish man who was a mutual close friend. What attracted me to Joel was that he was interested in *me*, as a person, my mind, what I thought about things. He wanted to talk to me—about a lot of different things—and he wasn't a chauvinist. He was very caring.

He was raised in a Conservative family. Originally, his family were Orthodox and had come from Poland. He had a very strong Hebrew upbringing, although his family was not extremely observant. His family is very knowledgeable about Judaism, and he learned a lot about it at home. His mother always tells about how he was the best *bar mitzvah* and did much more than he had to do.

When Joel started telling me about Judaism, a light went on for me and I said, "My God, I'm Jewish." I just felt like everything he said to me fit with my perception of the world and with what I wanted religion to do for me, and the way I felt about God. I always saw God as this huge universal force—a creative force. I believe that God doesn't manipulate people. God lives in us but doesn't control us. We have to find and cultivate God in our lives, in ourselves. And everything that Joel told me about Judaism supported that view.

The other thing about Joel that was very attractive to me was his love of family, and I knew *very* quickly that I wanted to marry him—much quicker than poor Joel knew. Although I was in the process of getting a master's degree in music and had always accepted the fact that if I had to live alone, I could make it, and I would be okay, the thing I wanted more than anything was to have a family. I wanted that to be the focal point in my life: to have kids and create a home and a loving atmosphere for other people. I saw in Joel and his family a devotion to family life that I considered extraordinary.

When you're twenty-five, though, you don't see the differences between two people as a problem. I learned to see it as a challenge. But even though everything I read and learned about Judaism seemed right to me, it was pretty blind on my part to think that it was all going to be easy. I can do without the Christmas tree, I thought, but it was harder than I expected. That feeling of loss is fading with time as I get more involved in Jewish celebrations each year. This year we built a *sukkah*—it is just the epitome of a beautiful Jewish home holiday ritual. And the symbols of the Jewish holidays to me are so replete with wonderful values. They're so beautiful that, believe me, I don't feel I suffer from giving up anything at all.

I have to admit, though, I've done things that have been good for me that didn't always start out in the most meaningful way. I took a fourteen-week conversion course; I learned a little Hebrew, and I enjoyed it. In six months, I converted. It was very short. It was no different than the kind of conversion that anybody that was just converting to marry their partner would have gone through. A lot of the symbolism was lost on me. For me the symbols are very important, so the "transfer" of my soul to Judaism was very gradual.

The difficult thing about being a convert is that you can't "be" Jewish without "doing" it. It's easy for Jews that have been Jews all their life to say, "I'm a Jew," whether they are observant or not. But it's impossible for non-Jews who convert to Judaism to say they're Jewish and feel spiritually connected to it unless they observe it in some way. I'm not sure how fully I understood that till I was in a congregation in which I could feel more comfortable about being active.

We shopped around for congregations. We tried a Reform temple, but there wasn't a real warm feeling there, and the music didn't draw me. Then we went to the Columbia Jewish Congregation. Their musical tradition is *hasidic* in style, which really appealed to me—talk about spiritual transference! I hadn't heard anything like *hasidic* music before, and I was very drawn in and excited. I liked the rabbi, Martin Siegel. He is very intellectual and has a wonderful knowledge and love of Torah. The way he talked about Torah really started to open my eyes.

About four or five years ago, we also joined the CJC's *havurah*. It's a group of about thirty to forty people who get together every Saturday morning. We don't have a rabbi lead that service. We take turns leading. Sometimes I bring my guitar, and there's more singing. Everybody takes a turn leading the *drash* (Torah discussion). That's been a very educational and spiritual experience for me.

I think another place where I've really found the connection, spiritually, is through studying Torah. I have come to believe so strongly in the divinity of the Torah, and this has really deepened my spirituality.

What CJC and the *havurah* have helped me to discover is that the Torah is so multidimensional. I have to compare it to a really great piece of music: every time you hear it it's different. And with the Torah, every time you study it, every time you read it, it is different, depending on where you are and who you are. Every year when you return to that same portion, the discussion is different. The truths are so profound, and relevant—as current today as they were 2,000 years ago. People haven't changed, the world hasn't changed, and so the truth doesn't change. And that's what's so incredible about it.

And what's so remarkable to me is how different the view is from a Jewish standpoint than from a Christian standpoint.

I may be wrong about this, because I was immature when I was a Christian, but I never got the impression that there was a very multidimensional attitude toward the Bible in Christianity, especially the Old Testament. I always heard how violent God was in the Old Testament—an antiquated view of God as opposed to the loving view of God in the New Testament. Just by virtue of the fact that Christians call the Torah the *Old* Testament connotes, to me, that it is no longer thought to be relevant. This lack of appreciation for the depth of Torah is a real stumbling block between Jews and Christians.

Just reading the words is not really Torah—it's the interpretation of those words that is Torah. The Torah is much more the *Midrash*, the oral tradition. *How* the language is used has implications for *what* it says. The English translation cannot adequately describe how one word can change a sentence. For example, when "you" is used in the plural in Hebrew versus "you" in the singular, different things are implied. In English "you" is used interchangably as plural or singular. It seems like a small thing, grammatically, but it can have great philosophical ramifications, of which the English, in bare translation, will give you no sense. Another example is the two words for "land," *eretz* and *adamah*. If it is just translated into English as "land," a lot of understanding is lost.

As a Christian I always questioned the divine inspiration of the Bible. As a Jew, the more I learn, the less I doubt it. We're all connected to God, and I think it was in moments of divine inspiration that the Torah was written by human beings. I don't know how that inspiration comes. I don't think that there's always an explanation for why things happen the way they do—whether in my own life or in the larger world. The fact is that if it inspires me, that's enough.

Knowing Torah is an enormous support in performing *mitzvot*—good deeds. Sometimes it seems so difficult to do them—there are so many things that pull us away from our spiritual development. Yet, people are not even aware of the good things they are doing that are actually following Jewish principles. You feed your dog before you sit down to eat yourself—that is Torah. It's so simple, and yet it's an act of loving-kindness toward a being who's more vulnerable than you are. The rabbis also teach that sometimes not doing a thing is also a good deed. The word held back as well as the word said. Every time you do something like that, you're building something. I think it makes you healthier. Jewish nonobservance is not healthy, and I agree with M. Scott Peck's *The Road Less Traveled*—a spiritual person is healthier than a nonspiritual person.

My path to Judaism is one major miracle. My life is also filled with smaller miracles—like this path that I've chosen to follow as a cantor. Being a cantor is so "me." I wasn't meant to be an opera singer. I chose to join a congregation that happens to have a natural singing style with guitar playing—and I happen to play the guitar. Suddenly a skill I had developed but had not used in years is so useful to me for directing the children's choir. I didn't even appreciate it until I was almost forty years old, and I married a guitarist. Go figure!

All along, the timing of everything I've done has been so perfect and the coincidences so amazing. For instance: I had just had my third child. I felt fulfilled as a mom—my first and foremost interest. I had been working in the family business as a bookkeeper, and that commitment was ending because the business was doing well enough to hire a bookkeeper. At that time, our associate rabbi introduced me to David Shneyer and Maalot.* All of a sudden it opened this door for me. If it had happened a year earlier, I couldn't have done it because I was working. And if it had happened a year later, it would have been a year wasted. But it happened just at the time that I was ready. And to me that was another miracle. Studying with David Shneyer and Sue Roemer and all of these incredible people with Maalot is opening new doors for me all the time.

The cantor emeritus of CJC, Siggi Rowe, is a good friend. He's from Germany also, from an Orthodox family. He's quite controversial for performing interfaith marriages. He feels it's very important to accept Jews in the community and not push them away. When he was in the war, he went to release Jews from prison camps in Austria. They asked the Americans, "Why did you betray us, why didn't you help us?" He told me, "I've always remembered that, and I've always felt I had to help Jews that needed to be helped. I swore I would never turn my back on a Jew." That's his perspective on a difficult issue.

He's ready to retire from doing weddings and has been very interested in involving me. A year ago I certainly wouldn't have been ready. But as a convert to Judaism, I feel that I can be very helpful in guiding people who are going to make the decision to marry regardless of what the Jewish community thinks. I can help them to at least take a realistic approach. They can at least make their marriages as strong as possible and make some good decisions about raising kids.

Many people convert after marriage. In Columbia Jewish Congregation, there are many interfaith marriages. Most of them are uncommitted Christians married to more committed Jews. As I said before, Christians are ignorant about Judaism, but so too are many Jews! I've found in my interviewing of couples that very many times the Christians are very supportive of the Jewish faith of their partner. I try to do a little bit of educating—of both partners—to open their minds and get them to see that maybe the Judaism that they were brought up in is not the entire picture of what Judaism is. I think that's so important.

Converts make an important statement to the Jewish community that people find Judaism very desirable without being born into it. The response of the Jewish com-

---

*Maalot is a new school and seminary in the Washington, D.C., area for cantors, educators, and lay persons interested in strengthening their background in Jewish music, liturgy, and ceremonial arts. The name Maalot comes from the *Shir HaMaalot* psalms, ancient songs of Jewish aspiration and celebration.

munity, however, is not always what I wish it would be. It's sad to me when someone puzzles over my conversion: "I can't believe anybody would choose to be Jewish."

Another somewhat odd response is from those born Jews who are defensive about
converts. There will be occasions in which it is relevant for me to mention that I am
a convert, and the response is, "You don't need to apologize for that." I wasn't apologizing! I was just explaining a fact about myself. Another person said, "You don't
need to tell me that. My husband converted to Judaism, and he never tells anybody
because it's not important." Or more chilling, in a discussion about intermarriage
led by a friend of mine, a woman sitting next to me said, "I know a married couple
who are both converts and they are living more like Jews than some of us." She thought
that was amazing.

It is true that some of my Jewish consciousness is still developing. I don't, for
example, feel as strong a conection as it seems to me other Jews feel toward Israel.
This year at *Selihot* (penitential prayers said before the High Holidays) a friend shared
that when she heard on the radio that the peace accords had been signed she just burst
into the *Shema*. I would never do that. I just don't feel as emotionally attached. She
cried when she retold the story, and I thought it was beautiful. And I felt a little bit
envious of her for feeling that way. Joel tells me to wait till we go to Israel because
that will help. Abba Eban's book *My People* helped. Studying the history of Israel
has helped because it is such a profoundly incredible history. Understanding what
happened through thousands of years gives you a better connection with Israel.

But I don't feel defensive about it, or apologetic, and I certainly don't feel inferior. I'm not offended by the terms "convert" or "Jew by Choice." I'm proud of the
choice I made and I'm comfortable both with being Jewish and with who I was before
I became Jewish. Actually, being a convert has sometimes given me opportunities
that born Jews don't always have.

It is helpful and gratifying to see Jewish identity through my children's eyes. I
think about what I would have loved as a child and try to keep their experiences in
mind when I'm trying to create a Jewish home with symbols that they will want to
continue in their own homes. One of the reasons I decided to take on the children's
choir at CJC was that I wanted my kids to be rooted musically in Judaism. They are
very receptive to it. The older two both sang in my choir, and my daughter still does.

We all love *Shabbat*. When we light candles, my son likes to turn off the lights.
The children fight over who's going to say the blessing over the bread each night.
My mother cried the first time she celebrated *Shabbat* with us and the kids sang the
Kiddush (blessing over wine) all the way through. She was very moved by it. It re-
minded her of her childhood when her family all sat around the table singing.

My son is going to be a *bar mitzvah* soon, and I'm tutoring him myself. He gets
very excited by the study of prayer when he has a good teacher, and the other night
was his first class with Rabbi Siegel. "It was cool! We talked about the first two lines
of another kid's portion—that's all we talked about for an hour. It was amazing."
I'm very excited about what Aaron is discovering about Judaism, because I think he
is discovering what is important.

I do see the differences between growing up Jewish and growing up as a gentile. You do feel different as a Jew, and my children have expressed that it would be easier to be a Christian. My son Aaron says that it is the "lazy part" of him that would like to be Christian. They resent the fact that they have to learn another language and that they have to spend a lot more time studying their religion than other kids do.

I don't want them to resent their Judaism, so we let our kids participate in soccer on Saturdays, which everyone does in the larger community here in Columbia. Sometimes I wish we were less assimilated than we are, because maybe the children don't feel the difference strongly and positively enough. I want them to see us practice Judaism. I want them to find the meaning in it, but I don't want them to see it as being something that pulls them away from other things that are good for them and that they want to do. I'm always afraid that they are going to bolt. I think it's difficult to be Jewish in this society. It's easy for Jews to get lost, and I want to see my children continue their Jewish heritage.

I also see it as a challenge to be observant without being judgmental. Rigid observance tends to lead to intolerance, and I don't think that is healthy. I constantly have to struggle to not be judgmental of people who don't observe at all. I see people who are less observant ritually, but who do a lot of good. There are so many ways to fulfill the commandments, and you may not be aware of how another person is doing that. It is more important to be involved in the process. Where you are on the continuum from totally observant to least observant is not so important. It is like a pendulum that swings in both directions, and we need balance.

Rabbi Hillel Baron, the Lubavitch rabbi in Columbia, once said that the Jewish people and the ways they practice their Judaism are like different parts of the body, and they all need each other to survive. I really believe that is true.

34

Little Miracles

Jim Poodiack

Jim looks as if he could be a member of the Olympic wrestling team, and at
first it seems believable when he tells of a troubled childhood as a tough kid.
But then this house-husband and father of three boys also shares that years of
living as an observant Jew have softened the rough edges; he is more relaxed,
he says, less cynical, nicer.

Although Jim's interest in Judaism initially came through his relationship
with Cathy, he soon realized that becoming a Jew was just as much a part
of his destiny as meeting his wife. Still, there have been challenges along the
way, from things as "simple" as observing the *mitzvot* to coping with the life-
threatening illnesses of two of his sons. Jim has come through these crises with
a belief that the answers to life's most difficult problems can be found in Judaism, and with patience and trust little miracles do happen.

I met Cathy when I was nineteen years old. She was a junior in high school and I
had just graduated. Up until I was nineteen I was not what you would call "nice"—
but since that time I've gotten nicer every year.

I never had a problem of *who* I was. I think I had a problem of *what* I was. I was
in serious trouble while I was growing up, but I never felt like I wasn't *somebody*.
No matter how you live, if you have a certain type of personality, you can feel you
are somebody. People didn't like the somebody I was, and so I was shuffled around
from my parents to grandparents to my aunts and uncles. And I would say that is
because I didn't know *what* I was.

Through the conversion, through marriage and living a Jewish life, I found what
I am. I had been so cynical about life. My personality has evolved, I deal differently
with other people. I've evolved as a human being. So much of it has to do with the
sense of what I am, or what I can be, what I'm striving for now. There is something
I can do. I can advance a certain way because I am on a path, a direction. And through
that, I think it's made things that otherwise I never would have been able to handle,
handleable—inside myself.

I've heard other people who have converted say that they never felt like they really
belonged in their family. I feel that. I didn't fit in at home, and I certainly didn't fit
in at church. And I've heard people say they always felt Jewish, or when they went
down for their last "dunk" in the *mikveh*, they felt something come into them. You
can take that any way you want. For myself, I think that people who look for miracles

look for big miracles. They don't look for the little ones. I've been able to appreciate the little miracles.

Until I met Cathy and we developed our relationship, I never had an anchor. I think of it now as destiny. I was meant to meet Cathy, and I was meant to become Jewish, and I was meant to raise a Jewish family. I really believe it—I don't believe there was any chance involved. It was all planned. It's *besheret*. And it's worked out, so far.

When Cathy went to Cornell, in her junior year of college, I also moved up to Ithaca. We knew then that we were going to get married. We're planners and plan everything in advance. We always talked about when we would have children, and I knew Cathy's faith meant a lot to her. I could see that, and I had no qualms about it—or about my converting. I was raised in a Catholic home but it wasn't a big deal. When I was growing up, I had Jewish friends and had been to their homes. I thought Judaism was a very nice religion.

When I was in seventh or eighth grade I had a friend whose family was Orthodox—*frum*. They'd come home from *shul* on Saturday, and I'd get a free lunch and listen to their conversations. I would ask the questions—questions that if you'd ask the local priest of my church or the nuns in the catechism, you couldn't really get an answer. The Catholic response was, "Well, that's faith. It's absolute; something we don't question." But when I was at this family's table—especially when they had company—I found nothing was absolute! There was always a lot of discussion and through that experience I started questioning. Once you start questioning Jesus and all that, it's not that hard to lose the belief in it.

That was during my growing up years in Binghamton, New York. It's an ethnic, working-class city, and it's very friendly. There were no real divisions among anyone. So Judaism was at the fringes of my life, and when I met Cathy I just became more involved.

After Cornell, Cathy was going to graduate school at Emory in Atlanta. By that time I had made the decision to convert. I just picked out some synagogues from the telephone book and made appointments to go see the rabbis. Each rabbi told me to go to the Hillel at the Emory campus. I learned later that they're supposed to turn you away. But they didn't just turn me away, they also told me where to go. The Hillel rabbi was Judah Mintz. He had a class for converts, which I joined, but most significantly, for one full year, he invited us to have *Shabbat* at his house—Friday night and Saturday, every week. I don't know if he was impressed with my devotion to changing my faith, as much as my devotion to Cathy.

I did not know what type of rabbi he was when I got there, but right off the bat he told me that it would be an Orthodox conversion and a lengthy process, with classes and *shomer Shabbat* lifestyle, keeping kosher. I probably just sat there saying, "Oh, no!" But Cathy and I had been living together for four years, knew we were going to get married, and knew we wanted to have children. For what may be a vain reason, I decided that I didn't want anyone to be able to question my children's Jewishness, and I had become aware of the differences between the branches of Judaism.

There were people in the conversion class who did opt for a Reform conversion. Rabbi Mintz said, "It's your choice." But he explained the difficulties that you could run into with a non-Orthodox conversion.

Getting used to being *Shomer Shabbat* was not easy. On Saturday, I was used to watching sports on television, or playing sports, or hopping in the car for a ride through the country. The things that you're used to doing are hard to give up. There were a couple times I remember thinking, I just need a break. I can count on one hand the times I've broken the *Shabbat*. I did it instead of feeling resentment, but I also came to realize that if you take a break, it's so easy to get out of it, and so I fought that urge. Because I knew myself. I figured I needed to keep right at it and do it until it was done, and at this point I really enjoy *Shabbat*.

What I found surprising was the depth of the Jewish community. Unless you're part of it, you don't know. All the organizations and all the services, the networks. It's just overwhelming. I was just amazed at how involved and how interconnected people are. As a Catholic, you go to church on Sunday, and class on Tuesday, your parents go to bingo, and that's basically it.

The rabbi's family took us under their wing. Somehow he knew things about me after meeting me only a few times. He certainly knew that we were going to get married—no matter what—and if something didn't work out with this conversion, I was going to do it another way, no matter what. He could also tell that Cathy's a spiritual person, and at that point of my life I was cynical. He must have known what type of personality I had and that if I wasn't pushed and given a direction, then it wasn't going to happen for me. "You come here every *Shabbat*, that way I know you're coming. If you don't come to my house, it's because you're going to someone else's house for *Shabbat*." And it worked for a full year. I learned the songs, the tunes, the order of the dinner, and I went to *shul* on Friday evenings and *Shabbat* mornings. It was like having a personal tutor. And there were the sessions with the conversion class. But I always felt a little special, because he seemed to be taking a special interest in me.

At that time the rabbi and his wife had two sons. Now they have another child. It was a vibrant family, and there was always company there. Not just for *Shabbat*, but every holiday. For someone who's a potential convert, Yom Kippur can be overwhelming. Rosh Hashanah and then Yom Kippur—the twenty-fifth hour in *shul*, you can sort of say, "Ohhhhh . . ." But having the rabbi right there and feeling his constant encouragement—if I hadn't gotten this warm embrace, I don't know if I would have been able to do it all. He is a tremendous rabbi, and we remain close to him and his family.

After about a year and a half, I went through the actual conversion rituals. Cathy was going to graduate her program in June, and we wanted to have a June wedding, so in April I met with the *Bet Din*.

At first I was very nervous, but because of the preparation I had, I felt confident. I think the rabbis could see that since I'd been at it such a long time, that even though it started out as a requirement for marriage, at this point, even if I wasn't going to get married, I was going to go through with this.

I would say about a good six months or so into the process it became something I was doing for myself. I started feeling comfortable going to *shul* all the time and could follow along in the prayer book, and people didn't think of me as a stranger. When you walk in and no one notices any difference, you're accepted. After the conversion, when I could wear my *tallit*—that was a good feeling.

The three rabbis of the *Bet Din* happened to be the three that I had seen to ask about conversion. The circumcision part was very interesting because the *mohel* must have been about eighty. And he was very nervous—nervous and so cute. But thank God I was already circumcised!

The *mikveh* was a totally different experience; it was very special. Perhaps because of my Catholic background, ritual did not seem to me to be a living experience. I anticipated the *mikveh* was going to be a formality because I already felt Jewish. I've talked with other converts, and they tell of feeling different during the process of the *mikveh*. All the time, you say, it's just water. It's not. My cynicism with *HaShem* was gone. Later, I felt a similar sensation standing in front of the open ark (where the Torah is kept) with the Torah scroll. I read from a paper that basically says you are throwing away your past and accepting Judaism. My hands were shaking—maybe it was a little nerves—but I got a warm rush. A rabbi I was sharing this with recently described it as a Jewish soul coming in. I can still remember, and I still get the goose bumps. It was very special.

Our wedding day was so hectic. I felt obligated to help my family through everything. Unless they'd seen it in a Barbra Streisand movie, they didn't know what was going on. At the wedding I felt Jewish but half the people who were there had no idea what was going on—and I was *from* them. It was a very strange sensation. When I went around to the tables at the reception, the Jewish people would have such a different feeling for our wedding, and then I would go to the other side and there's "Oh, I'm happy for you, but . . . they're Jews."

That didn't come from my parents or my grandmother. When I was growing up, my father's father referred to Jews as "yids." I'm sure that's how he was brought up. And I did have cousins who were just ignorant—anti-Semitic—yet they've never known any Jews. And, yes, they attended my wedding.

My presence in the family has absolutely changed that attitude. Now they know that "Jewish" is not just a thing. If someone hates Jews, I've shown them one of my children—*that's* who they would hate. That brings it close to home. If they watch something on TV now and see some anti-Semitism, they say, "That could be my nephew. How could people do that?" I think that makes a big difference.

Our first child was born ten months after we were married. We had a *bris*, of course, but it was very different from the *bris* of our third son. I have three boys and our celebration of each *bris* has evolved as our Jewishness has evolved. Our first son's *bris* was done in a *shul* in Atlanta to which we didn't belong, on a weekday morning, after *minyan*. They barely keep enough guys there for a *minyan*. It was just the *bris*—boom—and then we went home. That's how it was. It was more like an anxiety-ridden experience as opposed to something meaningful.

With my second son, we were back in Binghamton with family, and it was done in my mother-in-law's apartment on the kitchen table, with a house full of people. The people who attended were Jewish but not knowledgeable. It was a party atmosphere—a "typical" *bris*.

The third was done in our house—mainly because the *shul* was having a rummage sale that day. By then we belonged to an Orthodox *shul*, and most of the people who came were very Orthodox and knowledgeable. It was a completely different atmosphere because it was a celebration—with lots of singing and dancing.

For my first son, we didn't have a *pidyon haben* (redemption of the firstborn) because we didn't know about that ritual. Then when we moved back to Binghamton, Cathy was taking a class in the *Chabad* community with Rabbi Slonam's wife. A discussion in the class happened to touch on this, and Cathy said, "Wait, you're supposed to do that for the firstborn?" The *rebbetzin* (rabbi's wife) said, "Yes, and it's never too late." So Josh, at age seven, had a *pidyon haben*, and it was a community-wide celebration. The community really pulls together for things like this—Reform with the *hasidim*, together. In fact, I think some of the biggest sponsors of *Chabad* are the Reform in that community. They come together instead of pulling away from each other. And because we'd grown up in Binghamton, everyone knew our names.

During the years that we were living there, Cathy's father was sick. At that same time, her brother, who was thirty years old, passed away. We can't imagine what would have happened to the family if we hadn't been there during that time. Everything has a plan.

My brother-in-law's death was the result of complications following surgery for a brain tumor. There were a series of crises and it became apparent that even if he were to survive, he would not be functioning. Decisions had to be made, and Cathy's older brother distanced himself from the situation. Most of the responsibility for making arrangements fell on me, especially in the hospital. Should life support be used to keep him alive? My father-in-law and I would discuss the options. Of course we consulted with rabbis, and we followed a course of action based on *halakhah*. We disconnected him from the oxygen, and when he couldn't breathe on his own, he passed away.

Cathy and her father both have very strong faith and though it was very sad and painful for them, they were able to put the death in a religious perspective that gave them some solace. It was much more difficult for Cathy's older brother.

We sat *shivah* for her brother. That was my first experience with it except for when growing up we'd stop by at a *shivah* house when someone's grandmother passed away. With my brother-in-law's death I was able to go through the whole process. It's very healthy. (I never could understand the open casket of the Christian burial.) The cemetery is the most emotional time. Everything is so final at that point, and you must begin to let go. In the *shivah* process, you almost go through the stages of grieving. Then by the end of it, if you're able to, you let go. I appreciate the rules that you shouldn't go back to the cemetery for a certain amount of time. Grief can destroy a person, a family, if you don't learn to let go. In the *shivah* process, everyone's included. There's no "Leave me alone, I'm in my room crying," although a certain amount of that is healthy. People come, you sit, you grieve, you share. And by the end of the process, you're telling stories about the life lived and not about the death. That makes a big difference.

My father-in-law has since died also, and I still go to *shul* for both their *Yartzeits*, since I am the only male in the family who does that. While I am saying *Kaddish*, most of the time tears well up because it brings me back to the moment I came back from the cemetery. I have nearly the same type of sadness, if I'm saying it the right way, as if my brother or father-in-law had just left. My father-in-law and I were very close, since he was so instrumental in bringing me out of the mind-set I had when I was a teenager, and sometimes when I say *Kaddish*, I feel that if I were to turn my head, he would be right here.

My oldest son, Josh, started day school in New York. Up until that time we had attended the Conservative congregation in which Cathy had grown up—not too regularly, just a mainstream American Jewish family. It happened that most of the kids who went to the day school belonged to an Orthodox *shul*, and we were eager for Josh to have a group of friends.

Cathy went to the Orthodox *shul* and she said, "You have to come here. It's different." To me there was no difference between denominations, but I agreed to go. I enjoyed it. The people were so warm and so friendly; they just included newcomers right away. A skeptic might say, "Well, of course, they want more people to be like them so they're going to be extra friendly to get you to join them." But it was a genuine interest, in most cases. And we started going there.

Once the kids started in school and we were going to that *shul*, we started living that lifestyle and going to classes, studying with different people. Our Jewish observance just evolved, and we maintained it when we moved to Atlanta.

Part of our deepening commitment to Judaism was related to the experience of having a very ill child. When my middle son, Ben, was eighteen months old, we were told that we wouldn't see his second birthday. He had a spinal-cord tumor, and it was massive. After surgery and all the radiation treatments Ben had to learn how to walk all over again. It was about a year's process, and it was toward the end of that year that we started attending the Orthodox *shul*. We were also learning a little bit about Lubavitch and about a more spiritual aspect of Judaism that you don't really get from the mainstream.

At one point during Ben's illness Cathy went to the *Chabad* rabbi to ask, "What can I do Jewishly in my life to give my family more of a chance for health and well-being?" She found out that there was a way to live that actually encourages these things to happen to you—for example, keeping kosher, being *Shomer Shabbat*, keeping the laws of family purity. These had the effect of spiritually raising your family up. And she also learned of the *Rebbe*, Rabbi Menachem Schneerson.

Of course, I said, "If that stuff worked—if it was a 100-percent given—everyone would live like that and there'd be no sickness and everyone would live forever." But I've seen how the faith part helps. If you ever lived through something like the grave illness of a child, controlling your emotions is extremely hard. Maybe you're driving by yourself, stuck in traffic, you daydream, and you become very emotional, and you can't control yourself. But I could see how Cathy handled everything. Her faith helped, and I tried to develop that.

Thank God, for whatever reason, Ben is now fine, perfectly fine. He's now nine. And he has minimal side effects from everything, and if you were to see him, you wouldn't even know anything was ever wrong with him.

After Ben's illness we had written to the *Rebbe* to ask for a blessing to have a third child. You say to yourself, "I can't go through this again, if we are going to have another child who could be sick." At that point I believed, and I said, "Well, this doesn't hurt." The blessing was ". . . you'll have a son; may he have a full and healthy and happy life, and Amen. . . ." Then my youngest son, Avi, was born with what they thought was a heart murmur; then it turned out that he has a heart defect. We hope everything will be all right, but at some point he might need surgery. When I first heard that news, it threw me way off. "How can this be? Why is this happening to us? I can't deal with this!" I felt like rejecting everything, but Cathy stayed fast. My view of a full and happy life is a lot different from the *Rebbe's* view of a full and happy life. But who am I to say; I just have to go with the flow. I just have to accept it and move on. I think I did.

I don't try to look into the future. That's one of the things I gave up. I try to live day by day. Each day is different, and you just do the best you can every day. In our family, if you look too far ahead, it's a drag! There's no control, that's something I tried to learn when we were going through Ben's problems. I've developed an awareness of what *HaShem* has control of and what I have control of. That's where religious cynicism can develop: "If there was a God, why would this happen?" But as a result of living through these events, I have lost my earlier cynicism. I have developed a personal relationship with *HaShem* that is a part of my life now. It has also made a difference that we were part of a community. Community plays a role in making you feel connected to others and to God. I know that because of Judaism and the commitment I've developed for it, I've been able to handle the crises in our family.

We've lived a full cycle. But it's made us a lot stronger family. And I think it's made our commitment to *Yiddishkeit* a little stronger. You see the importance of observance, not just in an overview, but in the daily practice.

We're fairly observant, though at this point I would have no desire to become ultra-Orthodox. I'm comfortable with Orthodoxy, although in my own personal life I'm not as strict as my wife is in hers and my kids are in theirs. I do the best I can, for me. I don't do anything that would cause the kids to question, "If Daddy does this, why do I have to do that?" So I make sure that through my behavior, I don't cause a doubt in their minds. Other than that, we're pretty much *Shomer Shabbat*, strictly kosher.

There are some aspects of Orthodoxy that are harder for me to deal with than others.

About nine o'clock on a *Shabbat* evening in the summer, it's very hard not to say, "I think it's over!" The marriage-relationship laws and the fences that they put up to help you observe them—when we took that *mitzvah* into our life, I found it very difficult. It took some study and some counseling.

Another aspect of Judaism that I find works well for me is that it is easy talking to a rabbi—as opposed to talking to a priest. I'm grateful that I have friends who are rabbis, some of whom have lived their whole life *frum*, and some who took it on as adults. Some are my age, so I feel they can relate to me and understand what I am going through. You can talk to a rabbi about anything, because he's lived everything. They have a family, they have the problems, they have all the normal experiences of living. And, if you listen to them, and you're willing to accept their answers, I think they have the answers.

I do think Torah provides the answers to the difficult questions. And though you have free will, the answer is there if you're willing to accept it. Maybe right now I don't want to believe the answers and maybe I don't accept the answer, but the answer is there. It's just a personal problem if I don't accept it.

I enjoy the separation of sexes in *shul*. I have no problem with it, and neither does my wife. We have discussed this, because some modern Orthodox women say, "I don't agree with this." Especially if they are career women, in business, lawyers or doctors, then on *Shabbat*, they sit in the women's section. Some don't have the acceptance of their role in Judaism. It's not that women are unequal. They have a specific role. Cathy believes in that. She has no desire to take the man's part. And I enjoy it because I think that when you're with men and the women are separate, the level of prayer is better—not that men are perfect angels. It's a little more focused, and people are participating more. In a mixed congregation, when you're talking about what the kids did at breakfast, or talking about how hard it was to get to bed last night, then if someone else sits next to you, you get a whole conversation going through the whole line of seating instead of concentrating.

When we lived in Binghamton, I was the *"minyan*-maker." It was my job, as part of the men's club, to get the *minyan*. Mornings are no problem, it's the afternoon *minyans* that are hard to get. Now, in Atlanta, Cathy has to be at work, and since I am a house-husband and have to get the kids to school, I just don't have time to get over to the *minyan* and get back here in time to do everything. I still wake up, put on my *tefillin*, and say the morning prayers.

When my youngest son is in kindergarten, I'll go back to working outside the home. I usually work in the physical-education departments of alternative schools with behaviorally challenged children. I have experience in the public school system in New York. I can see the differences between that and the setting my children are in now. The big difference is that there is a real family feeling in our school. It sounds corny when you say the kids are all like a little family, but they really are. On a recent overnight field trip, the conversations I heard were amazing. They all know such details of each other's lives. And they have that rootedness in Judaism that is incorporated into their school day. I think my children are very self-confident. The feeling they have about going to school is, "I enjoy going to school. Everything is positive." I'm sorry to say it's not the way things are in public schools.

When we first contemplated sending the kids to Jewish day school, I thought maybe keeping them separate from other kids would not be good for them, but then I realized how important it is for Jewish kids. Ethnicity is not enough to carry you through. Kids need something more. They need to see what a Jewish lifestyle is, not just to *be* Jewish, but what it's like to *live* as a Jew. No matter what people say, no matter where you live, you'll always be a Jew, to other people, not just to yourself. So instead of just existing as a Jew, you are living as a Jew and developing a Jewish perspective and pride. Those are the things that carry you through.

I learn about Judaism vicariously through my kids. My biggest learning experience came when they were in the early primary grades. They would come home with their printouts on each holiday. They learn about being Jewish in a different way. So they learn, and I learn through them. It was a big source of pride when the kids said the *brakhot*. My oldest can say the Friday evening *Kiddush* in one breath.

There are some things, though, that you can study forever—like the Holocaust— and from the perspective of a convert, I don't think you can feel the hurt that must be inside the born Jew. I can't feel what blacks feel when they're insulted. I can feel *for* those people, but I can't feel what they feel. That is true also for the Holocaust. I can feel for that, and I can try to understand it, and I can be brought to tears by it. I can feel all the emotions and maybe I am feeling what any Jew would feel, but in my mind, because I wasn't born Jewish, I'm not sure it could ever be the same. What do my children feel because they are born Jews when they see on TV that someone hates you just because you are a Jew? There may be a line that divides us in that regard. It doesn't matter so much, but it's just there.

On the other hand, I'm not sure most Jews understand or even try to understand what a convert may have been through in order to become Jewish. What they may have to deal with in their own family. It's not like going into Woolworth's to the photo booth, put in a dollar and get three pictures of a conversion. Some born Jews may not understand what a big step it is, and what converts are willing to give up and take on to be Jewish, and I don't mean just Orthodoxy.

I've heard so many stories from converts about having a Jewish soul that I'm beginning to think there is something to that—like you are really not who you were born to be until you become a Jew. Even though I think I chose to convert for marriage, if I were to sit and be philosophical, I didn't choose to become Jewish. It was almost destiny. I was predisposed to become Jewish.

Nevertheless, I am a first-generation Jew. That is a different experience from those who have lived it all their lives, who come from observant parents and have genealogy that goes back forever. I have no basis to relate to that. There are always going to be people who, no matter what you do, will say, "Well, you weren't born Jewish, so you're not Jewish." That doesn't bother me because it's ignorance on their part.

In the Orthodox community, especially, once they know that your conversion was Orthodox, you're accepted right away. Not only that, they grab you and pull you into their lives because now that you're converted, they want you to get everything that you missed as a child. When we are invited to people's houses, even though they know I've been converted a long time, they want to offer me anything I may feel I've missed. "Is there something you want to learn? Is there something you've always wondered about?" A rabbi, especially, might say, "I don't want to be pushy, but can I call you? Do you want to study?" They always want to help. I've had so many invitations to study Torah that I think I could study with a different person every night. I feel their desire to include me, and I feel very included.

But it's all a matter of your commitment. It doesn't matter what kind of *shul* you join, if you go only once or twice a year and you're not involved in any aspect of *shul* activities except paying your dues, how Jewish are you going to feel? How can you expect those people to accept you? Really, you're not even accepting yourself.

In my kids' school I'm the soccer, basketball, and track and field coach, all on a volunteer basis. When we first moved here I wanted my children to be accepted and feel welcome right away. What better way than to become a coach, and that way the other kids who want to play sports will say, "Ah, this is the coach's son." It was a way to accelerate my kids' becoming a part of the community—and it worked!

I do not believe I could have the kind of family life I have now if it weren't for Judaism—not just because of who I married, but because of Judaism, itself. As I said, I get nicer every year, more relaxed. As the hair comes off your head, the more relaxed—or maybe humble—you get! But I wasn't always that way. Not when Cathy met me. I just can't imagine what she saw in me. She has a strong faith in God, and it gives her incredible patience. She is able to look at the big picture and the little things go like water off a duck's back. She looks at the big picture to the future.

One thing we've always shared is very similar beliefs in destiny—if it's meant to happen, it will happen. Why else would we be together? Why else would we go through what we have? It's all connected. Like when we joined the *shul*, you just walk in, and you have no idea what it's going to mean. But it's exactly what you're looking for. These things just happen. I always thank God that Cathy has such a good relationship with Him. I'm riding on her coattails.

35

In *Eretz Yisrael*

Marcia Chertok

When our friends and the founders of the East Bank Havurah, Myrna Lapides and Maurice Braverman, made *aliyah* to Israel a few years ago, they searched for just the right community in which to live and finally found it in the desert town of Yeroham. The community is unpretentious, even by Israeli standards, and often attracts hearty "pioneers" who want to feel close to the land and the heritage of our desert forebears.

At the time of this writing, Marcia Chertok and her family are about to celebrate their eighteenth year in Yeroham. The number eighteen corresponds to the numerical value of the Hebrew letters *het* and *yud*, which in combination spell *chai*, the Hebrew word meaning "life." For Marcia and her husband, Haim, moving their family to Israel marked the beginning of "life" for them as observant Jews finally able to live in Jewish community.

Their years together have seen Marcia and Haim living in an outpost in Japan where they created Jewish life practically from scratch, and then in the Central Valley of California where it was a 200-mile drive to the nearest kosher meat market. A trip to Israel and a chance meeting with a prophetic shopkeeper led the Chertoks to understand that their deepening commitment to an observant life along with their continuing concern with issues of social justice would achieve a more transcendent meaning in the Land of Israel.

I was born and grew up in Fresno, California, where I attended a Methodist church and was active in its youth group. Theology is not a Methodist strong point, but as a child I learned Bible stories, and I felt a positive connection to biblical Judaism. I remember my mother saying that the life Jesus lived was more important than the death he died. By the time I went to the University of California at Berkeley, I was doubting the divinity of Jesus. I think it fair to say that today no one of my then nuclear family is a believing Christian.

When I first met Haim back in August of 1961, I knew he was from New York City. He told me that his religion was important to him, but we didn't discuss it. Afterward I thought, "I hope he's Jewish and not Catholic." I may have ceased being a believing Christian, but the Protestant tenet that the man-God relationship is primary, without intermediary, was still basic, and the infallibility of the pope would have been impossible for me to accept. When, finally, we got around to the subject of religion he invited me to Rosh Hashanah services at Hillel House.

It was clear to us very early in our relationship that we would marry, and I had no difficulty accepting Judaism. I attended a conversion class in Oakland conducted by Reform and Reconstructionist rabbis. The classes were interesting though not intellectually challenging, and some parts, such as the discussion of Christianity, were very superficial. I would have been interested to hear a serious Jewish discussion of why Christianity is unacceptable, but they never rose above making light of the idea of a mother god, a father god, and a baby god.

I did some reading on my own and completed their process before Haim and I were married. Though the Reform movement purports to offer adherents a choice of what *mitzvot* to keep, they certainly didn't present potential converts with any alternatives. I was surprised that there was no mention of *mikveh*. I think I would have chosen that one. *Shabbat* was not explained, nor was traditional observance of holidays, to say nothing of *kashrut*.

Haim's family, not formally affiliated with any congregation, were very warm and accepting of me. My family accepted Haim, as well, though he didn't fit their image of the "ideal" son-in-law. My father and brother are building contractors. They work out of doors, and their recreation includes hunting, horses, and hiking. Haim shared none of these interests with them. He is an intellectual. There was, however, no shortage of goodwill. Both our families embody the American ideal of toleration and acceptance at its best.

My parents' families were both from the little town of Isabel, Kansas. As far as I know, everyone in Isabel was WASP. Before World War II my parents moved to Fresno, which, in addition to "unhyphenated" Americans, also included several minority communities: Armenians, Chicanos, and African-Americans as well as Japanese-Americans. (Needless to say, when I was growing up, some of these communities were not referred to in the terms that they prefer today.) On the block where I grew up were neighbors born in Italy and Norway, one family's grandfather was born in France, and, of course, there were lots of Midwesterners (from the dust-bowl era and other migrations). Everyone was accepted for what he was, even if at home we might smile about those "quaint" accents.

So, when faced with a Jewish potential son-in-law, my parents smiled at his quaint Bronx accent and overlooked the fact that his uncalloused hands lacked the skill to drive either a nail into a board or a car down the road. They welcomed him into the family. Haim learned to play cribbage, which he and my father still play every time they are together, less frequently now since we have moved to Israel. Haim has also learned to drive nails and cars.

Haim's parents accepted me, too, even though I have failed to push him to the heights of success in the law career they had envisioned for him. Nevertheless, they confided to us a few years ago that they could see that we make each other happy and have raised a family successfully. Most of their friends, on the other hand, can't take pride in the fact that their children are still happily married to their original spouses.

Before we married, I went with Haim to New York for two weeks to meet his family. I wanted to explain to them that I was taking classes and planned to convert. Haim's mother interrupted me: "We don't care what you believe, just cook Jewish." Learning to do that was fun! Later, when we lived in New York for a time, I worried that my interior-decorator mother-in-law would offer "encouragement" in the style of our decor, but she was wonderfully accepting of what we presented. Our personalities are very different; she is warm and exuberant, and I am much more reserved, but we have managed to get along fine.

At the time we married our level of observance was no cause for concern to either set of parents. We continued to eat with them, we just didn't eat pork. Our celebration of *Shabbat* consisted of lighting candles Friday night, sharing a leisurely meal, and attending services—nothing very confrontational about that.

Inherent in the course we have chosen for our lives is a distancing from our families. If, when we lived in New York City, we had not continued to eat with Haim's family, they would have been hurt. Now that he sees them only once a year or so in Florida, they willingly go to great lengths to satisfy his *kashrut* requirements. The advent of the microwave oven has also eased the problem, since it is easier to *kasher* than a stove. On a cross-country car trip a few years ago, we visited several of my aunts and uncles, who accepted our explanations of why we brought our own food. We were surprised to find bagels in Kansas!

Once we were married, Haim, who was in the U.S. Army at the time I met him, was stationed in Monterey, California. We enjoyed a three-and-a-half-month honeymoon. Monterey combines ideal weather, spectacular natural scenery (hills, ocean tide pools, beaches), and an interestingly preserved historical setting, the capital of "Spanish California." Haim's salary was $98 per month, and our rent was $75, but we could buy food cheaply at the PX (army post exchange) grocery store. I had time to catch up on reading and we enjoyed a steady stream of weekend guests, family, and friends who appreciated sharing our wonderful setting.

Then he drew a year-and-a-half "tour" in Japan, and I joined him there. We lived near a remote U.S. Army base on Hokkaido, the northernmost Japanese island, with a Jewish population of three couples and several single fellow soldiers.

Every other Friday night we met for services, and we celebrated holidays together. On our first Yom Kippur in Japan, we fasted and held services, and planned to break the fast with our little community. The other wives and I planned the menu and divided up the cooking. All afternoon of Yom Kippur I spent preparing blintzes (filled pancakes)—that's how little I knew about observance at the time. Everyone enjoyed the blintzes at the conclusion of the fast, and no one asked or cared *when* they had been prepared. Years later, I learned that cooking is a form of work that desecrates *Shabbat* and Yom Kippur.

Since Jewish cookbooks explained the details of *kashrut*, it was easier to learn about than other *mitzvot*. While still in Japan, we stopped eating shellfish at home and separated the cooking and eating of meat and dairy foods, and we bought two sets of dishes and pots and pans. There was, of course, no kosher meat available, although for Passover, *matzot* and kosher meat were flown in by the Jewish Welfare

Board.* I am sure that we avoided eating bread at Passover, but a true understanding of the concept of *hametz* would have to wait till we lived in a Jewish community, which for us meant till we came to Israel.

These first years together were a time of exploration and challenge. We continued to read everything we could get our hands on about anything Jewish. But in our remote outpost, whatever Jewish content our lives would have we had to fashion ourselves—and that was well before any *Jewish Catalog*! The base library was pretty well stocked with Jewish fiction, mainly Isaac Bashevis Singer, and some narratives and descriptions of the destruction of European Jewish life.

We ordered some books by mail. I was strongly affected by *Life Is with People* by Mark Zborowski and Elizabeth Herzog, a sociological study of *shtetl* life. What had been destroyed in the Holocaust seemed attractive to us—a way of life that didn't box religion up into one evening a week. When I studied with a rabbi years later for my Orthodox conversion, he could not believe that reading I. B. Singer could draw someone to Judaism. Singer, to him, was a detractor—and that is a tribute, of sorts, to Singer's ability to portray the ambivalence he felt. In *The Slave*, for example, Singer described Jewish life in Poland in some indefinite past time. Yes, the faith and integrity of those Jews is attractive, but at the same time Singer also describes faith closely associated with superstition. The Jews in the story are unable to accept Jacob's peasant wife (her conversion seemed an impossiblity to them), which would mean that she couldn't live with them or even be buried with them. Well, I, too, am sometimes troubled by the "exclusive" aspect in Judaism. Anyway, the rabbi I studied with focused on Singer's negative descriptions of Jewish life without seeing the tremendous affection the writer felt and conveyed for that lost world.

While we felt drawn to the possibility of living Jewish lives in a Jewish community, the first fourteen years of our marriage were spent in towns without Orthodox communities. Back in California after Japan, we continued to read, learn, and adjust our areas of observance at a pace that felt right—sometimes more, sometimes less. There were periods when what had made sense at one point in our lives failed to satisfy at another period. Sometimes we would "relax" our level of *Shabbat* and *kashrut* observance until we could refocus our lives and reorder our priorities. Until we made contact with the Orthodox community, our level of observance was whatever felt right. We had little idea if our observance approached Orthodoxy. Now we see that the spectrum of observance is a wide one; within Orthodoxy itself there are many degrees. But even before we learned about special ways of cooking before *Shabbat* and using a plata (a hot plate used to keep food warm), the spirit of *Shabbat* was there for our family.

---

*This organization is now known as the Jewish Community Centers Association of North America and among its many activities it provides support for Jewish military personnel through the Jewish Chaplaincy Council. It is the parent body of the Jewish Book Council, which awarded to Haim the National Jewish Book Award for *Stealing Home: Israel Bound and Rebound* in 1989.

For three years, we lived in Stockton, California, where we joined the Conservative congregation, and for years we were the youngest "new" members. More than one family "adopted" us, and everyone shared our excitement when we announced the news of my pregnancy. The older women, many of whom I hadn't met before, organized a baby shower–luncheon. After we had eaten and I had opened the gifts, someone took me home, and the rest of the ladies stayed to enjoy their regular card game!

Without a doubt, we felt warmly accepted by the community, but in that environment, there was little opportunity for learning. Most of the children and grandchildren of the congregation members, many of whom were from Eastern Europe, did not live in Stockton or at any rate did not attend that *shul*. Those our age whom we did meet seemed conventional and materialistic, happy to pursue goals represented by Madison Avenue, not people with whom we felt an affinity. We needed to find a way to connect our lives to some transcendent values, be they religious, artistic, or familial. One of our Stockton friends looked forward to the day when we would be "established," and actually commented, "You have nothing, how can you be so happy?" It was a measure of the gulf between us that many people we knew obviously didn't understand the verse from *Pirkei Avot*, "Who is rich? He who is satisfied with his lot."

Our next move was to New York City, where Haim was director of the Ben Salem Experimental College of Fordham University, a Jesuit institution. With some students, we organized a commune on City Island, a white, conservative enclave in New York City. We had a storefront where we made contact with local young people to expose them to values other than those represented by their parents. Besides antiwar activity, some of us worked at a special school in Harlem. Racial tensions were high, and there were riots in inner cities in several parts of the country.

Though we were the only Jews in the commune, the kitchen was kosher! And we were able to keep *Shabbat* as well. Perhaps because we shared a New Left social and political agenda, the Catholic Fordham students accepted and respected our religious preference. Within the Catholic community, there has been a tradition of combining social action and religious faith. On the other hand, the Jews we knew who were socially and politically active were not interested in combining politics with a religiously observant life, as we were doing.

After three years in New York City, we had had enough of city life and communal existence and were headed back to California for a more conventional family life. In 1969, college teaching positions were not as plentiful as they had been a few years before. We settled in Coalinga, a town of about 6,000 people with three Jewish families, counting us. We hadn't planned it that way, but that's where the job was. Also, we wanted to be near my family, and Fresno was not too far away.

As in Japan, we shared *seders* with the other families, because our house was kosher and everyone was content that we would host the *seder*. We took turns with another family driving our children the sixty miles to Fresno to attend Sunday school at the Conservative synagogue. As with the young Catholics in New York City, our religiously observant Protestant and Mormon neighbors in Coalinga could appreciate the motivations behind our practices, and they demonstrated their respect for our differences by being as pleased as could be to accommodate our preferences. Near the end of our seven years there, for example, our kids would bring their own cupcakes to friends' birthdays because we had stopped "eating out."

We continued to be involved in community and social action in Coalinga. I ran for and was elected to the school board. We organized a chapter of Amnesty International and worked to free prisoners in Malawi and Vietnam. I organized and led a Brownie troop. In short, we were happily involved in life in small town America.

The problem was that there was no Jewish context, something that had grown in importance to us with each passing year. Twice a year we would drive two hundred miles—either north to San Francisco or south to Los Angeles—to stock up on kosher meat. At Rosh Hashanah we would stay in Fresno or a community on the coast, but we didn't feel much at home in those places. Most importantly, our children were approaching junior-high age, and we realized that we were heading for trouble if we didn't make a change.

Over our *Shabbat* evening meal we could hear the cheers from the football stadium—such an important part of school social life in a small town. Even if Haim and I could manage our social lives to encompass non-Jewish friends and a *Shomer Shabbat* lifestyle, how would our children ever be able to do so?

These were questions we hadn't completely formulated when, in 1974, we had a chance to visit Israel as part of a Sister Cities tour. Fresno and the Israeli town of Afula were matched, and no one else from the Jewish community of Fresno was ready to accompany Fresno's mayor and his entourage, so we stepped up to take advantage of an eight-day tour of Israel. (Haim wrote of this trip in his book *Stealing Home: Israel Bound and Rebound*, published in 1988 by Fordham University Press.)

On the plane back to the States, Haim said to me, "We're coming back." I didn't realize he meant "for good." He related to me a particular definitive moment in, of all places, a hotel shop where he was looking for postcards. The only views were of Christian sights. He asked the shopkeeper if he had any cards of Jewish interest. When he brought them out, the man asked Haim, "Tell me, what are you doing in America that is so important that you couldn't do it here for Jews?" Maybe he asks that question of everyone who comes into his shop—it doesn't mattter. It was the right question, at the right time, to the right man. Haim couldn't answer, and so we spent the next two years preparing for *aliyah*.

The Jewish Agency representative put us in touch with a *garin aliyah* (settlement group). I flew to New York for a weekend convention they held, and it was good to talk to others who were planning the same move we were, and who knew more than we did what kinds of questions to ask.

These were modern Orthodox young families planning to start a *moshav shitufi* (semicommunal agricultural settlement) in the Negev. This sounded fine to us. And we felt we might define ourselves as "modern Orthodox"—we certainly didn't fit the mold of most Conservative families we knew. I discussed our history with the group and grew comfortable with them over *Shabbat*. They seemed happy enough with us, though they suggested that the children and I find an Orthodox rabbi and have Orthodox conversions *before* coming to Israel. "It will be much easier in America than in Israel," they said. Language alone made this true. We came to Israel not speaking Hebrew, and the *Bet Din* here doesn't speak English. And then religion here, like everything else, is politicized. The *Bet Din* here wields power, can be arbitrary, and doesn't often exhibit a very human face.

The Orthodox rabbi we saw in San Francisco wanted to know why we wanted an Orthodox conversion now, after all these years. We replied that we had gone about as far as we could go on our own down the road to religious observance. Now, we needed to be with others doing the same thing, and Israel was where we wanted to do it. He suggested that we read Rabbi Donin's book, *To Be a Jew*, and since we lived too far away to study with him, we could work with the semiretired Fresno rabbi who had been on the *Bet Din* in Manchester, England.

Our children, Jennifer and Ted, were ten and eight years old by then, young enough to be part of our decision and old enough to have to decide for themselves, too. On the matter of *Shabbat* observance, for example, Haim and I explained to the children that he and I would not use the telephone or watch TV or turn on or off electrical appliances, but we let them come to that decision for themselves. We felt that it would be counterproductive to tell them they could no longer watch Saturday cartoons. Instead of giving them "should not's," we tried to make *Shabbat* something they would like, too. We played games with them, we took walks to the library every week, and we spent the whole day together as a family. It was not long before they too joined us in *Shabbat* observance—and they remember making that decision themselves!

Our children had always considered themselves Jewish. So when we went through the *Bet Din*, *dam brit* (for my son), and *mikveh*, it was definitely a family observance, and it was neither the beginning nor the end of our journey. For myself, I felt somehow that I had more of an obligation to be observant now than if I had been born Jewish, and I took very seriously the promise to keep all the *mitzvot*.

Taharat hamishpahah was the *mitzvah* that we acquired at this time. As with most *mitzvot*, the prohibitions loom largest at first. The nearest *mikveh* was two hundred miles away, so I discussed with the San Francisco rabbi the possibility of using a nearby stream. Today, I'm not so sure it was kosher, but it was a temporary expedient. Once every month at dusk, Haim would drive with me half an hour west of town to a cattle ranch where a spring-fed stream ran. We would snake under the barbed wire fence through the pasture to a spot where the water was deep enough for immersion. Haim would watch me to see that the immersion was complete and "watch out" to make certain we were alone. It was a pleasant experience in summer, but the winter months were a test of faith and endurance. We used the stream for less than a year. Now, I can certainly appreciate the privacy and convenience of a real *mikveh*, not to mention the luxury of heated water! The significance this *mitzvah* has for me is that it, like *Shabbat*, is a periodic renewal, a bodily freshening, a way of bringing holiness to our sex lives that would otherwise be diminished.

In our town of Yeroham, a Coalinga-sized community, the population is primarily Moroccan. It is a distinct advantage to share the *mikveh* with these women. These immigrants and children of immigrants, from a society that was more observant than our modern American Jewish society, are reminiscent of the generation of immigrants from Eastern Europe—Haim's family and our Stockton friends. Most American Jews probably abandoned the *mikveh* before they junked *Shabbat* or *kashrut*. If our progress toward observance was a reverse journey along the path by which most *mitzvot* had previously been abandoned in America, then *mikveh*, *Shabbat*, and *kashrut* were lost in that order. Except for the largest cities, go find a *mikveh* west of New York. Even though according to *halakhah* it is forbidden to live in a town without a *mikveh* and communities are required to build a *mikveh* before a synagogue, it is rarely done these days.

But these "traditional" Moroccan neighbors of mine, who don't even define themselves as "religious"* continue to come to the *mikveh*. They have such a celebration for a bride's first immersion. The women escort her in a procession, singing and playing a big deep-toned drum. While the bride is preparing herself, there is more singing and dancing—more like belly dancing than anything else—and when she rejoins the women, there are refreshments and ululation. (The first time I heard this sound it reminded me of the sound track of an old-time Western movie with the Indians on the warpath. It is not inherently joyous, but over the years of hearing it at weddings and in the *bet knesset* at a boy's first *aliyah l'Torah* or at any other happy occasion, it has come to signify the sound of joy.) Later that evening there is a feast and party for family and friends. Of course, if I'm in a hurry this noisy throng can be annoying, but usually I enjoy the throbbing drums and happy crowd. Neither the celebrants nor the bride herself exhibit self-consciousness—no shame, no repression, no need for liberation—just joy in marking this feminine Jewish milestone.

When we left California for Israel in 1976, we thought we were headed to found a new settlement in the Negev. But upon our arrival, we learned our settlement group had accepted a site in the Gaza Strip. We knew that the Gaza Strip was already one of the most densely populated areas in Israel, with insufficient water for the needs of the then-present population. To us it was unconscionable to found an agricultural enterprise there, to use even more water, especially since Gaza is not considered part of the land of Israel from biblical to modern times. It was not to live there that we left Golden California. Politics hits hard and fast in this country.

It took us about a month to decide to start our own group around the basic tenets of religious observance, ecological awareness, social justice, and peace. Within a year, we had a group and a "temporary" place to live together in Yeroham, a development town south of Beerheva. The temporary has become permanent, and here we remain with a core of like-minded folk, still working on the problems that have, in truth, always occupied us.

---

*Of the three *mitzvot* mentioned above, *Shabbat* is the first to go. Those who aren't *Shomer Shabbat* still use the *mikveh* and observe *kashrut*.

Living in Israel, I can now understand more fully the meaning of the book title *Life Is with People*. Our son Shai was born at the end of our first year here. While in America, we had had our two children and stopped under the influence of the zero-population-growth imperative. We had taken in foster children and were planning to adopt more. Pnina, the mother of our first host family in Israel, told us confidentially, "You must have more children; two are not enough here." I have never seen so many pregnant women before. It didn't take much persuasion. After Shai arrived, everytime I'd get on a bus with my baby, some well-meaning "busybody" would tell me, "Hold him this way, not that. He could be hurt if the bus stops quickly," or "Where's his hat? It's so sunny today." So much unsolicited advice was hard to bear.

A few years later, when Shai was in about the second grade, we were supposed to go to Beersheva for a dental appointment. Shai wasn't outside the school where we'd agreed to meet. Some of his classmates whom I didn't recognize approached me: "You're Shai's mother. He went home on the school bus." These children had already learned to be aware of people and to offer assistance, even when not asked. Second graders in America, on the other hand, are trained not to talk to strangers.

Last year just before Purim, I was seated on a bus in Jerusalem and I noticed a child with a Purim noisemaker in his mouth. I said to him, "Take it out of your mouth," and to his mother, "He could be hurt if the bus lurches." I have become the old lady with the American accent admonishing strangers to put their candy wrappers in the trash bin instead of dropping them on the sidewalk. Looking as if no one had ever suggested it to them before, most comply willingly.

Over the years, our involvement in social-justice issues has framed many of the decisions we have made, and coming to Yeroham, in particular, was part of that process for us. Where one lives does make a statement about one's values. Yeroham is viewed in the Israeli media as being in the middle of nowhere, populated by the dregs of society. It is true that Yeroham has a high percentage of unemployment and families on welfare. Many Israelis serve time in the army in or near Yeroham; so these are the associations that "Yeroham" brings. On the other hand, because Yeroham has a high percentage of *olim*, people were more patient with my beginning Hebrew. The population is an interesting mix of Moroccans, Indians, native Israelis, and, more recently, Russians. Few skilled jobs are available, so many young people leave after the army and university.

Living here has been a challenge. We had concerns about education for our children, which is a problem in most parts of the country. Our two sons each spent at least a year learning at home when we couldn't find the right schools for them. We have otherwise not regretted our decision to live in Yeroham.

But what does social justice mean to us *in* Israel?

We have taken a stand for Bedouin rights when, for example, their water source was threatened, their cemetery was violated, or their flocks were confiscated.

Women's rights is another area of concern. Our efforts have focused on the social and religious spheres of that issue. We have explored ways within *halakhah* to expand women's participation. The *bet knesset* we founded is the only one in town that has women as voting members, or has women serving as board members. Our Rosh Hodesh group dates back to 1978. We began as a monthly discussion-learning group. One of our members, Leah Shakdiel, became the first woman member of a local religious council because she took the issue to the Supreme Court. Local religious councils administer government moneys for the burial society, the *mikveh*, and other religious services. In 1984, we began what has become an annual event, a women's reading of the *Megillat Esther* at Purim. Our weekly Talmud *shiur* (talmud class), now in its fourth year, began as a mixed class but has become a women's group, though occasionally a man will join us.

Of primary importance is that time here in Israel is Jewish time. Sunday is the first day of the workweek. January 1 is a workday like any other, as is December 25. We are in the process of shifting from a six-day workweek to five days. The weekend will consist of Friday and Saturday. On *Shabbat* nearly all businesses close from Friday afternoon until Saturday night or Sunday morning. Public transportation ceases. *Shabbat* feels different from the rest of the week. Most families, even secular ones, enjoy a special meal at home or with friends on Friday night.

Before Pesah, the entire *country* goes on a cleaning spree. Grocery stores put away all breads and *hametz* and sell only *matzot* and Pesah foods. No holiday here is as commercialized as Christmas in America. That is probably what I miss least. There is no shortage of holidays. The calendar is studded with them from Rosh Hashanah to Tisha B'Av. Of course, they are not all days off work and school, but they are observed from tree planting and fruit eating at Tu B'Shvat (New Year for Trees) to special music on the popular music stations and the siren calling the country to pause and remember on Memorial Day for fallen soldiers, the day before Independence Day.

Here in Yeroham there is a *shuk*, a produce market, on Tuesdays in the parking lot near the town center. I buy more fresh produce here and fewer canned or frozen foods than I did in America. There are also tents selling clothing and stalls with video-cassettes, housewares, toys, and so on. I always stop to chat with friends I meet there and come home with some bits of news. For daily supplies such as bread and milk I use the corner grocery, of which there are many in town in addition to the two supermarkets. Hot *pitot* (plural for *pitah*), baguettes, and croissants are delivered daily from the local bakery to the stores, and from Angel's Bakery in Jerusalem, crusty white or rye loaves without wrappers, which seemed unhygenic at first, but it tastes much better!

Of our four parents, my mother has really joined in our lives. She wants to understand what we are doing. She has come to appreciate *Shabbat* when she is with us, and when the children were small she was careful not to break *Shabbat* in their presence. For our visits with her in the States, she brings out the kosher dishes. She comes to Israel at least every other year for a month at a time, and she often chooses to join us in Pesah preparations and celebration. She has also challenged us sometimes. She has become a Unitarian-Universalist, and in their intellectual and social-justice traditions she poses some difficult questions. "What is this 'Chosen People' business? Is it racism? A way to divide people?" And she isn't satisfied with pat answers.

Even though we live on nearly opposite sides of the earth, Mother and I are still very close. She says that as long as each of us knows that the other is happy and doing what she wants to do, it is possible to live so far from each other. I know how she thinks and feels about almost everything. Sometimes I feel that I am her extension. We haven't quarreled in over thirty years—I simply can't imagine it. Now, I have the wonderful feeling of being the one in the middle because I am able to enjoy the same closeness with my daughter Jennifer, who, luckily for me, lives a five-minute walk away. She and I have the added pleasure of sharing even more holidays together as well as the women's activities in our community.

Raising a second pair of children in Israel has been a challenge. As opposed to our previous American experience, I felt here that it was an achievement just to find time with my toddlers to read them a story or cut out pictures for a scrapbook. There were always neighbors or neighbors' children dropping in to chat or play. This is probably a function of larger family size and smaller houses and yards. Israelis don't see time spent alone as positive. When our sons were each learning at home for a while, no one of our acquaintances worried that they might be missing out scholastically. The concern was that their social development would suffer. The peer group is seen as more essential than developing inner resources. I was recently pleased to hear my daughter Miriam confirm that in dressing modestly it is more important to do what you think is right than to worry about what people might say.

I feel I'm reaping the benefit of living in a family-oriented society. I see many fewer instances here than in America of adult children and parents who can't tolerate each other. During our first year in the country Jennifer and Ted learned, in the state religious-school system, about honoring their parents. They didn't go as far as standing each time we entered the room, but they stopped sitting in our chairs. They would not wake us up unless we had asked them to, and they became more respectful. The Israeli institution of boarding high schools also short-circuits the rebellious teenager syndrome. Miriam left home last fall to attend the same school Jennifer had gone to; so Haim and I have entered a new phase of life.

Our two sons have displayed their individuality in different ways. Ted, the older, went through a *hesder* program that combines army service with *yeshivah* study. He continued a few years afterward at the *yeshivah*, and today is married, the father of two sons, and teaching religious subjects in a high school in Beersheva. He and Ilana, his wife, recently bought a house in Yeroham and will soon be living nearby.

Our younger son, Shai, studies in a boarding school near us that specializes in environmental studies. Shortly after becoming *bar mitzvah* he decided that he no longer wanted to be "religious." At that time every conversation with him ended on the subject of how the religious political parties are corrupt. We don't disagree with him, but our perspective, of course, is different. The arrangement we worked out with him is that he goes to the nonreligious school of his choice but when he is at home he respects our religious sensibilities. Besides the regular course of studies, each student at this school chooses at least two extracurricular activities. For two years now, Shai has been a part of a group learning about Jewish mysticism. Our table conversation when he is at home—about every other weekend—is now more interesting than acrimonious.

I am sometimes troubled by the question posed by both my mother and I. B. Singer concerning the exclusivist aspect of the universal-exclusive tension that Judaism embodies. God is Lord of the world, Creator of the universe—how then to understand the exclusive relationship with the Jewish people? The "with-God-on-our-side" mentality of the nationalist religious element here in Israel is particularly hard to abide—though our children have managed to hold their own at school, where our position is a distinct minority. (Remember, we started a *garin* with a "peace with the Arabs and between Jews" ideal and several families joined us in Yeroham.) If Judaism is a religion for the Jewish people only, what is it that "the nations" are supposed to gain from our being "a light unto them"? I know that the way of life that strives to embody *Torat Israel* (the Torah of Israel) with *Am Israel* (the people of Israel) in *Eretz Yisrael* (the land of Israel) is the best for me. *Aliyah* has, in my case, taken the Jew out of America, but it's hard to take the American out of the Jew—I cannot *not* believe that all people are created equal, and a religion that emphasizes the special relationship of God with one particular tribe of humanity remains a paradox.

We are planning, soon, the celebration of the *hai* (eighteenth) year of our *aliyah*. We have felt for years now that, finally, we are in the right place. When we came, we didn't burn our bridges. We came on a sabbatical year (though the salary Haim got from the Coalinga college we put into a special fund that he could then return easily if we decided to stay in Israel), so he had a job to go back to. We didn't sell our house until we'd been in Israel over a year. When we came we told ourselves that if any of the four of us were unhappy and couldn't take it, we would return. By the end of the first year we knew we'd be staying. Haim had a couple of hard years teaching English in the local junior and senior high schools. During Rosh Hashanah in 1982, Haim was with the army in Beirut. He was on one of the last planes out. Trying to clarify to himself what he was doing there after years of anti–Vietnam War activity in America led him to his writing career. This is his "*aliyah* bonus." He still teaches part-time at Ben-Gurion University. I, too, work part-time for the university, as an English secretary for the Environmental Microbiology Unit at the Desert Research Institute at Sde Boker. We deal primarily with recycling water, and besides enjoying the work, I feel that it is significant both for Israel and for the world.

I think that one of the wonderful elements of our story is that Haim and I, together, have come this long and circuitous route to Israel and to a life of religious observance. Maybe it has worked because it was a leisurely trip, and we enjoy traveling!

36

From Seminary to *Shul*

"Matthew"

When faced with a life-threatening crisis, Matthew experienced, as many people do, a reexamination of his life. He realized that there was much that was not soul-satisfying, and he sought to correct that by leaving a high-powered job to work for the homeless. He applied to the Episcopal seminary and continued his religious studies.

But as he pursued a deepening involvement in Christianity, he found his way blocked by unbelief. At the same time, a work obligation provided him a chance encounter with a Jewish religious service, which he found strangely comforting and appealing. When he approached his mother, a devout Episcopalian, with the news of his interest in converting to Judaism, he faced a new crisis in her response.

M y mother was raised as an Episcopalian, and that was the religion in which I grew up. During my adolescent years, one of the only positive influences was my involvement with the church. I had a pretty close relationship with a priest who was a stable figure in my life.

My father was a businessman. His god was money. He was Greek, and technically, I guess, he was Greek Orthodox. He'd go to church maybe once a year with Mother. The only time I remotely saw him connect with anything in a spiritual sense, it was almost of mythic proportion. During a terrible storm in the middle of the winter, my father had taken a group of us fishing in the middle of the bay in a forty-six-foot boat. My father, who had been around water all his life, was absolutely gleeful, but the others on the boat, most of them grown men, were petrified. "Matt, we're going to die!" I can just see my father screaming out, "God, here's your chance!" A dare—that was about all I knew of religion from my father. That's the way he was at times.

My sister and I agree that, growing up, we had no childhood, and she eloped at age seventeen. I was lucky enough to go to college and then went on a merry-go-round of hard work and hard hours as an investment banker. That was not my choice, but that was what my father said I would be. My preference would have been to do graduate work in international relations. My father said, "No, you're going to work for a banking and investment firm. It's all been arranged. You are also going to get a scholarship to go to law school—that's part of the deal—and I really think, in the end, that's what you want to do. And here's your new car." The whole works.

So I went to law school and somewhere in the middle of all of that I got married. It lasted about two years. I was doing very well in the banking world, but I was miserable. I really didn't even know I had a problem, much less know how to solve the problem or where to go for help. I was also in the business world, where a few martinis at lunch were not frowned upon and a lot of liquor after work was just part of the routine.

Then, in the early 1980s, I was mugged on my front lawn, and I spent about ten minutes with one gun at the back of my head and one gun literally sitting on my lip. The fellow who had the gun on the front of my face was shaking so bad because he needed a fix that he could have blown my head off and never even known he had done it. That event jarred me, and some reality came rushing in.

If I lived through this—and it was iffy at that point—something was going to change in a major way, I said to myself. There was also a part of me that knew my lifestyle was completely irresponsible.

Right after that episode, I got a good case of religion, and I went to see the Episcopal bishop. I said, "Do you know what I really want to do? I want to go study theology." My father was out of the picture; he was very ill, and he was no longer controlling my life. My mother thought it was wonderful—her son was going to be a priest! So I left banking; I took a year off.

I had begun to become aware of how bad the situation for homeless and hungry people was becoming, but it really hit me one day when I was walking in the city with one of the clergy of the Episcopal diocese, and both of us stepped over a street person who was prone on the sidewalk. I turned to him and said, "You know, this is getting out of hand. It's an outrage. And another thing that is outrageous is the Roman Catholic Church does a whole lot for these people and the Episcopal Church doesn't do a damn thing. You're such a highly respected clergy person, why don't you do something about it?" That's how the Episcopal bishop found out about *me*.

And the bishop said, "Matthew, we need someone to put together a nonprofit corporation for us—to do shelters and soup kitchens. Are you by any chance crazy enough to do this?" And I said I'd love to do that! In that year, I founded one of the big soup kitchens downtown. It was a good time for me.

Everything was going great guns, but then one of the major churches in the southwest part of the city where the programs were run was taken over by radical charismatics—they are like the fundamentalists of the Episcopal Church. The social-service programs that I was running were basically just tenants at this parish and the charismatics came to me and said, "Matthew, we need to be more involved in your programs." And I said, "I'm not sure. I'm here to feed people and give them shelter, and you have a completely different agenda." They wanted to convert them or "heal" them or whatever. And I said, "No."

The next six months were absolute living hell. When you say no to these radical fundamentalists, you suddenly become an evil person. It became a very, very nasty battle, and the Episcopal Church doesn't do a good job of handling conflict. The end result was that I left, and I had an absolutely miserable feeling about anything to do with the church. Which on one level was very good for me, but on another level was very traumatic. "Linus" was losing his security blanket.

While I was in the last stages of my involvement in the feeding and shelter programs, a rabbi was looking for ways to involve his congregation's Outreach Project in programs in the inner city. So I was invited to make a presentation at their *Shabbat* services. This was strictly work, I thought, but when I got there, I loved it. The synagogue felt like a safe haven for me. It was religious, but it didn't have any of the baggage of the church. I just found it beautiful. A lot of it was just an emotional response, but I recognized that it was meaningful to me.

During this period, I had been studying, taking courses, and was not sure exactly when I would start seminary. One of the things that was a real crisis for me was the technical part of Christian theology called "Christology," which is the whole study of Jesus as the Messiah. Although I always believed in God, the creation, the order of the universe—those were more than just random events—I began to have doubts about the divinity of Jesus.

The first time I had this experience was at a seminar I was attending organized by Michael Ramsey, who was then the archbishop of Canterbury. In a liberal seminary, part of the academic study of theology involves the debunking of a lot of childhood "myths" about religion. The professor in the lecture I attended was raising all of the difficulties in Christian scripture, really tearing Christianity apart, in an analytical sense. A fellow sitting next to me had a pretty cut-and-dried notion of what scripture was all about. He completely came apart. He started screaming, ran out of the classroom, and said, "I won't listen to this anymore!"

For me, though, the bottom line was, "No, I don't believe this. No matter what. I don't believe in the divinity of Jesus."

That conclusion raised an interesting problem. I had left a good job in a bank in order to commit myself to working for the Church and eventually attend seminary, and all of a sudden, I determined, "If the truth be known, Matthew, you don't believe any of this." Not a nice place to be.

So after my experience at the synagogue, I talked to my current wife, who said, "You know, maybe you'd better try to sort all of this out. Something is going on." At that time she was working with a priest who was one of the leaders nationwide in Jewish–Christian dialogue. He referred me to another Episcopal priest, whom I had known from years before, and we talked. He said, "Matthew, maybe you shouldn't be talking to me. I know a rabbi you might like to talk to. Why don't we set up a meeting with him."

I was fortunate that the men in the church with whom I was discussing this issue were among the small minority of people who have been sensitized to the issue of Jewish–Christian relations and other religious experience. They don't confine their pastoral skills to keeping someone in the pew on Sunday morning. Liberal, academic Christian theologians don't have a lot of trouble with one person's embrace of Judaism. They were also aware that I was a serious student of theology, so they knew my struggles were not a mere whim.

Shortly thereafter, I happened to be visiting with my mother, telling her about these forays into Judaism. She became very distracted, which was distressing to me. I didn't have an easy relationship with either of my parents, but I sat there thinking, "What in the hell could be so controversial?" I could see my mother's anxiety level go up as I continued talking. She put her head down on the dining room table and started crying. I thought, "Yes, I have upset her over the years, but what is it about *this* discussion?" So I said, "Mother, what is going on?" She said, "Matthew, you know, there are a couple things in our family that you don't know about." And I thought, "Oh, brother, here we go again. Have I heard this story before!"

To make a long story short, at the age of thirty-seven I learned that my mother was the *foster* child of the prominent "Smith" family—all of whom I had considered my relatives while growing up. My mother was not "Elizabeth Mae Smith"; her maiden name was, in fact, "Isobel Rose," the daughter of a Jewish woman who died shortly after she had left her alcoholic husband and moved to this city with seven children. The children were placed in the hands of a secular social services agency.

When I told the rabbi this story he was quite amazed. After I had been studying with him for a while and taken the Introduction to Judaism course, and I was ready for the *mikveh*, the rabbi said, "First we have to figure out exactly what we're doing here. Matthew, you may not need to convert. You need to go and talk to your mother and see if you could produce some sort of family history." But it has been difficult to learn much more.

At first after she told me, I was angry with my mother. I felt my sister and I deserved to have known about this a long time ago. But I also appreciate the fact that she couldn't quite come to grips with it. She was embarrassed and torn by the fact that the Smith family had been good to her, but she was also upset because clearly she was "different."

On the other hand, Mother wasn't upset with me. Maybe she realized that this was something that she would eventually have had to deal with one way or another. But how strange it should come about this way. That just intrigued me more.

My mother has had help from a good friend in the church in feeling at ease with my decision to convert and to a certain degree with her acknowledgment of her own background. In fact, she recently called me and said, "Matthew, I was looking at a catalogue and there was this Hanukkah 'thing' for children, and I promised you I was going to send away for it, but I forgot. I apologize. I assume you will be lighting your Hanukkah candles beginning next week." She came to our house for the *seder* and was fascinated, and a few years ago I would have said that was impossible, since it would have really been a confrontation for her both with her ancestry and the fact that her son had left the church.

When it finally came time for me to decide about going to the *mikveh*, the rabbi asked me if I had any problems with going through with it, since in a legal sense I probably was Jewish already. But I needed that ceremonial as the dividing point. I'm a water person. If there has to be some sort of ritual entry point, there's no better point for me than water. So the water of the *mikveh* is the right image for me. It was very meaningful. Just a sense of coming home. A wonderful sense of peace.

The *Bet Din* beforehand was a disappointment. It was rushed and not very challenging. There were no serious questions, though I was certainly expecting there would be. Part of the problem is liberal Judaism's struggle over the *Bet Din*, and the other is just the time constraints of rabbis who have big congregations to attend to. From my experience on the institutional side of religion I know that can be pretty overwhelming. So I more or less shrugged it off and said, "That's the way it has to be. If you wanted it some other way you could have gone to a smaller *shul*." Or I could have sat down with the rabbi and discussed with him what I wanted, but I didn't. Happily for me, the *mikveh* was extraordinary.

Making the adjustments to my new status is a challenge. In the Episcopal Church I had a mastery of liturgical function. It was a natural; I didn't struggle with it all. Now, in *shul*, I sit back in a corner. I'm always invited to get more involved, but I'm still in process, and it's very unsettling for me because I'm not comfortable there. I'm still struggling with learning Hebrew. Just saying a *brakhah* in Hebrew in front of that whole crowd—"Oh, God! I can't do this." All my insecurities come to the fore.

Another thing that has been difficult for me to comprehend is my experience in *shul*. When I went to church, it was to worship, to have a religious experience. I would come to participate in the liturgy, not just be a casual observer. There was some idea that this is holy business and exploration of the divine. I carried this mind-set with me to *shul* and had begun to learn to appreciate the whole experience of *Shabbat* when one day right in the middle of the *Amidah* a fellow next to me pulls out his wallet, and takes out two Orioles tickets and hands them to the individual next to him. That fellow pulls out his wallet and pays him for them. I was so upset. From my understanding of Judaism, that is a clear desecration of the *Sabbath*—to interrupt the *Amidah* to transact business involving money! Doing the wrong thing at the worst time. And my rabbi said, "Matthew, first of all you're assuming that they know better. And they very well might not."

I've felt that synagogue services have become more of a community thing, a communal acknowledgment of Jewishness, than a religious experience. The man with the tickets had no problem with that. He was among friends. His real god is a baseball game and that's his liturgy—transacting business. The recipient was ecstatic that his friend was able to get him tickets.

It's been difficult for me that people don't take the religion more seriously. I have to put this in perspective because I am someone who has been intensely interested in theology. I need to find a serious adult education program in the Jewish community outside of the Orthodox community. I know a wonderful Orthodox rabbi, and I have been to a number of his lectures and talked with him extensively, but I have some problems with his idea of where the Torah came from and how we received it. It's strictly different from where I am.

Basically, I have a traditional, liberal interpretation of a holy people writing down their experience of God that went through a process of being handed down generation to generation and was eventually "canonized" and accepted as scripture. I do believe that the Torah is completely God-given, but through humans. The critical process of examining scripture makes total sense to me. I like the idea a people struggling for an understanding of the divine and the meaning of it all. The Torah is some of the deepest work of humans struggling with the whole issue of existence and the meaning of life.

There had been another issue, too, prior to my going to the *mikveh*. I am married to a woman who is Christian, and in one of the conversations the rabbi had said to me, "Matthew, I'm really not very comfortable about making a mixed marriage here." He and another rabbi from the *Bet Din* really struggled with that. Obviously, it resulted in the affirmative, although I'm not sure how they arrived at the decision. By this time, I was involved in the Jewish community, and it would have been nothing but harmful and hurtful not to have decided this way.

It has been a challenge to deal with the different practices in our home, especially because we have a child. My son, who is nearly school age, sees me *daven* every morning. My wife and I have not discussed very much about how he will be raised. She has concerns about how it would be received in her family if he were to be raised as a Jew. I believe that being exposed to both religions is fine, but it's very difficult to try to merge the two religious systems. The child becomes very confused. I talked with Daniel Mark Epstein about it.* I had read his book *Star of Wonder*, and I was asking him how he feels now, as an adult, about his mixed heritage, and he seems to have a craving for more and more Jewish life. It's not just balancing it all, but just living with the reality of the pull of the Christian side of his family.

A few years ago, for example, I said to my family, "Please, without causing a whole lot of ruckus—I'm not going to stand in the way of your Christmas celebration—but the family has to realize it is not my Christmas anymore. You don't have to agree with it, but at least respect my feelings. I appreciate that it's difficult, but you have to appreciate where I am." But even my mother, as sensitive as she has been, said, "Matthew, I'm going to give you a Christmas gift; I've always given you a Christmas gift." I said, "Mother, you of all people, don't have to give me a Christmas gift. That's my Christmas gift—don't give me anything." That has been a struggle for her. So, I now know what the "December dilemma" is.

I'm not sure you can balance it all. You can adapt to the tension. It can be a constructive tension or a destructive tension. On top of that, if you are struggling with this issue, there is a limited community that could offer support. It's not as though you can walk over to the Jewish neighborhood and talk to the Orthodox about this, and I've tried.

Dealing with friends and others in the non-Jewish community has had its own unique challenges. I find that most people just don't want to address the issue of my

---

*Mr. Epstein is a poet and author who has written of his experiences growing up with a Christian mother and Jewish father. Mr. Epstein converted to Judaism so that he might celebrate his *bar mitzvah* at age thirteen.

conversion. One time I had a close friend, my old college roommate, over for dinner, and he looked around and said, "Matthew, there's an awful lot of Jewish things in this house." "Yes," I said, "and one of them is me." And he said, "We're not going to talk about this tonight."

I am very involved in the black community, and recently at a meeting somebody made a terribly anti-Semitic remark. Not even thinking I was rude, I objected, and it was not well received. To be thrown into the middle of the increasingly tender ground of black-Jewish relations when you're still trying to figure out how to get comfortable in a big *shul*! When I think of how difficult some of these issues are I reflect back on some of the people that were involved in the Intro to Judaism course. For many of them, though perhaps not all, the pursuit of Judaism wasn't a spiritual journey; it was a romantic journey. I have seen how incredibly this change can impact your life; it takes all the strength of your conviction to see you through, sometimes.

So I am aware of the whole ongoing tension about what embracing Judaism means to one's life, personally and professionally. Communication is a central concern. I grew up in a family where there was silence on hot topics. My old tendency is to just sit on controversy and see what happens. There are mornings when I feel like saying, "Let's just be done with this. I'll go back. It really would be easier." But then I run into this wall that says, "You don't believe in Christianity; it's a religion based on faith." And I know this was a spiritual journey, like it or not, sometimes kicking and screaming along the way.

37

Comé con Gana

Marcy Franco

Most Jews do not realize what an impact their lives, especially their communal lives, have on non-Jews. Marcy grew up surrounded by Jewish people, attending their *simhahs*, sharing friendships, but her shyness prevented her from asking if she might attend synagogue with them. Perhaps it is not such a light thing to ask.

Eventually, Marcy did make the inquiries that led her to study for conversion, and shortly thereafter she met Lenny, her husband. The process of her conversion and inclusion in the Jewish community has not been without rough spots, but the balm for any of the slights she may have suffered has been the conviction that she was meant to be Jewish, that her soul has been Jewish— perhaps through the ages.

I grew up in Atlanta and when my parents moved here, they just happened to buy a house on the very edge of one of the oldest Jewish neighborhoods. In school, the majority was Jewish, mostly Sephardic. When I got older and found out that Jews were a minority, it was a surprise to me. So, I was surrounded by Judaism all my life, yet excluded from it, although as a young teen, I was invited to *bar mitzvahs*. As a matter of fact, I met my husband at a *bar mitzvah* when we were thirteen.

My first job was with a dentist who was Jewish and my first exposure to any kind of prejudice against Jews was when he was trying to join a country club, and they wouldn't accept him because he was Jewish. I was eighteen or nineteen.

I guess I was in my early twenties, when I finally decided that I would look into conversion. I called the Reform temple for information, and the reply was "Classes start next Thursday, and it's $120." That wasn't really what I wanted to hear. I wanted something a little more embracing than a date and a price. I'm a very shy person, and I didn't know that it was okay to say, "I'd like to go to synagogue with you sometime or I'd like to learn." I just didn't know how to find out more about it. A few years later, I was still living in very Jewish surroundings, all of my friends were Jewish, and everyone I dated was too, and I decided to try again.

"Comé con Gana" (Ladino for "Eat with an Appetite") is the subtitle of *The Sephardic Cooks*, a cookbook compiled and published by the Or VeShalom Synagogue in Atlanta, Georgia. Marcy is one of the editors of the latest edition of the cookbook.

My family's religion when I was growing up was Methodist. My father was a Methodist minister years ago, and my uncle still is. Surprisingly, though, anytime I had a religious question, I didn't get a satisfying answer. It was very frustrating to me.

When I finally got in touch with the Hillel at Emory University, I liked the fact that the rabbi there gave me a lot of information, besides suggesting I subscribe to the *Jewish Times*. He suggested I integrate myself a little more into Jewish life. I didn't even know if it was okay to go into a synagogue if I wasn't Jewish. I started going to services with friends, and in the meantime I met Lenny.

We knew a lot of the same people, but our circles had not crossed again since we first met at the *bar mitzvah* fifteen years earlier. We were living around the corner from each other. I told him that I was interested in Judaism and had just started to take classes. We started synagogue-shopping. Every Friday night we'd go to a different synagogue. We found a rabbi that we really liked here in Atlanta, and we both took classes. Lenny's been very supportive and helpful to me in my Jewish education, as well as when I later went to nursing school. He likes people to reach their potential.

Lenny is what I would call above-average religiously observant for this area. He grew up in a Sephardic family, and when we decided to join a synagogue it was the Sephardic congregation, Or VeShalom (Light and Peace). Rabbi Ichay had some concerns about my conversion, which I had begun with Rabbi Peterman from another synagogue. He wondered why Lenny hadn't brought me to Or VeShalom in the first place. But I had started the process before I met Lenny.

Lenny and I had been dating for about a year and a half and we wanted to be married. But Rabbi Ichay would not marry us because the conversion I was about to undergo was not Orthodox. At first we thought we would just go ahead and get married by someone else and then later I would go through another conversion to satisfy the requirements for our synagogue. But I did not feel comfortable with that, and finally, I went to Rabbi Peterman. He sent me to talk with several rabbis and an Orthodox *Bet Din* was convened to preside over my conversion.

Although everything worked out, just recalling that process brings back what an emotional time that was for me. On the morning before I knew that the rabbis were in accordance, I kept thinking, "What else can I do? What am I missing?" Two hours later the rabbi called and said, "You're there!" Everything finally was fitting into place, I really wasn't missing anything, I was "there." That was and still is a very moving moment for me. As a result, we have a nice life that has a really good core of Judaism.

My father was extremely supportive and very happy that I was getting back to religion. He specifically thanked Lenny for his influence in my return to a spiritual life. "You're bringing my daughter back to God" is what he said.

For my mother it has been more of a challenge. Since her core religion is based around Jesus Christ, she just naturally assumes that as her child I found it okay also. But it never was quite okay with me. Belief in the divinity of Jesus never quite seemed right. It seemed very contradictory when the Ten Commandments say "You should have no other gods before me." Well, what is this person doing in the middle, then? That was always a big question to me, and it was never explained to me to a point that made me a believer.

Although my mother has had a hard time, she respects what I'm doing, too. For the first few years, I would always invite my parents for *seders* or other holidays. Daddy enjoyed it—the stories, the religion—but for Mother, it just wasn't her cup of tea. So I don't make it a point to invite them anymore. When my kids visit them, she doesn't serve them food that they can't eat or doesn't mix meat and milk when we're there. She doesn't try to sneak around behind my back and feed the kids something that she knows I wouldn't like. Now, of course, they are old enough to say what they can and can't eat. On the Christian holidays, we still get together as a family. But it never really was a religious time in the house. It was like a family get-together and that's still what it is.

My parents are able to see that we have now been doing this for so many years. They see that it's working for me and that Lenny and I are happy and the kids are happy—what more can you want for your children? They don't push it one way or the other. Mother's kind of gotten used to it.

Right off the bat, I was totally accepted by Lenny's entire family: aunts, uncles, grandmothers, cousins. There was never any animosity or question of my sincerity or that I belonged. They were probably so happy because we were both thirty and finally getting married! I'm close to his family and he's extremely close to my family.

Although I am now completely accepted as a Jew by the Jewish community of which I am a part, it has not been a completely smooth transition. Initially, the response to me felt as if I were a stepchild, an outsider. When Lenny was with me I became visible, without him some people would look right through me. It does make me sad to recall how people behaved toward me until they found out who I was; then I was welcomed with open arms. I'm sure others have had this experience too. The interesting thing is that a friend of mine who is a born Jew and also blond-haired and blue-eyed had a similar experience when she first joined our synagogue.

I don't think that this is just the case in the Jewish community—probably the world as a whole responds this way to people who are different. Until you know for sure who somebody is or what worth they might have to you, an outsider is an outsider, as much as people like to say that's not so. In every community, people learn to know and recognize their own, especially with older people. But it was rough for me at first to get past being treated like a second-class citizen sometimes.

Some of this response comes from the fear of assimilation and intermarriage. The Jewish press reports that numbers are dwindling because of intermarriage, but what is anybody doing about it? Most people I know who are intermarried have become more involved in Judaism than a lot of couples we know that are both Jewish and are not affiliated with the synagogue, don't take their kids to Sunday school or Hebrew school and don't observe *Shabbat*. It's a complicated area. The community itself could be more aware of people who want to be Jewish. If somebody wants to come in, welcome them in. Don't assume someone is a stranger.

My husband and I laugh sometimes about what a non-Jew would think walking into a synagogue on Simhat Torah—all these people marching around, throwing candy! When I first came to Judaism, I didn't have any idea what went on, and I was scared. But something was calling me all my life; Judaism was calling me, and I felt it, and I'm not surprised that I'm Jewish now. It's where I belong, I feel more at home, more comfortable, less shy, less inhibited. And it was always right at my fingertips.

Christianity did not give me the feeling I wanted to get from religion. In Judaism, I was getting spiritually fulfilled. What was wonderful to me when I first started my Judaic studies was that when you asked a question, you didn't just get an answer, you got five answers and you could pick the one you liked the best. There are just so many angles. Everything I learned was just so comfortable, everything that just seemed to fit me spiritually, whereas before it was like I had my shoes on backward. Judaism is like a comfortable pair of bedroom slippers for me.

What I do kind of regret is not growing up Jewish, not getting to do the things I see my kids doing: Purim parties, first *seders*. When you get into Judaism as an adult, nobody tells you what a Purim carnival is. You don't get the fun things. You learn about *Sukkot* but you don't get to sit in a *sukkah*. These are all things I learned about through actively participating with other Jewish families.

I like the community feeling, the familiarity, the kinship of the community, the warmth—which was not exuded toward me at first, but is now. All the people that I go to synagogue with are my family. I've been there for sixteen years now and they have really accepted me. I've been on the sisterhood board for five or six years. We publish a traditional Sephardic cookbook, and I helped revise the last edition, along with the rabbi's wife and another woman who's been Sephardic all her life. It was a wonderful feeling for me to see my name in the front of the cookbook along with Lenny's grandmother! I really felt I belonged. The comfort, the tradition of Judaism feels like something that I've been doing for many lifetimes—and I never felt that before becoming Jewish.

I believe that I've been Jewish many, many times before. When I read a *midrash* that all the souls that would ever be Jewish were present at Sinai, I knew exactly what that meant. For some reason, in this lifetime I "caught the wrong bus." I had always had a strange feeling while growing up that I was a misplaced soul. When I began my conversion process and I talked to rabbis and others, they recognized it right away. They knew. They all were very open to what I was saying and what my concerns and interests were.

I enjoy the weekly cycle of *Shabbat*. The ongoing tradition is so important to me, especially the Sephardic traditions. The food is completely different. At the Hebrew Academy, where I work as a nurse, I was listening to some of the teachers telling what they were preparing for Rosh Hashanah, and I had to ask what they were talking about. *Kugel* and *matzah*-ball soup are not part of Sephardic tradition.

There's a lot of Spanish influence in Sephardic Judaism. We eat rice at Pesah, and we use a lot of tomato and lemon in our cooking. The melodies in our services are very different from Ashkenazic—some people complain that they are not as beautiful or are more difficult to follow. Some of our High Holiday services are done in Spanish. Instead of Yiddish, Spanish or French or Ladino is spoken. In the synagogue kitchen, cooking with the older ladies, especially, there is multilingual dialogue going on. Lenny likes to tell the story of visiting his Aunt Becky's when a houseful of women were all speaking in Spanish about someone they knew. Lenny said, "Oh, I didn't know that about so and so." So Aunt Becky says to the ladies, "Lenny can understand us," and they all switched to French. We've got people from . . . oh, I can't imagine how many different places, but everybody has that same core.

There was a time when the Sephardic and Ashkenazic communities kept more separate than they do now. If an Ashkenazic married a Sephardic, it was the worst thing that could happen. But what means so much to me is that we all worship in Hebrew, and these are the same words that people have been uttering over the years since time began. When you're in a synagogue and hearing these voices chanting, knowing that these are the same things that people have been saying for generations is a wonderful feeling.

Judaism has given us a wonderful, firm foundation for our family life. We all know we're Jewish, there's no doubt. I know that in some families in which there is no conversion, parents are raising children with what I consider the bogus idea that the children can decide for themselves what they want to be. First of all, you've got to give the children something to choose from in order for them to make a choice. And how are you going to give children a good Catholic upbringing and a good Jewish upbringing at the same time? Then when they're fifteen, their parents ask them, "What do you want to be?" It can't be. I don't think someone should convert just to get married, but I think that for the sake of the children, for the sake of the continuation of the Jewish people, a claim needs to be staked. On the other hand, the Jewish community has to cooperate more fully in that effort. My youngest son's Sunday school teacher last year kept telling him that his mother wasn't Jewish. She never consulted me.

I know that my children have peers of all different backgrounds who don't know what religion they are. One of my sons had a run-in with a child in his public school who was physically and verbally abusing Jake because we're Jewish. Jake tried to explain to this boy that although he believed in God, he didn't believe in Jesus. My children know from my explanations that Jesus was a man, probably a rabbi, but that he had no intention of starting his own religion. And the boy replied that he believed in Jesus but not in God. The counselor at school said that the boy's mother didn't know where her son got his ideas because they were never talked about in the home. I told Jake to just tell that boy that what he feels in his heart is okay, and what you feel in your heart is okay. The problem was finally resolved.

That's probably the first time I had experienced anything with the kids that was negative. My sons are proud of what they know of their long tradition. They really like the stories that they learn in Sunday school, and they like what we do and share with them at home. I feel I am giving them something more solid than I ever had as a child. I was only told, "You just have to believe because that is what we believe."

Children need answers and explanations, and if I can't give those to them, Lenny can. Lenny is very knowledgeable. He studies a lot of *midrash* and prays every day. I am more involved in the synagogue activities. So we have a good balance.

I know that genetically I'm not Jewish because my biological parents aren't, but I truly feel inside and out, every cell of me, every strand of DNA is definitely Jewish. When I see Jewish people that I don't even know, I'm connected to them. I am Jewish, I am connected to the Jewish community and religion. I just don't even think about it being any other way.

38

Judaism Is a Part of Every Moment

Yaakov Thompson

Scholarship has always been revered in Judaism, and throughout the generations, the epitome of the Jewish learned person has been the rabbi. Many Jews
study for the rabbinate, not as a vocation but only for the sake of deepening
their knowledge and understanding of the vast Jewish religious texts. Rabbi
Yaakov Thompson's initial interest in the pursuit of *semikhah*, rabbinical ordination, was to satisfy his yearning for a rich Jewish education.

Now, as rabbi of Congregation B'nai Israel in Fair Lawn, New Jersey,
Yaakov is at the center of his congregants' lives: probing with them questions
about the meaning of being a Jew and presiding over the life-cycle events that
are central to Jewish life. "A rabbi," he says, "lives in a perpetual state of crisis—
mine or someone else's!"

And this life, Yaakov affirms, is perfect for him. He can live each day fully
involved in the pursuit of Judaism—both the learning and the doing—that so
intrigued him as a college student in Ohio. And he is filled with gratitude that
"Judaism is a part of every moment of my life."

I was seventeen at the end of the Vietnam War, the last year of the draft. Like any
young person, I was aware, mostly through television and reading, of all that was
going on in America at that time. I saw the world as a place of great opportunity
for learning and exploring, though in the Ohio town of 8,000 people in which I grew
up, the norm after high-school graduation was to settle there with a job in a local
factory or farm.

But in the last two years of high school I became fascinated with history and classical cultures and wanted to pursue those disciplines on a college level—and beyond.
In the course of my studies at Ohio State, I took into consideration that there had
been another great ancient culture—the Hebrews. I had always been *aware* of it, of
course. Anybody who grows up in a Christian environment at least implicitly is aware
that if there is a *New* Testament there must be an *Old* Testament—whatever that may
mean to people who have little knowledge of the bigger picture of biblical history.

The household in which I grew up was nominally Christian but not terribly religious. Religion was not pushed or even discussed much. As a child I had been taken
to church and attended Sunday school and church events, but nothing about religion
particularly resonated with me at that time. I had known a couple of Jewish people
who weren't observant or had much of a Jewish education or background of any kind.

The only family I had was my mother, who died during my first year in rabbinical school. She had lived and worked and died all within the space of the same ten miles, and though she had very little concept of the life I was pursuing, she was supportive of me because of her intuitive realization that this was something that was giving me great happiness.

As a teenager, I felt increasing ambivalence about the culture in which I'd grown up—a Christian culture, de facto. An important experience for me was reading an essay by Bertrand Russell, "Why I'm not a Christian." In this essay, Russell notes his moral and ethical misgivings about the British Anglican tradition—which of course he'd taken for granted, having been raised in that culture—as the groundwork of what religion was. Reading this at seventeen pushed my ambivalence further. Yet I had a reverence for the *ideals* of religion, though certainly not from any one tradition—if anything, the opposite: anything that was "traditional" was suspect.

Now, part of my job as a rabbi is to speak *for* the tradition. I can recognize the change in me: who you are at eighteen is not who you are at forty. Though the disaffection of youth with regard to tradition is a particularly *human* problem, sometimes as Jews we tend to see it only as a Jewish problem. How do you direct people through the turmoils and the upheavals and the doubts of young adulthood, and, in addition, encourage participation in Jewish life and knowledge of what Judaism is? We all know of kids who go through the best of our educational programs who may not have a terribly good grip on what Judaism is really about or at best have an immature understanding of it. The Jewish education of many of the adults I encounter stopped at twelve or thirteen, and their theological sophistication and grasp of Judaism is at the level of a young teen. Their religious growth stops, and they may not come back to it until they have children and decide it's time for them to do something again.

My formal introduction to Judaism came when I discovered the Hillel on campus at Ohio State. One day I walked in and explained that I wasn't Jewish, but I wanted to learn more about Judaism, and I'd like to see the rabbi. It turned out to be a very good *shidukh* (match), and I began to study with Rabbi Chaim Siedler-Feller, who is now a Hillel rabbi in Los Angeles.

Mine was a gradual transformation. I was very excited intellectually by the study of Judaism, which contained, it seemed to me, such great wisdom. The more important change was the transformation from the study of a subject to the commitment to *be* Jewish and really understanding the implications of that choice.

At first Judaism was something I studied as a "subject," an "it" outside of me, something ancient, museumlike. A whole other step was to recognize that Judaism was alive and in the present: people live that way and do those things. One can learn all about what great minds have to say about the *parashah* on *tzitzit* in, say, Chills's book *The Mitzvot* or in Maimonides' *Sefer HaMitzvot*, but from there, it is a huge step—and a very different kind of step—to decide to *wear tzitzit*. "Where do I get them? What do I do with them?"

I benefited from meeting many people—both the professionals at Hillel and the other Jewish college students—who were very accepting of someone who wanted to learn and were encouraging and helpful as well. I decided early on that I wanted to convert, and by the time of my formal conversion, I'd already made up my mind that I would go to rabbinical school to continue my Jewish education. Most people advised, "Go to a graduate school." But it did not appeal to me to go to Brandeis for a Ph.D. in Jewish history or the University of Wisconsin for a doctorate in Hebrew. I wanted a *rabbinic* education—though not to become a congregational rabbi. That decision would come later.

It took me some time to discover where my place in Judaism would be. I didn't decide on Conservative Judaism when I first converted. My circle at Hillel included everyone—people identified themselves as Orthodox, Reform, Conservative. Rabbi Feller, my main teacher, was from YU (Yeshiva University); at the same time I was very friendly and studied with a last-year rabbinical student at HUC (Hebrew Union College). I also had contact with a Conservative rabbi in town. I think one of the things most bewildering and hard to sort out for people becoming Jewish is, "You can't just *be* 'Jewish,' you have to be *some kind* of 'Jewish.'" It's not the same thing as Protestant or Catholic or Episcopalian, because the "denomination" of Christian parlance is not the same as in Judaism. In a sense it is not the "label" with which you identify and are identified, but the way you live your life, especially in terms of ritual observance on a daily basis in community with other Jews.

In a Hillel environment rather than a *shul* environment, those labels had absolutely no meaning for me whatsoever—you were *just* "Jewish." It was very naive, because the reality of American Judaism, for political and other reasons, is that there are no "generic" Jews.

Deciding to identify myself as a Conservative Jew was a process that came about through my application to rabbinical schools. The last year in college I identified both HUC and JTS (Jewish Theological Seminary) as two places where I wanted to study. My first application to JTS was denied. As they do with many applicants for rabbinical school, they wanted me to come for a year as a graduate student. Instead, I chose to go to Israel for the HUC "Year in Israel" program. During the year in Israel, I came to the realization that I was not going to find a comfortable place in Reform Judaism. As much as I had said, "Jewish is Jewish," and even though I knew many Reform rabbis who are observant, Reform just didn't fit with my idea of the obligatory nature of Jewish law and Jewish observance.

I reapplied to JTS and did what I would have done a year before: I enrolled as a graduate student in the Talmud program. In that year, I again applied to the rabbinical school and was accepted. I spent a year as a master's student, four years in rabbinical school, then five years as a doctoral student.

I came to rabbinical school two years after my first conversion and more qualified academically than most students. In college, I had left the classics program and graduated as a major in Jewish studies, and although I obviously was not on the same level as people who had gone to day school their whole lives, there were many people who were accounting majors in college and now wanted to be rabbis.

So that there would be no question of my status as a Jew, I underwent a second conversion. My first *Bet Din*, sponsored by the Hillel, was ecumenical: a Reform rabbi, a Conservative rabbi, and a last-year HUC student, with all three of whom I had studied and been friends. Later, when it was clear to me that the rest of my life was going to be "something" Jewish, I began a process of learning and studying all over again, which culminated in an Orthodox-sponsored conversion.

During the first few years of rabbinical school, I had been undecided about what I would do once I had the title "Rabbi." There was still so much study ahead that the end result seemed too far off. I began to consider that the congregational rabbinate could and, indeed, should be the direction for my career during the course of the two years I spent as assistant to Rabbi I. Usher Kirschblum at the Jewish Center of Kew Gardens Hills, New York. With Rabbi Kirschblum I discovered that congregational work was something that I enjoyed and something I could, in time, do well.

Rabbi Kirschblum urged me to become involved in all rabbinic duties while I served with him. He guided my learning of the many practical aspects of congregational life, in particular the life cycle events, many of which I had never faced before. I would officiate and Rabbi Kirschblum, with great patience and concern for my growth, would explain later what I did "wrong." More than any other experience, it was the example Rabbi Kirschblum provided me and the faith that he had in me—even in the moments when I was fumbling in my new role—that shaped the kind of rabbi that I am and my personal "style."

The congregational rabbinate demands much of an individual and of the family of the rabbi. I was very fortunate to have had this opportunity to prepare for those demands. As a rabbi I am involved intimately on a daily basis with people's problems and personal private lives. Often, I live in a state of crisis—if it's not mine, it's someone else's. That is routine.

I've had to think about what it means to nurture people, not only in terms of nurturing my children but nurturing other people's children as a teacher and rabbi. How to nurture people spiritually and intellectually—always knowing that you are the "other," the father figure, the rabbi figure, the authority figure. Those aren't things that people discuss over the dinner table. Since I grew up without a father—I never met my father—I didn't have a role model. I've had to give some thought to this aspect of my role.

I had often thought that people would have a hard time relating to me as a rabbi because I was a convert. That, I supposed, might limit what I could do as a rabbi. At the same time, I have never made being a convert the center of my career, and happily, I find that as time passes the fact that I am a convert becomes less and less of an issue, and that is certainly the way that I prefer it to be.

There were times that, yes, certain things were difficult. I was breaking ground, since no convert had finished rabbinical school at the Seminary. There were troubles, just as there always will be. There is a dis-ease that certain people have with me, but I have discovered that it is more a reflection of the dis-ease *they* have with being Jewish—not with *me* being Jewish.

These things have affected me in trivial ways. I would call and say, "My name is Thompson; I'm applying for a Hebrew school job." And the reply would be, "This is a *Hebrew* school; we're *Jewish.*" One time I came in for the interview and everybody was laughing, "So, *Rabbi* Thompson. . . ." And I said, "What's so funny?" "Well, we have a black custodian in the synagogue. *His* name is Thompson, too. So, we couldn't wait to see what a "Rabbi" Thompson looked like." Very silly things like that. When I was younger and less secure, personally and professionally, those things would bother me.

Occasionally, I am reminded that I am from a "different" place. I now live in a town with a population of 35,000, 48 percent of which is Jewish. My kids are growing up thinking the whole world is Jewish. I have to remember, sometimes, that theirs is a different experience from my childhood. I grew up in a little town in the middle of nowhere with very few expectations. I was the first one in my family to go to college. My mother had a sixth-grade education.

I like to see my life as a continuum—not block it off into different eras, different lives. Some people have asked why, if I changed my name to "Yaakov," didn't I change my last name, too. But there was no need to do that. As much as Yaakov is a part of me, so is Thompson. I still enjoy listening to the same music I did when I was seventeen—Dylan. That is who I am, too. Some people are not comfortable with the story of my life; they are only looking at who and what I am now, and the function I serve now. Sometimes they say very dumb things like, "Gee, Rabbi, didn't you ever wish you could eat something not kosher?" That's not a thoughtful question. I spent the first twenty years of my life not knowing what kosher was.

I met my wife, Sarah, when I was in rabbinical school. She taught in a *yeshivah* that rented space during the day from the synagogue where I was principal of the Hebrew school, and we shared a classroom. It was never an issue in our relationship that I was a convert. Sarah grew up Orthodox in Manhattan, a part of the German community in Washington Heights—the "Yaki" community. A "Yak" is a German Jew. It comes from *yacquit*—"jacket." The German Jews were said to have "Yaki" ways—they were more formal, proper, more Americanized, and they always wore a suit jacket.

Labels don't mean too much to me, though. Some people tell me that I am really an Orthodox rabbi because I am more observant than they think a Conservative rabbi should be or because I am too traditional.

I *am* a traditional Conservative rabbi—somewhere on the far right of the Conservative movement. I do not call women to the Torah, for example. This stance comes from both my own nature and the nature of my congregation. There are three Conservative synagogues here in Fair Lawn: one is egalitarian, two are not. In my particular community, older and of European origin, there is not even a desire for egalitarian practices. And that is what I am comfortable with. But I am friendly with Orthodox rabbis *and* Reform rabbis, and our circle of friends includes people who are very *frum* and some who are totally nonobservant.

I've found that most Jewish people's experience with Judaism is radically different from mine. Their understanding of Judaism has come through the heart and through the stomach and through family events. Many people can't relate to a lot of my experiences or what I do in my life because they have never dealt with Judaism in an intellectual way.

I'm often invited to speak to groups, and I'll go on for an hour describing all these great concepts in Judaism. Then someone will raise his hand and say, "But Rabbi, we're just poor simple Jews. We don't have a Jewish education. We're not rabbis. We're not scholars. I grew up Jewish. I don't know much about it, but I *feel* very Jewish. What do you have to say to me?"

The first time that ever happened, I had to sit and think about where is that connecting link—for me and for everybody—between the mind and the heart, "between the study and the doing," we would say in classic rabbinic terms. What can I say to people who may be working the other way: they have the observance but they haven't had the study?

Perhaps because I came to Judaism as an "outsider" I have a fuller appreciation for the enormity of our history and the amazing depth of our faith. For me it was never (and I hope it will never be) enough to just "feel" Jewish. I constantly try to remind people that those "feelings" must serve as a catalyst to "do" things Jewish.

Some people consider that the rabbi should be the perfect role model when it comes to questions of personal observance. Often the most effective way for me to teach is to remind people that I, too, am a "Jew-in-progress," in other words, that I am still learning and growing as a Jew. To be a Jew, you *must* progress. I point to my own life and the process of my own development in order to remind others that no matter what may be your starting point, or how far along you may have come, you must continue to grow. I say to these people, "Please realize that I am not the Jew now that I was five or ten years ago. I hope five or ten years hence, I won't be the Jew that I am now." When we talk about making the right connection between Jewish learning and Jewish living, we are talking about urging people to continue to grow, to learn new things, to better understand what they already know.

I am very happy with the *baal teshuvah* movement. It is very good for Jews to be returning to Judaism—of course! But one of the potentially bad things, everyone will have to admit, is that it is all too easy to set people up for disappointment and failure. To say that within the course of some short period of time—sometimes only a few weeks—a person is going to radically alter his or her whole pattern of life, to go from being *Mehalel Shabbat* to *Shomer Shabbat*, going, for example, from eating whatever they want to the discipline of some level of *kashrut*, just can't happen overnight. When leaders of any denomination let people do this they are not really giving them the right tools. You have to *climb* up the mountain; it doesn't come in one "jump." It is true that we first have to find that niche where we fit in. Where is it that we find our community? Where is it that we find our level of observance that is comfortable and meaningful as a ground base from which we will work? We have to grow and mature into Judaism. All of Jewish life is a matter of growing. The problem is that too many Jews just stop growing.

The way I learned to be a Jew was as a young adult in a Hillel setting. It was a college environment, and we were all college age—learning about Judaism, making Jewish friends, being a support group for one another. It was religious and social learning all in one. But that setting is *not* the norm for most people who become Jewish. They come through the synagogue, and it is a whole different set of dynamics, a different way of finding a place for oneself in Judaism. It is a much more isolated way, and it is far more challenging to help people get involved in a community life that has a variety of focal points, than in college where Jewish life centers on one institution's integrated, though perhaps limited, options for involvement.

In my twelve years in the rabbinate, I've converted only perhaps five or six people. Not only do I take it a lot more seriously than most people, who often are not up for the long haul that I ask for, but also the task of integrating them into the community is a challenge. They sit in my office one-on-one and I have to *shlep* (carry or move) them into "Come to the synagogue and you'll meet people. . . ." In this environment, the responsibility is far greater on the individual rabbi as well as the individual convert to provide a deep and broad experience of Jewish life, and therefore requires a great deal of commitment and perseverance on the part of the convert.

When conferring with a potential convert, I always assume that the typical Christian doesn't know any more about Christianity than the typical Jew knows of Judaism. The person who says, "I don't want to be Christian anymore; I want to be Jewish," may know only that Christians believe in Jesus and Jews don't; Christians celebrate Christmas and Jews don't. But I want to see that they are asking themselves real questions about their belief in Christian ideas. Are they ready to rethink some of their basic assumptions between good and evil, individual sin versus "original" or collective sin? Can they accept that Judaism draws a very distinct line between human and divine?

One of the first things I do with people who come to me and want to know about being Jewish is to study Christianity with them—books such as *We Jews and Jesus* or *A Jewish Understanding of the New Testament* by Samuel Sandmel. In addition, where are they in terms of their development as a person?

Stage two is "This is Judaism. Where is this going to fit into your life?" What is their "ground zero," the first level where they are going to be comfortable observing Judaism? What can I, as the rabbi, reasonably and honestly accept as a stage two for them? I don't expect someone to become completely observant upon the *mikveh*, but I want them to know the ideals, and to make a goal for themselves based on these ideals. Yes, I know most born Jews don't work toward that, but I don't care. I don't have to answer for most Jews. If I am to be responsible for a person becoming Jewish, I tell people quite honestly, "There are enough wishy-washy Jews in the world, I don't need to make one more."

One of the dynamics that I often see is a person who became Jewish and is much more Jewishly educated and Jewishly committed than the people in their family who were born Jewish. That makes an opposite friction that is probably more the rule than the exception: the convert goes to class and the rabbi says, "You have to eat kosher."

The born Jew says, "Aw, come on, you don't have to do that to be Jewish." Or the rabbi will tell about the holidays, and the born Jew will say, "Oh, no, that's not what the holiday is about. Hanukkah, you get gifts; we have a Hanukkah bush." Yet, if we are successful in the conversion process, we have created a new soul that is going to *want* to be nourished by things Jewish. The message of conversion is that there is something very attractive and important about the Jewish tradition.

The common wisdom of the tradition as a whole is that we Jews have always been ambivalent, at best, about conversion. This attitude derives in part from events in Jewish history when the dominant gentile culture made it a capital offense to convert a person to Judaism. In addition, there are experiences of converts gone wrong who have done great damage. But, in part, Jews' ambivalence about other people becoming Jewish reflects *our* ambivalence about being Jewish. We have two competing value systems: the concept of *simhat shel mitzvah* ("the joy of the commandments"), which really means the joy of being Jewish. Vying with that is the concept of *kol malkhut shamayim* (the "yoke" of being Jewish). One says that Judaism is this terrible burden to bear; the other asserts that Judaism is a wonderful, unique thing to have. That ambivalence is built into our theology and is one of the reasons that we don't say, "Everyone should be Jewish."

We realize that it is not something you confer on somebody as a benefit, because when you make them Jewish you are obligating them, in a sense, putting them into "debt." Yet it is also a great blessing to be able to be Jewish. Of these two messages, some people are able to see only one and others only the other.

Any Jew who takes his or her Judaism seriously has this problem: on the one hand we always affirm, "We are not better than everybody else; the world doesn't need to be Jewish." *Sheva mitzvot b'nei Noah* (the seven Noahide laws); you don't have to be a Jew to be saved, redeemed—whatever words you want to use. However, if you are Jewish and it's important for you to be Jewish, you are saying, "It is better to be Jewish than not to be Jewish." That is something we haven't worked out in our theology or our self-definitions. It is one of the things that makes Judaism so different from the other religions. We hold tenaciously to our self-existence and yet we don't missionize and we don't say that everybody else must be like us. There is a paradox there. I say, "I am a Jew because it's the best thing there is and the best person I can be, but *you* don't have to be Jewish." That's ambiguous.

But Jews and Christians alike live in a very secularized culture in which religion is not the first resource for our values and not the first set of structures that we use to divvy up our time. One of the things I hear as a rabbi is, "Oh, nobody cares about religion. We have assimilation." People don't put this in a bigger picture. This is not a distinctly Jewish problem. Yes, it is a Jewish problem, but it's something that we have to assess within the larger question: How do people understand the function of religion in their lives?

One of the important messages that we have to offer as Jews is that life is more "holistic" than most people think. Life is not compartmentalized. Life and human experience are not made into a dichotomy between the secular and the religious, between the personal and the professional—it's *all* your life. Whatever you are doing at any particular moment—*that* is your *whole* life. Judaism is meant to be a part of every moment. Judaism is such an all-embracing way of life that all the other "isms" can grow out of your basic attitudes about living a Jewish life: secular humanism, behaviorism, cognitive therapy, and so on.

I think that psychology and theology are intimately bound up—self-actualization, for example. That is not a radical, new idea. It is very basic to the religious ideal, and not just of Judaism—being a *mensch* (responsible, ethical, compassionate, and so forth), living up to full potential. I'm very interested in Jung's idea that we are all both masculine and feminine. The well-balanced masculine personality, for example, has to have female ingredients. That is not a new idea. It is Jewish Kabbalah. It is classically *Zohar*, except the *Zohar* says it in much more physically sexual language, but it's the same thing: God is perfect because He's the comingling of the mercy and the judgment. It is an old idea.

One of the things I am always very excited to share with others is that in Judaism we have a radically different idea about what a human being is and what human potential is. There is no inherent evil or God-given good in any of us. We are a mixture of good and bad. As a Jew, and as a Jew who grew up with only Christian assumptions about the world, I feel that this view of the human self-worth is an important one, and it's one with which I feel much more comfortable.

For instance, I often vehemently attack Sigmund Freud because he is the epitome of the Christianized Jew. Modern American culture has been terribly influenced by Freudian assumptions. The Freudian concept of the human personality is one that is colored by assumptions that derive from Christianity and that are very counter to Judaism. A basic assumption of Christianity about the individual comes from the concept of "original sin"—the idea that humans are born eternally imperfect because of Adam's sin in the Garden of Eden. Original sin is a human being's destiny unless it is mitigated by a big act of grace by God. And what is Freud's basic assumption? That humans are driven by forces (instincts—"sins") we can't even identify, and redemption and salvation will come only through an act of grace that the psychotherapist can perform for us.

This Freudian understanding of human potential has become a part of modern American popular culture. The most blatant example is the criminal-justice system. With which model of humanity do you begin when looking at criminals? Are they born "bad" or born with the potential for either "bad" or "good"? In another area, as president of the board for the mental-health center in town, I face this issue every day. How is our potential for appropriately serving the community affected by our basic assumption about people? Do we approach people according to the sick model or the healthy model? Judaism starts with the assumption of the healthy model.

It is also important to me to speak out about the attitude that if you are religious you are "repressing" human desire. Again we have the Freudian model: religion and religious-based strictures are the product of repressive, obsessive personalities. "Why are you doing this to yourself? People don't live like that anymore." You can keep

Shabbat or keep kosher *only* if you have a medieval, repressed mentality, and you are just waiting like a butterfly to burst out and go shopping on Saturday and go to McDonald's for a Big Mac and Happy Meals. Somehow people can't grasp the idea that modernity and the enjoyment of modernity could somehow go hand-in-hand with an observant Jewish life. But these are not *Jewish* assumptions. These are the assumptions of Jews who are Americans.

Sociologically, Jewish life is a serious counterculture—if you want to call it that—and that counterculture does indeed reject much of what the larger culture is putting forth, but that's good! It should be rejected. It stinks!

What people don't see is that there are things that it's *good* to repress. Judaism is meant to teach restraints. It is not necessarily always good to come and go whenever you please or eat anything you want. There is something good, something to be learned, something to be gained from restraints and self-control. Nobody ever said that life can be exactly the way you want. That is an immature view of life, and immaturity has become a social disease. We speak of God as the divine parent, the divine father, but fathers—parents—set limits. In Judaism we are told to do the best we can, recognizing that our limits have a purpose. It is not just the faith in God—a Jew has to have faith in Judaism!

That is an important message, but how do we sugarcoat that and spoon-feed it to people in a way that they will get it?

It also makes no sense to create some kind of Jewish life without the traditional belief in a God that commands. If Jews ultimately don't have any greater purpose in their Jewishness than to express their cultural identity, then there is really no reason for their cultural identity, because it is completely relative and as good as any other.

I like to say that Judaism lives with *tension*. People have frustration that Judaism has a great deal of ambiguity. People come to me in times of crisis. They want to know, "Is there a Heaven and a Hell?" They want to know what is exactly the right thing to do or believe. They don't want to hear, "Well, some rabbis say this; some rabbis say that; some people believe this." People don't want that, sometimes even when they're not in crisis. That is one of the frustrations that Jews have with Judaism. There are times people want easy, definite answers. What's going to happen to me when I die? Is it like my Christian friends believe, that you go right up to heaven? What do Jews believe?"

But we don't have a pat answer. The biggest impact you can have as a teacher, a rabbi, is being honest about your own doubts, your own ability to say, "I don't know, and we don't know as a religion," without bringing people to total frustration or despair. The title of a book I am working on now is *Despair Is Not a Jewish Word*. Rebbe Nachman said this in Yiddish, already. Should this book ever see the light of day, what will it be? It's really just a collection of discourses—sermony-type things—about the cycle of *haftarah* readings. In dealing with kids preparing for *bar* and *bat mitzvahs*, the bottom line always becomes, "What is all this stuff about?" One of the central and ongoing messages is that the prophets were individuals who never gave in to despair, and they lived through some of the worst times that Jewish history ever saw. For me, on the personal, individual, psychological level is the message that there is never reason for ultimate despair—what philosophers call "existential despair" or what Viktor Frankl would call "the ultimate loss of meaning."

As I try to make sense of my life, and what other people describe as the "radical changes" that I have experienced, I don't see anything so "radical." I prefer to think of my life as a continuum of interests and growth. My first exposure to Judaism made me want to learn more. That would lead to my decision to pursue a full Jewish education for myself. Eventually I was able to begin to translate my experiences and perceptions into a language that could be shared with other Jews.

I consider myself to be that proverbial "luckiest person in the world." I have always been surrounded by people who believed in me and supported what I wanted to do. I feel very blessed to be who and what I am. Even if I had a chance to do it over, I know that there is nothing other than the rabbinate that I would choose for myself. Being a rabbi is not easy, sometimes it is not pleasant, but it is always important. I feel this most strongly when I have the chance to see that I have made an impact on someone's life, that I have helped someone else take a step forward.

I believe that every individual must, at some point, ask himself or herself some very difficult questions about life, about one's values, and about the ways in which one's life really mattered. I believe that we gain our greatest sense of purpose, our greatest sense of being alive to those around us, by reaching out with the desire to, if nothing else, be a *mensch*.

I continue to travel down my own road to Judaism. It is of ultimate importance in my life because Judaism informs and enriches every moment. It is the connecting link between what I believe and what I do. In the process, I hope that I have helped other people to find their way and speed their progress. I have great hope for my fellow human beings, and I trust that God will help all of us to reach for the best of what is in each of us. As a Jew, I always feel that the best is yet to come.

39

Eshet Hazon
Shonna Husbands-Hankin

I first met Shonna at a Jewish Renewal Movement retreat at Elat Chayyim. It was the family arts week and Shonna was leading a workshop on Judaic art. At week's end her class had a showing of the beautiful objects they had created—*mezuzot, menorahs, tallitot*—expressing each person's vision of Judaism's meaning to his or her own life.

Shonna believes that her coming to Judaism was something God "chose" for her—that in becoming Jewish she was answering a call that came from a voice deep within herself and from a different time. Giving heed to that voice and encouraging others to find theirs in the context of Judaism has informed every aspect of Shonna's life for the past twenty years.

In a life made more public by her husband's work as a rabbi and the cantor of their congregation, Shonna has found it essential to make a personal space for herself that enables her to continue to live her authentic life as a Jew and as an *"eshet hazon,"* a woman of vision.

My journey has had mystical elements that have guided me throughout my spiritual blossoming. I offer some pieces of my private journey here as a shimmering of light that will, I hope, illuminate others on their pathways to peace and inner wisdom, and offer my thanks to those who have served as teachers along the way.

As I look back at my life to see what shaped me on the path to become Jewish, I see things differently now than I saw originally. I was born here in Oregon, the oldest of four kids in a highly dysfunctional family, in which I had a lot of responsibility. My family is all of pioneer stock; our ancestors came here on wagon trains, not educated, a working-class family.

Growing up, I didn't know any Jewish people—didn't even *think* of knowing any Jewish people. I read books and had a very deep compassion and feeling, but where I grew up, there wasn't a community of Jews, so I had no reference point other than historical and emotional connections. I have a very striking memory about reading the *Diary of Anne Frank*, sitting in my pink-chiffon canopy bed; I couldn't put it down. I was completely enraptured with this story. And there was a power in it that stayed with me through subsequent experiences in my life.

When I was a young teenager, I did a lot of baby-sitting to earn money for school clothes and things like that. One family with a little daughter was about to move to

348

Germany, and they invited me to come live with them and baby-sit in exchange for room and board. They saw some of my family problems and, I think, they also saw my potential. It was a very special opportunity, but I didn't say anything to anybody about it. On the last night that I was baby-sitting for them, I asked, "Are you really serious about that?" And they said, "Yes!" My parents borrowed the money for the plane fare, and off I went.

I had just turned fifteen, and although in many ways I was very mature for my age, I had never been on an airplane before. I flew around the world by myself and lived in Munich with them for three and a half months. It was a fabulous opportunity for me to expand my horizon. Up until that time, my family had never traveled any place past Disneyland or Yellowstone Park. My trip to Munich opened up an international appetite for traveling and experiencing other cultures that continues to this day.

Munich in 1967 was still destroyed from World War II. The downtown was a disaster, still a complete mess. Twenty years later, and they still hadn't put things back together. I was an impressionable kid in a large, foreign, very old city, and I was shocked that the buildings were just toppled everywhere.

We would take a streetcar to a bakery to get special cookies and various other sweet little things—and then look up and see signs "To Dachau." It was a lot to filter in, with no guideposts. One day in my little room upstairs in our house, I was just snooping around, and I came across Nazi paraphernalia in a closet. It gave me the shivers. Obviously, the owner of the house was a Nazi and had kept all of his mementos. I was completely blown away. How could I look this person in the face? What kind of creep was he? It was just so shocking that I hadn't even considered: "They're probably on every street." This experience left a deep imprint in my memory.

After high school, at age seventeen, I became self-supporting, working my way through college. As a young woman in my early twenties, I worked two jobs and became very successful in the business world with a graphics-design company. Then I commuted to Portland to work with the legislature for a few years. But I felt a big emptiness inside and wondered, "Is this all there is to life? Working and doing well financially, you can buy things, and I can see how well I'm doing, but this can't be it. There's got to be more than this because this isn't completely fulfilling." There *was* a level of fulfillment in creating a home for myself; there wasn't a stable family home or parents to look back on to provide security. So I was doing *that* for myself, but there was a spiritual yearning for something more, a void that compelled me to ask: "Do I need a family? Do I need a husband? Do I need kids? Do I need God? Just earning money and running around—this isn't it, is it?" There was a hole inside of me.

As successful as I was, I felt that I got the message really early: "This isn't the point of being alive. Even if I am only twenty-four, I don't need to keep running around like a rat in a cage here for the next forty years." Ding! I got the picture. "This isn't what being here is for. This is a burnout, I'm not doing this anymore." I quit. I said, "I'm retiring!" In the spring of 1976, I gave myself permission to take a break.

I uprooted myself. I let go of everything material. I rented my house out for a year to somebody, and I let go of my jobs and my connections. I moved to California, but those plans didn't work out, and I was all alone. I had chosen to let my life crumble in a certain way, but I had my little Volkswagen and my tent.

As I was slowly traveling up the coast back to Oregon, trying to figure out what my next step might be, I began having an incredible experience with dreams. I was really low and feeling depressed, but at the same time, it was a very spiritually elevating opportunity to connect in really deep places. The series of dreams didn't stop for nearly a year and a half. They were very powerful, and I would wake up in the morning, and write them down for hours. I was undergoing a major spiritual transformation. After a while, I thought I was going crazy. "Who will take care of me? I'm losing my mind." At the same time, I knew that something really big was happening to me, and I wanted to honor that process. I wished I could be some place where people could understand what was happening. I wondered if there were a place—like a monastery—where people would just let me be and give me food, and I could just go through this process. Someplace where people wouldn't think I was crazy because I didn't want to be interacting in the regular world.

I can still remember some of those dreams very vividly, and though I am somewhat uncomfortable sharing such private visions in a public book, I offer them here as a gesture toward deeper understanding of some of the mystical paths that have brought some of us on our spiritual journeys to Judaism.

In one of the dreams I was sitting with people around a table. There were candles and people were singing songs. Everybody was going around introducing themselves and giving themselves new names. They were Hebrew names, but I didn't know what was going on because I had never seen a *Shabbat*. Then it was my turn, and I was trying to decide what my new name would be. The name that I gave myself was "Starbasket." I've since used that as my spirit name and translated it into Hebrew.

Salisha Kohav means "basket woman of the stars." Over the years I've looked back and tried to feel, "What is 'Starbasket'? A basket of stars or stars in a basket? What are all those symbols?" These were elements of my spirit past—a reflection of the deep connection I feel to Native Americans—and symbols of my inner self, the basket part being the artist, the native side, and the stars, my Jewish self, sparkling light. The basket also felt like a womb shape. I recognized this dream as a significant spiritual message and have tried to honor that.

Two weeks after this dream, I found myself back in Eugene, actually sitting around a table with candles, singing songs with people with all these Hebrew names I'd never heard of—a *Shabbat* dinner!

I had more dreams—one was about a journey on a huge pathway in the shape of the letter *J*, and the name of the city was "J—Salem." People coming from every direction going to "J," Jerusalem. Another dream in which Jewish people from all over the world came to Oregon to put together some kind of Jewish community (which later happened in real time). Many dreams. Many Jewish symbols. I was filling a dream journal each week recording my inner journey.

I had different powerful experiences around this period of my life—experiences that were coming from some very deep place inside of me. My inner and outer worlds began to fit together when I started making connections with this group of people that was doing *Shabbat*. These pursuits had nothing to do with earning a living, which had been such a focus for me for so many years. I was finding myself in another reality, and people who knew me before thought I was crazy: "What are you doing? You're not working; you're not living in your house." I was having this whole other journey—a spiritual journey—and I didn't have any guides for it; I didn't have any context for it. I knew it was deep and real and I wanted to honor the truth that was flowing through me.

At this time, Yitz, the man who was to become my husband, was just starting to get back into his Jewish life. He and some others had a Jewish household that was like a little *shul* where people would gather every *Shabbat*. My evolution was going on independently when I became a part of this group, and yet there was a sort of synchronicity in our lives as we came together.

It was at this house that I attended my first *seder*. As luck would have it, everyone was sick with the flu, so I prepared the whole thing. I had never seen a *matzah* ball in my life and there I was trying to figure out from a cookbook how you make them—for twenty-five people. But the whole experience felt very comfortable. I loved a lot of what I found in this Jewish gathering. I loved the dialogue and exchange of ideas, the familial feelings, the values, ethics, and spiritual flexibility that went with them.

My entrance into Judaism was with people who were very mystically oriented. That was my entire perception of Judaism. I had no other context. A year after my spiritual journey had begun, I arranged for a retreat led by Rabbi Zalman Schachter-Shalomi, and it was held in my house. I attended an international spiritual conference in Vancouver, B.C., where I met Rabbi Shlomo Carlebach. Later that year, Yitz and I coorganized a retreat with Jews and Native Americans to compare spiritual paths. All of my energy, previously devoted to my career, was redirected into a spiritual path—organizing all kinds of gatherings and retreats. Yitz and I had both had the vision of starting a rural Jewish community, and it began to be shaped by the convergence of ideas and people at this series of retreats.

Judaism had become my spiritual home, so it was a natural evolution to make a gesture of commitment. My first conversion was at a natural hot springs. There are seven sacred pools in beautiful misty mountains that can be reached only by hiking through the backwoods. We happened to be there for a healing of one of our group. My immersion happened in a way that was very mutually shared. It was wonderful.

Later that year, when Yitz and I finally decided to get married, I did another *mikveh*. I don't remember how it exactly was decided that I should do this, but I do recall there was pressure for me to have an Orthodox conversion with papers in order to protect me or my kids. A young Orthodox rabbi who had done some counseling with us when we were in a challenging position in our relationship flew out from New York City. We wanted to acknowledge the role he had played in our coming together, and he had all the right stamps of approval to be a witness for the *mikveh*.

I went through the second "conversion" experience in a "kosher" *mikveh* and later deeply regretted doing it. I felt it denied the spiritual process I had already been through once before that had been a pure moment for me. To do a second ritual for the sake of a piece of paper violated an understanding and wisdom about the spiritual power of that precious moment of *mikveh*. It made less of both experiences. It was more about rules and control over people instead of about spirit. There was a sense of *obligation* to go through this kind of conversion in order to protect yourself *politically*. That was a terrible rip-off spiritually. People shouldn't have to do that. Although I understood that this was supposed to be for my best well-being and my future kids' well-being, it was a terrible thing to do to somebody. People should be honored for the pure connection that they're making, based on their own commitment— whatever their *mikveh* looks like or wherever it takes place or whatever their process of coming to that moment is. Nothing more or less should be asked or offered. You can then sit down and have somebody sign a piece of paper.

Telling the story of conversion is hard because it's a private journey. We don't sit down and tell these stories to everybody and even when people ask, we wonder: "Do they really want to hear?" My impression is that they want a simple little two-sentence answer—maybe because they think that is all there is. The opportunity to share in a book is different because people will be able to carefully ponder what we say.

I am touched by the negativity that sometimes infuses the attitudes of born Jews about converts. The things that people say about Jews by Choice when they don't know that they're standing next to one. There's a lot of stereotyping, a lot of dumping, a lot of projecting negative energy. I've had that done to me over the years at different times, mostly by people who didn't know, and occasionally by people who were very confrontive, shocked to meet a Jew by Choice for the first time. What I came to understand was that I was a mirror for them and that, in fact, though my choosing may outwardly have appeared threatening to them somehow, it really was because they weren't owning their own Jewishness. They were at odds with their own inability to find what was beautiful or of value in their tradition and were confronted with someone who not only chose to be Jewish but was choosing it from a very high and spiritually motivated place. This was beyond them, and they were struggling with so much dark shadow energy and projecting that onto me. I was able to disengage from their anger or dark side enough to not take it on.

Those experiences have left an impression on me. I feel a sadness that so many Jews by birth haven't been given the treasures that Judaism has to offer and instead carry the burden of negativity and pain—and food—but it isn't based on the spiritual food that our generation is starving for. So many Jews by birth don't know where to "go" to find it, and it's right there. Judaism is a banquet, but they've never been able to share any of that. That's very sad.

I don't know why it is that I've been propelled through my life to devote myself to offering Judaism to other Jews. I've given my entire life over to creating Jewish artwork, to creating Jewish rituals, to creating a Jewish community. My entire last fifteen years has been my gift to the Jewish community. And again, it's coming from some place that's sort of unexplainable. It's a drive. There's something in me that's wanting to contribute toward the continuity of this culture and civilization and spiritual path and there's some reason why I've been chosen— rather than my choosing Judaism. I deeply feel that Judaism has chosen me. In spite of all my personal background or rational thinking or education, what has come to me has been very powerful. I can't deny that; it is so big. I need to offer myself for service because that's what is wanted of me, so I'm doing my best to live that out, though sometimes there are points where it doesn't really make sense. But it's what is.

In many of the dreams and experiences I have had I connect deeply, somehow, to the Holocaust. I feel on some level that I am a person reincarnated from the *Shoah*. Many Jews by Choice feel similarly, and for those people it's a very powerful part of them. The kinds of experiences I've had have been extraordinarily strong and come from no place in rational mind or no place that I was exposed to in my childhood. We didn't know any Jews. I do not fit in with the rest of my family in any way. I don't look like them, I don't have the same values. When we get together for Thanksgiving, I'm totally the odd person out by lifestyle, choices, all kinds of things.

An event occurred about five years ago that showed me how deep goes my sensation of connection to the Jewish people and to the past. We were up at a CAGE conference in Seattle, staying with hundreds of other families at a university in a multistory dorm building. In Eugene, ten people around the table for *Shabbat* is a crowd. So coming from such a small Jewish community, it was unusual for me to be amongst the hundreds of Jewish people at the conference. There we all were in this huge building when the fire alarm went off. Suddenly, there were hundreds of parents racing to get their children out of what could be a burning building. Usually, I am not an anxious person. Here, I was completely overwhelmed. It felt like I'd been there before. I had absolutely been there before—running. People were saying, "It's not a real fire; it's okay." But I was completely distraught and panicked. Racing for your life with your kids and you're all Jewish—to suddenly be in this panicked situation felt like it was coming out of some other experience.

I've had some other things like that—a sense of myself being this screaming crazy person in the back of a train car or truck or something, who can see what's coming ahead and other people can't get what's coming next; that sense of impending horror and doom. Those kinds of sensations that there's no way to explain in a rational place. My entire upbringing gave me no cues or clues for getting any of this. It has to come from some other part of reality that no one knows much about.

I feel there is a part of me that spiritually needed to marry a Jewish person. God had that in the plan. There was some healing that was meant for me to experience with somebody who also had a strong Jewish spiritual connection.

My husband's family lost hundreds of people in the Holocaust, but they never discussed it. I kept pressing and finally they spoke of it briefly—about Yitz's great-grandmother and her siblings, aunts and uncles and cousins. I've been the one who's worked to find out about this family history. I've been doing genealogy charts including those who had died in the Holocaust, those who've immigrated to Israel, and those who are still in Russia. Some part of me has a deep need to help reweave the fabric of this Jewish family, separated by time, history, and continents.

One of the other experiences that I've had that connects with the *Shoah* has occurred during communal *mikvehs*. I guess there have been maybe a half-dozen times at a retreat or a workshop when women have gathered together before *Shabbat* to have a communal *mikveh* in the swimming pool or lake. Standing there with all these naked women has been an extraordinarily powerful sensation for me, feeling like I've been there before—in the showers. It's very hard for me. It is so profound to stand there with forty naked women doing this beautiful ceremony, then seeing something that feels like a flashback, and I'm completely knocked over by the experience of being together in that way. Again, it's not a place that has any rational basis in my life. It has to come from some other, previous experience.

If you were to ask me if I believe in reincarnation—it's such a weird concept, I can't even say—it's not that I have some intellectual philosophy about it. But I have had so many of these experiences that I have to accept that they are a part of me. I can't explain them. They just *are*. It has opened up my panorama of things that were different than what I might have thought that I'm actually experiencing.

There's a new book out, *Beyond the Ashes* by Rabbi Yonassan Gershom, about people who feel they were born with the soul of someone who died in the Holocaust. This is a part of the experiences of our generation that isn't much known or talked about: "Where did all those people go?" The few people with whom I've spoken who've gone through this experience feel it strongly. They are generally converts. Jews by birth don't ever think of this that I know of. So this is new territory to be explored and to be offered into the communal possibility.

It will be shocking for people to read these stories of past life experiences because so many people who are Jewish by birth are carrying with them the pain and horror and distrust of others. There are certain patterns of behavior styles within the Jewish community that come from the loss (of the Holocaust victims) or having that loss handed down or the memory of that loss. Families never talking about it, but it is all being acted out nonverbally in other ways. The more it is shared that there are those of us who feel we are the souls of those who died, it will be a connection with others to grapple with the pain. It is our generation, the children of the late forties and fifties. We're the ones who had that possibility of reentering in some connected strand from that terrible time. Will it also be true of the children born in the 1990s? Maybe there are souls still needing to be reconnected.

When I came to Judaism, I decided that I couldn't go back and do the work I had been doing before in the same way. I needed to have a spiritual focus. My whole world has become completely Jewish. Our whole reality is filled with living our life on the rhythms of the Jewish holidays, and resonating with the spiritual teachings.

My graphics-design skills transformed into the Judaic artwork I've been engaged in for fifteen years, and I've contributed a lot of energy toward the synagogue and social services. For about ten years I was centrally involved in the planning and development of a *moshav* where we hoped to continue, in a more holistic way, the spiritual community that had been developing in a piecemeal fashion in town.

We bought the land; we moved there with seven families. We held more than fifty retreats there. We had women's conferences and international disability conferences and all the Jewish holidays there. There were organic gardens. We put our energy into this wonderful vision and dream.

Moshav is a tender subject for me because it represents a culmination of years of dreaming and working and visioning in the attempt to integrate spirituality and social, political, ecological balance for our lives. We moved in in 1983 and a lot of people thought we were past our prime for trying to do such an undertaking—after all, this wasn't the sixties anymore!—and to do it with a Jewish focus in a place that didn't have a nearby large Jewish community to support it in various ways.

I devoted my professional energies to being the director of a nonprofit organization to run the *moshav*, setting it up and arranging all the legalities and the financing, gathering a board of directors, acquiring the land and finding the families, then offering the *moshav* and community as a location for countless gatherings over the years. I was juggling the whole thing while having babies. We let go of a nice home in the city and lived in a very, very funky apartment above the main hall. We shared our resources because every family doesn't need to have its own lawnmower, washing machine, and so on.

Money was our main obstacle, and Oregon was going through a major recession at the time. Property values decreased. In the end, we couldn't even sell the land, and we ended up having to give the property back.

There's a part of me that feels a great deal of satisfaction that we took the risks, which were many, for a bunch of people with modest incomes. We tried to use our lives in the fullest way, because to live in a spiritual community, we were making a gesture of values, of trying to act out something in which we deeply believed, and though we lasted there only about three years, we did live the dream that many people carry in their hearts. There are lots of people who want to live in a community in the country, living a Jewish life and raising their kids in beautiful, safe surroundings. I still believe in it.

My husband's relatives, who went to Palestine in 1926 and were part of *kibbutz* from the first shovel of dirt, felt we didn't have the right impetus here—the motivating factors that forced people to look for a solution to the challenges of life through communal living were different in the beginnings of the State of Israel. As individuals in America, we have too many luxurious options. And it is true that we do have that luxury of all kinds of choices in how we go about our lives.

When I envision getting older and I look around and see the struggles that many people are having, I come to the same conclusion: communal life is an answer. We're not going to have money to retire, travel, and have a supported life. Why don't we all invest, buy a place on the coast and have all our friends come together and live as little seniors hobbling down the hallway together. It's good to live communally, sharing resources with a spiritual focus to your life that's bigger than just your own immediate nuclear family. There is the emotional connection of your extended spiritual family there for you. Who cares whether you have all those material things? It's time to shed all the materialism that this society is so chock-full of and to teach our kids there's something to do besides going shopping.

I look back on that time of the *moshav* as a period in my life when I felt most fully alive. I was using myself through all of my best gifts to try to offer things in ways that I believed in and fully expressed my values. There was a sense of purpose that I feel lacking in my life living in our little box in the city, where it is so easy to feel isolated and lonely. I don't feel connected to a larger vision. I believe that there is a social need for interaction different from going to your job and sitting at your computer stall. There's a need for connection on multidimensional levels that we're suffering the lack of in this society. The *moshav* served as a life gesture toward developing a communal spiritually based vision of community.

What called us from within to drop the security of our city living to live out a dream of community?

It's hard to know how to convey some of these kinds of experiences to other people or even to our own kids. It's very personal; sometimes it's beyond even my own understanding of it. The question is, how do you teach your kids to listen to those wise inner voices? What if their voices are something very different from your inner voice? God's wisdom speaking to them comes out in a different way. There's a level of emotionally wanting to accept what's God's will and just saying, okay, I get it, this is what I'm supposed to be doing. There's a level of being willing to offer your life to serve and move along the path that you're being guided to be on, regardless of rational thought and conscious decision making. You must be willing to hear an inner voice that's much bigger and allow your life to be guided from that place.

That's not something that I was taught to do, and it's hard to put that faith in yourself continually when there is no support and encouragement from society for that. You have to do it, therefore, from a very profound belief that you seek to strengthen just by your own inner listening and give credibility to hearing God's call in spite of how society really operates. I've tried to always be open to hearing that inner voice and acting on it. It's harder to hear when you have breakfast to cook and kids to drive to school and you're in a fast-paced life of keeping up with family. That makes finding a quiet time to listen more challenging for me. Joys, as well as disappointments, must be accepted so that we may resonate with that place that's bigger than we are.

I found a spiritual home for myself in Judaism that I didn't have in my Christian upbringing. I also feel powerfully connected to Native American traditions. Here again my pathway has often been through dreams and visions. Over the years, I've put together a number of retreats comparing the two because there are earth-based cycles in both that honor the truth of the seasons. There are sacred ceremonies that have a lot of similarity: sweat lodges and *mikvehs*, purification rites, ways of honoring the moon, ways of relating to women in their time of menstruation that can be looked at as sexist and discriminatory or as a community acknowledging powerful energy.

Women have a highly respected position in Native American tradition. My understanding is that when a woman is not included in a sweat lodge during her menstrual period, it is because her spiritual energy during that time is considered to be so powerful that it could somehow overwhelm the rest of what's going on. Instead of being considered dirty, it is acknowledged that the woman is in an extraordinary relationship with the Creator and with the cycles at that point and therefore is manifesting a different energy. I certainly have more powerful dreams and instincts at that time of my cycle. There's a greater emotional energy there and insightfulness and power.

The *mikvehs* I have done are "Oregonian" style. I take people to the hot springs and to the lakes and to the sides of the rivers, and we haul river water to people's bathtubs. I've done all kinds of things to create *mikvehs* here where there are none. We've taken Orthodox rabbis to go see what a true *mikveh* is in the woods and what it really is to go to a pool of living water. It's very astonishing for people who are used to traditional *mikvehs* enclosed in buildings.

To use *mikveh* as a spiritual tool is a wonderful opportunity, not just for women but for men as well. It is a way to acknowledge periods of spiritual transformation such as going to the *mikveh* in the evening after you've washed and prepared a body for a funeral. One can go to the *mikveh* to make a transformation in consciousness for a holiday or a stage in your development that requires you to be fully yourself. To make a physical gesture is very healing and transformative, and it helps on a lot of levels. So I see *mikveh* as more than just an opportunity for women to honor their menstrual cycles.

I feel like it's my responsibility—it's *our* responsibility—in this generation at this time to bring forward the voice of the women. We must be a part of ushering in this energy of the feminine in Judaism—to offer that to our daughters and to offer that to ourselves and to our husbands, to bring forth the feminine voice that's been missing. I have been very involved myself and with others in creating new rituals and ceremonies and *tefillah* for women. Another way of doing what I'm being called to do is through my artwork, creating new forms of women's *tallitot*, sacred garments for Jewish women in spiritual leadership positions that look different and feel different, enabling dance and movement. A woman can feel special and can be acknowledged as someone looking significantly different, empowered in her spiritual qualities, embodied in sacred garments.

An idea came to me at a retreat in the early 1980s that we needed to find a way to honor women spiritual leaders—an acknowledgment of what they are giving to their communities. So we created a ceremony called *"Eshet Hazon."* The first woman to be so recognized was Hannah Tiferet Siegal—an extraordinary woman who's a teacher and spiritual leader in her community, yet there isn't a format for acknowledging her and calling her "Rabbi." She's not proceeding along that traditional male path, now open to women. She's got a family, she's midwifing babies, weaving *tallitot*, creating ceremonies and rituals, and teaching people traditions. I wrote in *New Menorah* years ago about creating this ceremony for Hannah: we wrote her a document and made her a title and honored her as a Jewish spiritual woman teacher in our times.

Now ten years later, there have been twenty women—throughout the country and internationally—"ordained" by the will of the people, each being called "*Eshet Hazon*." Some of the women who have been so ordained by their own *minyan* circles have come together and have chosen other women to acknowledge, so it's a powerful web of connection—not through any organization, though. There is no course of study. And there's a significance to that. There are other ways to become a spiritual leader than the rabbinate track—though that works very well now for single women who are young. The path is cut for them to get going in that way. Women who are now forty, fifty, sixty years old, who have given their lives to women's spiritual development in all kinds of different ways, don't have a comparable way of being honored. There was a need to create such a ceremony, and it can be duplicated in everybody's creative imagination in their own communities.

My congregation is international. My sense of being fully at one with myself spiritually is in the Jewish Renewal Movement. I feel at home coming together with all of those people: sisters and brothers who are on the path, each in his or her own different way. Some with very strong Jewish backgrounds are taking that knowledge and experience into creative new modes of poetry or liturgy or music or other expressions. They are letting the sense of God's voice move through them in their work and in the deepest sense of themselves and are taking that to a new offering. The Tree of Life is alive and growing in this moment in time.

As a cantor for our congregation, Yitz is leading services that are more conservative and in larger groups of people than I am comfortable with. I feel stiff and cut off from myself in standard services. My spiritual fulfillment comes in intimate settings where it's more creative and on a smaller scale. This year for the High Holidays, Yitz led services for 1,000 people, and I led services in another spot simultaneously for a dozen people. I finally owned what I needed and did the right thing for me. It was the best I'd felt in years of going to services. It's not that I don't love the traditional singing and much of the *davening*—that power of sacred language also has its beauty that's very provocative and deep—but I can't handle sitting in a room with hundreds of other people reading out of an outmoded prayer book. I can't bear it. But that is what Yitz is being paid to do in that job. He's functioning in the whole rainbow from Orthodox to Jewish Renewal, and it is fine for him because he is able to find his own spiritual place. I am not. I'm happy only at one end of the continuum. There I feel really at peace and great in myself. When I'm pushed into that other sphere, I feel, "Oh, God, this is not for me." I can't stand it. It's very hard. I'm just bored with what feels to me to be lifeless expressions of Judaism.

All must be responsible for their spiritual well-being and contribute to the common well-being and health of the community by fully engaging themselves to their highest potential in that domain. Ideally we would find ourselves with like-minded people—a *havurah* of people like ourselves.

We live in a world that's not perfect, and multitudes are not taking any responsibility whatsoever for their spiritual path. There's a concern that the only way Judaism will continue is if there is some level of doing it *for* people. Family education is the new trend in the last years on how to ensure that Judaism will continue. "Don't just drop off your kid at Sunday school—you come too and we'll figure out what you can do at home with your family."

We need to reengage these adults who were so turned off to Judaism as kids. They must take the responsibility for their own spiritual development, and, rather than pass off to teachers the responsibility for transmitting that to their children, do it themselves. That's the huge transformation that has to take place because there are zillions of people in our age bracket who grew up in Judaism that for them was empty. For many postwar children, the Holocaust was the unifying factor. Judaism did not give them many guideposts for their lives.

Now we are so affluent that we have everything—everything but spirituality. We have absolutely everything material compared to any society through history and all through the rest of the world now. What is lacking, as Mother Teresa says, is wisdom—and we hunger for it. What are we doing with the time that's given to us? There are now so many people searching, but they don't even know to look to their own Judaism. Community leaders are doing an important *mitzvah* when they offer people a reminder that there might be something Jewish to pay attention to, to reconnect with.

My own feeling is that people can reconnect best by encouraging congregations to develop *havurot*. These are small intimate groups of people who can share *Shabbat* dinner with each other. Many groups of, say, five families will get together for holidays because people don't live near their families of origin anymore. People can empower each other to learn by having women's *davening* groups and children getting together to make up skits about the *parashah*. These little intimate groups can come together, maybe four times a year, for a retreat to spend a whole *Shabbat* with one another. Then when you come together for High Holidays, it has some connection, coherence, and relationship. You're not just walking in as blind sheep, knowing you're supposed to be there but not remembering why, and somebody is up there doing it for you. Getting together in *havurot* can become an active, engaging, alive process for people to live their lives on a Jewish cycle.

So many Jews by birth are still coming with a lot of their negative baggage and don't have an understanding about what wisdom lies within Judaism. Many converts are coming with the connection to their spirituality that really resonates with the teachings in Judaism that Jews by birth don't have a clue about. And they're missing something very important. My wish for the Jewish community would be that somehow there be an opening of hearts so that people could really learn from each other and hear of the wisdom of people that have opened themselves to a Jewish spiritual path. And to heal themselves in those places where they have been wounded. I don't think that can happen with masses of people just sitting in rows of chairs being "led," but with the intimacy that comes from sharing in safe and sacred settings.

Appendix

Questionnaire

I believe that the decision to convert to Judaism is most often far more complex and nonlinear, in a historical sense, than the following questions would suggest. The questions therefore are valuable only in stimulating you to think about your memories and feelings about the process of conversion. You do not need to write anything.

Family Background

• Think about your life with your family of origin. If your family had a "mission statement" (one for all/all for one; "Tradition!"; every man for himself, etc.) what would it have been?

• What place did religion have in your family life? What impact did your family's traditions have on you? Were there fundamental truths in which all family members believed?

• How does your family respond to diversity?

Adult Experiences That Led Up to Choosing Judaism

• What were your views about religion when you became an adult?

• Do you believe in God? Has your belief in God changed as you have become Jewish? Did you believe in Jesus as God and savior? In Mary as the mother of God? How have you transformed or left behind those beliefs? If belief in God is not part of your commitment to Judaism, how has that affected your Jewish life?

• If you came to Judaism seeking religious involvement, were you also considering traditions other than your own or Judaism?

• What did you hope to find in religion: spiritual fulfillment; community; a code by which to live; a closer relationship to and understanding of God, and so forth?

• Was there an event or series of events that led to your "discovery" of Judaism?

• What do you think makes Judaism uniquely suited to you?

The Process of Conversion

• Describe your decision to become Jewish. How did you act on that decision? What experiences were formative in this process?

• In what ways did you prepare for conversion? Who participated in this aspect of the process?

• What was the impact for you of the *Bet Din, dam brit* (if you are a man), and *mikveh*?
  • What ceremonies or celebrations surrounded this experience for you?
  • Were family dynamics intensified by your decision to convert?

Your Life as a Jew

• In your transition to a Jewish life, what have you found most meaningful? What expected and unexpected challenges have you faced and how have you accepted or resolved them?
  • Jewish ritual life (life-cycle ceremonies, the holidays, the Sabbath) is very rich and potentially overwhelming. Describe how you have incorporated ritual into your life.
  • Judaism can be divided into three major areas: religion, peoplehood, and culture. How has your identity merged into these areas?
  • How has your status evolved in the various communities to which you belong (family, work, religious, neighborhood, school, etc.)?
  • What is the effect of your conversion on your children?
  • How do you relate to Israel? Have your feelings changed since you became Jewish?
  • What does the Holocaust mean to you?
  • How do you feel you fit into the flow of generations from Abraham and Sarah?

Looking toward the Future

• What would you share with others considering conversion to help them in their process?
  • What is the significance of your conversion to Judaism as a whole? To the secular/Christian world?
  • How do you see yourself in the various life cycle events yet to come in your and your family's lives?

QUESTIONS FOR ADOPTEES

The experiences of adoptees as converts bear little similarity, at least on the surface, to those of adult converts. Most adoptees raised in a Jewish family have led only a Jewish life and in a sense have not "left" anything as some other converts do. However, since the purpose of my book is to explore as many avenues of the conversion experience as possible, I think it is valuable to know how adoptees feel about their status as Jews. Because the whole issue of adoption has become more open, adoptees have increasing access to information about their biological families, and may question their identities more freely than may have been the case in the past.

• What has it been like for you to integrate your Jewish identity, adoptive identity, and biological identity? Were the processes (if you went through them) of your acceptance of Judaism and acceptance of your adoption parallel processes, different, or converging?

• What questions did you ask your parents about your biological family and how you fit into your Jewish family and community?

• Do you feel connected to the Jewish "peoplehood," *l'dor vador*—"unto all generations"?

• Do you feel a stronger connection to some aspects of Judaism (religion, history, culture, language, Holocaust, etc.) than others and do you think this is a reflection of your experience as an adoptee?

• What responses have there been to your adoption and conversion? What responses from family, friends, and community were helpful/unhelpful in sustaining your Jewish identity?

• Was there a process of acceptance/rejection of Judaism at different phases of your life? As far as you can tell, how was your experience similar to or different from born Jews?

• Have you sought out your biological family? Did you ever feel an obligation to look into what you know of the religious heritage of your biological parents? If so, how did that contact affect your feelings about being Jewish, if at all?

• Describe what you know about your conversion. If you were old enough to participate, in what ways did you do so?

• At *bar/bat mitzvah* age, were you presented with the choice of whether to continue living a Jewish life?

• "Looking Jewish" is becoming less and less an issue as Jewish diversity is a more accepted fact. Was your physical appearance and fitting into stereotypes of Jewish looks ever an issue for you?

• What effect does knowing adult converts have on you? From your perspective, are there any similarities between the adult conversion experience and your own experience?

• What, if any, commentary, stories, laws, and so on from traditional Jewish sources concerning adoption have you found useful?

• How does Judaism's attitude toward adoption affect you in positive or negative ways?

• If you are now raising a family of your own, describe the thoughts and feelings you have about passing on the Jewish traditions to your children (biological or adoptive).

• Do you see a difference in the adoption climate in the Jewish community now that it appears adoption is becoming more common?

• What would you want to have people feel and understand about the experience of a child adopted into a Jewish family?

Glossary

Although this glossary contains more than the usual one-line definitions, it is merely a "taste" of the full dimension of each entry, many of which require whole chapters if not whole books to explain.

afikomen   Three *matzot* are placed in the *matzah* cover at the Passover *seder* table. The middle *matzah* is broken in half at the beginning of the *seder*, wrapped in a napkin, and by custom is hidden by children to be "ransomed" after the meal. In my husband's family the adults hide the *afikomen* and the children search for it. After the meal, once the *afikomen*, a symbol of the Paschal offering, is returned and eaten, no other food may be consumed. Then the rest of the *seder* proceeds.

agunah   (lit. "shut off") A woman whose husband refuses to give her a *get*, a religious divorce. According to Jewish law, a woman may not remarry if she does not have a religious divorce. The category of *agunah* also includes those women whose husbands have been killed, without witnesses, and the body has not been recovered.

Aleinu   Prayer at the end of the service that proclaims God the supreme ruler of the universe.

aliyah   (lit. "going up, ascent") Refers to being called up to the Torah. It is an honor in the synagogue to stand next to the person who reads from the Torah scroll. It is considered auspicious to be called to the Torah for momentous occasions, such as on the *Shabbat* before marriage. The first time a person "gets an *aliyah*" is on the occasion of his or her *bar/bat mitzvah*, and ever after he or she is eligible to get an *aliyah*. "Making *aliyah*" also refers to emigration to Israel.

Amidah   The silent series of prayers that is one of the centerpieces of the Jewish religious service. It is recited individually, while standing, and it is a custom that people will sit silently after they have finished. In some synagogues the service does not resume until everyone is again seated. In larger synagogues it is often the custom that people are not allowed to enter the sanctuary during this prayer in order not to break the concentration of those praying.

Ashkenaz   Originally referred to just that settlement of Jews in Northwest Europe along the banks of the Rhine. Now it denotes the entire Jewish cultural tradition of French, German, Polish-Lithuanian, Russian, Hungarian, Romanian, and Bulgarian Jews. Yiddish is the language associated with the *Ashkenazim*. Many of the cultural and social forms of the *Ashkenazim* are similar to the folkways of the European communities in which they lived, including dress, food, dance, and music—all given a unique Jewish twist and flavor.

baal teshuvah   (lit. "master of turning") Refers to those Jews who are returning to traditional Jewish religious observance after having lived a more secular life. This is such an important phenomenon in modern Jewish, Orthodox life that a whole network of institutions have been developed that are devoted to nurturing the needs and aspirations of the men and women who are rekindling their interest in traditional Jewish life.

bar/bat mitzvah   (lit. "son or daughter of the commandment") This rite of passage marks the entrance into full adult religious status for young Jewish men and women. Originally, the ceremony of *bar mitzvah* was celebrated only for thirteen-year-old boys, but in this century, the liberal branches of Judaism included girls. In traditional branches of Judaism, the *bat mitzvah* of girls occurred at age twelve and was a private marker of a girl's status as an adult with little or no public ceremony attached. Many Jews are concerned that the emphasis on the party usually associated with a *bar/bat mitzvah* has obscured the solemnity of the occasion. In my children's Jewish day school, young people are required to adopt a *tzedakah* project for a year as part of their preparation for their *bar/bat mitzvah* and as a reminder of the responsibility of Jewish adults to engage in *tikkun olam*—repair of the world.

BBYO   B'nai B'rith Youth Organization, founded in 1924 by B'nai B'rith, the world's oldest and largest Jewish service organization. Chapters throughout the world encourage Jewish teens to participate in programs of cultural, religious, community service, social, and athletic activities.

bentsch   The act of saying a blessing. Colloquially it refers to the grace after meals, the *Birkat HaMazon*, a series of blessings that thank God for providing us the goodness of food. Although we also say blessings before the meal, we reserve our greatest expression of gratitude till after we are sated, when we might be less likely to remember the Source of the bounty of which we have just partaken.

Bet Din   (lit. "house of judgment") The Jewish religious court, usually made up of three rabbis, but it may also consist of learned elders in the community. Modern *Batei Din* (plural) concern themselves mostly with issues of personal religous status, such as conversion or divorce, and the dietary laws, but in pre-Holocaust communities (and a few modern ultra-Orthodox communities) a *Bet Din* would preside over any matters concerning the relationship between Jewish people (e.g., commerce) that did not conflict with the authority of secular courts, as well as specifically religious matters.

bet knesset   (lit. "house of assembly") Synagogue.

bimah   (lit. "elevated place") The platform on which stands the desk from which the Torah is read.

blintzes   Crepelike pancakes filled with cheese or fruit, served with sour cream, applesauce, and cinnamon sugar.

bris board   A board onto which a baby is strapped to immobilize him for the circumcision. In a traditional *bris* the baby is placed on a pillow in the lap of the person who has the honor of being the *sandek*. This person, usually a male relative, will gently hold the baby's legs while the *bris* takes place.

brit milah (also **bris**) (lit. "covenant of circumcision") The removal of the foreskin of the penis, performed on the eighth day after the baby's birth, as commanded in Genesis 21:4, 17:12, and Leviticus 12:1–2, to mark the covenant that Abraham formed with God. The *bris* is performed by a *mohel*. Many people choose to have the *bris* done in their homes, where friends and family gather for this solemn and joyful occasion. After the operation is performed and honored family members or friends recite the various blessings, the rest of the crowd sings out *"Mazal Tov!"* and all partake in a festive meal.

bubbe (Yiddish) Grandmother, or a grandmother-aged person. A grandfather is a *zaide*.

Chabad The largest of the branches of the *hasidic* movement, founded in the eighteenth century by Rabbi Shneur Zalman of Liadi. The name *Chabad* is based on the initials of three of the highest of the ten *sefirot*, or spheres, which according to the Kabbalah emanate from God: *hokhmah* (wisdom), *binah* (reason), and *daat* (knowledge). Lubavitch is derived from the town in which Zalman's son Dov Baer lived. The most recent leader of the Chabad movement, Rabbi Menachem Mendel Schneerson, descendant of a dynasty of Chabad rabbis, was well educated in both secular and religious studies. Rabbi Schneerson was believed by his followers to be such a holy person that he could perform miracles. The very elderly Rebbe died in June 1994.

Chabad Lubavitchers have been very active in bringing Jews back to Judaism, sometimes setting up kiosks in shopping centers to invite Jewish people, and sometimes non-Jews as well, to eat *matzah* at Passover time, learn a little about Jewish customs, or get invited back to the "Chabad House" for a class, meal, or religious service. The men stand out in their distinctive garb: long black overcoats and fur-fringed hats or *shtreimels*, and *peyot* (earlocks) and full beards.

dam brit Drawing of blood from the penis in a symbolic *brit* for a man who is already circumcised. This is a part of the conversion ceremony for men in the traditional branches of Judaism.

daven To pray.

Dayenu (lit. "It would have been enough") This is the refrain for a song in the first part of the Passover *seder* that chronicles how God through His loving-kindness brought us step by step from the degradation of slavery to the redemption of Sinai.

Deuteronomy (Hebrew, *Devarim*, "words") The last of the five books of Moses contained in the Pentateuch or *Humash*, the Jewish Bible.

devar Torah (lit. "a word of Torah") A discussion of the Torah portion. A *devar Torah* can range from a minute discussion of the use and meaning of the words of the text, to a lecture on history, to an extrapolation of guidance for modern times, to a sharing of the interpretations made by scholars through the centuries. Anyone who takes the time to study the Torah portion and read supplementary materials can give a *devar Torah*, and *divrei Torah* are not reserved just for *Shabbat* but are offered in various settings in which Jews gather, from luncheons to meetings to joyful celebrations.

dreidl   A four-sided spinning top used in a game of chance associated with the Jewish holiday of Hanukkah. Each side is marked with a Hebrew letter. Each player gets a chance to spin the *dreidl*. If it lands with the *nun* up, the player gets nothing; with the *gimel* up, the player takes all the coins in the pot; with the *heh* up, the player takes half the coins; with the *shin* up, the player gives up one coin for the pot.

Eretz Yisrael   The land of Israel.

erev   ("eve") Used as a prefix: *erev Shabbat,* "*Shabbat eve,*" as in "I got the phone call about my new job '*erev Shabbat*' (just before *Shabbat* started)." "Everyone should drink a lot of water '*erev* Yom Kippur.'" There is an implication here of thinking ahead to get mundane things out of the way or make preparations before the holiday or Sabbath.

eshet hayil   The "woman of valor" (from Proverbs 31:10–31) is traditionally chanted by a husband to his wife on Friday night.

frum   (Yiddish, from German, "pious") Strictly observant of Jewish religious law.

ger (fem. **gioret**)   (lit. "stranger," but it is closer to "resident alien" or "sojourner") This has become synonymous with "proselyte" or convert.

get   The Jewish bill of divorce that must be presented by a Jewish husband to his Jewish wife or her representative. Without a *get*, a Jewish woman may not remarry. In Israel and in ultra-Orthodox communities elsewhere, women have no legal recourse in the religious courts. The issue of the *get* is a source of enormous controversy and great individual personal pain, since a vindictive or missing husband can withhold a *get*, whereas a husband whose wife refuses to accept the *get* may petition "one hundred rabbis" and gain permission to remarry.

haftarah   (lit. "concluding portion") A supplemental reading from the prophetic writings.

hag   Jewish holiday.

Haggadah   A book containing the service to be recited at the Passover *seder*. It includes the famous "four questions" (beginning with "Why is this night different from all other nights?), which are asked by the youngest person at the table. Through the course of the *seder*, the *Haggadah* describes the symbols on the *seder* plate and prescribes the four cups of wine to be drunk and the remembrance of the details of the exodus from Egypt, when the Israelites could have despaired but didn't. It is sung and chanted around the table on this most-observed Jewish holiday. It ends with the hope that next year we will be in Jerusalem.

hai   The Hebrew word meaning "life," it is made up of the two letters *het* and *yud*, which have a numerical value (as do all Hebrew letters) that adds up to eighteen. The number eighteen is therefore associated with "life" and auspicious occasions. When giving gifts of money or making donations, Jews often give in multiples of eighteen.

halakhah   The code of Jewish law that embraces all practices and observances of Judaism. Halakhah has been developed by learned Jews over centuries of study and discussion about the most minute details of daily life as well as global and transcendent concerns of human beings. The last major codification was the *Shulhan*

Arukh ("the prepared table") written by Joseph Caro in the sixteenth century. Interpretation of *halakhah* varies among the four main branches of Judaism: the Orthodox believes *halakhah* is absolutely binding; Reform believes Jews should be guided in some areas by *halakhah*; Conservative takes a middle path between the two and believes that *halakhah* should be binding but admits of a greater latitude in its application; Reconstruction eliminates *mitzvot* that are no longer relevant and believes that *halakhah* should be based on modern ethical standards.

hallah   The braided or round loaf of bread that graces the Sabbath table. When it is baked, a small portion (the *"hallah"*) is dropped to the bottom of the oven and a blessing is said, a symbol that in Temple days the *hallah* was given to the priests. Two loaves are used for the Sabbath to remind us of the two portions of *manna* that God gave the Israelites who followed Moses into the desert. The two portions made work unnecessary on the Sabbath.

hametz   Leavened bread or any leavened grain product. One of the time-honored traditions of *Pesah* or Passover preparations is the thorough cleaning of one's home to remove all traces of *hametz*, ending in the kitchen the night before *Pesah* begins, with a search through the cupboards using a candle and a feather. This is an especially delightful process with children, who are sometimes rewarded with small gifts or treats for finding the stray pieces of leaven. Whatever remains in the household that is not kosher for Passover, such as cans of soup, is put out of the way and "sold" to a non-Jew for a token amount of money, say a dollar. By around 10 A.M. on the morning of the first *seder*, one must burn any breakfast leftovers, and some communities have large bonfires for this purpose. As with other Jewish rituals, ridding ourselves of leaven so minutely is a physical exercise that is meant to have a spiritual effect. We are, among other things, reminded of the ephemeral nature of material possessions and the eternal nature of spiritual connections.

hamishe   (friendly; comfortable) A *hamishe* person fits in with people and makes you feel as though you have known them for a long time.

Hanukkah   (lit. "dedication") A minor holiday that commemorates the triumph of the Maccabees over the Syrians, which allowed the Jews to practice their religion. The story of the Hanukkah lights is fondly retold: when the Jews were once again able to go to their Temple there was enough oil for the ceremonial lamp to last only one day, but instead a miracle occurred and the oil lasted for eight days and nights. Celebrations include playing *"dreidl,"* receiving Hanukkah *gelt* (money) or small gifts, and eating potato *latkes* or *sufganiyot* (doughnuts), an Israeli tradition.

Because it often falls near the Christmas holidays, Hanukkah is often compared to Christmas. However, the attempt to equate the significance and celebration of Hanukkah with Christmas is troubling to many Jews.

HaShem   (lit. "the name") God.

hasidim   *Encyclopaedia Judaica* says of the *hasidim*, whose movement began in the eighteenth century and who adhere stringently to the Jewish religious laws: "Ecstasy, mass enthusiasm, close-knit group cohesion, and charismatic leadership . . . are the distinguishing socioreligious marks of Hasidim" (7:1390).

Havdalah   The ceremony at the end of *Shabbat* that marks the shift from sacred to everyday time.

havurah   (lit. "fellowship" or "group of friends") A *havurah* is a fellowship of Jews who come together for study, celebration, worship, and so forth, and is typically characterized by shared responsibility for leadership functions. The National Havurah Committee is a sort of umbrella organization that supports and promotes the hundreds of *havurot* across the United States and sponsors a yearly retreat.

Hebrew Union College   The Reform movement's seminary founded in Cincinnati, Ohio, in 1875, and merged with the Jewish Institute of Religion in New York in 1922. The HUC also has a center in Jerusalem.

heksher   (lit. "approbation" or "attestation") The mark on consumer goods, mainly food, that "attests" to the purchaser that the product is made in accordance with the laws of *kashrut*. There are many different *hekshers*, the most common of which is an *O* encircling a *u*, denoting the Union of Orthodox Jewish Congregations of America, but there are others such as *K* and *K* enclosed in a triangle. Some food produced locally will have a *heksher* known only to that community. While an "O-U" is generally accepted by every Jew, there are some *hekshers* not acceptable to the most observant communities.

Hillel House   The name of each campus location of the Hillel Foundation of the B'nai B'rith, the world's oldest and largest Jewish service organization. It serves the religious, cultural, and social needs of Jewish college students and is named after a famous ancient rabbi.

hol hamoed   Intermediate days of the festivals Pesah, Shavuot, and Sukkot.

Humash   (from the Hebrew *hamesh*, "five") Volume that contains the five books of the Jewish Bible; also "Pentateuch." The names of the five books are *Bereshit*, (Genesis), *Shemot* (Exodus), *VaYikra* (Leviticus), *BaMidbar* (Numbers), and *Devarim* (Deuteronomy). In the *Humash* the Hebrew of the Torah is written with vowels, and the English is alongside. It is footnoted in most editions with just a few of the thousands of explanations and commentaries that have been given throughout the ages.

huppah   The wedding canopy. It is also used to refer to the marriage ceremony, as in "We attended the *huppah*, but not the reception afterward." The *huppah* can be a self-supporting, ornate structure, or the groom's *tallit* held above the heads of the couple, its four corners usually attached to poles and supported by celebrants.

hutzpah   According to my mother-in-law, a native Yiddish-speaker, "a person with *hutzpah* has a lot of nerve, is very forward, doesn't always think of others."

JCC   Jewish Community Center; most Jewish communities large enough to support one have a JCC. In Baltimore we have two, which provide a variety of services and activities, including swimming and other sports, secular and religious classes, entertainment, children's programs and education, cultural exhibits, and performances.

Jewish Renewal Movement   As articulated by the Jewish Renewal organization ALEPH: "Jewish renewal is a diverse movement of individuals, groups and organizations engaged in the creation of a vital and relevant Judasim for our time. Jewish renewal draws on Jewish tradition, sacred texts, mysticism, culture and history as well as modern life experiences and our own inner truths. Jewish renewal is also characterized by the full inclusion of women, respect for other spiritual paths, and a commitment to *tikkun olam*, which we understand to mean deep healing of the world on personal, sociopolitical, and ecological levels."

Jewish Theological Seminary (JTS)   The Conservative movement's rabbinical college in New York City, with branches in Los Angeles (The University of Judaism) and in Jerusalem.

Kabbalah   Jewish mystical tradition, which started after the destruction of the second Temple and continues to this day. *Encyclopaedia Judaica* (10:489–490) says, generally, of Kabbalah: "It is mysticism in fact; but at the same time it is both esotericism and theosophy. . . . Kabbalah may be considered mysticism insofar as it seeks an apprehension of God and creation whose intrinsic elements are beyond the grasp of the intellect . . . through contemplation and illumination . . . and is far removed from the rational and intellectual approach to religion." More than a few Kabbalists have sought a direct human communion with God through annihilation of individuality.

One "user friendly" beginner's book about Kabbalah is *The Thirteen Petalled Rose*, by Adin Steinsaltz (New York: Jason Aronson, 1992).

Kaddish   (lit. "holy") The mourner's prayer, in Aramaic, the language of the Middle East 2,000 years ago. The *Kaddish* is a prayer in praise of God and not a prayer for the dead. It is said to honor the memory of the deceased. In traditional Judaism only men say *Kaddish*, since it must be said three times a day in a *minyan* (a group of ten or more men). In Jim's story, he refers to saying *Kaddish* for his father-and brother-in-law on his wife's behalf. In some synagogues it is traditional for only those who are in mourning to stand, but some have said that in post-Holocaust times we are all in mourning.

kasher   To make a food kosher, for example by salting and washing raw meat, or to make any object used in food production kosher, such as dipping metal utensils in boiling water.

kashrut   The dietary laws are minimally described in the Torah and have been expanded and refined over generations. In the Torah it is forbidden to "seethe a kid in its mother's milk," which is seen as a form of cruel usage and disrespect of animals. The rabbis took this a step further and said that no red meat or meat from fowl could be cooked or eaten with anything that derived from milk. Meat from animals that are domesticated, chew their cud, and have cloven hoofs are kosher. Only domesticated fowl is kosher. These animals must be slaughtered, in humane fashion, by a *shohet* (ritual slaughterer) who uses a very sharp knife to inflict a quickly fatal cut in an artery of the neck. The life-blood must be made to drain out. Originally, a *midrash* says, Israelites were to be vegetarian, but God allowed them to eat meat only if it was killed in the manner just described. Fish must have fins and scales and, along with eggs and all vegetables, are considered to be in a third category, *parve*—anything that is neither dairy nor meat. *Parve* may be eaten with dairy or meat meals.

ketubah   The marriage contract presented by a groom to the bride and signed by two *Shomer Shabbat* witnesses. "The ketubah was originally instituted (at the time of the Babylonian exile) to protect the rights of the Jewish married woman and to lend more dignity to the marriage. The text itself dates back to the second century B.C.E. and is written in Aramaic. It assures the woman that her husband will take care of her, provide for her, and cherish her, 'as is the way of Jewish husbands.' The ketubah text assures her that if the husband dies or divorces her, she will not be left without financial support" (Siegel, Strassfeld, and Strassfeld, *The First Jewish Catalog*, p. 195). Modern *ketubot* have been developed to provide rights and obligations for both partners in the marriage.

kibbutz   An Israeli communal settlement.

kike   A derogatory gentile term for "Jew."

kippah   A headcovering, like a skullcap, used principally by men. Also *yarmulke*.

klal Yisrael   "All of Israel," literally, all Jews.

kohen   A member of the priestly class. Jews were divided into "*kohanim*," the temple priests; "Levites," their assistants; and "Israelites," the rest of the Jewish people. The traditions of the *kohanim* are preserved almost exclusively by the Orthodox branches of Judaism. There is a special blessing over the congregation said on holidays, which only descendants of the priestly class may invoke. Men inherit this position from their fathers, but the daughter of a *kohen* does not pass it on to her sons. *Kohanim* still preside over the *pidyon haben*, the redemption of firstborn sons.

Kohanim were not allowed to marry converts, although a male convert may marry the daughter of a *kohen*. If the marriage between the female convert and the *kohen* had already taken place, however, it was recognized.

Kol Nidre   The prayer by this name in the first, evening service of the Yom Kippur holiday has given its name to the whole service. The prayer, which is rather short, is sung three times, first softly, then with increasing projection. It is an annulment of all vows between ourselves and God—note that it is only our vows with God; other vows must be negotiated between the people involved and are not absolved by this declaration.

kosher   (lit. "clean") This is meant in the ritual sense and customarily refers to food, but also refers to any Jewish ritual properly done or any ritual object properly made (e.g., a "kosher" *mikveh*; a "kosher" *mezuzah*, etc.).

kugel   Noodle and egg dish from Ashkenazic tradition, usually sweet and full of raisins.

kvell   To feel pleased and proud.

Ladino   The language of the Sephardic Jews who fled from Spain during the Spanish Inquisition of the late 1400s. Ladino is a mixture of medieval Castilian, Portuguese, Arabic, and Hebrew. Like Yiddish, it is written in Hebrew script.

latkes   Shredded potato pancakes usually associated with Hanukkah, but good anytime with sour cream, applesauce, and cinnamon sugar.

leyn   To chant the Torah.

Lubavitcher   (see *Chabad*) A branch of Hasidism.

Maariv   The evening service.

Mashiah   The Messiah.

matzah   The unleavened bread, much like a large cracker, that marks the observance of Passover. To be kosher or "proper" for the holiday, *matzot* must be made from specially prepared Passover flour mixed only with water. The process is carefully supervised so that the dough has no opportunity to rise. This makes a very dry and crumbly "bread" and the floors around the tables in Jewish homes are sprinkled with *matzah* crumbs at Passover time.

matzah ball   The dumpling made of *matzah* meal found in chicken soup that has come to typify Jewish cooking. Will the *Shabbat matzah* balls be light and fluffy, or sodden and leadlike?

Megillat Esther   The book of Esther, recited with much fervor and hilarity at Purim, the festival that marks the triumph of the Jews over the evil Haman (whose name, each time it is mentioned aloud in the story, is blotted out with raucous groggers —noisemakers) through the bravery and intellect of Queen Esther and her uncle, Mordehai.

mehitzah   The divider between men's and women's sections in traditional synagogues.

menorah   The traditional Jewish seven-branched candelabrum used in the synagogue. The Hanukkah *menorah* (more properly called *hanukkiah*) must have eight branches, with a ninth for the *shamash* or "service" candle used for lighting the others.

mezuzah   Nailed to the doorposts of Jewish homes, *mezuzot* (pl.) contain a scroll of the *Shema* prayer (Deuteronomy 6:4–9 and 11:13–21), reminding Jews in their comings and goings of God's unity.

midrash   Stories that are derived from and are explanations of Jewish religious texts. They fill in the blanks between the more austere narratives of those texts. The *Midrash* is a compilation of rabbinic commentaries on the Torah.

mikveh   The Jewish ritual bath. According to *halakhah*, a community must build a *mikveh* even before a synagogue. The waters of the *mikveh* are to be "living," that is, not piped in from the well or reservoir. The ideal, though fairly impractical, *mikveh* is a body of moving water such as an ocean or river. The *mikveh* is used whenever any ritual purification is needed—not only for people: a new set of dishes is dipped in the *mikveh* before it is used, for example. Although most closely associated with women who practice the *mitzvah* of *taharat hamishpahah* and with converts, the *mikveh* is also used by men before holidays and *Shabbat*, after caring for a dead body, and after experiencing a nocturnal emission.

Minha   The afternoon service.

minor fast   There are four minor fast days on the Jewish calendar and they are observed from dawn to nightfall. The injunction against eating or drinking on these days is somewhat more lenient than on Yom Kippur, when only the most infirm are permitted sustenance. As in many religious traditions, fasting serves the purpose of reminding us that only our bodies are part of the material world.

minyan   A group of ten (traditionally, men) required for the full service of prayers. Liberal traditions of Judaism allow women to be counted to make a *minyan*.

It is a special *mitzvah* (good deed) to be the "tenth" person, since that number is required for mourners to be able to say *Kaddish*.

Mishnah   In about 200 C.E. the *Mishnah* was completed. It is the codification of the oral law. The *Mishnah* and the *Gemara*, which is a commentary on and further expansion on the *Mishnah*, are contained in the Talmud.

mitzvah   This word means both "commandment" ("I observe the *mitzvah* of *kashrut*, and so I don't eat unkosher food") and "good deed" ("She did a *mitzvah* by driving the senior citizens to do their weekly shopping"). There are 613 *mitzvot* (pl.) in the Torah that are to be observed by Jews individually and collectively—this includes all the dietary laws, the laws surrounding birth, marriage, and death, as well as the injunction against wearing clothing made of cloth mixing wool and linen fibers. Some of these *mitzvot* are quite obscure or, in some cases, impossible in the modern day to perform, and in reality even the most observant Jew cannot "keep" all of the 613, since some of the *mitzvot* relate to activities to be carried on in the Temple.

mohel   (fem. *mohelet*) One who performs the *brit milah*, ritual circumcision. Although this person does not need to be a rabbi or a physician, he or she should be well versed in the religion and the ceremony as well as skilled in the physical procedure. Though traditionally men have been *mohels*, there is support in Torah for women to serve in this function, since Moses' wife Zipporah circumcised her sons (Exodus 4:24–26).*

moshav   A collective farm in Israel. People own land in common but may farm it individually or with others.

Musaf   The additional service added to the morning prayers on *Shabbat* and holidays.

Noahide laws   Seven laws that the rabbis hold binding upon all humankind. Six are negative: prohibiting idolatry, blasphemy, murder, adultery, robbery, and the eating of flesh cut from a living animal. The positive commandment requires the establishment of courts of justice.

olim   People who have made *aliyah*, immigration to Israel.

Oneg Shabbat   (lit. "Sabbath delight") Any celebration during the Sabbath, which might include a lecture, dancing, singing, and eating.

parashah   The Torah portion. In the *Humash* (Bible), the five books of Moses are divided into fifty-four sections or "*parashot.*" Each week of the year, except for festivals and holidays when special sections are read, a section of the Torah is *leyned* (chanted) in the synagogue or *minyan*. So much a part of Jewish life is the weekly *parashah* that people tend to link the remembrance of events in their lives with the *parashah* read that week: "My daughter was born *Shabbat Ki Tissa*" or "I remember it was *Shabbat VaYera* when we met because we were discussing how troublesome the story of Hagar is for me." Traditionally, a young person's celebration of his or

---

*Leo Trepp, *The Complete Book of Jewish Observance* (New York: Behrman House, 1980), p. 276.

her *bar/bat mitzvah*, based on the Sabbath of the Hebrew calendar birthdate, involves reciting the Torah and *haftarah* portion for that week.

PARVE   A group for adult children of intermarriage. The name indicates the feeling some have about being neither Christian nor Jew, because the word *parve* means any food that is neither dairy nor meat.

Passover seder   A religious service and festive meal that marks the Passover holiday. At the *seder* table we recline comfortably to remind us of the blessing of freedom. We eat *matzah* to remind us that the slaves fleeing from Egypt had no time to let their bread rise. We eat bitter herbs to remind us of the sorrow of enslavement and sing songs of celebration to remind us of God's blessings and redemption.

Pesadikh   Free of leaven and therefore kosher for Passover.

Pesah   (lit. "Passover") The commemoration of the liberation of the Israelite slaves from Egypt. This festival begins on the fifteenth of the month of Nisan and continues for eight days. It is marked by the Passover *seder* and the eating of unleavened bread during the eight days. We eat unleavened bread because the slaves in Egypt had to leave in such haste that their bread had no time to rise.

peyot   The earlocks worn by *hasidic* men.

pidyon haben   Ceremony for redemption of firstborn male children.

Pirkei Avot   (lit. "Chapters of the Fathers") Passages from the *Mishnah* containing sayings and religio-ethical teachings of the sages from the third century B.C.E. to the third century C.E. It is read during the summer months during *Shabbat* from Pesah to the Sabbath before Rosh Hashanah in Ashkenazic tradition and from Pesah to Shavuot among Sephardim.

pittur   Permission to remarry. After the *get* has been given by the husband to his wife, each receive a certificate allowing them to remarry.

pogrom   (Russian, "destruction") An organized massacre for the annihilation of any group or class, often with government collusion. Pogroms were chiefly directed at Jews.

Purim   (lit. "lots") Commemorates the rescue of Persian Jews, by the intervention of Esther and her uncle Mordehai, from the planned extermination orchestrated by the Persian prime minister, Haman. Jews celebrate this minor holiday by wearing costumes, reading the *Megillat Esther*, and using noisemakers (groggers) to blot out the name of Haman whenever it is mentioned in the narrative. Another lovely custom is the sending of gifts to friends and neighbors, called *mishlo'ah manot* (lit. "send gifts"), which usually include nuts and fruits and the special three-cornered cookie called "hamantaschen" (Haman's hats). It is also customary to give *tzedakah*.

Ramah   The name for the Conservative movement's summer camps for children, with an emphasis on Hebrew language and Israeli culture.

rebbe   Hasidic master or head of a hasidic dynasty.

Rosh Hashanah   (lit. "head of the year") The Jewish New Year is actually celebrated in the seventh month of the Jewish calendar, *Tishri*, and in fact there are actually four "new" years on the calendar: Rosh Hashanah; Tu B'Shvat, the New Year for trees; *Nisan*, the month of spring, the "first" month according to Torah; and the month of *Elul*, which in ancient times marked the cutoff for the tithing of cattle but has become a time to prepare ourselves for the celebration and soul-searching and spirit-focusing of Rosh Hashanah and Yom Kippur.

It is interesting that the Rosh Hashanah–Yom Kippur cycle begins with an uplifting holiday, which Rosh Hashanah is. We wish each other that we "may be inscribed for a good year." We gather friends and family for a celebratory meal, during which we all dip apples in honey for a "sweet year." Yet, during services on the two days of Rosh Hashanah we read some of the most troubling passages in the Bible: the binding of Isaac and the story of Ishmael and Hagar. We must grapple with how complicated life can become on the path toward truth. After services in the afternoon of the first day, we walk to a stream or the ocean for *tashlikh*, where we empty the crumbs from our pockets, a symbol for the "transgressions" of the year before.

Rosh Hodesh   New Moon, the beginning of the lunar month.

seder   (lit. "order") Generally refers to the Passover *seder*, although there are other *seders* for other holidays, such as Tu B'Shvat.

Selihot   Penitential prayers said before the High Holidays.

Sephardic   Refers to the Jews who were expelled from Spain in 1492 and settled primarily in Northern Africa, and also in Italy, Egypt, and Palestine, as well as Syria and the Balkans and in parts of the Turkish Empire. From the sixteenth century onward the distinctions between the Sephardim and the Ashkenazim became more pronounced, especially in synagogue practices but also in culture, social customs, and even the pronunciation of Hebrew.

seudah shlishit   The third meal eaten on *Shabbat* in the afternoon.

Shabbat   The Sabbath, a day of rest. *Shabbat* is observed from shortly before sunset on Friday night until after nightfall on Saturday night. The Sabbath is meant to be a delight and, although there are many prohibitions on activities, such as driving, writing, and cooking, there are also laws to enhance the celebratory nature of the day. On *Shabbat* it is said we get an extra soul and we feel the *Shekhinah*, God's presence, in our midst. So it is with regret that we say good-bye to the Sabbath with the *Havdalah* ceremony.

Shabbaton   A celebration of the entire Sabbath from sunset to sunset with a group of people.

shaliah   ("emissary") May refer to the leader of prayers in a synagogue, who is thereby serving as an emissary for the people; or an emissary from Israel to Jewish communities in the *Diaspora* for purposes of fundraising, education, and so forth.

shandeh   (Yiddish, "a shame") Something for which one should feel ashamed; to shame oneself.

Shavuot   The feast of weeks, a festival that occurs in late spring.

Sheheheyanu   A blessing said for all new things or on the first day of a seasonal holiday. "Blessed is God, Ruler of the Universe, who has kept us alive . . . to this season."

Shema   Probably the most widely known Hebrew prayer, it begins "Hear O Israel, the Lord our God, the Lord is One." It is repeated twice daily during prayers and is written on parchment to be put in the *tefillin* and in small containers called *mezuzot*, which are nailed to the doorposts of Jewish homes. The text follows:

> Hear O Israel, the Lord our God, the Lord is One.
> Blessed is the name of His Glorious Majesty for ever and ever.
> Love the Lord your God with all your heart, with all your soul, and with all your means. And these words which I command you this day shall be taken to your heart. Teach them diligently to your children, and talk of them when you sit in your house, when you walk on the road, when you lie down and when you rise up. Bind them for a sign upon your hand and for frontlets between your eyes. Write them on the doorposts of your house and on your gates. (Deut. 6:5–9)

Sheva Brachas   ("seven blessings") Celebration for the newlywed couple each of the seven nights following the wedding.

shidukh   Originally the preliminary conversations with a bride or her parents before the betrothal, it also has come to mean "making a match," the betrothal itself, and actual marriage.

shikseh   Female gentile (**shegetz**: male gentile) These are derogatory Yiddish words that derive from Hebrew. Edward L. Greenstein, quoted in *The Jewish Holidays*,* suggests that we must "wrestle free" of these words; "We need to break out of words and their poisonous associations just as we need to break out of ideas that prevent the free flow of the divine spirit in the world."

shivah   ("seven") The first seven days of mourning that follow the burial. During this period (which some liberal traditions of Judaism have reduced to five or three days), the mourners do no work, receive guests in their home for consolation and prayer. It is a *mitzvah* to visit a *shivah* house, especially to help make a *minyan* for services during which the mourner's *Kaddish* is recited.

shloshim   Thirty-day period of mourning following the death of a near relative. During the thirty days it is prohibited to participate in any joyful occasion. Parents are mourned for twelve months, other relatives for thirty days. *Kaddish* is said for eleven months (for a parent) and each year on the anniversary of the death.

Shomer Shabbat   (lit. "guardian of the Sabbath") Adhering to not only the laws governing the Sabbath but other *mitzvot*, such as *kashrut* and *taharat hamishpahah*.

shpiel   A play, or making a game out of something.

shtetl   Name for the small communities of Eastern Europe and Russia in which the majority of the world's Jews lived before the Holocaust. There were hundreds of these communities, none of which now exist.

shul   (Yiddish) Synagogue.

Shulhan Arukh   (lit. "the prepared table") The code of Jewish law.

siddur   The Jewish prayer book.

---

*Michael Strassfeld, *The Jewish Holidays: A Guide and Commentary* (New York: Harper & Row, 1985), p. 43.

simhahs   Celebrations, happy occasions. Weddings, baby namings, *brits*, and *bar/bat mitzvahs* are *simhahs*.

Simhat Torah   (lit. "rejoicing the Torah") It immediately follows the holiday of Sukkot and marks the ending of the reading of the whole Torah. The celebration includes a recitation of verses and a procession singing and dancing with the Torah. In some congregations the celebration goes on all night. The following *Shabbat* the Torah will have been rolled back to *Bereshit*–"In the beginning. . . ."

sukkah   (lit. "booth") These temporary shelters, erected during the festival of Sukkot, the feast of the tabernacles, are reminders that this was a harvest festival at one time. At Sukkot we are to eat, drink, even sleep in our *sukkahs*, and their roofs should be flimsy enough so that we may see the stars.

Sukkot   (lit. "tabernacles") One of the three pilgrim festivals (to Jerusalem). It begins after Yom Kippur and at its end we celebrate Simhat Torah (rejoicing of the Torah), a separate holiday. Besides dwelling in the *sukkah*, we celebrate Sukkot with the four species—the *lulav* (a "bouquet" made up of palm, citron, willow, and myrtle) and the *etrog* (citron)—which are carried in procession in the synagogue and over which blessings are recited in the *sukkah*.

taharat hamishpahah   The law of family purity. Couples who observe this *mitzvah* physically separate when the woman is menstruating and for seven clean days after she stops bleeding. (The end of this period, incidentally, coincides with the average woman's most fertile period in her cycle.) She then goes to the *mikveh*, where she prepares herself for immersion by soaking in a bathtub, washing her hair, brushing her teeth, and clipping fingernails and toenails. She wears no jewelry, even her wedding ring, so that there is no physical matter between her and the waters of the *mikveh*. After the immersion she says two blessings, one for the immersion itself and a second, the *Sheheheyanu*, in gratitude to God for bringing her to this new month, a new season of her life.

Although this *mitzvah* has been reviled by some women as insulting because of its inference of uncleanness, it has been held in esteem by many traditional Jewish women and is now finding adherents in a new generation of women who have come to see it not as punitive or derogatory but as an affirmation of woman's unique role in the life cycle. Some observant couples include a twin or sofa bed in addition to the marital bed for those times of the month when the man and woman may not sleep together.

tallit (or **tallis**)   Prayer shawl.

Talmud   The Talmud is a compilation of the codified oral law, *Mishnah*, and the commentary, *Gemara*, as well as other notes of historical, scientific, and social significance to Jews and Jewish life through the ages. One edition of the Talmud is printed in twenty volumes.

tefillin   (from Aramaic, "attachment," and Hebrew, *tefillah*, "prayer"). Two black leather boxes containing four portions of the Pentateuch (Exodus 13:1–16; Deuteronomy 6:4–9, 11:13–21), attached to leather straps that are wrapped, or "laid," around the weaker arm and around the head. Jewish men, and some women in liberal traditions, wear *tefillin* during morning prayers (except on *Shabbat* and holidays) along with a *tallit* (prayer shawl). Also called phylacteries.

teshuvah (lit. "return," "repentance") Basic to Judaism, *teshuvah* involves the renouncing of sin and the return to righteous living.

tevillah (lit. "immersion") Refers, generally, to immersion in the *mikveh*.

Thirty-six hidden saints (also *lamed-vav tzaddikim*, "thirty-six righteous people") Part folklore, part mystical tradition, in each generation there are said to be a minimum of thirty-six anonymous righteous people who through their merit and special relationship with the Source of Life maintain the world.

tikkun Volume containing the text of the Torah, both as it appears in the scroll and with pronunciation marks.

tikkun olam Repair of the world. It is the obligation of every Jew to take responsibility for making the world a better place because we are partners with God in perfecting the Divine creation. For many Jews, *tikkun olam* is *the* defining mission of life. As Abraham Joshua Heschel said, "In a free society, some are guilty, all are responsible." And from *Pirkei Avot*, "It is not for you to complete the work, but neither are you free to desist from it."

Tisha B'Av The solemn commemoration of the destruction of the Temple in Jerusalem in ancient times.

Torah (lit. "teaching," "law") The written law, but in its broadest meaning it also includes the "oral law" of the Talmud.

Torah U-Mesorah Society for Orthodox Hebrew Day Schools founded in 1944 in New York.

treif Not kosher.

Tu B'Shvat (fifteenth day of the month of *Shevat*) A New Year for Trees. Now celebrated as a sort of "Arbor Day" in Israel, it was originally the day that made a division between those fruit-bearing trees from which a tithe for the Temple could be taken. Tu B'Shvat is celebrated by eating new fruits, especially those from trees native to Israel. Tu B'Shvat has become for some Jews a Jewish "Earth Day."

tumah State of *ritual* impurity that occurs after a woman's menstrual period; after childbirth because of the blood flow (blood representing life) and "death" of the placenta; after seminal emission (loss of potential life-starting seed); and after handling a dead body in preparation for burial. Judaism solemnifies and makes very clear distinctions between life and death. When a person goes through a process that brings him or her into contact with that very powerful transition from life to death, then he or she must mark that change in ritual status by immersion in the *mikveh*.

tzedakah (lit. "righteousness") Means charity or philanthropy.

tzitzit (lit. "fringes") A special undergarment of light material with four corners on which are attached the "*tzitzit*," the fringes the Bible commands to be worn (Numbers 15:37–41). There are also *tzitzit* on the four corners of the *tallit*.

USY United Synagogue Youth, the Conservative movement's social and service organization for young people.

yarmulke   Skullcap worn for prayer, and by religious Jews at all times. Also *kippah*.

Yartzeit   (Yiddish, "year-time") The observance of the anniversary of death of a near relative. A twenty-four-hour candle is lit and *Kaddish* is recited.

yeshivah   A school devoted to the study of Torah, Talmud, and commentaries on the Bible.

Yiddish   Dialect associated with Ashkenazic Jews and originating perhaps a thousand years ago in the Jewish communities along the Rhine. Many Hebrew words are employed and the Hebrew alphabet is used to write Yiddish. There is a very extensive Yiddish literature that was at its peak in the years before the Holocaust. In his wonderful books on Yiddish (*The Joys of Yiddish* and *The Joys of Yinglish*), Leo Rosten entertains as he teaches about the language and the culture that inspired and was inspired by it.

Yiddishkeit   Jewish culture.

Yizkor   Memorial service originally observed only on Yom Kippur; in the eighteenth century, *Yizkor* services were added to Passover, Shavuot, and Sukkot.

Yom Kippur   The Day of Atonement. A solemn celebration that takes place ten days after Rosh Hashanah. On this day of fasting and prayer, we humans, having strayed from the path of God, have an opportunity to examine our souls: where have we "missed the mark" in our relationship with ourselves, our friends and family members, our community, and God. By being honest and thorough in our soul-searching, we can renew our "at-ONE-ment" with the source of life for another year.

yom tov   (lit. "good day") Jewish holiday.

Young Israel   An organization founded for the furtherance of Torah-based Judaism. It was established in 1915 to attract American and Canadian young people to Orthodoxy.

Zohar   A mystical commentary on the Bible. It contains a fairly complete system of kabbalistic theosophy dealing with the cosmology and cosmogony of the universe, the soul, good and evil, and so forth.

Bibliography

Included in this bibliography are the books referenced by the interviewees, some biographies of Jews by Choice, and some basic books on Judaism that will help the interested reader begin to pursue a deeper understanding of the Jewish way of life.

Baeck, Leo. *The Essence of Judaism*. New York: Schocken Books, 1948.
   A broad-ranging discussion of Judaism, how Jews think about themselves and the world.

Browne, Louis. *The Wisdom of the Jewish People*. Northvale, NJ: Jason Aronson, 1987.
   A broad-ranging book that begins with the Torah and goes through the beginning of the Christian era, through the talmudic period, and to the first half of the twentieth century, picking up on the highlights of Jewish thought and experience.

Buber, Martin. *I and Thou*. New York: Charles Scribner's Sons, 1958.
   Buber was a Jewish philosopher, poet, mystic, and humanist. How can one understand his or her relationship with God? Buber speaks of a direct relationship with God that occurs in the present moment and is possible for all human beings.

Carmel, Abraham. *So Strange My Path*. New York: Bloch Publishing, 1964.
   Born and raised in England, Carmel first left the Anglican Church to become a Catholic priest and later the priesthood to become a Jew.

Chertok, Haim. *Stealing Home: Israel Bound and Rebound*. Bronx, NY: Fordham University Press, 1988.
   Chertok describes his first trip to Israel, which became the seed for his family's decision to make *aliyah*; the state of mind about and commitment to Judaism that had been a spark in his and his wife Marcia's life; their adjustment to Israeli life in their desert town of Yeroham. Please see Marcia Chertok's story in this volume.

Cowan, Paul. *An Orphan in History*. New York: Bantam, 1983.
   Paul Cowan movingly recounts his return to Judaism.

Dershowitz, Alan. *Chutzpah*. Boston: Little, Brown, 1991.
   Dershowitz chronicles and comments on Jews in American culture and advocates that Jews confidently and assertively claim a place in American society instead of accepting a position like a "guest in someone else's house."

Dimont, Max. *Jews, God and History*. New York: Simon and Schuster, 1962.

Donin, Rabbi Hayim Halevy. *To Be a Jew: A Guide to Jewish Observance in Contemporary Life*. New York: Basic Books, 1972.
  Rabbi Donin describes in detail the basics of leading a Jewish life according to the Orthodox tradition.

Donin, Rabbi Hayim Halevy. *To Pray as a Jew: A Guide to the Prayer Book and the Synagogue Service*. New York: Basic Books, 1980.
  An excellent companion book to *To Be a Jew*. Rabbi Donin details the different parts of the prayer book and synagogue service.

Eichhorn, David Max. *Conversion to Judaism: A History and Analysis*. New York: KTAV, 1965.
  This discussion of conversion includes several short autobiographies of converts.

Encyclopaedia Judaica. Jerusalem: Keter Publishing House, 1972.

Epstein, Daniel Mark. *Star of Wonder: American Stories and Memoirs*, Woodstock, NY: Overlook Press, 1986.
  Essays of Epstein's childhood and youth growing up in an intermarried family.

Epstein, Lawrence J. *Conversion to Judaism: A Guidebook*. Northvale, NJ: Jason Aronson, 1994.
  A born Jew, Mr. Epstein writes a warm welcome to those who would choose to be Jewish and describes the essentials both for becoming Jewish and being Jewish.

Epstein, Lawrence J. *The Theory and Practice of Welcoming Converts to Judaism: Jewish Universalism*. Lewiston, NY: Edwin Mellen Press, 1992.
  This is a scholarly work. It has special significance because it is a departure from previous books on the subject. It advocates that the Jewish community embrace converts and potential converts much more actively, based on the author's view of Jewish Universalism.

Frankiel, Tamar. *The Voice of Sarah: Feminine Spirituality and Traditional Judaism*. San Francisco: Harper San Francisco, 1990.
  An observant Jewish woman and a feminist, Frankiel's doubts about women's role in traditional Judaism were allayed when she began "doing" Judaism with other strong, intelligent, observant women. Though there has always been a deep tradition of Jewish feminine spirituality, it has been in bits and pieces and never "codified." With her book, Frankiel begins this process, presenting traditional Judaism as a "living teaching."

Gershom, Rabbi Yonassan. *Beyond the Ashes: Cases of Reincarnation from the Holocaust*. Virginia Beach, VA: ARE Press, 1992.

Rabbi Gershom writes about people who believe they are reincarnated from those who died during the Holocaust. The chapter "Jewish Souls in Gentile Bodies" describes the feelings of many converts.

Gordon, Albert I., *The Nature of Conversion: A Study of Forty-five Men and Women Who Changed Their Religion*. Boston: Beacon Press, 1967.
This book includes discussions on the nature of conversion and interviews with people who have left their religion of birth for a different religion in adulthood.

Hersey, John. *The Wall*. New York: Bantam, 1967.
A fictional account, based on historical documents, of life in the Warsaw ghetto.

Heschel, Abraham Joshua. *The Earth Is the Lord's* and *The Sabbath*. Cleveland: World Publishing Company, 1963, and New York: Harper & Row, Torchbook Edition, 1963.
Heschel lyrically describes both the life of pre–World War II Eastern European Jewry and the celebration of the Sabbath.

Kellerman, Faye. *Ritual Bath* (and other titles). New York: Fawcett, 1987.
Kellerman has written a series of murder mysteries in which police detective Peter Decker becomes involved with the Jewish community, falls in love, begins the conversion process, and discovers that although adopted by a Christian family, he is a born Jew.

Kolatch, Alfred J. *The Jewish Book of Why*. Middle Village, NY: Jonathan David Publishers, 1981.
Explains Jewish religion through a question and answer format. Brief and concise.

Kotsuji, Abraham. *From Tokyo to Jerusalem*. New York: Bernard Geis Associates, 1964.
As a child Setschan Kotsuji was drawn away from Shinto by the Old Testament teachings of the Christian church of which he became a minister. Later in his life Kotsuji met and made friends with many Jews in China and through study realized that he was longing for conversion to Judaism. In Israel, at age sixty, he became a Jew.

Kukoff, Lydia. *Choosing Judaism: A Guide for Jews by Choice*. New York: Union of American Hebrew Congregations, 1982.
In a warm and very readable book, Ms. Kukoff describes her own conversion to Judaism and discusses how newly Jewish people can become more comfortable in the religion and culture. She provides an introduction to Jewish holidays, religious practices, Jewish life-cycle events, and so on.

Lamm, Maurice. *Becoming a Jew*. Middle Village, NY: Jonathan David Publishers, 1991.
Lamm describes the process of conversion from an Orthodox perspective.

Lester, Julius. *Lovesong*. New York: Henry Holt, 1988.

In the form of a diary, Julius Lester describes his life as it led him to convert to Judaism and his deep commitment to his chosen religion. Mr. Lester is of African-American ancestry, and his great-grandfather was a Jew.

Pirkei Avot

Our copy of the *Pirkei Avot* is a large, storybook-sized volume illustrated with etchings by Saul Raskin. The *Pirkei Avot* consists of paragraphs on ethical maxims attributed to sixty-five teachers covering a period of about two centuries B.C.E. and two centuries C.E.

Portnoy, Mindy; illustrated by Shelly O. Haas. *Mommy Never Went to Hebrew School*. Rockville, MD: Kar-Ben, 1989.

A young boy discusses why and how his mother converted to Judaism before he was born.

Romanoff, Lena. *Your People, My People: Finding Acceptance and Fulfillment as a Jew by Choice*. Philadelphia: Jewish Publication Society, 1990.

In this well-researched and compassionate book, Lena Romanoff provides comprehensive information on conversion. The book is both practical and anecdotal. Ms. Romanoff includes excerpts of interviews with converts and their families and uses these anecdotes to illustrate the various issues people face in the conversion process.

Rosen, James S., and Zaiman, Joel. *Syllabus for the Teacher of Choosing Jews*. New York: United Synagogue, 1992.

Rosten, Leo. *The Joys of Yiddish*. New York: McGraw-Hill, 1968.

Rosten, Leo. *The Joys of Yinglish*. New York: McGraw-Hill, 1989.

While defining Yiddish words and English words derived from Yiddish, Rosten uses humor to give the reader a flavor of this expressive language and the culture from which it was formed and gave form to. For even more fun, be sure to read it aloud with a native Yiddish speaker.

Roth, Cecil, ed. *The Standard Jewish Encyclopedia*. 3d. ed. Garden City, NY: Doubleday, 1966.

Scalamonti, John David. *Ordained to Be a Jew: A Catholic Priest's Conversion to Judaism*. Hoboken, NJ: KTAV, 1992.

Scalamonti converted to Orthodox Judaism.

Schwartzbaum, Avraham, *The Bamboo Cradle*. Spring Valley, NY: Philipp Feldheim, 1988.

While living in China, Schwartzbaum and his wife found an abandoned baby in a railway station. They adopted her and through the process of starting their family, they found their way back to Judaism. This is more an account of Schwartzbaum's somewhat strident embrace of Orthodoxy than the story of his daughter's life.

SH'MA: A Journal of Jewish Responsibility.
An eight-page biweekly publication of CLAL (National Jewish Center for Learning and Leadership, 47 W. 34th St., New York, N.Y. 10001). Diverse points of view on a wide range of issues.

SHOA. Claude Lanzmann, producer. New York: WNET, July 1988.
This eight-hour documentary of the Holocaust is unusual in that it powerfully portrays the experience of the Holocaust without using any archival footage. Instead Lanzmann and his film crew interviewed victims, perpetrators, rescuers, collaborators, and bystanders. Their off-camera reminiscences narrate the images on screen of villages, cattle cars, and concentration camps.

Singer, I. B. *The Slave*. New York: Fawcett Crest Books, 1962.
According to the book cover, "Jacob of the town of Josefov flees a massacre by Cossacks, is waylaid by robbers, and sold as a slave. Learned and pious, the son of rich parents, Jacob, a Jew, finds himself a cowherd, toiling among a semipagan people. He also finds himself passionately in love with Wanda, his master's daughter, a woman he is forbidden to wed. Through his love he learns the true meaning of religion and the essential holiness of all spirits."

Strassfeld, Michael, Strassfeld, Sharon, and Siegel, Richard. *The First Jewish Catalog: A Do-It-Yourself Kit*. Philadelphia: Jewish Publication Society, 1973.

Strassfeld, Michael, and Strassfeld, Sharon. *The Second Jewish Catalog: Sources and Resources*. Philadelphia: Jewish Publication Society, 1976.

Strassfeld, Michael, and Strassfeld, Sharon. *The Third Jewish Catalog: Creating Community*. Philadelphia: Jewish Publication Society, 1980.
All three Jewish catalogs are dog-eared in our house. They are a useful first reference for anything having to do with the practice of Judaism from both a traditional and an innovative point of view, and they are written in a compassionate, witty, and "user-friendly" way.

Wiesenthal, Simon. *The Sunflower*. New York: Schocken Books, 1976.
A Jew is taken from a death camp to the bed of a dying Nazi soldier who confesses to the Jew the atrocities he has committed and asks the Jew for forgiveness. What should the Jew have done? This question Weisenthal presented to, among others,

Abraham Joshua Heschel and Herbert Marcuse, and the book is composed of their responses to this moral issue.

Wigoder, Devorah. *Hope Is My House*. Englewood Cliffs, NJ: Prentice Hall, 1966.
    An American Irish-Catholic woman converts to Judaism and moves to Israel to live with her husband, who is a rabbi, just after the founding of the Israeli state.

Wouk, Herman. *This Is My God: The Jewish Way of Life*. New York: Pocket Books, 1974.
    A personal description of Judaism from the point of view of the author, who is a modern Orthodox Jew.

Zborowsky, Mark, and Herzog, Elizabeth. *Life Is with People*. New York: Schocken Books, 1953.
    These anthropologists take a look at what life was like in the pre-Holocaust small-town Eastern European Jewish communities known as *shtetls*, where the majority of the world's Jews lived before World War II.

About the Author

Catherine Hall Myrowitz is a convert to Judaism and for fifteen years has been an active member of the East Bank Havurah, an egalitarian *minyan* in Baltimore. As a clinical social worker, she has led groups for Jews by Choice for the Jewish Family Service. She is a contributor to the book *Lifecycles: Jewish Women on Life Passages and Personal Milestones*. She, her husband, Elliott, and their children, Rachel and David, live on a farm.